11th International Conference on Computational Semantics 2015

(IWCS 2015)

London, United Kingdom
15-17 April 2015

ISBN: 978-1-5108-0229-2

Printed from e-media with permission by:

Curran Associates, Inc.
57 Morehouse Lane
Red Hook, NY 12571

Some format issues inherent in the e-media version may also appear in this print version.

Printed by Curran Associates, Inc. (2015)

Association for Computational Linguistics
209 N. Eighth Street
Stroudsburg, Pennsylvania 18360

Phone: 1-570-476-8006
Fax: 1-570-476-0860

acl@aclweb.org

Additional copies of this publication are available from:

Curran Associates, Inc.
57 Morehouse Lane
Red Hook, NY 12571 USA
Phone: 845-758-0400
Fax: 845-758-2634
Email: curran@proceedings.com
Web: www.proceedings.com

Introduction

Welcome to IWCS 2015. IWCS is about all computational aspects of natural language semantics, and in this year's meeting we have a good representative subset thereof. This is reflected in the thematic structure of the sessions. On the one side, we have a range of papers on the statistical approaches to language: lexical, probabilistic, and distributional semantics (8 papers in total); on the other side, there are the formal logical and grammatical models of meaning (5 papers in total); we also have a number discussing the dynamic and incremental aspects of meaning in discourse and dialogue (9 papers in total). The short paper selection extends these topics in many different interesting directions, from quantifiers and compounds to multilinguality, crowdsourcing, and the combination of natural language with other modalities such as image and sound.

Our three keynote speakers also embody the range of approaches in today's natural language semantics world: Prof. Bengio's work shows how statistical models can become deeply embedded, with layers of meaning learnt by neural nets; Prof. Copestake shows the state of the art on compositionality in generative logical models and their corresponding automated tools; and last but not least, Prof. Barzilay's work shows how the meaning of language can be grounded in and learnt from tasks in order to control computer programs and guide intelligent software.

In total we accepted 22 long papers (36% of the submissions received) and 12 short papers (72%). The long papers will be presented in eight thematic sessions across the three days, with each day starting with a keynote talk. Along the way, we will also have poster session for the short papers, with each introduced by a lightning talk beforehand. We also have an afternoon for an open space (or "unconference") event, to allow anyone to propose and discuss topics that interest them. We enjoyed this approach at IWCS 2013 and hope you find it equally stimulating this time.

Before the conference, we have five workshops on various aspects of computational semantics: annotation, modality, ontologies, dialogue, and distributional semantics. This year, we also have a Hackathon preceding the main meeting and its workshops. This is a two day event, sponsored by a mix of academia and industry, where programmers from both venues gather to tackle three main tasks, also representative of the topics covered by the main meeting.

On the social side, we have a reception at Queen Mary's own Italian restaurant (Mucci's) at the end of the first day, and a dinner on a river boat cruising the Thames at the end of the second day. We hope you enjoy the conference!

Matthew Purver, Mehrnoosh Sadrzadeh and Matthew Stone

Organisation

Conference Chairs:

Matthew Purver, Queen Mary University of London
Mehrnoosh Sadrzadeh, Queen Mary University of London
Matthew Stone, Rutgers University

Local organization:

Local Chairs: Matthew Purver, Mehrnoosh Sadrzadeh
Website and Hackathon: Dmitrijs Milajevs
Proceedings and Handbook: Dimitri Kartsaklis
Facilities and Supplies: Sascha Griffiths, Esma Balkır

Program Committee:

Rodrigo Agerri, Nicholas Asher, Timothy Baldwin, Marco Baroni, Anja Belz, Emily M. Bender, Jonathan Berant, Raffaella Bernardi, Patrick Blackburn, Gemma Boleda, Johan Bos, Stefan Bott, António Branco, Chris Brew, Paul Buitelaar, Harry Bunt, Aljoscha Burchardt, Nicoletta Calzolari, Philipp Cimiano, Stephen Clark, Daoud Clarke, Paul Cook, Robin Cooper, Montse Cuadros, Dipanjan Das, Rodolfo Delmonte, Leon Derczynski, David DeVault, Georgiana Dinu, Dmitriy Dligach, Markus Egg, Katrin Erk, Arash Eshghi, Raquel Fernandez, Anette Frank, Claire Gardent, Dan Garrette, Jonathan Ginzburg, Edward Grefenstette, Aurélie Herbelot, Karl Moritz Hermann, Jerry Hobbs, Dimitri Kartsaklis, Lauri Karttunen, Ralf Klabunde, Alexander Koller, Emiel Krahmer, Shalom Lappin, Alex Lascarides, Kiyong Lee, Diana McCarthy, Louise McNally, Jeff Mitchell, Alessandro Moschitti, Shashi Narayan, Malvina Nissim, Diarmuid Ó Séaghdha, Ekaterina Ovchinnikova, Alexis Palmer, Martha Palmer, Laura Perez-Beltrachini, Manfred Pinkal, Paul Piwek, Massimo Poesio, Octavian Popescu, Stephen Pulman, James Pustejovsky, Allan Ramsay, German Rigau, Laura Rimell, Stephen Roller, Michael Roth, David Schlangen, Rolf Schwitter, Joanna Sio, Caroline Sporleder, Mary Swift, Stefan Thater, David Traum, Peter Turney, Kees van Deemter, Benjamin Van Durme, Jan van Eijck, Eva Maria Vecchi, Yannick Versley, Carl Vogel, Shan Wang, Roberto Zamparelli, Luke Zettlemoyer

Invited Speakers

Regina Barzilay, Massachusetts Institute of Technology:

Semantics of Language Grounding

Abstract: In this talk, I will address the problem of natural language grounding. We assume access to natural language documents that specify the desired behaviour of a control application. Our goal is to generate a program that will perform the task based on this description. The programs involve everything from changing the privacy settings on your browser, playing computer games, performing complex text processing tasks, to even solving math problems. Learning to perform tasks like these is complicated because the space of possible programs is very large, and the connections between the natural language and the resulting programs can be complex and ambiguous. I will present methods that utilize semantics of the target domain to reduce natural language ambiguity. On the most basic level, executing the induced programs in the corresponding environment and observing their effects can be used to verify the validity of the mapping from language to programs. We leverage this validation process as the main source of supervision to guide learning in settings where standard supervised techniques are not applicable. Beyond validation feedback, we demonstrate that using semantic inference in the target domain (e.g., program equivalence) can further improve the accuracy of natural language understanding.

Yoshua Bengio, Université de Montréal:

Deep Learning of Semantic Representations

Abstract: The core ingredient of deep learning is the notion of distributed representation. This talk will start by explaining its theoretical advantages, in comparison with non-parametric methods based on counting frequencies of occurrence of observed tuples of values (like with n-grams). The talk will then explain how having multiple levels of representation, i.e., depth, can in principle give another exponential advantage. Neural language models have been extremely successful in recent years but extending their reach from language modelling to machine translation is very appealing because it forces the learned intermediate representations to capture meaning, and we found that the resulting word embeddings are qualitatively different. Recently, we introduced the notion of attention-based neural machine translation, with impressive results on several language pairs, and these results will conclude the talk.

Ann Copestake, University of Cambridge:

Is There Any Logic in Logical Forms?

Abstract: Formalising the notion of compositionality in a way that makes it meaningful is notoriously complicated. The usual way of formally describing compositional semantics is via a version of Montague Grammar but, in many ways, MG and its successors are inconsistent with the way semantics is used in computational linguistics. As computational linguists we are rarely interested in model-theory or truth-conditions. Our assumptions about word meaning, and distributional models in particular, are very different from the MG idealisation. However, computational grammars have been constructed which produce empirically useful forms of compositional representation and are much broader in coverage than any grammar fragments from the linguistics literature. The methodology which underlies this work is predominantly syntax-driven (e.g., CCG, LFG and HPSG), but the goal has been to abstract away from the language-dependent details of syntax. The question, then, is whether this is 'just engineering' or whether there is some theoretical basis which is more consistent with CL than the broadly Montogovian approach. In this talk, I will start by outlining some of the work on compositional semantics with large-scale computational grammars and in particular work using Minimal Recursion Semantics (MRS) in DELPH-IN. There are grammar fragments for which MRS can be converted into a logical form with a model-theoretic interpretation but I will argue that attempting to use model theory to justify the MRS structures in general is inconsistent with the goals of grammar engineering. I will outline some alternative approaches to integrating distributional semantics with this framework and show that this also causes theoretical difficulties. In both cases, we could consider inferentialism as an alternative theoretical grounding whereby classical logical properties are treated as secondary rather than primary. In this view, it is important that our approaches to compositional and lexical semantics are consistent with uses of language in logical reasoning, but it is not necessary to try and reduce all aspects of semantics to logic.

Table of Contents

Conference Program

Wednesday 15th

09:00–09:30 ***Registration***

09:30–10:30 *Invited Talk 1: Semantics of Language Grounding*
Regina Barzilay

10:30–11:00 ***Coffee***

11:00–12:30 **Lexical Semantics**

11:00–11:30 *Leveraging a Semantically Annotated Corpus to Disambiguate Prepositional Phrase Attachment*
Guy Emerson and Ann Copestake

11:30–12:00 *Prepositional Phrase Attachment Problem Revisited: how Verbnet can Help*
Daniel Bailey, Yuliya Lierler and Benjamin Susman

12:00–12:30 *From Adjective Glosses to Attribute Concepts: Learning Different Aspects That an Adjective Can Describe*
Omid Bakhshandh and James Allen

12:30–13:00 ***Lightning talks***

13:00–14:00 ***Lunch***

Wednesday 15th (continued)

14:00–15:30 Poster Session (short papers)

Wednesday 15th (continued)

15:30–16:00 ***Coffee***

16:00–17:00 **Discourse and Generation**

16:00–16:30 *Hierarchical Statistical Semantic Realization for Minimal Recursion Semantics*
Matic Horvat, Ann Copestake and Bill Byrne

16:30–17:00 *Uniform Surprisal at the Level of Discourse Relations: Negation Markers and Discourse Connective Omission*
Fatemeh Torabi Asr and Vera Demberg

17:00–18:00 **Probabilistic Semantics**

17:00–17:30 *Efficiency in Ambiguity: Two Models of Probabilistic Semantics for Natural Language*
Daoud Clarke and Bill Keller

17:30–18:00 *On the Proper Treatment of Quantifiers in Probabilistic Logic Semantics*
Islam Beltagy and Katrin Erk

Thursday 16th

09:30–10:30 *Invited Talk 2: Deep Learning of Semantic Representations*
Yoshua Bengio

10:30–11:00 ***Coffee***

Thursday 16th (continued)

11:00–12:30 Distributional Methods

12:30–13:30 ***Lunch***

13:30–15:00 Reference and Incrementality

15:00–15:30 ***Coffee***

15:30–18:00 ***Open Space Event***

Friday 17th

09:30–10:30 *Invited Talk 3: Is There Any Logic in Logical Forms?*
Ann Copestake

10:30–11:00 ***Coffee***

11:00–12:30 **Parsing and Grammars**

11:00–11:30 *Semantic Dependency Graph Parsing Using Tree Approximations*
Željko Agić, Alexander Koller and Stephan Oepen

11:30–12:00 *Semantic construction with graph grammars*
Alexander Koller

12:00–12:30 *Layers of Interpretation: On Grammar and Compositionality*
Emily M. Bender, Dan Flickinger, Stephan Oepen, Woodley Packard and Ann Copestake

12:30–13:30 ***Lunch***

13:30–15:00 **Dialogue and Pragmatics**

13:30–14:00 *Pragmatic Rejection*
Julian J. Schlöder and Raquel Fernandez

14:00–14:30 *Feedback in Conversation as Incremental Semantic Update*
Arash Eshghi, Christine Howes, Eleni Gregoromichelaki, Julian Hough and Matthew Purver

14:30–15:00 *Dynamics of Public Commitments in Dialogue*
Antoine Venant and Nicholas Asher

15:00–15:30 ***Coffee***

Friday 17th (continued)

Leveraging a Semantically Annotated Corpus to Disambiguate Prepositional Phrase Attachment

Guy Emerson and Ann Copestake
Computer Laboratory, University of Cambridge
15 JJ Thomson Avenue, Cambridge CB3 0FD, United Kingdom
{gete2, aac10}@cam.ac.uk

Abstract

Accurate parse ranking requires semantic information, since a sentence may have many candidate parses involving common syntactic constructions. In this paper, we propose a probabilistic framework for incorporating distributional semantic information into a maximum entropy parser. Furthermore, to better deal with sparse data, we use a modified version of Latent Dirichlet Allocation to smooth the probability estimates. This LDA model generates pairs of lemmas, representing the two arguments of a semantic relation, and can be trained, in an unsupervised manner, on a corpus annotated with semantic dependencies. To evaluate our framework in isolation from the rest of a parser, we consider the special case of prepositional phrase attachment ambiguity. The results show that our semantically-motivated feature is effective in this case, and moreover, the LDA smoothing both produces semantically interpretable topics, and also improves performance over raw co-occurrence frequencies, demonstrating that it can successfully generalise patterns in the training data.

1 Introduction

Ambiguity is a ubiquitous feature of natural language, and presents a serious challenge for parsing. For people, however, it does not present a problem in most situations, because only one interpretation will be sensible. In examples (1) and (2), fluent speakers will not consciously consider a gun-wielding dog or a moustache used as a biting tool. Both of these examples demonstrate syntactic ambiguity (the final prepositional phrase (PP) could modify the preceding noun, or the main verb), rather than lexical ambiguity (homophony or polysemy).

(1) The sheriff shot a dog with a rifle.

(2) The dog bit a sheriff with a moustache.

In many cases, parse ranking can be achieved by comparing syntactic structures, since some constructions are more common. In the above examples, however, the same set of structures are available, but the best parse differs: the PP should modify the verb "shot" in (1), but the noun "sheriff" in (2). Dealing with such cases requires semantic information.

A promising approach to represent lexical semantics assumes the distributional hypothesis, which was succinctly stated by Turney and Pantel (2010): "words that occur in similar contexts tend to have similar meanings". Our method uses corpus data to estimate the plausibility of semantic relations, which could then be exploited as features in a maximum entropy parser. In section 3, we first describe the general framework, then explain how it can be specialised to tackle PP-attachment.

To overcome data sparsity, we introduce a generative model based on Ó Séaghdha (2010)'s modified version of Latent Dirichlet Allocation (LDA), where two lemmas are generated at a time, which we use to represent the two arguments of a binary semantic relation. The probabilities produced by the LDA model can then be incorporated into a discriminative parse selection model, using our general framework.

Proceedings of the 11th International Conference on Computational Semantics, pages 1–11,
London, UK, April 15-17 2015.

This LDA model can be trained unsupervised using a semantically annotated corpus. To clarify what this means, it is helpful to distinguish two notions of "labelled data": linguistic annotations, and desired outputs. Following Ghahramani (2004), supervised learning requires both a set of inputs and a set of desired outputs, while unsupervised learning requires only inputs. Although we use a corpus with linguistic annotations, these are not desired outputs, and learning is unsupervised in this sense. Since our training data was automatically produced using a parser (as explained in section 4.2), our method can also be seen as self-training, where a statistical parser can be improved using unlabelled corpus data.

Because of its central role in linguistic processing, parse ranking has been extensively studied, and we review other efforts to incorporate semantic information in section 2. To evaluate our framework, we consider the special case of PP-attachment ambiguity, comparing the model's predictions with hand-annotated data, as explained in section 4. Results are presented in section 5, which we discuss in section 6. Finally, we give suggestions for future work in section 7, and conclude in section 8.

2 Related Work

The mathematical framework described in section 3.3 follows the "Rooth-LDA" model described by Ó Séaghdha (2010). However, he uses it to model verbs' selectional preferences, not for parse ranking. The main difference in this work is to train multiple such models and compare their probabilities.

The use of lexical information in parse ranking has been explored for some time. Collins (1996) used bilexical dependencies derived from parse trees, estimating the probabiliity of a relation given a sentence. We consider instead the plausibility of relations, which can be included in a more general ranking model.

Rei and Briscoe (2013) consider re-ranking the output of a parser which includes bilexical grammatical relations. They use co-occurrence frequencies to produce confidence scores for each relation, and combine these to produce a score for the entire parse. To smooth the scores, they use a semantic vector space model to find similar lexical items, and average the scores for all such items. From this point of view, our LDA model is an alternative smoothing method. Additionally, both our approach and theirs can be seen as examples of self-training. However, their re-ranking approach must be applied on the output of a parser, while we explain how such scores can be directly integrated as features in parse ranking.

Hindle and Rooth (1993) motived the use of lexical information for disambiguating PP-attachment. More recently, Zhao and Lin (2004) gave a state-of-the-art supervised algorithm for this problem. Given a new construction, they use a semantic vector space to find the most similar examples in the training data, and the most common attachment site among these is then assigned to the new example.

Unlike Zhao and Lin, and many other authors tackling this problem using the Penn Treebank, our model is unsupervised and generative. The first fact makes more data available for training, since we can learn from unambiguous cases, and the second plays an important role in building a framework that can handle arbitrary types of ambiguity. This provides a significant advantage over many discriminative approaches to PP-attachment: despite Zhao and Lin's impressive results, it is unclear how their method could be extended to cope with arbitrary ambiguity in a full sentence.

Clark et al. (2009) use lexical similarity measures in resolving coordination ambiguities. They propose two similarity systems, one based on WordNet, and the other on distributional information extracted from Wikipedia using the C&C parser. Hogan (2007) also consider similarity, both of the head words and also in terms of syntactic structure. However, while similarity might be appropriate for handing coordination, since conjuncts are likely to be semantically similar, this does not generalise well to other relations, where the lexical items involved may be semantically related, but not similar.

Bergsma et al. (2011) approach coordination ambiguity using annotated text, aligned bilingual text, and plain monolingual text, building statistics of lexical association. However, this method works at the string level, without semantic annotations, and there is no clear generalisation to other semantic relations.

Agirre et al. (2008) use lexical semantics in parsing, both in general and considering PP-attachment in particular. They replace tokens with more general WordNet synsets, which reduces data sparsity for standard lexicalised parsing techniques. Our LDA approach essentially provides an alternative method to back-off to semantic classes, without having to deal with the problem of word sense disambiguation.

3 Generative Model

3.1 Modelling an Arbitrary Relation

Despite the vast variety of syntactic frameworks, many parsers will produce semantic or syntactic relations in some form. We might therefore rephrase parse ranking as follows: given a set of candidate parses, choose the one with the most plausible relations.

Given a binary relation $x \xrightarrow{r} y$ between lexical items x and y, we can consider the joint probability distribution $P(r, x, y)$, which is the chance that, if we are given a random instance of any binary relation, we observe it to be the relation r between items x and y. However, rare lexical items will have low probabilities, even if they are a close semantic fit, so we should normalise by the words' overall probability of occurrence, $P(x)$ and $P(y)$, as shown in (3). The denominator can be interpreted as co-occurrence of x and y under the null hypothesis that they are generated independently, according to their overall frequency. We do not normalise by $P(r)$, so that the frequency of the relation is still taken into account, which is important, as we will see in section 3.2.

$$score\,(r, x, y) = \frac{P(r, x, y)}{P(x)\,P(y)} \tag{3}$$

A Maximum Entropy parser (MaxEnt; Berger et al., 1996) relies on a set of features $f_1, \ldots, f_m$ with corresponding weights $\lambda_1, \ldots, \lambda_m$. The probability of a parse t for a sentence s is given in (4), where Z is a normalisation constant which can often be neglected. The values of the weights λ_i are chosen to maximise the likelihood of training data, sometimes including a Gaussian prior for regularisation.

$$P(t|s) = \frac{1}{Z} \exp \sum_{i=1}^{m} \lambda_i f_i(t) \tag{4}$$

To incorporate the above scores into a MaxEnt parser, we could define a feature which sums the scores of all relations in a parse. However, the scores in (3) are always positive, so this would bias us towards parses with many relations. Instead, we can take the logarithm of the score, so that plausible relations are rewarded, and implausible ones penalised.[1] For a parse t containing k relations $x_i \xrightarrow{r_i} y_i$, we define f to be the sum of the log-scores, as shown in (5). Given a grammar and decoder that can generate candidate parses, this feature allows us to exploit semantic information in parse ranking.

$$f(t) = \sum_{i=1}^{k} \log\left(score\,(r_i, x_i, y_i)\right) \tag{5}$$

3.2 Application to PP-attachment

The effect of such a model on a wide-coverage parser will be complicated by interactions with other components. To evaluate it independently, we restrict attention to PP-attachment in four-lemma sequences $w = (v, n_1, p, n_2)$, of the form (*verb, noun, preposition, noun*), where (p, n_2) forms a PP which could attach to either the verb v, or the verb's direct object n_1. Surrounding context is not considered. For example, we could have the sequence (*eat, pasta, with, fork*).

We consider two relations, both mediated by the preposition p: for nominal attachment, a relation $r_{p,N}$ between n_1 and n_2; and for verbal attachment, a relation $r_{p,V}$ between v and n_2.

Given a sequence w, we seek the probability of attachment to n_1 or v, which we denote as $P(N|w)$ and $P(V|w)$, respectively. Taking their ratio and applying Bayes rule yields (6). To use the scores defined in (3), we first make two independence assumptions: if the PP is attached to n_1, then v is independent, and if the PP is attached to v, then n_1 is independent. We then make the approximation that the probabilities $P(N|p)$ and $P(V|p)$ for this particular ambiguity are proportional to the probabilities of observing $r_{p,N}$ and $r_{p,V}$ in general.[2] This precisely gives us a ratio of plausibility scores, shown in (9).

[1] The expected value of the log-score is equal to the mutual information of x and y, minus the conditional entropy of r given x and y. A smaller bias would therefore remain, depending on which of these two quantities is larger.

[2] Technically, as we move from (7) to (8), we shift from considering a probability space over four-lemma sequences to a probability space over binary relations. We abuse notation in using the same P to denote probabilities in both spaces.

$$\frac{P(N|w)}{P(V|w)} = \frac{P(N|p)\,P(v,n_1,n_2|p,N)}{P(V|p)\,P(v,n_1,n_2|p,V)} \tag{6}$$

$$\approx \frac{P(N|p)\,P(n_1,n_2|p,N)\,P(v)}{P(V|p)\,P(v,n_2|p,V)\,P(n_1)} \tag{7}$$

$$\approx \frac{P(r_{p,N})\,P(n_1,n_2|r_{p,N})\,P(v)\,P(n_2)}{P(r_{p,V})\,P(v,n_2|r_{p,V})\,P(n_1)\,P(n_2)} \tag{8}$$

$$= \frac{score\,(r_{p,N},n_1,n_2)}{score\,(r_{p,V},v,n_2)} \tag{9}$$

In the context of a MaxEnt parser, suppose we have defined f, as in (5), with weight λ. For parses t_N and t_V representing nominal and verbal attachment, whose features are identical except for f, the ratio in their probabilities is shown in (10). This depends precisely on the ratio of plausbility scores, hence using f is equivalent to making the above independence assumptions and approximations.

$$\frac{P(t_N)}{P(t_V)} = \left(\frac{score\,(r_{p,N},n_1,n_2)}{score\,(r_{p,V},v,n_2)}\right)^{\lambda} \tag{10}$$

In the following section, we describe a generative model to produce better estimates of the probabilities $P(n_1,n_2|r_{p,N})$ and $P(v,n_2|r_{p,V})$. Note that a discriminative model would have to consider all three lemmas v, n_1, and n_2, which would both reduce the amount of training data (since unambiguous cases only using two lemmas must be discarded), and increase the number of model parameters (since we must account for three lemmas, not two). These two facts combined could strongly encourage overfitting.

3.3 Latent Dirichlet Allocation

In its original formulation, Latent Dirichlet Allocation (LDA; Blei et al., 2003) models the topics present in a collection of documents. Ó Séaghdha (2010) adapted this framework to model verb-object collocations. Instead of considering a document and the words it contains, we consider a relation (such as the verb-object relation) and all instances of that relation in some corpus (verbs paired with their objects). The aim is to overcome data sparsity, generalising from specific corpus examples to unseen collocations. This is achieved using latent variables, or "topics".

Intuitively, each topic should correspond to two sets of lemmas, whose members have a strong semantic connection via the given relation. For example, the sets {*run, walk, stroll, gallop*} and {*road, street, path, boulevard*} are semantically related via a preposition like *down*. A rare combination such as *gallop* and *boulevard* might not be observed in training, but should still be considered plausible.

Although LDA was first introduced as a clustering algorithm, we are interested in the probability of generation, and the topic assignments themselves can be discarded.

3.3.1 Formal Description

A pair (v,n) is generated from a relation r in two stages. First, we generate a topic z from the relation, and then independently generate v and n from the topic. To do this, we associate with each relation a distribution $\theta^{(r)}$ over topics, and with each topic a pair of distributions $\varphi^{(z)}$ and $\psi^{(z)}$ over words. Symbolically, we can write this as in (12), where Cat denotes a categorical[3] distribution, i.e. one where each probability is defined separately.

To prevent overfitting, we define Bayesian priors, to specify the kinds of distribution for θ, φ and ψ that we should expect. The most natural choice is a Dirichlet distribution, as it is the conjugate prior of a categorical distribution, which simplifies calculations. We have three priors, as shown in (11), with hyperparameters α, β and γ. The entire generative process is shown using plate notation in figure 1, where R relations are generated, each with M instances, using T topics.

[3]Sometimes known as *multinomial* or *unigram*.

$$\theta \sim \text{Dir}(\alpha), \quad \varphi \sim \text{Dir}(\beta), \quad \psi \sim \text{Dir}(\gamma) \tag{11}$$

$$z \sim \text{Cat}\left(\theta^{(r)}\right), \quad v \sim \text{Cat}\left(\varphi^{(z)}\right), \quad n \sim \text{Cat}\left(\psi^{(z)}\right) \tag{12}$$

We apply this framework to PP-attachment by replacing the pair (v, n) with either: (n_1, n_2) for nominal attachment, or (v, n_2) for verbal attachment. Each preposition is therefore associated with two LDA models, which yield probabilities $P(v, n_2 | r_{p,V})$ and $P(n_1, n_2 | r_{p,N})$ for use in equation (8).

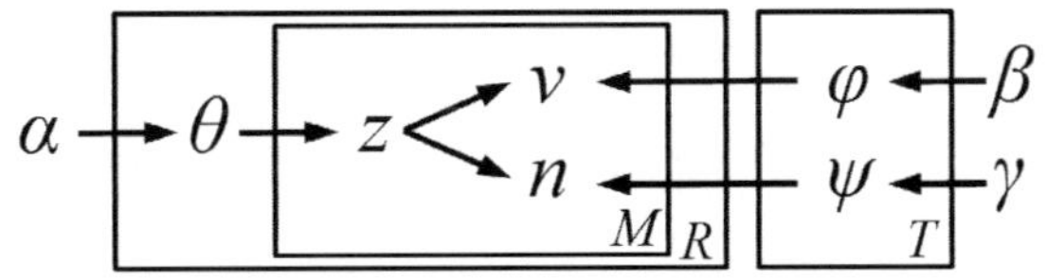

Figure 1: The modified LDA model

3.3.2 Inference

Defining the LDA model requires fixing four hyperparameters: the number of latent topics T, and the three Dirichlet priors α, β, and γ. Given these, and some training data, we can infer latent topic assignments z, and categorical distributions θ, φ, and ψ. However, for new instances, the distributions are semantically informative, while the topic assignments are not. Hence, we would like to sum over all topic assignments to obtain the marginal posterior distributions for θ, φ, and ψ. Calculating this is intractable, but we can approximate it using Gibbs sampling, applied to LDA by Griffiths and Steyvers (2004). This assigns a topic to each token (each pair of lemmas), and iteratively changes one topic assignment, conditioning on all others. Given a sample set of topic assignments, we can estimate the distributions θ, φ, and ψ, as shown in (13). Finally, we estimate the marginal probability of generating a pair (x, y), as shown in (14). The formulae also make clear the effect of the Dirichlet priors - compared to a maximum likelihood estimate, they smooth the probabilities by adding virtual samples to each $f_{\cdot\cdot}$ term.

$$\hat{\theta}_z = \frac{f_{zr} + \alpha_z}{f_{\cdot r} + \sum_{z'} \alpha_{z'}} \quad , \quad \hat{\varphi}_x^{(z)} = \frac{f_{zx} + \beta}{f_{z\cdot} + V\beta} \quad , \quad \hat{\psi}_y^{(z)} = \frac{f_{zy} + \gamma}{f_{z\cdot} + V\gamma} \tag{13}$$

$$\hat{P}(x, y) = \sum_z \hat{\theta}_z \hat{\varphi}_x^{(z)} \hat{\psi}_y^{(z)} \tag{14}$$

A single Gibbs sample will not be representative of the overall distribution, so we must average the probabilities from several samples. However, the topics themselves are labelled arbitrarily, so we cannot average the statistics $\hat{\theta}$, $\hat{\varphi}$, and $\hat{\psi}$. Nonetheless, the statistic $\hat{P}$ is invariant under re-ordering of topics and can therefore be meaningfully averaged. This gives us a better approximation of the true value, and the standard deviation provides an error estimate, which we explore in section 5.3.

3.3.3 Model Selection

Training requires fixing the hyperparameters T, α, β and γ in advance. Griffiths and Steyvers (2004) recommend setting parameters to maximise the training data's log-likelihood L. However, this could result in overfitting, if more parameters are used than necessary; intuitively, some topics may end up matching random noise. One alternative is the Akaike Information Criterion (AIC; Akaike, 1974), which penalises the dimensionality k of the parameter space, and is defined as $2k - 2\log(L)$. Bruce and Wiebe (1999) demonstrate that such a criterion in natural language processing can avoid overfitting.

We have $T - 1$ independent parameters from θ, and $T(V-1)$ from each of φ and ψ, where V is the vocabulary size.[4] Neglecting lower order terms, this gives $k = 2TV$. However, rare lemmas appear in few topics, giving sparse frequency counts, so k is effectively much lower. We are not aware of a method to deal with such sparse values. However, a simple work-around is to pretend V is smaller, for example $V = 1000$, effectively ignoring parameters for rare lexical items.

[4]Reordering topics only represents a finite number $T!$ of symmetries, and therefore does not reduce the dimensionality.

4 Experimental Setup

4.1 Choice of Prepositions

We trained models for the following prepositions: *as, at, by, for, from, in, on, to, with*. They were chosen for their high frequency of both attachment sites. Rare prepositions (such as *betwixt*) were discarded because of limited data. Prepositions with a strong preference of attachment site (such as *of*) were discarded because choosing the more common site already provides high performance.

	Instances	Proportion N
as	1,119,000	20.3 %
at	1,238,000	37.4 %
by	612,000	29.3 %
for	2,236,000	55.7 %
from	1,056,000	43.6 %

	Instances	Proportion N
in	5,288,000	37.6 %
on	1,628,000	49.7 %
to	1,411,000	46.1 %
with	1,638,000	37.4 %

Table 1: Number of training instances, with proportion of nominal attachment

4.2 Training Data

We trained the model using the WikiWoods corpus (Flickinger et al., 2010), which is both large, and also has rich syntactic and semantic annotations. It was produced from the full English Wikipedia using the PET parser (Callmeier, 2000; Toutanova et al., 2005) trained on the gold-standard subcorpus WeScience (Ytrestøl et al, 2009), and using the English Resource Grammar (ERG; Flickinger, 2000). Of particular note is that the ERG incorporates Minimal Recursion Semantics (MRS; Copestake et al., 2005), which can be expressed using dependency graphs (Copestake, 2009).

The relations mentioned in section 3.2 are not explicit in the ERG, since prepositions are represented as nodes, with edges to mark their arguments. To produce a set of training data, we searched for all preposition nodes[5] in the corpus, which either had both arguments ARG1 and ARG2 saturated, or, if no ARG1 was present, was the ARG1 of another node. We split the data based on nominal or verbal attachment, discarding PPs attached to other parts of speech. Each training instance was then a tuple of the form (v, p, n) or (n_1, p, n_2), for verbal or nominal attachment, respectively. We used lemmas rather than wordforms, to reduce data sparsity. The WeScience subcorpus was withheld from training, since it was used for evaluation (see section 4.3). In total, 16m instances were used, with a breakdown in table 1.

4.3 Evaluation Data

Two datasets were used in evaluation. We produced the first from WeScience, the manually treebanked portion of the Wikipedia data used to produce WikiWoods. This dataset allows evaluation in the same domain and with the same annotation conventions as the training data. We extracted all potentially ambiguous PPs from the DMRS structures: for PPs attached to a noun, the noun must be the object of a verb, and for PPs attached to a verb, the verb must have an object. Duplicates were removed, since this would unfairly weight those examples: some repeated cases, such as (*store metadata in format*), are limited in their domain. If the same tuple occurred with different attachment sites, the most common site was used, which happened twice, or if neither was more common, it was discarded, which happened four times. This produced 3485 unique sequences, of which 2157 contained one of the nine prepositions under consideration. The data is available on `https://github.com/guyemerson/WeSciencePP`.

The second data set was extracted from the Penn Treebank by Ratnaparkhi et al. (1994). This dataset has been widely used, allowing a comparison with other approaches. We extracted tuples with one of

[5]The ERG includes some prepositions in the "sense" field of a verb, rather than as a separate node. This is done for semantically opaque constructions, such as *rely on a friend*, where the meaning cannot be described in terms of *rely* and *on a friend*. We may wish to ignore such cases for two reasons: firstly, the preposition often appears either immediately following the verb or sentence-finally, which makes ambiguous sentences less common; secondly, the semantics is often idiosyncratic and hence less amenable to generalisations across lemmas. We discuss these cases further in section 6.1.

the relevant prepositions, lemmatised all words, and removed out of vocabulary items. This gave 1240 instances from the evaluation section of the corpus. We note that the data is noisy: it contains 'nouns' such as *the* (98 times), *all* (10 times), and *'s* (10 times), which are impossible under the annotation conventions of WikiWoods. We discuss limitations of evaluating against this dataset in section 6.1.

4.4 Baselines

We give results compared to two baselines. The low baseline chooses the most common attachment site for each preposition, as seen in the training data, regardless of the other lexical items. The high baseline is the maximum likelihood estimate, using Laplace smoothing with parameter 0.01. Comparing to the low baseline shows the effect of our framework using the feature defined in (5), while comparing to the high baseline shows the effect of the LDA smoothing. Additionally, we can consider an LDA model with a single topic, which is equivalent to the simpler smoothing method of backing off to bigram frequencies.

5 Results

5.1 Model Selection

We varied T to find the effect on the log-likelihood and the AIC (taking $V = 1000$), either fixing $\alpha = 50/T$, and $\beta = \gamma = 0.01$, which follows the recommendations of Steyvers and Griffiths (2007), or using hyperparameter optimisation, which allows asymmetric α. The results are shown in figure 2. For unoptimised models, using the log-likelihood suggests $T \approx 70$, and the AIC suggests $T \approx 35$. For the optimised model, the AIC suggests $T \approx 40$; however, the log-likelihood has not yet found its maximum, suggesting a much larger value, exactly what AIC is designed to avoid.

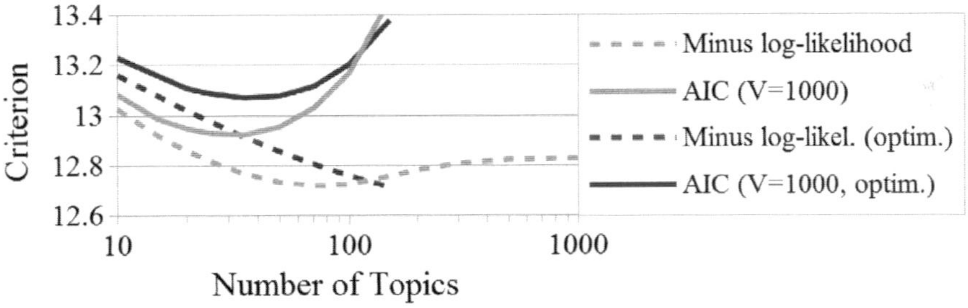

Figure 2: Model selection for LDA

5.2 Evaluation

Overall accuracy in choosing the correct attachment site is given in table 2. The large gap between the high and low baselines shows the importance of lexical information. The high baseline and the 1-topic model (i.e. backing off to bigrams) show similar performance. The best performing LDA models achieve 3 and 7 percentage point increases for WeScience and the Penn Treebank, demonstrating the effectiveness of this smoothing method. The higher gain for the Penn Treebank suggests that smoothing is more important when evaluating across domains.

The choices of hyperparameters suggested by the log-likelihood and AIC closely agree with the best performing model. The results also suggest that the LDA smoothing is robust to choosing too high a value for T. As we can see in table 2, there is only a small drop in performance with larger values of T. This result agrees with Wallach et al. (2009), who show that LDA, as applied to topic modelling, is reasonably robust to large choices of T, and that it is generally better to set T too high than too low.

Surprisingly, hyperparameter optimisation (allowing α to be asymmetric) did not provide a significant change in performance, even though we might expect some topics to be more common.

			Accuracy	
T	Samp.	Optim.?	WeSci	PTB
1	-	-	0.708	0.659
35	10	no	0.744	**0.701**
50	10	no	0.745	0.697
50	30	no	**0.747**	0.698
50	10	yes	0.741	0.695
70	10	no	0.736	0.694
70	30	no	0.738	0.696
70	10	yes	0.741	0.700
100	10	no	0.735	0.700
300	10	no	0.738	0.680
High baseline			0.718	0.629
Low baseline			0.609	0.571

Table 2: Performance of our model, varying number of topics T, number of Gibbs samples, and hyper-parameter optimisation. The highest scores for each dataset are shown in bold.

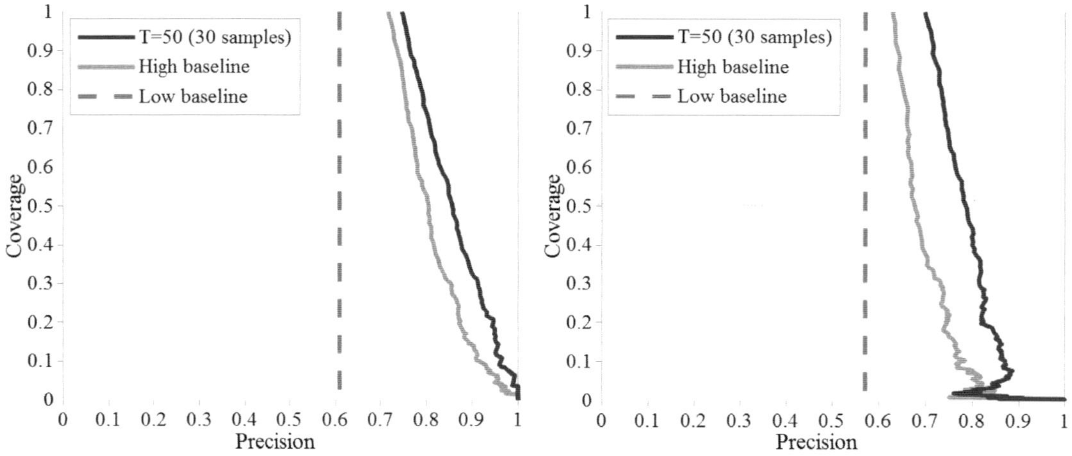

Figure 3: Coverage against precision (left WeScience, right Penn Treebank)

Since the model is probabilistic, we can interpret it conservatively, and only predict attachment if the log-odds are above a threshold. This reduces coverage, but could increase precision. We can be more confident when Gibbs samples produce similar probabilities, so we make the threshold a function of the estimated error, as in (15).[6] Here, ε_N and ε_V denote the standard error in log-probability for the nominal and verbal models - for k samples with standard deviation s, the standard error in the mean is $\varepsilon = \frac{1}{\sqrt{k}}s$. When summing independent errors, the total error is the square root of the sum of their squares.

$$|\log P\left(N|w\right) - \log P\left(V|w\right)| > \lambda \left(1 + \sqrt{\varepsilon_N^2 + \varepsilon_V^2}\right) \tag{15}$$

Graphs of coverage against precision are given in figure 3, for both datasets. As the threshold increases, the curve moves down (lower coverage) and to the right (higher precision). The increase in precision shows that the estimated probability does indeed correlate with the probability of being correct. The difference between the two solid curves shows the effect of the LDA smoothing.

5.3 Variability of Gibbs Samples

To explore how stable the probability estimates are, we evaluated the individual Gibbs samples of the $T = 50$ model. If the standard deviation s is larger than the difference in log-probability Δ, then the

[6]More complicated functions did not appear to offer any advantages; we omit results for brevity.

attachment site predicted by a single sample is not reliable - this was true for 18% of the WeScience data. If the standard error $\varepsilon = \frac{1}{\sqrt{30}}s$ is larger than Δ, then the attachment site predicted by the averaged model is not reliable - this was true for 3% of the WeScience data. Furthermore, the average accuracy of a single $T = 50$ sample on the WeScience dataset was 0.734 (standard deviation 0.0035) Hence, averaging over 30 samples reduces the number of unreliable cases by a factor of six, and increases accuracy by 1.3 percentage points.

5.4 Semantic Content of Topics

Figure 4 shows that genuine semantic information is inferred. We could characterise the first topic as describing a BUILDING in an AREA. However, the second topic reminds us that, since the topics are unsupervised, there may not always be a neat characterisation: the n_2 lemmas are all war-related, except for *election*. There is still a plausible connection between *election* and most of the n_1 lemmas, but we leave the reader to decide if elections are indeed like wars.

For large T, many topics are completely unused (with no tokens assigned to the topic), agreeing with the above conclusions that the optimal value of T is around 50.

n_1	*school, building, station, house, church, home, street, center, office, college*
n_2	*area, city, town, district, country, village, state, neighborhood, center, county*

n_1	*preparation, plan, time, way, force, date, support, responsibility, point, base*
n_2	*invasion, war, attack, operation, battle, campaign, deployment, election, landing, assault*

Figure 4: Most likely lemmas in two inferred topics (from $T = 50$ samples). Top: *in*. Bottom: *for*.

6 Discussion

6.1 Comparison with Other Approaches to PP-attachment

Our reported accuracy on the Penn Treebank data appears lower than state-of-the-art approaches, such as Zhao and Lin (2004)'s nearest-neighbour algorithm (described in section 2), which achieves 86.5% accuracy. However, the figures cannot be directly compared, for three main reasons.

Firstly, there will be a performance drop due to the change of domain - for instance, the PTB has more financial content. To quantify the domain difference, we can find the probability of generating the test data. For the $T = 50$ model, the average probability of a tuple is 8.9 times lower for the PTB than for WeScience, indicating it would be unlikely to find the PTB instances in the WikiWoods domain.

Secondly, we considered only nine prepositions, which cover just 40% of the test data. Many other prepositions are easier to deal with; for example, *of* constitutes nearly a third of all instances (926 out of 3097), but 99.1% are attached to the noun. If we simply choose the most frequent attachment site for prepositions not in our model, we achieve 79.0% accuracy, which is 7.5% lower than state-of-the-art, but this difference is well within the cross-domain drops in performance reported by McClosky et al. (2010), which vary from 5.2% to 32.0%, and by MacKinlay et al. (2011), which vary from 5.4% to 15.8%.

Thirdly, there are annotation differences between WikiWoods and the PTB, which would cause a drop in performance even if the domain were the same. As a striking example, *to* is the best performing preposition in WeScience (94% accuracy, over a baseline of 74%), but has mediocre performance on the PTB (70% accuracy, over a baseline of 61%). Much of this drop can be explained by the fact that *to* is often subcategorised for, both by verbs (*give to, pay to, provide to*), and by nouns (*exception to, damage to*). For such cases, the ERG includes *to* in the verb or noun's lexical entry, and there is no preposition in the semantics, so they do not appear in the WikiWoods training data. As a result, these cases in the PTB are often misclassified.

Finally, it may appear that performance on WeScience is also lower than state-of-the-art, but this dataset may in fact be more difficult than the PTB dataset. To quantify how useful each slot of the 4-tuple is for predicting the attachment site, we can use the conditional entropy of the attachment site given a slot.[7] A value of 0 would imply it is perfectly predictive. For the verb slot, and both of the noun slots, the WeScience data has higher conditional entropy than the PTB[8] (1% higher for v, 17% higher for n_1, and 11% higher for n_2), suggesting that predicting attachment in the PTB data is an easier task.

6.2 Quality of Training Data

Flickinger et al. (2010) estimate the quality of the automatic WikiWoods annotations by sampling 1000 sentences and inspecting them manually to find errors. They judge "misattachment of a modifying prepositional phrase" to be a minor error, which is particularly of note considering such errors provide us with inaccurate training data. In their sample, 65.7% of sentences contained no minor errors. They do not give a breakdown of error types, so it is not possible to determine the accuracy for PP-attachment, but it is clear that a significant number of such errors were present. The results therefore indicate that our model enjoys some robustness to errors in its training data.

7 Future Work

PP-attachment ambiguities represent a fraction of all syntactic ambiguities. The most important future step is therefore to confirm the effectiveness of our framework in a wide-coverage parser, as explained in section 3.1. Additionally, the LDA smoothing could be integrated with other approaches, such as Rei and Briscoe (2013)'s reranking method, described in section 2.

The LDA model could be trained on multiple relations simultaneously, to account for cases where more than one preposition is possible, as shown in (16). This could reduce data sparsity and hence improve performance, particularly for rare prepositions. This requires no change to the mathematical formalism, simply involving multiple samples from the same Dirichlet distribution α.

(16) They walked {along, across, down} the road.

To simplify model selection, we could use a Hierarchical Dirichlet Process (Teh et al., 2006), which modifies LDA to allow an arbitrary number of topics.

8 Conclusion

We have described a novel framework for incorporating distributional semantic information in a maximum entropy parser. Within this framework, we used a generative model based on Latent Dirichlet Allocation, in order to overcome data sparsity. We evaluated this approach on the specific task of resolving PP-attachment ambiguity, explaining how this problem relates to the general case. The LDA model successfully extracted semantic information from corpus data, and outperformed a maximum likelihood baseline. Furthermore, we demonstrated that training the model is robust to various hyperparameter settings, which suggests that this method should be easy to apply to new settings. These results indicate that this is a promising approach to integrating distributional semantics with parse ranking.

References

Agirre, E., T. Baldwin, and D. Martinez (2008). Improving parsing and PP attachment performance with sense information. In *Proc. ACL.*

Akaike, H. (1974). A new look at the statistical model identification. *Automatic Control, IEEE.*

Berger, A. L., V. J. D. Pietra, and S. A. D. Pietra (1996). A maximum entropy approach to natural language processing. *Computational Linguistics.*

[7] Ideally, we would calculate conditional entropy given the entire 4-tuple. However, almost all tuples are unique in the dataset, making estimates of entropy very error prone. Hence, we report conditional entropy given only one slot.

[8] No unbiased estimator of entropy exists for discrete distributions (Paninski, 2003). To mitigate against the effect of sample size, we averaged entropy estimates for subsamples of the WeScience dataset, to match the size of the PTB dataset.

Bergsma, S., D. Yarowsky, and K. Church (2011). Using large monolingual and bilingual corpora to improve coordination disambiguation. In *Proc. ACL*.

Blei, D. M., A. Y. Ng, and M. I. Jordan (2003). Latent Dirichlet allocation. *The Journal of Machine Learning Research*.

Bruce, R. F. and J. M. Wiebe (1999). Decomposable modeling in natural language processing. *Computational Linguistics*.

Callmeier, U. (2001). Efficient parsing with large-scale unification grammars. Master's thesis, Universität des Saarlandes, Saarbrücken, Germany.

Clark, S., A. Copestake, J. R. Curran, Y. Zhang, A. Herbelot, J. Haggerty, B.-G. Ahn, C. Van Wyk, J. Roesner, J. Kummerfeld, et al. (2009). Large-scale syntactic processing: Parsing the web final report of the 2009 JHU CLSP workshop.

Collins, M. J. (1996). A new statistical parser based on bigram lexical dependencies. In *Proc. ACL*.

Copestake, A. (2009). Slacker semantics: Why superficiality, dependency and avoidance of commitment can be the right way to go. In *Proc. EACL*.

Copestake, A., D. Flickinger, C. Pollard, and I. A. Sag (2005). Minimal recursion semantics: An introduction. *Research on Language and Computation*.

Flickinger, D. (2000). On building a more efficient grammar by exploiting types. *Natural Language Engineering*.

Flickinger, D., S. Oepen, and G. Ytrestøl (2010). WikiWoods: Syntacto-semantic annotation for English Wikipedia. In *Proc. LREC*.

Ghahramani, Z. (2004). Unsupervised learning. In *Advanced Lectures on Machine Learning*. Springer.

Griffiths, T. L. and M. Steyvers (2004). Finding scientific topics. *Proceedings of the National Academy of Sciences of the United States of America*.

Hindle, D. and M. Rooth (1993). Structural ambiguity and lexical relations. *Computational linguistics*.

Hogan, D. (2007). Coordinate noun phrase disambiguation in a generative parsing model. In *Proc. ACL*.

MacKinlay, A., R. Dridan, D. Flickinger, and T. Baldwin (2011). Cross-domain effects on parse selection for precision grammars. *Research on Language and Computation*.

McClosky, D., E. Charniak, and M. Johnson (2010). Automatic domain adaptation for parsing. In *Proc. NAACL*.

Ó Séaghdha, D. (2010). Latent variable models of selectional preference. In *Proc. ACL*.

Paninski, L. (2003). Estimation of entropy and mutual information. *Neural computation*.

Ratnaparkhi, A., J. Reynar, and S. Roukos (1994). A maximum entropy model for prepositional phrase attachment. In *Proc. Workshop on Human Language Technology*. ACL.

Rei, M. and T. Briscoe (2013). Parser lexicalisation through self-learning. In *Proc. NAACL-HLT*.

Steyvers, M. and T. Griffiths (2007). Probabilistic topic models. *Handbook of latent semantic analysis*.

Teh, Y. W., M. I. Jordan, M. J. Beal, and D. M. Blei (2006). Hierarchical Dirichlet processes. *Journal of the American Statistical Association*.

Toutanova, K., C. D. Manning, D. Flickinger, and S. Oepen (2005). Stochastic HPSG parse selection using the Redwoods corpus. *Journal of Research on Language and Computation*.

Turney, P. D. and P. Pantel (2010). From frequency to meaning: Vector space models of semantics. *Journal of Artificial Intelligence Research*.

Wallach, H., D. Mimno, and A. McCallum (2009). Rethinking LDA: Why priors matter. *Advances in Neural Information Processing Systems*.

Ytrestøl, G., S. Oepen, and D. Flickinger (2009). Extracting and annotating Wikipedia sub-domains. In *Proceedings of the 7th International Workshop on Treebanks and Linguistic Theories*.

Zhao, S. and D. Lin (2004). A nearest-neighbor method for resolving PP-attachment ambiguity. In *Natural Language Processing–IJCNLP 2004*. Springer.

Prepositional Phrase Attachment Problem Revisited: How VERBNET Can Help

Dan Bailey
University of Nebraska at Omaha
dbailey@unomaha.edu

Yuliya Lierler
University of Nebraska at Omaha
ylierler@unomaha.edu

Benjamin Susman
University of Nebraska at Omaha
bsusman@unomaha.edu

Abstract

Resolving attachment ambiguities is a pervasive problem in syntactic analysis. We propose and investigate an approach to resolving prepositional phrase attachment that centers around the ways of incorporating semantic knowledge derived from the lexico-semantic ontologies such as VERBNET and WORDNET.

1 Introduction

Syntactic parsing is a process of uncovering the internal structure of sentences, in particular, articulating what the constituents of a given sentence are and what relationships are between them. Software systems that perform this task are called *(syntactic) parsers*. Parsing technology has seen striking advances. Wide-coverage off-the-shelf parsers are freely available and ready to use. Yet, modern parsers are not at the level of human-expert agreement. One of the notorious problems in parsing technology is determining prepositional phrase attachment. For example, the following phrase by Ray Mooney:

eat spaghetti with chopsticks. (1)

is syntactically ambiguous allowing for two syntactic structures: in one, the prepositional phrase *with chopsticks* modifies (attaches to) the verb *eat* and in another, it modifies the noun *spaghetti*. The latter is erroneous as it suggests that *spaghetti with chopsticks* constitutes a meal. The phrase

eat spaghetti with meatballs (2)

is syntactically ambiguous in a similar manner. Modern advanced parsers do not produce proper syntactic representations for these phrases: instead they favor the same structure for both statements (Lierler and Schüller, 2013).

These "spaghetti" examples illustrate the necessity to incorporate semantic knowledge into the parsing process, in particular, one has to take into account *selectional restrictions* (Katz and Fodor, 1963) — the semantic, common-sense restrictions that a word imposes on the environment in which it occurs. For instance, the fact that chopsticks are an instrument suggests that *with chopsticks* modifies *eat spaghetti* in phrase (1) as a tool for eating. Current statistical methods, dominant in the field of syntactic analysis, take into account selectional restrictions *implicitly* by assigning the most probable syntactic structure based on observed co-occurrences of words and structures in training corpora. As mentioned, this is often not sufficient. In this work we propose and investigate an approach to the prepositional phrase attachment problem that incorporates explicit semantic knowledge available in the lexico-semantic dataset VERBNET into the decision process for resolving the ambiguity of prepositional statements. Machine learning forms a backbone of the decision procedure that we investigate.

Proceedings of the 11th International Conference on Computational Semantics, pages 12–22,
London, UK, April 15-17 2015.

This work targets to bring knowledge representation techniques into syntactic parsing. Indeed, lexical ontologies VERBNET and WORDNET are at heart of this project. Lierler and Schüller (2013) advocated a framework for parsing that results in what they call semantically-coherent syntactic parses. These parses account for selectional restrictions. On the one hand, that work suggests a promising direction. On the other hand, it outlines the need for automatic methods for acquiring lexico-semantic information that relates to parsing a sentence. Present work takes a step in the direction of establishing principles to mine existing lexico-semantic resources and incorporate found information into parsing process.

The importance of taking semantic information, including selectional restrictions, into account during parsing has long been recognized. Ford (1982), Jensen and Binot (1987), Hirst (1988), Dahlgren (1988), and Allen (1995) devised methods for parsing that performed selectional restrictions analysis. These methods assume that a systematic word taxonomy as well as a database of selectional restrictions is available. Developments in the field of Lexical semantics have made such systematic large scale datasets, including WORDNET (Miller et al., 1990) and VERBNET (Kipper et al., 2000), a reality. The WORDNET project provides a taxonomy that organizes words into a coherent representation that reflects some lexical relationships between them. The VERBNET project provides a domain-independent, broad-coverage verb lexicon that includes selectional restriction information. Also recent research illustrates the benefits of lexico-semantic information in tasks closely related to parsing. Zhou et al. (2011) illustrate how web-derived selectional preferences improve dependency parsing. Zapirain et al. (2013) show that selectional preferences obtained by means of WORDNET-based similarity metrics improve semantic role labeling. Srikumar and Roth (2013) illustrate how selectional restrictions posed by prepositions improve relation prediction performance. Agirre et al. (2008, 2011) also suggest the necessity of incorporating semantic information into parsing by providing evidence that word sense information stemming from WORDNET improves parsing and prepositional phrase attachment.

These findings support the importance of developing parsing algorithms that can handle semantic information effectively. We view the decision procedure for resolving prepositional phrase attachment developed in this paper as complementary to above mentioned methods. The main driving vehicle of this work is the VERBNET ontology. To the best of our knowledge no current approach relies on the use of VERBNET in compiling selectional preferences information.

The prepositional phrase attachment problem has received a lot of attention as a stand alone task. Lapata and Keller (2005) provide a summary of systems attempting to solve this problem. All of the reported systems have centered on machine learning approaches such as a maximum entropy model (Ratnaparkhi et al., 1994), a back-off model (Collins and Brooks, 1995), a transformation based approach (Brill and Resnik, 1994), a memory-based learning approach (Zavrel et al., 1997), and unsupervised approaches (Ratnaparkhi, 1998) or (Pantel and Lin, 2000). The reported accuracy of the systems ranged from 81.60% to 88.10%. The average human precision on the task is reported to be 88.20%.

The outline of the paper follows. We begin by introducing the relevant resources and concepts, in particular, VERBNET and WORDNET along with the concept of selectional restriction. Following that, we introduce the problem of prepositional phrase attachment. Once these foundations have been laid, we provide the details of a machine-learning based algorithm that makes use of the VERBNET and WORDNET resources in a systematic way. We then evaluate a system that implements the outlined algorithm and discuss our plans for its future.

2 The VERBNET, WORDNET Lexicons and Selectional Restrictions

Levin classes (Levin, 1993) are groups of verbs that share usage patterns and have semantic similarity. For instance, the Levin class for the verb *hit* includes the words *bang*, *bash*, *click* and *thwack*. These words can be used alike and suggest similar sentence structures. Organizing verbs into groups according to the similarity of their syntactic behavior is the basis of Levin classes. It is supported by an extensive study suggesting that similar syntactic behavior translates into common semantic features of verbs (Levin, 1993). The VERBNET ontology (Kipper et al., 2000) is an English-language verb lexicon that collects verbs into extended Levin classes and provides information about the sentence structure that these classes share.

The VERBNET dataset is composed of basic structures, called *frame syntax*. For example, a frame syntax for a *hit*-verb class follows:

$$\text{AGENT}_{intControl}\ \text{V}\ \text{PATIENT}\ \{\texttt{with}\}\ \text{INSTRUMENT}_{concrete} \tag{3}$$

This frame syntax suggests that one possible structure for the use of a verb in the *hit*-class is to have an AGENT followed by the verb itself, then a PATIENT, the preposition *with* and an INSTRUMENT. The AGENT, PATIENT and INSTRUMENT are called *thematic roles*. VERBNET allows 23 such roles including THEME, RECIPIENT, SOURCE.[1] The thematic roles in VERBNET are augmented further by *restrictions*. VERBNET maintains a hierarchy of restrictions based on the top-level entries in EuroWordNet (Kipper-Schuler, 2005, Section 3.1.2) consisting of 37 entries. This hierarchy allows VERBNET to specify that the AGENT thematic role for the verbs in class *hit* is of the type *intelligent control* (*intControl*) and the INSTRUMENT role in *hit* is *concrete*. In other words, an entity that serves an INSTRUMENT role of *hit* possesses a property of being *concrete* – some concrete physical object.

The WORDNET system is a comprehensive manually developed lexical database from Princeton University (Miller et al., 1990). In WORDNET, nouns, verbs, and adjectives are organized into synonym sets each representing one underlying lexical concept. Several semantic relations among words are incorporated into WORDNET as links between the synonym sets. These semantic relations include super/subordinate relations — *hypernymy, hyponymy or ISA relation*; and part-whole relation — *meronymy*. Thus we can investigate relationships between various concepts by following links within WORDNET. For instance, by following the ISA links, one may easily establish that synonym set containing a noun *boy* is in ISA relation with a synonym set for the *intelligent control* concept. The WORDNET lexicon has been extensively used for developing metrics and procedures for determining the relatedness/similarity of lexical concepts. The task of identifying whether and how given words are related has many applications in natural language processing (NLP) (e.g., word sense disambiguation, information extraction). Budanitsky and Hirst (2006) present a comprehensive study that compares five different measures of relatedness based on WORDNET including a measure by Leacock and Chodorow (1998). In this work we also use WORDNET for similar purposes. For example, with the help of WORDNET we define what it means that a noun "matches" a restriction or a thematic role. Section 4 presents the definition of matching.

Selectional restrictions (Katz and Fodor, 1963) are the semantic, common-sense restrictions that a word imposes on the environment in which it occurs. A *selectional construct* is a tuple $[w, t, r, p]$ where (i) w is a word, (ii) t is a thematic role that the word w allows, (iii) r is a restriction on the thematic role t with respect to the word w (by the empty set we denote no restrictions), (iv) p is a set of prepositions that can be used to realize the thematic role t of the word w (this set may be empty suggesting that no preposition is necessary to realize this thematic role). Selectional construct is meant to capture the selectional restrictions (sometimes we use these terms interchangeably). The VERBNET lexicon can be viewed as a systematic, wide-coverage knowledge base about selectional restrictions of verbs. Recall a frame syntax (3) for the verb *hit*. We now present three selectional constructs that follow from the frame:

$$(hit, \text{AGENT}, intControl, \emptyset),\quad (hit, \text{PATIENT}, \emptyset, \emptyset),\quad (hit, \text{INSTRUMENT}, concrete, \{with\}).$$

3 Prepositional Phrase Attachment

Resolving prepositional phrase (PP) attachment ambiguities is a pervasive problem in NLP exemplified by phrases (1) and (2). They look "identical" modulo one word, yet the proper syntactic analyzer will process (1) differently from (2). Indeed, the "instrumental" use of the preposition *with* — as in phrase (1)

[1] Table 2 of the VERBNET website `http://verbs.colorado.edu/~mpalmer/projects/verbnet.html` lists the thematic roles and brief explanations.

should be parsed into dependency structure of the form:

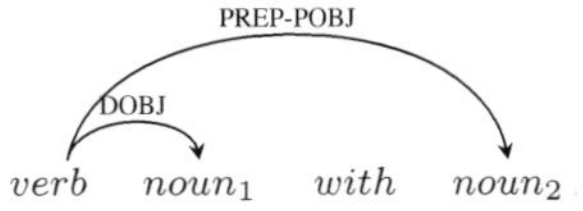

(4)

This parse structure reveals the prepositional phrase attachment describes the action being undertaken.

"Comitative" use of *with* such as in phrase (2) leads to a structure of the form

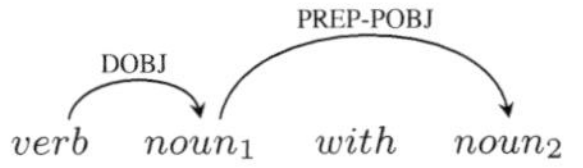

(5)

We call (4) and (5) $\mathcal{P}$-parse structures. We call a phrase, $\mathcal{P}$*-phrase*, when it has the form

verb noun-phrase preposition noun-phrase.

In the introduction, we argued that selectional restrictions provide sufficient information to disambiguate many PP attachments. We now incorporate selectional restrictions into syntactic parsing of $\mathcal{P}$-phrases. We say that a selectional construct *justifies* an edge annotated by PREP-POBJ from w to n if it has the form (w, t, r, p), where thematic role t and restriction r on t are "matched" by word n. Section 4 presents the definition of matching for different thematic roles and restrictions. A $\mathcal{P}$-parse structure is *semantically coherent* if its edge annotated by PREP-POBJ is justified by some selectional construct triggered by the words occurring in a $\mathcal{P}$-parse structure.

For example, $\mathcal{P}$-phrase (1) triggers the selectional construct

$$(eat, \text{INSTRUMENT}, concrete, \{with\}). \tag{6}$$

Intuitively, this construct justifies the PREP-POBJ edge between $spaghetti$ and $chopsticks$. $\mathcal{P}$-parse of the form (4) is thus semantically coherent.

We can view selectional restrictions as conditions that must be satisfied in the process of parsing. In other words, semantically coherent parse structures are the ones that satisfy these conditions. It is clear that at times more than one parse structure is semantically coherent for a phrase. Similarly, more than one selectional construct may justify a PREP-POBJ edge.

4 PP-attachment Selection Algorithm

The dataset by Ratnaparkhi et al. (1994) is often used to devise and evaluate PP-attachment resolution systems. We use it in this work also. For the rest of the paper we refer to the Ratnaparkhi et al. dataset as $\mathcal{R}$. The $\mathcal{R}$ dataset is a collection of $\mathcal{P}$-phrases stemming from Penn Treebank. Each data entry in $\mathcal{R}$ is a tuple of the form

$$(verb,\ noun_1,\ prep,\ noun_2). \tag{7}$$

Intuitively, each tuple corresponds to a $\mathcal{P}$-phrase. Figure 1 presents the basic statistics on ten most occurring prepositions in the dataset. The second row titled *Total* gives the number of tuples contained in $\mathcal{R}$ that mention the respective preposition. The third row presents the ratio of the number of occurrences of a preposition (the second row) over the size of the $\mathcal{R}$ dataset. Overall $\mathcal{R}$ contains 23898 $\mathcal{P}$-phrases. The last row represents the frequencies of the verb attachment for the respective prepositions. We note how by far the most frequent preposition of is also very bias in a sense that 99% of the time it triggers the attachment to a noun. This is why we present the column named *All-of* that gives the statistics for all tuples that do not contain the preposition of.

Machine learning methods are commonly used for implementing decision/classification procedures called classifiers. In supervised learning, the classifier is first trained on a set of labeled data (training data) that is representative of the domain of interest. Typically labeled data consists of pairs of

Preposition	All	All - of	of	in	to	for	on	from	with	at	as	by
Total	23898	17395	6503	3973	3005	2522	1421	1059	1049	780	564	526
% of $\mathcal{R}$	100	72.8	27.2	16.6	12.6	10.6	5.9	4.4	4.4	3.3	2.4	2.2
% Verb Attachment	46.9	64.2	0.9	54.6	80.1	51.2	53.8	68.6	64.4	80.4	81.2	72.2

Figure 1: Basic statistics on the Ratnaparkhi et al. (1994) dataset.

input objects and a desired output. An input object is often summarized by so called feature vector. A classifier of choice analyzes the training data and produces a model that can be used to evaluate unlabeled input objects. In this work we rely on Logistic Regression classification algorithm as the vehicle for implementing the decision procedure for the PP-attachment selection problem. To implement this procedure we used the Logistic Regression classifier with a ridge estimator of 10^{-7} available in Weka[2] (Hall et al., 2009) – software by University of Waikato which contains tools for data preprocessing, classification, and clustering. We call our system PPATTACH, which is available at `http://www.unomaha.edu/nlpkr/software/ppattach/`.

In our settings we used the $\mathcal{R}$ dataset to produce training data. Each $\mathcal{P}$-phrase (7) in $\mathcal{R}$ is mapped to a feature vector composed of five elements:

- the preposition $prep$ of the tuple (7);
- the VERBNET verb class of the $verb$ in (7). If the verb class is unavailable in VERBNET then lemmatized $verb$ serves the role of a feature itself. We call this feature *Verbclass*;
- Features named VERBNET$[noun_1, noun_2]$, VERBNET$[noun_2]$, and *Nominalization*, which encode information that some selectional constructs stemming from VERBNET are "applicable" to the tuple (7).

We now speak about the rationale behind choosing these features. Figure 1 clearly indicates that prepositions are bias to one or another attachment decision. Lapata and Keller (2005) present a generic baseline for the prepositional phrase attachment decision by choosing noun attachment in all cases, which achieves correct attachment 56.9% of the time. They further present that this baseline can be improved simply by choosing the most likely attachment decision for each preposition reaching 72.2% accuracy. These observations provide strong evidence for the necessity of the first feature. As discussed verbs impose selectional restrictions. The second feature in combination with the first one allows us to use the $\mathcal{R}$ dataset to collect the statistical information about verb classes and their usage. The last three features are based on the information stemming from VERBNET. These features allow us to incorporate explicit information on selectional restrictions available in VERBNET into the decision procedure for the PP-attachment selection problem. We now proceed towards the description of how these three VERBNET-based features are computed.

To describe the computation of the VERBNET-based features precisely, we define a concept of matching. We say that a noun *matches* a thematic role (a restriction) listed in Figure 2 if one of its WORDNET senses has a path in WORDNET justified by the ISA links to a corresponding lexical concept depicted in Figure 2. We also say that a noun *matches* the thematic role INSTRUMENT if the definition (gloss) of one of the noun's WORDNET senses contains a string "used". Likewise, we establish a *match* with the restriction $pointy$ by finding the string, "sharp" within the definition for one of the noun's senses. Accounting for parts of word's definition stems from the work by Jensen and Binot (1987). Figure 2 contains all 23 thematic roles of the VERBNET dataset.

Descriptions of the computation procedures of VERBNET-based features follow. Each procedure is given a tuple of the form (7) as its input. These features are binary, their default values are 0.

Feature VERBNET$[noun_1, noun_2]$: We start by searching for all verb-classes that include $verb$ from tuple (7). Frame syntax structures of the form

$$\texttt{THEMROLE verb THEMROLE}_{1\,restriction_1}\ \{\texttt{prep}\}\ \texttt{THEMROLE}_{2\,restriction_2} \quad (8)$$

[2] `http://www.cs.waikato.ac.nz/ml/weka/`

Thematic Role	WORDNET Concept
THEME, PATIENT, RECIPIENT, OBLIQUE, DESTINATION, EXPERIENCER, SOURCE, BENEFICIARY, AGENT, PRODUCT, MATERIAL, TOPIC, PREDICATE, ASSET, EXTENT, PROPOSITION, CAUSE, VALUE	entity.n.01
ACTOR	causal_agent.n.01
LOCATION	location.n.01, location.n.03
INSTRUMENT	instrumentality.n.03, act.n.02, communication.n.02, body_part.n.01
ATTRIBUTE	attribute.n.02
STIMULUS	stimulation.n.02

Restriction	WORDNET Concept
abstract	abstraction.n.06
communication	communication.n.02
body_part	body_part.n.01
force	entity.n.01
pointy, concrete, refl, solid	physical_entity.n.01
organization	group.n.01
region	region.n.01

Restriction	WORDNET Concept
location	location.n.01, location.n.03
animal	animal.n.01
animate	causal_agent.n.01, living_thing.n.01
currency	currency.n.01
machine	machine.n.01
scalar	scalar.n.01
comestible	comestible.n.01

Figure 2: WORDNET ISA-Parent

are extracted from these classes. Frame syntax (8) translates into selectional constructs that include

$$(verb, \text{THEMROLE}_1, restriction_1, \emptyset) \tag{9}$$
$$(verb, \text{THEMROLE}_2, restriction_2, \{prep\}) \tag{10}$$

For each frame syntax, we (i) verify whether $noun_1$ matches the thematic role THEMROLE$_1$ as well as the restriction $restriction_1$, which suggests that selectional construct (9) justifies an edge between $verb$ and $noun_1$, and (ii) verify whether $noun_2$ matches THEMROLE$_2$ as well as $restriction_2$, which suggests that selectional construct (10) justifies a PREP-POBJ edge between $verb$ and $noun_2$. If this test is positive for at least one frame syntax we assign value VERB to the feature VERBNET$[noun_1, noun_2]$.

Feature VERBNET$[noun_2]$: This procedure is similar to the previous method. Frame syntax structures of the form

$$\text{THEMROLE v } \{\text{prep}\} \text{ THEMROLE}_{2\,restriction_2} \tag{11}$$

are extracted from the verb-classes in VERBNET that include $verb$ from tuple (7). The frame syntax (11) translates into selectional constructs that include restriction (10). We then verify whether $noun_2$ matches THEMROLE$_2$ as well as $restriction_2$, which suggests that selectional construct (10) justifies an edge between $verb$ and $noun_2$. Subsequently we assign value VERB to the feature VERBNET$[noun_2]$.

Feature *Nominalization*: *Nominalization* is the use of a verb, an adjective, or an adverb as a noun, with or without morphological transformation. In this work, we are especially interested in nouns derived from verbs. Such nouns typically behave as nouns grammatically, yet semantically they carry information of a respective verb. For example, a noun "conversation" is derived from a verb "to converse", which informally suggests at least two participants in the event of conversation. Given tuple (7), the *Nominalization* method starts by identifying whether $noun_1$ is derived from a verb. The WORDNET lexicon contains edges between nouns and verbs that are called *derivationally related forms*. We search WORDNET for connections via these edges between $noun_1$ and some verb. We require that the root word remains the same between $noun_1$ and a found verb. If such verb exists we consider $noun_1$ to be a nominalization. If $noun_1$ is derived from some verb, the VERBNET lexicon is searched for all verb-classes that include this verb. Frame syntax structures of the form (11) are extracted. We then verify whether $noun_2$ matches THEMROLE$_2$ as well as $restriction_2$, which suggests that selectional construct (10) justifies a NOUN assignment for the feature.

5 Evaluation

We use various metrics to gauge the overall performance of the PPATTACH system. First we consider a baseline which consists of the most likely attachment on a per preposition basis. We also construct a PPATTACH- system by dropping the *Verbclass* feature from PPATTACH. We construct a GENERIC system by dropping the VERBNET-based features from the PPATTACH system.

We train and test each system on the whole $\mathcal{R}$ dataset and subsets of $\mathcal{R}$ on a preposition-by-preposition basis. Given that each resultant dataset is of limited size (see the second row in Figure 1), we use 10-fold cross-validation to evaluate the methods. The cross-validation was done in Weka. The main idea is to randomly select instances that constitute the test set. Subsequently we train a classifier on the remaining instances and evaluate the model on the selected test set. This is conducted ten times (with different test-training set pairs). Figure 3 summarizes the classification accuracy (the number of correct classifications over the number of classifications) of the system using Logistic Regression classifier.

Preposition	All	All - of	of	in	to	for	on	from	with	at	as	by
Baseline	74.6	65.4	99.1	54.6	80.1	51.2	53.8	68.6	64.4	80.4	81.2	72.2
PPATTACH-	79.3	72.7	99.0	64.6	87.8	66.6	68.5	75.5	70.9	81.8	79.8	80.0
GENERIC	79.0	72.3	99.0	64.7	87.8	67.0	68.2	76.3	69.7	82.9	79.8	82.3
PPATTACH	79.3	72.5	99.0	64.7	88.0	66.9	69.6	75.4	70.7	81.9	78.5	81.7

Figure 3: Evaluation Data on PPATTACH using Logistic Regression.

We see substantial improvements from Baseline across most prepositions. Figure 4 presents data that can be used to explain this. For each VERBNET-based feature, this figure presents two rows. The row named *Recall* gives a percentage that describes the frequency at which the feature is assigned a value different from default; the row named *Precision* gives a percentage of relevant instances such that the feature assignment agrees with the correct attachment decision. For six out of ten prepositions the precision for the VERBNET$[noun_1, noun_2]$ feature is at least 83.6%. For five out of these prepositions the recall ranges from 10.3% to 37.6%. There are two prepositions at and as that have high precision, yet the performance of PPATTACH is comparable to that of Baseline. We also find that in this case the verb class does not play a role in improving the classification accuracy (Baseline and GENERIC behave practically identical). Figure 1 illustrates that the prepositions at and as have strong attachment bias for verb. Most of the features in PPATTACH also favor such attachment. Gaining evidence for the other decision shall improve the situation.

VERBNET-based features		of	in	to	for	on	from	with	at	as	by
VERBNET$[noun_1, noun_2]$	Recall	4.1	12.9	37.6	25.5	9.4	25.3	15.7	10.3	22.3	0.8
	Precision	6.0	66.0	91.5	59.6	71.6	83.6	92.7	93.8	98.4	100.0
VERBNET$[noun_2]$	Recall	1.2	7.5	27.5	3.8	10.6	7.0	9.2	1.7	0.0	5.5
	Precision	0.0	59.8	89.7	60.4	85.3	82.4	88.5	100	N/A	96.6
Nominalization	Recall	1.5	12.8	9.8	3.9	3.7	2.8	10.3	0.3	0.0	1.0
	Precision	100.0	70.2	27.8	66.3	64.2	56.7	66.7	50.0	N/A	60.0

Figure 4: Features Evaluation for PPATTACH.

We now note on the difference that changing the classification algorithm can make to PPATTACH performance. Figure 5 summarizes the classification accuracy of PPATTACH using the Naïve Bayes classifier of Weka. In this case, PPATTACH- markedly lags behind GENERIC and PPATTACH, indicating the importance of the classification algorithm selection.

The PPATTACH system lags behind its peers (see Introduction). The top performing system for disambiguating prepositional attachment on $\mathcal{R}$ by Stetina and Nagao (1997) reported in (Lapata and Keller, 2005) incorporates manual word sense disambiguation. Also, let us take a closer look at several samples from $\mathcal{R}$. Consider tuples $(held, talks, with, parties)$ and $(establish, relation, with, institution)$.

They were annotated in Penn Treebank as having verb attachment suggesting errors in this corpus[3].

Preposition	All	All - of	of	in	to	for	on	from	with	at	as	by
PPATTACH-	74.5	67.7	99.1	59.8	80.1	54.5	57.0	69.2	67.9	80.3	81.2	71.9
GENERIC	79.0	71.3	99.1	64.5	86.2	66.5	68.3	76.1	69.9	80.4	81.0	80.0
PPATTACH	78.9	71.2	99.1	65.3	87.9	66.5	68.5	76.5	72.8	80.5	81.0	80.0

Figure 5: Evaluation Data on PPATTACH using Naïve Bayes.

6 Beyond VERBNET: Preposition *with* Case-Study

This section focuses on a specific preposition, *with*. We investigate whether and how *with*-specific features improve classification accuracy. We start by noting that VERBNET often omits information. Consider sentence (1). There is nothing in VERBNET that suggests the selectional construct (6). This construct is intuitively triggered by the preposition *with* itself. Indeed, there are three main uses of *with*: *instrumental*, *adverbial*, and *comitative*. The instrumental use of *with* indicates that the prepositional phrase conveys details in which the object serves the role of an instrument while executing the action suggested by the verb. Phrase (1) illustrates the instrumental use of *with*. In contrast, the phrase *eat spaghetti with enthusiasm* illustrates an adverbial use of *with*. Here, the prepositional phrase answers the question of *how* the action was undertaken. To accommodate for common instrumental and adverbial uses of *with* we propose the following generic selectional constructs

$$(v, \text{INSTRUMENT}, \textit{concrete}, \{\textit{with}\}) \tag{12}$$

$$(v, \text{MANNER}, \emptyset, \{\textit{with}\}), \tag{13}$$

where v is a variable that can be substituted by *any* verb including *eat* or *hit*.

The grammatical case *comitative* denotes accompaniment. In English this case is often realized by *with* and captures the sense of *together with* or *in company with*. Expressions *spaghetti with meatballs* and *boat with an engine* illustrate the comitative case. In the former example, words *spaghetti* and *meatballs* are closely *related* to each other as they both denote food entities. In the later example, *boat* and *engine* are in lexical relation meronymy. We propose two selectional constructs that account for such examples

$$(w, \text{COMPANION}, \textit{related}(w), \{\textit{with}\}) \tag{14}$$

$$(w, \text{COMPANION}, \textit{meronym}(w), \{\textit{with}\}) \tag{15}$$

where w is a variable that can be substituted by *any* word, e.g., *spaghetti* or *boat*; *related*(w) stands for any word w' such that w and w' are related (according to a certain metric); *meronym*(w) stands for any word w' such that w' is a meronym of w.

In describing selectional constructs (14) and (15) we identified the need not only for a metric to establish relatedness between words, but also for a wide-coverage meronym relation database. The WORDNET lexicon records meronymy relations between synonym sets. However, it is not flawless and questions arise when attempting automatic methods for identifying meronymy. For example, in WORDNET *arm* is listed as a direct meronym of *human*, but *leg* is not. Thus to identify that *leg* is a meronym of *human*, deeper mining of WORDNET becomes a necessity. Later in this section we describe an algorithm that we devised for this purpose. To establish relatedness between words we rely on WORDNET and the metric developed by Leacock and Chodorow (1998).

Below we present features that capture the aforementioned reasoning as well as several other observations. We use these features to augment the PPATTACH system to construct the system PPATTACH+.

[3] *Held talks* represents the case of light verb construction; *establish* is an aspectual verb: both cases hint a noun attachment.

Feature *Instrumentality*: This method accounts for "instrument" selectional construct (12). We verify whether $noun_2$ matches the thematic role INSTRUMENT, which suggests that selectional construct (12) justifies an edge between $verb$ and $noun_2$. We assign VERB to the feature.

Feature *Adverbial Use*: We proposed to characterize an adverbial use of $with$ by selectional construct (13). We say that a noun *matches* the thematic role MANNER if there exists an adverbial derivation from a noun to some verb in WORDNET. The "derivationally related forms" edges of WORDNET are used to establish an adverbial derivation. If $noun_2$ in the given tuple (7) matches the thematic role MANNER then selectional construct (13) justifies an edge between $verb$ and $noun_2$. We assign VERB to the feature.

Feature *Similarity*: This procedure accounts for "related" selectional construct (14). We verify whether $noun_1$ and $noun_2$ of the given tuple (7) are related using the Leacock-Chodorow algorithm (1998).If the value produced by the Leacock-Chodorow procedure exceeds 2, we assume that the nouns are related. This translates into the fact that selectional construct (12) justifies an edge between $noun_1$ and $noun_2$. We assign a value NOUN to the feature.

Feature *Meronymy*: This procedure accounts for "meronymy" selectional construct (15). For a given tuple (7), we verify whether $noun_2$ is a meronym of $noun_1$ using a WORDNET-based method that we propose. First, we take the $noun_1$ and construct a set containing its full hypernymy and hyponymy tree for all of its WORDNET synsets. Second, we construct a set consisting of the full hyponymy for $noun_2$ for all of its WORDNET synsets. If an element from the set for $noun_2$ is a meronym, as defined by WORDNET, of an element in the set for $noun_1$, then we conclude that $noun_2$ is a meronym of $noun_1$. If the meronymy selectional construct justifies an edge between $noun_1$ and $noun_2$, the feature is assigned NOUN.

Feature *Relational Noun*: Phrases such as $developed\ a\ relationship\ with\ people$ contain a relational noun $relationship$. Relational nouns suggest that there is a possessive relation between "individuals" participating in an utterance. To accommodate for relational nouns we propose the following generic selectional construct $(n, \text{POSSESSOR}, \emptyset, \{with\})$, where n is a relational noun. Given tuple (7), the *Relational Noun* method identifies whether $noun_1$ is a relational noun by observing if one of its WORDNET senses has a path justified by the ISA links in WORDNET to a lexical concept *relation*. Currently, we assume that any noun matches the thematic role POSSESSOR. We assign the feature NOUN if we establish that $noun_1$ is relational.

Feature *Idiom*: Some verb/noun combinations represent an idiomatic use, such as "make hay". The WORDNET lexicon contains entries representing idioms. We verify whether $verb$ and $noun_1$ of the given tuple (7) form an idiom by means of WORDNET. If this is the case, we assign VERB to the feature.

We analyzed performance of each described feature. Figure 6 presents the data in a similar fashion as Figure 4. On the left, we list higher precision features. We note the high recall of *Instrumentality* and rather reliable precision. This is a positive indication that we may address the limitations encountered for VERBNET and to generally improve classification. On the right, we list the lower precision features. The "right" results suggest that the ways to refine algorithms for implementing low-precision features should be sought out. Also, it is possible that the semantic information carried by the verb outweighs the information available from *Similarity* and *Meronymy*. In the future we plan to investigate these possibilities. The classification accuracy of the PPATTACH+ system is 71.2% for $with$. Due to the

Instrumentality	Recall	48.0
	Precision	70.6
Relational Noun	Recall	5.8
	Precision	75.4
Adverbial Use	Recall	2.3
	Precision	75.0

Similarity	Recall	15.7
	Precision	38.8
Meronymy	Recall	3.1
	Precision	48.5
Idiom	Recall	1.6
	Precision	35.3

Figure 6: Features Evaluation for PPATTACH+.

poor precision we witnessed for the "right" features, we retested the PPATTACH+ after removing these features. We subsequently achieve a classification accuracy of 72.0%, outperforming the PPATTACH accuracy of 70.7%. Overall, the results appear to be promising, suggesting that preposition-specific selectional constructs will lead to better classification as a whole.

7 Discussion and Future Work

In this work we proposed a principled method for incorporating wide-coverage lexical resources VERBNET and WORDNET into decision making for the task of resolving prepositional phrase attachment. Our preliminary system PPATTACH illustrates the feasibility and promise of the approach.

The proposed method relies on a number of features that are suggestive of why a particular attachment is reasonable. For instance, consider the feature *Instrumentality*. In cases when the value of this feature is VERB, we are urged to believe that the second noun of a given $\mathcal{P}$-phrase tuple can be labeled as an instrument of the action indicated by the verb of the tuple (following from the fact that the "instrument" selectional construct is applicable to this $\mathcal{P}$-phrase tuple). A long-term goal of this project is to incorporate elements of the proposed decision procedure into modern parsing technology and, in particular, into semantic role labeling methods. Work by Zhou et al. (2011), Srikumar and Roth (2013), Agirre et al. (2008, 2011), and Belinkov et al. (2014) encourages research in this direction.

As we continue development of this project, we hope to improve the presented method in several ways. We will use WORDNET to a greater extent to determine selectional restrictions on nouns. For example, the current method does not draw any distinction between AGENT and ASSET. We also intend to incorporate a semantic ontology called NOMLEX (Macleod et al., 1998) that incorporated noun-based selectional restrictions. Figure 1 illustrates that all but one preposition *of* prefer verb attachment. Most of the features we investigated also favor such attachment. Gaining evidence for the other decision will be helpful. We illustrated how we improve on preposition *with* by augmenting available lexico-semantic ontologies with knowledge specific to this preposition. We will pursue similar effort for other prepositions in the future. We also intend to go beyond the development and evaluation geared by the $\mathcal{R}$ dataset. Our discussion in the Evaluation section suggests such necessity.

Acknowledgments

Thanks to A. Artsymenia, J. Beavers, C. Bonial, M. Chernyshevich, S. Erdogan, A. Harrison, V. Lifschitz, J. Michael, M. Palmer, D. Postanogov, P. Schüller, Q. Zhu, and the anonymous reviewers for useful discussions and comments. Daniel Bailey was supported by a FIRE-2013: Fund for Investing in the Research Enterprise Grant of the University of Nebraska. Ben Susman was partially supported by FIRE-2013.

References

Agirre, E., T. Baldwin, and D. Martínez (2008). Improving parsing and pp attachment performance with sense information. In *46th Annual Meeting of the Association for Computational Linguistics (ACL)*, pp. 317–325.

Agirre, E., K. Bengoetxea, K. Gojenola, and J. Nivre (2011). Improving dependency parsing with semantic classes. In *49th Annual Meeting of the Association for Computational Linguistics (ACL, Short Papers)*, pp. 699–703.

Allen, J. (1995). *Natural Language Understanding (2Nd Ed.)*. Redwood City, CA, USA: Benjamin-Cummings Publishing Co., Inc.

Belinkov, Y., T. Lei, R. Barzilay, and A. Globerson (2014). Exploring Compositional Architectures and Word Vector Representations for Prepositional Phrase Attachment. *Transactions of the Association for Computational Linguistics 2*, 561–572.

Brill, E. and P. Resnik (1994). A rule-based approach to prepositional phrase attachment disambiguation. In *15th conference on Computational linguistics-Volume 2*, pp. 1198–1204.

Budanitsky, A. and G. Hirst (2006, March). Evaluating wordnet-based measures of lexical semantic relatedness. *Computional Linguistics 32*(1), 13–47.

Collins, M. and J. Brooks (1995). Prepositional phrase attachment through a backed-off model. In *Proceedings of the Third Workshop on Very Large Corpora*, pp. 27–38.

Dahlgren, K. (1988). *Naive Semantics for Natural Language Understanding*. Norwell, MA, USA: Kluwer Academic Publishers.

Ford, Bresnan, K. (1982). A competence-based theory of syntatic closure. In Bresnan (Ed.), *The Mental Representation of Grammatical Relations*, pp. 727–796. The MIT Press.

Hall, M., E. Frank, G. Holmes, B. Pfahringer, P. Reutemann, and I. H. Witten (2009, November). The weka data mining software: An update. *SIGKDD Explor. Newsl. 11*(1), 10–18.

Hirst, G. (1988, March). Semantic interpretation and ambiguity. *Artificial intelligence 34*(2), 131–177.

Jensen, K. and J.-L. Binot (1987). Disambiguating prepositional phrase attachments by using on-line dictionary definitions. *Computational Linguistics 13*(3-4), 251–260.

Katz, J. J. and J. A. Fodor (1963). The structure of a semantic theory. *Language 39*(2), pp. 170–210.

Kipper, K., H. T. Dang, and M. Palmer (2000). Class-based construction of a verb lexicon. In *7th National Conference on Artificial Intelligence and Twelfth Conference on Innovative Applications of Artificial Intelligence*, pp. 691–696. AAAI Press / The MIT Press.

Kipper-Schuler, K. (2005). *VerbNet: A Broad-Coverage, Comprehensive Verb Lexicon*. Ph. D. thesis, University of Pennsylvania.

Lapata, M. and F. Keller (2005). Web-based models for natural language processing. *ACM Transactions on Speech and Language Processing (TSLP) 2*(1), 3.

Leacock, C. and M. Chodorow (1998). Combining local context and wordnet similarity for word sense identification. In C. Fellbaum (Ed.), *WordNet: An Electronic Lexical Database*, Cambridge, MA, USA, pp. 265–283. The MIT Press.

Levin, B. (1993). *English verb classes and alternations : a preliminary investigation*. University Of Chicago Press.

Lierler, Y. and P. Schüller (2013). Towards a tight integration of syntactic parsing with semantic disambiguation by means of declarative programming. In *10th International Conference on Computational Semantics (IWCS)*.

Macleod, C., R. Grishman, A. Meyers, L. Barrett, and R. Reeves (1998). Nomlex: A lexicon of nominalizations. *Proceedings og EURALEX 98*, 187–193.

Miller, G. A., R. Beckwith, C. Fellbaum, D. Gross, and K. Miller (1990). Wordnet: An on-line lexical database. *International Journal of Lexicography 3*, 235–244.

Pantel, P. and D. Lin (2000). An unsupervised approach to prepositional phrase attachment using contextually similar words. In *38th Annual Meeting on Association for Computational Linguistics (ACL)*, Stroudsburg, PA, USA, pp. 101–108.

Ratnaparkhi, A. (1998). Statistical models for unsupervised prepositional phrase attachment. In *36th Annual Meeting of the Association for Computational Linguistics and 17th International Conference on Computational Linguistics - Volume 2 (ACL)*, Stroudsburg, PA, USA, pp. 1079–1085.

Ratnaparkhi, A., J. Reynar, and S. Roukos (1994). A maximum entropy model for prepositional phrase attachment. In *Workshop on Human Language Technology*, pp. 250–255.

Srikumar, V. and D. Roth (2013). Modeling semantic relations expressed by prepositions. *TACL 1*, 231–242.

Stetina, J. and M. Nagao (1997). Corpus based pp attachment ambiguity resolution with a semantic dictionary. In *5th Workshop pn Very Large Corpora*, pp. 66–80.

Zapirain, B., E. Agirre, L. Màrquez, and M. Surdeanu (2013). Selectional preferences for semantic role classification. *Computational Linguistics 39*(3), 631–663.

Zavrel, J., W. Daelemans, J. Veenstra, et al. (1997). Resolving PP attachment ambiguities with memory-based learning. In *Workshop on Computational Language Learning (CoNLL'97), ACL, Madrid*.

Zhou, G., J. Zhao, K. Liu, and L. Cai (2011). Exploiting web-derived selectional preference to improve statistical dependency parsing. In *49th Annual Meeting of the Association for Computational Linguistics (ACL)*, pp. 1556–1565.

From Adjective Glosses to Attribute Concepts: Learning Different Aspects That an Adjective Can Describe

Omid Bakhshandeh[1] and James F. Allen[1,2]

[1]Computer Science Department, University of Rochester, Rochester, New York
[2]Institute for Human and Machine Cognition, Pensacola, Florida ,
omidb@cs.rochester.edu, james@cs.rochester.edu

Abstract

Adjectives are one of the major contributors to conveying subjective meaning to sentences. Understanding the semantics of adjectives is essential for understanding natural language sentences. In this paper we propose a novel approach for learning different properties that an adjective can describe, corresponding to the 'attribute concepts', which is not currently available in existing linguistic resources. We accomplish this by reading adjective glosses and bootstrapping attribute concepts from a seed of adjectives. We show that we can learn new attribute concepts using adjective glosses of WordNet adjectives with high accuracy as compared with human annotation on a test set.

1 Introduction

Adjectives have not been studied in lexical semantics as much as verbs and nouns. However, they have a very interesting polymorphic behavior in adding subtle meaning to a sentence. The main function of adjectives is the modification of words, such as nouns, by describing some properties of them. For instance, the adjective *fast* in the sentence 'a fast car' is describing the *speed* property of a car. Another example is the adjective *tall* in the sentence 'he is tall' which describes the 'stature' property of someone. Adjectives can describe a different value for the same property. For instance, *large* and *small* each describe the 'size' property of something. Such properties can be associated with an abstract scale, on which some adjectives are ordered by their semantic intensity. Generally, is it possible for an entity to have a quality which lies somewhere in the middle of a scale associated with a property. For instance, assuming a scale for size, it is possible to grade new adjectives so that they describe some new spot on the size scale. Such adjectives are called 'gradable adjectives'. We generally determine whether an adjective is gradable by deciding whether or not graded usages with comparative modifiers (more, less, etc) is possible for it (Rusiecki, 1985). Gradable adjectives imply the existence of an underlying semantic scale (pertaining to a property). It has been argued that gradable adjectives denote functions from objects to intervals or points on a scale (Kennedy, 1999).

Not all adjectives are intended to be interpreted in a gradable sense. A famous example of the class of non-gradable adjectives is the set of color adjectives such as *red*. It is argued that when someone says 'His tie is red' it would scarcely make sense to follow up with the question 'how red is the tie?' (Young, 1984). However, we can all understand gradable usages of 'red' in sentences such as 'the reddest I have ever seen', which is because 'red' is being used as a quality adjective (Young, 1984). Many of the classic non-gradable adjectives can be seen to be used with degree-modifiers and comparatives or superlatives in various contexts, such as 'This dog is the wildest'. By observing such adjectives deeper, one can see that there are some adjectives which specifically define a property, but that property does not really have other adjectives related to it. For instance, the adjective 'intermural' which means 'between two or more institutions' can be associated with 'institution' property, as one can say 'some organization is more intermural than the other'. However, there are no other adjectives talking about 'institution' property.

Proceedings of the 11th International Conference on Computational Semantics, pages 23–33,
London, UK, April 15-17 2015.

Another example is the adjective *feminine*, which modifies the 'femininity' property, as someone can say 'someone is more feminine than the other'.In language understanding knowing the underlying properties being modified by the adjective in a gradable sense is useful, so we try to come up with a property denoting attribute concept for all of the adjectives in general. We use 'attribute identification' to refer to the task of assigning a set of "attribute concepts" to an adjective. Hence, in the earlier examples, 'size' is the attribute concept of 'large/small/tiny', and 'institution' is the attribute concept of the 'intermural' adjective. Furthermore, there are adjectives that modify more than one property of an entity. For instance, the adjective *gangling* means "tall and thin and having long slender limbs". It is evident from the meaning that *gangling* can modify the noun it is describing with respect to two different properties: 'height' and 'thickness'. Another example is the adjective 'squab' which means 'short and fat' which again describes two distinct properties. Hence, the set of attribute concepts for both 'gangling' and 'squab' is {height, thickness}.

Determining the attribute concepts of adjectives can improve our understanding of the natural language sentences. For instance, consider a sentence such as 'The tap water here is lukewarm, but it is usually freezing uptown'. By having the knowledge of attributes and scales, one can have ordering of adjectives regarding their intensities, and then can understand how different the temperature property of tap water is in uptown. In general, learning the set of attribute concepts and associating adjectives to them is a pre-requisite for ordering adjectives and their polarity magnitude on scales. Moreover, having attribute concepts, one can disambiguate among various senses of an adjective such as *hot* in the sentence 'our debate is so boring, but this topic is hot.', by knowing that two adjectives usually pertain to the same attribute concept in order to be comparable.

Existing linguistic resources (dictionaries, WordNet (Miller, 1995), and thesauri) rarely contain information on adjectives being part of a scale, relating to an attribute concept, or being of a particular strength. In this paper, we present a novel approach for finding all the attribute concepts including scales that an adjective synset (here in WordNet 3.0) is graded on. Our approach is based on reading adjective glosses and bootstrapping attribute concepts from a seed of adjectives. Our approach builds on the fact that there are redundant syntactic and semantic patterns in definitions of words which enables bootstrapping (Yarowsky, 1995).To our knowledge, none of the earlier works have attempted to find more than one scale that an adjective can describe. In Section 4 we show that we can learn attribute concepts using adjective glosses with high accuracy as compared with human annotation on a sub-set of adjectives. Moreover, none of the earlier approaches have had as good coverage as our method, which is about 77% of WordNet adjectives. Last but not least, our bootstrapping algorithm can be generally employed in learning any kind of property from definitional texts for different parts of speech, not only adjectives. We focus on adjectives as property-denoting lexical entities, since they are valuable for acquiring concept representations for areas such as ontology learning. The result of this work can lead towards describing the semantics of adjectives contained in as part of a larger effort to develop new techniques for automatically acquiring deep lexical knowledge for capturing knowledge about concepts.

2 Adjectives in WordNet

The semantic organization of adjectives in the WordNet is not similar to the organization of nouns and verbs, as adjectives do not show a hierarchical organization (Mendes, 2006). In general, adjectives in WordNet are divided into *descriptive* and *relational* classes. Descriptive adjectives are the ones that ascribe a value of an attribute to a noun, i.e, they describe a property of a noun they modify. WordNet has links between some of the descriptive adjectives expressing a value of an attribute and the noun with which that attribute is lexicalized. For example, the adjective 'tall' is linked to the noun attribute 'stature'.

Among all 18,156 adjective synsets in WordNet, only about 620 of them have the attribute link. Instead of the hypernymic relation that is used among nouns, the main relation used for descriptive adjectives is antonymy. Binary opposition of adjectives, which shows contrary values of an attribute, is represented by pointers with the meaning of 'IS-ANTONIMOUS-TO'. For adjectives that do not seem

Class	Total in WordNet	Examples
Descriptive (head of dumbbell structures, with attribute links)	620	tall, warm, beautiful, heavy
Descriptive (similar to a head of a dumbbell, with indirect attribute links)	3,541	damp, scorching, lukewarm, massive
Descriptive (have antonyms, but no attribute links)	3,226	cheap, poor, dry, valuable
Relational (no direct or indirect antonym)	4,951	oxidized, racial, rat-like, beaten

Table 1: Statistics of different classes of adjectives in WordNet

to have a direct antonym, WordNet has a pointer with the meaning of 'IS-SIMILAR-TO' which points to an adjective which is similar in meaning, through which an indirect antonym is inherited. For example, wet and dry are direct antonyms and an indirect antonymic pointer exists between damp and dry since damp is similar to wet. WordNet encodes such structures in the form of clusters (adjective-sets), which are often called *dumbbells* or satellites. In dumbbells two antonymous synsets (head-words) are linked to a noun which they describe (attribute) and each head-word is linked to its similar adjectives. Dumbbells seemed well motivated psycho-linguistically and distributionally, but they are not sufficiently informative for detecting and quantifying meaning similarities among adjectives. For instance, there is no specific semantic distinction between all the similar-to links of a particular head-word, i.e., they are all treated in the same way. Moreover, only 3,541 adjectives are encoded in dumbbell structure, which is a limited coverage on all adjectives. There are 3,226 descriptive adjectives in WordNet which have antonyms and inherently ascribe a value to an attribute, but are not linked to any attributive nouns, e.g. 'cheap' and 'expensive', none of which has an attribute link in WordNet. Our main goal in this paper is to expand the set of attribute concepts to all WordNet adjectives, proposing a methodology for high coverage attribute learning. As will be explained in Section 4, our approach covers about 14,104 adjectives (77%) on average.

Relational adjectives (pertainyms) are the ones that do not have an antonym and are related by derivation to specific nouns. If an adjective does not have a direct or indirect antonym, then it is relational and it has a pointer to the noun it relates to, i.e., is derived from. Relational adjectives are mostly known not to be gradable (Mendes, 2006), e.g., *atomic*, however, there are relational adjectives which pass the linguistic test for gradability, such as 'nutritional'. We apply our approach to relational adjectives as well, and try to find a property-defining attribute concept for them. The results of this experiment can be found in section 4. Table 1 summarizes some statistics on adjectives in WordNet. The sum of total adjectives in this table is larger than 18,156, which is due to the intersection between adjectives with pertainym link and descriptive adjectives with no direct or indirect attribute link.

3 The Approach

Glosses, as a short meaning explanations for words, provide a rich pieces of information about the words they describe. In this paper, we present our novel approach on using WordNet glosses for understanding the semantics of adjectives, specifically the properties they can describe. As mentioned earlier, we aim to identify all the attribute concepts (including scales) that an adjective can be associated with. We propose a semi-supervised method for learning attribute concepts. The idea is to use the already encoded attribute links of 620 adjectives in WordNet as the initial seed and bootstrap attribute concept of the rest of adjectives by learning patterns. The high-level iterative bootstrapping algorithm is described in the Algorithm 1. In the upcoming subsections we will describe each phase of this algorithm in detail.

Algorithm 1 Algorithm for learning attribute concepts

Require: set J = All adjectives
set Θ^T = Features in iteration T
set S = Seed adjectives with known attributes
set X_j = Candidate attributes for adjective j

// Pre-processing and Candidate Attribute Extraction
for adjective *j* in *J* **do**
  Process *j*'s gloss, and get back its link-augmented-dependency tree (LAD)
  Process *j*'s gloss, and get back its set of candidate attributes, X_j
end for
while not converged **do**
  //Feature Extraction and Model Training
  Θ^t = Extract features from S
  Train a classifier F, using features Θ^t
  //Decoding and Updating the Seed
  for adjective $j \in J$ and $j \notin S$ **do**
    Using F, tag all candidates attributes in *j*
    if Any of the candidates is tagged as 'attribute' **then**
      add *j* to S
    end if
  end for
end while

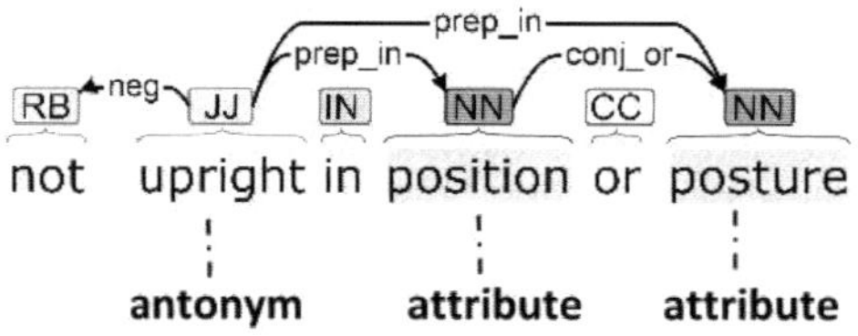

Figure 1: The link-augmented graph of the gloss of the adjective 'unerect'

3.1 Pre-processing

For each adjective we should process its gloss first. The idea is to enrich the dependency structure of the gloss with the semantic links. First, we parse the gloss using Stanford dependency parser (de Marneffe et al., 2006). Here we use Collapsed CC-processed dependencies, which produces a graph for a sentence with a node for some of the words in the sentence and an edge for some predefined relations between the nodes. Second, we extract all the semantic links (such as 'IS-ANTONIMOUS-TO, 'IS-SIMILAR-TO' and 'ATTRIBUTE') that the adjective has and incorporate it as links into the dependency tree. We call the resulting data structure a 'link-augmented-dependency tree' (LAD). As an example, consider the adjective *unerect*, which means 'not upright in position or posture'. Figure 1 shows the resultant LAD structure for this adjective. As you can see, the node *upright* is tagged as 'IS-ANTONIMOUS-TO' with directive $antonym$, and both nodes *position* and *posture* are tagged as 'ATTRIBUTE' with directive $attribute$.

3.2 Candidate Attribute Extraction

For each adjective, we need to have a set of candidate attributes, X_j. As all seed attribute concepts are nouns, we restrict our candidate set to only nouns. Experimenting on an initial development set, we found the following criteria for the candidate attributes of a given adjective j:

- All nouns appearing in the gloss of j.
- All nominalizations of the adjectives appearing in the gloss of j.
- All hypernyms of nouns appearing in gloss, up to two levels in WordNet hierarchy. For example, for the candidate 'tallness' we extract 'height'.
- All hypernyms of nominalizations of the adjectives appearing in the gloss, up to two levels in WordNet hierarchy.
- All candidates of the adjectives appearing in the gloss of j. For example, for the adjective *gangling* which is defined as 'tall and thin' we recursively include all the candidates of 'tall' and 'thin' as the candidates for 'gangling'.

Using all these criteria, we extract a set X_j for each j, which will be used in the training phase.

3.3 Feature Extraction

After pre-processing all glosses and making a LAD, in each iteration we extract features from our seed set. We mainly extract the syntactic and semantic features which are counted as evidence for pinpointing the attribute concepts. The rationale behind the forthcoming feature extraction is the observation that the glosses tend to look alike, so there are some hidden syntactic and semantic patterns among glosses. We use the paths of a given LAD for finding general lexical and semantic patterns in the glosses. The resulting patterns make our feature set. Following are the four types of features, each of which provides a different kind of information.

- **Lexical-semantic Features**: These are the features which use both lexical and semantic aspects of a path in LAD.
- **Semantic Features**: These are the features which only use semantic aspects of a path.
- **Lexical Features**: These features only use lexical aspects of a path.
- **POS Features**: These rules only use part of speech information of a path.

From Figure 1 consider the example path: not $\xleftarrow{neg}$ upright $\xrightarrow{prep\_in}$ position. Following is the four types of feature that we extract for this path:

- Lexical-semantic Feature: not(RB) $\xleftarrow{neg}$ upright(ANT-JJ) $\xrightarrow{prep\_in}$?(NN).
- Semantic Feature: not(RB)$\xleftarrow{neg}$ *(ANT-JJ) $\xrightarrow{prep\_in}$?(NN).
- Lexical Feature: not(RB)$\xleftarrow{neg}$ upright(JJ) $\xrightarrow{prep\_in}$?(NN).
- POS Feature: *(RB)$\xleftarrow{neg}$ *(JJ) $\xrightarrow{prep\_in}$?(NN).

In all of the above features, the '?' indicates the noun attribute concept for which we are extracting features. Also, the '*' shows any lexical item which satisfies the constraints provided inside the parentheses.

3.4 Model Training

For each adjective j, there is a set of candidates X_j, each of which should be tagged as either *attribute* or *non-attribute*. Therefore, the task of finding attribute concepts of an adjective becomes a tagging problem, where X is the set of candidates and Y is the set of possible tags. The two models we experiment with here are Logistic Regression and Conditional Random Fields:

Logistic Regression: The first model we experimented with is a binary classifier which attempts to tag each candidate attribute either as an *attribute* or *non-attribute*. The features used for training the model are the extracted features in the previous phase. Here we use a Logistic Regression model, which has one attribute candidate as its input. The probability of tagging attribute candidate x with tag y is as follows:

$$p_\theta(\mathbf{y}|\mathbf{x}) = \frac{1}{Z_\theta(\mathbf{x})} \exp\left\{\sum_{k=1}^{K} \theta_k f_k(y, x)\right\} \tag{1}$$

where f is the feature function and $Z_\theta(\mathbf{x})$ is defined as follows:

$$Z_\theta(\mathbf{x}) = \sum_{\mathbf{y} \in Y^T} \exp\left\{\sum_{k=1}^{K} \theta_k f_k(y, x)\right\} \tag{2}$$

The results of training a classifier using a logistic regression model are presented in Section 4.

Conditional Random Fields: In order to better estimate the tag for each attribute candidate it is essential to know the other candidates. The Logistic Regression model does not take into account the set of specific candidates derived from the gloss of one specific adjective. A common approach for taking into account such a sequential tagging is to model the problem with Conditional Random Fields (CRF) (Lafferty et al., 2001). We decided to use a linear chain CRF, which produces promising results. The results of training a classifier using a CRF model are presented in Section 4.

3.5 Decoding and Updating the Seed

The bootstrapping algorithm described earlier iterates until convergence, which is until the seed set gets stabilized. At each iteration, we try to find all attribute concepts for some new adjectives which are not covered in the seed, decoding using the trained model parameters. At each iteration, the seed gets updated with a new set of adjectives, the ones which have at least one of their attribute candidates tagged as *attribute* by the decoder. Changes in seed set result in extracting new features for the next iterations, hence making a more general classifier. Table 2 shows some of the adjectives classified under the attribute concepts 'size', 'magnet', 'price' and 'moisture' using our algorithm. We will discuss the evaluation results of our approach in the next section.

Attribute	Adjective	Gloss
Size	minor	limited in size or scope
	great	relatively large in size or number or extent
	mountainous	like a mountain in size and impressiveness
Magnet	attractable	capable of being magnetized or attracted by a magnet
	magnetic	having the properties of a magnet
Price	cheap	relatively low in price or charging low prices
	expensive	high in price or charging high prices
Moisture	dry	lacking moisture or volatile components
	wet	containing moisture or volatile components

Table 2: Example of the learned attribute concepts for adjectives using our algorithm

4 Evaluation and Experimental Results

We evaluate the quality of our extracted attribute concepts in two stages: evaluation of the tagging and the full iterative approach.

4.1 Evaluation of the Tagging

The first stage attempts to evaluate the classifiers together with feature sets independent from the bootstrapping method. In order to compare the classifiers' performance standalone, we sampled a test set from the set of gold-standard attribute links of WordNet, which have not been used as in the initial seed set. We compared our learned attribute concepts with this gold-standard test set. As discussed earlier, we mainly use two classifiers for finding attribute concepts. The first method is Logistic Regression (LR) and the second method is (CRF). We measure precision, recall and F1-score for each of these classifiers, for both *attribute* and *non-attribute* tags. The results of this experiment are depicted in tables 3 and 4.

Method	Precision	Recall	F1-Score
CRF	87%	62%	72%
LR	79%	63%	70%

Table 3: Attribute Tagging Results

Method	Precision	Recall	F1-Score
CRF	71%	91%	80%
LR	70%	83%	76%

Table 4: Non-Attribute Tagging Results

As the results show, the classification method using our feature set has high accuracy for both *attribute* and *non-attribute* tagging. The CRF classifier outperforms the LR classifier mainly in tagging as *attribute*. This was expected, as the CRF model takes into account the set of candidates for a given adjective, which results in better predictions. Overall, the classifiers have higher accuracy on assigning *attribute* tag, i.e., true positive cases. Also, the lower recall in attribute-tagging is affected by the fact that most of the candidates are non-attributes and only one or few candidates for each adjective are tagged as attribute.

4.2 Evaluating the Full Iterative Approach

The second scenario aims at evaluating the full approach, including the iterative bootstrapping. For this purpose, we made a dataset of randomly selected 250 WordNet adjectives (either descriptive or relational) which did not have an attribute link and were associated with an attribute concept by our approach. We attempted to manually annotate this dataset with a gold-standard attribute concept. We asked 20 human judges to perform the evaluation task. The judges were provided with a guideline defining the notions of attribute-concept and gradability for adjectives. Then for each adjective, we provided the human judges with a few lines of information regarding the adjective in question, together with our extracted attribute concept for that adjective. As an example, the evaluation task for the adjective *'dry'* is as follows:

```
* [Synset: dry (lacking moisture or volatile components)
  example usage: "dry paint"]
>> Is this a gradable adjective? (y,n)
* ATTRIBUTE CONCEPT: moisture
>> Does the above attribute concept sound correct to you? (y,n)
>> If not, what is your suggestion? ...
>> Was it vague to assign an attribute to this adjective? (y,n)
```

The annotation agreement using Fleiss' kappa measure (Fleiss, 1981) was $\kappa = 74\%$, which shows a substantial agreement. Only the adjectives with substantial agreements on all annotation questions were included in the gold-standard set, resulting in about 210 adjectives. Given the fact that our algorithm has found an attribute concept for all the gold-standard data, we only report on Precision score. Also, it is important to note that the bootstrapping algorithm is sensitive to the adjectives added to the seed on every iteration, so we tune our classifiers to have better precision than recall. That is, we would rather have a robust feature extraction phase which accounts for true positives and fewer false positives. Table 5 summarizes the results of evaluation of the two methods LR and CRF against the created gold-standard dataset under $Precision_{all}$ column.

As the results show, 57% of our approach's decisions on determining the attribute concepts were correct. Among the adjectives for which the system has determined wrong answers, 82% were annotated as vague or hard to annotate by the human judges, most of which were relational adjectives. An example of an incorrect answer of the algorithm is for the adjective *abdominal*, in a noun phrase such as 'abdominal muscles'. In order to correctly determine the scalability and gradability of such adjectives, we need to have world knowledge about various concepts, knowing that abdominal refers to a part of body. The algorithm's selected attribute for this adjective was *abdomen*, which does not seem natural to a human annotator, but from the algorithm's viewpoint it is the main property that this adjective is modifying. Most such adjectives are classified as being vague and mostly non-gradable by the human annotators.

We compute the descriptive precision ($Precision_{descriptive}$) score by removing the adjectives which have been tagged as vague. As the results in Table 5 show, the accuracy of finding the attribute concepts on mostly descriptive adjectives is high. This shows that our approach performs very well on pinpointing the gradable adjectives, learning new attribute concepts for about 77% of adjectives in WordNet. As mentioned earlier in section 2, many of the relational adjectives can be considered gradable, e.g., for the adjective 'nutritional' it is plausible to say 'Milk is more nutritional than soda'. Hence, including relational adjectives in the attribute concept dataset can be very useful.

Method	$Precision_{all}$	$Precision_{descriptive}$
CRF	57%	**85%**
LR	48%	72%

Table 5: Evaluation results on hand annotated random test set.

5 Related Work

Typically adjectives play a significant role in conveying opinion and subjectivity of language. There have been many works concerning the semantics of adjectives in the field of opinion mining which can relate to our work. Hatzivassiloglou and McKeown (1993) performed the first attempt towards automatic identification of adjective scales. They presented an approach for clustering adjectives in the same scale based on their positive or negative orientation. Another work (Hatzivassiloglou and McKeown, 1997) proposes to classify the semantic polarity of adjectives based on their behavior in conjunction with other adjectives in a news corpus. They employ the existing clustering algorithms for this task.Turney and Littman (2003) decide on semantic orientation of a word (positive, negative combined with mild or strong) using statistical association with a set of positive and negative paradigm words. OPINE (Popescu and Etzioni, 2005), a system for product review mining, ranks opinion words by their strength. Our work differs fundamentally from these works in that it does not attempt to assign positive or negative polarities to adjectives. All such works focus on detection of semantic orientation of adjectives, and do not report on extracting attribute concepts or scales for adjectives. The information on orientation of adjectives is very helpful for understanding their semantics, but it is not sufficient for deep understanding which can enable further inference.

Another ongoing research project is on adjective intensity ordering, where researchers aim at ordering/ranking similar adjectives based on their intensity, such as lukewarm $<$ warm $<$ hot. Sheinman and Tokunaga (Sheinman and Tokunaga, 2009a) attempt to automatically learn adjective scaling patterns using seed adjectives and Web hits. They collect lexico-semantic patterns via bootstrapping from seed adjective pairs to obtain pairwise intensities. AdjScale (Sheinman and Tokunaga, 2009a,b) proposes a new semantic relation for gradable adjectives in WordNet, which encodes the information on the intensity of different adjectives which share the attribute link. They use lexical-semantic patterns for mining the Web for evidence of the relative strength of adjectives such as 'large' and 'gigantic' with respect to their attribute 'size'. Then they can derive pairwise partial ordering on adjectives which share an attribute. They apply the extracted patterns on WordNet dumbbells, for which they get new intensity relation links among the similar adjectives in the dumbbells. Finally, Melo and Bansal (de Melo and Bansal, 2013) present an unsupervised approach that uses semantics from Web-scale data (patterns such as 'good but not excellent') to rank words by assigning them positions on a continuous scale. They use Mixed Integer Linear Programming to determine the ranks on scales, as opposed to pairwise ranking in earlier works. All the mentioned works have only taken into account the descriptive adjectives in WordNet, i.e., the ones having an attribute link in the dumbbell structures – which provides a limited coverage, only about 22% of all adjectives. These works come short on extracting non-existing attribute concepts for naming new scales. Our work can find attribute concepts for all WordNet adjectives and associate relevant adjectives to the same attribute concept, which is a big step towards high quality ordering of adjective intensities. Moreover, none of these works investigate finding more than one scale that an adjective is graded on. Our work determines not only one, but all different aspects that an adjective could describe.

Another close body of work is the research on assigning attributes to adjective-noun phrases. The compositional semantics of adjective-noun phrases can be modeled in terms of selective binding (Pustejovsky, 1995), i.e., the adjective selects one of possibly several roles or attributes from the semantics of the noun. For example, given the phrase *(1) warm weather*, the semantic representation is '$TEMPERATURE(weather) = warm$'. Hartung and Frank (Hartung and Frank, 2010a) attempt to extract the attribute for adjective-noun phrases, by selecting the semantics of the noun that is selected by the adjectiveMainly, this kind of knowledge has been extracted from corpora by searching for patterns (Almuhareb, 2006; Cimiano, 2006). An instance of pattern is [the x of the y is z], where x is an attribute, y is a noun, and z is an adjective that paraphrases (1), e.g. *the color of the car is blue*. However, linguistic patterns that explicitly relate triplet co-occurrences of nouns, adjectives, and attributes are very rare – and in many cases, may not even provide sufficient evidence to determine an attribute for a given noun-adjective pair. Hartung and Frank (Hartung and Frank, 2010b) propose an alternative method which is doublet co-occurrences. They first search for noun-attribute co-occurrences, then adjective-attribute co-occurrences. However, doublet co-occurrences do not result in significant boost in web hits for patterns and their approach still lacks breadth in identifying adjective attributes.

6 Conclusion

In this paper we presented a new approach for comprehensive identification of the attribute concepts of adjectives in WordNet. The main idea is to learn the attribute concepts by bootstrapping using the adjective glosses. Our results show that our approach can identify the attribute concepts of about 77% of WordNet adjectives with high accuracy. Our algorithm can be generalized in order to be applied to various applications which require finding certain properties from definitional texts. Our work on determining the adjective attribute concepts could also benefit the research on sentiment orientation (positive/negative) of adjectives.

Another semantic relation between adjectives that is not considered by WordNet is gradation, i.e, the intensity of adjectives as compared with one another, going from a weak strength to a strong one. Once we have the extensive attribute concepts for most of the WordNet adjectives, we can attempt to order the adjectives classified under the same concept based on their degree of intensity. Our work aims at producing a large, unrestricted number of individual intensity scales (attribute concepts) for different qualities and hence can help in fine-grained sentiment analysis with respect to very particular aspects. As the next step of this work, we are planning to order all adjectives associated with the attribute concepts that we identified in this work. Also, given the promising results using linear chain CRF, we are planning to experiment with other structured CRF models as a future work. Moreover, we are planning to release the derived attribute concepts dataset, which could be helpful for various language understanding tasks.

Acknowledgments

We would like to thank anonymous reviewers for their valuable feedback. This work is sponsored by Nuance Foundation and The Office of Naval Research under grant number N000141110417.

References

Almuhareb, A. (2006). *Attributes in Lexical Acquisition*. Ph. D. thesis.

Cimiano, P. (2006). *Ontology Learning and Population from Text: Algorithms, Evaluation and Applications*. Secaucus, NJ, USA: Springer-Verlag New York, Inc.

de Marneffe, M.-C., B. MacCartney, and C. D. Manning (2006). Generating typed dependency parses from phrase structure parses. In *In Proc. INTL Conf. On Language Resource and Evaluation (LREC)*, pp. 449–454.

de Melo, G. and M. Bansal (2013). Good, great, excellent: Global inference of semantic intensities. *TACL 1*, 279–290.

Fleiss, J. L. (1981). *Statistical Methods for Rates and Proportions* (2nd ed.). New York: Wiley-Interscience.

Hartung, M. and A. Frank (2010a). A semi-supervised type-based classification of adjectives: Distinguishing properties and relations. In N. Calzolari, K. Choukri, B. Maegaard, J. Mariani, J. Odijk, S. Piperidis, M. Rosner, and D. Tapias (Eds.), *LREC*. European Language Resources Association.

Hartung, M. and A. Frank (2010b). A structured vector space model for hidden attribute meaning in adjective-noun phrases. In *Proceedings of the 23rd International Conference on Computational Linguistics*, COLING '10, Stroudsburg, PA, USA, pp. 430–438. Association for Computational Linguistics.

Hatzivassiloglou, V. and K. R. McKeown (1993). Towards the automatic identification of adjectival scales: Clustering adjectives according to meaning. In *Proceedings of the 31st Annual Meeting on Association for Computational Linguistics*, ACL '93, Stroudsburg, PA, USA, pp. 172–182. Association for Computational Linguistics.

Hatzivassiloglou, V. and K. R. McKeown (1997). Predicting the semantic orientation of adjectives. In *Proceedings of the 35th Annual Meeting of the Association for Computational Linguistics and Eighth Conference of the European Chapter of the Association for Computational Linguistics*, ACL '98, Stroudsburg, PA, USA, pp. 174–181. Association for Computational Linguistics.

Kennedy, C. (1999). Projecting the adjective: The syntax and semantics of gradability and comparison. In *In Proc. INTL Conf. On Language Resource and Evaluation (LREC)*. New York: Garland Press.

Lafferty, J. D., A. McCallum, and F. C. N. Pereira (2001). Conditional random fields: Probabilistic models for segmenting and labeling sequence data. In *Proceedings of the Eighteenth International Conference on Machine Learning*, ICML '01, San Francisco, CA, USA, pp. 282–289. Morgan Kaufmann Publishers Inc.

Mendes, S. (2006). Adjectives in wordnet.pt. In *In: Proceedings of the GWA 2006, Global WordNet Association Conference, Jeju Island, Korea*.

Miller, G. A. (1995, November). Wordnet: A lexical database for english. *Commun. ACM 38*(11), 39–41.

Popescu, A.-M. and O. Etzioni (2005). Extracting product features and opinions from reviews. In *Proceedings of the Conference on Human Language Technology and Empirical Methods in Natural Language Processing*, HLT '05, Stroudsburg, PA, USA, pp. 339–346. Association for Computational Linguistics.

Pustejovsky, J. (1995). *The Generative Lexicon*. Cambridge, MA: MIT Press.

Rusiecki, J. (1985). Adjectives and comparison in english. Longman.

Sheinman, V. and T. Tokunaga (2009a). Adjscales: Differentiating between similar adjectives for language learners. In J. A. M. Cordeiro, B. Shishkov, A. Verbraeck, and M. Helfert (Eds.), *CSEDU (1)*, pp. 229–235. INSTICC Press.

Sheinman, V. and T. Tokunaga (2009b). Adjscales: Visualizing differences between adjectives for language learners. *IEICE Transactions 92-D*(8), 1542–1550.

Turney, P. D. and M. L. Littman (2003, October). Measuring praise and criticism: Inference of semantic orientation from association. *ACM Trans. Inf. Syst. 21*(4), 315–346.

Yarowsky, D. (1995). Unsupervised word sense disambiguation rivaling supervised methods. In *Proceedings of the 33rd Annual Meeting on Association for Computational Linguistics*, ACL '95, Stroudsburg, PA, USA, pp. 189–196. Association for Computational Linguistics.

Young, D. J. (1984). *Introducing English Grammar*. Howard Jackson.

Exploiting Fine-grained Syntactic Transfer Features to Predict the Compositionality of German Particle Verbs

Stefan Bott and Sabine Schulte im Walde
Institut für Maschinelle Sprachverabeitung, Universität Stuttgart
{stefan.bott,schulte}@ims.uni-stuttgart.de

Abstract

This article presents a distributional approach to predict the compositionality of German particle verbs by modelling changes in syntactic argument structure. We justify the experiments on theoretical grounds and employ GermaNet, Topic Models and Singular Value Decomposition for generalization, to compensate for data sparseness. Evaluating against three human-rated gold standards, our fine-grained syntactic approach is able to predict the level of compositionality of the particle verbs but is nevertheless inferior to a coarse-grained bag-of-words approach.

1 Introduction

In German, particle verbs (PVs) such as *aufessen* (*to eat up*) are a frequent and productive type of multiword expression composed of a base verb (BV) and a prefix particle. We are interested in predicting the degrees of compositionality of German PVs, which exhibit a varying degree of compositionality with respect to their base verbs, as illustrated in (1) vs. (2). The meaning of the highly compositional PV *nachdrucken* (*to reprint*) is closely related to its BV *drucken* (*to print*), while the PV *nachgeben* (*to give in*) has little in common with the BV *geben* (*to give*).

(1) *Der Verlag druckte das Buch nach.*
The publisher printed the book again-PRT.
'The publisher reprinted the book.'

(2) *Peter gab ihrer Bitte nach.*
Peter gave her request in-PRT.
'Peter gave in to her request.'

In previous work we demonstrated that the compositionality level of PVs can be predicted by using a simple Word Space Model which represents local word contexts as a bag-of-words extracted from a symmetric window around the target PV instances (Bott and Schulte im Walde, 2014a). The approach worked well because compositional PVs tend to co-occur locally with the same words as their corresponding base verbs.

The compositionality of German PVs is, however, also influenced by syntactic factors. While semantically similar verbs in general tend to have similar subcategorization frames (Merlo and Stevenson, 2001; Joanis et al., 2008), PV-BV pairs may differ in their syntactic properties, even if the PV is highly compositional. We refer to this linguistic phenomenon as "syntactic transfer problem". We understand transfers as regular changes in subcategorization frames of PVs by transfer, incorporation or addition of complements in comparison to the BV (Stiebels, 1996; Lüdeling, 2001). For example, the semantic role expressed by the subject of the BV *leuchten* in (3) is "transferred" to an instrumental PP of the highly compositional PV *anleuchten* in (4). In addition, the patient of *anleuchten* (i.e., the direct object) has no correspondence for *leuchten*. We call this a case of argument extension. The opposite case (i.e., a PV does not realize a semantic role used by its BV) is called argument incorporation.

Proceedings of the 11th International Conference on Computational Semantics, pages 34–39,
London, UK, April 15-17 2015.

(3) *Die Lampe leuchtet.*
'The lamp-SBJ shines.'

(4) *Peter leuchtet das Bild mit der Lampe an.*
Peter-SBJ shines the picture-OBJ$_{ACC}$ with the lamp-PP$_{DAT}$ at-PRT.
'The man beams at the picture with the lamp.'

Our hypothesis is that the degree of reliability of the prediction of such syntactic transfers represents an indirect indicator of semantic transparency: If many of the complements of a PV correspond to a complement of its BV, the PV is regarded as highly compositional, even if the PV complements are not realized as the same syntactic argument types. Conversely, if few of the PV complements correspond to BV complements, this is an indicator of low compositionality.

To explore our hypothesis, we rely on the distributional similarity between PV–BV complements, to model argument correspondences in order to predict PV compositionality. For example, identifying strong distributional similarity between the instrumental PPs of *anleuchten* and the subjects of *leuchten* (see examples (3) and (4) above) would allow us to predict strong PV compositionality, even though the distributional similarity of identical complement types (e.g., the subjects) is low.

Our novel approach exploits fine-grained syntactic transfer information which is not accessible within a window-based distributional approach, while it should preserve an essential part of the information contained in context windows, since the head nouns within subcategorization frames typically appear in the local context. To compensate for the inevitable data sparseness, we employ the lexical taxonomy *GermaNet* (Hamp and Feldweg, 1997), *Topic Models* (Blei et al., 2003) and *Singular Value Decomposition (SVD)* to generalize over individual complement heads. All of them have proven effective in other distributional semantics tasks (Joanis et al. (2008), Ó Séaghdha (2010), Guo and Diab (2011), Bullinaria and Levy (2012), among others).

The variants of our fine-grained syntactic approach are able to predict PV compositionality, but even though our model is (a) theoretically well-grounded, (b) supported by sophisticated generalization methods and (c) successful, a conceptually much simpler bag-of-words approach to the distributional representation of PVs cannot be outperformed.

2 Related Work & Motivation

The problem of predicting degrees of PV compositionality is not new and has been addressed previously, mainly for English (Baldwin et al., 2003; McCarthy et al., 2003; Bannard, 2005). For German, Schulte im Walde (2005) explored salient features at the syntax-semantics interface that determined the semantic nearest neighbors of German PVs. Relying on the insights of this study, Kühner and Schulte im Walde (2010) used unsupervised clustering to determine the degree of compositionality of German PVs. They hypothesized that compositional PVs tend to occur more often in the same clusters with their corresponding BVs than opaque PVs. Their approach relied on nominal complement heads in two modes, (1) with and (2) without explicit reference to the syntactic functions. The explicit incorporation of syntactic information (mode 1) yielded less satisfactory results, since a given subcategorization slot for a PV complement does not necessarily correspond to the same semantic type of complement slot for the BV, thus putting the syntactic transfer problem in evidence, again.

In our previous approach, we relied on word window information with no access to syntactic information (Bott and Schulte im Walde, 2014a), with a focus on PV frequency and ambiguity. For the current work, we started out from the idea that syntactic information should be more useful than window information if the distributional similarity is measured over individual salient slot correspondences rather than across all slots as in earlier approaches. Therefore, a pre-processing step automatically determines the distributionally most similar complement slot pairs for a given PV-BV pair and their subcategorization frames, in order to measure the similarity between PVs and their BVs. In Bott and Schulte im Walde (2014b) we already showed that the prediction of syntactic transfers with distributional methods is feasible. In the present work we exploit the prediction of syntactic transfer patterns as an intermediate step for the assessment of compositionality levels.

Through dividing up the local context among different subcategorization slots we expected a problem of data sparseness more severe than for window-based approaches which represent all the context words in the same vector and are less likely to result in sparse representations. For this reason, we apply a series of generalization techniques utilizing a lexical taxonomy and Topic Models, as well as SVD as a dimensionality reduction technique.

3 Experiments

3.1 Syntactic Slot Correspondence

In order to build a model of syntactic transfer to predict PV compositionality, a pre-processing step determined a measure of *syntactic slot correspondence*. We selected the 5 most common subcategorization frames of each PV and each BV induced from dependency parses of the German web corpus *SdeWaC* containing approx. 880 million words (Bohnet, 2010; Faaß and Eckart, 2013). From these 5 most probable verb frames, we used all noun and prepositional phrase complement slots with nominal heads, except for adjuncts. Each PV slot was compared against each BV slot, by measuring the cosine between the vectors containing the complement heads as dimensions, and head counts[1] within the slots as values. E.g. (see examples (3) and (4)), we found the nouns *Licht* and *Taschenlampe* (among others) both as instrumental PP (DAT-mit)[2] of *anleuchten* and as subject (SBJ) of *leuchten*, and the cosine of this slot correspondence over all nouns was 0.9898.

3.2 Syntactic Transfer Strength

In order to use the syntactic slot correspondence scores to predict the degree of PV-BV compositionality, we first selected the best matching BV slot for each PV complement slot, as suggested in Bott and Schulte im Walde (2014b) and then calculated the average score over these best matches across all PV slots. This average value is considered as a confidence measure for the assumption that the PV–BV complement slots correspond to each other and realize the same semantic roles. Regarding our hypothesis, we rely on the average cosine value to predict the degree of PV compositionality.

To account for possible null correspondences in argument incorporation and argument extension cases, we applied a variable threshold on the cosine distance ($t = 0.1/0.2/0.3$, and $t = 0$ referring to no threshold). If the best matching BV complement slot of a PV complement slot had a cosine below this threshold, it was not taken into account.

3.3 Generalization

The major problem of this approach is data sparseness. We thus applied three generalization techniques to the head nouns:

1. ***GermaNet (GN)*** is the German version of WordNet (Hamp and Feldweg, 1997). We use the nth topmost taxonomy levels in the GermaNet hierarchy as generalizations of head nouns. In the case of multiple inheritance the counts of a subordinate node are distributed over the superordinated nodes.
2. ***LDA***: We use the MALLET tool (McCallum, 2002) to create LDA topic generalizations for the head nouns, in a similar way as Ó Séaghdha (2010). While LDA is usually applied over text documents, we consider as document the set of noun heads in the same subcategorization slot.
3. ***SVD***: We use the DISSECT tool (Dinu et al., 2013) to apply dimensionality reduction to the vectors of complement head nouns.

[1]We used *Local Mutual Information (LMI)* (Evert, 2005).

[2]PP slots are marked with case and preposition.

3.4 Evaluation

We evaluated our models against three gold standards (GS). Each of them contains PVs across different particles and was annotated by humans for the degree of compositionality:
GS1: A gold standard collected by Hartmann (2008), consisting of 99 randomly selected PVs across 11 particles, balanced over 8 frequency ranges and judged by 4 experts on a scale from 0 to 10.
GS2: A gold standard of 354 randomly selected PVs across the same 11 verb particles, balanced over 3 frequency ranges while taking the frequencies from three corpora into account. We collected ratings with Amazon Mechanical Turk on a scale from 1 to 7.[3]
GS3: A subset of 150 PVs from GS2, after removing the most frequent and infrequent PVs as well as prefix verbs, because we concentrate on the empirically challenging separable PVs. [4]

In the actual evaluation, we compared the rankings of the system-derived PV–BV cosine scores against the human rankings, using Spearman's ρ (Siegel and Castellan, 1988).

4 Results & Discussion

In the following, we describe and discuss our results across methods, across cosine threshold values, and across gold standards. Figure 1 presents the ρ values for the threshold $t = 0.3$ (which in the majority of cases outperformed the other threshold levels) and across gold standards. Across all syntactic models, we obtained the best results when evaluating against GS3. This was expected given that this gold standard excludes prefix verbs and very infrequent and very frequent PVs which are hard to assess in terms of PV-BV compositionality: Infrequent verbs are highly affected by data sparseness; highly frequent verbs have a tendency towards lexical ambiguity(Bott and Schulte im Walde, 2014a). In the same vein, the particularly low results[5] obtained with GS1 can be explained by its large proportion of low-frequent and high-frequent PVs.

Figure 1 also shows that the syntactic approach (a) provides poor results when it relies on raw frequency counts or LMI values; (b) is better for GermaNet level 2 than level 1 and the levels >2;[6] (c) provides the best results with SVD and (d) relying on LDA is most robust against low and high frequency and obtains the best results for GS2, which are however outperformed by GermaNet and SVD models.

Finally, Figure 1 demonstrates that, against our expectations, our new approach was not able to perform better than our previous bag-of-words models extracted from local windows. Even if the window models are conceptually simple, they seem to carry a lot of salient information which is also more robust against low frequency and ambiguity (obtaining better results for GS1 vs. GS2 vs. GS3). The virtues of bag-of-words models can apparently not even be outperformed by generalizing over nouns or by dimensionality reduction. Hoping that our novel syntactic information is in some way complementary to window information, we carried out an additional experiment where we computed a weighted average of the cosine values obtained from both feature types. Comparing the combined predictions with the human rankings, the system was however still beaten by window information alone.

Figure 2 provides a deeper look into our results across thresholds, now focusing on GS3. The plot shows that for the most successful generalization models (GN level 2 and SVD), the results improve with an increasing threshold. Excluding subcategorization complement slots of PVs that do not correspond to a distributionally similar subcategorization slot of its BV thus seems to support the identification of PV syntactic argument changes. This is an interesting theoretical result because it corroborates the influence of argument incorporation and argument extensions.

Error analysis in combination with theoretical considerations revealed that, overall, data sparseness appears to remain a central problem. The representation of each verb as a series of vectors, one for each

[3] `https://www.mturk.com`

[4] We do not treat non-separable prefix verbs like *ver|lieben*, but note that a series of verbs, such as *um|fahren* do exists as PVs and prefix verbs, with different readings.

[5] Negative ρ values are omitted in the plot.

[6] GN results for levels >3 are omitted for space reasons.

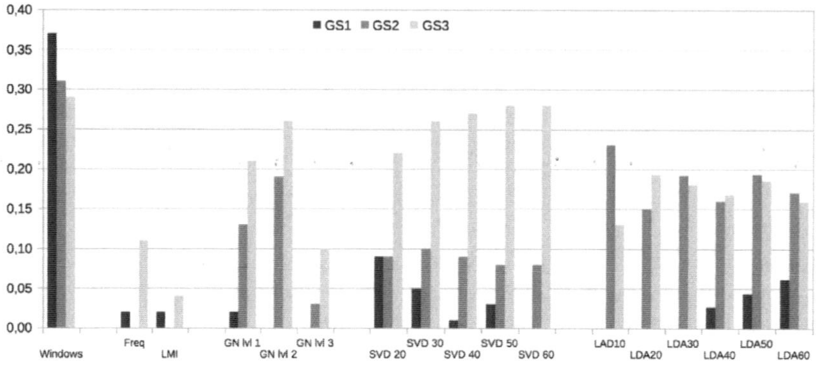

Figure 1: Results across gold standards, for t=0.3.

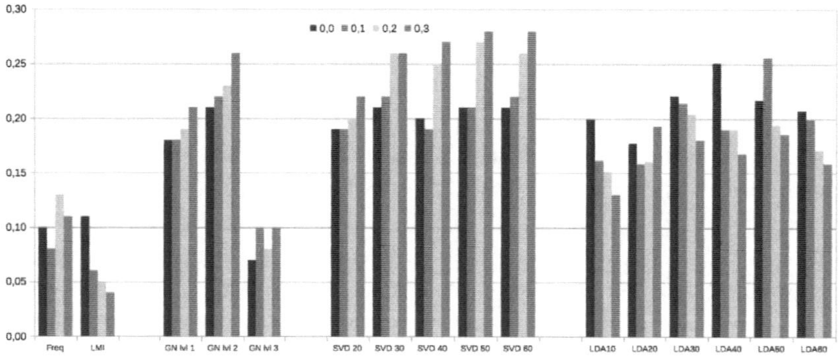

Figure 2: Results across thresholds, for GS3.

subcategorization complement, splits up the mass of counts in comparison to a verb window vector. Our syntax-based approach may need much more data to perform on an equal level as the window approach.

5 Conclusions

In this article we described a novel distributional approach to predict the degree of compositionality of German particle verbs. Our approach exploited syntactic information and involved a direct modeling of the syntactic transfer phenomenon. Relying on various gold standards, and varying complement similarity thresholds and generalization methods, we successfully predicted PV compositionality. Threshold variation indicated that we indeed capture PV-BV syntactic argument changes, and generalization by GermaNet high taxonomy levels and SVD helped with the apparent data sparseness. Nevertheless, information provided by context windows outperforms our fine-grained syntactic approach.

Acknowledgments

The research was supported by the DFG Research Grant SCHU 2580/2 (Stefan Bott) and the DFG Heisenberg Fellowship SCHU-2580/1 (Sabine Schulte im Walde).

References

Baldwin, T., C. Bannard, T. Tanaka, and D. Widdows (2003). An Empirical Model of Multiword Expression Decomposability. In *Proceedings of the ACL Workshop on Multiword Expressions: Analysis, Acquisition and Treatment*, Sapporo, Japan, pp. 89–96.

Bannard, C. (2005). Learning about the Meaning of Verb–Particle Constructions from Corpora. *Computer Speech and Language 19*, 467–478.

Blei, D., A. Ng, and M. Jordan (2003). Latent Dirichlet Allocation. *Journal of Machine Learning Research 3*, 993–1022.

Bohnet, B. (2010). Top Accuracy and Fast Dependency Parsing is not a Contradiction. In *Proceedings of the 23rd International Conference on Computational Linguistics*, Beijing, China, pp. 89–97.

Bott, S. and S. Schulte im Walde (2014a). Optimizing a Distributional Semantic Model for the Prediction of German Particle Verb Compositionality. In *Proceedings of the 9th International Conference on Language Resources and Evaluation*, Reykjavik, Iceland, pp. 509–516.

Bott, S. and S. Schulte im Walde (2014b). Syntactic Transfer Patterns of German Particle Verbs and their Impact on Lexical Semantics. In *Proceedings of the 3rd Joint Conference on Lexical and Computational Semantics*, Dublin, Ireland, pp. 182–192.

Bullinaria, J. A. and J. P. Levy (2012). Extracting Semantic Representations from Word Co-Occurrence Statistics: Stop-Lists, Stemming, and SVD. *Behavior Research Methods 44*, 890–907.

Dinu, G., N. The Pham, and M. Baroni (2013). DISSECT – DIStributional SEmantics Composition Toolkit. In *Proceedings of the 51st Annual Meeting of the Association for Computational Linguistics: System Demonstrations*, Sofia, Bulgaria.

Evert, S. (2005). *The Statistics of Word Co-Occurrences: Word Pairs and Collocations*. Ph. D. thesis, IMS, Universität Stuttgart.

Faaß, G. and K. Eckart (2013). SdeWaC – a Corpus of Parsable Sentences from the Web. In *Proceedings of the International Conference of the German Society for Computational Linguistics and Language Technology*, Darmstadt, Germany, pp. 61–68.

Guo, W. and M. Diab (2011). Semantic Topic Models: CombiningWord Distributional Statistics and Dictionary Definitions. In *Proceedings of the Conference on Empirical Methods in Natural Language Processing*, Edinburgh, UK, pp. 552–561.

Hamp, B. and H. Feldweg (1997). GermaNet – A Lexical-Semantic Net for German. In *Proceedings of the ACL Workshop on Automatic Information Extraction and Building Lexical Semantic Resources for NLP Applications*, Madrid, Spain, pp. 9–15.

Hartmann, S. (2008). Einfluss syntaktischer und semantischer Subkategorisierung auf die Kompositionalität von Partikelverben. Studienarbeit. IMS, Universität Stuttgart.

Joanis, E., S. Stevenson, and D. James (2008). A General Feature Space for Automatic Verb Classification. *Natural Language Engineering 14*(3), 337–367.

Kühner, N. and S. Schulte im Walde (2010). Determining the Degree of Compositionality of German Particle Verbs by Clustering Approaches. In *Proceedings of the 10th Conference on Natural Language Processing*, Saarbrücken, Germany, pp. 47–56.

Lüdeling, A. (2001). *On German Particle Verbs and Similar Constructions in German*. CSLI.

McCallum, A. K. (2002). MALLET: A Machine Learning for Language Toolkit.

McCarthy, D., B. Keller, and J. Carroll (2003). Detecting a Continuum of Compositionality in Phrasal Verbs. In *Proceedings of the ACL Workshop on Multiword Expressions: Analysis, Acquisition and Treatment*, Sapporo, Japan, pp. 73–80.

Merlo, P. and S. Stevenson (2001). Automatic Verb Classification Based on Statistical Distributions of Argument Structure. *Computational Linguistics 27*(3), 373–408.

Ó Séaghdha, D. (2010). Latent Variable Models of Selectional Preference. In *Proceedings of the 48th Annual Meeting of the Association for Computational Linguistics*, Uppsala, Sweden, pp. 435–444.

Schulte im Walde, S. (2005). Exploring Features to Identify Semantic Nearest Neighbours: A Case Study on German Particle Verbs. In *Proceedings of the International Conference on Recent Advances in Natural Language Processing*, Borovets, Bulgaria, pp. 608–614.

Siegel, S. and N. J. Castellan (1988). *Nonparametric Statistics for the Behavioral Sciences*. Boston, MA: McGraw-Hill.

Stiebels, B. (1996). *Lexikalische Argumente und Adjunkte. Zum semantischen Beitrag von verbalen Präfixen und Partikeln*. Berlin: Akademie Verlag.

Multilingual Reliability and "Semantic" Structure of Continuous Word Spaces

Maximilian Köper, Christian Scheible, Sabine Schulte im Walde
Institut für Maschinelle Sprachverarbeitung, Universität Stuttgart
{koepermn,scheibcn,schulte}@ims.uni-stuttgart.de

Abstract

While continuous word vector representations enjoy increasing popularity, it is still poorly understood (i) how reliable they are for other languages than English, and (ii) to what extent they encode deep semantic relatedness such as paradigmatic relations. This study presents experiments with continuous word vectors for English and German, a morphologically rich language. For evaluation, we use both published and newly created datasets of morpho-syntactic and semantic relations. Our results show that (i) morphological complexity causes a drop in accuracy, and (ii) continuous representations lack the ability to solve analogies of paradigmatic relations.

1 Introduction

Until recently, the majority of research on semantic spaces concentrated on vector spaces relying on context counts (*count vector spaces*). However, increasing attention is being devoted to low-dimensional continuous word vector representations. Unlike count vectors, these continuous vectors are the result of supervised training of context-predicting models (*predict vector spaces*).[1]

Mikolov et al. (2013) reported that a predict vector space trained with a simplified neural language model (cf. Bengio et al. (2003)) seemingly encodes syntactic and semantic properties, which can be recovered directly from the space through linear translations, to solve analogies such as

$$\overrightarrow{\text{king}} - \overrightarrow{\text{man}} = \overrightarrow{\text{queen}} - \overrightarrow{\text{woman}}.$$

Baroni et al. (2014) presented experiments where predict vectors outperform count vectors on several semantic benchmarks involving semantic relatedness, word clustering, and selectional preferences.

Several open questions regarding predict vectors remain. In this paper, we focus on two shortcomings of previous analyses. First, the analogies in the "syntactic" and "semantic" benchmark datasets by Mikolov et al. (2013) in fact cover mostly morpho-syntactic relations – even in the semantic category. Consequently, it is still unknown to what extent predict vector spaces encode deep semantic relatedness, such as paradigmatic relations. Rei and Briscoe (2014) offered some insight by testing hypernymy relations through similarity; Melamud et al. (2014) investigated synonymy, hypernymy, and co-hyponymy relations. However, no systematic evaluation of deep semantic analogies has been performed so far.

Second, it remains unclear whether comparable performance can be achieved for a wider range of relations in morphologically rich languages, as most previous work on predict vectors worked with English data. A notable exception is Zuanović et al. (2014), who achieved strong performance for superlative and country-capital analogies in Croatian. Wolf et al. (2013) learned mappings of predict vectors between English, Hebrew, and Arabic, but provided no deeper insight into the model's capabilities on a direct evaluation of semantic relations. Faruqui and Dyer (2014) trained predict vectors using two languages, but evaluated only in English.

We present a systematic exploration of morpho-syntactic and semantic relatedness in English and the morphologically richer language German. We show detailed results of the continuous bag-of-words model (CBOW) by Mikolov et al. (2013), which we apply to equivalent morpho-syntactic tasks for both

[1] The terminology follows Baroni et al. (2014).

Proceedings of the 11th International Conference on Computational Semantics, pages 40–45,
London, UK, April 15-17 2015.

languages. Pertaining to the question of deep semantic relatedness, we evaluate on existing benchmarks on general semantic relatedness, and on newly created paradigmatic semantic analogies. To make the models for the two languages as comparable as possible, they are trained on web corpora which were obtained with the same crawling technique, and which we subsample to comparable size.

We present evidence that – while general semantic relatedness is captured well by predict models – paradigmatic relations are problematic for count vector spaces. Moreover, our experiments on German show that its morphological richness does indeed make the prediction of analogies more difficult.

2 Data

2.1 Morpho-Syntactic and Semantic Tasks

We evaluate a variety of analogy and semantic relatedness tasks, 23 for English and 21 for German. They are in part taken from the literature and in part newly constructed.[2]

The **Google semantic/syntactic** analogy datasets *(Google-Sem/Syn)* were introduced in Mikolov et al. (2013). The datasets contain analogy questions of the form A:B::C:D, meaning A is to B as C is to D, where the fourth word (D) is unknown. We constructed German counterparts of the datasets through manual translation and subsequent cross-checking by three human judges. We omitted the relation type "adjective–adverb" for both languages, because it does not exist in German. The final task set contains five *Google-Sem* and eight *Google-Syn* relation types with 18 552 analogy tasks per language.

The **paradigmatic semantic relation** dataset *(Sem-Para)* also contains analogy tasks. Here, the paradigmatic relation between A and B is the same as between C and D. The dataset was constructed from antonymy, synonymy, and hypernymy relation pairs collected by Lenci & Benotto for English and by Scheible & Schulte im Walde for German, using the methodology described in Scheible and Schulte im Walde (2014): Relying on a random selection of target nouns, verbs and adjectives from WordNet/GermaNet – balanced for semantic class, degree of polysemy, and frequency according to the WaCKy corpora (Baroni et al., 2009) –, antonyms, synonyms, and hypernyms were collected in an experiment hosted on Amazon Mechanical Turk. We constructed analogy questions by selecting only those target-response pairs that were submitted by at least four out of ten turkers. Then, we exhaustively combined all pairs for each word class and relation type.[3] The resulting English dataset contains 7 516 analogies; the German dataset contains 2 462 analogies.

In the same way, we created an analogy dataset with 10 000 unique analogy questions from the hypernymy and meronymy relations in *BLESS* (Baroni and Lenci, 2011), by randomly picking semantic relation pairs. BLESS is available only for English, but we included it in *Sem-Para* as it is a popular semantic benchmark.

Overall, the *Sem-Para* dataset constitutes a deep semantic challenge, containing very specific, domain-related and potentially low-frequent semantic details that are difficult to solve even for humans. For example, the tasks include antonyms such as *biblical:secular::deaf:hearing* or *screech:whisper::ink:erase*; hypernyms such as *groove:dance::maze:puzzle*; and synonyms such as *skyline:horizon::rumor:gossip*.

The **general semantic** dataset *(Sem-Gen)* does not require to solve analogies but to predict the degree of semantic relatedness between word pairs. It contains three semantic benchmarks:

1. *RG* (Rubenstein and Goodenough, 1965) and its German equivalent *Gur65* (Gurevych, 2005).
2. *WordSim353* (Finkelstein et al., 2001) and its translation into German *WordSim280* by Schmidt et al. (2011): As Schmidt et al. did not re-rate the German relation pairs after translation (which we considered necessary due to potential meaning shifts), we collected new ratings for the German pairs from 10 subjects, applying the same conditions as the original WordSim353 collection task. To ensure identical size for both languages, we reduced the English data to the common 280 pairs.

[2]The new datasets are available at `http://www.ims.uni-stuttgart.de/data/analogies/`.

[3]Regarding hypernymy and meronymy (see BLESS below), we restricted the pair combination such that the word to be predicted is always the hypernym or holonym, respectively. The reason for this restriction is that there are too many correct choices for the corresponding hyponyms and meronyms.

	Google-Sem			Google-Syn			Sem-Gen			Sem-Para w/o BLESS			TOEFL		
	CBOW	SKIP	BOW	CBOW	SKIP	BOW	CBOW	SKIP	BOW	CBOW	SKIP	BOW	CBOW	SKIP	BOW
EN W	68.8	**71.8**	39.5	**81.9**	80.5	57.9	**77.9**	77.8	77.8	**19.3**	16.4	15.6	**96.2**	**96.2**	72.2
EN L	68.3	**71.8**	40.3	47.1	**47.4**	29.3	**80.5**	78.6	66.4	18.4	**15.9**	15.8	**90.0**	87.5	66.2
DE W	42.4	**45.9**	27.3	**48.4**	47.1	31.0	**75.6**	73.3	58.9	14.7	14.4	**14.8**	**69.0**	68.3	54.4
DE L	43.5	**45.9**	28.9	**31.8**	31.5	23.7	73.3	**75.7**	64.7	**15.1**	13.8	14.9	**69.4**	68.5	55.8

Table 1: Results (ρ for Sem-Gen, accuracy for others) by task category across models.

3. 80 *TOEFL* (Test of English as a Foreign Language) questions by Landauer and Dumais (1997) for English, and 426 questions from a similar collection by Mohammad et al. (2007) for German. Each semantic similarity question is multiple choice, with four alternatives for a given stem. Unlike the original English TOEFL data, the German dataset also contains phrases, which we disregarded.

2.2 Corpora

We obtain vectors using the *COW* web corpora *ENCOW14* for English and *DECOW12* for German (Schäfer and Bildhauer, 2012). The corpora contain lemma and part-of-speech annotations. In addition, we applied some basic pre-processing: we removed non-alphanumeric tokens and sentences with fewer than four words, and we lowercased all tokens. In order to limit effects of corpus size, we subsampled the English corpus to contain approximately the same number of tokens as the German corpus, 7.9 billion.

3 Experiments

3.1 Setup and Evaluation

Our setups vary model type (two predict models and one count model), language (English and German), and word forms vs. lemmas in the training data – leading to a total of $3\times2\times2$ models. Our predict models are the standard CBOW and SKIP-gram models, trained with the `word2vec` toolkit (Mikolov et al., 2013). We use negative sampling with 15 negative samples, 400 dimensions, a symmetrical window of size 2, subsampling with $p = 10^{-5}$, and a frequency threshold of 50 to filter out rare words.

Our count model is a standard bag-of-words model with positive point-wise mutual information weighting and dimensionality reduction through singular value decomposition. The dimensionality and the window size were set identical to the predict vectors.

We solve analogy tasks with the 3COSMUL method (Levy and Goldberg, 2014), and similarity tasks with cosine similarity. For the *Google*, *TOEFL*, and *Sem-Para* tasks, we report accuracy; for *RG* and *WordSim* we report Spearman's rank-order correlation coefficient ρ.

3.2 Results

Table 1 compares the word-based (W) and lemma-based (L) results of the English (EN) and the German (DE) ***predict vs. count models***. We first confirm previous insight (Baroni et al., 2014) that the predict models (CBOW; SKIP) in most cases outperform the count models (BOW). Second, we also confirm that the SKIP-gram model outperforms CBOW only on *Google-Sem* (Mikolov et al., 2013). Third, we find that lemmatized models generally perform slightly better on semantic tasks, whereas full word forms are necessary for morpho-syntactic tasks. Table 2 presents a breakdown by task for the overall best model (CBOW). Based on this, we will now discuss our two main questions.

(i) Morphological richness of target language: For the *Google-Sem/Syn* analogies, the level of performance is generally higher in English than in German. The only exceptions are the tasks *nationality-adjective* (L), and *plural-verbs* (both W+L). Our experiments demonstrate that, compared to English, the *Google* analogies are more difficult to solve for the morphologically richer language German. Using full

	Google-Sem (Acc)					Google-Syn (Acc)								Sem-Para (Acc)							Sem-Gen (ρ)		Sem-Gen (Acc)
	common-countries	capital-world	currency	city-in-state	family	opposite	nationality-adjective	comparative	superlative	plural-nouns	plural-verbs	present-participle	past-tense	adj-ant	verb-ant	noun-ant	noun-syn	noun-hyp	BLESS-hyp	BLESS-mer	RG/Gur65	WordSim280	TOEFL
EN W	94.0	74.6	19.5	67.5	83.3	50.2	85.5	95.4	94.8	92.4	80.9	77.6	68.6	11.6	1.3	0.4	4.3	0.8	1.0	0.0	82.3	73.6	96.2
EN L	92.6	73.1	21.4	70.0	71.9	49.5	84.8	56.0	46.3	67.3	15.8	39.1	6.6	12.5	3.8	0.0	7.3	1.3	1.9	0.0	84.3	76.7	90.0
DE W	82.0	55.8	14.9	17.7	60.5	23.1	40.3	69.8	37.9	73.8	83.9	15.4	53.5	4.2	0.0	5.0	5.9	1.1	–	–	75.1	76.1	69.0
DE L	81.8	58.8	17.5	17.5	60.7	21.4	85.1	14.8	7.9	63.0	37.7	17.7	1.3	5.3	0.3	3.6	8.6	1.1	–	–	79.1	76.7	69.4

Table 2: Results by task for the English and German CBOW models.

word forms, these differences are consequently the strongest for the *Google-Syn* morpho-syntactic tasks[4] *opposite, comparative, superlative, plural-nouns, present-participle*, and *past-tense*, where considerably more word forms per lemma exist in German than in English. As a consequence, the German search space is larger, and it becomes more difficult to predict the correct form. For example, while English only uses three adjective word forms per lemma, i.e., positive, comparative and superlative (e.g., *fast, faster, fastest*), German inflects adjectives for case, gender and number (e.g., *schneller(e|en|er|es)* are all valid translations of *faster*). The results for *nationality-adjective* confirm this insight, because the lemma-based (L) German data with a reduced search space (i.e., only offering one adjective lemma instead of the various inflected forms) clearly improves over the word-based German version (40.3% $\rightarrow$ 85.1%). Regarding *plural-verbs*, we assume that the German task is not more difficult than the English task, because even though German verbs are also inflected, written language predominantly uses two verb forms (third person singular and plural), as in English.

(ii) Deep semantic tasks: First, we contrast the *Google* tasks with varying morpho-syntactic and light semantic content against the semantic relation tasks *Sem-Gen* and the deep semantic tasks *Sem-Para*. We observe that performance across models and languages is still high when addressing semantic relatedness on a coarse-grained level (*Sem-Gen*): This is true when the number of related pairs is comparably low, and the relation types differ more strongly (*RG* and *WordSim*), or when the search space is very restricted (*TOEFL*, which is a multiple choice task). However, accuracy is dramatically low when deep semantic knowledge is required, as in *Sem-Para*. Only *adj-ant* and *noun-syn* achieve accuracy scores of over 5.0% for both languages. In most cases, lemmatization slightly helps by reducing the search space, because distinguishing between word forms is not required by the tasks. Yet, the gain is lower than we had expected due to lemmatization errors on the web data, which led to a considerable set of full inflected forms still being part of the search spaces.

Data analysis reveals the following major error types in the *Sem-Para* task category: Next to a minority of clearly wrong solutions, the CBOW model suggested wrong words/lemmas that are nevertheless related to the requested solution, either morphologically or semantically. An example for a wrong but morphologically similar solution is *Freiheit (freedom)* instead of *gefangen (caught)* as the prediction for *unfruchtbar:fruchtbar::frei:? (sterile:fertile::free:?)*. Examples for wrong but semantically similar solutions are the hyponym *Holzstuhl (wooden chair)* instead of the hypernym *Möbel (furniture)* for *Atomwaffe:Waffe::Stuhl:? (atomic weapon:weapon::chair:?)*; the synonym *erhöhen (increase)* instead of the antonym *abfallen (decrease)* for *verbieten:erlauben::ansteigen:? (forbid:allow::increase:?)*; and the synonym *undetermined* instead of the antonym *known* for *manual:automatic::unknown:?*. Overall, wrong semantic suggestions are most often synonyms (instead of hypernyms or antonyms).

Morphological variation is again a more serious problem for the German data, not only regarding inflection but also regarding composition: many wrong solutions are compounds suggested for their heads (as in the *Stuhl–Holzstuhl* example above). Further examples of this type of error are *Cayennepfeffer (cayenne pepper)* instead of *Salz (salt)* as the antonym of *Pfeffer (pepper)*; and *Lufttemperatur (air temperature)* instead of *Wärme (warmth)* as the synonym of *Temperatur (temperature)*.

[4]The performance gap on the *Google-Sem* tasks is smaller. An exception is *city-in-state*, where this gap may be attributed to better coverage of American cities in English.

	Sem-Para (Rec10)						
	adj-ant	verb-ant	noun-ant	noun-syn	noun-hyp	BLESS-hyp	BLESS-mer
				CBOW			
EN W	25.5	7.7	3.9	**29.1**	7.9	4.6	0.6
EN L	23.6	**9.1**	4.3	26.8	9.0	5.6	0.6
DE W	14.4	4.2	17.5	27.3	4.9	–	–
DE L	15.1	7.1	16.1	27.1	6.2	–	–
				SKIP			
EN W	**25.7**	7.2	3.4	21.6	5.0	4.0	0.6
EN L	23.7	6.7	3.2	21.9	5.7	5.4	0.8
DE W	15.2	2.9	17.1	24.2	5.8	–	–
DE L	**15.5**	2.9	16.8	22.3	3.9	–	–
				BOW			
EN W	24.9	7.1	6.1	21.0	18.6	6.1	1.9
EN L	16.4	6.4	**6.7**	20.3	**19.6**	**8.5**	**2.4**
DE W	6.3	**7.8**	**28.3**	26.8	4.9	–	–
DE L	8.5	5.8	22.8	**31.0**	**6.8**	–	–

Table 3: *Sem-Para* results across models, for recall at ten.

Table 3 compares the *Sem-Para* results across models, now relying on recall of the target being in the top 10 (Rec10). We consider this measure a fairer choice than accuracy because (a) the *Sem-Para* dataset contains considerably more difficult tasks, and (b) the higher proportions allow a better comparison across conditions. Bold font indicates the best results per column and language. Similar to before, the best results are reached for *adj-ant* and *noun-syn*, as well as for *noun-ant*, with Rec10 between 25.7% and 31.0%. Performance on *noun-hyp* reaches $> 15\%$ in only two cases, and the *verb-ant* and *BLESS* results are always $< 10.0\%$ for both languages and W/L conditions. Furthermore, there is no clear tendency for one of the languages or W vs. L to outperform the other. It is clear, however, that the superiority of the CBOW model in comparison to BOW vanished: in most cases, the BOW models outperform the CBOW (and SKIP) models, most impressively for *noun-ant* and *noun-hyp*.

4 Conclusion

We presented a systematic cross-lingual investigation of predict vectors on morpho-syntactic and semantic tasks. First, we showed that their overall performance in German, a morphologically richer language, is lower than in English. Second, we found that none of the vector spaces encodes deep semantic information reliably: In both languages, they lack the ability to solve analogies of paradigmatic relations.

Acknowledgments

The research was supported by the DFG Collaborative Research Centre SFB 732 (Maximilian Köper) and the DFG Heisenberg Fellowship SCHU-2580 (Sabine Schulte im Walde).

References

Baroni, M., S. Bernardini, A. Ferraresi, and E. Zanchetta (2009). The WaCky Wide Web: A collection of very large linguistically processed web-crawled corpora. *Language Resources and Evaluation 43*(3), 209–226.

Baroni, M., G. Dinu, and G. Kruszewski (2014). Don't count, predict! A systematic comparison of context-counting vs. context-predicting semantic vectors. In *Proceedings of the 52nd Annual Meeting of the Association for Computational Linguistics*, pp. 238–247.

Baroni, M. and A. Lenci (2011). How we BLESSed distributional semantic evaluation. In *Proceedings of the EMNLP Workshop on Geometrical Models for Natural Language Semantics*, pp. 1–10.

Bengio, Y., R. Ducharme, P. Vincent, and C. Jauvin (2003). A neural probabilistic language model. *Journal of Machine Learning Research 3*, 1137–1155.

Faruqui, M. and C. Dyer (2014). Improving vector space word representations using multilingual correlation. In *Proceedings of the 14th Conference of the European Chapter of the Association for Computational Linguistics*, pp. 462–471.

Finkelstein, L., E. Gabrilovich, Y. Matias, E. Rivlin, Z. Solan, G. Wolfman, and E. Ruppin (2001). Placing search in context: The concept revisited. In *Proceedings of the 10th International Conference on the World Wide Web*, pp. 406–414.

Gurevych, I. (2005). Using the structure of a conceptual network in computing semantic relatedness. In *Proceedings of the 2nd International Joint Conference on Natural Language Processing*, pp. 767–778.

Landauer, T. K. and S. T. Dumais (1997). A solution to Plato's problem: The latent semantic analysis theory of acquisition, induction and representation of knowledge. *Psychological Review 104*(2), 211–240.

Levy, O. and Y. Goldberg (2014). Linguistic regularities in sparse and explicit word representations. In *Proceedings of the 18th Conference on Computational Natural Language Learning*, pp. 171–180.

Melamud, O., I. Dagan, J. Goldberger, I. Szpektor, and D. Yuret (2014). Probabilistic modeling of joint-context in distributional similarity. In *Proceedings of the 18th Conference on Computational Natural Language Learning*, pp. 181–190.

Mikolov, T., K. Chen, G. Corrado, and J. Dean (2013). Efficient estimation of word representations in vector space. In *Proceedings of the International Conference on Learning Representations*.

Mikolov, T., I. Sutskever, K. Chen, G. S. Corrado, and J. Dean (2013). Distributed representations of words and phrases and their compositionality. In *Advances in Neural Information Processing Systems 26*, pp. 3111–3119.

Mikolov, T., W.-t. Yih, and G. Zweig (2013). Linguistic regularities in continuous space word representations. In *Proceedings of the Conference of the North American Chapter of the Association for Computational Linguistics: Human Language Technologies*, pp. 746–751.

Mohammad, S., I. Gurevych, G. Hirst, and T. Zesch (2007). Cross-lingual distributional profiles of concepts for measuring semantic distance. In *Proceedings of the Joint Conference on Empirical Methods in Natural Language Processing and Computational Natural Language Learning*, pp. 571–580.

Rei, M. and T. Briscoe (2014). Looking for hyponyms in vector space. In *Proceedings of the 18th Conference on Computational Natural Language Learning*, pp. 68–77.

Rubenstein, H. and J. B. Goodenough (1965). Contextual correlates of synonymy. *Communications of the ACM 8*(10), 627–633.

Schäfer, R. and F. Bildhauer (2012). Building large corpora from the web using a new efficient tool chain. In *Proceedings of the 8th International Conference on Language Resources and Evaluation*, pp. 486–493.

Scheible, S. and S. Schulte im Walde (2014). A database of paradigmatic semantic relation pairs for German nouns, verbs, and adjectives. In *Proceedings of the COLING Workshop on Lexical and Grammatical Resources for Language Processing*, pp. 111–119.

Schmidt, S., P. Scholl, C. Rensing, and R. Steinmetz (2011). Cross-lingual recommendations in a resource-based learning scenario. In *Towards Ubiquitious Learning, Proceedings of the 6th European Conference on Technology Enhanced Learning*, pp. 356–369.

Wolf, L., Y. Hanani, K. Bar, and N. Dershowitz (2013). Joint `word2vec` networks for bilingual semantic representations. In *Proceedings of the 15th International Conference on Intelligent Text Processing and Computational Linguistics*.

Zuanović, L., M. Karan, and J. Šnajder (2014). Experiments with neural word embeddings for Croatian. In *Proceedings of the 9th Language Technologies Conference*, pp. 69–72.

Clarifying Intentions in Dialogue: A Corpus Study*

Julian J. Schlöder and Raquel Fernández
Institute for Logic, Language and Computation
University of Amsterdam
julian.schloeder@gmail.com, raquel.fernandez@uva.nl

Abstract

As part of our ongoing work on grounding in dialogue, we present a corpus-based investigation of intention-level clarification requests. We propose to refine existing theories of grounding by considering two distinct types of intention-related conversational problems: *intention recognition* and *intention adoption*. This distinction is backed-up by an annotation experiment conducted on a corpus assembled with a novel method for automatically retrieving potential requests for clarification.

1 Introduction

Dialogue is commonly modelled as a *joint activity* where the interlocutors are not merely making individual moves, but actively collaborate. A central coordination device is the *common ground* of the dialogue participants, the information they mutually take for granted (Stalnaker, 1978). This common ground is changed and expanded over the course of a conversation in a process called *grounding* (Clark, 1996). We are interested in the mechanisms used to establish agreement, *i.e.*, in the conversational means to establish a belief as *joint*. To investigate this issue, in this paper we examine cases where grounding (partially) fails, as indicated by the presence of clarifications requests (CRs). In contrast to previous work (*i.a.*, Gabsdil, 2003; Purver, 2004; Rodríguez and Schlangen, 2004), which has mostly focused on CRs triggered by acoustic and semantic understanding problems, we are particularly concerned with problems related to intention *recognition* (going beyond semantic interpretation) and intention *adoption* (*i.e.*, mutual agreement). The following examples, from the AMI Meeting Corpus (Carletta, 2007), are cases in point:

(1) A: I think that's all.
B: **Meeting's over?**

(2) A: Just uh do that quickly.
B: **How do you do it?**

(3) A: I'd say two.
B: **Why?**

In these examples, it cannot be said that B has fully grounded A's proposal, but also not that B rejects A's utterance. Rather, B asks a question that is conducive to the grounding process. In (1), B has apparently understood A's utterance, but is unsure as to whether A's intention was to conclude the session. We therefore consider CRs like B's question in (1) as related to *intention recognition*. In contrast, in (2) and (3), B displays unwillingness or inability (but no outright refusal) to ground A's proposal, and requests further information she needs to establish common ground, *i.e.*, to *adopt* A's intention *as joint*. Requests for instructions have also been related to clarification in Benotti's (2009) work on multiagent planning.

In this paper, we present a corpus-based investigation of intention-level clarification, part of an ongoing project that aims to analyse the grounding process beyond semantic interpretation. In the next section, we introduce some theoretical observations and refine existing theories of grounding (Clark, 1996; Allwood, 1995) by distinguishing between *intention recognition* and *intention adoption*. We then present a systematic heuristic to retrieve potential clarification requests from dialogue corpora and discuss the results of a small-scale annotation experiment.[1] We end with pointers for future work.

*The research presented in this paper has been funded by the European Community's Seventh Framework Programme (FP7/2007-2013) under grant agreement no. 567652 *ESSENCE: Evolution of Shared Semantics in Computational Environments* (http://www.essence-network.com/).

[1] We will make our annotated data freely available.

Proceedings of the 11th International Conference on Computational Semantics, pages 46–51,
London, UK, April 15-17 2015. ©2015 Association for Computational Linguistics

	Level		Joint Action	Example Clarification
1	contact		A and B pay attention to each other	*Are you talking to me?*
2	perception		A produces a signal and B perceives it	*What did you say?*
3	understanding		A conveys a meaning and B recognises it	*What did you mean?*
4.1	uptake	intention recognition	A intends a project and B understands it	*What do you want?*
4.2		intention adoption	A proposes a project and B accepts it	*Why should we do this?*

Table 1: Grounding hierarchy for speaker A and addressee B with refined uptake level.

2 Theoretical Observations

As extensively discussed by Hulstijn and Maudet (2006), the intentional level we are interested in is commonly denoted with the term *uptake*. In particular, in Clark's (1996) stratification of the grounding process into four distinct levels (see Table 1 for our take on it), the fourth level, "proposal and consideration (uptake)," is related to the speaker's intentions. When discussing joint projects at level 4, Clark introduces the notion of *joint construals*: the determination and consideration of speaker meaning, including the intended illocutionary force (Clark, 1996, pp. 212–213). However, he also points out that uptake may fail due to unwillingness or inability: "when respondents are unwilling or unable to comply with the project as proposed, they can *decline* to take it up" (Clark, 1996, p. 204). We contend that this difference between construal and compliance—between intention recognition and intention adoption—has been obscured in the literature so far.[2] For example, in their annotation scheme for CRs, Rodríguez and Schlangen (2004) reproduce the underspecification in labelling their level 4 CRs as "recognising or evaluating speaker intention."

Since we, with Clark (1996), consider such intentional categories to be part of the grounding hierarchy, we expect problems on an intentional level to be evinced in much the same way as other conversational mishaps: in particular by CRs aimed at fixing these different types of conversational trouble. When studying the CRs annotated as intention related in the corpus of Rodríguez and Schlangen (2004) we indeed find examples related to *recognition* and others which aim at *adoption*:[3]

(4) K: okay, again from the top
I: **from the very top?**
K: no, well, [. . .]

(5) K: for me that is in fact below this
I: **why below?**
K: yes, it belongs there, all okay.

In (4), speaker I has evidently not fully understood what K's question is, despite having successfully parsed and understood the propositional content of K's utterance. On the other hand, I displays no such problem in (5), but rather some reluctance to adopt K's assertion as common ground. We consider (4) to be a clarification question related to *intention recognition* whereas the one in (5) relates to *intention adoption*. A particularly striking class of intention recognition CRs are *speech act determination* questions as in the following example:[4]

(6) A: And we're going to discuss [. . .] who's gonna do what and just clarify
B: **Are you asking me whether I wanna be in there?**

Our hypothesis is that the classes of clarification requests related to intention recognition and intention adoption, respectively, are distinct and discernible. In particular, we propose to improve upon Clark's (1996) hierarchy by splitting his uptake-level into two, separating recognition from adoption. Table 1 shows our amended hierarchy and constructed examples for clarification requests evincing failure at a certain level. To test this hypothesis, we have surveyed existing corpora of CRs and assembled a novel corpus of intention-related CRs to check if annotators could reasonably discern the two classes.

[2] While DIT++ (Bunt, 2012) stratifies the grounding hierarchy into "attention / perception / interpretation / evaluation / execution," it is similarly underspecified: To us, evaluation (*e.g.*, checking an asserted proposition for consistency) relates to intention adoption, whereas (semantic) understanding and (pragmatic) intention retrieval (*e.g.*, recognising on level 4.1 that an indicative was intended as an *inform* act and hence requires a consistency check on level 4.2) are again distinct categories.

[3] We thank the authors for providing us with their annotated corpus; in the dialogues, I is explaining to K how to assemble a paper airplane. We had the German-language examples translated to English by a native speaker of German.

[4] Retrieved from the British National Corpus (BNC) (Burnard, 2000) using SCoRE (Purver, 2001).

3 Corpus Study

3.1 Previous Studies

Our work builds on previous corpus studies of CRs (Purver et al., 2003; Rodríguez and Schlangen, 2004; Rieser and Moore, 2005). However, existent studies are not perfectly suited for investigating grounding at the level of intentions.[5] Firstly, the annotation scheme of Purver et al. (2003; 2004), which the authors apply to a section of the BNC (Burnard, 2000), makes use of semantic categories that cannot easily be mapped to the intention-level distinctions introduced in the previous section. Secondly, while the schemes employed by Rodríguez and Schlangen (2004) and Rieser and Moore (2005) (both based on Schlangen, 2004) do include a category for intention-level CRs, the corpora they annotate—the Bielefeld Corpus and the Carnegie Mellon Communicator Corpus, respectively—are highly task-oriented and hence the intentions of the interlocutors are to a large degree presupposed: the participants intend to fulfil the task. Finally, in all cases, the focus of the authors did not lie with intentional clarification and therefore they might have left out questions in their annotations that are interesting to us, in particular more complex intention adoption CRs (which may not have been considered CRs to begin with, given the lack of well established theoretical distinctions discussed in the previous section).

For our study, we have chosen to extract questions from the AMI Meeting Corpus (Carletta, 2007), a collection of dialogues amongst four participants role-playing a design team for a TV remote control. The dialogues are loosely task- and goal-oriented, but the conversation is mostly unconstrained. Due to this setting, we expect a larger amount of discussion and decision making, which should give rise to more intention-level CRs. In addition, the rich annotations distributed with the AMI Corpus enabled us to apply a sophisticated heuristic to automatically extract potential CRs, which we describe next.

3.2 Data

The AMI Corpus is annotated with dialogue acts, including a class of '`Elicit-*`' acts denoting different kinds of information requests/questions, but without specifically distinguishing CRs. However, the corpus is also annotated with relations between utterances, loosely called *adjacency pair* annotation,[6] which indicates whether or not an utterance is considered a direct reply to another one. We utilise observations on the sequential nature of CRs ("other-initiated repair") in group settings made by Schegloff (2000) to assemble a set of possible clarification requests as follows. Take all utterances Q where:

a. Q is turn-initial and annotated as an '`Elicit-`' type of dialogue act, spoken by a speaker B.

b. Q is the second part of an adjacency pair; the first part (the *source*) is spoken by another speaker A.

c. Q is the first part of another adjacency pair; the second part (the *answer*) is spoken by A as well.

This heuristic is based on the intuition that CRs are proper questions (*i.e.*, utterances that demand an answer) with a backward-looking function (*i.e.*, related to an earlier source utterance) that are typically answered by the speaker of the source. We expect this heuristic to have a sufficiently high recall to be quantitatively applicable, but are aware that it cannot find each and every CR.[7]

There are 338 utterances Q in the AMI Corpus satisfying the criteria above. We note that the annotation manual for the AMI Corpus states that CRs are usually annotated as '`Elicit-`' acts, but that some very simple CRs (*e.g.*, *'huh?'*) can instead be tagged as '`Comment-about-Understanding (und)`.' However, this class also contains some backchannel utterances: positive comments about understanding. If we apply the same heuristic to the utterances annotated as 'und,' we find 195 additional possible CRs. We confirmed that our heuristic successfully separates CRs from backchannels, and that these CRs are

[5] We have carefully studied the annotated data described in Purver et al. (2003) and Rodríguez and Schlangen (2004), which was kindly provided to us by the authors upon request.

[6] See `http://mmm.idiap.ch/private/ami/annotation/dialogue_acts_manual_1.0.pdf`.

[7] In particular, previous work indicates that some CRs are simply not answered; Rodríguez and Schlangen (2004) report 8.7% unanswered CRs in their corpus. Our heuristic does not find these.

indeed related to levels 1–3 of Clark's (1996) hierarchy. However, these utterances are not the primary subject of our study. We henceforth refer to CRs on levels 1–3 collectively as *low-level.*

3.3 Annotation Procedure

As indicated above, we are primarily interested in the 338 possible CRs annotated as '`Elicit-`' dialogue acts and therefore included only these in our annotation. Since our main interest is in intention-level CRs and our primary ambition is the investigation of intention adoption *vs.* intention recognition, we used the following simple annotation scheme: Each question found by our heuristic is annotated as one of {`not`, `low`, `int-rec`, `int-ad`, `ambig`}, where the categories are defined as follows.

- **not CR.** Select this category if you are sure that the question is not a clarification request. That is, if it does *not* serve to better the askers understanding of the previous highlighted utterance. For instance if the question is requesting novel information, moving the dialogue forward.
- **low CR.** Select this category if the question indicates that the asker has not fully understood the *semantic / propositional content* of the previous highlighted utterance. This includes, for example, *word meaning* problems, *acoustic* problems, or *reference resolution.*
- **intention recognition CR.** Select this category if the question indicates semantic understanding, but that the CR utterer *has not fully understood (or is trying to guess)* the speaker's goal/intention (the intended function of the previous highlighted utterance). The prototypical case is *speech act determination.*
- **intention adoption CR.** Select this category if the question indicates the CR utterer *has understood/recognised* the speaker's main goal (their intention), *but does not yet accept it because he wants/needs more information or he has incompatible beliefs.* For instance, if the CR utterer asks about the reason behind the speaker's utterance before accepting it, or requests information needed to carry out her proposal.
- **ambiguous.** Sometimes it may not be possible to decide what function a CR has precisely, maybe due to a lack of context. In those cases, annotate the question as ambiguous.

We instructed our annotators to follow a decision tree where they first decide whether a question is clearly *not* a CR, and only otherwise consider the different categories of CRs. This is because in a pilot study we found that the distinction between '`not CR`' and '`intention adoption CR`' was difficult for some annotators. To reduce the confusion, we defined the '`not CR`' class as only clear-cut cases of not-CR questions, at the risk of incurring a higher amount of ambiguity when the decision tree bottoms out, *i.e.*, when a question that was not definitely not a CR could not be matched to a CR-category after all. Our annotation scheme only refines one dimension (namely, '`source`') of the multi-dimensional schemes applied by Rodríguez and Schlangen (2004) and Rieser and Moore (2005). Since our main ambition in this work is to establish the two levels of intentionality, we leave a fuller annotation with further dimensions—such as syntactic categories like Schlangen's (2004) '`form`'—for future work.

Nevertheless, this is a difficult annotation task: Annotators can only play the role of overhearer and therefore have a more indirect access to the intentions of the interlocutors. In addition, CRs in particular can be fragmented and ambiguous. Therefore, annotators were shown a substantial dialogue excerpt starting 10 utterances before the source and ending with either the 10th utterance after the answer to the CR or with the CR-asker's next reply (the *follow-up*). We found that answer and follow-up are particularly helpful in determining the function of a CR: the answer gives hints towards the speaker's interpretation of the CR, and the follow-up can show whether the asker agrees with that construal.[8]

In the full study, the corpus was annotated by 2 expert annotators, since we deemed the task to be too complex and fine-grained for naïve annotators. One third of the corpus was annotated by both annotators, the remaining two thirds by one annotator each. To create a gold-standard on the overlapping segment, the annotators discussed the utterances where their initial judgement differed and mutually agreed on the appropriate annotation.

[8]Rodríguez and Schlangen (2004) include the CR asker's '`happiness`' (as evinced by the follow-up) in their annotation.

Category	Count	including 'und'	Example
not CR	90 (27%)	-	A: *'You can call me Peter.' – B: 'And you are? In the project?'*
low-level	78 (23%)	273 (62%)	A: *'Seventy-five percent of users find it ugly.' – B: 'The LCD?'*
intent. recognition	53 (16%)	53 (12%)	A: *'I think that's all.' – B: 'Meeting's over?'*
intent. adoption	77 (23%)	77 (17%)	A: *'That's a very unnatural motion.' – B: 'Do you think?'*
ambiguous	40 (12%)	40 (9%)	
Total	338 (100%)	443 (100%)	

Table 2: Distribution of clarification requests in our corpus with examples for each category.

3.4 Results

In the five-way classification task described above, our annotators had an agreement (Cohen's κ, 1960) of $\kappa = 0.76$ on the overlapping third of the corpus;[9] of $\kappa = 0.85$ in the boolean task of determining whether an utterance is a CR; and of $\kappa = 0.82$ in the boolean task of retrieving intention-related CRs from all other questions. The distribution of categories is shown in Table 2. In order to compare our distribution to previous work, we have also recorded the distribution we obtain when dropping the items annotated as '`not CR`' and adding the questions annotated as '`Comment-about-Understanding (und)`' as low-level CRs. Then the total number of CRs in our corpus is 443.

The AMI Corpus contains about 42,000 turns, so we found that roughly 1.1% of turns receive clarification according to our heuristic. Previous studies have indicated a higher number: Purver (2004) reports about 4% and Rodríguez and Schlangen (2004) about 5.8%. Rodríguez and Schlangen (2004) themselves conjecture that their corpus might contain an unusually high amount of CRs due to the setting (an instructor guiding a builder). For comparison, we have manually extracted CRs from a 2500-turn subset of the AMI Corpus: We found 52 CRs in that segment, indicating that about 2% of turns prompt a CR. It is to be expected that our heuristic misses some CRs, *e.g.*, ones that do not receive an answer, and its coverage is dependent on how systematic the adjacency pair annotation in the AMI Corpus is.

While our heuristic only retrieves an estimated 50% of CRs,[10] the distribution of classes we found is comparable to the results described by Rodríguez and Schlangen (2004) and Rieser and Moore (2005): They report 63.5% and 75%, respectively, of low-level CRs and 22.2% / 20% on intention-level. Rodríguez and Schlangen (2004) mark the remaining 14.3% as ambiguous, whereas Rieser and Moore (2005) report 5% "other/several" and do not mention an ambiguity class.[11] By and large, this is comparable to the distribution we found. We have low ambiguity (9%) compared to Rodríguez and Schlangen (2004) because we conflated different categories of lower-level CRs into one '`low CR`' category. As we had hoped, we find a larger amount (29%) of intention-level CRs than the previous studies. We take the similarity in distributions as tacitly confirming the viability of our heuristic for quantitative evaluation.

4 Conclusion

We have theoretically motivated a distinction within grounding hierarchies between *intention recognition* and *intention adoption* and have created a novel corpus of intention-level CRs to investigate its tenability. Our corpus is not only novel in its contents, but also in its construction: unlike previous studies, we have developed and applied a suitable heuristic that exploits rich existing annotations to automatically find possible clarification requests. A small-scale annotation experiment on our corpus showed that the theoretical distinction we propose is viable. Our immediate next step in this project is a deeper investigation into the form and problem sources of the intention-level CRs in our corpus, including a more fine-grained annotation.

[9] Rodríguez and Schlangen (2004) report $\kappa = 0.7$ in the task of determining the level of understanding that the CR addresses. However, their categorisation is different from ours. In particular, they do not include a '`not CR`' category.

[10] We surveyed the CRs not found by our heuristic and attribute this mostly to the adjacency pair annotation; however, in addition to CRs that are not answered at all, there are also CRs that are answered by a different person than the source speaker.

[11] Their category "ambiguity" refers to a class of CRs dubbed "ambiguity refinement" and not to uncertainty in the annotation.

References

Allwood, J. (1995). An activity based approach to pragmatics. *Gothenburg papers in theoretical linguistics* (76), 1–38.

Benotti, L. (2009). Clarification potential of instructions. In *Proceedings of the 10th Annual Meeting of the Special Interest Group on Discourse and Dialogue (SIGdial)*.

Bunt, H. (2012). The semantics of feedback. In *Proceedings of the 16th SemDial Workshop on the Semantics and Pragmatics of Dialogue (SeineDial)*.

Burnard, L. (2000). *Reference Guide for the British National Corpus (World Edition)*. Oxford University Computing Services.

Carletta, J. (2007). Unleashing the killer corpus: experiences in creating the multi-everything ami meeting corpus. *Language Resources and Evaluation 41*(2), 181–190.

Clark, H. H. (1996). *Using language*. Cambridge University Press.

Cohen, J. (1960). A coefficient of agreement for nominal scales. *Educational and Psychological Measurement 1*(20), 37–46.

Gabsdil, M. (2003). Clarification in spoken dialogue systems. In *Proceedings of the 2003 AAAI Spring Symposium. Workshop on Natural Language Generation in Spoken and Written Dialogue*, Stanford, CA, pp. 28–35.

Hulstijn, J. and N. Maudet (2006, June). Uptake and joint action. *Cognitive Systems Research 7*(2-3), 175–191.

Purver, M. (2001, October). SCoRE: A tool for searching the BNC. Technical Report TR-01-07, Department of Computer Science, King's College London.

Purver, M. (2004). *The Theory and Use of Clarification Requests in Dialogue*. Ph. D. thesis, King's College, University of London.

Purver, M., J. Ginzburg, and P. Healey (2003). On the means for clarification in dialogue. In *Current and new directions in discourse and dialogue*, pp. 235–255. Springer.

Rieser, V. and J. D. Moore (2005). Implications for generating clarification requests in task-oriented dialogues. In *Proceedings of the 43rd Annual Meeting of the Association for Computational Linguistics (ACL)*.

Rodríguez, K. J. and D. Schlangen (2004). Form, intonation and function of clarification requests in German task-oriented spoken dialogues. In *Proceedings of the 8th SemDial Workshop on the Semantics and Pragmatics of Dialogue (Catalog)*.

Schegloff, E. A. (2000). When 'others' initiate repair. *Applied Linguistics 21*(2), 205–243.

Schlangen, D. (2004). Causes and strategies for requesting clarification in dialogue. In *Proceedings of the 5th SIGdial Workshop on Discourse and Dialogue*.

Stalnaker, R. (1978). Assertion. In P. Cole (Ed.), *Pragmatics*, Volume 9 of *Syntax and Semantics*, pp. 315–332. New York Academic Press.

From distributional semantics to feature norms: grounding semantic models in human perceptual data

Luana Făgărășan, **Eva Maria Vecchi** and **Stephen Clark**
University of Cambridge
Computer Laboratory
{luana.fagarasan | eva.vecchi | stephen.clark}@cl.cam.ac.uk

Abstract

Multimodal semantic models attempt to ground distributional semantics through the integration of visual or perceptual information. Feature norms provide useful insight into human concept acquisition, but cannot be used to ground large-scale semantics because they are expensive to produce. We present an automatic method for predicting feature norms for new concepts by learning a mapping from a text-based distributional semantic space to a space built using feature norms. Our experimental results show that we are able to generalise feature-based concept representations, which opens up the possibility of developing large-scale semantic models grounded in a proxy for human perceptual data.

1 Introduction

Distributional semantic models (Turney and Pantel, 2010; Sahlgren, 2006) represent the meanings of words by relying on their statistical distribution in text (Erk, 2012; Bengio et al., 2006; Mikolov et al., 2013; Clark, 2015). Despite performing well in a wide range of semantic tasks, a common criticism is that by only representing meaning through linguistic input these models are not grounded in perception, since the words only exist in relation to each other and are not in relation to the physical world. This concern is motivated by the increasing evidence in the cognitive science literature that the semantics of words is derived not only from our exposure to the language, but also through our interactions with the world. One way to overcome this issue would be to include perceptual information in the semantic models (Barsalou et al., 2003). It has already been shown, for example, that models that learn from both visual and linguistic input improve performance on a variety of tasks such as word association or semantic similarity (Bruni et al., 2014).

However, the visual modality alone cannot capture all perceptual information that humans possess. A more cognitively sound representation of human intuitions in relation to particular concepts is given by semantic property norms, also known as semantic feature norms. A number of property norming studies (McRae et al., 2005; Vinson and Vigliocco, 2008; Devereux et al., 2013) have focused on collecting feature norms for various concepts in order to allow for empirical testing of psychological semantic theories. In these studies humans are asked to identify the most important attributes of a concept; *e.g.* given AIRPLANE, its most important features could be `to_fly`, `has_wings` and `is_used_for_transport`. These datasets provide a valuable insight into human concept representation and have been successfully used for tasks such as text simplification for limited vocabulary groups, personality modelling and metaphor processing, as well as a proxy for modelling perceptual information (Riordan and Jones, 2011; Andrews et al., 2009; Hill et al., 2014). Feature norms provide an interesting source of semantic information because they capture higher level conceptual knowledge in comparison to the low level perceptual information represented in images, for example.

Despite their advantages, semantic feature norms are not widely used in computational linguistics, mainly because they are expensive to produce and have only been collected for small sets of words; moreover there is no finite list of features that can be produced for a given concept. In Roller and Schulte im

Proceedings of the 11th International Conference on Computational Semantics, pages 52–57,
London, UK, April 15-17 2015. ©2015 Association for Computational Linguistics

SHRIMP	CUCUMBER	DRESS
is_edible, 19	a_vegetable, 25	clothing, 21
is_small, 17	eaten_in_salads, 24	worn_by_women, 15
lives_in_water, 12	is_green, 23	is_feminine, 10
is_pink, 11	is_long, 15	is_formal, 10
tastes_good, 9	eaten_as_pickles, 12	is_long, 10
has_a_shell, 8	has_skin, 9	different_styles, 9
lives_in_oceans, 8	grows_in_gardens, 7	made_of_material, 9

Table 1: Examples of features and production frequencies for concepts from the McRae norms

Walde (2013), the authors construct a three-way multimodal model, integrating textual, feature and visual modalities. However, this method is restricted to the same disadvantages of feature norm datasets. There have been some attempts at automatically generating feature norms using large text corpora (Kelly et al., 2014; Baroni et al., 2010; Barbu, 2008) but the generated features are often a production of carefully crafted rules and statistical distribution of words in text rather than a proxy for human conceptual knowledge. Our work focuses on predicting features for new concepts, by learning a mapping from a distributional semantic space based solely on linguistic input to a more cognitively-sound semantic space where feature norms are seen as a proxy for perceptual information. A precedent for this work has been set in Johns and Jones (2012), but whilst they predict feature representations through global lexical similarity, we infer them through learning a cross-modal mapping.

2 Mapping between semantic spaces

The integration of perceptual and linguistic information is supported by a large body of work in the cognitive science literature (Riordan and Jones, 2011; Andrews et al., 2009) that shows that models that include both types of information perform better at fitting human semantic data.

The idea of learning a mapping between semantic spaces appears in previous work; for example Lazaridou et al. (2014) learn a cross-modal mapping between text and images and Mikolov et al. (2013) show that a linear mapping between vector spaces of different languages can be learned by only relying on a small amount of bilingual information from which missing dictionary entries can be inferred. Following the approach in Mikolov et al. (2013), we learn a linear mapping between the distributional space and the feature-based space.

2.1 Feature norm datasets

One of the largest and most widely used feature-norm datasets is from McRae et al. (2005). Participants were asked to produce a list of features for a given concept, whilst being encouraged to write down different kinds of properties, *e.g.* how the concept feels, smells or for what it is used (Table 1). The dataset contains a total of 2526 features for 541 concrete concepts, with a mean of 13.7 features per concept. More recently, Devereux et al. (2013) collected semantic properties for 638 concrete concepts in a similar fashion. There are also other property norms datasets which contain verbs and nouns referring to events (Vinson and Vigliocco, 2008). Since the semantic property norms in the McRae dataset have been used extensively in the literature as a proxy for perceptual information, we will report our experimental results on this dataset.

2.2 Semantic spaces

A feature-based semantic space (**FS**) can be represented in a similar way to the co-occurrence based distributional models. Concepts are treated as target words, features as context words and co-occurrence counts are replaced with production frequencies, *i.e.* the number of participants that produced the feature for a given concept (Table 2). We build two such feature-based semantic spaces: one using all the 2526

	has_fur	has_wheels	an_animal	a_pet
cat_FS	22	0	21	17
	dog	black	book	animal
cat_DS	4516	3124	1500	2480

Table 2: Example representation of CAT in the feature-based and distributional spaces

features in the McRae dataset as contexts (FS1) and one obtained by reducing the dimensions of FS1 to 300 using SVD (FS2).

For the distributional spaces (**DS**), we experimented with various parameter settings, and built four spaces using Wikipedia as a corpus and sentence-like windows together with the following parameters:

- DS1: contexts are the top 10K most frequent content words in Wikipedia, values are raw co-occurrence counts.
- DS2: same contexts as DS1, counts are re-weighted using PPMI and normalised as detailed in Polajnar and Clark (2014).
- DS3: perform SVD to 300 dimensions on DS2.
- DS4: same as DS3 but with row normalisation performed after dimensionality reduction.

We also use the context-predicting vectors available as part of the word2vec[1] project (Mikolov et al., 2013) (DS5). These vectors are 300 dimensional and are trained on a Google News dataset (100 billion words).

2.3 The mapping function

Our goal is to learn a function f: **DS** $\rightarrow$ **FS** that maps a distributional vector for a concept to its feature-based vector. Following Mikolov et al. (2013), we learn the mapping as a linear relationship between the distributional representation of a word and its featural representation. We estimate the coefficients of the function using (multivariate) partial least squares regression (PLSR) as implemented in the R pls package (Mevik and Wehrens, 2007), with the latent dimension parameter of PLSR set to 50.

3 Experimental results

We performed all experiments using a training set of 400 randomly selected McRae concepts and a test set of the remaining 138.[2] We use the featural representations of the concepts in the training set in order to learn a mapping between the two spaces, and the featural representations of the concepts in the test set as gold-standard vectors in order to analyse the quality of the learned transformation.

For each item in the test set, we computed the concept's predicted vector, $f(\vec{x})$, by applying the learned mapping, f, to the concept's representation in **DS**, $\vec{x}$. We then retrieved the top neighbours of the predicted vector in **FS** using cosine similarity. We were interested in observing, for a given concept, whether the gold-standard featural vector was retrieved in the topN neighbours of the predicted featural vector. Results averaged over the entire test set are summarised in Table 3. We also report the performance of a random baseline (RAND), where a concept's nearest neighbours are randomly ranked, and we note that our model outperforms chance by a large margin.

For the experiments in which the feature space dimensions are interpretable, *i.e.* not reduced (FS1), we also report the MAP (Mean Average Precision). This allows us to measure the learnt mapping's ability to assign higher values to the gold features of a McRae concept (those properties that have a non-zero production frequency for a particular concept in the McRae dataset) than to the non-gold features.

[1]https://code.google.com/p/word2vec/

[2]Out of the 541 McRae concepts, we discarded three (AXE, ARMOUR and DUNEBUGGY) because they were not available in the pre-trained word2vec vectors.

DS	FS	top1	top5	top10	top20	MAP
RAND	-	0.37	0.74	1.85	3.70	-
DS1	FS1	0.72	14.49	29.71	49.28	0.30
DS2	FS1	2.90	12.32	23.91	47.10	0.29
DS3	FS1	2.90	13.04	24.64	49.28	0.37
DS3	FS2	2.17	15.22	26.09	50.00	-
DS4	FS2	3.62	15.22	25.36	49.28	-
DS5	FS1	1.45	14.49	24.64	44.20	0.29
DS5	FS2	1.45	19.57	26.09	46.38	-

Table 3: Percentage (%) of test items that retrieve their gold-standard vector in the topN neighbours of their predicted vector.

Word	Nearest neighbours of predicted vector	Result	Top weighted predicted features
JAR	bucket, strainer, pot, spatula	not top20	made_of_plastic, is_round*, made_of_metal, found_in_kitchens*
JEANS	shawl, shirt, blouse, sweater	not top20	clothing, different_colours, worn_by_women*
BUGGY	skateboard, truck, scooter, cart	in top20	has_wheels, made_of_wood*, is_large*, used_for_transportation
SEAWEED	shrimp, perch, trout, salmon	in top20	is_edible, lives_in_water*, is_green, swims*, is_small*
HORSE	cow, ox, sheep, donkey	in top10	an_animal, has_4_legs, is_large, has_legs, lives_on_farms
PLATYPUS	otter, salamander, turtle, walrus	in top10	an_animal, is_small*, lives_in_water, is_long*,
SPARROW	starling, finch, partridge, sparrow	in top5	a_bird, flies, has_feathers, has_a_beak, has_wings
SPATULA	strainer, spatula, grater, colander	in top5	made_of_metal, found_in_kitchens, made_of_plastic
HATCHET	hatchet, machete, sword, dagger	in top1	made_of_metal, is_sharp, has_a_handle, a_tool, a_weapon*
GUN	gun, rifle, bazooka, shotgun	in top1	used_for_killing, a_weapon, made_of_metal, is_dangerous

Table 4: Qualitative analysis of predicted vectors (obtained by mapping from DS3 to FS1) for 10 concepts in the test set. Features annotated with an asterix(*) are not listed in the gold standard feature vector for the given concepts.

We compute the MAP score as follows: for each concept in the test set, we rank the features from the predicted feature vector in terms of their values, and measure the quality of this ranking with IR-based average precision, using the gold-standard feature set as the "relevant" feature set. The MAP score is then obtained by taking the mean average precision over the entire test set. Overall, the model seems to rank gold features highly, but the MAP score is certainly affected by the features which have not been seen in training (these account for 18.8% of the total number of features), because these will have a zero weight assigned to them, and so will be found at the end of the ranked feature list for that concept.

A qualitative evaluation of the top neighbours for predicted featural vectors can be found in Table 4. Overall, the mapping results look promising, even for items that do not list the gold feature vector as one of the top neighbours. However, overall the mapping looks too coarse. One reason could be the fact that the feature-based space is relatively sparse (the maximum number of features for a concept is 26, whereas there are over 2500 dimensions in the space). The reason why, for example, the predicted vector for JAR does not contain its gold standard in the top 20 neighbours might simply be that there are not enough discriminating features for the model to learn that a jar usually has a lid and a bucket does not; or that jeans are worn on the lower body, as opposed to shawls which are worn on the shoulders. It is important to note that a production frequency of zero for a concept-feature pair in the McRae dataset does not necessarily mean that the feature is not a plausible property of the concept, but only that it is not one of the most salient features, since it was not produced by any of the human participants (*e.g.* the feature `has_teeth` has not been listed as a property of CAT in the McRae dataset, but it is clearly a plausible property of the CAT concept). Many of the top-predicted features for the concepts in the test set are plausible, even if they are not listed in the gold data (*e.g* `lives_in_water` for SEAWEED). This is yet another indication that the concept-feature pairs listed in the McRae dataset are not complete, meaning that there are salient features that apply to some concepts which have not been spelled out by the participants.

The ability to generalise feature representations to unseen concepts also means that these can now be evaluated on standard NLP tasks since we can obtain full coverage on the evaluation datasets. In order to show that the quality of the predicted vectors is in line with the state of the art on modelling concept similarity and relatedness, we computed the correlation on a subset of 1288 noun-noun pairs (485 words) from the MEN dataset (Bruni et al., 2014), leaving it to future work to test such transformations on different parts of speech like verbs or adjectives. It is important to mention that in the construction of this subset we also excluded all McRae concepts from MEN, because we didn't want any of that training data to occur in the test set. The mapping function was trained on all the concepts in the McRae dataset and then used to predict featural vectors for words in the MEN subset described above. A qualitative analysis of the predicted vectors show that they contain highly plausible features for words that are highly perceptual (*e.g.* the top predicted features for COOKIE are `is_round`, `is_edible`, `tastes_good`, `eaten_by_baking`), as opposed to words that are more abstract or don't rely on perceptual information (*e.g.* the top predicted features for LOVE are `an_animal`, `made_of_metal`, `is_sharp`). We obtain the best Spearman correlation (0.71) for the predicted featural vectors by training the mapping on the Mikolov vectors (DS5), the Spearman correlation of these vectors on the MEN subset being 0.75. The high correlation with the MEN scores shows that the featural vectors capture lexical similarity well, but suggest that rather than using them in isolation to construct a semantic model, they would be most helpful as an added modality in a multimodal semantic model.

4 Conclusion

Feature norms have shown to be potentially useful as a proxy for human conceptual knowledge and grounding, an idea that has been the basis of numerous psychological studies despite the limited availability of large-scale data for various semantic tasks. In this paper, we present a methodology to automatically predict feature norms for new concepts by mapping the representation of the concept from a distributional space to its feature-based semantic representation.

Clearly much experimental work is yet to be done, but in this initial study we have demonstrated the promise of such a mapping. We see two major advantages to our approach. First, we are no longer limited to the sparse datasets and expensive procedures when working with feature norms, and second, we can gain a better understanding of the relationship between the distributional use of a word and our cognitive and experiential representation of the corresponding concept. We envisage a future in which a more sophisticated computational model of semantics, integrating text, vision, audio, perception and experience, will encompass our full intuition of a concept's meaning.

In future work, we plan to pursue this research in a number of ways. First, we aim to investigate ways to improve the mapping between spaces by exploring different machine learning approaches, such as other types of linear regression or canonical-correlation analysis. We are also interested in comparing the performance of non-linear transformations such as neural network embeddings with that of linear mappings. In addition, we wish to perform a more qualitative investigation of which distributional dimensions are particularly predictive of which feature norms in feature space.

Acknowledgments

LF is supported by an EPSRC Doctoral Training Grant. EMV is supported by ERC Starting Grant DisCoTex (306920). SC is supported by EPSRC grant EP/I037512/1 and ERC Starting Grant DisCoTex (306920). We thank Douwe Kiela and the anonymous reviewers for their helpful comments.

References

Andrews, M., G. Vigliocco, and D. Vinson (2009). Integrating experiential and distributional data to learn semantic representations. *Psychological review 116*(3), 463.

Barbu, E. (2008). Combining methods to learn feature-norm-like concept descriptions. In *Proceedings of the ESSLLI Workshop on Distributional Lexical Semantics*, pp. 9–16.

Baroni, M., B. Murphy, E. Barbu, and M. Poesio (2010). Strudel: A corpus-based semantic model based on properties and types. *Cognitive Science 34*(2), 222–254.

Barsalou, L. W., W. Kyle Simmons, A. K. Barbey, and C. D. Wilson (2003). Grounding conceptual knowledge in modality-specific systems. *Trends in cognitive sciences 7*(2), 84–91.

Bengio, Y., H. Schwenk, J.-S. Senécal, F. Morin, and J.-L. Gauvain (2006). Neural probabilistic language models. In *Innovations in Machine Learning*, pp. 137–186. Springer.

Bruni, E., N.-K. Tran, and M. Baroni (2014). Multimodal distributional semantics. *Journal Artificial Intelligence Research (JAIR) 49*, 1–47.

Clark, S. (2015). Vector space models of lexical meaning. *Handbook of Contemporary Semantics–second edition. Wiley-Blackwell.*

Devereux, B. J., L. K. Tyler, J. Geertzen, and B. Randall (2013). The centre for speech, language and the brain (cslb) concept property norms. *Behavior research methods*, 1–9.

Erk, K. (2012). Vector space models of word meaning and phrase meaning: A survey. *Language and Linguistics Compass 6*(10), 635–653.

Hill, F., R. Reichart, and A. Korhonen (2014). Multi-modal models for concrete and abstract concept meaning. *Transactions of the Association for Computational Linguistics 2*, 285–296.

Johns, B. T. and M. N. Jones (2012). Perceptual inference through global lexical similarity. *Topics in Cognitive Science 4*(1), 103–120.

Kelly, C., B. Devereux, and A. Korhonen (2014). Automatic extraction of property norm-like data from large text corpora. *Cognitive Science 38*(4), 638–682.

Lazaridou, A., E. Bruni, and M. Baroni (2014, June). Is this a wampimuk? cross-modal mapping between distributional semantics and the visual world. In *Proceedings of the 52nd Annual Meeting of the Association for Computational Linguistics (Volume 1: Long Papers)*, Baltimore, Maryland, pp. 1403–1414. Association for Computational Linguistics.

McRae, K., G. S. Cree, M. S. Seidenberg, and C. McNorgan (2005). Semantic feature production norms for a large set of living and nonliving things. *Behavior research methods 37*(4), 547–559.

Mevik, B.-H. and R. Wehrens (2007). The pls package: principal component and partial least squares regression in r. *Journal of Statistical Software 18*(2), 1–24.

Mikolov, T., K. Chen, G. Corrado, and J. Dean (2013). Efficient estimation of word representations in vector space. *arXiv preprint arXiv:1301.3781.*

Mikolov, T., Q. V. Le, and I. Sutskever (2013). Exploiting similarities among languages for machine translation. *arXiv preprint arXiv:1309.4168.*

Mikolov, T., W.-t. Yih, and G. Zweig (2013). Linguistic regularities in continuous space word representations. In *HLT-NAACL*, pp. 746–751. Citeseer.

Polajnar, T. and S. Clark (2014, April). Improving distributional semantic vectors through context selection and normalisation. In *Proceedings of the 14th Conference of the European Chapter of the Association for Computational Linguistics*, Gothenburg, Sweden, pp. 230–238. Association for Computational Linguistics.

Riordan, B. and M. N. Jones (2011). Redundancy in perceptual and linguistic experience: Comparing feature-based and distributional models of semantic representation. *Topics in Cognitive Science 3*(2), 303–345.

Roller, S. and S. Schulte im Walde (2013, October). A multimodal LDA model integrating textual, cognitive and visual modalities. In *Proceedings of the 2013 Conference on Empirical Methods in Natural Language Processing*, Seattle, Washington, USA, pp. 1146–1157. Association for Computational Linguistics.

Sahlgren, M. (2006). *The Word-Space Model.* Dissertation, Stockholm University.

Turney, P. D. and P. Pantel (2010). From frequency to meaning: Vector space models of semantics. *Journal of artificial intelligence research 37*(1), 141–188.

Vinson, D. P. and G. Vigliocco (2008). Semantic feature production norms for a large set of objects and events. *Behavior Research Methods 40*(1), 183–190.

Obtaining a Better Understanding of Distributional Models of German Derivational Morphology

Max Kisselew* Sebastian Padó* Alexis Palmer* Jan Šnajder†
*Institut für maschinelle Sprachverarbeitung, Stuttgart University, Germany
†Faculty of Electrical Engineering and Computing, University of Zagreb, Croatia
{kisselmx,pado,palmeras}@ims.uni-stuttgart.de jan.snajder@fer.hr

Abstract

Predicting the (distributional) meaning of derivationally related words (*read* / *read+er*) from one another has recently been recognized as an instance of distributional compositional meaning construction. However, the properties of this task are not yet well understood. In this paper, we present an analysis of two such composition models on a set of German derivation patterns (e.g., *-in*, *durch-*). We begin by introducing a rank-based evaluation metric, which reveals the task to be challenging due to specific properties of German (compounding, capitalization). We also find that performance varies greatly between patterns and even among base-derived term pairs of the same pattern. A regression analysis shows that semantic coherence of the base and derived terms within a pattern, as well as coherence of the semantic shifts from base to derived terms, all significantly impact prediction quality.

1 Introduction

Derivation is a major morphological process of word formation (e.g., *read* → *read+er*), which is typically associated with a fairly specific *semantic shift* (*+er*: agentivization). It may therefore be surprising that the semantics of derivation is a relatively understudied phenomenon in distributional semantics. Recently, Lazaridou et al. (2013) proposed to consider the semantics of a derived term like *read+er* as the result of a compositional process that combines the meanings of the base term *read* and the affix *+er*. This puts derivation into the purview of *compositional distributional semantic models* (CDSMs). CDSMs are normally used to compute the meaning of phrases and sentences by combining distributional representations of the individual words. A first generation of CDSMs represented all words as vectors and modeled composition as vector combination (Mitchell and Lapata, 2010). A second generation represents the meaning of predicates as higher-order algebraic objects such as matrices and tensors (Baroni and Zamparelli, 2010; Coecke et al., 2010), which are combined using various composition operations.

Lazaridou et al. predict vectors for derived terms and evaluate their approach on a set of English derivation patterns. Building on and extending their analysis, we turn to German derivation patterns and offer both qualitative and quantitative analyses of two composition models on a state-of-the-art vector space, with the aim of better understanding where these models work well and where they fail. Our contributions are as follows. First, we perform all analyses in parallel for six derivation patterns (two each for nouns, adjectives, and verbs). This provides new insights, as we can cross-reference results from individual analyses. Secondly, we evaluate using a rank-based metric, allowing for better assessment of the practical utility of these models. Thirdly, we construct a regression model that is able to explain performance differences among patterns and word pairs in terms of differences in *semantic coherence*.

2 Modeling Derivation as Meaning Composition

Morphological derivation is a major morphological process of word formation that combines a *base term* with functional morphemes, typically a single affix, into a *derived term*, and may additionally involve

Proceedings of the 11th International Conference on Computational Semantics, pages 58–63,
London, UK, April 15-17 2015.

stem changes. In contrast to inflection, derivation produces new lexical items, and it is distinct from composition, which combines two bases. Derivation comprises a large number of distinct *patterns*. Some cross part-of-speech boundaries (nominalization, verbalization, adjectivization), but many do not (gender indicators like *actor / actress* or (de-)intensifiers like *red / reddish*). In many languages, such as German or the Slavic languages, derivational morphology is extremely productive (Štekauer and Lieber, 2005).

Particularly relevant from a semantic perspective is that the meanings of the base and derived terms are often, but not always, closely related to each other. Consequently, derivational knowledge can be used to improve semantic processing (Luong et al., 2013; Padó et al., 2013). However, relatively few databases of derivational relations exist. CELEX (Baayen et al., 1996) contains derivational information for several languages, but was largely hand-written. A recent large-coverage resource for German, DErivBase (Zeller et al., 2013), covers 280k lemmas and was created from a rule-based framework that is fairly portable across languages. It is unique in that each base-derived lemma pair is labeled with a sequence of derivation patterns from a set of 267 patterns, enabling easy access to instances of specific patterns (cf. Section 3).

Compositional models for derivation. Base and derived terms are closely related in meaning. In addition, this relation is coherent to a substantial extent, due to the phenomenon of productivity. In English, for example, the suffix *-er* generally indicates an agentive nominalization (*sleep / sleeper*) and *un-* is a negation prefix (*well / unwell*). Though Mikolov et al. (2013) address some inflectional patterns, Lazaridou et al. (2013) were the first to use this observation to motivate modeling derivation with CDSMs. Conceptually, the meaning of the base term (represented as a distributional vector) is combined with some distributional representation of the affix to obtain a vector representing the meaning of the derived term. In their experiments, they found that the two best-motivated and best-performing composition models were the *full additive model* (Zanzotto et al., 2010) and the *lexical function model* (Baroni and Zamparelli, 2010). Botha and Blunsom (2014) use a related approach to model morphology for language modeling.

The additive model (ADD) (Mitchell and Lapata, 2010) generally represents a derivation pattern p as a vector computed as the shift from base term vector $\boldsymbol{b}$ to the derived term vector $\boldsymbol{d}$, i.e., $\boldsymbol{b} + \boldsymbol{p} \approx \boldsymbol{d}$. Given a set of base-derived term pairs (b, d) for p, the best $\hat{\boldsymbol{p}}$ is computed as the average of the vector difference, $\hat{\boldsymbol{p}} = \frac{1}{N}\sum_i(\boldsymbol{d_i} - \boldsymbol{b_i})$.[1] The lexical function model (LEXFUN) represents the pattern as a matrix $\boldsymbol{P}$ that encodes the linear transformation that maps base onto derived terms: $\boldsymbol{Pb} \approx \boldsymbol{d}$. The best matrix $\hat{\boldsymbol{P}}$ is typically computed via least-squares regression between the predicted vectors $\hat{\boldsymbol{d}}_i$ and the actual vectors $\boldsymbol{d}_i$.

3 Experimental Setup

Distributional model. We build a vector space from the SdeWaC corpus (Faaß and Eckart, 2013), part-of-speech tagged and lemmatized using TreeTagger (Schmid, 1994). To alleviate sparsity arising from TreeTagger's lexicon-driven lemmatization, we back off for unrecognized words to the MATE Tools (Bohnet, 2010), which have higher recall but lower precision than TreeTagger. We also reconstruct lemmas for separated prefix verbs based on the MATE dependency analysis. Finally, we get a word list with 289,946 types (content words only). From the corpus, we extract lemmatized sentences and train a state-of-the art predictive model, namely CBOW (Mikolov et al., 2013). This model builds distributed word vectors by learning to predict the current word based on a context. We use lemma-POS pairs as both target and context elements, 300 dimensions, negative sampling set to 15, and no hierarchical softmax.

Selected patterns and word pairs. We investigate six derivation patterns in German and the word pairs associated with them in DErivBase (see Table 1). We consider only patterns where base and derived terms have the same POS, and we prefer patterns encoding straightforward semantic shifts. Such patterns tend to encode meaning shifts without corresponding argument structure changes; thus they are represented appropriately in composition models based on purely lexical vector spaces. Per pattern, we randomly select 80 word pairs for which both base and derived lemmas appear at least 20 times in SdeWaC.[2]

[1]Lazaridou et al. (2013) use a slightly different formulation of the additive model. We experimented with both theirs and the standard version of the additive model. Since we obtained best results with the latter, we use the standard version.

[2]We replace a small number of erroneous pairs (e.g., *Log* $\longrightarrow$ *Login* for NN02) found by manual inspection.

ID	Pattern	Sample word pair	English translation	BL	ADD	LEXFUN
AA02	*un-*	*sagbar* → *unsagbar*	*sayable* → *unspeakable*	42.5% (.46)	41.25% (.49)	18.75% (.31)
AA03	*anti-*	*religiös* → *antireligiös*	*religious* → *antireligious*	7.5% (.51)	37.5% (.58)	47.5% (.58)
NN02	*-in*	*Bäcker* → *Bäckerin*	*baker* → *female baker*	35.0% (.56)	66.25% (.65)	26.25% (.51)
NN57	*-chen*	*Schiff* → *Schiffchen*	*ship* → *small ship*	20.0% (.55)	28.75% (.57)	15.0% (.49)
VV13	*an-*	*backen* → *anbacken*	*to bake* → *to stick, burn*	18.75% (.43)	18.75% (.43)	5% (.27)
VV31	*durch-*	*sehen* → *durchsehen*	*to see* → *to peruse*	3.75% (.40)	7.5% (.40)	1.25% (.27)
Mean				21.25% (.49)	33.33% (.52)	18.96% (.41)

Table 1: Derivation patterns, representative examples (and translations), and prediction performance in terms of R_{oof} percentages and mean similarity between derived and gold vectors, 10-fold cross-validation.

Experimental design and baseline. We experiment with the two composition models described in Section 2 (ADD and LEXFUN) as implemented in the DISSECT toolkit (Dinu et al., 2013). As baseline (BL), again following Lazaridou et al. (2013), we predict the base term of each word pair as the derived term. With six derivation patterns, our investigation thus includes 18 experiments. In each experiment, we perform 10-fold cross-validation on the 80 word pairs for each pattern.

All these models predict some point in vector space for the derived term, and we compare against the gold standard position of the derived term with cosine similarity. Like Lazaridou et al. (2013), we consider this average similarity directly, but believe that it is not informative enough since it does not indicate concretely how many correct derivations are found. Therefore, we adopt as our primary evaluation metric the R_{oof} (*Recall out of five*) metric proposed by McCarthy and Navigli (2009) for lexical substitution. It counts how often the correct derived term is found among the five nearest neighbors of the prediction (selected from all words of the same POS). R_{oof} is motivated by rank-based evaluation metrics from IR (such as Precision at n), but our setup differs in that there can be at most one true positive in each list.

4 Results and Discussion

Global observations. Table 1 shows R_{oof} performance and mean similarities, pattern-by-pattern, of the two composition models (ADD and LEXFUN) and the baseline. Measured by R_{oof} score, ADD strongly outperforms BL for four patterns; for the other two, it achieves (nearly-)equivalent performance. LEXFUN, on the other hand, beats BL for one pattern (AA03) and in all other cases is much worse. ADD outperforms LEXFUN for all but one pattern. A comparison of R_{oof} and mean similarity indicates that similarity alone is not a good indicator of how reliably a model will include the actual derived vector in the nearest neighbors of its prediction. This validates our call for a more NLP-oriented evaluation.

The mean similarities are sufficient to make some comparisons across languages, though. Lazaridou et al. (2013) find that both additive and lexical function models yield higher mean similarities than the baseline. For our German data, this is true only for ADD. This shows that the semantic shifts underlying derivation patterns are, to some extent, expressible as vector addition in the CBOW space, while it is more difficult to capture them as a lexical function. The overall worse performance is, in our view, related to some specific characteristics of German. First, due to the general capitalization of nouns, named entities are not orthographically recognizable. Consequently, for *Strauß* (*bouquet*), BL and ADD return terms related to the composers Richard (e.g., *Alpensinfonie*) or Johann (e.g., *Walzerkönig* (waltz king)) Strauss. Secondly, nominal compounds introduce higher sparsity and more confounders. For example, for the derived term *Apfelbäumchen* (*~apple treelet*), LEXFUN's closest returned neighbor is the noun *Bäumchen*, which is a case of *combined* derivation and composition, yet is counted as incorrect. In English, compounds such as *apple tree(let)* are considered neither as base nor as potential derived terms.

Semantic coherence appears to be an important determinant of prediction quality. The best-performing pattern for ADD is NN02, the gender affix *-in* (turning masculine into feminine nouns), which applies to fairly coherent classes of people (nationalities, roles, and professions). We see a similar effect for the

Norweger → ***Norweger+in*** (*male* → *female Norwegian*)		NN02	***pluralistisch*** → ***anti+pluralistisch*** (*pluralistic* → *antipluralistic*)		AA03
BL	ADD	LEXFUN	BL	ADD	LEXFUN
1. Norweger	*Norweger*	*Schwed+in*	*1. pluralistisch*	*pluralistisch*	*anti+demokratisch*
2. Däne	*Schwed+in*	*Australier+in*	*2. plural*	*plural*	*anti+liberal*
3. Schwede	***Norweger+in***	***Norweger+in***	*3. demokratisch*	*demokratisch*	*anti+modernistisch*
4. Isländer	*Däne*	*Dän+in*	*4. säkular*	*anti+totalitär*	***anti+pluralistisch***
5. Solberg	*Dän+in*	*Landsfrau*	*5. freiheitlich*	*säkular*	*anti+modern*

Table 2: Five nearest neighbors to the predicted vector for the derived term. Correct derived term appears in bold; + marks instances of the relevant derivational affix.

best-performing pattern for LEXFUN, AA03 (the adjectival affix *anti-*). While the base term meanings of this pattern vary quite a bit, the meanings of the derived terms are distributionally coherent, with many shared typical context words (*demonstration*, *protest*, etc.). In contrast, the more difficult diminutive affix *-chen* (NN57) can be applied to nearly any noun, leading to less coherent sets of base and derived terms.

Both models have the most difficulty with verb-verb patterns. Analysis of word pairs for patterns VV13 and VV31, both of which are *prefix verbs*, indicates that the semantic shifts expressed by verb prefixation are often highly ambiguous (Lechler and Roßdeutscher, 2009) and therefore difficult to capture.

Nearest-neighbor analysis. We next examined the five nearest neighbors (5-NN) produced by the different models, as shown in Table 2. Interestingly, ADD and LEXFUN appear to capture different aspects of the semantic composition. The neighbors of LEXFUN are not random, despite its bad R_{oof} performance, but largely composed of morphologically complex words combining semantically related bases with the derivational affix in question. ADD generally finds terms that are semantically related to the base, both morphologically simple and complex. Analysis of the 5-NNs for each model confirms these impressions: (a), ADD always returns the base term as the nearest neighbor. That is, in an evaluation considering only the top neighbor, BL and ADD would have identical performance; (b), 54% of the LEXFUN 5-NNs are other derived terms of the same derivation pattern. This is quite high in comparison to BL (8%) and ADD (14%); (c), both ADD (48%) and BL (46%) are much more likely than LEXFUN (11%) to return neighbors that include the base term or its stem, as *plural (pluralistic)* above.

Regression analysis of ADD. Finally, we perform a quantitative analysis of the performance of ADD, our best model. Based on the discussion above, our hypothesis is that the additive model works best for patterns that are *coherent*. We operationalize this by defining four *coherence features* at the word pair level (cf. Figure 1): (a) Coherence of base terms (*BCoh*) – cosine similarity between a base term and the centroid of all base terms of the pattern; (b) Coherence of derived terms (*DCoh*) – cosine similarity between a derived term and the centroid of all derived terms of the pattern; (c) Similarity between base and derived term (*BDSim*) – cosine similarity between the two vectors of the base and derived terms; (d) Coherence of difference vectors (*DiffCoh*) – cosine similarity between the difference vector for a base-derived term pair (its semantic shift) and the centroid of all difference vectors of the pattern.

For our analysis, we use a mixed effects logistic regression (MELR, Jaeger (2008)). Logistic regression is used in linguistics to investigate quantitative relationships (Bresnan et al., 2007). It predicts the probability of a binary response variable y depending on a set of predictors $\mathbf{x}$ as $P(y = 1) = \sigma(\mathbf{bx})$ where σ is the sigmoid function. Its coefficients are interpretable as *log odds*: given a positive coefficient of size b_i, every one-unit increase of x_i increases the odds of $y = 1$ by a factor of e^{b_i}; correspondingly, negative values increase the odds of $y = 0$. MELR is a generalization that distinguishes traditional *fixed effects* from a novel category of predictors, so-called *random effects*, $\mathbf{x}'$, so that $P(y = 1) = \sigma(\mathbf{bx} + \mathbf{cx'})$. The coefficients $\mathbf{c}$ of random effects are drawn from a normal distribution with zero mean, which is appropriate for many predictors (Clark, 1973) and makes the model generalizable to unseen values.

In our MELR model, each word pair is a datapoint. We use 0/1 (success in the R_{oof} evaluation) as y, the coherence features as fixed effects, and the pattern identity as random effect. The resulting coefficients are shown in Figure 1. The negative intercept results from the overall predominance of failures. The next

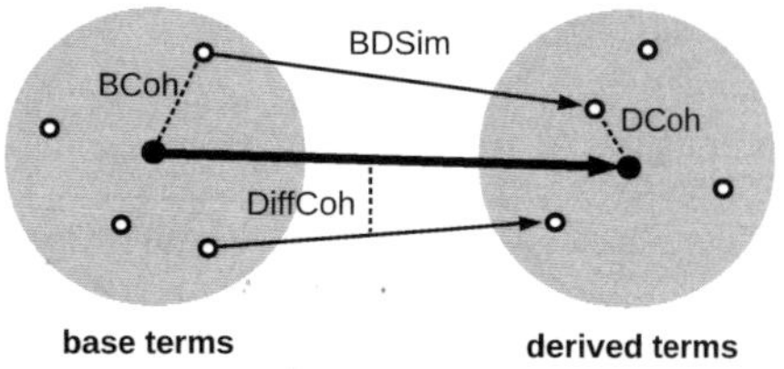

Feature name	Coefficient	p-value
Intercept	-15.0	<0.0001
BCoh	-4.6	<0.01
DCoh	$+2.0$	n.s.
BDSim	$+6.7$	<0.0001
DiffCoh	$+26.8$	<0.0001

Figure 1: Illustration of coherence in vector space (left) and regression coefficients (right)

two features are somewhat surprising: We find a negative coefficient for BCoh, indicating semantically more coherent base terms are correlated with more difficult derivation patterns. Indeed, the most difficult pattern for the model (VV31) has the highest average base term coherence (0.40), and the simplest pattern (NN02) the lowest (0.29). DCoh, the coherence among derived terms, does have a positive coefficient, but it is too small to reach significance. We tend to see these two results as artefacts of our small sample.

The remaining two features (BDSim, and DiffCoh) have strong positive coefficients, indicating that patterns where (a) base terms and derived terms are similar within pairs, or (b) the difference vectors all point into the same direction, are easier to model. The last feature is particularly strong – not surprising, given that ADD uses the centroid of the difference vectors to make predictions. Finally, the random effect coefficients of the patterns are small (between -0.7 and $+0.7$), indicating the model's robustness.

We also evaluate the regression model by predicting the R_{oof} percentages from Table 1, simply counting the number of successes for each pattern. The mean difference to the actual numbers is 2.5%. The highest individual difference is 3.75 (32.5 vs. 28.75 for NN57), the lowest 0% (for NN02). This means that the regression model does quite a good job at predicting top-5 accuracy. We take this as evidence that the features' coefficients capture a relevant and substantial aspect of the phenomenon.

5 Conclusion

In this paper, we have analyzed compositional distributional models for predicting the meaning of derived terms from their base terms with a focus on in-depth analysis. We found that this prediction task is challenging, at least for the derivation patterns we considered. This may not be surprising, given the relatively subtle semantic differences introduced by some patterns (e.g., the gender of the term, or the polarity), which may be hard to recover distributionally. In that sense, our choice of (putatively easy) within-POS derivations may actually have worked against us: in cross-POS derivations, base and derived terms should have more clearly distinguished distributional profiles. At any rate, it seems that additional modeling efforts are necessary to produce more robust models of derivational morphology.

We believe that two results of our analyses are particularly noteworthy. The first is the correlation between the coherence of the derivation patterns and the performance of the additive composition model. While the existence of such correlations may seem obvious given the way the additive model works, we hope, on account of their strength, that we can predict the difficulty of modeling novel derivations, as well as link this approach to theoretical work on (ir-)regularity (Plank, 1981). The second result is the complementarity of the additive and lexical function models, which capture the base meaning and the affix meaning well, respectively. This suggests combining the two models as an interesting avenue.

References

Baayen, H. R., R. Piepenbrock, and L. Gulikers (1996). *The CELEX lexical database. Release 2. LDC96L14.* Philadelphia, PA: Linguistic Data Consortium, University of Pennsylvania.

Baroni, M. and R. Zamparelli (2010). Nouns are vectors, adjectives are matrices: Representing adjective-noun constructions in semantic space. In *Proceedings of EMNLP*, Cambridge, MA, USA.

Bohnet, B. (2010). Top accuracy and fast dependency parsing is not a contradiction. In *Proceedings of COLING*, Beijing, China.

Botha, J. A. and P. Blunsom (2014). Compositional morphology for word representations and language modelling. In *Proceedings of ICML*, Beijing, China.

Bresnan, J., A. Cueni, T. Nikitina, and H. Baayen (2007). Predicting the dative alternation. In *Cognitive Foundations of Interpretation*. Royal Netherlands Academy of Science.

Clark, H. H. (1973). The language-as-fixed-effect fallacy: A critique of language statistics in psychological research. *Journal of verbal learning and verbal behavior 12*(4).

Coecke, B., M. Sadrzadeh, and S. Clark (2010). Mathematical foundations for a compositional distributional model of meaning. *Linguistic Analysis 36*.

Dinu, G., N. T. Pham, and M. Baroni (2013). DISSECT – DIStributional SEmantics Composition Toolkit. In *Proceedings of ACL*, Sofia, Bulgaria.

Faaß, G. and K. Eckart (2013). SdeWaC – a corpus of parsable sentences from the web. In *Language Processing and Knowledge in the Web*, Lecture Notes in Computer Science. Springer.

Jaeger, T. (2008). Categorical data analysis: Away from ANOVAs and toward logit mixed models. *Journal of Memory and Language 59*(4).

Lazaridou, A., M. Marelli, R. Zamparelli, and M. Baroni (2013). Compositional-ly derived representations of morphologically complex words in distributional semantics. In *Proceedings of ACL*, Sofia, Bulgaria.

Lechler, A. and A. Roßdeutscher (2009). German particle verbs with *auf-*. Reconstructing their composition in a DRT-based framework. *Linguistische Berichte 220*.

Luong, M.-T., R. Socher, and C. D. Manning (2013). Better word representations with recursive neural networks for morphology. In *Proceedings of CoNLL*, Sofia, Bulgaria.

McCarthy, D. and R. Navigli (2009). The English lexical substitution task. *Language Resources and Evaluation 43*(2).

Mikolov, T., K. Chen, G. Corrado, and J. Dean (2013). Efficient estimation of word representations in vector space. In *Proceedings of ICLR*, Scottsdale, AZ, USA.

Mikolov, T., W.-T. Yih, and G. Zweig (2013). Linguistic regularities in continuous space word representations. In *Proceedings of HLT-NAACL*, Atlanta, GA.

Mitchell, J. and M. Lapata (2010). Composition in distributional models of semantics. *Cognitive Science 34*(8).

Padó, S., J. Šnajder, and B. Zeller (2013). Derivational smoothing for syntactic distributional semantics. In *Proceedings of ACL*, Sofia, Bulgaria.

Plank, F. (1981). *Morphologische (Ir-)Regularitäten. Aspekte der Wortstrukturtheorie*. Tübingen: Narr.

Schmid, H. (1994). Probabilistic part-of-speech tagging using decision trees. In *Proceedings of NeMLaP*, Manchester, UK.

Štekauer, P. and R. Lieber (Eds.) (2005). *Handbook of Word-Formation*, Volume 64 of *Studies in Natural Language and Linguistic Theory*. Springer.

Zanzotto, F. M., I. Korkontzelos, F. Fallucchi, and S. Manandhar (2010). Estimating linear models for compositional distributional semantics. In *Proceedings of COLING*, Beijing, China.

Zeller, B., J. Šnajder, and S. Padó (2013). DErivBase: Inducing and evaluating a derivational morphology resource for German. In *Proceedings of ACL*, Sofia, Bulgaria.

Semantic Complexity of Quantifiers and their Distribution in Corpora

Camilo Thorne
IBM CAS Trento - Trento RISE
Povo di Trento, Italy
c.thorne.email@trentorise.eu

Jakub Szymanik
Institute for Logic, Language, and Computation
Amsterdam, The Netherlands
j.k.szymanik@uva.nl

Abstract

The semantic complexity of a quantifier can be defined as the computational complexity of the finite model checking problem induced by its semantics. This paper describes a preliminary study to understand if quantifier distribution in corpora can be to some extent predicted or explained by semantic complexity. We show that corpora distributions for English are significantly skewed towards quantifiers of low complexity and that this bias can be described in some cases by a power law.

1 Introduction

Quantification is an essential feature of natural languages. It is used to specify the (vague) number or quantity of objects satisfying a certain property. Quantifier expressions are built from *noun phrases* (whether definite or indefinite, names or pronouns) and *determiners* resulting in expressions such as "a subject", "more than half of the men", "the queen of England", "John", "some", "five" or "every" (see Peters and Westerståhl (2006) for an overview).

More recently, interest has arisen regarding *semantic complexity*, that is, the complexity of reasoning with (and understanding) fragments of natural language. One model that has been proposed to study natural language semantic complexity is to consider the computational properties that arise from formal semantic analysis, see e.g., Ristad (1993); van Benthem (1987); Kontinen and Szymanik (2008). One could wonder whether speakers (due to their restricted cognitive resources) are naturally biased towards low complexity expressions, see Szymanik and Zajenkowski (2010); Schlotterbeck and Bott (2013). Additionally, related work by Thorne (2012) shows that, when one considers *the satisfiability problem* of specific fragments of English then computationally tractable combinations of constructs occur more frequently than intractable ones.

This paper extends such work by showing that: *(i)* quantifiers can be ranked w.r.t. to their semantic complexity, viz., their computational complexity w.r.t. the *model-checking* problem, and their expressiveness; *(ii)* within a selected set of corpora quantifier distribution is skewed towards computationally easier quantifiers; and *(iii)* such distribution describes a power law.

2 Generalized Quantifiers and Semantic Complexity

Generalized Quantifiers. Generalized quantifiers are usually taken to denote relations holding between subsets of the universe. For instance, in a given model $\mathcal{I} = (\mathbb{D}_{\mathcal{I}}, \cdot^{\mathcal{I}})$ the statement "most As are B" says: $\#(A^{\mathcal{I}} \cap B^{\mathcal{I}}) > \#(A^{\mathcal{I}} \setminus B^{\mathcal{I}})$, where $A^{\mathcal{I}}, B^{\mathcal{I}} \subseteq \mathbb{D}_{\mathcal{I}}$ and $\#(A)$ stands for the cardinality of set

Proceedings of the 11th International Conference on Computational Semantics, pages 64–69,
London, UK, April 15-17 2015.

Table 1: Top: Base FO (Aristotelian and counting) and proportional generalized quantifiers studied in this paper, ranked by semantic complexity; $> k$ and $< k$ comprise by abuse the superlative quantifiers "at least k" and "at most k". Bottom, left: Sample English sentences realizing Ramsey quantifiers; notice the use of the reciprocal "each other". Bottom, right: Semantic complexity of Ramsey quantifiers by quantifier class.

Q	Model Class	S. C.		Example
some	$\{\mathcal{I} \mid A^{\mathcal{I}} \cap B^{\mathcal{I}} \neq \emptyset\}$	$\mathbf{AC}^0$	*ari*	some men are happy
all	$\{\mathcal{I} \mid A^{\mathcal{I}} \subseteq B^{\mathcal{I}}\}$	$\mathbf{AC}^0$	*ari*	all humans are mammals
the	$\{\mathcal{I} \mid \#(A^{\mathcal{I}} \cap B^{\mathcal{I}}) = 1\}$	$\mathbf{AC}^0$	*cnt*	the third emperor of Rome was deranged
$> k$	$\{\mathcal{I} \mid \#(A^{\mathcal{I}} \cap B^{\mathcal{I}}) > k\}$	$\mathbf{AC}^0$	*cnt*	more than 5 men are happy
$< k$	$\{\mathcal{I} \mid \#(A^{\mathcal{I}} \cap B^{\mathcal{I}}) < k\}$	$\mathbf{AC}^0$	*cnt*	fewer than 100 violins are Stradivari
k	$\{\mathcal{I} \mid \#(A^{\mathcal{I}} \cap B^{\mathcal{I}}) = k\}$	$\mathbf{AC}^0$	*cnt*	50 MPs voted against the war in Irak
most	$\{\mathcal{I} \mid \#(A^{\mathcal{I}} \cap B^{\mathcal{I}}) > \#(A^{\mathcal{I}} \setminus B^{\mathcal{I}})\}$	**P**	*pro*	most trains are safe
few	$\{\mathcal{I} \mid \#(A^{\mathcal{I}} \cap B^{\mathcal{I}}) < \#(A^{\mathcal{I}} \setminus B^{\mathcal{I}})\}$	**P**	*pro*	few people are trustworthy
$> p/k$	$\{\mathcal{I} \mid \#(A^{\mathcal{I}} \cap B^{\mathcal{I}}) > p \cdot (\#(A)/k)\}$	**P**	*pro*	more than $2/3$ of planets are lifeless
$< p/k$	$\{\mathcal{I} \mid \#(A^{\mathcal{I}} \cap B^{\mathcal{I}}) < p \cdot (\#(A)/k)\}$	**P**	*pro*	less than $1/3$ of Americans are rich
p/k	$\{\mathcal{I} \mid \#(A^{\mathcal{I}} \cap B^{\mathcal{I}}) = p \cdot (\#(A)/k)\}$	**P**	*pro*	$1/3$ of Peru's population lives in Lima
$> k\%$	$\{\mathcal{I} \mid \#(A^{\mathcal{I}} \cap B^{\mathcal{I}}) > k \cdot (\#(A)/100)\}$	**P**	*pro*	more than 10% of Peruvians are poor
$< k\%$	$\{\mathcal{I} \mid \#(A^{\mathcal{I}} \cap B^{\mathcal{I}}) < k \cdot (\#(A)/100)\}$	**P**	*pro*	less than 5% of the Earth is water
$k\%$	$\{\mathcal{I} \mid \#(A^{\mathcal{I}} \cap B^{\mathcal{I}}) = k \cdot (\#(A)/100)\}$	**P**	*pro*	15% of Muslims are Shia

R_Q	Example
R_{some}	some children like each other
$R_{>p/k}$	more than $2/3$ of female MPs sit next to each other
R_{most}	most people help each other
$R_{>k}$	at least 2 men married each other in the UK last year

Quantifier Class R_Q	S.C.
Aristotelian (*ari+recip*)	$\mathbf{AC}^0$
counting (*cnt+recip*)	$\mathbf{AC}^0$
proportional (*pro+recip*)	**NP**-complete

A. Going a step further, we can take a generalized quantifier Q to be a functional relation associating with each model $\mathcal{I}$ a relation between relations on its universe, $\mathbb{D}_{\mathcal{I}}$. This is actually equivalent to their standard Lindström (1966) model-theoretic definition as classes of models:

Definition 2.1 (Generalized Quantifier). Let $t = (n_1, \ldots, n_k)$ be a k-tuple of positive integers. A *generalized quantifier* of type t is a class Q of models of a vocabulary $\tau_t = \{R_1, \ldots, R_k\}$, such that R_i is n_i-ary for $1 \leq i \leq k$, and Q is closed under isomorphisms, i.e. if $\mathcal{I} \in Q$ and $\mathcal{I}'$ is isomorphic to $\mathcal{I}$, then $\mathcal{I}' \in Q$. It gives rise to a *query* $\overline{Q}(R_1, \ldots, R_n)$ such that $\mathcal{I} \models \overline{Q}(R_1, \ldots, R_n)$ iff $\mathcal{I} \in Q$.

Semantic Complexity. An important consequence of this definition is the notion of *semantic complexity*, which refers to the computational complexity[1] of the finite model checking problem that it induces, namely the question: does $\mathcal{I} \models \overline{Q}(R_1, \ldots, R_n)$? When considering such problem we are interested in its complexity w.r.t. the size of the model $\mathcal{I}$, that is, in *data complexity*, see Immerman (1998). Semantic complexity induces a partial ordering (ranking) of quantifiers. Furthermore, it induces a partition into *tractable* and *intractable* generalized quantifiers. Respectively: quantifiers, for which model checking is *at most* **P**, and quantifiers for which model checking is *at least* **NP**-hard.

Tractable Quantifiers. Tractable quantifiers come in two flavors: first-order (FO) and proportional:

1. **FO.** FO quantifiers Q of type t over $\tau_t = \{R_1, \ldots, R_n\}$, are quantifiers which give rise to FO queries (with identity). They are those with the lowest semantic complexity, viz. $\mathbf{AC}^0$ (the data complexity of model checking in FO with identity is in $\mathbf{AC}^0$, see Immerman (1998)). See Table 1, top. They are typically split in the literature into:

[1] Please refer to Papadimitrou (1994) for the basics of computational complexity.

- *Aristotelian* quantifiers (*some*, *all*), which are the quantifiers dealt with in traditional syllogistic logic.
- *Counting* quantifiers (*the*, $< k$, $> k$, k), in which the number of individuals in the domain verifying a given property is specified. Counting quantifiers while sharing the same semantic complexity of Aristotelian quantifiers, are nevertheless more expressive and can be distinguished via their associated language problem (van Benthem (1987)): given a model $\mathcal{I}$ and query $\overline{Q}(R_1, \ldots, R_1)$ one can construct a finite state automaton $A_{\mathcal{I}}$ for $\mathcal{I}$ and a word w_Q over the alphabet $\{0, 1\}$ s.t. $\mathcal{I} \models \overline{Q}(R_1, \ldots, R_1)$ iff $w_Q \in L(A_{\mathcal{I}})$ where $L(A_{\mathcal{I}})$ denotes the language recognized by $A_{\mathcal{I}}$. The automaton $A_{\mathcal{I}}$ will have 2 states whenever Q is Aristotelian, and at most $k + 2$ states whenever Q is a counting quantifier[2].

2. **Proportional.** More interesting are *proportional* quantifiers, e.g., *most* ("most men") and $> p/k$ ("more than one third of men"). They are used often by speakers when referring to collections (the denotation of collective or plural nouns) and their quantitative properties. Proportional quantifiers are strictly more expressive than Aristotelian or counting quantifiers. Indeed, as Barwise and Cooper (1980) showed, they are not FO expressible. This is reflected by their higher semantic complexity, in **P** (Szymanik, 2010).

Intractable Quantifiers. Intractable quantifiers can be derived from tractable ones via various model-theoretic operations. One such operation is *Ramseyfication*, that turns a monadic quantifier of type $(1, 1)$ into a polyadic quantifier of type $(1, 2)$. Ramseyfication is expressed by the reciprocal expression "each other" under the default (strong) interpretation of Dalrymple et al. (1998). It intuitively states that the models of the resulting Ramseyfied quantifiers are graphs with connected components. Intractability arises when it is applied to proportional quantifiers, giving rise to so-called "clique" quantifiers (Szymanik, 2010). See Table 1, bottom.

3 Pattern-based Corpus Analysis

Semantic complexity and expressiveness can be leveraged to induce both a partition and a ranking of quantifiers[3], where Aristotelian quantifiers occupy the lowest and Ramseyfied proportional quantifiers the highest end of the spectrum. Such theoretical results are reflected by their distribution in (English) corpora.

Quantifier Patterns. We identified generalized quantifiers indirectly, via part-of-speech (POS) patterns that reasonably approximate their surface forms and lexical variants. The POS tags were required to filter out contexts in which quantifier words do not express a quantifier such as "no" in "you cannot say no" (an interjection) –as opposed to "no" in "no tickets were left" (a determiner). Each such pattern defined a quantifier *type*. This done, we counted the number of times each type is instantiated within a sentence in the corpus, that is, its number of *tokens* (lexical variants). We considered Penn Treebank/Brown corpus POSs (Francis and Kucera, 1979)[4]. We present two such patterns (the others were defined analogously):

1. to identify the Aristotelian quantifier *all*, we considered its lexical variants "all", "everybody", "everything", "every", "each", "everyone" and "the N" (where N is a plural noun), and built the regex: .*(*every/at* | *Every/at* | *all/abn* | *All/abn* | *the/at .*/nns* | *The/at ./nns* | *everything/pn* | *Everything/pn* | *everyone/pn* | *Everyone/pn* | *everybody/pn* | *Everybody/pn* | *each/dt* | *Each/dt*).*;
2. to identify Ramsey quantifiers, we checked for sentences that match *at the same time* the regular expressions of the base (FO, counting or proportional) quantifiers and the following pattern for the reciprocal: .* *each/dt other/ap* .*.

Using such patterns we observed the frequency of *(i)* generalized quantifiers, and *(ii)* tractable and intractable Ramsey quantifiers, to see whether such distribution was skewed towards low complexity quan-

[2]More in general, the class REG of regular languages corresponds to the class of quantifiers definable in so-called divisibility logic, see Mostowski (1998).

[3]Note that $\mathbf{AC}^0 \subseteq \mathbf{P} \subseteq \mathbf{NP}$-complete and $\text{REG}_2 \subseteq \text{REG}_{\leq k+2}$.

[4]For the POS tagging, we relied on the NLTK 3-gram tagger, see `http://www.nltk.org/`.

tifiers in the former case, and towards tractable quantifiers in the latter case.

Corpora. To obtain sufficiently large, balanced and representative samples of contemporary English, we considered two corpora covering multiple domains and sentence types (declarative and interrogative). Specifically, we considered the well-known Brown corpus by Francis and Kucera (1979) ($\sim$60,647 sentences and 1,014,312 word tokens). We also considered a sizeable sample of a large web corpus, the ukWaC corpus ($\sim$280,001 sentences and 100,000,000 word tokens) from Baroni et al. (2009), built from a 2006-2007 crawl of the (complete) .uk domain.

Power Laws. Power laws, first discussed by Zipf (1935), relate the frequency of linguistic tokens to their rank, viz., to the ordering induced by their frequency. They typically predict that frequency is proportional to rank (modulo two real-valued parameters a and b^{-1}), giving rise to non-normal, skewed distributions where the topmost (w.r.t. rank) 20% words in a corpus concentrate around 80% of the probability mass or frequency. They are widespread in natural language data (Baroni, 2009). More recent work (Newman, 2005) has shown that power laws can be variously modified and extended to cover wider spectra of natural language phenomena and rankings. One such possible extension is to consider, as we do in this paper, power laws relating the frequency of a quantifier Q to its semantic complexity rank:

Definition 3.1 (Complexity Power Law). The power law between *quantifier frequency* $fr(Q)$ and *quantifier complexity rank* $rk(Q)$ is described by the equation: $fr(Q) = a/rk(Q)^b$, with $a, b \in \mathbb{R}$.

To approximate the distribution parameters a and b we ran (Newman, 2005) a least squares linear regression, since power laws are equivalent to linear models on the log-log scale[5]. We measured also the ensuing R^2 coefficient, that captures how well the observations fit the inferred power law equation and that ranges from 0 (no fit) to 1 (perfect fit). To validate further our models we ran a χ^2 test (at $p = 0.01$ significance) w.r.t. the uniform distribution as our null hypothesis.

Results and Interpretation. The distributions observed are summarized by Figure 1. The top left corner describes the contingency (raw frequency) tables used for the figures. The top right figures describe relative frequency by quantifier class. The bottom figures, by quantifier: the reader will find to the left the average and cumulative relative frequency plots, and to the right the log-log (power law) regressions.

As expected by the theory, Aristotelian and counting —$\mathbf{AC}^0$— quantifiers occur more frequently than proportional —**P**— quantifiers, and (proportional) Ramsey —**NP**-hard— quantifiers. See Figure 1 (top right). This bias is statistically significant: their distribution significantly differs from uniform or random distributions, as $p < 0.01$.

Furthermore, when we consider separately the distribution of, on the one hand, base quantifiers, and on the other hand, Ramseyfied quantifiers, we can infer power laws skewed towards Aristotelian quantifiers and bounded Ramsey quantifiers: see Figure 1 (bottom). In both cases a high goodness-of-fit coefficient was obtained: $R^2 = 0.94$ for base quantifiers and $R^2 = 0.92$ for Ramseyfied quantifiers (mean distribution).

Finally Figure 1 (top left) shows that tractable quantifiers occur significantly more often than intractable quantifiers. Furthermore, the same observation applies to FO and proportional quantifiers vis-à-vis their Ramseyfications. Actually, Ramseyfications, whether tractable or intractable, appear to be in general rare ("sparse") in natural language data. We conjecture that this is due to an increase in expressiveness and complexity relatively to proportional and FO quantifiers, that cannot be easily captured through the techniques used to build Table 1, and merits further investigation.

The method described was relatively noisy (the POS tagger had an accuracy of around 80%) and not fully exhaustive (the patterns did not cover all quantifier surface forms). However, we believe that our datasets were large and representative enough, and our rule patterns adequate enough to derive reasonable approximations to the distribution of quantifiers in English.

[5]I.e., $y = a/x^b$ iff $\log(y) = \log(a/x^b) = a - b \cdot \log(x)$.

	pro+ recip	*cnt+ recip*	*ari+ recip*
Brown	4	17	186
ukwack	5,732	10,484	33,107
total	5,736	10,501	33,293

pro	*cnt*	*ari*
20,362	64,846	687,915
1,306,971	1,983,694	8,650,650
1,327,333	2,048,540	9,338,565

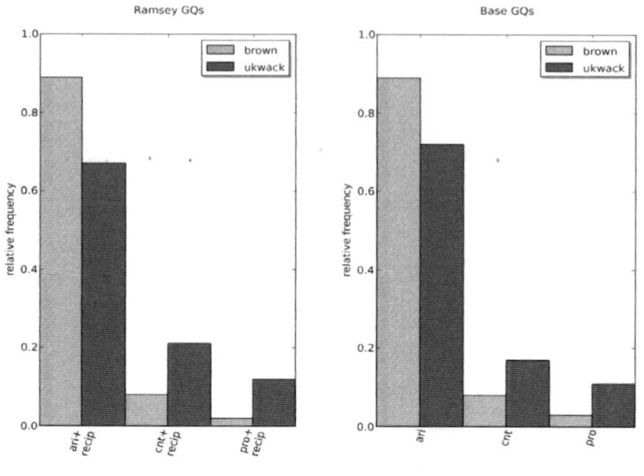

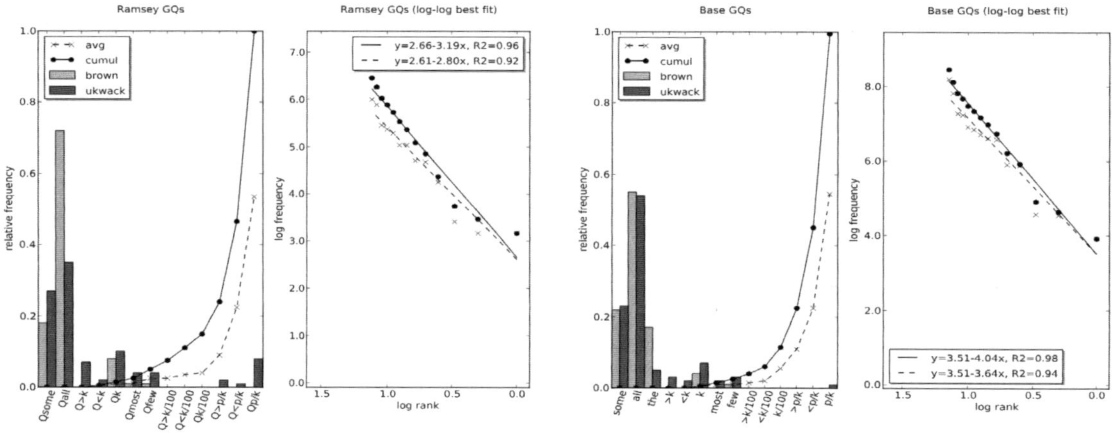

Figure 1: Top, left: Ramsey quantifier (raw) frequencies, and base quantifier (raw) frequencies. Top, right: Ramsey and base quantifier distribution by quantifier class. Bottom, left: Ramsey quantifier distribution and log-log power law regression. Bottom, right: Base quantifier distribution and log-log power law regression.

4 Conclusions

We have studied the semantic complexity and corpora distribution of natural language quantifiers. The computationally easier quantifiers occur more frequently in everyday communication, i.e., their distributions satisfy power laws. Moreover, we have empirically shown—as suggested by Ristad (1993); Mostowski and Szymanik (2012)—that: although everyday English may contain computationally hard constructions, they are infrequent. These results, together with Thorne (2012), suggest that abstract computational properties of natural language expressions can be used to explain their distribution in corpora. Indeed, one of the linguistic reasons to expect power laws in natural language data is the *principle of least effort in communication*: speakers tend to minimize the communication effort by generating "simple" messages (Zipf, 1935).

As ongoing and further research, we envision several axes. Firstly, to refine our patterns to better cover the lexical variants of the quantifiers considered in this paper. Secondly, to consider much larger corpora. Thirdly, to refine our complexity analysis to explain the frequency gap induced by Ramseyfication. Finally, to run cross-language experiments to address the *equivalent complexity* question: does the complexity of quantification imply a distribution similar accross languages?

References

Baroni, M. (2009). Distributions in text. In *Corpus linguistics: An International Handbook*, Volume 2, pp. 803–821. Mouton de Gruyter.

Baroni, M., S. Bernardini, A. Ferraresi, and E. Zanchetta (2009). The WaCky Wide Web: A collection of very large linguistically processed web-crawled corpora. *Language Resources and Evaluation 43*(3), 209–226.

Barwise, J. and R. Cooper (1980). Generalized quantifiers and natural language. *Linguistics and Philosophy 4*(2), 159–219.

van Benthem, J. (1987). Towards a computational semantics. In P. Gärdenfors (Ed.), *Generalized Quantifiers*, pp. 31–71. Reidel Publishing Company.

Dalrymple, M., M. Kanazawa, Y. Kim, S. Mchombo, and S. Peters (1998). Reciprocal expressions and the concept of reciprocity. *Linguistics and Philosophy 21*, 159–210.

Francis, W. N. and H. Kucera (1979). Brown corpus manual. Technical report, Department of Linguistics, Brown University, Providence, Rhode Island, US.

Immerman, N. (1998). *Descriptive Complexity*. Texts in Computer Science. New York, NY: Springer.

Kontinen, J. and J. Szymanik (2008). A remark on collective quantification. *Journal of Logic, Language and Information 17*(2), 131–140.

Lindström, P. (1966). First order predicate logic with generalized quantifiers. *Theoria 32*, 186–195.

Mostowski, M. (1998). Computational semantics for monadic quantifiers. *Journal of Applied Non-Classical Logics 8*, 107–121.

Mostowski, M. and J. Szymanik (2012). Semantic bounds for everyday language. *Semiotica 188*(1-4), 363–372.

Newman, M. E. J. (2005). Power laws, Pareto distributions and Zipf's law. *Contemporary Physics 46*(5), 323–351.

Papadimitrou, C. (1994). *Computational Complexity*. Addison Wesley - Longman.

Peters, S. and D. Westerståhl (2006). *Quantifiers in Language and Logic*. Oxford: Clarendon Press.

Ristad, E. S. (1993, March). *The Language Complexity Game*. Artificial Intelligence. The MIT Press.

Schlotterbeck, F. and O. Bott (2013). Easy solutions for a hard problem? The computational complexity of reciprocals with quantificational antecedents. *Journal of Logic, Language and Information 22*(4), 363–390.

Szymanik, J. (2010). Computational complexity of polyadic lifts of generalized quantifiers in natural language. *Linguistics and Philosophy 33*(3), 215–250.

Szymanik, J. and M. Zajenkowski (2010). Comprehension of simple quantifiers. Empirical evaluation of a computational model. *Cognitive Science: A Multidisciplinary Journal 34*(3), 521–532.

Thorne, C. (2012). Studying the distribution of fragments of English using deep semantic annotation. In *Proceedings of the ISA8 Workshop*.

Zipf, G. (1935). *The Psychobiology of Language: An Introduction to Dynamic Philology*. Cambridge, Mass.: M.I.T. Press.

Sound-based distributional models

Alessandro Lopopolo
VU University Amsterdam
a.lopopolo@vu.nl

Emiel van Miltenburg
VU University Amsterdam
emiel.van.miltenburg@vu.nl

Abstract

Following earlier work in multimodal distributional semantics, we present the first results of our efforts to build a perceptually grounded semantic model. Rather than using images, our models are built on sound data collected from freesound.org. We compare three models: one bag-of-words model based on user-provided tags, a model based on audio features, using a 'bag-of-audio-words' approach and a model that combines the two. Our results show that the models are able to capture semantic relatedness, with the tag-based model scoring higher than the sound-based model and the combined model. However, capturing semantic relatedness is biased towards language-based models. Future work will focus on improving the sound-based model, finding ways to combine linguistic and acoustic information, and creating more reliable evaluation data.

1 Introduction

This paper explores the possibility of creating distributional semantic models (Turney et al. 2010) from a large dataset of tagged sounds.[1] Traditionally, distributional models have solely relied on word co-occurrences in large corpora. Recently, Bruni et al. (2012a) have started to combine visual features with textual ones, resulting in a performance increase for tasks focusing on the use of color terms. Sound has received relatively little attention in the distributional semantics literature, but we believe that it may be a useful source of information, especially for the representation of actions or events like *talking, shattering*, or *barking*. We propose three models: a tag-based model, a model based on bags-of-auditory words, and a model combining both kinds of information. We evaluate these models against human similarity and relatedness judgments, and show that while the tag-based model performs better than the others, the sound-based model and the combined model still correlate well with the judgment data. Based on our results, we suggest a number of future improvements. All of our code is available on GitHub.[2]

2 Three distributional models

In the following sections, we present three distributional models: a tag-based model (SoundFX-tags), a bag-of-auditory-words model (SoundFX-BoAW), and a model based on both kinds of information (SoundFX-combined). We base our models on a subset of 4,744 sounds from the Freesound database (Font et al. 2013, total 225,247 sounds) that were manually categorized as SoundFX by Font et al. (2014). We chose to focus on this subset because these sounds represent real-life events (e.g. opening and closing doors, barking dogs, and leaking faucets), rather than e.g. music. All sounds are tagged and provided with descriptions by the uploaders. General statistics of this data set are given in Table 1. Some examples of tags associated with particular sounds are {*lawn-mower, machine, motor, mower*}, and {*laundromat, laundry, machine, vibration*}. We downloaded the sounds and the metadata through the Freesound API.[3]

[1]This work was carried out in the *Understanding Language by Machines* project, supported by the Spinoza prize from the Netherlands Organisation for Scientific Research (NWO). We wish to thank three anonymous reviewers for their feedback, which has noticeably improved this paper. All remaining errors are, of course, our own.

[2]https://github.com/evanmiltenburg/soundmodels-iwcs

[3]http://www.freesound.org/docs/api/

Proceedings of the 11th International Conference on Computational Semantics, pages 70–75,
London, UK, April 15-17 2015.

Total number of tags	43277	Average number of tags per sound	9
Number of different tags	4068	Average number of sounds per tag	11
Total number of sounds	4744	Average duration (seconds)	29

Table 1: General statistics about the SoundFX dataset.

2.1 A tag-based distributional model

We used Latent Semantic Analysis (Landauer & Dumais 1997) to create a tag-based distributional model (SoundFX-tags) . In our implementation, we used Scikit-learn (Pedregosa et al. 2011) to transform the tag×tag co-occurrence matrix (using TF-IDF), reduce the dimensionality of the matrix (using SVD, singular value decomposition), and to get a distance matrix using the cosine similarity measure. In our setup, we only use tags occurring more than 5 times that do not only contain digits (which are typically used to categorize files (by year, track number, etc.) rather than to describe their contents).

2.2 A sound-based distributional model

The tag-based model above provides an example of the *bag-of-words* approach, where the meaning of a word is inferred from co-occurrence data with other words. This idea has recently been extended to the domain of images; in the *bag-of-visual-words* approach, the meaning of a word is computed on the basis of visual features extracted from the images it occurs with (Bruni et al. 2012a,b, 2014). Inspired by this image-based work, researchers in the field of sound event detection have started to implement models using a *bag-of-audio-words* (BoAW) approach (Liu et al. 2010, Pancoast & Akbacak 2012). Following these authors, we set up a pipeline to create a BoAW-model. Our pipeline consists of the following stages:

1. **Preprocessing**: we convert all the sounds to WAV-format, resample them to 44100 Hz, and normalize the sounds using RMS (root mean square).
2. **Populating the feature space**: we populate a feature space by extracting acoustic descriptors from a training database of sounds. We partition each sound in partially overlapping windows of a fixed size, and compute descriptors on the basis of each window.[4] As the descriptor, we use mel-frequency cepstral coefficients (Fang et al. 2001) concatenated with log spectral energy.
3. **Building the audio vocabulary**: we cluster the descriptors using k-means. The centroids of the clusters are chosen as the audio words of our vocabulary, and thus we end up with k audio words.
4. **Creating a [sound × audio-word] matrix**: we again partition each sound in windows, and for each window we compute an acoustic descriptor. We then create a count matrix, based on which audio word is closest (using Euclidean distance) to each descriptor.
5. **Creating a [tag × audio-word] matrix**: we take the previous matrix to compute the tag×audio-word matrix. Every tag is represented by a vector that is the grand average of all the sound-vectors associated with that tag.

For our model (SoundFX-BoAW), we randomly selected 400 sounds from the set of SoundFX files. These sounds constitute the training set of the vocabulary building phase. For both the vocabulary building and the encoding phase, descriptors are extracted from each sound using windows of 250ms starting every 100ms. The BoAW model was created using 100 audio words. We transformed the values in the [tag×audio-word] matrix using Positive Local Mutual Information (plmi). The [tag×audio-word] matrix is obtained by averaging all the sound-vectors associated with each single tag (mean number of sound per tag = 39.71). Its dimensionality is reduced using SVD in order to avoid sparcity and reduce noise.

[4]The total number of windows (and thus the number of descriptors extracted) depends on the actual length of the sound.

2.3 A combined model

To combine tag information with audio word information, for this paper we propose to concatenate the TF-IDF-transformed SoundFX [tag × tag] matrix with a PLMI-transformed [tag × audio-word] matrix, and then reduce the resulting matrix using SVD. This is similar to Bruni et al.'s (2012a) approach. As an alternative to concatenation-based approaches, we can imagine creating a shared embedding model with both sound and language data (cf. Socher et al.'s (2013) work with images), but we leave the construction of such a model to future research.

3 Evaluation Procedure

We evaluated our models on the MEN Test Collection (Bruni et al. 2014) and on SimLex-999 (Hill et al. 2014). The former provides a test of semantic relatedness, i.e. how strongly two words are associated. The latter tests semantic similarity, which is a measure of how *alike* two concepts are. Hill et al. (2014) show that similarity ratings are more difficult to predict on the basis of text corpus data.

To evaluate our models, we took the tag pairs from both benchmarks, and we compared the similarity/relatedness ratings with the cosine similarity between the tags in each model. The correlation between the cosine similarity values and the actual ratings are reported in the next section. Our expectations for the performance of our models are as follows:

1. We expect the tag-based model (SoundFX-tags) to perform better on MEN than on SimLex-999, because (i) tag co-occurrence can only tell us something about which actions and entities typically occur together in a given event. But that does not tell us how alike the tags are; and (ii) language-based models typically perform better on measures of relatedness.
2. We expect the sound-based model (SoundFX-BoAW) to perform worse than SoundFX-tags on both tasks. This would parallel Bruni et al.'s results with bag-of-visual-words models.
3. We expect SoundFX-BoAW to perform better on SimLex-999 than on MEN, because the model clusters sounds (and thus tags) by their likeness.
4. We expect the combined model (SoundFX-combined) to perform better on both tasks than SoundFX-BoAW, because it is enriched with information from SoundFX-tags (which we expect to be a better approximator of human semantic judgment, see expectation 1).

In addition, we also created a tag-based model using the full Freesound database (Freesound-tags) because we were curious to see the effects of quantity versus quality (i.e. homogeneity) of tags. We were hoping that the two would balance each other out, yielding a performance on par with SoundFX-tags. In future work, we hope to be able to provide a better benchmark for sound-based distributional models. For example, MEN is based on tags from an image dataset. Clearly this is not ideal for models of sound domain, and a more balanced test collection is needed.

4 Results

Table 2 shows the results for our models. Each row shows the correlation scores on MEN and SimLex-999 for our models. We have selected the models with the optimal number of dimensions, which is why we report two models for SoundFX-tags: with 100 dimensions it produces the best score on SimLex, while with 400 dimensions it produces the best score on MEN. Our other models did not differ as much in their 'high-scores' for MEN and SimLex, which is why we do not report different versions of these. The results confirm our first two expectations, while the latter two expectations are not borne out.

SoundFX-tags scores better on MEN than on SimLex. The correlations show that our tag-based models are also more robust in capturing relatedness: optimizing on SimLex rather than on MEN is not as detrimental to the MEN-results as optimizing on MEN is to the SimLex-results. Our results also show that adding more data does not improve our model: when we use all the tags in the full Freesound database, the results are only slightly worse on the MEN task, and average on the SimLex task.

Model	Dimensions	MEN	SimLex-999
SoundFX-tags	100	0.675	**0.489**
SoundFX-tags	400	**0.689**	0.397
Freesound-tags	3000	0.643	0.426
SoundFX-BoAW	60	0.402	0.233
SoundFX-combined	1000	0.404	0.226

Table 2: Spearman correlations between our models and the MEN and Simlex-999 datasets.

SoundFX-tags scores better on both evaluation sets than SoundFX-BoAW. As noted in the previous section, this parallels Bruni et al.'s (2012a) results with bag-of-visual-words models. To further compare SoundFX-tags (optimized on MEN) with SoundFX-BoAW, we computed the pairwise distance for all combinations of tags in both models. A Spearman rank correlation between these sets of distances returns a value of 0.23. This means that both models are not strongly correlated with each other. In other words: they encode different information.

Counter to our expectations, SoundFX-BoAW does *not* perform better on SimLex than on MEN. Why is this? We believe that the reason lies in the tags provided with the sounds. For a good performance on SimLex, the tags should be close descriptions of the sounds, so that we know how similar two tags are on the basis of the similarity between the sounds they denote. We know that sounds seem to be good at capturing *events* (e.g. walking), but it is often hard or even impossible to recognize the objects present in those events (e.g. shoes vs. sandals). Ideally for our purposes, the sounds in the Freesound database would only be tagged with event-descriptions or with low-level descriptions of the sounds (*walking, sniffing, barking, scratching, beeping*). However, the tags are provided by the producers of the sounds. This has the result that the tags are typically very high-level descriptions, including all the objects involved in the production of the sound. This is detrimental to the performance on SimLex. Meanwhile, because on average there are so many tags per sound, there are many tags that get clustered together based on co-occurrence. This boosts the performance on the MEN-task.

Also counter to our expectations, Table 2 shows that the combined model is equivalent (rather than superior) to the sound-based model, i.e. combining the tag data with the audio-word data does not improve performance. Following the suggestions of two reviewers, we experimented with normalizing the matrices before concatenation. We tried two methods: (i) MAXDIVIDE: Divide all values in each matrix by their respective maximum value in that matrix; (ii) LOGMAXDIVIDE: to prevent extreme values in the BoAW-matrix from marginalizing the other values, we first took the log of all values in the matrix before dividing all values in both matrices by their respective maximum values. Table 3 provides a comparison of all concatenation methods.

Model	Dimensions	MEN	SimLex-999
SoundFX-combined	1000	0.404	0.226
SoundFX-MaxDivide	150	**0.688**	0.450
SoundFX-MaxDivide	100	0.678	**0.493**
SoundFX-LogMaxDivide	150	0.442	0.232
SoundFX-LogMaxDivide	100	0.435	0.239

Table 3: Spearman correlations between different concatenation models and the MEN and Simlex-999 datasets.

We conclude that the low performance of the old concatenation model is due to the fact that the relatively high values in the BoAW matrix (between 0 and 106312) had a marginalizing effect on the low values in the tag matrix (between 0 and 1), dominating the SVD. The LOGMAXDIVIDE method delivers models that are slightly better than the BoAW model and the old concatenation model, but worse than the others. Normalization using MAXDIVIDE delivers a competitive model on the MEN dataset, and the best model overall on SimLex, beating SoundFX-tags-400 by a margin of 0.004. With such a small difference, we should be wary of concluding that audio information (rather than chance) helped improve SimLex performance (as we predicted). More research on the possible contributions of audio data to semantic models is required.

5 Discussion and conclusion

We presented the first (to our knowledge) attempt to create a sound-based semantic space based on user-generated and -tagged sounds. The database used for our models is less controlled and much noisier as compared to other audio datasets used to test acoustic event recognition pipelines [5] or for studying auditory perception (Cotton & Ellis 2011, Capilla et al. 2013). The Freesound database (Font et al. 2013) provides a huge collection of sounds recorded by different human users, in different conditions and using different equipments. Moreover, all the linguistic metadata (tags, titles, and descriptions) are provided by the users who recorded and uploaded the sounds without any overt supervision or strict guidelines.[6] Moreover, the number of sounds per tag (i.e. the number of sounds used to encode each tag in the SoundFX-BoAW model) varies between 6 and 2050, with an average number of sound per tag equal to 39.71. What might seem like limitations at first sight, might turn out to be strong points in favor of our analyses. The strong correlations of both tag-based and sound-based families of models with the MEN and SimLex benchmarks proves that, even with uncontrolled data, the models are still able to capture semantic regularities in the auditory domain.

The sound-based model implemented the BoAW-paradigm using mel frequency cepstral coefficients sampled in partially overlapping windows over the sound signals. This captures short-term distribution of energy over the sound spectrum. BoAW encoding thus capture distributions of features across sounds, but completely ignores the development of the sound over a span of time larger than the sampling time windows. To combat this issue, we plan to assess other features or combination of features in the future (see Breebaart & McKinney 2004 for a list). Other possible improvements are using a different clustering algorithm for vocabulary creation, and using different sound encoding techniques. We plan to look at Gaussian Mixture Models and Fisher encoding (also used successfully by Bruni et al. (2012b, 2014) for their image-based models). Nonetheless, we are planning to overtake the feature selection step by exploring the possibility of using unsupervised methods for learning feature representations provided by deep learning algorithms (Bengio 2009, Mohamed et al. 2009, Hinton et al. 2012).

The evidently better performance of SoundFX-tags as compared to SoundFX-BoAW in the quantitative evaluation may simply be due to the nature of the benchmarks that we used. MEN and SimLex are both linguistic tasks, and so they may very well be biased towards language-based models. Furthermore, as mentioned in Section 3, MEN was based on a collection of image tags. Thus we may question the reliability of MEN as a test for sound-based models, which may very well stand out once sound-related tags are considered as well. In the short term, we plan to collect a controlled set of such tags, along with human similarity ratings for both the tags as well as the sounds labeled with those tags. A longer-term goal is to create other kinds of benchmarks that are better equipped to test the quality of perceptually grounded models.

Moreover, we are aware of the limitations of the simple concatenation technique employed to obtain SoundFX-combined. In order to try to overcome this, we are planning to explore deep-learning techniques to learn shared text-sound embeddings similar to what has been already proposed by Socher et al. (2013) and Ngiam et al. (2011). Our results are an encouraging first step to incorporate sound information in distributional semantic models. We hope that this development will parallel the success of image-based models, and that all kinds of perceptually grounded models may ultimately be unified in a single model that captures the semantics of human experience.

[5] `http://c4dm.eecs.qmul.ac.uk/sceneseventschallenge/description.html`

[6] Note that descriptions are moderated, and users may receive a warning that their sounds have a "bad description". There are some description guidelines, which can be found at: `http://www.freesound.org/help/faq/#sounds-2`. However, this does not mean that all sounds have a clear and uniform description.

References

Bengio, Yoshua. 2009. Learning deep architectures for ai. *Found. Trends Mach. Learn.* 2(1). 1–127. doi:10.1561/2200000006. http://dx.doi.org/10.1561/2200000006.

Breebaart, J. & M. McKinney. 2004. Features for audio classification .

Bruni, Elia, Gemma Boleda, Marco Baroni & Nam-Khanh Tran. 2012a. Distributional semantics in technicolor. In *Proceedings of the 50th annual meeting of the association for computational linguistics: Long papers-volume 1*, 136–145. Association for Computational Linguistics.

Bruni, Elia, Nam Khanh Tran & Marco Baroni. 2014. Multimodal distributional semantics. *Journal of Artificial Intelligence Research* 1. 1–47.

Bruni, Elia, Jasper Uijlings, Marco Baroni & Nicu Sebe. 2012b. Distributional semantics with eyes: Using image analysis to improve computational representations of word meaning. In *Proceedings of acm multimedia*, 1219–1228. Nara, Japan.

Capilla, Almudena, Pascal Belin & Joachim Gross. 2013. The early spatio-temporal correlates and task independence of cerebral voice processing studied with MEG. *Cerebral cortex (New York, N.Y. : 1991)* 23(6). 1388–95. doi:10.1093/cercor/bhs119.

Cotton, Courtenay V. & Daniel P. W. Ellis. 2011. Spectral vs. spectro-temporal features for acoustic event detection. In *Ieee workshop on applications of signal processing to audio and acoustics, waspaa 2011, new paltz, ny, usa, october 16-19, 2011*, 69–72.

Fang, Zheng, Zhang Guoliang & Song Zhanjiang. 2001. Comparison of different implementations of mfcc. *J. Comput. Sci. Technol.* 16(6). 582–589. doi:10.1007/BF02943243. http://dx.doi.org/10.1007/BF02943243.

Font, Frederic, Gerard Roma & Xavier Serra. 2013. Freesound technical demo. In *Proceedings of the 21st acm international conference on multimedia*, 411–412. ACM.

Font, Frederic, Joan Serrà & Xavier Serra. 2014. Audio clip classification using social tags and the effect of tag expansion. In *Audio engineering society conference: 53rd international conference: Semantic audio*, Audio Engineering Society.

Hill, Felix, Roi Reichart & Anna Korhonen. 2014. Simlex-999: Evaluating semantic models with (genuine) similarity estimation. *arXiv preprint arXiv:1408.3456* .

Hinton, Geoffrey E., Li Deng, Dong Yu, George E. Dahl, Abdel-rahman Mohamed, Navdeep Jaitly, Andrew Senior, Vincent Vanhoucke, Patrick Nguyen, Tara N. Sainath & Brian Kingsbury. 2012. Deep neural networks for acoustic modeling in speech recognition: The shared views of four research groups. *IEEE Signal Process. Mag.* 29(6). 82–97.

Landauer, Thomas K & Susan T Dumais. 1997. A solution to plato's problem: The latent semantic analysis theory of acquisition, induction, and representation of knowledge. *Psychological review* 104(2). 211.

Liu, Yang, Wanlei Zhao, Chong-Wah Ngo, Changsheng Xu & Hanqing Lu. 2010. Coherent bag-of audio words model for efficient large-scale video copy detection. In Shipeng Li, Xinbo Gao & Nicu Sebe (eds.), *Civr*, 89–96. ACM.

Mohamed, Abdel-rahman, George E. Dahl & Geoffrey E. Hinton. 2009. Deep belief networks for phone recognition. In *Nips workshop on deep learning for speech recognition and related applications*, .

Ngiam, Jiquan, Aditya Khosla, Mingyu Kim, Juhan Nam, Honglak Lee & Andrew Y Ng. 2011. Multimodal Deep Learning. *Proceedings of The 28th International Conference on Machine Learning (ICML)* 689–696.

Pancoast, Stephanie & Murat Akbacak. 2012. Bag-of-audio-words approach for multimedia event classification. In *Interspeech*, ISCA.

Pedregosa, F., G. Varoquaux, A. Gramfort, V. Michel, B. Thirion, O. Grisel, M. Blondel, P. Prettenhofer, R. Weiss, V. Dubourg, J. Vanderplas, A. Passos, D. Cournapeau, M. Brucher, M. Perrot & E. Duchesnay. 2011. Scikit-learn: Machine learning in Python. *Journal of Machine Learning Research* 12. 2825–2830.

Socher, Richard, Milind Ganjoo, Christopher D Manning & Andrew Ng. 2013. Zero-shot learning through cross-modal transfer. In *Advances in neural information processing systems*, 935–943.

Turney, Peter D, Patrick Pantel et al. 2010. From frequency to meaning: Vector space models of semantics. *Journal of artificial intelligence research* 37(1). 141–188.

Alignment of Eye Movements and Spoken Language for Semantic Image Understanding

Preethi Vaidyanathan, Emily Prud'hommeaux, Cecilia O. Alm,
Jeff B. Pelz, and Anne R. Haake
Rochester Institute of Technology
(pxv1621|emilypx|coagla|jbppph|arhics)@rit.edu

Abstract

Extracting meaning from images is a challenging task that has generated much interest in recent years. In domains such as medicine, image understanding requires special expertise. Experts' eye movements can act as pointers to important image regions, while their accompanying spoken language descriptions, informed by their knowledge and experience, call attention to the concepts and features associated with those regions. In this paper, we apply an unsupervised alignment technique, widely used in machine translation to align parallel corpora, to align observers' eye movements with the verbal narrations they produce while examining an image. The resulting alignments can then be used to create a database of low-level image features and high-level semantic annotations corresponding to perceptually important image regions. Such a database can in turn be used to automatically annotate new images. Initial results demonstrate the feasibility of a framework that draws on recognized bitext alignment algorithms for performing unsupervised automatic semantic annotation of image regions. Planned enhancements to the methods are also discussed.

1 Introduction

The ability to identify and describe the important regions of an image is useful for a range of vision-based reasoning tasks. When expert observers communicate the outcome of vision-based reasoning, spoken language is the most natural and convenient instrument for conveying their understanding. This paper reports on a novel approach for semantically annotating important regions of an image with natural language descriptors. The proposed method builds on prior work in machine translation for bitext alignment (Vogel et al., 1996; Liang et al., 2006) but differs in the insight that such methods can be applied to align multimodal visual-linguistic data. Using these methods, we report on initial steps to integrate eye movements and transcribed spoken narratives elicited from expert observers inspecting medical images.

Our work relies on the fact that observers' eye movements over an image reveal what they consider to be the important image regions, their relation to one another, and their relation to the image inspection objectives. Observers' co-captured narrations about the image naturally express relevant meaning and, especially in expert domains, special knowledge and experience that guide vision-based problem-solving and decision-making. Despite being co-captured, precise time synchronization between eye movement and narrations cannot be assumed (Vaidyanathan et al., 2013). Therefore, techniques are needed to integrate the visual data with the linguistic data. When meaningfully aligned, such visual-linguistic data can be used to annotate important image regions with appropriate lexical concepts.

We treat the problem of integrating the two data streams as analogous to the alignment of a parallel corpus, or bitext, in machine translation, in which the words of a sentence in one language are aligned to their corresponding translations in another language. For our problem, eye movements on images are considered to be the visual language comprising visual units of analysis, while the transcribed narratives contain the linguistic units of analysis. Previous work has investigated the association of words with pictures, words with videos, and words with objects and image regions (Forsyth et al., 2009; Kuznetsova et al., 2013; Kong et al., 2014). But the combination of perceptual information (via eye movements) and

Proceedings of the 11th International Conference on Computational Semantics, pages 76–81,
London, UK, April 15-17 2015.

more naturally obtained conceptual information (via narratives) will greatly improve the understanding of the semantics of an image, allowing image regions that are relevant for an image inspection task to be annotated with meaningful linguistic descriptors. In this ongoing work, we use dermatological images as a test case to learn the alignments between the two types of units of analysis. We primarily seek to determine whether a bitext alignment approach can be used to align multimodal data consisting of eye movements and transcribed narratives.

2 Prior Work

Automatic semantic annotation of images and image regions is an important but highly challenging problem for researchers in computer vision and image-based applications. Algorithms employing low-level image features have succeeded somewhat in capturing the statistics of natural scenes, identifying faces, and recognizing objects (Zhang et al., 2012). Some researchers have proposed sophisticated models for semantic annotation through object recognition that while successful on certain types of images either failed to capture the semantics of the image and the relations between regions or fared poorly in expert domains such as medicine (Müller et al., 2004; Vinyals et al., 2014). Multiple approaches have been developed for generating image captions (Kuznetsova et al., 2013; Kong et al., 2014). The method we propose here differs from these earlier approaches in its use of spoken language descriptions and eye movement data. In addition to being more natural than approaches such as labeling of images by drawing or eliciting image descriptions on Mechanical Turk, our approach has the potential to provide more information (Vaidyanathan et al., 2013).

Empirical experiments have shown that eye movements are closely time-locked with human language processing (Ferreira and Tanenhaus, 2007). Roy (2000) proposed a technique for integrating vision and language elicited from infants using a mutual information model. Although useful in infant-directed interactions it is unlikely that this would translate successfully to complex scenarios containing multiple objects/concepts such as viewing medical images. Researchers have used techniques such as Latent Dirichlet Allocation to address the multimodal integration problem (Li and Wang, 2003). Machine translation approaches have been used with image features to recognize and annotate objects in scenes, to automatically match words to the corresponding pictures, and to describe scenes and generate linguistic descriptions of image regions (Duygulu et al., 2002; Berg et al., 2004; Yu and Ballard, 2004). While prior work supports the feasibility of integrating the visual and linguistic modalities, it also leaves open the question of whether multimodal integration is feasible in more complex scenarios such as medical image annotation. Moreover, eye movements in complex scenarios are usually not considered in this work. We make a key contribution by focusing on integrating experts' gaze data, known to encode their perceptual knowledge for vision-based problem solving in their domain (Li et al., 2013).

3 Data Collection

Twenty-nine dermatologists were eye tracked and audio recorded while they inspected and described 29 images of dermatological conditions. A Sensomotoric Instruments (SMI) eye tracking apparatus and a TASCAM audio recording equipment were used. The participants were asked to describe the image to the experimenter, using a modified version of the Master-Apprentice method (Beyer and Holtzblatt, 1997), a data elicitation methodology from human-computer interaction for eliciting rich spoken descriptions (Womack et al., 2012). Certain data were missing or excluded for quality reasons, leaving a multimodal corpus consisting of 26 observers and 29 images.

4 Aligning eye movements and transcribed narratives

The goal of this research is to develop a method for aligning an observer's eye movements over an image (the visual units) with his spoken description of that image (the linguistic units). Our first step is

SIL of um SIL uh SIL serpiginous SIL uh erythematous SIL uh SIL this plaque uh extending from the SIL interdigital space between the right SIL great toe and first toe SIL uh just distal though looks like there's a few erythematous pap- s- f- ca- small papules SIL uh SIL uh SIL so differential SIL would be SIL uh SIL cutaneous larva migrans SIL uh SIL two scabes SIL three some other SIL uh SIL trauma or SIL external insult SIL uh i would say about SIL um SIL final diagnos- be cutanea larva SIL migrans SIL which i'd say ninety SIL um SIL percent certain SIL next SIL

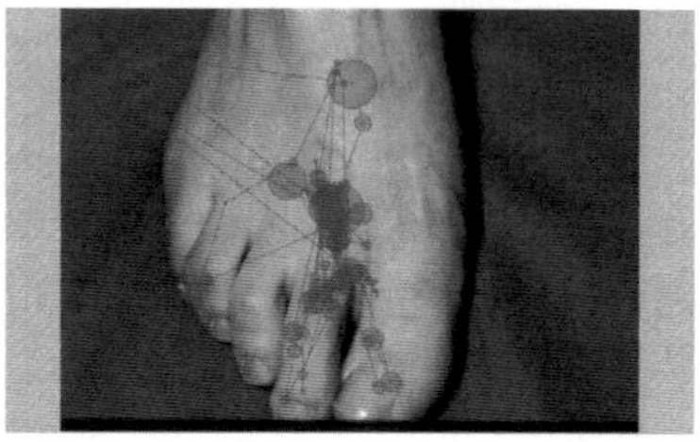

Figure 1: **A multimodal data example**. *Left*: Transcribed narrative with speech disfluencies, silent (SIL) pauses, and no utterance boundaries. *Right*: Eye movements overlaid on the corresponding image. The circles represent locations where the observer gazed, with the size of the circle reflecting gaze duration. The lines connecting the circles indicate changes of gaze location. Image courtesy:Logical Images

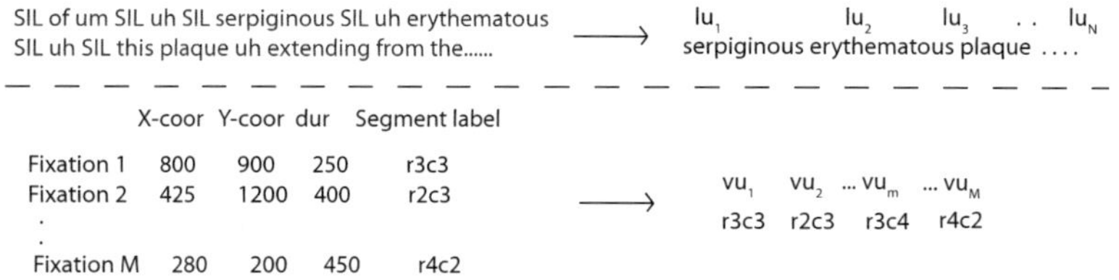

Figure 2: The top panel shows an excerpt of a transcribed narrative and the resulting linguistic units after filtering based on parsing evidence. The bottom panel shows eye movement data and the resulting gaze-filtered image regions or visual units. The linguistic and visual units jointly act as input to the Berkeley aligner. Linear order of the units is maintained and reflected in the parallel data windows.

therefore to extract these visual and linguistic units from the eye-tracking data and audio recordings. The audio recordings of the observers were transcribed verbatim, as shown in Figure 1. Most dermatological concepts present in an image tend to involve either noun phrases or adjectives. Accordingly, the linguistic units for alignment are nouns and adjectives, which we identify using the following process. Utterance boundaries are added and silent and filled pauses are removed before parsing the data with the Berkeley parser (Petrov and Klein, 2007). From the parsed output, tokens in noun phrases and adjective phrases are extracted. The linear order of the data is maintained. Following the extraction process, we filter out regular stopwords along with a set of tokens reflecting the data collection scenario (e.g., *differential, certainty, diagnosis*).[1] Names of diagnoses (*psoriasis, basal cell carcinoma*, etc.) are also removed since such words do not correspond to any particular image region but instead reflect the disease that an image depicts as a whole. The resulting filtered and linearly ordered sequences of linguistic units serve as one of the inputs to the bitext alignment algorithm. An example is shown in Figure 2.

The eye movement data consists of fixation locations indicating where in the image observers gazed, as shown in Figure 1. We use fixation locations in conjunction with image regions to obtain the visual units. The images are of size 1680 x 1050 pixels. We divide each image into a grid of 5 rows (*r*) and 5 columns (*c*). Each cell in the grid is associated with a label that encodes the row and column number for that cell, for example *r3c9, r4c12.* The fixations of an observer are overlaid on this grid, and each fixation is labeled according to the grid cell it falls within. In this way, we obtain a linearly ordered sequence of visual units consisting of fixated image regions, encoded using the grid labels, for the other input to the alignment algorithm. An example is shown in Figure 2.

In machine translation, an alignment model is trained on a parallel corpus of sentences rendered in two different languages. In our case, each observers' entire narrative and entire set of fixations is one training sentence pair. For each image, this would yield a corpus of only 26 parallel sentences, which would be insufficient to generate a reliable alignment model. To increase the amount of training data, we

[1] Observers were supposed to provide a differential, a final diagnosis, and to indicate diagnostic certainty.

Image	Precision	Recall	F-measure
1	0.71	0.65	0.68
2	0.65	0.44	0.52
3	0.28	0.32	0.30
4	0.44	0.36	0.40
5	0.24	0.32	0.28
Overall	0.42	0.40	0.41

Table 1: Alignment precision, recall, and F-measure for 5 images. Higher values indicate better alignment.

use a moving window of 5 seconds, extracting linguistic and visual units within each sliding timeframe and adding that pair of unit sequences as a "sentence" pair in the corpus. The time window is applied incrementally over a narrative, resulting in a much larger parallel corpus. In order to ensure that the two sequences in a given sentence pair are of roughly equal length, we merge contiguous identical visual units. (For example *r2c3, r3c3, r3c3* is converted into *r2c3, r3c3*.) We then randomly select visual units, still maintaining the linear order, such that the number of visual units is equal to number of linguistic units within that time window. We leave optimization of the parameters relating to grid segmentation, time window size, and visual unit selection for future work.

The pairs of sequences of linguistic and visual units, organized as described above, serve as a parallel corpus for training the aligner. We use the Berkeley aligner, recognized for its accuracy and flexibility in testing and training alignment models (Liang et al., 2006). Following standard approaches to word alignment for machine translation, the Berkeley aligner uses expectation maximization to learn an alignment model in an unsupervised manner. To generate gold standard reference alignments for evaluating the aligner, a researcher with reasonable knowledge of the regions in the image and the vocabulary used by the observers to describe the images manually produced alignments for 5 of the 29 images. Future work will involve more images.

5 Results

Word alignment output for building machine translation models is typically formatted as a set of paired indices for each input sentence pair being aligned. Each index pair represents an alignment between the words at the locations indicated by the indices. The standard metric used to evaluate word alignment for machine translation is the word alignment error rate (AER), which compares the index pairs output by the aligner to the manually derived reference index pairs. Knowing the locations of the words being aligned is necessary for subsequent steps in the MT pipeline, such as building the phrase table. In contrast, our end goal is to learn which words are being used to describe the various regions in the image, independently of when the words were uttered and when the fixations occured. Thus, rather than evaluate the accuracy of the index pairs output by the aligner, we instead evaluate our aligner in terms of how accurately it identifies the correct correspondences between words and regions indicated by those index pairs.

In Table 1, we report the precision, recall, and F-measure of our aligner output, calculated as described above, for the 5 images for which we produced manual reference alignments. We see that although the performance of the aligner varies depending on the image, we achieve strong performance values in some cases and reasonable performance overall. Figure 3 shows one of the images in our evaluation set overlaid with the 5x5 grid. In addition, the figure includes a randomly selected subset of words from the observers' narratives overlaid on the regions with which they were associated by the alignment model. Many of the words were correctly aligned with the regions they depict.

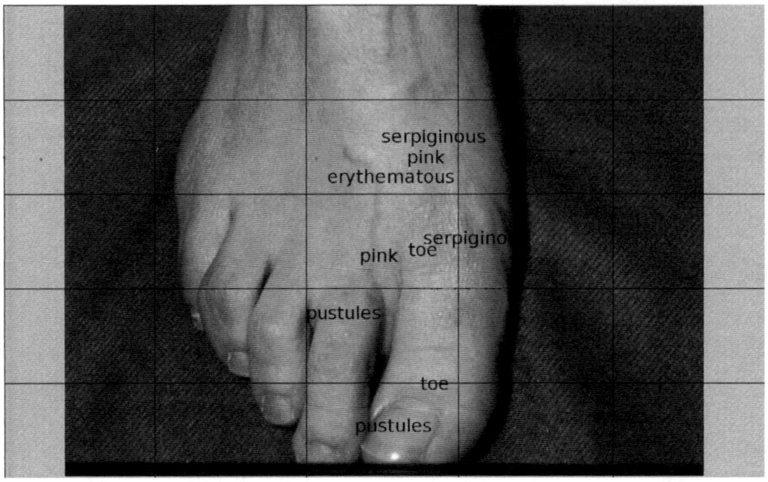

Figure 3: Some occurrences of a set of randomly selected lingusitic units (word tokens) overlaid on the visual units (image regions) with which they were aligned by the alignment model.

6 Discussion and Conclusion

The reasonably high precision, recall, and F-measure alignment results for images 1 and 2 indicate that a bitext alignment model can be used to align eye movements and transcribed narratives. Visual inspection of the aligner output might explain why the results are not as high for images 3, 4, and 5. In particular, some abstract linguistic units that are not physically present in the image (e.g., *unusual, thought*) but tagged as noun and adjective tokens by the parser, are included in the input to the aligner. These abstract units are not, however, included in the manually derived reference alignments, thereby lowering the precision of the alignment output for these images. We also note that the reference alignments generated by the researcher could be different from those generated by a dermatology expert.

The next phase in the development of our system for automated semantic annotation of images will be to use these alignments to map the low-level image features of these images and the image regions to the lexical items and semantic concepts with which they are associated via alignment. A model built on these mapping could be used to generate semantic annotations of previously unseen images. In addition, further collection of visual-linguistic information could be made more efficient using automatic speech recognition adapted to the medical or dermatological domain.

There are many improvements that can be made to the existing system, particularly in the way that the various parameter values were selected. The size of the time window used to expand the parallel corpus, the image segmentation approach, and the selection of the visual units all can be tuned in order to optimize alignment performance. In addition, our method for extracting the linguistic units relies on parsing output, which could be improved by training the parser on spoken language data from the biomedical domain. In future work, we also intend to use a more sophisticated image segmentation algorithm together with a medical ontology such as the Unified Medical Language System (UMLS) to learn even more meaningful relations between important image regions and lexical concepts.

In summary, the work presented here introduces a new approach for obtaining semantic annotations for images by creatively integrating visual and linguistic information. These preliminary results highlight the potential of adapting existing NLP methods to problems involving multimodal data.

References

Berg, T. L., A. C. Berg, J. Edwards, and D. Forsyth (2004). Who's in the picture? *Advances in neural information processing systems 17*, 137–144.

Beyer, H. and K. Holtzblatt (1997). *Contextual design: Defining customer-centered systems.* San Diego: Elsevier.

Duygulu, P., K. Barnard, J. F. de Freitas, and D. A. (2002). Object recognition as machine translation: Learning a lexicon for a fixed image vocabulary. In *Computer Vision-ECCV 2002*, pp. 97–112.

Ferreira, F. and M. K. Tanenhaus (2007). Introduction to the special issue on language–vision interactions. *Journal of Memory and Language 57*(4), 455–459.

Forsyth, D. A., T. Berg, C. O. Alm, A. Farhadi, J. Hockenmaier, N. Loeff, and G. Wang (2009). Words and pictures: Categories, modifiers, depiction, and iconography. In S. J. Dickinson (Ed.), *Object Categorization: Computer and Human Vision Perspectives*. Cambridge: Cambridge University Press.

Kong, C., D. Lin, M. Bansal, R. Urtasun, and S. Fidler (2014). What are you talking about? Text-to-image coreference. In *IEEE Conference on Computer Vision and Pattern Recognition*, pp. 3558–3565.

Kuznetsova, P., V. Ordonez, A. C. Berg, T. L. Berg, and Y. Choi (2013). Generalizing image captions for image-text parallel corpus. In *Proceedings of ACL*, pp. 790–796.

Li, J. and J. Z. Wang (2003). Automatic linguistic indexing of pictures by a statistical modeling approach. *IEEE Transactions on Pattern Analysis and Machine Intelligence 25*(9), 1075–1088.

Li, R., P. Shi, and A. R. Haake (2013). Image understanding from experts' eyes by modeling perceptual skill of diagnostic reasoning processes. In *Proceedings of the IEEE Conference on Computer Vision and Pattern Recognition (CVPR)*, pp. 2187–2194.

Liang, P., B. Taskar, and D. Klein (2006). Alignment by agreement. In *Proceedings of NAACL-HLT*, pp. 104–111.

Müller, H., N. Michoux, D. Bandon, and A. Geissbuhler (2004). A review of content-based image retrieval systems in medical applications? Clinical benefits and future directions. *International Journal of Medical Informatics 73*(1), 1–23.

Petrov, S. and D. Klein (2007). Improved inference for unlexicalized parsing. In *Proceedings of HLT-NAACL*, pp. 404–411.

Roy, D. (2000). Integration of speech and vision using mutual information. In *Proceedings of ICASSP*, pp. 2369–2372.

Vaidyanathan, P., J. B. Pelz, C. O. Alm, C. Calvelli, P. Shi, and A. R. Haake (2013). Integration of eye movements and spoken description for medical image understanding. In *Proceedings of the 17th European Conference on Eye Movements*.

Vinyals, O., A. Toshev, S. Bengio, and D. Erhan (2014). Show and tell: A neural image caption generator. *arXiv preprint arXiv:1411.4555*.

Vogel, S., H. Ney, and C. Tillmann (1996). HMM-based word alignment in statistical translation. In *Proceedings of the 16th conference on Computational Linguistics-Volume 2*, pp. 836–841.

Womack, K., W. McCoy, C. O. Alm, C. Calvelli, J. B. Pelz, P. Shi, and A. R. Haake (2012). Disfluencies as extra-propositional indicators of cognitive processing. In *Proceedings of the Workshop on Extra-Propositional Aspects of Meaning in Computational Linguistics*, pp. 1–9.

Yu, C. and D. H. Ballard (2004). A multimodal learning interface for grounding spoken language in sensory perceptions. *ACM Transactions on Applied Perception (TAP) 1*(1), 57–80.

Zhang, D., M. M. Islam, and G. Lu (2012). A review on automatic image annotation techniques. *Pattern Recognition 45*(1), 346 – 362.

From a Distance: Using Cross-lingual Word Alignments for Noun Compound Bracketing

Patrick Ziering
Institute for NLP
University of Stuttgart, Germany

Lonneke van der Plas
Institute of Linguistics
University of Malta, Malta

Patrick.Ziering@ims.uni-stuttgart.de
Lonneke.vanderPlas@um.edu.mt

Abstract

We present a cross-lingual method for determining NP structures. More specifically, we try to determine whether the semantics of tripartite noun compounds in context requires a left or right branching interpretation. The system exploits the difference in word position between languages as found in parallel corpora. We achieve a bracketing accuracy of 94.6%, significantly outperforming all systems in comparison and comparable to human performance. Our system generates large amounts of high-quality bracketed NPs in a multilingual context that can be used to train supervised learners.

1 Introduction

k-partite noun compounds, i.e., compositions of k bare common nouns that function as one unit, (kNCs), such as *air traffic control system*, usually have an implicit structure that reflects semantics. While a LEFT-branching *[world banana] market* is very unlikely, for *luxury cattle truck*, both structures make sense and context is necessary for disambiguation: *[luxury cattle] truck* is a truck for luxury cattle whereas *luxury [cattle truck]* is a luxury truck for (any) cattle. Therefore, a proper structural analysis is a crucial part of noun compound interpretation and of fundamental importance for many tasks in natural language processing such as machine translation. The correct French translation of *luxury cattle truck* depends on the internal structure. While [*luxury cattle*] *truck* is translated as *camion pour bétail de luxe*, the preferred translation for *luxury* [*cattle truck*] is *camion de luxe pour bétail*.

Previous work on noun compound bracketing has shown that supervised beats unsupervised. The latter approaches use N-gram statistics or lexical patterns (Lauer, 1995; Nakov and Hearst, 2005; Barrière and Ménard, 2014), web counts (Lapata and Keller, 2004) or semantic relations (Kim and Baldwin, 2013) and evaluate on carefully selected evaluation data from encyclopedia (Lauer, 1995; Barrière and Ménard, 2014) or from general newspaper text (Kim and Baldwin, 2013). Vadas and Curran (2007a,b) manually annotated the Penn Treebank and showed that they improve over unsupervised results by a large margin. Pitler et al. (2010) used the data from Vadas and Curran (2007a) for a parser applicable on base noun phrases (NPs) of any length including coordinations. Barker (1998) presents a bracketing method for k-partite NPs that reduces the task to three-word bracketings within a sliding window. One advantage of supervised approaches for this task is that kNCs are labeled in context so contextual features can be used in the learning framework. These are especially useful when dealing with ambiguous kNCs.

The need for annotated data is a drawback of supervised approaches. Manual annotations are costly and time-consuming. To circumvent this need for annotated data, previous work has used cross-lingual supervision based on parallel corpora. Bergsma et al. (2011) made use of small amounts of annotated data on the target side and complement this with bilingual features from unlabeled bitext in a co-trained classifier for coordination disambiguation in complex NPs. Previous work on using cross-lingual data for the analysis of multi-word expressions (MWEs) of different types include Busa and Johnston (1996); Girju (2007); Sinha (2009); Tsvetkov and Wintner (2010); Ziering et al. (2013).

Proceedings of the 11th International Conference on Computational Semantics, pages 82–87,
London, UK, April 15-17 2015.

Ziering and Van der Plas (2014) propose an approach that refrains from using any human annotation. They use the fact, that languages differ in their preference for open or closed compounding (i.e., multiword vs. one-word compounds), for inducing the English bracketing of 3NCs. English open 3NCs like *human rights abuses* can be translated to partially closed phrases as in German *Verletzungen der Menschenrechte*, (*abuses of human rights*), from which we can induce the LEFT-branching structure. Although this approach achieves a solid accuracy, a crucial limitation is coverage, because restricting to six paraphrasing patterns ignores many other predictive cases. Moreover, the system needs part of speech (PoS) tags and splitting information for determining 2NCs and is therefore rather language-dependent.

In this paper, we present a precise, high-coverage and knowledge-lean method for bracketing kNCs (for $k \geq 3$) occurring in parallel data. Our method uses the distances of words that are aligned to kNC components in parallel languages. For example, the 3NC *human rights violations* can be bracketed using the positions of aligned words in the Italian fragment ... *che le* ***violazioni*** *gravi e sistematiche dei* ***diritti umani*** .... The fact, that the alignment of the third noun, *violations* (**violazioni**), is separated from the rest, points us in the direction of LEFT-branching. Using less restricted forms of cross-lingual supervision, we achieve a much higher coverage than Ziering and Van der Plas (2014). Furthermore, our results are more accurate. In contrast to previous unsupervised methods, our system is applicable in both token- and type-based modes. Token-based bracketing is context-dependent and allows for a better treatment of structural ambiguity (as in *luxury cattle truck*). We generate large amounts of high-quality bracketed kNCs in a multilingual context that can be used to train supervised learners.

2 Aligned Word Distance Bracketing

The aligned word distance bracketing (AWDB) is inspired by Behaghel's First Law saying that elements which belong close together intellectually will also be placed close together (Behaghel, 1909).

$c_1, \ldots, c_n \Leftarrow \mathrm{N}_1, \ldots, \mathrm{N}_k$
$AW_i \Leftarrow$ set of content words c_i aligns to
while $|\{c_1, \ldots, c_n\}| > 1$ **do**
  $(c_m, c_{m+1}) \Leftarrow c$-pair with minimal AWD
  merge c_m and c_{m+1} to $c_{[m,\, m+1]}$
  $AW_{[m,\, m+1]} = AW_m \cup AW_{m+1}$
end while

Figure 1: AWDB algorithm for kNCs

For each language l, we apply the AWDB algorithm on a kNC as shown in Figure 1: we start bottom-up with one constituent per noun. For each constituent c_i, we create a set of content words[1] c_i aligns to, AW_i. We merge the two consecutive constituents c_m and c_{m+1} with the smallest aligned word distance (AWD) based on the minimum distance from all words in AW_m to all words in AW_{m+1}:

$$\mathrm{AWD}(c_m, c_{m+1}) = \min_{x \in AW_m, y \in AW_{m+1}} |pos(x) - pos(y)|$$

where $pos(\alpha)$ is the position of a word α in a sentence. In the case of (c_m, c_{m+1}) being aligned to a common closed compound, AWD(c_m, c_{m+1}) is zero. If the smallest AWD is not unique but the related constituents do not overlap (e.g., (c_1,c_2) and (c_3,c_4) aligning to two different closed compounds) we merge both constituent pairs in one iteration. If they overlap (e.g., (c_1,c_2) and (c_2,c_3) aligning to a common closed compound), no bracketing structure can be derived from the word positions in l. Similarly, if there is an empty set AW_e, i.e., there is no alignment from c_e to a content word in l, AWDB cannot bracket the kNC using the translation to l. If no structure can be derived from any aligned language, AWDB refuses to answer.

For example, the 4NC *air transport safety organization* is aligned to four words in the French fragment *Nous devons mettre en place cette* ***organisation***$_7$ *européenne chargée de la* ***sécurité***$_{12}$ *du* ***transport***$_{14}$ ***aérien***$_{15}$ *qui* ... (*We need to establish this European* ***organization*** *responsible for the* ***safety*** *of* ***air transport*** *that* ...). The aligned word sets are: $AW_1 = \{$aérien$\}$, $AW_2 = \{$transport$\}$, $AW_3 = \{$sécurité$\}$ and

[1] These are words tagged as noun, adjective or verb. They can be identified with corpus frequency to remain knowledge-lean.

$AW_4 = \{\text{organisation}\}$. c_1 and c_2 have the smallest AWD and thus are merged. In the next iteration, the smallest AWD is between $c_{[1,\ 2]}$ and c_3. As last step, we merge $c_{[[1,\ 2],\ 3]}$ and c_4. The resulting constituent corresponds to the 4NC structure [[[*air transport*] *safety*] *organization*].

To determine the final bracketing for a given kNC, we use the majority vote of all structures derived from all aligned languages. In the case of a tie, AWDB does not produce a final bracketing. Although this decision leads to lower coverage, it enables us to measure the pure impact of the cross-lingual word distance feature. For practical purposes, an additional back-off model is put in place. In order to mitigate word alignment problems and data sparseness, we additionaly bracket kNCs in a type-based fashion, i.e., we collect all kNC structures of a kNC type from various contexts.

3 Experiments

Tools and data. While AWDB is designed for bracketing NPs of any length, we first experiment with bracketing 3NCs, the largest class of 3^+NCs (93.8% on the basic dataset of Ziering and Van der Plas (2014)), for which bracketing is a binary classification (i.e., LEFT or RIGHT). For bracketing longer NCs we often have to make do with partial information from a language, instead of a full structure. In future work, we plan to investigate methods to combine these partial results. Moreover, in contrast to previous work (e.g., Vadas and Curran (2007b)), we take only common nouns as components into account rather than named entities. We consider the task of bracketing 3NCs composed of common nouns more ambitious, because named entities often form a single concept that is easy to spot, e.g., ***Apple II*** *owners*. Although AWDB can also process compounds including adjectives (e.g., ***active*** *inclusion policy* aligned to the Dutch *beleid voor actieve insluiting* (*policy for active inclusion*)), for a direct comparison with the system of Ziering and Van der Plas (2014), that analyses 3NCs, we restrict ourselves to noun sequences.

We use the Europarl[2] compound database[3] developed by Ziering and Van der Plas (2014). This database has been compiled from the OPUS[4] corpus (Tiedemann, 2012) and comprises ten languages: Danish, Dutch, English, French, German, Greek, Italian, Portuguese, Spanish and Swedish. We use the initial version (basic dataset), that contains English word sequences that conform PoS chunks and their alignments. We select English word sequences whose PoS pattern conforms three nouns.

Extraction errors are a problem, since many adjectives have been tagged as nouns and some 3NCs occur as incomplete fragments. For increasing the effectiveness of human annotation, we developed a high-confidence noun filter $P_{noun}(word) = P(noun \mid word)$. It is trained on the English Wikipedia[5] tagged by TreeTagger (Schmid, 1995). We inspect all 3NCs in the context of one token to the left and right, $w_0\{N_1 N_2 N_3\}w_4$. If $P_{noun}(N_i) < \theta$ or $P_{noun}(w_j) \geq \theta$, we remove the 3NC from our dataset. We inspected a subset of all 3NCs in the database and estimated the best filter quality to be with $\theta = 0.04$. This threshold discards ***increasing*** *land abandonment* but keeps ***human*** *rights abuse*. Our final dataset contains 14,941 tokens and 8824 types.

Systems in comparison. We compare AWDB with the bracketing approach of Ziering and Van der Plas (2014). For both systems, we use the majority vote across all nine aligned languages, in a token- and type-based version. We implemented an unsupervised method based on statistics on bi-grams extracted from the English part of the Europarl corpus.[6] As scorer, we use the *Chi squared* (χ^2) measure, which worked best in previous work (Nakov and Hearst, 2005). We consider both the *adjacency* (i.e., (N_1, N_2) vs. (N_2, N_3), (Marcus, 1980)) and the *dependency* (i.e., (N_1, N_2) vs. (N_1, N_3), (Lauer, 1995)) model. We created a back-off model for the bracketing system of Ziering and Van der Plas (2014) and for AWDB that falls back to using χ^2 if no bracketing structure can be derived (*system* $\rightarrow \chi^2$). Finally, we compare with a baseline, that always predicts the majority class: LEFT.

Human annotation. We observed that there is only a very small overlap between test sets of previous work on NP bracketing and the Europarl database. The test set used by Ziering and Van der Plas (2014) is very small and the labeling is less fine-grained. Thus, we decided to create our own test set.

---

[2]statmt.org/europarl

[3]ims.uni-stuttgart.de/data/NCDatabase.html

[4]opus.lingfil.uu.se

[5]en.wikipedia.org

[6]For a fair comparison, we leave systems that have access to external knowledge, such as web search engines, aside.

A trained independent annotator classified a set of 1100 tokens in context with one of the following labels: LEFT, RIGHT, EXTRACTION (for extraction errors that survived the high-confidence noun filter $P_{noun}(word)$), UNDECIDED (for 3NCs that cannot be disambiguated within the one-sentence context) and SEMANTIC INDETERMINATE (for 3NCs for which LEFT and RIGHT have the same meaning such as *book price fixing* (i.e., *price fixing for books* is equivalent to *fixing of the book price*)). We consider the full dataset to compare the coverage of the systems in comparison. For the accuracy figures, in order to keep annotation efforts small, we asked evaluators to annotate just those tokens that our system provides an answer to, because tokens that our system has no answer to will not be evaluated in the comparative evaluation on accuracy anyhow. Two additional trained independent annotators each classified one half of the dataset for checking inter-annotator agreement. For the classes LEFT/RIGHT (308 tokens), we achieve an agreement rate of 90.3% and $\kappa = 0.717$ (Cohen, 1960), which means good agreement (Landis and Koch, 1977). We use the LEFT/RIGHT consensus of the 3NC tokens as final test set (278 tokens).

Evaluation Measure. We measure accuracy (Acc $_\Omega$) for a set of 3NC tokens, Ω, as correct LEFT/RIGHT labels divided by all LEFT/RIGHT labels. Coverage is measured as LEFT/RIGHT labels divided by all 3NC tokens in the full dataset. We refer to the harmonic mean of Acc $_\Omega$ and Coverage as $harmonic(\Omega)$.

4 Results and Discussion

System	Coverage
AWDB$_{token}$ / AWDB$_{type}$	87.9% / 91.2%
AWDB$_{type}$ $\rightarrow \chi^2$	100%
χ^2	100%
Zier.v.d.Plas14$_{token}$ / Zier.v.d.Plas14$_{type}$	29.9% / 48.1%
Zier.v.d.Plas14$_{type}$ $\rightarrow \chi^2$	100%
LEFT baseline	100%

Table 1: Evaluation results on coverage

As it turned out that the *adjacency* model outperforms the *dependency* model, we only report results for the first. Table 1 presents the coverage of each system, based on the full dataset. Our first result is that type-based cross-lingual bracketing outperforms token-based and achieves up to 91.2% in coverage. As expected, the system of Ziering and Van der Plas (2014) does not cover more than 48.1%. The χ^2 method and the back-off models cover all 3NCs in our dataset. The fact that AWDB$_{type}$ misses 8.8% of the dataset is mainly due to equal distances between aligned words (e.g., *crisis resolution mechanism* is only aligned to closed compounds, such as the Swedish *krislösningsmekanism* or to nouns separated by one preposition, such as the Spanish *mecanismo de resolución de crisis*). In future work, we will add more languages in the hope to find more variation and thus get an even higher coverage.

System	Acc$_{com}$	$harmonic(com)$	com
AWDB$_{token}$ / AWDB$_{type}$	94.4% / 94.4%	91.0% / **92.8%**	270
Zier.v.d.Plas14$_{token}$ / Zier.v.d.Plas14$_{type}$	**87.8%** / 87.2%	44.6% / **62.0%**	180
AWDB$_{type}$	**94.6%**†	**92.9%**†	184
Zier.v.d.Plas14$_{type}$	86.4%	61.8%	
AWDB$_{type}$	**94.1%**†	92.6%	273
χ^2	87.9%	**93.6%**	
AWDB$_{type}$ $\rightarrow \chi^2$	**93.5%**†	**96.6%**†	278
Zier.v.d.Plas14$_{type}$ $\rightarrow \chi^2$	86.7%	92.9%	
χ^2	87.4%	93.3%	
LEFT baseline	80.9%	89.4%	

Table 2: Direct comparison on common test sets; † = significantly better than the systems in comparison

Table 2 directly compares the systems on common subsets (com), i.e., on 3NCs for which all systems in the set provide a result. The main reason why cross-lingual systems make bracketing errors is the quality of automatic word alignment. AWDB outperforms Ziering and Van der Plas (2014) significantly[7]. This can be explained with the flexible structure of AWDB, which can exploit more data and is thus more robust to word alignment errors. AWDB significantly outperforms χ^2 in accuracy but is inferior in $harmonic(com)$. The last four lines of Table 2 show all systems with full coverage. AWDB's back-off model achieves the best $harmonic(com)$ with **96.6%** and an accuracy comparable to human performance. For AWDB, types and tokens show the same accuracy. The harmonic mean numbers for the system of Ziering and Van der Plas (2014) illustrate that coverage gain of types outweighs a higher accuracy of tokens. Our intuition that token-based approaches are superior in accuracy is hardly reflected in the present results. We believe that this is due to the domain-specificity of Europarl. There are only few instances, where the bracketing of a 3NC type differs from token to token. We expect to see a larger difference for general domain parallel corpora.

Language	**Acc**$_{com}$	**Coverage**	$harmonic(com)$	com
Romance	86.6%	**86.2%**	**86.4%**	201
Germanic	**94.0%**	68.0%	78.9%	

Table 3: Evaluation of language families for AWDB$_{type}$

Table 3 shows the contribution of the Romance (i.e., French, Italian, Portuguese and Spanish) and Germanic (i.e., Danish, Dutch, German and Swedish) language families for AWDB$_{type}$. Romance languages have a higher coverage than Germanic languages. This is because many 3NCs are aligned to a closed Germanic compound, which gives no information on the internal structure. Since Romance languages use open compounds, coverage is higher. On the other hand, Romance languages are worse in accuracy. One reason for this is that they can also produce constructions that violate Behaghel (1909)'s First Law, e.g., *state health service* can be translated to the Portuguese *serviços de saúde estatais* (lit.: *[service of health] state*$_{adj}$). While Ziering and Van der Plas (2014) excluded the pattern NOUN + PREP + NOUN + ADJ, we observed that excluding results with this pattern worsens the overall performance of AWDB. Test set instances with this pattern in any Romance language have significantly[8] more LEFT labels than the total test set. Furthermore, many instances of these cases can be disambiguated using morphosyntactic information such as number, e.g., *world fishing quotas* aligned to the French *quotas de pêche mondi**aux*** (*quotas*$_{pl}$ *of fishing*$_{sg}$ *world*$_{adj,pl}$).

As a result, we have 13,622 3NC tokens in context annotated with bracketing structures that are comparable to human annotation. The manual annotation by Vadas and Curran (2007a) resulted in 5582 three-word NPs, that were successfully used to train supervised learners.

5 Conclusion

In this paper, we presented a method for the automatic bracketing of k-partite noun compounds by using the surface structure (i.e., various word positions) in parallel translations as supervision. In an experiment, we extracted 3NCs from a noun compound database comprising ten languages derived from a parallel corpus. Our bracketing system outperforms all systems in comparison with an accuracy of 94.6% and is comparable with human performance.

In future work, we will investigate how to combine partial bracketing results from different languages and how to make the approach independent from parallel data. Along with this paper, we publish[9] the processed dataset and our test set, which can be used as training and test data for supervised learners.

Acknowledgements

We thank the anonymous reviewers for their helpful feedback and Alaeddine Haouas for the discussions on French. This research was funded by the German Research Foundation (Collaborative Research Centre 732, Project D11).

[7]Approximate randomization test (Yeh, 2000), $p < 5\%$

[8]z-test for proportions; $p < 5\%$

[9]www.ims.uni-stuttgart.de/data/AWDB.data.tgz

References

Barker, K. (1998). A Trainable Bracketer for Noun Modifiers. In *Canadian Conference on AI*, Volume 1418 of *Lecture Notes in Computer Science*.

Barrière, C. and P. A. Ménard (2014). Multiword Noun Compound Bracketing using Wikipedia. In *ComAComA 2014*.

Behaghel, O. (1909). Beziehungen zwischen Umfang und Reihenfolge von Satzgliedern. *Indogermanische Forschungen*.

Bergsma, S., D. Yarowsky, and K. Church (2011). Using Large Monolingual and Bilingual Corpora to Improve Coordination Disambiguation. In *ACL-HLT 2011*.

Busa, F. and M. Johnston (1996). Cross-Linguistic Semantics for Complex Nominals in the Generative Lexicon. In *AISB Workshop on Multilinguality in the Lexicon*.

Cohen, J. (1960). A Coefficient of Agreement for Nominal Scales. *Educational and Psychological Measurement 20*.

Girju, R. (2007). Improving the Interpretation of Noun Phrases with Crosslinguistic Information. In *ACL 2007*.

Kim, S. N. and T. Baldwin (2013). A Lexical Semantic Approach to Interpreting and Bracketing English Noun Compounds. *Natural Language Engineering 19*(3).

Landis, J. R. and G. G. Koch (1977). The Measurement of Observer Agreement for Categorical Data. *Biometrics 33*.

Lapata, M. and F. Keller (2004). The Web as a Baseline: Evaluating the Performance of Unsupervised Web-based models for a range of NLP tasks. In *HLT-NAACL 2004*.

Lauer, M. (1995). *Designing Statistical Language Learners: Experiments on Noun Compounds*. Ph. D. thesis, Macquarie University.

Marcus, M. (1980). *A Theory of Syntactic Recognition for Natural Language*. MIT Press.

Nakov, P. and M. Hearst (2005). Search Engine Statistics Beyond the N-gram: Application to Noun Compound Bracketing. In *CONLL 2005*.

Pitler, E., S. Bergsma, D. Lin, and K. W. Church (2010). Using Web-scale N-grams to Improve Base NP Parsing Performance. In *COLING 2010*.

Schmid, H. (1995). Improvements in Part-of-Speech Tagging with an Application to German. In *ACL SIGDAT-Workshop*.

Sinha, R. M. K. (2009). Mining Complex Predicates In Hindi Using A Parallel Hindi-English Corpus. In *Workshop on Multiword Expressions: Identification, Interpretation, Disambiguation and Applications*.

Tiedemann, J. (2012). Parallel Data, Tools and Interfaces in OPUS. In *LREC 2012*.

Tsvetkov, Y. and S. Wintner (2010). Extraction of Multi-word Expressions from Small Parallel Corpora. In *Coling 2010: Posters*, Beijing, China.

Vadas, D. and J. Curran (2007a). Adding Noun Phrase Structure to the Penn Treebank. In *ACL 2007*.

Vadas, D. and J. R. Curran (2007b). Large-scale Supervised Models for Noun Phrase Bracketing. In *PACLING 2007*.

Yeh, A. (2000). More Accurate Tests for the Statistical Significance of Result Differences. In *COLING 2000*.

Ziering, P. and L. Van der Plas (2014). What good are 'Nominalkomposita' for 'noun compounds': Multilingual Extraction and Structure Analysis of Nominal Compositions using Linguistic Restrictors. In *COLING 2014*.

Ziering, P., L. Van der Plas, and H. Schütze (2013). Multilingual Lexicon Bootstrapping - Improving a Lexicon Induction System Using a Parallel Corpus. In *IJCNLP 2013*.

Unsupervised Learning of Meaningful Semantic Classes for Entity Aggregates

Henry Anaya-Sánchez
NLP & IR Group, UNED
Juan del Rosal, 16
28040 Madrid, Spain
henry.anaya@lsi.uned.es

Anselmo Peñas
NLP & IR Group, UNED
Juan del Rosal, 16
28040 Madrid, Spain
anselmo@lsi.uned.es

Abstract

This paper addresses the task of semantic class learning by introducing a new methodology to identify the set of semantic classes underlying an aggregate of instances (i.e, a set of nominal phrases observed as a particular semantic role in a collection of text documents). The aim is to identify a set of semantically coherent (i.e., interpretable) and general enough classes capable of accurately describing the full extension that the set of instances is intended to represent. Thus, the set of learned classes is then used to devise a generative model for entity categorization tasks such as semantic class induction. The proposed methods are completely unsupervised and rely on an (unlabeled) open-domain collection of text documents used as the source of background knowledge.

We demonstrate our proposal on a collection of news stories. Specifically, we model the set of classes underlying the predicate arguments in a Proposition Store built from the news. The experiments carried out show significant improvements over a (baseline) generative model of entities based on latent classes that is defined by means of Hierarchical Dirichlet Processes.

1 Introduction

The problem of identifying semantic classes for words in Natural Language Processing (NLP) has been shown useful to address many text processing tasks, mainly in the context of supervised and semi-supervised learning, in which the development of systems suffers from data scarcity.

Although some semantic dictionaries and ontologies do exist such as WordNet (Miller, 1995) or DBPedia (Mendes et al., 2011), their coverage is rarely complete, especially for large open classes (e.g., very specific classes of people and objects), and they fail to integrate new knowledge. Thus, it helps a lot to firstly learn word categories or classes from a large amount of (unlabeled) training data and then to use these categories as features for the supervised tasks.

The general task of semantic class learning, which can be broadly defined as the task of learning classes of words and their instances from text corpora, has been addressed in a variety of forms that correspond to different application scenarios. Among these forms, we can find two that have been termed as *semantic class mining* (Shi et al., 2010; Huang and Riloff, 2010; Kozareva et al., 2008) and *semantic class induction* (Iosif et al., 2006; Grave et al., 2013). These have to do respectively with (i) the expansion of (seed) sets of instances labeled with class information (Knowledge Base population), and with (ii) automatic annotation of individual instances with their semantic classes in the context of a particular text.

In our research, we are more focused on the later. Specifically, we center on the task of providing a collection of instances with class information (what an entity is) in a given textual context, and then to eventually enrich the context with properties inherited from the semantic class.

Thus, an important issue addressed in our work is that of learning a set of *meaningful classes* to label a collection of instances composing a semantic aggregate. By *meaningful classes*, we refer to a set of classes showing the following two properties:

Proceedings of the 11th International Conference on Computational Semantics, pages 88–93,
London, UK, April 15-17 2015.

- be a general enough class so that it can represent other entity occurrences in similar contexts, but also
- be a specific enough and coherent class so that it directly reflects the most important entity properties that can be inherited from the textual context in which the instance occurs.

For example, in the context "*x1* throws a touchdown pass", entity *x1* should be assigned with classes entailing football *players* rather than just a generic class *person*, and more likely, receive the class *quarterback*.

With the term *semantic aggregate* we refer to a set of instances not completely chosen at random, but sharing some contextual relationships (e.g., a set of nominal phrases observed in a given syntactic/semantic relationship with a specific verb in a text corpus).

In this way, this paper proposes a new methodology to identify/learn the set of semantic classes underlying an aggregate of entity instances. The aim is to learn a set of semantically meaningful classes capable of accurately describing the full extension that the set of entity instances is intended to represent for a posterior application to semantic class induction.

Thus, we also go beyond and propose a generative model of instances based on the set of learned classes for the aggregates to allow the classification of individual occurrences of instances.

We evaluate our proposal from a collection of news. Specifically, we model the set of semantic classes underlying the predicate arguments in a Proposition Store (Peñas and Hovy, 2010) built from the news texts.

So far, it has said little about the quality of automatically learned classes beyond their coverage; which is traditionally measured when evaluating approaches in application scenarios related to the task of semantic class mining, for expanding seed sets of words. By taking advantage of the generative method proposed to model instances, we rely on a recently introduced coherence measure to evaluate the coherence of the learned classes to classify instances. Also, we measure the generalization of instances by means of the likelihood of generating held-aside data.

The experiments carried out show significant improvements over a (baseline) generative model of instances based on latent classes that is defined by means of Hierarchical Dirichlet Processes (HDP) (Teh et al., 2006).

2 Learning semantic classes

We propose to learn the set of semantic classes underlying a (finite) semantic aggregate of entities instances A from a global set of candidate classes $C_0 = \{c_1, \ldots, c_{|C_0|}\}$ by relying on a learned value of Pointwise Mutual Information (PMI) between each possible class $c \in C_0$ and a model $\{p(c|A)\}_{c \in C_0}$ of posterior probabilities of classes conditioned on the aggregate. All statistics are learnt from a background text corpus in which the instances in A occur.

Specifically, we define by $Dom(A) = \{c | c \in C_0 \wedge pmi(c, A) > \theta_0 \wedge p(c|A) > \theta'_0\}$ the set of semantic classes underlying A; where θ_0 and θ'_0 are minimum thresholds, and $pmi(c, A)$ is the PMI value between c and A. [1] This value is calculated as follows:

$$pmi(c, A) = \log\left(\frac{p(c, A)}{p(c)p(A)}\right) = \log\left(\frac{p(c|A)}{p(c)}\right) \tag{1}$$

where both the model component $p(c|A)$ and prior $p(c)$ are learned relying on the following parameters:

- a $|C_0| \times |C_0|$ stochastic matrix $T = \{p(c_i|c_j)\}_{1 \le i \le |C_0|, 1 \le j \le |C_0|}$ representing a statistical mapping between possible classes in C_0 ($\forall j \in \{1, \ldots, |C_0|\}$, $\sum_{i=1}^{|C_0|} p(c_i|c_j) = 1$),
- a $|C_0| \times |I|$ stochastic matrix $Q = \{p(c_j|e_k)\}_{1 \le j \le |C_0|, 1 \le k \le |I|}$ that represents the distribution of possible classes conditioned on instances in the corpus (not only instances appearing in A but all instances in the corpus), and

[1] In our experiments, we set up to 1 and 0.001 the values of parameters θ_0 and θ'_0 respectively.

- a stochastic column vector $P(A) = \langle p(e_1|A), \ldots, p(e_{|I|}|A) \rangle^\top$ representing the distribution of observed instances in A.

From the above elements, the model of posterior class probabilities is estimated as:

$$p(c_i|A) = (T \cdot Q \cdot P(A))_i \quad (2)$$

being Q and $P(A)$ learned from maximum likelihood estimations; whereas the stochastic mapping T is learned by relying on infinite Markov chains between candidate classes as follows:

$$p(c_i|c_j) = \left((1-\alpha)(I_{|C_0|\times|C_0|} - \alpha T_0)^{-1}\right)_{i,j} \quad (3)$$

where $I_{|C_0|\times|C_0|}$ is the $|C_0| \times |C_0|$ identity matrix, T_0 is an $|C_0| \times |C_0|$ matrix whose element $(T_0)_{i,j}$ is defined as:

$$p_0(c_i|c_j) = \sum_{e \in I} p(c_i|e)p(e|c_j) \quad (4)$$

and α is the probability of adding a new candidate class to the Markov chain being generated. The idea of applying Markov chains is to obtain a "semantic-transitive" smoothing of mapping p_0 to define the mapping between classes. Note that such a mapping in turn applies a smoothing to the model of class posteriors given by $Q \cdot P(A)$.

Priors $p(c_1), \ldots, p(c_{|C_0|})$ correspond to the stationary distribution of candidate classes learned from the Markov chains.

2.1 Candidate classes

Assuming that Proposition Stores can be easily built in a unsupervised manner from the text corpus used as background (for example, such as in (Peñas and Hovy, 2010) that include class-instances observations in the one hand and propositions in the other), the process of obtaining candidate classes and class-instance counts to estimate the above models is straightforward.

Nevertheless, we additionally consider as candidate classes all common nominal phrases that do not appear as classes in the class-instance relation, but that appear as argument of propositions. These classes are considered to be singletons, whose entity instances are observed each time they occur as the argument of a proposition. Besides, we consider each (common) nominal phrase as instance of its head noun.

3 A generative model of instances

We consider a Probabilistic Topic Modeling (PTM) approach to model the intended extension of the classes underlying an aggregate as a realization from a generative model based on the learned classes.

Thus, similar to traditional PTM approaches such as LDA, we model each aggregate of instances $A = e_1, \ldots, e_{N_A}$ as a mixture:

$$p(e|A) = \sum_{i=1}^{k} p(e|c_{A_i})\, p(c_{A_i}) \quad (5)$$

where e is an arbitrary instance, for all $i \in \{1, \ldots, k\}$, c_{A_i} is a class, $p(c_{A_i})$ is the prior for c_{A_i} in the generation of instances for A ($\langle p(c_{A_1}), \ldots, p(c_{A_k}) \rangle \sim \text{Dirichlet}_k(\alpha_C)$), and $p(e|c_{A_i})$ is the probability of instantiating class c_{A_i} with instance e.

However, different from traditional PTM approaches, classes in Equation 5 do not correspond to true latent distributions of instances. Instead, each class in the mixture is actually a class in $Dom(A)$.

The probability value $p(e|c_{A_i})$ in learning time is estimated from the parameters learned in the previous section to set up the model of class posteriors conditioned on the individual instances; whereas for applying the learned model to instance classification, the value is estimated from the counts of class assignments to entities in the text corpora in a similar way as LDA does (i.e., by applying a Dirichlet smoothing to the distribution of instances labeled with class c_{A_i} when learning the model). The aim is to allow applying the model to unseen instances for semantic class induction, while respecting the class-instance distribution learned in previous section.

Table 1: Averaged values of UMass coherence obtained (using ϵ=1.0e-50) for the clustering-based distributions of instances induced by the generative models.

Method	n=5	n=10	n=15	n=20
HDP	-217.051	-1271.62	-3665.42	-8073.6
Our proposal	-1.9693	-8.3945	-18.8997	-33.4624

4 Experiments

In order to evaluate our proposal, we consider a collection of 30,826 New York Times articles about US football, from which we build two proposition stores: one for training (based on the first 80% of the published articles) and the other one for testing (based on the remainder articles). The aim was to learn the semantic classes underlying each predicate argument taken as semantic aggregate of instances.

Specifically, documents in the training set were parsed using a standard dependency parser De Marneffe and Manning (2008); Klein and Manning (2003) together with TARSQI Verhagen et al. (2005), and after collapsing some syntactic dependencies following Clark and Harrison (2009); Peñas and Hovy (2010), we select the collection of 1,646,583 propositions corresponding to the top 1500 more frequent verb-based predicates (i.e., about the 90 percent of the total number of propositions in the training) to set up the input proposition store. The same procedure was applied to gather propositions from the test set, but they were held-aside for testing purposes.

We applied our approach to learn the classes underlying each predicate argument from the proposition store used for training, and evaluate the obtained models by conducting two experiments. In each experiment, we choose to compare the results obtained by our proposal to a baseline produced by applying HDP Teh et al. (2006) to infer latent distributions of distributions of instances, instead of using the PTM approach described in Section 3. [2]

4.1 Evaluating coherence

Thus, the first experiment was aimed at measuring the coherence or degree of interpretability of each distribution of instances induced from the class-based generative models. For this purpose, we rely on the UMass measure of coherence as defined in Stevens et al. (2012), that in this case was defined by regarding the co-occurrence frequencies of instances across the predicate arguments.

The UMass measure of coherence is intrinsic in nature. Significantly, it computes its counts from the training corpus used to train the models rather than a test corpus Stevens et al. (2012). So that, it attempts to confirm that the models learned data known to be in the corpus. This measure has been shown to be in agreement with coherence judgments by experts Mimno et al. (2011) in PTM.

In Table 1, we show the averaged values of UMass coherence obtained by each approach. As can be seen, the greatest values of the coherence measure correspond to the distributions of instances underlying the classes learned by our approach. This directly corroborates the good performance of the proposed model to learn coherent classes of entities to semantically label the aggregates of instances. In all cases, HDP significantly performs the worst in this experiment. To illustrate how the obtained values of coherence are representative enough of actual coherent distributions of instances, we show in Table 2 the classes learned for some predicate arguments. As can be seen, our approach accurately capture the more likely meaning of each argument.

4.2 Evaluating the generalization performance

The second experiment was focused on evaluating the generalization performance of our proposal, which we measure in terms of the generation of the held-aside argument instances in the test set. The average

[2] HDP is a fully bayesian, unsupervised PTM approach that differently from LDA and related (traditional) PTM approaches does not need to known the number of topics (in our case, instance distributions) to be discovered beforehand. Besides, HDP has been shown to optimize the generative approach of LDA in terms of the likelihood of predicting data.

Table 2: Examples of the classes learned by our approach for some predicate arguments.

Predicate	Arg.	Classes learned
win	x win -	team, group, no., person, champion,[football,team], host, giants, defeat, 49er, opponent, [defend,champion], victory,[super bowl,champion], [only,team],[other,team]
win	- win y	game,championship,title,[national,championship], [first,game], [last,game],[football,game],bowl,victory,job,[playoff,game],[straight,game],award, [consecutive,game], one,[division,title],division,[final,game],[home,game],[big,game], [championship,game],[run,game],[super,bowl],[regular-season,game],[national,title],battle
pass	x pass -	touchdown, group, person, [first,touchdown]
pass	- pass y	yard, season, test, play, touchdown, record, interception, ball, situation, examination, physical, [big,play], attempt, efficiency, rush, mark, downs, [last,season], yardage, offense, completion, [total,yard], more, rusher, person, protection, one
make	x make -	team, group, person, that, kicker
make	- make y	play, decision, mistake,[big,play],catch, playoff, start, change, move, difference, appearance, call, offer, deal, choice, money, debut, sense, statement,score, progress,trip, one, interception

Table 3: Averaged values and standard deviation of log-likelihood on the generation of instances for predicate arguments in the test data.

Method	Avg. likelihood	Std. dev.
HDP	-2009.77	169.52
Our approach	-1638.55	95.0238

log-likelihood on the generation of instances from each predicate argument was adopted to measure the performance in this case.

Table 3 summarizes the results obtained in this experiment. As it is shown, our approach, again, largely outperforms the approach based on HDP. All these results suggest that the classes learned by our approach can be properly applied to perform the identification of semantic classes, specially to address the task of semantic class induction.

5 Conclusions

In this paper, a new methodology to identify the set of semantic classes underlying an aggregate of instances (namely, a set of nominal phrases observed as predicate arguments in a collection of text documents) has been introduced. The aim of the methodology is to identify a set of semantically coherent (i.e., interpretable) and general classes capable of accurately describing the full extension that the set of instances is intended to represent. The set of learned classes was then used to devise a generative model for entity categorization tasks such as semantic class induction. The experiments carried out over a collection of news show significant improvements over a (baseline) generative model of instances (in terms of coherence and generalization) that is based on latent classes defined by means of Hierarchical Dirichlet Processes. Future work includes the application of our proposal to model generalized propositions as tuples of classes to directly address the task of semantic class induction.

Acknowledgments

This work was partially funded by MINECO (PCIN-2013-002-C02-01) and EPSRC (EP/K017845/1) in the framework of CHIST-ERA READERS project, and by project Voxpopuli (TIN2013-47090-C3-1).

References

Clark, P. and P. Harrison (2009). Large-scale extraction and use of knowledge from text. In *Proceedings of the fifth international conference on Knowledge capture*, pp. 153–160. ACM.

De Marneffe, M.-C. and C. D. Manning (2008). The stanford typed dependencies representation. In *Coling 2008: Proceedings of the workshop on Cross-Framework and Cross-Domain Parser Evaluation*, pp. 1–8.

Grave, E., G. Obozinski, F. Bach, et al. (2013). Hidden markov tree models for semantic class induction. In *CoNLL-Seventeenth Conference on Computational Natural Language Learning*.

Huang, R. and E. Riloff (2010). Inducing domain-specific semantic class taggers from (almost) nothing. In *Proceedings of the 48th Annual Meeting of the Association for Computational Linguistics*, pp. 275–285. Association for Computational Linguistics.

Iosif, E., A. Tegos, A. Pangos, E. Fosler-Lussier, and A. Potamianos (2006). Unsupervised combination of metrics for semantic class induction. In *Spoken Language Technology Workshop, 2006. IEEE*, pp. 86–89. IEEE.

Klein, D. and C. D. Manning (2003). Accurate unlexicalized parsing. In *Proceedings of the 41st Annual Meeting on Association for Computational Linguistics-Volume 1*, pp. 423–430.

Kozareva, Z., E. Riloff, and E. H. Hovy (2008). Semantic class learning from the web with hyponym pattern linkage graphs. In *Proceeding of the ACL*, Volume 8, pp. 1048–1056.

Mendes, P. N., M. Jakob, A. García-Silva, and C. Bizer (2011). Dbpedia spotlight: shedding light on the web of documents. In *Proceedings of the 7th International Conference on Semantic Systems*, pp. 1–8. ACM.

Miller, G. (1995). Wordnet: A lexical database for english. *Communications of the ACM 38*(11), 39–41.

Mimno, D., H. Wallach, E. Talley, M. Leenders, and A. McCallum (2011). Optimizing semantic coherence in topic models. In *Proceedings of the Conference on Empirical Methods in Natural Language Processing*, pp. 262–272.

Peñas, A. and E. Hovy (2010). Filling knowledge gaps in text for machine reading. In *Proceedings of the 23rd International Conference on Computational Linguistics: Posters*, pp. 979–987. Association for Computational Linguistics.

Shi, S., H. Zhang, X. Yuan, and J.-R. Wen (2010). Corpus-based semantic class mining: distributional vs. pattern-based approaches. In *Proceedings of the 23rd International Conference on Computational Linguistics*, pp. 993–1001. Association for Computational Linguistics.

Stevens, K., P. Kegelmeyer, D. Andrzejewski, and D. Buttler (2012). Exploring topic coherence over many models and many topics. In *Proceedings of the 2012 Joint Conference on Empirical Methods in Natural Language Processing and Computational Natural Language Learning*, pp. 952–961. Association for Computational Linguistics.

Teh, Y., M. Jordan, M. Beal, and D. Blei (2006). Hierarchical dirichlet processes. *Journal of the American Statistical Association 101*(476), 1566–1581.

Verhagen, M., I. Mani, R. Sauri, R. Knippen, S. B. Jang, J. Littman, A. Rumshisky, J. Phillips, and J. Pustejovsky (2005). Automating temporal annotation with tarsqi. In *Proceedings of the ACL 2005 on Interactive poster and demonstration sessions*, pp. 81–84.

Crowdsourced Word Sense Annotations and Difficult Words and Examples

Oier Lopez de Lacalle
University of the Basque Country
oier.lopezdelacalle@ehu.eus

Eneko Agirre
University of the Basque Country
e.agirre@ehu.eus

Abstract

Word Sense Disambiguation has been stuck for many years. The recent availability of crowdsourced data with large numbers of sense annotations per example facilitates the exploration of new perspectives. Previous work has shown that words with uniform sense distribution have lower accuracy. In this paper we show that the agreement between annotators has a stronger correlation with performance, and that it can also be used to detect problematic examples. In particular, we show that, for many words, such examples are not useful for training, and that they are more difficult to disambiguate. The manual analysis seems to indicate that most of the problematic examples correspond to occurrences of subtle sense distinctions where the context is not enough to discern which is the sense that should be applied.

1 Introduction

Word sense ambiguity is a major obstacle for accurate information extraction, summarization and machine translation, but there is still a lack of high performance Word Sense Disambiguation systems (WSD). The current state-of-the-art is around the high 60s accuracy for words in full documents (Zhong and Ng, 2010), and high 70s for words with larger number of training examples (lexical sample). The lack of large, high-quality, annotated corpora and the fine-grainedness of the sense inventories (typically WordNet) are thought to be the main reasons for the poor performance (Hovy et al., 2006). The situation of WSD is in stark contrast to the progresses made on Named-Entity Disambiguation, where performance over 80% accuracy is routinely reported (Hoffart et al., 2012).

In this paper we focus on the recent release of crowdsourced data with large numbers of sense annotations per example (Passonneau and Carpenter, 2014), and try to shed some light in the factors that affect the performance of a supervised WSD system. In particular, we extend the analysis set up in (Yarowsky and Florian, 2002), and show that the agreement between annotators has a strong correlation with the performance for a particular word, stronger than previously used factors like the number of senses of the word and the sense distribution for the word.

In addition, we show that crowdsourced data can be used to detect problematic examples. In particular, our results indicate that, for many words, such examples are not useful for training, and that they are more difficult to disambiguate. The last section shows some examples.

2 Previous work on factors affecting WSD performance

WSD is a problem which differs from other natural language processing tasks in that each target word is a different classification problem, in contrast to, for instance, document classification, PoS tagging or parsing, where one needs to train one single classifier for all. Furthermore, it is already known that, given a fixed amount of training data, the performance of a supervised WSD algorithm varies from one word to another (Yarowsky and Florian, 2002).

Yarowsky and Florian (2002) did a thorough analysis of the behaviour of several WSD systems on a variety of factors: (a) target language (English, Spanish, Swedish and Basque); (b) part of speech; (c)

Proceedings of the 11th International Conference on Computational Semantics, pages 94–100,
London, UK, April 15-17 2015. ©2015 Association for Computational Linguistics

sense granularity; (d) inclusion and exclusion of major feature classes; (e) variable context width (further broken down by part-of-speech of keyword); (f) number of training examples; (g) baseline probability of the most likely sense; (h) sense distributional entropy; (i) number of senses per keyword; (j) divergence between training and test data; (k) degree of (artificially introduced) noise in the training data; (l) the effectiveness of an algorithms confidence rankings. Their analysis was based on the annotated examples for a handful of words, as released in the SensEval2 lexical sample task (Edmonds and Cotton, 2001).

In particular they found that the performance of all systems decreased for words with higher number of senses (as opposed to words with few senses) and for those with more uniform distributions of senses (as opposed to words with skewed distributions of senses). The distribution of senses was measured using the entropy of the probability distribution of the senses, normalized by the number of senses[1] $H_r(P) = H(P)/log_2(\#senses)$, where $H(P) = -\sum_{i \in senses} p(i) log_2 p(i)$ (Yarowsky and Florian, 2002).

In this paper we quantify the correlation of those two factors with the performance of a WSD system, in order to compare their contribution. In addition, we analyse a new factor, agreement between annotators, which can be used not only to know which words are more difficult, but also to characterize which examples are more difficult to disambiguate. To our knowledge, this is the first work which quantifies the contribution of each of these factors towards the performance on WSD, and the only one which analyses example difficulty for WSD on empirical grounds.

Our work is also related to (Plank et al., 2014), which showed that multiple crowdsourced annotations of the same item allow to improve the performance in PoS tagging. They incorporate the uncertainty of the annotators into the loss function of the model by measuring the inter-annotator agreement on a small sample of data, with good results. Our work can be seen as preliminary evidence that such a method can be also applied to WSD.

3 Measuring annotation agreement

The corpus used in the experiments is a subset of MASC, the Manually Annotated Sub-Corpus of the Open American National Corpus (Ide et al., 2008), which contains a subsidiary word sense sentence corpus consisting of approximately one thousand sentences per word annotated with WordNet 3.0 sense labels (Passonneau et al., 2012). In this work we make use of a publicly available subset of 45 words (17 nouns, 19 verbs and 9 adjectives, see Table 4) that have been annotated, 1000 sentences per target word, using crowdsourcing (Passonneau and Carpenter, 2014). The authors collected between 20 and 25 labels for every sentence.

We measured annotation agreement using the multiple annotations in the corpus and calculate the annotation entropy of an example and word sense distribution entropy as follows. In annotation entropy, we use directly the true-category probabilities from Dawid and Sekene's model (Passonneau and Carpenter, 2014) associated to each example to measure its entropy (as defined in the previous section). The annotation entropy for a word is the average of the entropy for each example. In sense entropy, on the other hand, we measure the overall confusion among senses and based on confusion distribution we calculate the entropy of each word sense. Similarly, the sense entropy of a word is averaged over all word sense entropy measures.

4 Annotation agreement explains word performance

We created a gold standard with a single sense per example, following (Passonneau and Carpenter, 2014), which use a probabilistic annotation model (Dawid and Skene, 1979). We split the 1000 examples for each word into development and test, sampling 85% (and 15% respectively) at random, preserving the overall sense distribution.

[1]The normalization ensures that the figure is comparable across words, as we divide by the maximum entropy for a word with that number of senses.

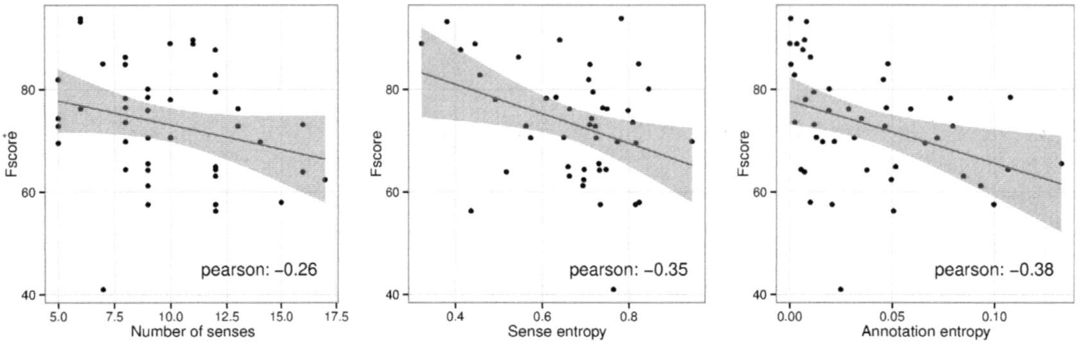

Figure 1: Scatterplots that show the correlation between the factors and accuracy. Each point corresponds to a word.

Regression Model	R^2	F-test
Number of senses	0.067	$p = 0.085$
Sense entropy	0.105	$p = 0.017$
Annotation entropy	0.123	$p = 0.011$
Full model	0.357	$p = 0.0001$
Full interaction	0.330	$p = 0.002$

Table 1: Regression analysis summary. The first three rows refer to the simplest models, where each factor (annotation entropy, sense entropy and number of senses) is taken in isolation. The full model takes all three factors with no interaction, and the full interaction includes all three factors and interactions. R^2 and F-test indicate whether the model is fitted.

The Word Sense Disambiguation algorithm of choice is *It Makes Sense* (IMS) (Zhong and Ng, 2010), which reports the best WSD results to date. We used it out-of-the-box, using the default parametrization and built-in feature extraction. The system always returned an answer, so the accuracy, precision, recall and F1 score are equal.

As explored in (Yarowsky and Florian, 2002), the variability of the accuracy across words can be related to many factors, including the distribution of senses and the number of senses of the word in the dataset. In this work, we introduce annotation agreement to the analysis. Figure 1 shows how each factor is correlated with the performance of the IMS WSD system, along with the Pearson product-moment. The highest correlation with the performance is for annotation entropy (-0.38) and the lowest for the number of senses (-0.26), whilst sense entropy has slightly lower correlation (-0.35) than annotation entropy.

Table 4 shows the number of senses, entropy of sense distribution and the entropy of the annotation agreement for each of the 45 target words.

In addition, we performed regression analysis of the three factors, alone, and in combination. All in all, we fit 5 linear models: the simplest models take each factor alone in a simple linear model;[2] the full model uses the three factors as a linear combination with no interaction between the factors; the full interaction model also models pairwise and three-wise multiplications of the factors.[3]

Table 1 shows the main figures of the analysis. Regarding models with only one factor, the entropy of annotation agreement explains performance better than sense entropy and number of senses (the higher R^2 the better the model fits the data). Actually, the number of senses alone is not a significant factor that explains the difficulty of a word (t-test $p > 0.05$), although in combination with the other factors it is a valuable information. Annotation agreement and the sense distribution do have a significant correlation according to the t-test.

[2]The simplest linear regression model is typically formalized as follows: $f = B_0 + B_1 \cdot factor_i + \epsilon$

[3]This can be generalized as follows: $f = B_0 + \sum_i B_i \cdot factor_i + \sum_j B_j \cdot interaction_j + \epsilon$

no-filt	train-filt	test-filt	t&t-filt
70.4	71.0	72.2	73.3

Table 2: Average results for the 30 words which get improvement using thresholds. Legend (cf. Section 5): no-filt for using full train and test data, train-filt for filtered train, test-filt for filtered test, and t&t-filt for filtered train and test. See table 4 for statistics and results of individual words.

The results for the "full model" show that the three models are complementary, and that in combination they account for 35.7% of the variance of the WSD performance measured in Fscore (according to adjusted R^2), with high significance. The analysis shows, as well, that the "full interaction" model does not explain the performance any better. Although this model is also significant (F-test $p = 0.002$), the adjusted R^2 is lower than in the "full model" (0.357 vs 0.330), showing that combining the factors without interactions is sufficient.[4]

5 Annotation agreement characterizes problematic examples

Contrary to the sense distribution of a word, annotation agreement can be used to detect problematic examples. In particular, we show that, for many words, such examples are not useful for training, and that they are more difficult to disambiguate.

We explored the use of thresholds to ignore the training examples with highest annotation entropy per example. 15% of the train data was set aside for development, and the rest was used to train IMS. We tried several thresholds: 0.5,0.25,0.1,0.05,0.01,0.001. The lower the threshold the fewer examples to train (difficult examples have high entropy values). Table 4 in the appendix shows the thresholds which yield the best results on development data. Overall, In 15 out of the 45 words, the best results on development were obtained using all the data, but for the remaining 30, removing examples improved results on development. Incidentally, those 15 words tend to have lower annotation entropy than the 30 words.

Table 2 shows the results on test data for the 30 words that improve on development. The train-filt column shows the results when we remove the examples with less agreement from train. Note that the threshold was only applied to 30 words. The performance improvement over using the full train data is on 0.6 absolute for these 30 words. The improvement is concentrated on 12 words, as 9 words get equal, and 9 words get a decrease in performance. When we use the threshold set in development to remove examples with less agreement from test, the performance increases 1.8 (test-filt column in Table 2). In this case, 23 words get better performance, 4 equal, and 3 words get a decrease. Finally, when we train and test on examples below the threshold, the improvement on the 30 words amount to 2.9. 24 words get better performance, 4 equal, and only 2 words get a decrease.

6 Examples

We sampled some problematic examples for the three words which attain the best improvement when removing examples from train with respect to the baseline: *tell*, *level* and *window*, in this order. Table 3 shows the 5 examples with highest annotation entropy for *tell*. The examples correspond to uses of *tell* where two fine-grained distinctions in WordNet[5] are hard to differentiate. A similar trend was observed for *level* and *window* (cf. Table 3), where the examples with high annotation entropy where also annotated with two fine-grained closely related senses. In all three words the examples corresponded to the two most frequent senses.

We had hypothesized two factors which could explain the high annotation entropy for some examples: the confusability among two senses of the word, and poor context for disambiguation. The manual

[4]Note that we also tried using specific interactions, and none improved over not using interactions.

[5]`http://wordnetweb.princeton.edu/perl/webwn`

A university spokesperson *told#1* the Michigan Daily that the library ...
On Monday, Naumann *told#2* a Berlin radio station that he opposed the ...
He *told#1* me that there is a "three strikes and you're out ...
Rumsfeld *told#2* Bob Woodward that he had no recollection of Wolfowitz's ...
When teams made decisions about how to do their work, employees *told#1* us ...
tell#1: express in words
tell#2: let something be known
An even more striking *level#1* of B-cell clonal dominance and expansion ...
... can turn into anaphylaxis , where toxic *levels#2* of histamines ...
The expression *level#1* of the EP 2 receptor mRNA in these vessels was ...
... was found to be approximately 1.6 times the *level#2* of control.
... the mean expression *level#1* of all genes was adjusted so that ...
level#1: a position on a scale of intensity or amount or quality
level#2: a relative position or degree of value in a graded group
The *windows#6* to the rear of its faded Art Deco ground floor were designed by ...
we actually took a screen uh door *window#6* off one of windows to try and allow ...
... is relieved by a shot of yellow flowers, visible through the *window#1*.
... and the neon bakery sign I can see from my office *window#6* often calls out to me ...
... a small brush and uh try to keep the paint from dripping on the *windows#6* and ...
window#1: a framework of wood or metal that contains a glass window pane ...
window#6: a pane of glass in a window

Table 3: Five examples with highest annotation entropy for *tell*, *level* and *window*, annotated with senses. Corresponding definitions are also given.

inspection seems to indicate the the former is the main factor in play here, confounded by the fact that the context does not allow to properly distinguish the specific sense, leaving it underspecified.

7 Conclusions and future work

The recent availability of crowdsourced data with large numbers of sense annotations per example allows to explore new perspectives in WSD. Previous work has shown that words with uniform sense distribution have lower accuracy. In this paper we show that the agreement between annotators has a stronger correlation with performance, and that it can be used to detect problematic examples. In particular, we show that, for many words, such examples are not useful for training, and that they are more difficult to disambiguate. Manual analysis seems to indicate that most of the problematic examples correspond to occurrences of subtle sense distinctions, where the context is not enough to discern which is the sense that should be applied.

In the future, we would like to explore methods that exploit problematic examples. On the one hand removing problematic examples could improve sense clustering, and vice-versa, clustering could help reduce the number of problematic examples. On the other hand detecting problematic examples could be used to improve WSD systems, for instance, using more refined ML techniques like Plank et al. (2014) to treat low agreement examples sensibly, or detecting underspecified examples in test.

Acknowledgements

This work was partially funded by MINECO (CHIST-ERA READERS project - PCIN-2013-002- C02-01) and the European Commission (QTLEAP - FP7-ICT-2013.4.1-610516).

References

Dawid, A. P. and A. M. Skene (1979). Maximum likelihood estimation of observer error-rates using the em algorithm. *Applied Statistics 28*(1), 20–28.

Edmonds, P. and S. Cotton (2001). Senseval-2: Overview. In *The Proceedings of the Second International Workshop on Evaluating Word Sense Disambiguation Systems*, SENSEVAL '01, Stroudsburg, PA, USA, pp. 1–5. Association for Computational Linguistics.

Hoffart, J., S. Seufert, D. B. Nguyen, M. Theobald, and G. Weikum (2012). Kore: Keyphrase overlap relatedness for entity disambiguation. In *Proceedings of the 21st ACM international conference on Information and knowledge management*, pp. 545554.

Hovy, E., M. Marcus, M. Palmer, L. Ramshaw, and R. Weischedel (2006). Ontonotes: The 90 In *Proceedings of HLT-NAACL 2006*, pp. 57–60.

Ide, N., C. Baker, C. Fellbaum, C. Fillmore, and R. Passonneau (2008, may). MASC: the Manually Annotated Sub-Corpus of American English. In *Proceedings of the Sixth International Conference on Language Resources and Evaluation (LREC'08)*, Marrakech, Morocco. European Language Resources Association (ELRA). http://www.lrec-conf.org/proceedings/lrec2008/.

Passonneau, R. J., C. F. Baker, C. Fellbaum, and N. Ide (2012, may). The MASC word sense corpus. In N. C. C. Chair), K. Choukri, T. Declerck, M. U. Doan, B. Maegaard, J. Mariani, A. Moreno, J. Odijk, and S. Piperidis (Eds.), *Proceedings of the Eight International Conference on Language Resources and Evaluation (LREC'12)*, Istanbul, Turkey. European Language Resources Association (ELRA).

Passonneau, R. J. and B. Carpenter (2014). The benefits of a model of annotation. *Transactions of the Association for Computational Linguistics 2*(1-9), 311–326.

Plank, B., D. Hovy, and A. Søgaard (2014, April). Learning part-of-speech taggers with inter-annotator agreement loss. In *Proceedings of the 14th Conference of the European Chapter of the Association for Computational Linguistics*, Gothenburg, Sweden, pp. 742–751. Association for Computational Linguistics.

Yarowsky, D. and R. Florian (2002). Evaluating sense disambiguation across diverse parameter spaces. *Natural Language Engineering 8*(4), 293–310.

Zhong, Z. and H. T. Ng (2010). It makes sense: A wide-coverage word sense disambiguation system for free text. In *Proceedings of the ACL 2010 System Demonstrations*, Uppsala, Sweden, pp. 78–83.

Appendix: statistics for individual words

word	pos	ns	s-ent	a-ent	thr	no-filt	train-filt	test-filt	t&t-filt
common	j	1	0.72	0.03	None	70.5			
fair	j	11	0.45	0.00	0.1	88.8	89.8	88.8	89.8
full	j	9	0.63	0.11	0.5	78.5	77.8	78.6	78.6
high	j	8	0.55	0.01	None	86.3			
late	j	8	0.71	0.00	None	84.9			
long	j	1	0.49	0.01	None	78.0			
normal	j	5	0.71	0.05	0.5	81.9	79.9	82.3	80.1
particular	j	7	0.82	0.05	None	85.0			
poor	j	6	0.75	0.06	None	76.2			
board	n	1	0.32	0.00	0.001	88.9	88.9	89.5	89.5
book	n	12	0.43	0.05	0.5	56.3	56.3	58.3	58.3
color	n	9	0.73	0.13	0.25	65.5	66.2	68	69.7
control	n	12	0.72	0.01	None	79.5			
date	n	9	0.85	0.02	0.25	80.1	80.1	80.4	81.2
family	n	9	0.73	0.04	0.001	64.3	64.3	64.8	66.7
image	n	1	0.65	0.01	None	70.6			
land	n	12	0.81	0.02	None	57.6			
level	n	9	0.57	0.07	0.05	70.5	71.9	70.4	77.8
life	n	15	0.82	0.01	0.5	58	58.7	58	58.7
number	n	12	0.41	0.01	0.25	87.7	87.7	87.6	87.6
paper	n	8	0.74	0.05	0.05	76.4	75	78	76.3
sense	n	6	0.78	0.00	None	93.8			
time	n	11	0.64	0.01	0.25	89.6	88.5	90.0	88.9
way	n	13	0.56	0.05	None	72.8			
window	n	5	0.8	0.02	0.05	75.9	78.6	77.4	80.3
work	n	8	0.95	0.02	0.001	69.8	66.3	75.9	74.1
add	v	7	0.77	0.03	0.01	41	41	41	41
appear	v	8	0.75	0.11	0.25	64.4	63	68.5	67.7
ask	v	8	0.61	0.08	0.01	78.3	76.2	86.7	86.7
find	v	17	0.69	0.05	0.01	62.4	64.5	65.8	67.5
fold	v	6	0.38	0.01	None	93.2			
help	v	9	0.69	0.09	0.001	61.2	64	67.1	71.4
kill	v	16	0.52	0.01	0.001	63.9	66.7	65	67.9
know	v	12	0.66	0.09	0.5	63.1	67.2	63.9	68.3
live	v	8	0.81	0.00	0.001	73.5	74.8	74.1	75.5
lose	v	12	0.7	0.01	0.001	64.4	64.4	67.2	66.4
meet	v	14	0.77	0.02	0.5	69.7	69	69.7	69
read	v	12	0.46	0.00	None	82.8			
say	v	12	0.66	0.05	0.1	64.9	64.9	68.7	69.5
serve	v	16	0.71	0.01	0.5	73.1	73.1	72.9	72.9
show	v	13	0.66	0.03	None	76.2			
suggest	v	5	0.71	0.04	None	74.3			
tell	v	9	0.73	0.1	0.1	57.6	65.3	59.8	65.7
wait	v	5	0.82	0.07	0.5	69.5	74	71.1	76
win	v	9	0.72	0.08	0.05	72.8	72.1	76.3	77.2

Table 4: Statistics for 45 words, with results across different evaluation conditions. Legend: ns for number of senses, s-ent for sense entropy, a-ent for annotation entropy, thr for threshold (cf. Section 5). The remaining columns report results on the following conditions (cf. Section 5): no-filt for using full train and test data, train-filt for filtered train, test-filt for filtered test, and t&t-filt for filtered train and test.

Curse or Boon? Presence of Subjunctive Mood in Opinionated Text

Sapna Negi and Paul Buitelaar
Insight Centre for Data Analytics
National University of Ireland
Galway
firstname.lastname@insight-centre.org

Abstract

In addition to the expression of positive and negative sentiments in the reviews, customers often tend to express wishes and suggestions regarding improvements in a product/service, which could be worth extracting. Subjunctive mood is often present in sentences which speak about a possibility or action that has not yet occurred. While this phenomena poses challenges to the identification of positive and negative sentiments hidden in a text, it can be helpful to identify wishes and suggestions. In this paper, we extract features from a small dataset of subjunctive mood, and use those features to identify wishes and suggestions in opinionated text. Our study validates that subjunctive features can be good features for the detection of wishes. However, with the given dataset, such features did not perform well for suggestion detection.

1 Introduction

In the context of Sentiment Analysis, presence of a variety of linguistic phenomena poses challenges for the identification of underlying sentiment in an opinionated text. Subjunctive mood is one such phenomena (Liu et al. (2013); Bloom (2011)). It is a commonly occurring language phenomenon in Indo-European languages, which is a verb mood typically used in subordinate clauses to express action that has not yet occurred, in the form of a wish, possibility, necessity etc. (Guan, 2012). Oxford dictionary defines it as, *Relating to or denoting a mood of verbs expressing what is imagined or wished or possible*. Sentiment terms present in such sentences may not necessarily contribute to the actual sentiment of the sentence, for example 'I wish it tasted as amazing as it looked' is not positive. While this is considered as a challenge for sentiment analysis, we adopt a different perspective, and discover benefits of the presence of subjunctive mood in opinionated text.

Apart from the expression of criticism and satisfaction in customer reviews, reviews might include suggestions for improvements. Suggestions can either be expressed explicitly (Brun, 2013), or by expressing wishes regarding new features and improvements(Ramanand et al., 2010) (Table 1). Extraction of suggestions goes beyond the scope of sentiment analysis, and also complements it by providing another valuable information that is worth analyzing. Table 1 presents some examples of occurrence of subjunctive mood collected from different forums on English grammar[1]. There seems to be a high probability of the occurrence of subjunctive mood in wish and suggestion expressing sentences. This observation can be exploited for the tasks of wish detection (Ramanand et al., 2010), and suggestion extraction (Brun, 2013). To the best of our knowledge, subjunctive mood has never been analysed in the context of wish and suggestion detection.

We collect a sample dataset comprising of example sentences of subjunctive mood, and identify features of subjunctive mood. We then employ a state of the art statistical classifier, and use subjunctive features in order to perform two kind of tasks on a given set of sentences: 1. Detect wish expressing sentences, and 2. Detect suggestion expressing sentences.

[1] http://grammar.about.com/od/rs/g/subjuncterm05.htm

Proceedings of the 11th International Conference on Computational Semantics, pages 101–106,
London, UK, April 15-17 2015.

Description	Examples
Suggestion bearing wishes in product reviews	I wanted a dvd player that had basic features and would be able to play dvd or format discs that I had made myself. I wish canon would work out some way for that issue.
Direct suggestions in product reviews	They should improve their user interface.
Wishes in political discussions	I wish someone said that to teddy at the meeting yesterday. Perhaps I should have stopped at 8 or 9 years old. I would like to know if you re a purist or a hypocrite.
Sentences containing subjunctive mood	I wish it were summer. I suggest that Dawn drive the car. But if it weren't so big, it wouldn't be nearly so fun.

Table 1: Examples of Suggestions, Wishes, and Subjunctive Mood

2 Related work

Mood and Modality: Modality is a grammatical category that allows the expression of aspects related to the attitude of a speaker towards his statement, in terms of degree of certainty, reliability, subjectivity, sources of information, and perspective (Morante and Sporleder, 2012). Subjunctive mood originated from the typological studies of modality (Palmer, 1986; Dudman, 1988; Portner, 2009). Some works equate its presence with 'counterfactuality'(Palmer, 1986), while some do not (Anderson, 1951). Other concepts like 'event modality', 'irrealis' (Palmer, 1986), have definitions similar to that of subjunctive mood.

Benamara et al. (2012) studied modality and negation for French language, with an objective to examine its effect on sentiment polarity. Narayanan et al. (2009) performed sentiment analysis on conditional sentences. Our objective however is inclined towards wish and suggestion detection, rather than sentiment analysis.

Wish Detection: Goldberg et al. (2009) performed wish detection on datasets obtained from political discussion forums and product reviews. They automatically extracted sentence templates from a corpus of new year wishes, and used them as features with a statistical classifier.

Suggestion Detection: Ramanand et al. (2010) pointed out that wish is a broader category, which might not bear suggestions every time. They performed suggestion detection, where they focussed only on suggestion bearing wishes, and used manually formulated syntactic patterns for their detection. Brun (2013) also extracted suggestions from product reviews and used syntactico-semantic patterns for suggestion detection. None of these works on suggestion detection used a statistical classifier.

None of these works aligned the problem of wish and suggestion detection with subjunctive mood, or identified features related to it. Wish and suggestion detection remain young problems, and our work contributes towards the same.

3 Datasets

Following are the datasets which we use for our experiments.

- **Wish Detection**
  Oxford dictionary defines the noun wish as, *A desire or hope for something to happen.* Goldberg et al. (2009) follow this definition of wish and provide manually annotated datasets, where each sentence is labelled as wish or non-wish. Following two datasets are made available:
  a. Political Discussions: 6379 sentences, out of which 34% are annotated wishes.
  b. Product Reviews: 1235 sentences, out of which 12% are annotated as wishes.
  Table 1 presents some examples from these datasets.
  Ramanand et al. (2010) worked on product review dataset of the wish corpus, with an objective to extract suggestions for improvements. They considered suggestions as a subset of wishes, and

thus retained the labels of only suggestion bearing wishes. They also annotated additional product reviews, but their data is not available for open research.

- **Suggestion Detection**
  Product reviews (new): We re-annotated the product review dataset from Goldberg et al. (2009), for suggestions. This also includes wishes for improvements and new features. Out of 1235 sentences, 6% are annotated as suggestions. Table 1 presents some examples from this dataset.
  Annotation Details: We had 2 annotators annotate each sentence with a suggestion or non-suggestion tag. We support the observation of Ramanand et al. (2010) that wishes for improvements and new features are implicit expression of suggestions. Therefore, annotators were also asked to annotate suggestions which were expressed as wishes. For inter-annotator agreement, a kappa value of 0.874 was obtained. In the final dataset, we only retained the sentences where both the annotators agree.

Subjunctive Feature Extraction
Subjunctive Mood Dataset (new): Since we did not come across any corpus of subjunctive mood, we collected example sentences of subjunctive mood from various grammar websites and forums[2], which resulted in a sample dataset of 229 sentences. Table 1 shows examples from this dataset. We use this dataset for manual and automatic identification of features of subjunctive mood.

4 Approach

We use a statistical classifier to detect wishes and suggestions in corresponding datasets. We obtain the following set of features from the subjunctive mood dataset.

Lexical Features:

- **Condition indicator 'if':** This is a binary feature, whose value depends on the presence and absence of 'if' in a sentence.
- **Suggestion and Wish Verbs:** We collect some suggestion and wish indicator verbs observed in the subjunctive mood dataset. We then expand this set of verbs by using VerbNet 3.2 (Schuler, 2005). VerbNet is a wide coverage verb lexicon, which places verbs into classes whose members have common syntactic and semantic properties. We collect all members of the VerbNet verb classes *advice, wish, want, urge, require*; 28 different verbs were obtained. Ramanand et al. (2010) also used a similar but much smaller subset {*love, like, prefer and suggest*} in their rules.

Syntactic Features:

- **Frequent POS sequences:** This is a set of 3,4 length sequences of Part Of Speech (POS) tags, which are automatically extracted from the subjunctive mood dataset. Words in the sentences are replaced by their corresponding POS tag, and top 200 sequences are extracted based on their weight. The weight of each sequence is a product of Term Frequency (TF) and Inverse Document Frequency (IDF). In order to apply the concept of TF and IDF to POS tag sequences, every 3 and 4 length tag sequence occurring in the corpus is treated as a term. We separate tags within a sequence with an underscore. An example of a sequence of length 3 would be PRP_VB_PRP ie. Personal Pronoun_Base form of Verb_Personal pronoun.
- **Frequent Dependency Relations:** These are a set of dependency relations (Marneffe and Manning, 2008). Using the same method as the part of speech tags, we identify 5 most frequent dependency relations which occur in the subjunctive mood dataset. In order to apply the concept of TF/IDF, each dependency relation occurring in the corpus is treated as a term. The top 5 relations were: *advmod, aux, ccomp, mark* and *nsubj*.

[2] http://grammar.about.com/od/rs/g/subjuncterm05.htm

Data	Experiment	Features	Precision	Recall	AUC
Politics	Ours	unigrams	0.73	0.65	0.76
		subjunctive	0.70	0.34	0.63
		unigrams,subjunctive	0.75	0.67	0.78
	Goldberg et.al (2009)	templates	n/a	n/a	0.73
		unigrams,templates	n/a	n/a	**0.80**
Products	Ours	unigrams	0.78	0.21	0.60
		subjunctive	0.59	0.31	**0.64**
		unigrams,subjunctive	0.82	0.25	0.62
	Goldberg et.al (2009)	templates	n/a	n/a	0.47
		unigrams,templates	n/a	n/a	0.56

Table 2: Results of Wish Detection and Comparison with Goldberg et. al. 2009

Data	Features	Precision	Recall	AUC
	unigrams	0.29	0.02	0.51
products	subjunctive	**0.29**	**0.11**	**0.54**
	unigrams,subjunctive	0.33	0.02	0.51

Table 3: Results of Suggestion Detection

We also obtain classification results of the combination of these features with the standard unigram features (Table 2, 3).
To obtain the part of speech and dependency information, we use Stanford Parser 3.3.1 (Klein and Manning, 2003). Word stemming is not performed. We use the LibSVM implementation of SVM classifier (EL-Manzalawy and Honavar, 2005). The parameter values of SVM classifiers are: SVM type = C-SVC, Kernel Function = Radial Basis Function. Features are ranked using the Info- Gain feature selection algorithm (Mitchell, 1997). Top 1000 features are used in all the experiments ie. the size of feature vector is not more than 1000.

5 Subjunctive Feature Evaluation

Goldberg et al. (2009) evaluated their approach using a 10 fold cross validation on their datasets. In order to compare subjunctive features against their wish template features, we also perform 10 fold cross validation on their wish datasets (politics and products). The evaluation metrics include Precision, Recall, and Area Under Curve (AUC) for the positive class. AUC was also used by Goldberg et al. (2009).
To the best of our knowledge, statistical classification based approach have not yet been employed to detect suggestions in reviews. Our experiment which uses subjunctive features for suggestion detection, is the first in this regard.

Results and Discussion

Table 2 compares the AUC values obtained with unigrams, subjunctive features, a combination of both, and the results from Goldberg et al. (2009) for wish detection. Table 3 compares the AUC values obtained with unigrams, subjunctive features, and a combination of both for suggestion detection. Table 4 presents some of the top features used by the classifier.

Wish Detection:
Unigrams vs Subjunctive: One probable reason for the better performance of subjunctive features over unigrams in the case of product dataset, could be the small size of the dataset. In the case of politics dataset, similar reason (big dataset) can be attributed for the better performance of unigrams over subjunctive features.

Classification	Data	Unigrams	Subjunctive
Wish	Politics	hope, please, wish, hopefully, I, you, should, want, your, all	hope, want, nsubj, wish, MD_VB_VBN, advmod, PRP_VBP_IN, PRP_VBP_PRP, VB_DT_NN, PRP_VBP_DT
	Products	hope, wish, hoping, now, would, hopefully, sell, should, want, get	hope, wish, want, MD_VB_VBN, aux, ccomp, RB_PRP_MD, RB_PRP_MD_VB, if, nsubj
Suggestion	Products	if, you, your, now, recommend, I , better, waste, display, want	if, IN_PRP_VBP,IN_PRP_VB, recommend, suggest, DT_NN_VBZ, PRP_VBP_DT, PRP_MD_VB, IN_PRP_VB_DT, NN_PRP_MD

Table 4: Top 10 Unigram and Subjunctive features used by the Classifier

Wish templates vs Subjunctive: The wish templates of Goldberg et al. (2009) perform better than our subjunctive features for the politics data. However, subjunctive features perform much better with product data as compared to the wish templates (Table 3). This may lead to the conclusion that wish templates need larger training corpus, since they failed for the smaller dataset of product reviews (AUC less than 0.5). One additional benefit of subjunctive features could be that subjunctive mood appears in many languages, and thus such features can be easily extended to multi-lingual wish detection.

Suggestion Detection:
Subjunctive features perform better than unigrams in this case too. An overall decrease in classifier performance for the task of suggestion detection can be attributed to the fact that not all wishes are suggestions, and therefore are not tagged in this dataset. Some of these untagged wishes would contain subjunctive mood, which reduced the performance of subjunctive features, as compared to the task of wish detection.

6 Conclusion

From the results of feature evaluation, we conclude that subjunctive features are not effective for suggestion detection, but are considerably effective for the task of wish detection. This work contributes towards both, analysis and methodology for wish detection. On the analysis part, we validate that a considerable amount of wishes in opinionated text contain subjunctive mood. On the methodology part, we use subjunctive mood features as effective features for the detection of wishes. We also provide datasets for this kind of study.
Since we only deal with 2 domains here, further experiments can be performed over data from different domains. In the continuation of this work, we intend to extend the datasets and explore more syntactic and semantic features for wish and suggestion detection.

Acknowledgement

This work has been funded by the the European Union's Horizon 2020 programme under grant agreement No 644632 MixedEmotions, and Science Foundation Ireland under Grant Number SFI/12/RC/2289.

References

C. Brun and C. Hagege (2013). *Suggestion Mining: Detecting Suggestions for Improvements in Users Comments*.

Anderson, A. R. (1951). A note on subjunctive and counterfactual conditionals. *JST 12*.

Benamara, F., B. Chardon, Y. Mathieu, V. Popescu, and N. Asher (2012). How do negation and modality impact on opinions? In *Proceedings of the Workshop on Extra-Propositional Aspects of Meaning in Computational Linguistics*, ExProM '12, pp. 10–18. Association for Computational Linguistics.

Bloom, K. (2011). *Sentiment analysis based on appraisal theory and functional local grammars*. Ph. D. thesis, Illinois Institute of Technology.

Dudman, V. H. (1988). Indicative and subjunctive. *Analysis*, 113–122.

EL-Manzalawy, Y. and V. Honavar (2005). *WLSVM: Integrating LibSVM into Weka Environment.*

Goldberg, A. B., N. Fillmore, D. Andrzejewski, Z. Xu, B. Gibson, and X. Zhu (2009). May all your wishes come true: A study of wishes and how to recognize them. In *Proceedings of Human Language Technologies: The 2009 Annual Conference of the North American Chapter of the Association for Computational Linguistics*, NAACL '09, Stroudsburg, PA, USA, pp. 263–271. Association for Computational Linguistics.

Guan, X. (2012). A study on the formalization of english subjunctive mood. Academy Publisher.

Klein, D. and C. D. Manning (2003). Accurate unlexicalized parsing. In *Proceedings of the 41st Annual Meeting on Association for Computational Linguistics - Volume 1*, ACL '03, Stroudsburg, PA, USA, pp. 423–430. Association for Computational Linguistics.

Liu, Y., X. Yu, Z. Chen, and B. Liu (2013). Sentiment analysis of sentences with modalities. In *Proceedings of the 2013 International Workshop on Mining Unstructured Big Data Using Natural Language Processing*, UnstructureNLP '13, New York, NY, USA, pp. 39–44. ACM.

Marneffe, M.-C. D. and C. D. Manning (2008). Stanford typed dependencies manual.

Mitchell, T. M. (1997). *Machine Learning* (1 ed.). New York, NY, USA: McGraw-Hill, Inc.

Morante, R. and C. Sporleder (2012). Modality and negation: An introduction to the special issue. *Computational Linguistics 38*(2), 223–260.

Narayanan, R., B. Liu, and A. Choudhary (2009). Sentiment analysis of conditional sentences. In *Proceedings of the 2009 Conference on Empirical Methods in Natural Language Processing*, EMNLP '09, pp. 180–189. Association for Computational Linguistics.

Palmer, F. R. (1986). *Mood and Modality*. Cambridge University Press.

Portner, P. (2009). *Modality*. Oxford University Press.

Ramanand, J., K. Bhavsar, and N. Pedanekar (2010, June). Wishful thinking - finding suggestions and 'buy' wishes from product reviews. In *Proceedings of the NAACL HLT 2010 Workshop on Computational Approaches to Analysis and Generation of Emotion in Text*, Los Angeles, CA, pp. 54–61. Association for Computational Linguistics.

Schuler, K. K. (2005). *Verbnet: A Broad-coverage, Comprehensive Verb Lexicon*. Ph. D. thesis, Philadelphia, PA, USA. AAI3179808.

Hierarchical Statistical Semantic Realization for Minimal Recursion Semantics

Matic Horvat
Computer Laboratory
University of Cambridge
mh693@cam.ac.uk

Ann Copestake
Computer Laboratory
University of Cambridge
aac10@cam.ac.uk

William Byrne
Department of Engineering
University of Cambridge
wjb31@cam.ac.uk

Abstract

We introduce a robust statistical approach to realization from Minimal Recursion Semantics representations. The approach treats realization as a translation problem, transforming the Dependency MRS graph representation to a surface string. Translation is based on a Synchronous Context-Free Grammar that is automatically extracted from a large corpus of parsed sentences. We have evaluated the new approach on the Wikiwoods corpus, where it shows promising results.[1]

1 Introduction

Realization from Minimal Recursion Semantics (MRS) representations has traditionally used a chart-based approach governed by a resource grammar. Introduced by Carroll et al. (1999) and Carroll and Oepen (2005), the chart-based approach is lexically-driven and is able to produce a large number of candidate surface strings which may be ranked using an N-gram language model or using discriminative machine learning (Velldal and Oepen, 2005; Velldal, 2009).

As the chart-based realization relies on a resource grammar, it tends to perform well when realizing from MRS representations that were created by a parser using the same resource grammar. However, the chart-based approach may fail to produce any output when the MRS representation has missing or incorrect parts. This is a significant issue for the MRS representations produced as a result of semantic transfer in semantic transfer translation systems such as LOGON (Lø nning et al., 2004) due to the difficulty of the translation problem. Consequently, the realization component is unable to produce any output and, in turn, translation fails.

In this paper we describe a first attempt at statistical realization from MRS representations. The approach treats realization as a translation problem, transforming the Dependency MRS graph representation to a surface string. The approach draws inspiration from Statistical Machine Translation, namely the hierarchical phrase-based approach to translation introduced by Chiang (2005, 2007). We will refer to the new approach as Hierarchical Statistical Semantic Realization or HSSR.

As part of the HSSR system, we present an approach for the automatic extraction of salient hierarchical rules for realization. The approach creates rules by considering DMRS subgraphs and corresponding surface substrings. The rules are created in two stages, first creating terminal rules, followed by nonterminal rules. The latter are created by 'subtracting' terminal rules from each other. The realization rules are extracted from a large parsed corpus to form a Synchronous Context-Free Grammar (SCFG).

We build on the ideas behind HiFST, a hierarchical phrase-based decoder introduced by Iglesias et al. (2009), to create a realization decoder. The decoder represents realization rules as Weighted Finite State Acceptors (WFSA). It uses WFSA operations to create a lattice encoding all possible realizations under a given SCFG. An N-gram language model is applied to the lattice to encourage fluency in surface realizations. The best realization is selected by finding the shortest path through the lattice.

[1]This research was partially supported by Qualcomm Research Scholarship and Churchill College Scholarship. The authors would also like to thank Juan Pino and Aurelien Waite for their help with software and experiments.

Proceedings of the 11th International Conference on Computational Semantics, pages 107–117,
London, UK, April 15-17 2015.

The long term goal of the HSSR system is to provide a robust alternative to chart-based realization that would be especially useful for realization in semantic transfer-based translation systems. However, in this paper we focus on presenting the main ideas behind HSSR and not on providing a direct alternative to the traditional approach. The system in its current stage of development lacks maturity and efficiency required by its potential applications. Consequently, we make some simplifying assumptions during evaluation, which we discuss in the relevant parts of the paper.

The HSSR approach is suitable for realization in any language, provided that there is a resource grammar of the language available. We evaluated its performance on the Wikiwoods corpus (Flickinger et al., 2010), a large deep parsed corpus of English Wikipedia which provides a large collection of MRS representations aligned with surface realizations that are suitable for learning the realization grammar.

We measure the performance of the HSSR system using BLEU and discuss its strengths and weakness using example output. The system shows promising results, with the main issues stemming from the lack of efficiency.

2 Minimal Recursion Semantics

Minimal Recursion Semantics (MRS) is a framework for computational semantics introduced by Copestake et al. (1995) and formally described in Copestake et al. (2005). As discussed there, MRS is a meta-language for describing semantic structures in some underlying object language: the object language usually discussed is predicate calculus with generalized quantifiers.

MRS was designed to be a tractable representation for large-scale parsing and generation, while not sacrificing expressiveness. It provides flat semantic representations that enable underspecification and can be integrated with grammatical representation in a number of frameworks. While MRS has been used in a wide variety of grammars, we concentrate here on MRS output by the English Resource Grammar (ERG, (Flickinger, 2000)), which we refer to as English Resource Semantics (ERS). The ERS is constructed compositionally in parallel with the syntactic analysis of a sentence.

To illustrate MRS/ERS, consider the sentence shown in (1) and the corresponding ERS in (2):[2]

(1) No generally accepted formal definition of algorithm exists yet.

(2) LTOP: l2,
RELS: < l4: _no(x, h7, _), l8: _general(e1, e2), l8: _accept(e2, _, x), l8: _formal(e3, x), l8: _definition(x, y), l5: udefq(y, h6, _), l3: _algorithm(y), l2: _exist(e4, x), l2: _yet(e5, e4), >
HCONS: $< h7 =_q l8, h6 =_q l3 >$

The main part of the representation is the RELS list, a bag of elementary predications (EPs). Each EP has an associated label, which is used for indicating scope (e.g., l8: _definition(x, y) has label l8). Predicates corresponding directly to word stems (i.e., lemmas) are indicated with a leading underscore. HCONS is a set of constraints which relate the labels to argument 'holes' in quantifiers and other scopal predicates. Local top (LTOP) is the topmost label in the MRS that is not the label of a quantifier. Note that there is a 'placeholder' quantifier, udefq, for the bare singular *algorithm*.[3] (3) shows the scoped readings in the object language:

(3) udefq(y, algorithm(y), _no(x, _general(e1, e2) $\wedge$ _accept(e2, _, x) $\wedge$ _formal(e3, x) $\wedge$ _definition(x, y), _exist(e4, x) $\wedge$ _yet(e5, e4)))
_no(x, udef(y, _algorithm(y), _general(e1, e2) $\wedge$ _accept(e2, _, x) $\wedge$ _formal(e3, x) $\wedge$ _definition(x, y)) _exist(e4, x) $\wedge$ _yet(e5, e4))

To show the relationship between these structures and MRS, first observe that through nesting of arguments each forms a tree, and that elements at each level of the tree are always combined with conjunctions. The root of the tree corresponds to the topmost quantifier. The MRS representation uses a

[2]From the 1214 version of the ERG: this is the top-ranked analysis produced, but the only other analysis is very similar. We have simplified the ERS in a number of respects for expository purposes.

[3]A kind term here, but the ERG does not distinguish kinds from ordinary entities since the syntax does not differentiate.

list of predications instead of the explicit conjunction. We can add an element to each predication to express its position in the tree: this is the MRS label. Instead of expressing the relationship between the quantifier (or other scopal predicate) and its arguments by embedding, we use a 'hole' argument to the quantifier and equate it to a label, as shown in (4):

(4) l5: udefq(y, h6, l4), h6=l3, l4: _no(x, h7, l2), h7=l8, l8: _general(e1, e2), l8: _accept(e2, _, x), l8: _formal(e3, x), l8: _definition(x, y), l3: _algorithm(y), l2: _exist(e4, x), l2: _yet(e5, e4)

If we specify an LTOP and put the hole-label equalities into HCONS, this is now formally an MRS but it only corresponds to the first reading shown in (3). Scope underspecification in MRS is a generalization of the trees corresponding to the different scopes, maintaining the constraints between the elements via qeq constraints ($=_q$, equality modulo quantifier) between hole arguments and labels. Intuitively, a qeq constraint, $h =_q l$, enables one or more quantifiers to float between the label l and handle h but we will not explain the details here. Replacing the equalities with qeq constraints in the example above underspecifies scope, giving the MRS shown in (2).

Robust Minimal Recursion Semantics (RMRS) is a modified MRS representation that also allows underspecification of relational information (Copestake, 2007). The transformation process between MRS and RMRS splits off most of arguments of elementary predicates and refers to them using anchors (*a*). e.g., in (4), l8: _accept(e2, _, x) becomes l8:a4:_accept(e2), ARG2(a4, x).

Dependency MRS (DMRS) (Copestake, 2009) is an alternative representation interconvertible with MRS or RMRS. It has minimal redundancy in its structure and was developed for the purpose of readability and ease of use for both humans and computational applications. A DMRS is a directed graph with elementary predicates as nodes. It is constructed from a RMRS representation by combining 3 subgraphs: (1) Label equality graph, connecting EPs with shared labels; (2) Handle-to-label qeq graph, connecting handles and labels; (3) Variable graph, connecting EPs with their arguments. Upon merging the three subgraphs, the redundant links are deterministically removed to form a DMRS graph. The DMRS graph for our example is shown in (5):

(5)

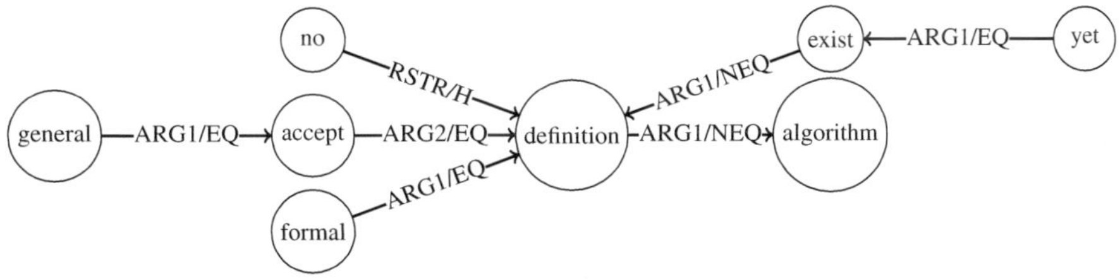

Note that the udefq is missing in this DMRS, because we systematically ignore these placeholder predicates in the realization algorithm. For readability, we have not shown the leading underscores.

3 Hierarchical Statistical Semantic Realization

Hierarchical Statistical Semantic Realization (HSSR) is an approach that treats realization as a translation problem from a semantic representation to the surface string. As the input to realization is a DMRS graph, we define realization as transformation of a graph structure to a sequence of symbols. Transformation between the two is conducted using hierarchical rules, each rule realizing a part of the source graph. This approach draws inspiration from hierarchical phrase-based translation by Chiang (2005, 2007).

We refer to the collection of realization rules as a realization grammar. The realization grammar is automatically acquired from a large collection of MRS representations which are aligned with their sentence realizations.

We obtain a string realization of a previously unseen DMRS graph representation by applying a sequence of realization rules (a derivation) that transform all parts of the original DMRS graph. For any realization grammar of significant size, there will be many derivation candidates to choose from. We define a log-linear model over the derivations that assigns probabilities based on rule features and

N-gram language model probability. We obtain the final string realization by applying the most probable derivation to the source DMRS graph.

In the remainder of the section we describe the aspects of HSSR outlined above in more detail. Our description is accompanied by a realization example, whose source DMRS graph was shown in (5). In (6), the source graph is aligned with the string realization symbols:

(6)

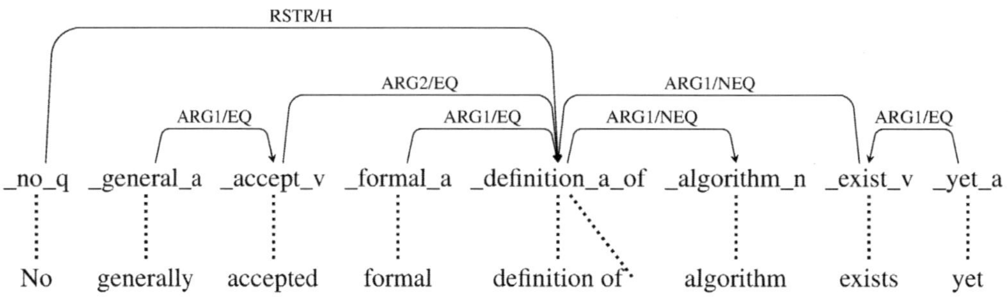

3.1 Grammar

HSSR grammar is formally a Synchronous Context-Free Grammar (SCFG) consisting of rewrite rules of the form:

$$X \rightarrow \langle \gamma, \alpha, \sim \rangle \quad (1)$$

where X is the nonterminal left-hand side, γ is a partial DMRS graph, α is a sequence of symbols, and $\sim$ is a one-to-one correspondence between nonterminal occurrences in γ and α. Consider the example rules extracted from (6):

(7) $X \rightarrow \langle$ _algorithm_n , algorithm $\rangle$

(8) $X \rightarrow \langle$ _definition_a_of _algorithm_n , definition of algorithm $\rangle$
ARG1/NEQ

(9) $X \rightarrow \langle$ _definition_a_of $X_{\boxed{1}}$, definition of $X_{\boxed{1}}$ $\rangle$
ARG1/NEQ

(10) $X \rightarrow \langle$ _no_q $X_{\boxed{1}}$ _exist_v _yet_a , no $X_{\boxed{1}}$ exists yet $\rangle$
RSTR/H ARG1/NEQ ARG1/EQ

We can interpret the rule in (8) as 'when encountering a subgraph consisting of two nodes, *_definition_a_of* and *_algorithm_n*, and an edge with label *ARG1/NEQ* originating in the former node and ending in the latter node, translate that subgraph as a sequence of symbols *definition of algorithm*.'

The rules shown in (7) and (8) consist of terminal nodes and terminal symbols. Additionally, a rule can contain one or more nonterminals X, represented as a nonterminal node on the source side and a nonterminal symbol on the target side. Two nonterminal rules extracted from (6) are shown in (9) and (10). The one-to-one correspondence $\sim$ between source and target side nonterminals is shown implicitly through the use of indexes on nonterminal symbols.

The presence of nonterminals in grammar rules enables hierarchical application of rules. Since every left hand side is the nonterminal X, any rule can be nested within any other rule with a nonterminal.

3.2 Rule extraction

HSSR rule extraction is an automatic procedure that extracts SCFG rules from a corpus to create a grammar. A grammar provides rules for translating previously unseen MRS representations. We define the basic unit of rule extraction as an *example*, consisting of (1) a DMRS graph, (2) a sequence of symbols, and (3) the alignment between nodes and the symbols.

We can obtain such an example by parsing a sentence using a parser with a resource grammar. We used the ACE parser[4] combined with the English Resource Grammar. The parser produces an MRS representation, which we convert to a DMRS graph using the pyDelphin library[5]. Finally, we derive the alignment between nodes of the DMRS graph and symbols of the original sentence. Therefore, constructing a corpus suitable for rule extraction does not require any manual annotation. Instead, parsing a monolingual corpus with an MRS parser is sufficient.

The rule extraction procedure from a single example extracts terminal and nonterminal rules:

Terminal rules are extracted first for a given example and have the following properties:

1. The source side is a connected subgraph of the source graph consisting of terminal nodes.
2. The target side is a subsequence of terminal symbols.
3. No node outside the subgraph is aligned to a symbol in the target side and no symbol outside the target side is aligned to a node in the subgraph.
4. The rule contains at least one node aligned to at least one symbol.
5. The source side is a *valid* subgraph of the source graph. A valid subgraph contains a set of nodes such that no outgoing edge of any node is omitted. This ensures that only rules with all argument nodes present are extracted.

Nonterminal rules are extracted by subtracting a terminal rule from an existing rule. Rule subtraction replaces the subrule's subgraph and symbol sequence with a nonterminal symbol in the enclosing rule. Nonterminal rules have the following properties:

1. The source side is a connected subgraph of the source graph consisting of terminal and non-terminal nodes.
2. The target side is a sequence of terminal and nonterminal symbols.
3. No node outside the subgraph is aligned to a symbol in the target side and no symbol outside the target side is aligned to a node in the subgraph.
4. The rule contains at least one terminal node aligned to at least one terminal symbol.
5. Any pair of nonterminal nodes in the source subgraph does not share an edge.
6. A nonterminal node assumes no structure, i.e. the subtracted subgraph has a single node to which other unsubtracted nodes potentially connect to.
7. No edge originates from a nonterminal node.

(7) and (8) are terminal rules. The entire input graph shown in (6) can also form a terminal rule. (9) and (10) are examples of nonterminal rules. (9) was constructed by subtracting the terminal rule in (7) from the terminal rule in (8).

Nonterminal rules are extracted iteratively - in the first iteration, pairs of terminal rules are considered, while in the subsequent iterations, pairs of terminal rules and existing nonterminal rules are considered. This procedure produces rules with multiple nonterminals.

Manipulation of graphs, including enumerating subgraphs and comparing them, is inherently computationally intensive. To ensure that the rule extraction procedure is computationally tractable for sentences of reasonable length, we introduce two heuristic constraints on the rules in the final grammar: a) the size of the subgraph node set is at most five nodes; b) a rule contains at most two nonterminals.

Limiting the graph size to five nodes is a heuristic decision as we believe that five nodes are sufficient to capture most semantic locality in DMRS representations. We will verify this in future experiments. Limiting the number of nonterminals to two is a practical limitation to limit the size of extracted grammar and improve decoder efficiency.

[4]The ACE parser by Woodley Packard is available at http://sweaglesw.org/linguistics/ace/

[5]The pyDelphin library by Michael Goodman is available at https://github.com/goodmami/pydelphin

3.3 Model

A derivation is a sequence of translation rules that produces the full realization of an input representation. Any SCFG of significant size is able to produce many different derivations and consequently many different realizations of an input representation. A mechanism for choosing the best derivation is therefore needed. We define a log-linear model over derivations D:

$$P(D) \propto \prod_i \theta_i(D)^{\lambda_i} \tag{2}$$

where θ_i are features defined over rules used in derivation D and λ_i are feature weights. We define four features to aid realization: bidirectional conditional translation probabilities $P(\text{source}|\text{target})$ and $P(\text{target}|\text{source})$, N-gram language model probability, and word insertion penalty. The bidirectional probability features are trained by performing rule extraction and using rule frequency counts to estimate the probabilities. The feature weights λ_i of the log-linear model are tuned using grid search over the parameter space using BLEU (Papineni et al., 2002) as the measure of performance.

3.4 Decoder

The task of the decoder is to generate a string realization for a (previously unseen) MRS representation. The decoder uses a grammar estimated on a training corpus as the source of translation rules. We base the HSSR decoder on the ideas behind the HiFST hierarchical phrase-based translation system, presented in Iglesias et al. (2009).

Following the description in Allauzen et al. (2014), our decoder operates in three stages:

1. **Realization**: The decoder constructs a Weighted Finite State Acceptor (WFSA) encoding all possible realizations under a given synchronous context-free grammar G.

2. **Language Model application**: The decoder composes the realization WFSA with a weighted regular grammar defined by an N-gram language model. The resulting WFSA contains paths weighted by combined realization and language model scores.

3. **Search**: The decoder finds the shortest path through the combined WFSA.

We perform the **realization** stage in two distinct parts: (1) rule application, and (2) realization WFSA construction. Its implementation makes use of the OpenFST library[6] (Allauzen et al., 2007).

Given an input graph I and grammar G, our goal in rule application is to find the set of all rules R_I from grammar G, that can be used to realize graph I. Instead of checking all rules of grammar G against the graph I, we reverse the process. We generate all possible subgraphs I_s of the graph I that respect the same constraints we impose on the rules of grammar G in the rule extraction algorithm. Nevertheless, this process is less constrained than rule extraction due to the lack of a surface string. The set of subgraphs I_S forms a query against grammar G that retrieves the rules whose source side γ equals one of the subgraphs in the set I_S to form the set of all applicable rules R_I.

The query procedure requires matching of graphs against one another. This problem is commonly known as graph isomorphism problem, which belongs to the class of NP problems (Read and Corneil, 1977). We devised an efficient heuristic solution for DMRS graphs that works in the vast majority of cases. The heuristic solution fails only in the case of a completely symmetrical subgraph (in terms of node's adjacent and 1-removed neighbors), which is rarely encountered. When such a graph is encountered, the consequence is that some rules from the grammar that could have been applied to the subgraph are not recognized.

In an SMT environment using SCFGs a modified CYK algorithm operating over word spans is usually used to aid efficient construction of the translation WFSA. In contrast, instead of word spans HSSR decoder depends on the concept of *graph coverage*. A source side subgraph of a rule R covers a certain

[6] http://www.openfst.org

part of the input graph I. A graph coverage can be represented with a bit vector g_R of length n, where n is the size of the input graph's node set. Each position in g_R corresponds to a single node in the graph I. A particular position in g_R has a value of 1 if that node occurs in the subgraph of rule R, otherwise the value is 0. For instance, rule R in (9) has a node coverage bit vector $g_R = 00001100$, assuming that the order of nodes in the bit vector corresponds to the order they are displayed in (6). Graph coverage information is a byproduct of the rule application algorithm. Graph coverage with bit vectors resembles bit coverage of bag of words described in de Gispert et al. (2014).

While the size of the CYK grid of word spans grows in $\mathcal{O}(n^2)$ space with input size, the size of the grid of graph coverages grows in $\mathcal{O}(2^n)$. In general, however, the space of possible graph coverages of a given input graph is severely constrained by the rules present in the SCFG grammar.

In the second part of the realization stage, we use the set of applicable rules R_I and associated graph coverages g_R to create a WFSA which contains all possible realizations of the input graph I.

In a bottom-up process, the decoder groups rules into cells so that each cell corresponds to a single graph coverage bit vector. The decoder then encodes each R_i rule's target side as a Recursive Transition Network (RTN), treating each nonterminal arc as a pointer to a cell with a corresponding graph coverage g_R lower in the hierarchy. Based on rule features, a log-linear model assigns weights to arcs in RTNs.

A cell RTN is created as a union of all RTNs within that cell. Finally, the decoder performs a recursive RTN expansion, starting from the top most cell - the cell with the highest graph coverage (i.e. graph coverage with the largest number of nodes covered). RTN expansion replaces the nonterminal pointers to other cells lower in the hierarchy with the RTNs of those cells until reaching the bottom of hierarchy. RTN expansion produces the final realization WFSA encoding all realizations of the input graph I under grammar G.

The remaining two stages of the decoder are **language model application** and **search**. Language model application is conducted by composing the realization WFSA and language model WFSA using the *applylm* tool of the HiFST system[7] (Iglesias et al., 2009). The shortest path through the combined WFSA, found using the OpenFST shortest path operation, is the most probable realization under the given grammar and log-linear model, and therefore, the output of the decoder. In addition to finding a single shortest path through the WFSA, N-shortest paths can be extracted to produce an N-best list of realizations. An N-best list of realizations can be re-ranked using various strategies to improve the performance of the realizer. The strategies include re-ranking with a stronger language model and re-ranking using discriminative machine learning with a larger set of features.

4 Evaluation

We evaluated the HSSR approach by realizing a set of parsed MRS representations and comparing the realized surface strings against the original sentences. We use the BLEU metric for comparison of surface strings. Espinosa et al. (2010) have investigated the use of various automatic evaluation metrics to measure the quality of realization output. They have found that several standard Statistical Machine Translation evaluation metrics, including BLEU, correlate moderately well with human judgment of adequacy and fluency for the string realization task. The authors conclude that these metrics are useful for measuring incremental progress of a realization system, but advise caution when comparing different realization systems.

4.1 Experimental setup

We trained and evaluated the HSSR system on a subset of the Wikiwoods corpus. The Wikiwoods corpus, introduced by Flickinger et al. (2010), contains close to 1.3 million deep-parsed content articles, extracted from a snapshot of English Wikipedia in July 2008.

We randomly sampled chunks of the corpus to create our training, tuning, and test sets. The training set consists of around 1 million DMRS-sentence pairs. Tuning and test sets consist of 500 and 1000

[7] HiFST and related tools are available as open source: http://ucam-smt.github.io/

DMRS-sentence pairs respectively. Due to efficiency reasons, we selected input pairs of up to 20 tokens in the training set, and up to 15 DMRS graph nodes in the tuning and test sets. In future, we plan to address the efficiency of rule extraction and decoding with regards to input size by introducing an input graph splitting strategy, a graph equivalent to the standard practices of sentence splitting in SMT.

In the preprocessing stage, we performed general predicate node filtering from DMRS graphs to remove nodes that would introduce unnecessary complexity in rule extraction and decoding. On the other hand, we augmented the DMRS representations with explicit punctuation nodes and links, as the graphs otherwise do not contain information regarding punctuation.

We evaluated the system using 2-gram, 3-gram, and 4-gram language models. We estimated the language models on the entire Wikiwoods corpus, consisting of 800 million words (excluding tuning and training sets). The language models were estimated using KenLM toolkit (Heafield, 2011) with interpolated modified Kneser-Ney smoothing (Chen and Goodman, 1998).

Rule extraction on the training set of 1 million DMRS graph-surface string pairs produced 7.3 million realization rules. Practical limitations mentioned above apply: we extracted rules with at most 2 nonterminals, and the size of source side is at most five nodes.

We tuned the log-linear model weights using simple grid search over several iterations against the BLEU evaluation metric (Papineni et al., 2002). A mature system could instead be optimized using standard tuning approaches from SMT, for example MERT (Och, 2003) and LMERT (Macherey et al., 2008; Waite et al., 2011).

The decoding times of the current system implementation can be relatively long. We enforced reasonable computation time by terminating decoding of a DMRS graph after 300 seconds. This occurred for 96/1000 examples in the test set. As BLEU significantly penalizes short or omitted output using the brevity penalty, we computed the BLEU scores only on decoded examples. The final evaluation example set is the same between all systems in order to keep the scores comparable between them.

4.2 Results and discussion

We obtain the following results on decoded DMRS graphs of the test set:

Language model	BLEU
2-gram	46.02
3-gram	46.66
4-gram	46.63

We hypothesized that a strong language model will have a significant impact on the performance of the system. The hypothesis is partially confirmed by the increase in BLEU score from 2-gram to 3-gram. However, using a 4-gram language model yields no improvement over the 3-gram language model. The lack of improvement is unexpected, as 4-gram language models often yield good performance increases in SMT applications. The results warrant additional experiments with language models in future, including varying the size of training data for language model estimation and expanding the training data to other domains.

We list example output of the HSSR realization system in Table 1. In the first example, we show a successful instance of realization. The meaning is preserved by the realization process, although we could argue that '*grand falmouth hotel*' is not equivalent to '*grand hotel falmouth*'. The second example of realization is less successful, in part due to incorrect PP-attachment during parsing that produces a somewhat broken DMRS graph, and in part due to the application of incorrect realization rules.

As described in §3.4, the decoder produces the realization with the highest sum node coverage bit vector. In practical terms, this means that when it is not able to cover the entire source graph using hierarchical realization rules, it attempts to realize the largest part of the graph it can. This can be seen in the third realization example, where the substring '*, for instance ,*' was omitted from the realization as the grammar did not include a rule joining it with the rest of the sentence.

A more severe case of partial realization is shown in example four. The predicate *colour* has three arguments in the original DMRS representation. As we limit the number of nonterminals in rules to

	Source	Surface string
1.	original	the grand falmouth hotel was opened in 1865 just outside the station .
	realization	in 1865 the grand hotel falmouth was opened just outside the station .
2.	original	the railway would also open up areas of kazahstan for exploration of minerals and oil .
	realization	would also the railway to open up areas of kazahstan for exploration of minerals and oil .
3.	original	the direction also functioned as an inferior court in case of , for instance , theft .
	realization	the direction also functioned as an inferior court in case of theft .
4.	original	the false killer is uniformly coloured a dark grey to black .
	realization	a dark grey to black .
5.	original	although abuye survived this threat unharmed , sources differ on the details .
	realization	unharmed abuye survived this threat although sources differ on the details , .

Table 1: Output examples of the HSSR system with a 4-gram language model.

two, the only way to realize a predicate with three arguments is by using a rule that includes one of its arguments directly. Such a rule does not occur in the current grammar, and consequently the decoder is unable to realize the predicate *colour*. As the predicate node is the main verb of the sentence, it connects other parts of the the input graph together. For this reason, only the largest subgraph can be realized, producing '*a dark grey to black .*', despite the fact that a realization for '*the false killer*' is produced during decoding. We recognize three strategies of combating such errors: (1) increasing the maximum number of nonterminals to three, which would considerably increase the size of the realization grammar and the load on the decoder; (2) introducing glue rules which would combine realized parts of subgraphs despite missing connecting predicates; (3) increasing the size of the grammar in hope that such rules would be extracted from examples. We find the second preferable to others as it also enables realization in other instances of missing rules (not to mention that there are instances of predicates with four arguments). However, introduction of glue rules is nontrivial as it can create spurious ambiguity in the decoder - a situation where many distinct derivations with the same model features and realizations are produced (Chiang, 2007). An increase in spurious ambiguity would affect the decoder efficiency and cause problems for advanced tuning procedures depending on n-best lists, such as MERT.

The fifth and final example realization demonstrates the variability of output that the realization system is able to produce. This highlights the deficiencies of using N-gram precision measures such as BLEU for evaluating realization (and translation) output.

5 Related Work

In this paper we described a first attempt at statistical realization from MRS representations using synchronous context-free grammar. In this section we discuss similar approaches to realization.

One way of categorizing realization systems is according to the type of input assumed. Some authors have worked on the problem of word ordering, where the input is a bag of words, possibly combined with partial ordering information (e.g., Zhang and Clark (2011), de Gispert et al. (2014), Horvat and Byrne (2014)). Other systems take as input some form of meaning representation designed for a limited domain: such systems may be tested on the GEOQUERY corpus, for instance. Of particular relevance to us is Wong and Mooney (2007) which investigates SMT based techniques: they experiment with a phrase-based SMT method, a system that inverts an SMT-based semantic parser and a third approach which is a hybrid of these. Other systems take as input a structured representation which is intended to be flexible enough to cover general language: most such systems are associated with bidirectional approaches, and they have generally been tested with representations produced by parsers or with trees from manually-annotated treebanks. For instance, a number of systems have been built that take LFG f-structures as input (Cahill and van Genabith, 2006): others work on syntax trees, dependencies or logical representations.

These different assumptions about input make it extremely difficult to compare realization systems directly. The structural properties of the input determine which algorithms will be suitable for realization. While MRS has a logical object language, structurally the syntax of MRS is quite unlike a conventional logic. The earlier work on MRS (i.e., Carroll et al. (1999) and subsequent papers listed in the introduction) used the flatness of its structure to facilitate the use of a chart generation approach, while in our work on generation from DMRS, the input is a graph.

In terms of methodology, our work is perhaps closest to (Cahill and van Genabith, 2006) whose PCFG system for robust probabilistic generation is based on approximations to a LFG automatically extracted from a treebank. However, the nature of the input and the techniques employed are very different. White (2011) investigates an approach which has some similarities with ours, using MT-style glue rules for robustness in conjunction with a realizer based on CCG, but his approach is directed at patching up failed realizations.

6 Conclusions and Future Work

In this paper, we presented a first attempt at statistical realization from MRS representations. The approach treats realization as a translation problem, transforming the Dependency MRS graph representation to a surface string. The HSSR approach draws inspiration from Statistical Machine Translation. We evaluated the performance of the new approach on a subset of the Wikiwoods corpus. We measured the performance of the HSSR system using BLEU and discussed its strengths and weakness using example output. The system shows promising results, with the main issues stemming from the lack of efficiency.

There are several areas of possible improvement. As mentioned above, the main area to address is decoder efficiency for larger input sizes and realization grammars. Additional heuristic constraints and WFSA pruning can be introduced to help decrease computational cost of realization. Realization of large DMRS graph representations (i.e. DMRS graphs with more than 20 nodes) may require a graph splitting strategy analogous to sentence splitting commonly performed in SMT. The performance of the realization system can likely be increased by extracting a larger realization grammar, engineering more features, and implementing an advanced tuning procedure such as MERT.

In addition to realization we are working to expand the HSSR system to an SMT system using semantic structures to aid the translation process. In this framework, DMRS graph representations in source language will be translated into surface strings in the target language.

References

Allauzen, C., B. Byrne, A. de Gispert, G. Iglesias, and M. Riley (2014). Pushdown Automata in Statistical Machine Translation. *Computational Linguistics 40*(3), 687–723.

Allauzen, C., M. Riley, J. Schalkwyk, W. Skut, and M. Mohri (2007). OpenFst : A General and Efficient Weighted Finite-State Transducer Library. In *Implementation and Application of Automata*, pp. 11–23.

Cahill, A. and J. van Genabith (2006, July). Robust PCFG-Based Generation Using Automatically Acquired LFG Approximations. In *Proceedings of COLING-ACL (2006)*, Sydney, Australia, pp. 1033–1040. Association for Computational Linguistics.

Carroll, J., A. Copestake, D. Flickinger, and V. Poznanski (1999). An efficient chart generator for (semi-) lexicalist grammars. In *European workshop on natural language generation*, pp. 86–95.

Carroll, J. and S. Oepen (2005). High Efficiency Realization for a Wide-Coverage Unification Grammar. In *IJCNLP*, pp. 165–176.

Chen, S. F. and J. T. Goodman (1998). An Empirical Study of Smoothing Techniques for Language Modeling. Technical report, Harvard University.

Chiang, D. (2005). A Hierarchical Phrase-Based Model for Statistical Machine Translation. In *Proceedings of ACL 2005*, Michigan, USA, pp. 263–270.

Chiang, D. (2007). Hierarchical phrase-based translation. *Computational Linguistics 33*(2), 201–228.

Copestake, A. (2007). Semantic Composition with (Robust) Minimal Recursion Semantics. In *ACL 2007 Workshop on Deep Linguistic Processing*, pp. 73–80.

Copestake, A. (2009). Slacker semantics: why superficiality, dependency and avoidance of commitment can be the right way to go. In *Proceedings of EACL 2009*, Athens, Greece, pp. 1–9.

Copestake, A., D. Flickinger, R. Malouf, S. Riehemann, and I. Sag (1995). Translation using Minimal Recursion Semantics. In *Proceedings of the 6th International Conference on Theoretical and Methodological Issues in Machine Translation (TMI-95)*, Leuven, Belgium.

Copestake, A., D. Flickinger, C. Pollard, and I. Sag (2005, July). Minimal Recursion Semantics: An Introduction. *Journal of Research on Language and Computation 3*(2-3), 281–332.

de Gispert, A., M. Tomalin, and W. Byrne (2014). Word Ordering with Phrase-Based Grammars. In *Proceedings of EACL 2014*, pp. 259–268.

Espinosa, D., R. Rajkumar, M. White, and S. Berleant (2010). Further Meta-Evaluation of Broad-Coverage Surface Realization. In *Proceedings of EMNLP 2010*, pp. 564–574.

Flickinger, D. (2000). On building a more effcient grammar by exploiting types. *Natural Language Engineering 6*(1), 15–28.

Flickinger, D., S. Oepen, and G. Ytrestø l (2010). WikiWoods: Syntacto-Semantic Annotation for English Wikipedia. In *Proceedings of LREC 2010*, Valletta, Malta, pp. 1665–1671.

Heafield, K. (2011). KenLM : Faster and Smaller Language Model Queries. In *Proceedings of the EMNLP 2011 Sixth Workshop on Statistical Machine Translation*, Edinburgh, UK, pp. 187–197.

Horvat, M. and W. Byrne (2014). A Graph-Based Approach to String Regeneration. In *Student Research Workshop at EACL 2014*, Gothenburg, Sweden, pp. 85–95.

Iglesias, G., A. de Gispert, E. R. Banga, and W. Byrne (2009). Hierarchical Phrase-Based Translation with Weighted Finite State Transducers. In *Proceedings of HLT-NAACL 2009*, Boulder, USA, pp. 433–441.

Lø nning, J. T., S. Oepen, D. Beermann, L. Hellan, J. Carroll, H. Dyvik, D. Flickinger, J. B. Johannessen, P. Meurer, T. r. Nordgard, V. Rosen, and E. Velldal (2004). LOGON - A Norwegian MT Effort. In *Proceedings of the Workshop in Recent Advances in Scandinavian Machine Translation*, Uppsala, Sweden.

Macherey, W., F. J. Och, I. Thayer, and J. Uszkoreit (2008). Lattice-based minimum error rate training for statistical machine translation. In *Proceedings of EMNLP 2008*, Honolulu, USA, pp. 725–734.

Och, F. J. (2003). Minimum error rate training in statistical machine translation. In *Proceedings of ACL 2003*, pp. 160–167.

Papineni, K., S. Roukos, T. Ward, and W.-j. Zhu (2002). BLEU: a Method for Automatic Evaluation of Machine Translation. In *Proceedings of ACL 2002*, Philadelphia, USA, pp. 311–318.

Read, R. C. and D. G. Corneil (1977). The graph isomorphism disease. *Journal of Graph Theory 1*(4), 339–363.

Velldal, E. (2009). *Empirical Realization Ranking*. Ph. D. thesis, University of Oslo.

Velldal, E. and S. Oepen (2005). Maximum Entropy Models for Realization Ranking. In *Machine Translation Summit*, pp. 109–116.

Waite, A., G. Blackwood, and W. Byrne (2011). Lattice-based minimum error rate training using weighted finite-state transducers with tropical polynomial weights. In *Proceedings of the 9th International Workshop on Finite-State Methods and Natural Language Processing (FSMNLP 2011)*, Blois, France, pp. 116–125.

White, M. (2011). Glue rules for robust chart realization. In *Proceedings of the 13th European Workshop on Natural Language Generation*, pp. 194–199.

Wong, Y. W. and R. J. Mooney (2007). Generation by Inverting a Semantic Parser that Uses Statistical Machine Translation. In *HLT-NAACL*, pp. 172–179.

Zhang, Y. and S. Clark (2011). Syntax-Based Grammaticality Improvement using CCG and Guided Search. In *Proceedings of EMNLP 2011*, pp. 1147–1157.

Uniform Information Density at the Level of Discourse Relations: Negation Markers and Discourse Connective Omission

Fatemeh Torabi Asr & Vera Demberg
Saarland University
fatemeh|vera@coli.uni-saarland.de

Abstract

About half of the discourse relations annotated in Penn Discourse Treebank (Prasad et al., 2008) are not explicitly marked using a discourse connective. But we do not have extensive theories of when or why a discourse relation is marked explicitly or when the connective is omitted. Asr and Demberg (2012a) have suggested an information-theoretic perspective according to which discourse connectives are more likely to be omitted when they are marking a relation that is expected or predictable. This account is based on the Uniform Information Density theory (Levy and Jaeger, 2007), which suggests that speakers choose among alternative formulations that are allowed in their language the ones that achieve a roughly uniform rate of information transmission. Optional discourse markers should thus be omitted if they would lead to a trough in information density, and be inserted in order to avoid peaks in information density. We here test this hypothesis by observing how far a specific cue, negation in any form, affects the discourse relations that can be predicted to hold in a text, and how the presence of this cue in turn affects the use of explicit discourse connectives.

1 Introduction

Discourse connectives are known as optional linguistic elements to construct relations between clausal units in text: in the Penn Discourse Treebank (PDTB Prasad et al. 2008), only about half of the annotated discourse relations are marked in the text by a discourse connective. In the remaining cases, the discourse relation can still be recovered without an explicit marker. Consider for example the sentences below, which stand in a causal relationship:

(1) a. John did not go to the concert. He was ill.
  b. John did not go to the concert, because he was ill.

The question we would like to discuss in this paper is whether there is a principled explanation of when such optional discourse markers are inserted by speakers / writers, and when they are omitted.

In Grician pragmatics the *maxim of quantity* holds that speakers should make their contribution as informative as is required for the listeners to grasp the message, but not more informative than is required (Grice, 1975). The *Uniform Information Density* theory (UID, Levy and Jaeger 2007) further refines this notion with respect to how information can be transferred optimally from a speaker to a hearer: in order to optimally use the comprehenders channel capacity, the speaker should distribute the information uniformly across the utterance, in a manner that approximates channel capacity. In particular, among alternative linguistic formulations of the same content, the one formulation that conveys the information more uniformly should be preferred.

The amount of information conveyed by a word is quantified in terms of its *Surprisal* (Hale, 2003). Surprisal of a word w_i in a sentence is calculated based on its conditional probability given the preceding context:

$$s(w_i) = -\log p(w_i|w_{1...i-1}) \tag{1}$$

Proceedings of the 11th International Conference on Computational Semantics, pages 118–128,
London, UK, April 15-17 2015.

From the perspective of the speaker, the Uniform Information Density hypothesis predicts that the amount of surprisal should be held roughly equal from word to word. If information is transmitted at a rate close to channel capacity, information transmission is optimal because the maximal amount of information can be transmitted while avoiding comprehension problems.

Evidence that speakers indeed behave in this way, and choose among meaning-equivalent alternatives the ones that correspond to a more uniform rate of information transmission has been provided by a range of experimental and corpus-based studies at the level of spoken word duration and articulation (Aylett and Turk, 2004; Buz et al., 2014), morphology (Kurumada and Jaeger, 2013), syntax (Jaeger, 2010), lexical choices (Piantadosi et al., 2011; Mahowald et al., 2013), referring expressions (Tily and Piantadosi, 2009; Kravtchenko, 2014), and across levels, e.g., effect from syntax on spoken word durations (Demberg et al., 2012). We here investigate whether UID can also explain discourse-level phenomena, such as the insertion vs. omission of discourse connectives.

Some first evidence for this hypothesis comes from Asr and Demberg (2012a), who looked into the discourse-relation annotated Penn Discourse Treebank (PDTB, Prasad et al. 2008) corpus to explore **what relation senses** tend to be expressed without discourse connectives. Asr and Demberg observe that discourse relations which are predictable given general cognitive biases in relation interpretation, such as continuity and causality are more likely to be expressed without an explicit discourse connective, while unpredictable (discontinuous, adversative or temporally backward) relations tend to be marked with an explicit connective.

These observations are in line with the general predictions of theories about efficient language production such as Grice's maxim of quantity and the UID account. However, the UID more specifically suggests that even markers of generally unexpected relations may be subject to omission if there are other strong cues in the local context, which make the relation predictable. The present paper addresses this gap by specifically looking into how far a generally unexpected discourse relation, `chosen alernative`, can be expressed without its typical discourse connective *instead* when a good cue is present in the first argument of the discourse relation (the "good cue" here will be negation).

After providing some background about the Penn Discourse Treebank and discourse connectives in section 2, we propose how to calculate surprisal for discourse relations in section 3. Our experiments in section 4 first focus on the relational information encoded in negation. We investigate what types of relations benefit from negation as a statistically licensed marker. Second, under the notion of UID, we predict that the optional marker of a discourse relation (*instead* for the `Chosen alternative` relation) should be dropped as a function of linguistic features in the first argument (here, negative polarity), which are predictive of the relation sense. We find not only that the polarity of a sentence changes the distribution of the discourse relations that it makes with the context, but also that the relational surprisal calculated based on this feature is a predictor of the connective ellipsis.

2 Background and related work

This section introduces discourse relations, specifically according to the definition employed in annotation of the PDTB. We also sketch an overview of the studies on the linguistic markers of discourse relations such as sentence connectives and clausal features. Finally, we focus on the studies that look at the question of implicitness.

2.1 Discourse relations in PDTB

PDTB is the largest resource for discourse related studies published so far. It contains about fifty thousand annotated relations on text from Wall Street Journals. Relations are considered for pairs of clauses connected by a discourse connective, as well as between neighboring sentences which are not connected by any discourse cue. If two clauses are joined by a discourse connective the boundaries of the arguments are annotated and a label indicating the relation sense is assigned. Otherwise, the annotators were asked to first see whether any discourse connective could artificially be inserted between the two arguments

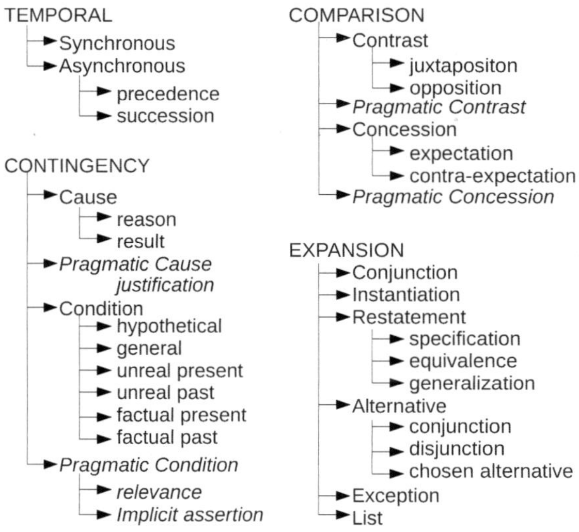

Figure 1: Hierarchy of relation senses in PDTB (Prasad et al., 2008)

and then apply the same procedure to annotate a relation sense accordingly. In the latter case the relation is called *implicit* given that the discourse connective is absent from the original text [1]. Annotation of the relation senses is according to a hierarchy of coarse to fine-grained semantic categories depicted in Figure 1. For example, a `chosen alternative` relation is a very specific sense located in depth three of the hierarchy, and it is used when the connective indicates that its two arguments denote alternative situations but only one (Arg2) has occurred.

(2) *[No price for the new shares has been set.] Instead, [the companies will leave it up to the marketplace to decide.]* — `EXPANSION.Alternative.chosen alternative`

Some relations are annotated with less specificity due to the disagreement between annotators, or with two different sense labels when both relations are conveyed simultaneously [2].

2.2 Discourse connectives

Discourse connectives are words or expressions which connect neighboring sentences and clauses in a text. Starting by the work of Halliday and Hasan (1976) these linguistic elements have been identified as cohesion devices. Later researchers argue that in addition to the surface connectivity, discourse connectives provide constraints on how readers should relate the content of the linked sentences (Trabasso et al., 1982; Blakemore, 1992; Sanders and Noordman, 2000). Experimental studies have proven the effect of these cues on various aspect of sentence processing (Caron et al., 1988; Millis and Just, 1994; Murray, 1995; Köhne and Demberg, 2013). For example, Murray (1995) showed that each category of connectives, such as causal vs. adversative, triggers a different expectation of the text continuation and if a relation is expressed with an infelicitous connective, readers face comprehension difficulty. Köhne and Demberg (2013) carried out an online reading study that revealed such effects show up very early during reading the second argument of a relation and confirmed that the online influence of a sentence connective can be as fine grained as triggering lexical predictions.

While discourse connectives are know as the best markers of discourse relations, empirical studies such as Knott (1996) and Asr and Demberg (2012b; 2013) indicate that connective types vary a lot in

[1] Other than explicit and implicit discourse relations, PDTB contains a set of other types of relations which are not considered here.

[2] Interested readers are referred to Prasad et al. (2008) for more details on the annotation guidelines.

terms of the granularity and amount of relational information they encode and this goes beyond the typical coarse-grained categorization of connectives. In particular, Asr and Demberg (2013) show that *instead* and *because* are highly informative (or strongly constraining) markers which should play an important role in identification of very specific discourse relations, whereas *and* and *but* occur in a wide range of contexts, thus do not disambiguate the relation down to a very specific sense.

2.3 Other relational cues

Even when connectives are absent or do not exhibit enough information about the relation sense between two consecutive discourse units, readers can still infer relations by relying on their world-knowledge and the information encoded in the arguments of the relation; See an implicit *reason* relation in the following example.

(3) John admires Mary. She plays the piano very well.

Rohde and Horton (2010, 2014) provide more evidence for the incrementality of discourse relation processing within a novel visual world experiment, which specifically shows that people predict the relation between two sentences as soon as they encounter a cue, be it the discourse connective or other linguistic cues yet within the first clause. Implicit causality verbs, such as *admire* in the above example, trigger expectation for a causal continuation and given the time course of the effect in Rohde and Horton's experiment one can infer that the connective (in this case *because*) would then be a redundant operator. Recently, a few systematic corpus studies have been conducted on the discovery of other types of relational markers in natural text (Prasad et al., 2010; Das and Taboada, 2013; Duque, 2013; Webber, 2013). The obtained annotations throughout these studies indicate that, in fact, a lot of discourse relations benefit from other types of cues besides explicit discourse connectives. Furthermore, machine learning attempts for detection of implicit discourse relations reveal that lexical, syntactic and clause-level properties of the arguments can determine the relation sense with good accuracy, at least for a coarse-grained classification (Pitler et al., 2009; Lin et al., 2009; Zhou et al., 2010; Park and Cardie, 2012; Rutherford and Xue, 2014).

2.4 Implicitness

Regarding the question of implicitness, Asr and Demberg (2012a, 2013) study causal and continuous discourse relations which based on cognitive theories and lab experiments tend to be eagerly inferred by readers when sentences are encountered consecutively. In both studies, Asr and Demberg extract different senses of relations from PDTB and find a higher degree of implicitness (proportion of the implicit to the explicit occurrences) for causal and continuous relation senses compared with other types of relations, e.g. comparison or backward temporal relations. This finding has been interpreted as an evidence that writers consider the reader side default inferential biases during language production. Asr and Demberg (2012a) also investigate the effect of implicit causality verbs as a linguistic cue in Arg1 of the relation. Regarding the observations of Rohde and Horton (2010) about the comprehension of causal relations, they predict a higher degree of implicitness for `CONTINGENCY.Cause.reason` relations containing implicit causality verbs. Analysis of these relations in PDTB fails to show any significant correlation between the two factors which is attributed to the noise involved with the automatic extraction and sense disambiguation of the targeted verbs. Beside that, the verb type can simply be a non-salient feature at the discourse level and in particular implicit causality verbs might generate expectation for causal relations only in a particularly constrained context. In fact, the lab experiments regarding the effect of these verbs on comprehension have benefited from very specific form of text, i.e., a simple and short narration about two protagonists like in 2.3 which makes the stimuli very different from sentences in expository text. Furthermore, the majority of previous lab findings about this class of verbs support the predictability of a following referent rather than the relation sense.

Patterson and Kehler (2013) train a classifier on the linguistic features of the arguments of PDTB relations to distinguish between implicit and explicit occurrences. The results suggests that implicit and explicit relations are indeed different, i.e., it is possible to predict based on the arguments whether a connective is required or not. Nevertheless, their findings lack interpretability: while the classifier can suggest with acceptable accuracy when a discourse connective is necessary (86.6% in binary classification), it does not provide any insight why this either case is preferred. They also run a comparison task on Amazon Mechanical Turk to see how human judgment differs from the automatic classification on the same test data set. They find that human preference in selecting between implicit/explicit variations of the relations aligns with the original text even less often (68% accuracy). The authors propose that it could be due to genre-specific editorial regulations that is applied in Wall Street Journal, e.g., use of sentence initial *but*, that is not recommended in prescriptive grammar books and, in turn, not preferred by Amturk subjects. From a psycholinguistic perspective, there is always a difference between decisions that human language users subconsciously make in writing and what they might prefer in an explicit judgment task, because a different cognitive mechanism is activated in each task.

2.5 Our focus: Sentence polarity

This paper presents an attempt to investigate the interaction of strong discourse relation cues (which are not considered as traditional discourse markers) with presence/absence of the sentence connectives. We look into the use of negation words in the first argument of a relation as an incrementally available cue for predicting the relation between a sentence and the upcoming discourse unit.

Webber's manual analysis of the `chosen alternative` relations in PDTB, as well as a corpus of *instead sentences*, reveals that the first argument of this type of relation usually contains some type of negation or a downward entailing verb (Webber, 2013). Based on this observation and the fact that negation (as long as the scope is not resolved) is a relatively easy feature to automatically detect in text, we decided to look into this feature as a case study of UID at the level of inter-sentential coherence relations. Another motivation for studying negation comes from the emphasized importance given to the relation polarity as a cognitively plausible dimension for classification of discourse relations (Sanders, 1997)[3]. Hence, in Section 5, we will examine:

- whether the presence of explicit negation words in a sentence changes the distribution of the discourse relations and in particular is statistically licensed as a feature of the `chosen alternative` relations.
- whether the presence/absence of the connectives can be explained according to the UID, i.e., predicted by relational surprisal which in turn is calculated based on the negation feature extracted from Arg1.

3 Surprisal at the discourse connective

The standard formulation of surprisal at a particular word w is its negative log probability in context: $-\log P(w|context)$. We can then calculate, for example, the syntactic surprisal of a word in context as the difference between the sum of the probabilities of all syntactic trees spanning words $w_1..w_{i-1}$ and the sum of the probabilities of all trees additionally including word w_i:

$$S_{syntactic}(w_i) = -\log \sum_{T \in Trees} P(T, w_1..w_i) - -\log \sum_{T \in Trees} P(T, w_1..w_{i-1})$$

(see Levy, 2008; Demberg and Keller, 2008). Similarly, we can define discourse relation surprisal as

$$S_{relational}(w_i) = -\log \sum_{R \in DiscRels} P(R, w_1..w_i) - -\log \sum_{R \in DiscRels} P(R, w_1..w_{i-1})$$

[3]Note, however, that negation in the surface is not necessarily equivalent to negative relational polarity. For example, "Mary loves John, but she pretends to ignore him." is a negative polarity relation without utilizing any covert negation, whereas, "Mary doesn't love John and she pretends to ignore him" is a positive polarity relation including some negation.

General Intuition. Discourse relation surprisal quantifies how much a word w_i changes the distribution of all possible instances of discourse relations R. In this conceptualisation, all words can potentially convey some information about the discourse relations in the text. Discourse connectives and adverbials like *but*, *since* or *because* are treated the same way as other cues in the text — while they are generally very informative cues about upcoming discourse relations, almost all of the discourse connectives are ambiguous, i.e. they can occur as a marker of several discourse relations, and are therefore best treated probabilistically, just like other cues. The perspective of all words being potential cues for discourse relations allows us to account for how words in the arguments of a discourse relation can affect discourse relation inference beyond the connective. Cues such as negation, event modals, coreference patterns, temporal phrases, verb tense and modality are also known to play a role for discourse relation inference. We hypothesise that humans have certain general expectations about upcoming discourse relations (i.e., a preference for causal and continuous relations), and that these expectations are updated by incoming words that contribute to shape the anticipation of a discourse relation. For example, a negation would convey the discourse-relation relevant information that a likely upcoming discourse relation could be a chosen alternative, a contrast or an explanation.

Conceptual Simplification for Avoiding Data Sparsity. In this paper, we focus on information conveyed by a cue in the first argument and its effect on the presence of a discourse connective like *instead*. The connective should be omitted if the information it conveys is highly predictable given previous context, or if its presence would otherwise make non-optional words in the second argument highly predictable and non-informative. The latter effect is much harder to estimate with the amount of data that we have; therefore, we will concentrate on the first part.

The information conveyed by a connective is thus:

$$S(connective) = -\log \sum_{R \in DiscRels} P(R, connective, arg1) - -\log \sum_{R \in DiscRels} P(R, arg1)$$

If the distribution of expected discourse relations does not change much by observing the connective, then surprisal at the discourse connective is very small, leading to a trough in information density. The connective should then be omitted. Hence, the interesting component in the above formula is $P(R|arg1)$, indicative of the information already available to predict the relation before encountering the discourse connective.

4 Experiment

In general, $P(R|arg1)$ can be computed for all possible values of relations R based on a set of features extracted from the first argument of the discourse relations in a reference corpus. In this study, we start off with a single feature within Arg1 of the relation. If as we predicted, connectives are used as modulator of relational surprisal, we should find for a given relation sense $R \in DiscRels$ that the connective $Conn$ marking R is present where $P(R|arg1)$ is small and that it should be omitted when $P(R|arg1)$ is high.

4.1 Negation in the arguments of discourse relations

A binary feature is defined indicating whether any of the following negation words is present in the Arg1 of a relation: {*not, n't, no, without, never, neither, none, non , nor, nobody, nothing*}. In PDTB, the Arg1 of an implicit relation is always the one that appears first in the text. In case of explicit relations, the order of arguments is reversed, when a sentence initial subordinating connective is used (that is, Arg2 is always the one directly following the connective in explicitly marked relations). Since our argument is based upon incremental processing of the relational cues, the analysis presented in this paper excludes relations with reversed arguments, 1920 instances in the corpus – we'd like to note however that same analysis leads to very similar results when reversed relations included. Among all implicit and explicit relations under analysis about 14% turn out to have some negation in their Arg1.

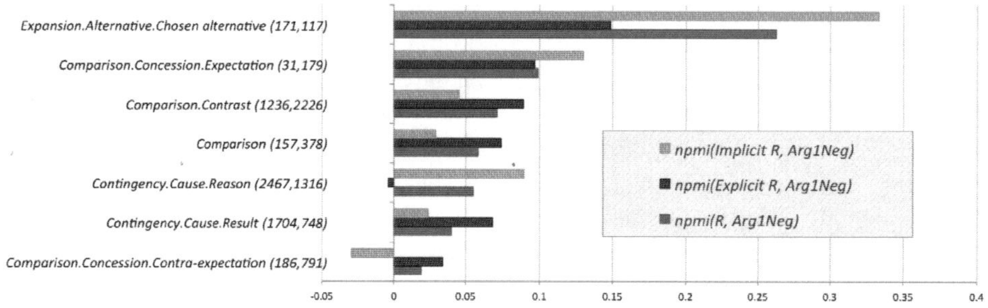

Figure 2: Relation senses showing positive $npmi$ with negation in Arg1 (all significant at $p < 0.001$ except the `contra-expectation`). Frequency of implicit and explicit occurrences of every relation sense is indicated in brackets.

To test the reliability of the automatic procedure in discovery of negative words, we compared our list of explicit `chosen alternative` relations with the list manually analyzed by Webber (2013) and discovered only 1 difference where our algorithm found a negation in the first argument but it was not considered by Webber as a marker of the relation. Webber also detected 5 influential negation words in the attribution of the relations, as well as, 5 negations in a larger context rather than in the Arg1 boundaries. We do not consider such cases for the matter of consistency, i.e., we focus on the linguistic cues inside Arg1. Finally, all relations are considered with their fine-grained senses annotated in the PDTB and if a relation is annotated with more than one sense in the corpus, we count it for every sense separately. We only look into the relations that have 30 or more implicit and 30 or more explicit instances in the corpus.

4.2 Correlation bw. polarity and relation senses

Regarding the investigation of the UID hypothesis, we first need to make sure that negation is statistically licensed as a feature of the `chosen alternative` relation. Merely knowing that such a cues occurs frequently with this type of relation is not enough, because negation might be a strong marker of some other relation(s) too. If other relation senses turn out to be more likely given the presence of negation, the connective in `chosen alternative` would not be subject to omission in order to keep a uniform discourse-level information density, or such a correlation would be expected to a lesser extent. If on the other hand, `chosen alternative` turns out to be the most likely relation sense given the negation cue, then it would make a perfect test case for investigation of the UID.

Similar to Asr and Demberg's analysis of discourse connectives strength, we calculate the normalized point-wise mutual information (Bouma, 2009) between the polarity of the first argument of a relation as a binary cue, and its sense:

$$npmi(R|C) = \frac{\log p(R)p(C)}{\log p(R, C)} - 1 \tag{2}$$

This removes the unwanted effect of the raw frequency of the relations and provides us with a scaled measure to see what relations benefit from negation as a cue. Figure 2 shows the relation senses obtaining a positive $npmi$ with the *negation* cue in Arg1. Other relation senses either obtain a significantly negative score (e.g., `synchronous` which indicates that a negative polarity sentence in a text would least likely be followed by this relation) or a closed to zero score, i.e., no correlation. The `chosen alternative` relation, in particular, is located at the top, meaning that negation in Arg1 is highly predictive of this relation sense. Running the same analysis by considering only the implicit relations in the corpus reveals an even stronger pattern.

4.3 Relational surprisal as a predictor of implicitness

The posterior probability of the `chosen alternative` given the presence of a negation cue, $3.45 * 10^{-2}$, is much higher than its prior which is $8.44 * 10^{-3}$. Among the `chosen alternative` relations, absence of the discourse connective is positively correlated with the presence of negation: the likelihood of the connective being dropped is 75.6% for relations with some negation in Arg1, whereas, it is only 39% for the rest of `chosen alternative` relations ($p < 0.001$). This observation is consistent with our hypothesis: if a cue like negation is helpful to human comprehenders (or affects what speakers do) in order to infer a discourse relation, then the relation should be marked less often in presence of that cue.

Figure 2 indicates that two other relation senses, i.e., `expectation` and `reason` show similar patterns (though the UID effect is only significant for `reason`). On the other hand, `COMPARISON` and `COMPARISON.Contrast` relations show an opposite trend, i.e., while negation in Arg1 increases the likelihood of these relations, the connectives marking these relations tend to be dropped in the presence rather than absence of the negation feature (not a significant difference though). This raises a question: why should the presence of negation in Arg1 of `chosen alternative` correlate with its implicitness but not for some other relation types? It is quite possible that the necessity of the connective is affected by other factors not included in our analysis. An alternative explanation would be that negation is not a similarly salient feature for `contrast` relations as it is for `chosen alternative` relations. In fact, the `Contrast` relation is much more common, and negation does not affect its distribution (prior $1.01 * 10^{-1}$, posterior $1.34 * 10^{-1}$) as much as it affects the distribution of the `chosen alternative` relation. Finally, as pointed out before, discourse connectives differ a lot in terms of their relational information content, hence, presence/absence of the highly informative connectives such as *instead* and *because* is more of a UID related question compared with relatively less informative, i.e., ambiguous connectives such as *but* which is typically used in `Contrast` relations.

5 Discussion

Our analysis here was based on the predictability of a discourse relation given a local cue in the first argument of a discourse relation. Considering only a single feature in the first argument is a rather poor measure of estimating the real predictive effect of the words in the first argument of a discourse relation on the identity of the discourse relation, in particular in the absence of more sophisticated methods for determining negation scope in our approach. This method on average hence seriously under-estimates the predictability of discourse relations. Nevertheless, we found support for the hypothesis that negation is a good cue for the `chosen alternative` relation (Webber, 2013), and were furthermore able to show that the distribution of the discourse connectors marking this relation is consistent with the predictions of the Uniform Information Density hypothesis.

A second point to take into account when thinking about these results is that the insertion or omission of a discourse connector should not only depend on the amount of new information it conveys with respect to earlier cues in the text, but rather that its presence might also be determined by whether it is redundant with respect to information contained in the second argument (which may not be left out due to reasons of grammaticality): the prediction is that the optional linguistic element (the connector) should be omitted if that leads to a more uniform distribution of information across the utterance. It would be particularly interesting to connect this observation with the speaker's planning capacities: such considerations should be more difficult to take into account during language production, when the distance between two words that are partially redundant with respect to one another is larger.

6 Conclusions

Following the Uniform Information Density hypothesis, we predicted that optional markers of discourse relations should be used in cases when they convey a substantial amount of new information, and should be left out if the information they convey is predictable given other cues in the incrementally available context. In order to investigate this hypothesis, we proposed a formula for calculating surprisal at the level of discourse relations. As a test case, we measured the relational surprisal according to a simple linguistic feature, i.e., presence/absence of negation in the first argument of a discourse relation.

Our analysis of the relations extracted from PDTB reveals that:

1. Sentence polarity affects the distribution of discourse relations and in particular increases the likelihood of a `chosen alternative` relation, as well as 6 other (among 44) relations. This result motivates an experimental investigation of the expectations generated by a negated sentence.

2. The sentence connective *instead* that is a strong marker of `chosen alternative` tends to be dropped in cases with lower relational surprisal, i.e., when the relation is highly predictable due to the presence of negation in Arg1. This result provides supporting evidence for UID at the level of discourse, i.e., suggesting that the writers of the WSJ text subconsciously marked instances of inter-sentential relations that are less predictable given their linguistic context.

In the future, we would like to construct a model with a high-coverage set of clausal, syntactic and semantic features predictive of relation sense classes to examine whether the relational information content of the connectives used for an instance of a relation is correlated with the predictability of the relation sense according to the features of the arguments. In a more accurate setup, it would be interesting to look into the word-by-word prediction of the model and the distance between a strong relational cue and the possibly present discourse connective.

Acknowledgments

We would like to thank Florian Jaeger for the valuable discussions on the UID theory and his helpful comments. Thanks to Bonnie Webber for sharing the details of her analysis of the PDTB chosen alternative relations and for her thoughtful revision of the initial version of this paper. This research was funded by the German Research Foundation (DFG) as part of SFB 1102 "Information Density and Linguistic Encoding".

References

Asr, F. T. and V. Demberg (2012a). Implicitness of discourse relations. In *Proceedings of the 25th International Conference on Computational Linguistics COLING*, Mumbai, India, pp. 2669 –2684.

Asr, F. T. and V. Demberg (2012b). Measuring the strength of the discourse cues. In *Proceedings of the workshop on the Advances in Discourse Analysis and its Computational Aspects*, Mumbai, India.

Asr, F. T. and V. Demberg (2013). On the information conveyed by discourse markers. In *Proceedings of the workshop on Computational Modeling and Cognitive Linguistics, ACL*, Sofia, Bulgaria.

Aylett, M. and A. Turk (2004). The smooth signal redundancy hypothesis: A functional explanation for relationships between redundancy, prosodic prominence, and duration in spontaneous speech. *Language and Speech 47*(1), 31–56.

Blakemore, D. (1992). *Understanding utterances: An introduction to pragmatics*. Blackwell Oxford.

Bouma, G. (2009). Normalized (pointwise) mutual information in collocation extraction. In *Proceedings of the Biennial GSCL Conference*, pp. 31–40.

Buz, E., F. Jaeger, and M. K. Tanenhaus (2014). Contextual confusability leads to targeted hyperarticulation. In *Proceedings of the 36th annual conference of the cognitive science society*.

Caron, J., H. C. Micko, and M. Thuring (1988). Conjunctions and the recall of composite sentences. *Journal of Memory and Language 27*(3), 309–323.

Das, D. and M. Taboada (2013). Explicit and implicit coherence relations: A corpus study.

Demberg, V. and F. Keller (2008). Data from eye-tracking corpora as evidence for theories of syntactic processing complexity. *Cognition 109*(2), 193–210.

Demberg, V., A. B. Sayeed, P. J. Gorinski, and N. Engonopoulos (2012). Syntactic surprisal affects spoken word duration in conversational contexts. In *Proceedings of the 2012 Joint Conference on Empirical Methods in Natural Language Processing and Computational Natural Language Learning*, pp. 356–367.

Duque, E. (2013). Signaling causal coherence relations. *Discourse Studies*.

Grice, H. P. (1975). Logic and conversation. *Reprinted in Studies in the Way of Words 1985*, 2240.

Hale, J. (2003). The information conveyed by words in sentences. *Journal of Psycholinguistic Research 32*(2), 101–123.

Halliday, M. and R. Hasan (1976). *Cohesion in English*. Longman (London).

Jaeger, F. (2010). Redundancy and reduction: Speakers manage syntactic information density. *Cognitive psychology 61*(1), 23–62.

Knott, A. (1996). A data-driven methodology for motivating a set of coherence relations.

Köhne, J. and V. Demberg (2013). The time-course of processing discourse connectives. In *Proceedings of the 35th Annual Meeting of the Cognitive Science Society*.

Kravtchenko, E. (2014). Predictability and syntactic production: Evidence from subject omission in russian. In *Proceedings of the 36th annual conference of the cognitive science society*.

Kurumada, C. and T. F. Jaeger (2013). Communicatively efficient language production and case-marker omission in japanese. In *The 35th Annual Meeting of the Cognitive Science Society*, pp. 858–863.

Levy, R. (2008). Expectation-based syntactic comprehension. *Cognition 106*(3), 1126–1177.

Levy, R. and T. F. Jaeger (2007). Speakers optimize information density through syntactic reduction. In *Advances in Neural Information Processing Systems*.

Lin, Z., M. Kan, and H. Ng (2009). Recognizing implicit discourse relations in the penn discourse treebank. In *Proceedings of the 2009 Conference on Empirical Methods in Natural Language Processing*, pp. 343–351.

Mahowald, K., E. Fedorenko, S. T. Piantadosi, and E. Gibson (2013). Info/information theory: Speakers choose shorter words in predictive contexts. *Cognition 126*(2), 313–318.

Millis, K. and M. Just (1994). The influence of connectives on sentence comprehension. *Journal of Memory and Language*.

Murray, J. (1995). Logical connectives and local coherence. *Sources of Coherence in Reading*, 107–125.

Park, J. and C. Cardie (2012). Improving implicit discourse relation recognition through feature set optimization. In *Proceedings of the 13th Annual Meeting of the Special Interest Group on Discourse and Dialogue*, pp. 108–112. Association for Computational Linguistics.

Patterson, G. and A. Kehler (2013). Predicting the presence of discourse connectives. In *Proceedings of the conference on Empirical Methods in Natural Language Processing EMNLP*, pp. 914–923.

Piantadosi, S. T., H. Tily, and E. Gibson (2011). Word lengths are optimized for efficient communication. *Proceedings of the National Academy of Sciences 108*(9), 3526–3529.

Pitler, E., A. Louis, and A. Nenkova (2009). Automatic sense prediction for implicit discourse relations in text. In *Proceedings of the Joint Conference of the 47th Annual Meeting of the ACL and the 4th International Joint Conference on Natural Language Processing of the AFNLP: Volume 2-Volume 2*, pp. 683–691.

Prasad, R., N. Dinesh, A. Lee, E. Miltsakaki, L. Robaldo, A. Joshi, and B. Webber (2008). The Penn Discourse Treebank 2.0. In *Proceedings of the 6th International Conference on Language Resources and Evaluation*, pp. 2961–2968.

Prasad, R., A. Joshi, and B. Webber (2010). Realization of discourse relations by other means: alternative lexicalizations. In *Proceedings of the 23rd International Conference on Computational Linguistics: Posters*, pp. 1023–1031.

Rohde, H. and W. Horton (2010). Why or what next? eye movements reveal expectations about discourse direction. In *Proceedings of 23rd Annual CUNY Conference on Human Sentence Processing*, pp. 18–20.

Rohde, H. and W. S. Horton (2014). Anticipatory looks reveal expectations about discourse relations. *Cognition 133*(3), 667–691.

Rutherford, A. T. and N. Xue (2014). Discovering implicit discourse relations through brown cluster pair representation and coreference patterns.

Sanders, T. (1997). Semantic and pragmatic sources of coherence: On the categorization of coherence relations in context. *Discourse Processes 24*(1), 119–147.

Sanders, T. J. and L. G. Noordman (2000). The role of coherence relations and their linguistic markers in text processing. *Discourse processes 29*(1), 37–60.

Tily, H. and S. Piantadosi (2009). Refer efficiently: Use less informative expressions for more predictable meanings. In *Proceedings of the workshop on the production of referring expressions: Bridging the gap between computational and empirical approaches to reference*.

Trabasso, T., T. Secco, and P. Van Der Broek (1982). Causal cohesion and story coherence. *Learning and comprehension of text*.

Webber, B. (2013). What excludes an alternative in coherence relations? In *Proceedings of the International Workshop on Computational Semantics*.

Zhou, Z., Y. Xu, Z. Niu, M. Lan, J. Su, and C. Tan (2010). Predicting discourse connectives for implicit discourse relation recognition. In *Proceedings of the 23rd International Conference on Computational Linguistics: Posters*, pp. 1507–1514.

Efficiency in Ambiguity:
Two Models of Probabilistic Semantics for Natural Language

Daoud Clarke
University of Sussex, Brighton
daoud.clarke@gmail.com

Bill Keller
University of Sussex, Brighton
billk@sussex.ac.uk

Abstract

This paper explores theoretical issues in constructing an adequate probabilistic semantics for natural language. Two approaches are contrasted. The first extends Montague Semantics with a probability distribution over models. It has nice theoretical properties, but does not account for the ubiquitous nature of ambiguity; moreover inference is NP-hard. An alternative approach is described in which a sequence of pairs of sentences and truth values is generated randomly. By sacrificing some of the nice theoretical properties of the first approach it is possible to model ambiguity naturally; moreover inference now has polynomial time complexity. Both approaches provide a compositional semantics and account for the gradience of semantic judgements of belief and inference.[1]

1 Introduction

This paper explores theoretical issues in developing an expressive and computationally tractable, probabilistic semantics for natural language. Our general approach is situated within the formal, compositional semantics developed by Richard Montague, which is augmented to allow for probabilistic judgements about truth and inference. The present work takes as a point of departure a number of key assumptions. First, an adequate semantics should provide an account of both lexical and phrasal (i.e. compositional) meaning. Second, it should provide for judgements about degrees of belief. That is, a semantics should account for beliefs that statements are more or less likely to be true, or that one statement may entail another to a certain degree. Third, an adequate computational semantics should support effective procedures for learning semantic representations and for inference.

Vector space models of meaning have become a popular approach to computational semantics. Distributional models represent word meanings as vectors of corpus-based distributional contexts and have been successfully applied to a wide variety of tasks, including, *inter alia*, word sense induction and disambiguation (Khapra et al., 2010; Baskaya et al., 2013), textual entailment (Marelli et al., 2014), coreference resolution (Lee et al., 2012) and taxonomy induction (Fountain and Lapata, 2012). The success of vector-space models is due to several factors. They support fine-grained judgements of similarity, allowing us to account for semantic gradience, for example, that the lexeme *pear* is more similar to *banana* than to, say, *cat*. Moreover, distributional vectors can be learnt in an unsupervised fashion from corpus data, either by counting occurrences of distributional contexts for a word or phrase, or by performing more sophisticated analysis on the data (Mikolov et al., 2013; Pennington et al., 2014).

Vector-based approaches differ in many regards from compositional, model-theoretic treatments of meaning such as Montague semantics or Discourse Representation Theory (Kamp and Reyle, 1993). It has proved challenging to extend vector space models to account for the way in which meanings may be composed and to support inference. The problem of developing a fully compositional, distributional semantics has recently become a very active area of research (Widdows, 2008; Mitchell and Lapata, 2008; Baroni and Zamparelli, 2010; Garrette et al., 2011; Grefenstette et al., 2011; Socher et al., 2012;

[1]The authors are grateful for the comments of a number of anonymous reviewers on earlier drafts. The work was funded as part of EPSRC EP/I037458/1, *A Unified Model of Compositional and Distributional Semantics: Theory and Applications.*

Proceedings of the 11th International Conference on Computational Semantics, pages 129–139,
London, UK, April 15-17 2015.

Lewis and Steedman, 2013) and efforts made to find a theoretical foundation (Clarke, 2012; Kartsaklis et al., 2014). Researchers have also begun to address the problem of combining the strengths of both the distributional and model-theoretic approaches (Clarke, 2007; Coecke et al., 2010; Garrette et al., 2011; Lewis and Steedman, 2013).

This paper considers an alternative strategy for developing a computational semantics. Starting with a compositional, model-theoretic semantics, this is augmented with ideas drawn from probabilistic semantics (Gaifman, 1964; Nilsson, 1986; Sato, 1995). Probabilistic semantics provides a rich seam of ideas that can be applied to the construction of a compositional semantics with desirable properties such as gradience and learnability. Below, we explore two different ways in which this might be achieved. Our objective is to map out some of the territory, to consider issues of representational adequacy and computational complexity and to provide useful guidance for others venturing into this landscape.

2 Background

2.1 Montague Semantics

In the early 1970s, Richard Montague detailed a formal treatment of natural language semantics (Montague, 1970a,b, 1973). Montague's conception of semantics was truth-conditional and model-theoretic. He considered that a fundamental aim of any adequate theory of semantics was "to characterise the notions of a true sentence (under a given interpretation) and of entailment" (Montague, 1970b). A central methodological component of Montague's approach was the *Principle of Compositionality*: the meaning of an expression is a function of the meanings of its parts and the way they are combined syntactically.

Following Montague, we assume that natural language expressions are parsed by a categorial grammar. Further, every word has an associated function with a type. Let $\mathcal{T}$ be the smallest set such that:

Basic types: $e, t \in \mathcal{T}$

Complex types: if $\alpha, \beta \in \mathcal{T}$, then $\alpha/\beta \in \mathcal{T}$.

Note that type α/β is the type of a function from type β to type α.

The set B of *basic expressions* comprises symbols denoting meanings of words. Each $b \in B$ has a type τ_b. The set Λ of *well-formed expressions*, and the extension of τ to Λ are defined as follows. Let Λ be the smallest set such that:

- $B \subseteq \Lambda$
- For every pair $\gamma, \delta \in \Lambda$ such that $\tau_\gamma = \alpha/\beta$ and $\tau_\delta = \beta$, then $\gamma(\delta) \in \Lambda$ and $\tau_{\gamma(\delta)} = \alpha$

Let Λ_τ denote the set of well-formed expressions of type τ. A *sentence* is a well-formed expression of type t.

The set D_τ of *possible denotations* of type τ is defined by:

$$\begin{aligned} D_e &= E \\ D_t &= \{\bot, \top\} \\ D_{\alpha/\beta} &= {D_\alpha}^{D_\beta} \end{aligned}$$

where E is a set of *entities*. Thus the denotation of a complex type is a function between the denotations for the types from which it is composed. An *interpretation* is a pair $\langle E, F\rangle$ such that E is a non-empty set and F is a function with domain B such that $F(b) \in D_{\tau_b}$ for all $b \in B$. A well-formed expression γ has the value $[\![\gamma]\!]$ in the interpretation $\langle E, F\rangle$, where:

- $[\![b]\!] = F(b)$ for $b \in B$
- $[\![\gamma(\delta)]\!] = [\![\gamma]\!]([\![\delta]\!])$ for $\gamma \in \Lambda_{\alpha/\beta}$ and $\delta \in \Lambda_\beta$.

subject	*verb*	*object*	m_1	m_2	m_3	m_4
john	likes	john	1	1	1	1
john	likes	mary	0	1	1	1
mary	likes	john	1	0	0	1
mary	likes	mary	0	0	1	1
john	loves	john	1	1	1	1
john	loves	mary	1	0	1	1
mary	loves	john	1	1	1	1
mary	loves	mary	1	0	1	1

Table 1: Four possible models describing relationships between John and Mary.

John likes Mary
$\mu(\{m_2, m_3, m_4\}) == 0.9$

Mary likes John or Mary
$\mu(\{m_1, m_3, m_4\}) == 0.8$

John likes Mary given that he loves her
$\mu(\{m_3, m_4\})/\mu(\{m_1, m_3, m_4\}) = 0.7/0.8$

Table 2: Statements and their probabilities given the models in Table 1.

A sentence s is *true* in interpretation $\langle E, F\rangle$ if $[\![s]\!] = \top$, otherwise it is *false*. A *theory* T is a set of pairs $(s, \hat{s})$, where s is a sentence and $\hat{s} \in \{\top, \bot\}$ is a truth value. A *model* for a theory T is an interpretation $\langle E, F\rangle$ such that $[\![s]\!] = \hat{s}$ for every sentence $s \in T$. In this case we say that the model *satisfies* T, and write $\langle E, F\rangle \models T$.

2.2 Probabilistic Semantics

The idea of attaching probabilities to propositional truth is an old one and related to the foundation of probability itself (Keynes, 1921; Łoś, 1955). Gaifman (1964) discusses probability measures for first order calculus; the work of Sato (1995) concerns probability measures for logic programs. The idea we adopt is to associate probability measures with the space of models. Our approach is closely related in motivation to work by Cooper et al. (2014) and Goodman and Lassiter (2014).

In model-theoretic semantics, a way to view the meaning of a statement s is as the set of all interpretations $\mathcal{M}_s$ for which s is true. Probabilistic semantics extends this idea by assuming that models occur randomly. Formally, probabilities are defined in terms of a probability space $\langle \Omega, \sigma, \mu\rangle$, where Ω is the set of all models, σ is a sigma algebra associated with theories and μ is a probability measure on σ. We can then estimate the probability of a sentence s as the sum of the probabilities of all models $\mathcal{M}_s$, for s.

In general, the set of models will be infinite, but for purposes of exposition, consider a simple example with a small number of models, as in Table 1. Each column defines a different model of the relationship between John and Mary. We assume a probability distribution over models, with $P(m_1) = 0.1$, $P(m_2) = 0.2$, $P(m_3) = 0.3$, $P(m_4) = 0.4$ (all other possible models have probability zero). We can then deduce the probability of statements about John and Mary, as shown in Table 2.

3 A Probabilistic Montague Semantics

Let Ω be the set of all Montague-style interpretations, $M(T)$ the set of all models for the theory T and σ_0 the set of all sets of models that satisfy some theory: $\sigma_0 = \{M(T) : T \text{ is a theory}\}$. In general, σ_0 is not a sigma algebra, as it is not guaranteed for any two theories T_1, T_2 that $M(T_1) \cup M(T_2) \in \sigma_0$. For any Montague grammar containing a propositional fragment this would hold, but even if this is not the case we can still define a probability space by considering the sigma algebra σ generated by σ_0: the smallest sigma algebra containing σ_0. For μ a probability measure on σ, $\langle \Omega, \sigma, \mu\rangle$ is a probability space describing the probability of theories. The probability of T is defined as $\mu(M(T))$. For sentences s_1 and s_2 such that $\mu(M(\{(s_2, \top)\}) > 0$, the conditional probability $P(s_1|s_2)$ is interpreted as the *degree to which s_2 entails s_1* and defined as

$$P(s_1|s_2) = \frac{\mu(M(\{(s_1, \top), (s_2, \top)\}))}{\mu(M(\{(s_2, \top)\}))}$$

Note too that for $\mu(M(\{(s_2, \top)\})) > 0$, if s_2 *logically entails* s_1, then $P(s_1|s_2) = 1$.

3.1 Restricting the Space of Models

A key objective is to be able to learn semantics from corpus data. We describe one way this may be achieved within our framework. The central idea is to limit the number of denotations under consideration and define a probabilistic generative model for interpretations. Assume E is fixed. Let $\phi_\tau = \{[\![\lambda]\!] : \lambda \in \Lambda_\tau\}$ be the set of denotations occurring with type τ. Assume F is constrained s.t. $|\phi_\tau| = n_\tau$, where n_τ is a constant for each type satisfying $n_\tau \leq |D_\tau|$. Note that $\phi_\tau \subseteq D_\tau$ and ϕ_τ can be a lot smaller than D_τ if the range of F restricted to Λ_τ does not cover all of D_τ. We also assume that the occurring denotations are ordered, so we can write $\phi_\tau = \{d_{\tau,1}, d_{\tau,2}, \ldots d_{\tau,n_\tau}\}$. The restriction in the number of occurring denotations makes learning a distribution over models practicable, since the space of exploration can be made small enough to handle in a reasonable amount of time.

We assume that denotations are generated with probabilities conditionally independent given a random variable taking values from some set H. This gives us the following process to generate F:

- Generate a hidden value $h \in H$
- Generate $F(b) \in \phi_{\tau_b}$ for each $b \in B$ where $P(d_{\tau_b,i}|b,h) = \theta_{b,i,h}$
- Generate $d_{\alpha/\beta,i}(d_{\alpha,j}) \in \phi_\beta$ for each $d_{\alpha/\beta,i}$, $d_{\alpha,j}$, where $P(d_{\beta,k}|d_{\alpha/\beta,i}, d_{\alpha,j}, h) = \theta_{\beta,i,j,k,h}$

The parameters to be learnt are the probability distributions $\theta_{b,i,h}$ over possible values $d_{\tau_b,i}$, for each basic expression b and hidden value h, and $\theta_{\beta,i,j,k,h}$ over values $d_{\beta,k}$ for each function $d_{\alpha/\beta,i}$, argument $d_{\alpha,j}$ and hidden value h.

3.2 Learning and Inference

For a theory T and parameters θ, we compute $P(T|\theta)$ as follows. For each hidden variable h:

- Iterate over models for T. This can be done bottom-up by first choosing the denotation for each basic expression, then recursively for complex expressions. Choices must be remembered and if a contradiction arises, the model is abandoned.
- The probability of each model given h can be found by multiplying the parameters associated with each choice made in the previous step.

We can use Maximum Likelihood to estimate the parameters given a set of observed theories $\mathcal{D} = \{T_1, T_2, \ldots T_N\}$. We look for the parameters θ that maximize the likelihood

$$P(\mathcal{D}|\theta) = \prod_{n=1}^{N} P(T_i|\theta)$$

This can be maximised using gradient ascent or expectation maximisation. We have verified that this can be done for small examples with a simple Python implementation.

4 Stochastic Semantics

Our formulation of Probabilistic Montague Semantics does not adequately account for ambiguity in natural language. Although we have a probability distribution over interpretations, in any given interpretation each occurrence of a word must have the same denotation. This is unsatisfactory, as a word may exhibit different senses across a theory. For example, consider two sentences, each containing an occurrence of the word *bank*, but with different senses. In our current formulation both occurrences of *bank* are forced to have the same denotation. To allow a word's meaning to vary across a theory, one possibility is to represent different occurrences of a word by different predicates. For example, we might perform word sense disambiguation on each sentence and decide that the two occurrences of *bank* are unrelated. In this case, the first occurrence might be represented by the predicate *bank*$_1$ and the second by *bank*$_2$.

```
% Hidden variable
values(hidden, [h0, h1]).

% Types
values(word(noun, Word, Hidden), [n0, n1]).
values(word(verb, Word, Hidden), [v0, v1]).
values(word(det, Word, Hidden), [d0, d1]).
values(function(s, Value1, Value2, Hidden), [t0, t1]).
values(function(np, Value1, Value2, Hidden), [np0, np1]).
values(function(vp, Value1, Value2, Hidden), [vp0, vp1]).

evaluate(w(Word, Type), Hidden, Result) :-
  msw(word(Type, Word, Hidden), Result).
evaluate(f(Type, X, Y), Hidden, Result) :-
  evaluate(X, Hidden, XResult),
  evaluate(Y, Hidden, YResult),
  msw(function(Type, XResult, YResult, Hidden), Result).

theory([], _).
theory([truth(Sentence, Result)|Tail], Hidden) :-
  evaluate(Sentence, Hidden, Result),
  theory(Tail, Hidden).

theory(T) :-
  msw(hidden, Hidden),
  theory(T, Hidden).
```

Figure 1: A PRISM program describing probability distributions over natural language models used for our examples.

We consider an alternative which incorporates *degrees of ambiguity* into the representation of a word's meaning. This is consistent with many distributional frameworks, where a word is often represented as a vector of all of its contexts of occurrence, regardless of sense. We drop the requirement that in any given interpretation, each occurrence of a word must have the same denotation. Generalising this idea to denotations for all types results in an entirely different semantic model. It turns out that this model can be formulated in a straightforward way within the framework due to Sato and Kameya (1997). We call our new framework *Stochastic Semantics*. We no longer associate a set of models with a sentence, but instead assume that pairs of sentences and truth values are randomly generated in sequence. The probability of each pair being generated is conditionally independent of previous pairs given the hidden variable.

An illustrative implementation of Stochastic Semantics is shown in Figure 1. The code is written in PRISM (Sato and Kameya, 1997), a probabilistic extension of the Prolog logic-progamming language that incorporates probabilistic predicates and declarations. In particular, PRISM allows *random switches*. In the code, the predicate `values` is used to declare a named switch and associate with it a number of possible outcomes. The probabilistic predicate `msw` allows a random choice to made amongst these outcomes at execution time. To simplify the code, complex types of the grammar are referred to by their corresponding natural language categories: type t is represented by `s`, type (t/e) by `vp` and type $t/(e/t)$ by `np`.

The program defines how sentences are randomly assigned truth values. For example, the switch `values(word(noun,Word,Hidden),[n0,n1])` introduces a switch for nouns having two possible outcomes, `n0` and `n1`. The outcomes are conditioned on the particular choice of noun (`Word`) and on the choice of hidden variable (`Hidden`). Similarly, switches are associated with complex types. For example the values associated with a sentence (`s`) switch are conditioned on the choices of its component parts and a hidden variable, and so on.

The probability of a theory is derived by evaluating the truth conditions of its component sentences. For example, a query returning the probability of the sentence *the cat likes the dog* would be expressed as a theory $\{(likes(the(dog))(the(cat)), \top)\}$, which can be translated into a Prolog expression in a straightforward manner.

5 Complexity

We focus on determining the probability of a sentence, as this is needed for both learning and inference.

5.1 Complexity of Probabilistic Montague Semantics

We first consider the problem of *Probabilistic Montague Semantics satisfiability* (PM-SAT) and then show that the problem of computing the probability of a sentence must be at least as hard.

Definition (PM-SAT). Given a restricted set of denotations ϕ_τ for each type τ and probability distributions defined by θ, determine whether the probability of a given sentence taking the value $\top$ is non-zero.

Theorem. PM-SAT *is NP-complete with respect to the length of the input sentence.*

Proof. We first show NP-hardness by reduction from SAT. Construct a special language for propositional logic with symbols P_i of type t, $\wedge$ and $\vee$ of type $(t/t)/t$ and $\neg$ of type t/t. For example $\vee(P_1)(\neg(P_2))$ is a sentence of this language. Using a more familiar and suggestive notation it might be written as $P_1 \vee \neg P_2$. We fix a generative model for interpretations of the language as follows. Hidden values are not needed, so assume H has a single element. Further assume distributions defined by θ such that the P_i take values in $\{\top, \bot\}$ with equal probability, while the symbols $\wedge$, $\vee$ and $\neg$ simply reproduce the familiar logical truth functions for conjunction, disjunction and negation respectively, with probability 1. Note for example that there is an interpretation for which $\vee(P_1)(\neg(P_2))$ has value $\top$. On the other hand, the sentence $\wedge(P_1)(\neg(P_1))$ will have value $\bot$ for all interpretations.

It follows from the construction above that a sentence has truth value $\top$ with non-zero probability if and only if it is satisfiable. Hence we can solve SAT if we can solve PM-SAT, and so PM-SAT is NP-hard. Finally, to show NP-completeness we note that PM-SAT can be solved by a non-deterministic machine in time linear in sentence length. This is achieved by choosing a value from H, assigning every possible value to all basic expressions and then recursively to complex expressions. Any assignment that gives a non-zero probability for the sentence taking the value $\top$ will return true. So PM-SAT is in NP and is thus NP-complete. □

Let us call the problem of computing the probability of a sentence in Probabilistic Montague Semantics PM-PROB. Clearly PM-PROB is at least as hard as PM-SAT, since if we knew the probability of a sentence we would know whether it was non-zero. It follows that PM-PROB is NP-hard.

5.2 Complexity of Stochastic Semantics

Let us call the problem of computing the probability of a sentence for Stochastic Semantics, SS-PROB. We show that SS-PROB is computationally easier than PM-PROB. Note that for Stochastic Semantics there is no dependency between different parts of a sentence. Dynamic programming can then be used to store the probability distribution over possible denotations associated with each expression, so that they are computed once for each hidden value. Let L be the number of expressions in a sentence and n the maximum number of denotations for all types, i.e. the greatest value of n_τ for all types τ. The algorithm to compute the probability of a sentence is as follows. For each $h \in H$:

- For each basic expression of type τ, compute the probability distribution over ϕ_τ; this can be computed in maximum $O(n)$ time.
- Recursively for each complex expression of type τ, compute the probability distribution over ϕ_τ, this requires maximum $O(n^2)$ time since we need to iterate over possible values of the expression and the type it acts on.

For a given hidden value in H, computing the probability of a sentence requires L computations each of complexity at most n^2. The total worst-case time complexity for SS-PROB is thus $O(|H|Ln^2)$. This is linear in the number of expressions L and so linear in the length of the sentence.

Text	Hypothesis	Ent.
some cats like all dogs	some animals like all dogs	Yes
no animals like all dogs	no cats like all dogs	Yes
some dogs like all dogs	some animals like all dogs	Yes
no animals like all dogs	no dogs like all dogs	Yes
some men like all dogs	some people like all dogs	Yes
no people like all dogs	no men like all dogs	Yes
no men like all dogs	no people like all dogs	No

Table 3: Example Text and Hypothesis sentences, and whether entailment holds. Both our systems are able to learn from the data above the line that the determiner "no" reverses the direction of entailment.

Noun	Hidden	n0	n1
animals	h0	0.00	1.00
animals	h1	0.67	0.33
cats	h0	1.00	0.00
cats	h1	0.47	0.53
dogs	h0	0.70	0.30
dogs	h1	0.55	0.45
men	h0	1.00	0.00
men	h1	0.60	0.40
people	h0	0.00	1.00
people	h1	0.53	0.47

Table 4: Learnt probabilities obtained using the Stochastic Semantics implementation.

6 Discussion

A learning system such as those we have described can be adapted to the task of recognising textual entailment (Dagan et al., 2005). This task is to determine whether one natural language sentence (the "text") entails another (the "hypothesis") and thus generalizes some important natural language problems, including question answering, summarisation and information extraction. For example, a pair for which entailment holds could be translated to the following set of theories:

$$\{(s_T, \top), (s_H, \top)\}, \{(s_T, \bot), (s_H, \top)\}, \{(s_T, \bot), (s_H, \bot)\}$$

where s_T is the sentence associated with the text and s_H the sentence associated with the hypothesis.

We verified that our two systems were able to learn some simple logical features of natural language semantics on toy textual entailment examples. In particular, determiners such as "no" reverse the direction of entailment, so that while "some cats" entails "some animals", "no animals" entails "no cats" (see Table 3). As an aside, we note that while our formalism does not employ explicit representations of lexical semantics, such representations can be recovered from the learnt models. The representation of a word is a tensor rather than a vector, because there is a distinct probability distribution over possible values for each hidden value. Table 4 shows the learnt values for the nouns obtained using the Stochastic Semantics implementation. If we want to compare words we can consider the matrix entries as a flat vector and use any of the standard similarity measures (e.g. cosine).

The flexibility granted by Stochastic Semantics results in the loss of certain nice properties. A necessary consequence of incorporating stochastic ambiguity into the formalism is the failure of logical entailment. If we do not disambiguate, then a sentence may not entail itself to degree 1 since it may mean different things in different contexts. We argue that it makes sense to sacrifice some properties which are expected when handling logical expressions in order to account for ambiguity as as an inherent property of language.

It is notable that the approach that accounts for ambiguity has lower complexity. Intuitively, this is because we do not have to keep track of the interpretation previously assigned to an expression: we are free to assign a new one. This also means that the expressive power of Probabilistic Montague Semantics is greater than that of Stochastic Semantics. In the latter, the meaning of a sentence can be viewed as simply a distribution over hidden variables, whereas in the former, the meaning also includes, for example, a record of all the words contained in the sentence. It is possible that Probabilistic Montague Semantics can be made more computationally efficient by placing further restrictions on the nature of distributions over models. For example, if we have no hidden variables, then the distribution can be described efficiently using Markov Logic Networks. Again, this restriction comes at the expense of expressive power.

7 Related Work

van Eijck and Lappin (2012) presents a framework for probabilistic semantics that is motivated by the need to account for gradience effects as an intrinsic part of a model of linguistic competence. They outline a compositional semantics for a propositional language in which the probability of the truth of a sentence is defined in terms of a probability distribution over possible states of affairs (worlds). Whilst the importance of providing a computationally adequate explanation of semantic learning is emphasised, issues of the tractability of inference are not addressed.

In a computational setting, an important objection to the appeal to possible worlds is that they are not tractably representable. Cooper et al. (2014) proposes a rich type system with records in which the judgment about whether a given situation is of a given type is probabilistic. Unlike worlds, situation types (Barwise and Perry, 1983) are not maximal consistent sets of propositions, but may be as small or as large as necessary. A schematic theory of semantic learning is outlined, based on an individual's observations of situations and their types, modelled probabilistically. This account of meaning provides the basis for a compositional semantics employing a probabilistic interpretation function.

In contrast to (Cooper et al., 2014), the present work assumes a generative process over interpreting structures. In particular, this means that interpretation with respect to a given model is categorical, while meaning is defined in terms of the probability distribution over all models. By restricting the space of possible models we show that semantic learning is possible, where the primary data for learning are pairs of sentences and truth values (rather than probabilistic type judgments). A result of our learning is the ability to determine degrees of entailment between pairs of sentences.

The present work shares motivation with Goodman and Lassiter (2014), who argue for the role of uncertainty in cognition and language understanding whilst preserving a compositional, truth conditional semantics. They show how probability may be used to formalise uncertainty and the gradience of judgements about belief and inference. The approach introduces a stochastic λ-calculus to provide compositional tools for probabilistic modelling, but has not yet addressed the problem of learning.

Coecke et al. (Coecke et al., 2010) propose a framework based on category-theoretic similarities between vector spaces and pregroup grammars. Their approach is closely related to ours since it is also founded in Montague semantics: words are treated as linear functions between vector spaces. It was recently demonstrated that this approach can be extended to allow the simulation of predicate calculus using tensors (Grefenstette, 2013). Garrette et al. (2011) describe an approach to combining logical semantics with distributional semantics using Markov Logic Networks (Richardson and Domingos, 2006). Sentences are parsed into logical form using Boxer (Bos et al., 2004) and probabilistic rules are added using the distributional model of Erk and Padó (2010). Lewis and Steedman (2013) take a standard logical approach to semantics except that the relational constants used are derived from distributional clustering.

8 Conclusion

This paper has explored theoretical properties of models of meaning. The reader may question the value of a paper whose contributions are mainly theoretical in nature. Whilst we fully intend to further explore our ideas in an experimental setting, we believe that readers interested in probabilistic approaches to natural language semantics will benefit from the theoretical ideas presented here. In particular:

- We take a standard approach to natural language semantics (Montague semantics) and augment it using a standard approach (probabilistic semantics). We are thus in an area that seems natural to explore.

- We are able to demonstrate deficiencies of this approach, both in representational adequacy and computational complexity, that may provide useful guidance for others considering venturing into this landscape.

- We identify an alternative area for exploration that alleviates the difficulties associated with the first approach.

We have shown that:

1. It is possible to learn probability distributions over models directly from data by restricting the set of models, whilst retaining many of the desirable properties of full Montague semantics.
2. The problem of computing the probability that a sentence is true in this framework is NP-hard.
3. Taking account of lexical ambiguity suggests a new approach in which pairs of sentences and truth values are generated randomly. The probability that a sentence is true can then be computed in polynomial time.
4. Both models are able to learn from a few examples that quantifiers such as "no" reverse the direction of entailment.

In future work, we plan to apply our ideas to the general task of recognising textual entailment. This would involve learning from much larger datasets and provide a more stringent test of the practical application of the approach. We also plan to further investigate the relationship between our models and vector space representations of meaning. This, together with a development of the theory, may lead to interesting new ways to describe probabilistic semantics that combine logical aspects of meaning with those which are better represented distributionally.

We have so far restricted ourselves to Montague semantics, and we are thus constrained by the well-known limitations of this formalism with respect to expressing aspects of discourse. It would be interesting to investigate how well our ideas could be incorporated into a formalism such as Discourse Representation Theory.

Finally, the examples presented here deal with a very small fragment of natural language. There are many complex natural language phenomena that have been dealt with successfully within the framework of Montague semantics. This suggests that it should be possible to apply probabilistic semantics to learn about a wide range of phenomena such as quantifier scope ambiguity, intensional contexts, time and tense and indexicals, amongst others.

References

Baroni, M. and R. Zamparelli (2010). Nouns are vectors, adjectives are matrices: Representing adjective-noun constructions in semantic space. In *Proceedings of the 2010 Conference on Empirical Methods in Natural Language Processing*.

Barwise, J. and J. Perry (1983). *Situations and Attitudes.* Cambridge, Mass.: Bradford Books. MIT Press.

Baskaya, O., E. Sert, V. Cirik, and D. Yuret (2013, June). Ai-ku: Using substitute vectors and co-occurrence modeling for word sense induction and disambiguation. In *Second Joint Conference on Lexical and Computational Semantics (*SEM), Volume 2: Proceedings of the Seventh International Workshop on Semantic Evaluation (SemEval 2013)*, Atlanta, Georgia, USA, pp. 300–306. Association for Computational Linguistics.

Bos, J., S. Clark, M. Steedman, J. R. Curran, and J. Hockenmaier (2004). Wide-coverage semantic representations from a ccg parser. In *Proceedings of the 20th international conference on Computational Linguistics*, pp. 1240. Association for Computational Linguistics.

Clarke, D. (2007). *Context-theoretic Semantics for Natural Language: an Algebraic Framework.* Ph. D. thesis, Department of Informatics, University of Sussex.

Clarke, D. (2012). A context-theoretic framework for compositionality in distributional semantics. *Computational Linguistics 38*(1), 41–71.

Coecke, B., M. Sadrzadeh, and S. Clark (2010). Mathematical foundations for a compositional distributional model of meaning. *CoRR abs/1003.4394*.

Cooper, R., S. Dobnik, S. Lappin, and S. Larsson (2014). A probabilistic rich type theory for semantic interpretation. In *Proceedings of the EACL 2014 Workshop on Type Theory and Natural Language Semantics (TTNLS)*, pp. 72–79. Association for Computational Linguistics.

Dagan, I., O. Glickman, and B. Magnini (2005). The pascal recognising textual entailment challenge. In *Proceedings of the PASCAL Challenges Workshop on Recognising Textual Entailment*, pp. 1–8.

Erk, K. and S. Padó (2010). Exemplar-based models for word meaning in context. In *Proceedings of the ACL 2010 conference short papers*, pp. 92–97. Association for Computational Linguistics.

Fountain, T. and M. Lapata (2012, June). Taxonomy induction using hierarchical random graphs. In *Proceedings of the 2012 Conference of the North American Chapter of the Association for Computational Linguistics: Human Language Technologies*, Montréal, Canada, pp. 466–476. Association for Computational Linguistics.

Gaifman, H. (1964). Concerning measures in first order calculi. *Israel J. Math. 2*, 1–18.

Garrette, D., K. Erk, and R. Mooney (2011). Integrating logical representations with probabilistic information using markov logic. In *Proceedings of the Ninth International Conference on Computational Semantics*, pp. 105–114. Association for Computational Linguistics.

Goodman, N. and D. Lassiter (2014). Probabilistic semantics and pragmatics: Uncertainty in language and thought. In S. Lappin and C. Fox (Eds.), *Handbook of Contemporary Semantic Theory*. Wiley-Blackwell.

Grefenstette, E. (2013). Towards a formal distributional semantics: Simulating logical calculi with tensors. In *Proceedings of the Second Joint Conference on Lexical and Computational Semantics*. Proceedings of the Second Joint Conference on Lexical and Computational Semantics.

Grefenstette, E., M. Sadrzadeh, S. Clark, B. Coecke, and S. Pulman (2011). Concrete sentence spaces for compositional distributional models of meaning. *Proceedings of the 9th International Conference on Computational Semantics (IWCS 2011)*, 125–134.

Kamp, H. and U. Reyle (1993). *From Discourse to Logic: Introduction to Modeltheoretic Semantics of Natural Language, Formal Logic and Discourse Representation Theory*, Volume 42 of *Studies in linguistics and philosophy*. Kluwer, Dordrecht.

Kartsaklis, D., M. Sadrzadeh, S. Pulman, and B. Coecke (2014). Reasoning about meaning in natural language with compact closed categories and frobenius algebras. In J. Chubb, A. Eskandarian, and V. Harizano (Eds.), *Logic and Algebraic Structures in Quantum Computing and Information*. Cambridge University Press (to appear).

Keynes, J. M. (1921). *A treatise on probability*. Cambridge University Press.

Khapra, M., A. Kulkarni, S. Sohoney, and P. Bhattacharyya (2010, July). All words domain adapted WSD: Finding a middle ground between supervision and unsupervision. In *Proceedings of the 48th Annual Meeting of the Association for Computational Linguistics*, Uppsala, Sweden, pp. 1532–1541. Association for Computational Linguistics.

Lee, H., M. Recasens, A. Chang, M. Surdeanu, and D. Jurafsky (2012, July). Joint entity and event coreference resolution across documents. In *Proceedings of the 2012 Joint Conference on Empirical Methods in Natural Language Processing and Computational Natural Language Learning*, Jeju Island, Korea, pp. 489–500. Association for Computational Linguistics.

Lewis, M. and M. Steedman (2013). Combined distributional and logical semantics. *Transactions of the Association for Computational Linguistics 1*, 179–192.

Łoś, J. (1955). On the axiomatic treatment of probability. *Colloq. Math 3*, 125–137.

Marelli, M., L. Bentivogli, M. Baroni, R. Bernardi, S. Menini, and R. Zamparelli (2014, August). Semeval-2014 task 1: Evaluation of compositional distributional semantic models on full sentences through semantic relatedness and textual entailment. In *Proceedings of the 8th International Workshop on Semantic Evaluation (SemEval 2014)*, Dublin, Ireland, pp. 1–8. Association for Computational Linguistics and Dublin City University.

Mikolov, T., K. Chen, G. Corrado, and J. Dean (2013). Efficient estimation of word representations in vector space. *ICLR Workshop*.

Mitchell, J. and M. Lapata (2008, June). Vector-based models of semantic composition. In *Proceedings of ACL-08: HLT*, Columbus, Ohio, pp. 236–244. Association for Computational Linguistics.

Montague, R. (1970a). English as a formal language. In B. V. et al. (Ed.), Linguaggi nella Societ e nella Tecnica, pp. 189–223.

Montague, R. (1970b). Universal grammar. *Theoria 36*, 373–398.

Montague, R. (1973). The proper treatment of quantification in ordinary english. In J. Hintikka, J. Moravcsik, and P. Suppes (Eds.), *Approaches to Natural Language*, pp. 221–242. Reidel, Dordrecht.

Nilsson, N. (1986). Probabilistic logic. *Artificial Intelligence 28*, 71–87.

Pennington, J., R. Socher, and C. Manning (2014, October). Glove: Global vectors for word representation. In *Proceedings of the 2014 Conference on Empirical Methods in Natural Language Processing (EMNLP)*, Doha, Qatar, pp. 1532–1543. Association for Computational Linguistics.

Richardson, M. and P. Domingos (2006). Markov logic networks. *Machine learning 62*(1-2), 107–136.

Sato, T. (1995). A statistical learning method for logic programs with distribution semantics. In *Proceedings of the 12th International Conference on Logic Programming (ICLP95)*.

Sato, T. and Y. Kameya (1997). Prism: a language for symbolic-statistical modeling. In *IJCAI*, Volume 97, pp. 1330–1339. Citeseer.

Socher, R., B. Huval, C. D. Manning, and A. Y. Ng (2012). Semantic compositionality through recursive matrix-vector spaces. In *Proceedings of the 2012 Joint Conference on Empirical Methods in Natural Language Processing and Computational Natural Language Learning*, pp. 1201–1211. Association for Computational Linguistics.

van Eijck, J. and S. Lappin (2012). Probabilistic semantics for natural language. In Z. Christoff, P. Galeazzi, N. Gierasimszuk, A. Marcoci, and S. Smets (Eds.), *Logic and Interactive Rationality (LIRA)*, Volume 2, pp. 17–35. ILLC, University of Amsterdam.

Widdows, D. (2008). Semantic vector products: Some initial investigations. In *Proceedings of the Second Symposium on Quantum Interaction, Oxford, UK*, pp. 1–8.

On the Proper Treatment of Quantifiers in Probabilistic Logic Semantics

Islam Beltagy
The University of Texas at Austin
Computer Science Department
beltagy@cs.utexas.edu

Katrin Erk
The University of Texas at Austin
Linguistics Department
katrin.erk@mail.utexas.edu

Abstract

As a format for describing the meaning of natural language sentences, probabilistic logic combines the expressivity of first-order logic with the ability to handle graded information in a principled fashion. But practical probabilistic logic frameworks usually assume a finite domain in which each entity corresponds to a constant in the logic (domain closure assumption). They also assume a closed world where everything has a very low prior probability. These assumptions lead to some problems in the inferences that these systems make. In this paper, we show how to formulate Textual Entailment (RTE) inference problems in probabilistic logic in a way that takes the domain closure and closed-world assumptions into account. We evaluate our proposed technique on three RTE datasets, on a synthetic dataset with a focus on complex forms of quantification, on FraCas and on one more natural dataset. We show that our technique leads to improvements on the more natural dataset, and achieves 100% accuracy on the synthetic dataset and on the relevant part of FraCas.

1 Introduction

Tasks in natural language semantics are becoming more fine-grained, like Textual Entailment (Dagan et al., 2013), Semantic Parsing (Kwiatkowski et al., 2013; Berant et al., 2013), or fine-grained opinion analysis. With the more complex tasks, there has been a renewed interest in phenomena like negation (Choi and Cardie, 2008) or the factivity of embedded clauses (MacCartney and Manning, 2009; Lotan et al., 2013) – phenomena that used to be standardly handled by logic-based semantics. Bos (2013) identifies the use of broad-coverage lexical resources as one aspect that is crucial to the success of logic-based approaches. Another crucial aspect is the ability to reason with uncertain, probabilistic information (Garrette et al., 2011; Beltagy et al., 2013). Lexical information typically comes with weights, be it weights of paraphrase rules (Lin and Pantel, 2001; Ganitkevitch et al., 2013), confidence ratings of word sense disambiguation systems, or distributional similarity values, and reasoning with such information and finding the overall best interpretation requires the ability to handle weights. This is possible in the framework of probabilistic logic (Nilsson, 1986).

In this paper we do not talk about *why* one should use probabilistic logic for natural language semantics (we argue for the need for probabilistic logic in previous work (Beltagy et al., 2013) which is summarized in section 2.4), we focus on the *how*, as it turns out that some practical design properties of probabilistic reasoning systems make it necessary to make changes to the meaning representations. One characteristic of practical probabilistic logic frameworks such as Markov Logic (Richardson and Domingos, 2006) is that they assume a finite domain, in particular they assume that the entities in the domain correspond to the constants mentioned in the set of formulas at hand. This is the *domain closure assumption (DCA)*, a strong assumption that reduces any inference problem to the propositional case. It also has far-reaching consequences on the behavior of a system. For example, suppose we know that *Tweety is a bird that flies*: $bird(T) \wedge fly(E) \wedge agent(T, E)$ (There is a flying event of which Tweety is the agent. We use this Neo-Davidsonian representation throughout the paper, as it is also produced by the wide-coverage semantic analysis system we use). Then we can conclude that *every bird flies*, because

Proceedings of the 11th International Conference on Computational Semantics, pages 140–150,
London, UK, April 15-17 2015. ©2015 Association for Computational Linguistics

by the DCA we are only considering models with a domain of size one. Of that single entity, we know both that it is a bird and that it flies. In a natural language inference setting, such as Textual Entailment, this is not the conclusion we would like to draw. So we need to use a nonstandard encoding to ensure that existential and universal quantifiers behave in the way they should.

Another issue that we face is that practical probabilistic logic frameworks usually have to construct all groundings of the given formulas before doing inference. The *closed-world assumption (CWA)* – the assumption that nothing is the case unless stated otherwise – helps to keep memory use for this grounding step in check (Beltagy and Mooney, 2014). However, the CWA comes with inference problems of its own, for example it would let us infer from *The sky is blue* that *No girl is dancing* because by the CWA we assume that no entity is dancing unless we were told otherwise.

In this paper, we concentrate on entailment, one of the fundamental criteria of language understanding. We show how to formulate probabilistic logic inference problems for the task of Recognizing Textual Entailment (RTE, Dagan et al. (2013)) in a way that takes the domain closure assumption as well as the closed-world assumption into account. We evaluate our approach on three RTE datasets. The first is a synthetic dataset that exhaustively tests inference performance on sentences with two quantifiers. We get 100% accuracy on this dataset. We also evaluate on the first section of the FraCas dataset (Cooper et al., 1996), a collection of Textual Entailment problems tailored focusing on particular semantic phenomena. We restrict our analysis to sentences with determiners that our current system handles (excluding "few", "most", "many" and "at least"), and we get 100% accuracy on them. Also, we evaluate on the RTE part of the SICK dataset (Marelli et al., 2014) and show that our approach leads to improvements.

2 Background and Related Work

2.1 Recognizing Textual Entailment

Recognizing Textual Entailment (RTE) (Dagan et al., 2013) is the task of determining whether one natural language text, the *Text* T, *Entails*, *Contradicts*, or is *Neutral* with respect to another, the *Hypothesis* H. Here are examples from the SICK dataset (Marelli et al., 2014):

- Entailment

T: A man and a woman are walking together through the woods.
H: A man and a woman are walking through a wooded area.

- Contradiction

T: A man is jumping into an empty pool
H: A man is jumping into a full pool

- Neutral

T: A young girl is dancing
H: A young girl is standing on one leg

2.2 Statistical relational learning

Statistical Relational Learning (SRL) techniques (Getoor and Taskar, 2007) combine logical and statistical knowledge in one uniform framework and provide a mechanism for coherent probabilistic inference. They typically employ weighted formulas in first-order logic to compactly encode complex probabilistic graphical models. Weighted rules allow situations in which not all clauses are satisfied. These frameworks typically operate on the set of all groundings of a given set of formulas. A probabilistic logic program defines a probability distribution over the possible values of the ground atoms where they are treated as random variables. In addition to a set of rules R, a probabilistic logic program takes an evidence set E asserting some truth values about some of the random variables. Then, given a query formula Q, probabilistic logic inference calculates the probability $P(Q|R, E)$ which is the answer to the query.

2.3 Markov Logic Networks

Markov Logic Networks (MLN) (Richardson and Domingos, 2006) are one of the statistical relational learning frameworks. MLNs work as templates to build graphical models that define probability distributions over worlds (equivalently, truth assignments to ground atoms), where a world's probability increases exponentially with the total weight of the ground clauses that it satisfies. Probability of a given world x is denoted by:

$$P(X = x) = \frac{1}{Z} \exp\left(\sum_i w_i n_i(x)\right) \tag{1}$$

where Z is the partition function, i ranges over all formulas F_i is the MLN, w_i is the weight of F_i and $n_i(x)$ is the number of true groundings of F_i in the world x. The marginal inference of MLNs calculates the probability $P(Q|E, R)$, where Q is a query, E is the evidence set, and R is the set of weighted formulas.

Alchemy (Kok et al., 2005) is the most widely used MLN implementation. It is a software package that contains implementations of a variety of MLN inference and learning algorithms. However, developing a scalable, general-purpose, accurate inference method for complex MLNs is an open problem.

2.4 Markov Logic Networks for Natural Language Semantics

Logic-based natural language semantics follows the framework of Montague Grammar as laid out in Montague's "Proper Treatment of Quantification in Ordinary English" (Montague, 1973). Recent wide-coverage tools that use logic-based sentence representations include Copestake and Flickinger (2000), Bos (2008), and Lewis and Steedman (2013).

In this work, we build on the approach of Beltagy et al. (2013) and Beltagy and Mooney (2014). Beltagy et al. (2013) use Bos' system Boxer to map English sentences to logical form, then use Markov Logic Networks to reason over those meaning representations, evaluating on two tasks, RTE and sentence similarity (semantic textual similarity, STS (Agirre et al., 2012)). Weighted clauses are used to encode distributional similarity of words or phrases as a set KB of weighted inference rules. An RTE problem of whether Text T entails Hypothesis H given the set of inference rules KB is transformed into the question of the probability of the hypothesis given the text and the rules, $P(H|T, KB)$. The Alchemy tool (Kok et al., 2005) is used to estimate this probability. Then a classifier is trained to convert the probabilities into judgments of Entailment, Contradiction, or Neutral. However, because of lack of adaptation to domain closure and other problems, the approach of Beltagy et al. (2013) is not able to make use of universal quantifiers in the Hypothesis H. In this paper, we address this problem.

Beltagy and Mooney (2014) propose an inference algorithm that can solve the inference problem $P(H|T, KB)$ efficiently for complex queries. They enforce a closed-world assumption that significantly reduces the problem size. However, this closed-world assumption makes negated hypotheses H come true regardless of T. In this paper, we also address this issue.

3 Approach

A significant difference between standard logic and probabilistic logic comes from the fact that practical probabilistic logic frameworks typically make the Domain Closure Assumption (DCA, Genesereth and Nilsson (1987); Richardson and Domingos (2006)): The only models considered for a set F of formulas are those for which the following three conditions hold. (a) Different constants refer to different objects in the domain, (b) the only objects in the domain are those that can be represented using the constant and function symbols in F, and (c) for each function f appearing in F, the value of f applied to every possible tuple of arguments is known, and is a constant appearing in F. Together, these three conditions entail that *there is a one-to-one relation between objects in the domain and the named constants of* F.

For working with Markov Logic Networks in practice, this means that constants need to be explicitly introduced in the probabilistic logic program. Constants are used to ground the predicates, and build the

MLN's graphical model. Different sets of constants result into different graphical models. If no constants are explicitly introduced, the graphical model is empty (no random variables). A more serious problem is that the DCA affects the behavior of universal quantifiers, as illustrated with the Tweety example in the introduction. We address this problem by adding more constants to the system.

While the DCA is not commonly made outside of probabilistic logic systems, the Closed World Assumption (CWA) is widely used in inference systems. However, in the context of Textual Entailment, it, too, leads to problems, as it assumes that all negative information is true a priori – but in RTE we do not want to assume anything to be true unless stated in the Text, neither positive nor negative information.

This section discusses the changes that we make to the representations of natural language sentence meaning in order to deal with the DCA and CWA. We focus on the Textual Entailment task as these changes will be different for the evidence given (the Text T) and the query (the Hypothesis H).

3.1 Skolemization

Skolemization (Skolem, 1920) transforms a formula $\forall x_1 \ldots x_n \exists y.F$ to $\forall x_1 \ldots x_n.F^*$, where F^* is formed from F by replacing all free occurrences of y by a term $f(x_1, \ldots, x_n)$ for a new function symbol f. If $n = 0$, f is called a *Skolem constant*, otherwise a *Skolem function*. Although Skolemization is a widely used technique when using standard first-order logic, it is typically not used in the context of probabilistic logic because typical probabilistic logic applications do not require existential quantifiers. In addition, the standard way of dealing with an existential quantifier in probabilistic logic is by replacing it with a disjunction over all constants in the domain (Richardson and Domingos, 2006). In our case, Skolemization plays a role for existential quantifiers in the text T. Take for example *T: A man is driving a car*, which in logical form is

$$T : \exists x, y, z.\, man(x) \wedge agent(y, x) \wedge drive(y) \wedge patient(y, z) \wedge car(z)$$

Because of the DCA, we need to explicitly introduce constants into the domain. Skolemization solves this problem. Non-embedded existentially quantified variables like in the example above are replaced with Skolem constants

$$T : man(M) \wedge agent(D, M) \wedge drive(D) \wedge patient(D, C) \wedge car(C)$$

where M, D, C are constants introduced into the domain. Standard Skolemization would replace an embedded existentially quantified variable y with a Skolem function depending on all universally quantified variables x under which y is embedded. For example, here is the logical form of *T: All birds fly*.

$$T : \forall x.\, bird(x) \Rightarrow \exists y.\, agent(y, x) \wedge fly(y)$$

It is Skolemized as follows:

$$T : \forall x.\, bird(x) \Rightarrow agent(f(x), x) \wedge fly(f(x))$$

By condition (c) of the DCA, if we used a Skolem function, it would need to map its argument to a constant. In particular, it would need to map each argument to a new constant to state that for every known bird (i.e., for any constant that is a bird) there is a separate flying event. To achieve this, we introduce a new predicate $skolem_f$ that we use instead of the Skolem function f, and for every constant that is a bird, we add an extra constant that is a flying event. The example above then becomes

$$T : \forall x.\, bird(x) \Rightarrow \forall y.\, skolem_f(x, y) \Rightarrow agent(y, x) \wedge fly(y)$$

Assume that we have evidence of a single bird B_1. Then we introduce a new constant C_1 and an atom $skolem_f(B_1, C_1)$ to simulate that the Skolem function f maps the constant B_1 to the constant C_1.

3.2 Existence

Suppose we have a sentence *T: All birds with wings fly*. Its representation will yield an empty graphical model because there are no constants in the system. However, pragmatically this sentence presupposes that there are, in fact, birds with wings (Strawson, 1950; Geurts, 2007). By default, probabilistic logic and standard first-order logic do not capture this existential presupposition. We add it here to avoid the problem of empty graphical models. In a simplification of the account of Geurts (2007), we assume that the domain of almost all quantifiers is presupposed to be nonempty.

"Existence" deals with universal quantifiers in the text T. Each universal quantifier $all(restrictor,$ $body)$ has a body and restrictor. From the parse tree of a sentence, bodies and restrictors of each quantifier can be identified. We add an existence rule for the entities in the restrictor of each universal quantifier. For example, *T: All birds with wings fly*,

$$T : \forall x, y.\, bird(x) \wedge with(x, y) \wedge wing(y) \Rightarrow \exists z.\, agent(z, x) \wedge fly(z)$$

is changed to *T: All birds with wings fly, and there is a bird with wings.*

$$T : (\ \forall x, y.\, bird(x) \wedge with(x, y) \wedge wing(y) \Rightarrow \exists z.\, agent(z, x) \wedge fly(z)\ )$$
$$\wedge\ (\ \exists u, v.\, bird(u) \wedge with(u, v) \wedge wing(v)\ )$$

Then we leave it to the Skolemization to generate constants and evidence representing the *bird with wings*, $bird(B) \wedge with(B, W) \wedge wing(W)$.

Here is another example, for a universal quantifier that comes from a negated existential, *T: No bird flies*, which in logic is:

$$T : \neg\exists x, y.\, bird(x) \wedge agent(y, x) \wedge fly(y)$$

or equivalently (by rewriting it as restrictor and body)

$$T : \forall x, y.\, bird(x) \Rightarrow \neg(fly(y) \wedge agent(y, x))$$

The Existence assumption is applied to the restrictor *bird*, so it modifies this sentence to *T: No bird flies, and there is a bird.*

$$T : (\ \neg\exists x, y.\, bird(x) \wedge agent(y, x) \wedge fly(y)\ ) \wedge (\ \exists v.\, bird(v)\ )$$

Again, Skolemization generates the constants and evidence $bird(B)$.

One special case that we need to take into consideration is sentences like *T: There are no birds*, which in logic is

$$T : \neg\exists x.\, bird(x)$$

Although $bird(x)$ has a universally quantified variable, we do not generate an existence rule for it. In this case the nonemptiness of the domain is not assumed because the sentence explicitly negates it.

3.3 Universal quantifiers in the hypothesis

Under the DCA, it is possible to conclude from *T: Tweety is a bird that flies* that *H: all birds fly*, as discussed above, because H is true for all constants *in the domain*. While we used Skolemization and Existence to handle issues in the representation of T, this problem affects universally quantified variables in H. Similar to what we do for universal quantifiers in T, we introduce new constants to handle universal quantifiers in H, but for a different rationale.

Consider T_1: *There is a black bird*, T_2: *All birds are black*, and *H: All birds are black.* These sentences are represented as

$$T_1 : \exists x.\, bird(x) \wedge black(x)$$
$$Skolemized\, T_1 : bird(B) \wedge black(B)$$

$$T_2 : \forall x.\, bird(x) \Rightarrow black(x)$$
$$Skolemized\, T_2 : \forall x.\, bird(x) \Rightarrow black(x)$$

$$H : \forall x.\, bird(x) \Rightarrow black(x)$$

We want H to be judged true only if there is evidence that all birds will be black, no matter how many birds there are in the domain, as is the case in T_2 but not T_1. So we introduce a new constant D and assert $bird(D)$ to test if it follows that $black(D)$. The new evidence $bird(D)$ prevents the hypothesis from being judged true given T_1. Given T_2, the new bird D will be inferred to be black, in which case we take the hypothesis to be true.[1]

As with Existence, the same special case need to be taken into consideration. For sentences like *H: There are no birds*, which in logic is

$$H : \neg\exists x.\, bird(x)$$

we do not generate any hard evidence for $bird(x)$.

3.4 Negative hypotheses and the closed-world assumption

As discussed above, practical probabilistic logic systems typically operate on ground formulas, and the grounding step can require significant amounts of memory. Making the closed-world assumption (CWA) mitigates this effect (Beltagy and Mooney, 2014). In a probabilistic logic system, the CWA takes the form of a statement that everything has a very low prior probability. The problem here is that a negated hypothesis H could come true just because of the CWA, not because the negation is explicitly stated in T. Here is an example that demonstrates the problem, *H: There is no young girl dancing*:

$$H : \forall x, y.\, young(x) \wedge girl(x) \Rightarrow \neg(agent(y,x) \wedge dance(y))$$

As in section 3.3, we generate from H evidence of a young girl $young(G) \wedge girl(G)$ because it is in the restrictor of the universal quantifier (stating that an additional *young girl* exists in the world in general, not in this particular situation). For H to be true, inference needs to find out that G is not dancing. We need H to be true only if T is explicitly negating the existence of a young girl that dances, but because of the CWA, H could become true even if T is uninformative.

To make sure that H becomes true only if it is entailed by T, we construct a new rule R which, together with the evidence generated from H, states the opposite of the negated parts of H. R is formed as a conjunction of all the predicates that were not used to generate evidence before, and are *negated* in H. This rule R gets a positive weight indicating that its ground atoms have high prior probability. This way, the prior probability of H is low, and H cannot become true unless T explicitly negates R. Here is a Neutral RTE example adapted from the SICK dataset, *T: A young girl is standing on one leg*, and *H: There is no young girl dancing*. Their representations are

T: $\exists x, y, z.\, young(x) \wedge girl(x) \wedge agent(y,x) \wedge stand(y) \wedge on(y,z) \wedge one(z) \wedge leg(z)$
H: $\forall x, y.\, young(x) \wedge girl(x) \Rightarrow \neg(agent(y,x) \wedge dance(y))$
E: $young(G) \wedge girl(G)$
R: $agent(D,G) \wedge dance(D) | w = 1.5$

[1]Note that this strategy can fail, for example given *T: There is a black bird, and if there are exactly two birds, then all birds are black.* If we were to handle quantifiers like *exactly two*, which we are not doing yet, we would mistakenly conclude that all birds are black. However, we expect that sentences like this will be extremely rare in naturally occurring text.

E is the evidence generated for the restrictor of the universal quantifier in H, and R is the weighted rule for the remaining negated predicates. The relation between T and H is Neutral, as T does not entail H. This means, we want $P(H|T, E) = 0$, but because of the CWA, $P(H|T, E) \approx 1$. Adding R solves this problem and $P(H|T, E, R) \approx 0$ because H is not explicitly entailed by T.

In case H contains existentially quantified variables that occur in negated predicates, they need to be universally quantified in R for H to be false by default. For example, *H: There is some bird that is not black*:

$$H : \exists x.\, bird(x) \wedge \neg black(x)$$
$$R : \forall x.\, black(x) | w = 1.5$$

Without R, the prior probability of H is $P(H) \approx 1$ because by default any bird is not black. However, with R, $P(H|R) \approx 0$. If one variable is universally quantified and the other is existentially quantified, we need to do something more complex. Here is an example, *H: The young girl is not dancing*:

$$H : \exists x.\, young(x) \wedge girl(x) \wedge \neg(\ \exists y.\, agent(y, x) \wedge dance(y)\ )$$
$$R : \forall v.\, agent(D, v) \wedge dance(D) | w = 1.5$$

If H is a negated formula that is entailed by T, then T (which has infinite weight) will contradict R, allowing H to be true. Any weighted inference rules in KB will need weights high enough to overcome R. So the weight of R is taken into account when computing inference rule weights.

4 Evaluation

We evaluate on three RTE datasets. The first is a synthetic dataset that exhaustively tests inference performance on sentences with two quantifiers. The second is the RTE part of the SICK dataset (Marelli et al., 2014). The third is FraCas (Cooper et al., 1996).

4.1 Synthetic dataset

We automatically generate an RTE dataset that exhaustively test inferences on sentences with two quantifiers. Each RTE pair (T, H) is generated following this format:

$$T : Q_{t1}(L_{t1}, Q_{t2}(L_{t2}, R_{t2}))$$
$$H : Q_{h1}(L_{h1}, Q_{h2}(L_{h2}, R_{h2}))$$

where

- $Q_x \in$ {some, all, no, not all}
- $L_{t1}, L_{h1} \in$ {man, hungry man} and $L_{t1} \neq L_{h1}$
- $L_{t2}, L_{h2} \in$ {food, delicious food} and $L_{t2} \neq L_{h2}$
- $R_{t2}, R_{h2} =$ eat

Informally, the dataset has all possible combinations of sentences with two quantifiers. Also it has all possible combinations of monotonicity directions – upward and downward – between L_{t1} and L_{h1} and between L_{t2} and L_{h2}. The dataset size is 1,024 RTE pairs. Here is an example of a generated RTE pair:

T: No man eats all food

H: Some hungry men eat not all delicious food

The dataset is automatically annotated for entailment decisions by normalizing the logical forms of the sentences and then using standard monotonicy rules on the bodies and restrictors of the quantifiers. 72 pairs out of the 1,024 are entailing pairs, and the rest are non-entailing.

Our system computes $P(H|T)$. The resulting probability between 0 and 1 needs to be mapped to an Entail/Non-entail decision. In this dataset, and because we do not have weighted inference rules, all output probabilities close to 1 denote Entail and probabilities close to 0 denote Non-entail.

	Synthetic dataset			SICK dataset	FraCas dataset	
System	Accuracy	FP	FN	Accuracy	Gold parses	System parses
Baseline(most common class)	92.96%	0	72	56.36%	47.82%	47.82%
Skolem	50.78%	472	32	68.10%	50.00%	43.48%
Skolem + Existence	57.03%	440	0	68.10%	43.48%	36.96%
Skolem + ($\forall$ in H)	82.42%	140	40	68.14%	63.04%	50.00%
Skolem + ($\forall$ in H) + CWA	96.09%	0	40	76.48%	100.0%	84.78%
Full system	**100%**	0	0	**76.52%**	**100.0%**	84.78%

Table 1: Results of all datasets on different configurations of the system. The most common class baseline is Non-entail for the synthetic dataset, Neutral for SICK and Entail for FraCas. False positives (FP) and False negatives (FN) statistic are reported only for the synthetic dataset because it is a binary classification task. FP/FN results are counts out of 1,024.

Results The leftmost part of Table 1 summarizes the results on the synthetic dataset in terms of accuracy. The baseline always judges non-entailment. Ablation tests are as follows. *Skolem* is a system that applies Skolemization to existentially quantified variables in the Text T (Sec. 3.1) but none of the other adaptations of Section 3. *Existence* is a system that makes the existence assumption for universal quantifiers in T (Sec. 3.2). *($\forall$ in H)* is constant introduction for universal quantifiers in the Hypothesis (Sec. 3.3). Finally, *CWA* is a system that handles negation in the Hypothesis H in a way that takes the closed-world assumption into account (Sec. 3.4). The results in Table 1 show the importance of each part of the proposed system. Skolemization and the Existence assumption eliminate some false negatives from missing constants. All false positives are eliminated when constants are introduced for universal quantifiers in the Hypothesis ($\forall$ in H) and when the effects of the closed-world assumption are counteracted (*CWA*). The full system achieves 100% accuracy, showing that our formulation is perfectly handling the DCA and CWA on these complex quantified sentences.

Note that a pure logic system such as Boxer (Bos, 2008) can also achieve 100% on this dataset. But again, the aim of this paper is not to argue that probabilistic logic is preferable to standard first order logic. This can only be done by showing that weighted, uncertain knowledge leads to better inferences. Rather, this paper constitutes a necessary prerequisite, in that it is necessary first to determine how to achieve the correct (hard) inferences with probabilistic logic before we measure the effect of weighting.

4.2 The SICK dataset

Sentences Involving Compositional Knowledge (SICK, Marelli et al. (2014)) is an RTE dataset collected for the SemEval 2014 competition. It consists of 5,000 T/H pairs for training and 5,000 for testing. Pairs are annotated for both RTE and STS (sentence similarity). For the purpose of this paper, we only use the RTE annotation.

Pairs in SICK (as well as FraCas in the next section) are classified into three classes, Entailment, Contradiction, and Neutral. This means that computing the probability $P(H|T)$ alone is not enough for this threeway classification. We additionally compute $P(\neg T|H)$. Entailing pairs have $P(H|T) \approx 1$, $P(\neg T|H) \approx 0$, Contradicting pairs have $P(H|T) \approx 0$, $P(\neg T|H) \approx 1$, and Neutral pairs have $P(H|T) \approx P(\neg T|H)$. We use these two conditional probabilities as input features to an SVM classifier trained on the training set to mapped them to an Entail/Neutral/Contradict decision.

Results The middle panel of Table 1 reports results on the SICK dataset, again in terms of accuracy. Almost all sentences in the SICK dataset are simple existentially quantified sentences except for a few sentences with an outer negation. Accordingly, the system with Skolemization basically achieves the same accuracy as when Existence and ($\forall$ in H) are added. Handling negation in H effectively improves the accuracy of our system by reducing the number of false positives resulting from the CWA.

4.3 The FraCas dataset

FraCas (Cooper et al., 1996)[2] is a dataset of hand-built entailments pairs. The dataset consists of 9 sections, each of which is testing a different set of phenomena. For this paper, we use sentences from the first section, which tests quantification and monotonicity. However, we exclude pairs containing the determiners "few", "most", "many" and "at least" because our system does not currently have a representation for them. We evaluate on 46 pairs out of 74.[3][4] Because of that, we cannot compare with previous systems that evaluate on the whole section (MacCartney and Manning, 2008; Lewis and Steedman, 2013).

To map sentences to logical form, we use Boxer as discussed in section 2.4. By default, Boxer relies on C&C (Curran et al., 2009) to get the CCG parses of the sentences. Instead, we run Boxer on CCG parses produced by EasyCCG (Lewis and Steedman, 2014) because it is more accurate on FraCas. Like Lewis and Steedman (2013) we additionally test on gold-standard parses to be able to evaluate our technique of handling quantifiers in the absence of parser errors. Also, as we do with the SICK dataset, we add the inference $P(\neg T|H)$ for the detection of contradictions.

For multi-sentence examples, we add a simple co-reference resolution step that connects definite NPs across sentences. For example, *the right to live in Europe* in T1 and T3 should corefer in the following example:

T1: Every European has the right to live in Europe
T2: Every European is a person
T3: Every person who has the right to live in Europe can travel freely within Europe

We also added two rules encoding lexical knowledge, paraphrased as "a lot of $x \Rightarrow x$" and "one of $x \Rightarrow x$" to handle one of the examples, as lexical coverage is not the focus of our analysis.

Results The rightmost panel in Table 1 summarizes the results of our system for gold parses and system parses. We see that the Existence assumption is not needed in this dataset because it is constructed to test semantics and not presupposition. Results with Existence are lower because without Existence, three cases (the previous example is one of them) are correctly classified as Entail, but with Existence they are classified as Neutral. Without Existence the domain is empty, and $P(\neg T|H) = 0$ because $\neg T$, which is existentially quantified, is trivially false. With Existence added, $P(\neg T|H) = 1$ because the domain is not empty, and the CWA is not handled. Also we see that, as in the two previous experiments, adding the approach that handles the CWA has the biggest impact. With all components of the system added, and with gold parses, we get 100% accuracy. With system parses, all results are lower, but the relative scores for the different subsystems are comparable to the gold parse case.

5 Future Work

One important extension to this work is to support generalized quantifiers in probabilistic logic. Some determiners, such as "few" and "most", cannot be represented in standard first-order logic. But it could be possible to represent them using the probabilistic aspect of probabilistic logic. With support for generalized quantifiers, we would be able to evaluate on the pairs we skipped from the FraCas dataset (Cooper et al., 1996). Another important next step is to refine the closed world assumption such that it assumes fewer things to be false. In particular we want to use (hard or soft) typing to distinguish between impossible propositions on the one hand and possible but unsupported ones on the other hand.

[2]We use the version by MacCartney and Manning (2007)

[3]The first section consists of 80 pairs, but like MacCartney and Manning (2007) we ignore the pairs with an undefined result.

[4]The gold standard annotation for pair number 69 should be Neutral not Entail. We changed it accordingly.

6 Conclusion

In this paper we showed how to do textual entailment in probabilistic logic while taking into account the problems resulting from the domain closure assumption (DCA) and the closed-world assumption (CWA). This paper is not concerned with *why* one should use probabilistic logic for natural language semantics (we argue for the need for probabilistic logic in previous work (Beltagy et al., 2013)), it only addresses the *how*. Our formulation involves Skolemization of the text T, generating evidence for universally quantified variables in T to simulate the existential presupposition, generating evidence to test universal quantifiers in H, and preventing negated H from being judged true independently of T because of the CWA. We evaluate our formulation on a synthetic dataset that has complex forms of quantifications and on the relevant part of the FraCas dataset and get a 100% accuracy on both. We also evaluate on the SICK dataset and show improved performance.

Acknowledgments

This research was supported by the DARPA DEFT program under AFRL grant FA8750-13-2-0026 and by the NSF CAREER grant IIS 0845925. Any opinions, findings, and conclusions or recommendations expressed in this material are those of the author and do not necessarily reflect the view of DARPA, DoD or the US government. Some experiments were run on the Mastodon Cluster supported by NSF Grant EIA-0303609. We are grateful to Raymond Mooney, as well as the anonymous reviewers, for helpful discussions.

References

Agirre, E., D. Cer, M. Diab, and A. Gonzalez-Agirre (2012). SemEval-2012 task 6: A pilot on semantic textual similarity. In *Proceedings of the 6th International Workshop on Semantic Evaluation (SemEval-2012)*.

Beltagy, I., C. Chau, G. Boleda, D. Garrette, K. Erk, and R. Mooney (2013). Montague meets Markov: Deep semantics with probabilistic logical form. In *Proceedings of the Second Joint Conference on Lexical and Computational Semantics (*SEM-2013)*.

Beltagy, I. and R. J. Mooney (2014). Efficient Markov logic inference for natural language semantics. In *Proceedings of AAAI 2014 Workshop on Statistical Relational AI (StarAI-2014)*.

Berant, J., A. Chou, R. Frostig, and P. Liang (2013). Semantic parsing on Freebase from question-answer pairs. In *Proceedings of Conference on Empirical Methods in Natural Language Processing (EMNLP-2013)*.

Bos, J. (2008). Wide-coverage semantic analysis with Boxer. In *Proceedings of Semantics in Text Processing (STEP-2008)*.

Bos, J. (2013). Is there a place for logic in recognizing textual entailment? *Linguistic Issues in Language Technology 9*.

Choi, Y. and C. Cardie (2008). Learning with compositional semantics as structural inference for subsentential sentiment analysis. In *Proceedings of the Conference on Empirical Methods in Natural Language Processing (EMNLP-2008)*.

Cooper, R., D. Crouch, J. Van Eijck, C. Fox, J. Van Genabith, J. Jaspars, H. Kamp, D. Milward, M. Pinkal, M. Poesio, et al. (1996). Using the framework. Technical report, Technical Report LRE 62-051 D-16, The FraCaS Consortium.

Copestake, A. and D. Flickinger (2000). An open-source grammar development environment and broad-coverage english grammar using HPSG. In *Proceedings of the International Conference on Language Resources and Evaluation (LREC-2000)*.

Curran, J., S. Clark, and J. Bos (2009). Linguistically motivated large-scale nlp with c&c and boxer. In *Proceedings of the 45th Annual Meeting of the Association for Computational Linguistics Companion Volume Proceedings of the Demo and Poster Sessions*.

Dagan, I., D. Roth, M. Sammons, and F. M. Zanzotto (2013). Recognizing textual entailment: Models and applications. *Synthesis Lectures on Human Language Technologies 6*(4), 1–220.

Ganitkevitch, J., B. Van Durme, and C. Callison-Burch (2013). PPDB: The paraphrase database. In *Proceedings of the Conference of the North American Chapter of the Association for Computational Linguistics: Human Language Technologies(NAACL-HLT-2013)*, pp. 758–764.

Garrette, D., K. Erk, and R. Mooney (2011). Integrating logical representations with probabilistic information using Markov logic. In *Proceedings of International Conference on Computational Semantics (IWCS-2011)*.

Genesereth, M. R. and N. J. Nilsson (1987). *Logical foundations of artificial intelligence*. San Mateo, CA: Morgan Kaufman.

Getoor, L. and B. Taskar (2007). *Introduction to Statistical Relational Learning*. Cambridge, MA: MIT Press.

Geurts, B. (2007). Existential import. In I. Comorovski and K. van Heusinger (Eds.), *Existence: syntax and semantics*, pp. 253–271. Dordrecht: Springer.

Kok, S., P. Singla, M. Richardson, and P. Domingos (2005). The Alchemy system for statistical relational AI. `http://www.cs.washington.edu/ai/alchemy`.

Kwiatkowski, T., E. Choi, Y. Artzi, and L. Zettlemoyer (2013). Scaling semantic parsers with on-the-fly ontology matching. In *Proceedings of Conference on Empirical Methods in Natural Language Processing (EMNLP-2013)*.

Lewis, M. and M. Steedman (2013). Combined distributional and logical semantics. *Transactions of the Association for Computational Linguistics (TACL-2013) 1*, 179–192.

Lewis, M. and M. Steedman (2014). A* ccg parsing with a supertag-factored model. In *Proceedings of the Conference on Empirical Methods in Natural Language Processing (EMNLP-2014)*.

Lin, D. and P. Pantel (2001). DIRT - discovery of inference rules from text. In *In Proceedings of the ACM SIGKDD Conference on Knowledge Discovery and Data Mining*.

Lotan, A., A. Stern, and I. Dagan (2013). Truthteller: Annotating predicate truth. In *Proceedings of the Conference of the North American Chapter of the Association for Computational Linguistics: Human Language Technologies(NAACL-HLT-2013)*.

MacCartney, B. and C. D. Manning (2007). Natural logic for textual inference. In *Proceedings of the ACL-PASCAL Workshop on Textual Entailment and Paraphrasing*, pp. 193–200.

MacCartney, B. and C. D. Manning (2008). Modeling semantic containment and exclusion in natural language inference. In *Proceedings of the 22nd International Conference on Computational Linguistics (Coling-2008)*.

MacCartney, B. and C. D. Manning (2009). An extended model of natural logic. In *Proceedings of the International Workshop on Computational Semantics (IWCS-2009)*.

Marelli, M., S. Menini, M. Baroni, L. Bentivogli, R. Bernardi, and R. Zamparelli (2014, may). A SICK cure for the evaluation of compositional distributional semantic models. In *Proceedings of the Ninth International Conference on Language Resources and Evaluation (LREC-2014)*.

Montague, R. (1973). The proper treatment of quantification in ordinary English. In K. Hintikka, J. Moravcsik, and P. Suppes (Eds.), *Approaches to Natural Language*, pp. 221–242. Dordrecht: Reidel.

Nilsson, N. J. (1986). Probabilistic logic. *Artificial intelligence 28*(1), 71–87.

Richardson, M. and P. Domingos (2006). Markov logic networks. *Machine Learning 62*, 107–136.

Skolem, T. (1920). Logisch-kombinatorische Untersuchungen über die Erfüllbarkeit oder Beweisbarkeit mathematischer Sätze. *Skrifter utgit av Videnskapselskapet i Kristiania 4*, 4–36.

Strawson, P. F. (1950). On referring. *Mind 59*, 320–344.

Mr Darcy and Mr Toad, gentlemen: distributional names and their kinds

Aurélie Herbelot
University of Cambridge
aurelie.herbelot@cantab.net

Abstract

This paper investigates the representation of proper names in distributional semantics. We define three properties we expect names to display: uniqueness (being a unique entity), instantiation (being an instance of a relevant kind) and individuality (being separable from the subspace of concepts). We show that taking a standard distribution as the representation of a name does not satisfy those properties particularly well. We propose an alternative method to compute a name vector, which relies on re-weighting the distribution of the appropriate named entity type – in effect, producing an individual out of a kind. We illustrate the behaviour of such representations over some characters from two English novels.

1 Introduction

Distributional semantics (DS) rests on the idea that the meaning of words is given by their linguistic context (Harris, 1954). While DS has been very successful in modelling a range of phenomena – in particular those linked to similarity – the scope of the theory remains unclear. Some have called it a semantics of the lexicon, i.e. not a fully formed theory of meaning but an aspect of lexical knowledge, with influence over other parts of semantics (Baroni et al., 2014; Erk, 2014). This view is supported by the fact that by nature, distributional information is an aggregate of all contexts in which a word appears, and therefore some kind of average representation tending towards generic, conceptual meaning. In turn, it has been suggested that, as conceptual representations, they might be linked to a traditional notion of intension (Erk, 2013).

While a lot of work in DS has focused on noun phrases, one particular type has been mostly neglected: those phrases classically referred to as **proper names** in philosophy of language. Mill (1843) defines a proper name as 'a word that answers the purpose of showing what thing it is that we are talking about but not of telling anything about it'. Under that category fall proper nouns (*Alice, Carroll*), noun phrases containing proper nouns (*Lewis Carroll*) and even noun phrases denoting unique objects but consisting solely of (in English, usually capitalised) common nouns (*the Tower Bridge*).

Proper names are an interesting test-bed for distributional semantics for several reasons. First, although they are fully part of the lexicon, they refer to uniquely referenced objects: to our knowledge, this type of linguistic entity has never been studied in DS. Second, their semantics is contested and some have claimed that they do not, in fact, have intension and are purely extensional – while others support various types of intensional notions, ranging from minimalist accounts where e.g. *Smith* means 'the individual named Smith' to complex clusters of definite descriptions. Thirdly, they are good examples of lexical items which, often, are previously unknown to the hearer (i.e. we may have no preconception of the meaning of *Anna Pavlovna* until we encounter the corresponding character in *War and Peace*).

This paper is an exploration of proper names in distributional settings. We introduce three properties that are expected from names: uniqueness (being a unique entity), instantiation (being an instance of a relevant kind) and individuality (being separable from the subspace of concepts). We argue that the distributional representation of individuals is badly modelled by a standard co-occurrence vector in a static corpus: not only does it fail to satisfy the above properties, but it amounts to an unrealistic view of

Proceedings of the 11th International Conference on Computational Semantics, pages 151–161,
London, UK, April 15-17 2015. ©2015 Association for Computational Linguistics

the lexicon where all items are *a priori* present. While this view is defensible with regard to a general representation of an adult's lexical knowledge, it does not hold for proper names, neologisms, etc.

In the following, we contrast 'standard' vectorial representations of names with a model based on the contextualisation of a more general distribution. For instance, we assume that upon encountering the name *Mr Darcy* for the first time in the novel *Pride and prejudice*, a reader will attribute it the representation of the concept *man* and subsequently specialise it as per the linguistic contexts in which the name appears. We show that this approach performs better in modelling the expected properties.

The resulting model can be described in terms of kinds and individuals. Distributions obtained in the standard way from large corpora represent generic, conceptual information about a kind. The contextualisation process produces an individual from the relevant kind. Although the focus of this paper is on names, it will be clear that the proposed method is applicable to common nouns, so that the individual referred to as *my cat* can be generated from the concept *cat* across relevant contexts in a discourse. To finish, we tentatively show that the created individuals can be added up to form pluralities which stand between concepts and their instances in the semantic space.

2 Related work

2.1 Proper names

There is an extensive philosophical literature on proper names, which we will not attempt to summarise here (see Cumming, 2013 for an overview). We will instead focus on the particular approach which we can best relate to distributional theories.

Mill (1843) started the debate on the semantics of proper names with a purely extensional view, stating that the meaning of a name is its referent in a world – and only its referent. This view came under attack from proponents of both sense theories and so-called 'descriptivism'. The sense theory (Frege, 1892) relies on a notion of 'sense' or 'intension' to describe the cognitive content of a name. This notion allows us to explain the semantic difference between *Evening Star* and *Morning Star*, while acknowledging that their referents in the real world are one same object, the planet Venus. Similarly, descriptivists took the stance that a name has the semantics of a definite description which, by proxy, provides its meaning (be it through its intension or any other device). For instance, the meaning of *Aristotle* might be equated with the meaning of *the teacher of Alexander the Great* (Russell, 1911).

When trying to relate a distributional description of proper names to standard philosophical theories, the most natural correspondence is probably 'cluster' descriptivism (Searle, 1958), which states that the semantics of a name is a complex definite expression potentially including several predicates, i.e. the semantics of *Aristotle* might be that of *the teacher of Alexander the Great and most famous pupil of Plato*. Distributionally, we might say that the meaning of *Aristotle* is a distribution where contexts are complex predications and the predicates *teacher of Alexander* and *pupil of Plato* are highly weighted. Note that the distribution does not, at first glance, encapsulate the definiteness which makes the individual unique. In §3.2, we will discuss how to assess the uniqueness and individuality of a name.

2.2 Distributional meaning in context

Various distributional methods have been proposed to compute the meaning of a word in context (this work is summarised in Dinu et al., 2012). Proposals can be classified in two groups: those which consist, roughly, in 'reweighting' a target vector using its close syntactic context (e.g. Erk and Padó, 2008; Thater et al., 2011), and those which build the contextualised vector by selecting corpus occurrences of the target word that are 'similar' to the context under consideration (e.g. Rapp, 2004).

Contextualisation methods have been mainly studied from the point of view of disambiguation and selectional preference, showing they could solve a range of lexical problems. We build on this work by applying the technique further in order to separate, not various senses of a word, but various instances of a concept (§5).

3 Building distributional names: corpora and experimental design

3.1 Corpora

In this work, we use three different corpora:

- the British National Corpus (BNC), a balanced corpus of British English totalling 100M words, which we use for the purpose of obtaining a 'general' semantic space for English. This gives us distributional representations for the most frequent words in the language.
- *Pride and prejudice* by Jane Austen (1813), a novel of around 13,000 tokens (henceforth *P&P*).
- *The wind in the willows* by Kenneth Grahame (1908), a children's novel of around 6000 tokens (henceforth *WitW*).

We will be analysing the behaviour of a range of names occurring in the above novels. One natural question that arises is whether their distributions should be computed from the relevant novel only, or from its concatenation with the BNC. Insofar as a novel creates a different world from the real one – potentially creating or altering word meanings – it seems more reasonable to create a semantic space for the book in isolation. This has however the disadvantage of extracting vectors from very sparse data: the counts obtained for the names' contexts may not reflect their general distributions.

Following preliminary experimentation, we decided to create semantic spaces for each book separately. Indeed, extracting name distributions from the concatenated corpora resulted in vectors heavily biased towards book-specific contexts (with e.g. Mr Darcy showing high weights against other *P&P* names and rarer words like *parsonage* or *to-morrow*). In §5, we will show how to make use of the lexical information in the BNC as a complement to the novel-specific distributions.

We build a distributional space for each corpus, using the DISSECT toolkit (Dinu et al., 2012). We select Positive Pointwise Mutual Information (PPMI) as weighting measure and word windows of size 10 as context. We apply sum normalisation to the vectors. We tune the size of each space by evaluating it against a standard similarity task: we take the MEN dataset[1] (Bruni et al., 2012), which consists of word pairs annotated with human similarity judgements, and calculate the Spearman (ρ) correlation between the cosine distances for those pairs in the semantic space and the human annotations. When a pair contains a word that does not occur in the corpus, it is discarded.

For the BNC, we tune both the number of dimensions and vocabulary size in the range 1000-10000. We obtain a correlation of 0.689 for the BNC with 4000 dimensions and a vocabulary consisting of the 5000 most frequent words in the corpus. This is in line with state-of-the-art results for the MEN dataset. We note, however, that this space does not contain the words *toad, badger* and *mole*, which are crucial to our analysis. We add them to our best space, with no significant reduction to the correlation ($\rho = 0.688$).

For the novels, we tune the number of dimensions over a range from 500 to 5500 and the vocabulary size from 500 to 2000. *P&P* gets its highest correlations with 500 dimensions and a vocabulary made of the 1000 most frequent words in the corpus. At $\rho = 0.376$, the correlation is much lower than that obtained on the BNC, but this is expected given the size of the corpus. *WitW* performs best with 1500 dimensions and a smaller vocabulary of the top 500 items in the novel ($\rho = 0.358$).

3.2 Design

For clarity reasons, we adopt a somewhat arbitrary terminology in the following, where we use the word 'concept' to refer solely to the (distributionally modelled) intensions of *non*-proper names (e.g. *aardvark, blue, think*) (see Erk, 2013; McNally, 2014 for accounts of distributions as concepts). Further, we will also abide by the idea that concept vectors express some sort of 'generic' information. It is worth considering why this is a reasonable assumption for common nouns. We recall that a noun's distribution is a statistical representation of its usages, which normally gives more weight to contexts

[1] http://clic.cimec.unitn.it/ elia.bruni/MEN.

that are characteristic for it. It is calculated over a large number of tokens which themselves partake in references to a) individuals (*my dog*), b) pluralities (*the neighbour's dogs*) and c) kinds (*the dog is a mammal*). There is perhaps little intuition as to how those referent types contribute to the distribution. We attempted to gain some understanding of this by consulting previous work on the annotation of generic noun phrases. Herbelot and Copestake (2011) produced a small dataset[2] consisting of 300 randomly selected noun phrases, annotated (amongst other things) with kinds.[3] From this data, we extrapolate that around 10% of noun phrases in text refer to kinds, with the overwhelming majority denoting individuals or (existential) plurals. This indicates that in the distribution of a common noun, a context with high weight is one which is characteristic of individuals or groups, rather than of the concept itself.

We can then say that a distribution is a representation of the type of things *generally* said of the *instances* of a particular concept. In other words, the distribution is generic (a kind) not by virtue of collecting contexts associated with kind references but by virtue of generating a model of the concept's 'supremum', i.e. of all its instances, as given by a closed corpus (for an account of kinds as supremums, see e.g. Chierchia, 1998). In what follows, we will assume that 'kind' and 'concept' can be used interchangeably (McNally, 2014 follows a similar argument).

Having clarified our notion of concept, we can turn to individuals. In an ideal semantic space, name distributions would have the following properties:

1. **Uniqueness:** the intension of a proper name should let us capture its unique extension in a given world. This implies that intensions themselves should be separable within the distributional space. In other words, two Smiths referring to separate individuals should also have separate intensions, i.e. occupy different points in the semantic space.

2. **Instantiation:** names should stand in a learnable relationship to the concept they are instantiating. For instance, Mr Darcy should clearly be an instance of *man, person*, etc.

3. **Individuality:** proper names should be distinguishable from concepts. This is related to the uniqueness property but not identical to it. Let's for instance assume a world with exactly one dodo named Dolly. If the intension of *Dolly* were the same as the intension of *dodo*, this would make Dolly unique (because there is only one dodo in that world) but wouldn't stress her individuality, i.e. that she is *a* dodo and not the kind *dodo*.

Assuming that different individuals do not occur exactly in the same contexts in corpora, the **uniqueness** property is satisfied by selecting only those occurrences of a name which refer to the same entity.[4] In other words, the 'relevant' contexts for building a name distribution are the ones surrounding mentions in a co-reference chain. We note that this context selection is similar to the method used by e.g. Rapp (2004) for dealing with polysemy. In the following, for simplicity reasons and to avoid noise, we do not run co-reference resolution over our corpora. Rather, we only consider unambiguous proper names and build a distribution over their occurrences (this is in keeping with the standard way to build distributions, where e.g. pronominal anaphors are ignored).

Instantiation is testable by borrowing distributional measures which have been shown to perform well in the task of hyponymy detection. That is, given a distributional name, we can attempt to extract the concept(s) it most likely instantiates by assuming they partake in the same kind of relation as nouns to their hypernyms. In our experiments, we use the invCL measure (Lenci and Benotto, 2012), which takes into account how much a hyponym occurs in a subset of the contexts in which its hypernym appears, and how much the hypernym occurs in a superset of the contexts associated with the hyponym. For each name, we calculate its invCL score with respect to its 50 nearest neighbours (specifically, the 50

[2]Available at `http://www.cl.cam.ac.uk/~ah433/underquantification.kind.annot`.

[3]In the related paper, a kind is defined as a noun phrase which can be paraphrased in context as either a bare plural or a singular: *(A/The) Scottish fiddler(s) emulating 18th century playing styles sometimes use a replica of this type of bow.*

[4]We can imagine the extreme case of two Smiths described in exactly the same contexts but referring to two different individuals. But we would argue that, given the linguistic contexts only, a human would not be able to capture their extensional difference.

common nouns which are closest to it in the semantic space). We output the highest scores as potentially instantiated concepts and manually verify the results.

The **individuality** property is not trivial to capture. One clear-cut test, from the generics literature, would be to inspect how a name's distribution interacts with those predicates which are only applicable to kinds (*extinct, widespread, common* – see Carlson and Pelletier, 1995). We would expect that the composition of an individual with, say, *widespread* would result in a semantically anomalous sentence: **Mr Toad is widespread.* Unfortunately, there are very few such 'kind predicates', making them inadequate for a quantitative study. More promisingly perhaps, some predicates – typically those with so-called 'positive alternatives' – are known to be unsuitable for kinds but appropriate for individuals: **Badgers are male/Mr Badger is male* (the generic sentence is blocked by the positive alternative **Badgers are female*, see Leslie, 2008). Testing the felicity of generic statements, however, is non-trivial as it is dependent on many factors, from human inter-annotator agreement to the distributional composition function used to combine the subject and predicate. So instead, we propose in what follows a related but straightforward test.

We note that, while the most characteristic contexts of a kind can be extensionally exclusive, those of an individual (at least the static predicates) should be less so. For instance, both *rich* and *poor* may appear in the top contexts of *man* (making the corresponding **Men are rich/poor* infelicitous), but we would only expect one or the other at the top of an individual's distribution. More generally, we suggest that the characteristic contexts of an individual will be significantly more coherent than those of a kind. That is, the linguistic items strongly associated with an individual should be on the whole related to each other because that individual cannot embody the range of experiences covered by many members of a group. To test individuality, we thus propose to calculate the coherence of the top 50 characteristic contexts for each name distribution and compare it to the coherence of the kind(s) it instantiates. As in Newman et al. (2010), we define the coherence of a set of words $w_1...w_n$ as the mean of their pairwise similarities (where similarity is the cosine distance between two vectors):

$$Coherence(w_{1...n}) = mean\{Sim(w_i, w_j), ij \in 1...n, i < j\}$$

We illustrate our claims by closely inspecting the distributions of a small range of individuals in the two novels under study. These include some major and more minor protagonists in *Pride and prejudice* (Mr Darcy, Mr Bingley, Elizabeth and Jane Bennett, Mr Collins and Mr Denny) and the main protagonists in *The wind in the willows* (Mr Toad, Mole, Rat, Badger).

4 Individuals as they come

The obvious way to start building distributions for names is simply to regard them as any other lexical item and output their vector in the standard way. Here are the top characteristic contexts of Mr Darcy (*P&P*) and Mr Toad (*WitW*):

Darcy (Mr, acquaint, Miss, interest, eye, Pemberley, degree, stand, wholly, walk, nephew, sake, civility, surprise)

Toad (Hall, sternly, ho, paddock, smash, whack, popular, nonsense, trot, seize, disguise, cushion, terror, necessaries)

The problem with such a representation is that it is typically very sparse. *Darcy* occurs 416 times in *Pride and prejudice*, but *Denny*, for example, only occurs 11 times. In the following, we show how such representations fare against the design requirements highlighted in §3.2.

4.1 Analysis

4.1.1 Instantiation

Tables 1 and 3 report the top 5 invCL scores for various characters. Relevant concepts are shown in bold. For *P&P*, we note that Darcy and Bingley are correctly classified as gentlemen, at the top of the table,

Darcy	Elizabeth	Bingley	Jane	Collins	Denny
0.47 **gentleman**	0.47 moment	0.48 **gentleman**	0.48 feeling	0.50 daughter	0.47 news
0.47 word	0.46 subject	0.48 lady	0.47 **sister**	0.48 house	0.47 intention
0.46 manner	0.46 feeling	0.46 sister	0.46 pleasure	0.47 family	0.47 aunt
0.46 feeling	0.46 pleasure	0.46 party	0.46 aunt	0.46 **cousin**	0.45 journey
0.46 conversation	0.45 house	0.46 answer	0.46 letter	0.46 lady	0.44 home

Table 1: Top invCL scores for various characters in *Pride and prejudice* – standard distributions

Toad	Rat	Mole	Badger
0.41 **animal**	0.40 water	0.40 **animal**	0.43 time
0.38 **toad**	0.39 **animal**	0.38 time	0.43 **animal**
0.38 time	0.39 time	0.37 thing	0.40 thing
0.37 way	0.37 thing	0.36 way	0.39 friend
0.36 thing	0.36 way	0.35 water	0.38 toad

Table 2: Top invCL scores for various characters in *Wind in the willows* – standard distributions

and that other characters have a relevant hypernym amongst the highest scores: Jane is a sister, Collins a cousin. However, two characters (Elizabeth and Denny) fail to return any concept relevant to their actual status. Moreover, we observe a high proportion of irrelevant gendered/family relations (Mr Collins is no daughter or lady, Mr Denny no aunt), and even non-human items in the lists. The characters of *WitW* present similar issues, although all are classified as 'animals'. Only Toad, however, returns the common noun *toad* as hypernym.

4.1.2 Individuality

We report the individual coherence of all characters under consideration, and compare them to the coherence of the concepts they (should) instantiate. In order to get good conceptual representations, we use the BNC vectors which we take to average many more instances of a kind than are available in either novel. For the same reason, BNC distributions are taken as representations of the characteristic contexts. These choices mean that in effect, we are comparing the characteristic contexts of a character, as given in the corpus where s/he appears, with the characteristic contexts of a generic man/woman/toad, etc. as given by a large, all-purpose corpus. Table 3 shows all results. Humans in *P&P* are compared with both *man/woman* and *gentleman/lady*.

We note that in general, names are a little less coherent than the concepts they instantiate, indicating that their distributions do not satisfy the individuality property very well.

	Individual coherence	Kind coherence								
		woman	lady	man	gentleman	toad	rat	mole	badger	animal
Darcy	0.22	-	-	0.24	0.25	-	-	-	-	-
Elizabeth	0.24	0.24	0.28	-	-	-	-	-	-	-
Bingley	0.23	-	-	0.24	0.25	-	-	-	-	-
Jane	0.23	0.24	0.28	-	-	-	-	-	-	-
Collins	0.22	-	-	0.24	0.25	-	-	-	-	-
Denny	0.23	-	-	0.24	0.25	-	-	-	-	-
Toad	0.21	-	-	-	-	0.24	-	-	-	0.22
Rat	0.23	-	-	-	-	-	0.24	-	-	0.22
Mole	0.22	-	-	-	-		-	0.22	-	0.22
Badger	0.21	-	-	-	-		-	-	0.23	0.22

Table 3: Coherence values for some characters and the concepts they instantiate – standard distributions

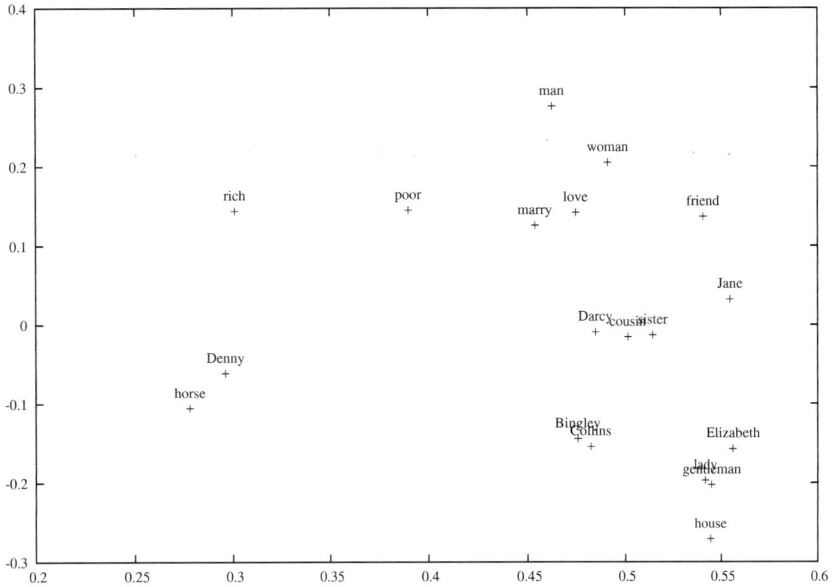

Figure 1: The *Pride and prejudice space* – standard distributions. The figure was produced by selecting relevant names and concepts from the semantic space and applying SVD dimensionality reduction to 'flatten' the space to two dimensions.

4.1.3 Discussion

Our results suggest that standard distributional representations of proper names model instantiation to some extent, but fail to show the individuality of the referents.

As a further qualitative analysis of the obtained representation, we show a 2D visualisation of the semantic space for *P&P* in Fig. 1. We observe that there is no principled separation between names and concepts: although individuals tend to roughly occupy the same portion of the space, they are situated in the midst of concepts. We can expect that learning a function that separates kinds from individuals would be extremely challenging.

5 Names as contextualised kinds

We observed in §4.1 that standard distributions do not model instantiation well. But we would expect that in virtue of being called *Badger* or *Mr Darcy*, an individual would naturally acquire the properties of the kind *badger* or the kind *man/gentleman* – without, in fact, needing any context. In this section, we try out another model of names which relies on the contextualisation of a distributional kind.

5.1 System description

We suggest that a speaker of English already has an extensive lexical knowledge when coming to *P&P* or *WitW*. That is, her interpretation of the words in the books relies on prior assumptions with regard to their meaning. For proper names, it is expected that conventions, the context surrounding the first mention and/or world knowledge will anchor them as a named entity of a certain type (*Mr Darcy* is a male person in virtue of his title, the *Tower Bridge* explicitly refers to its nature via a common noun, *London* is supposedly known to be a city and *Pemberley* is understood to be a place name in the sentence *she will always be at Pemberley with you* (*P&P*, Chap. 6)). In computational linguistics, this process is performed via named entity recognition (NER).

In this work, we assume that NER has taken place over our corpus and that the *P&P* characters have been classed as either *man* or *woman*. We also presuppose, trivially, that *Toad* has been recognised as a toad, *Rat* as a rat, etc. We propose that on encountering Mr Darcy for the first time, a reader might simply attribute him the properties of the lexical item *man*, as given by the relevant distribution in a large corpus, and then specialise the representation as per the contexts where *Darcy* occurs.

We note that in this setup, the individuality property is at odds with instantiation. In order to make Darcy a unique individual, more weight must be given to the features that distinguish him from the kind *man*. Doing so, however, may result in a vector that does not stand anymore in a principled relationship with the concept it instantiates.

We formalise a name distribution as follows. Let N be a proper name, instance of kind K. N has a 'standard' distribution $\boldsymbol{v}(N)$, as obtained in §4, with m characteristic contexts $c_1...c_m \in C$ (i.e. the m most highly weighted dimensions in the vector) . K also has a distribution $\boldsymbol{v}(K)$ which lives in a space S with dimensions $d_{1...n} \in D$, as obtained from a large background corpus (in our example, the BNC). We define $\boldsymbol{v}(K)$ in terms of S's basis vectors $\{\boldsymbol{e}_{d'}|d' \in D\}$ and a weighting function w (in our case, PPMI):

$$\boldsymbol{v}(K) = \sum_{d' \in D} w(K, d').\boldsymbol{e}_{d'} \tag{1}$$

We could contextualise $\boldsymbol{v}(K)$ with respect to each context in which the name appears. For efficiency reasons, however, we simply perform the contextualisation with respect to each of the characteristic contexts $c' \in C$ in $\boldsymbol{v}(N)$, using the following function:

$$C(K, c') = \sum_{d' \in D} cos(c', d')^p w(K, d').\boldsymbol{e}_{d'} \tag{2}$$

This is equivalent to one of the models proposed by Thater et al. (2011), but without taking into account the nature of the syntactic relation between K and c'. Further, we introduce a weight p acting on the cosine function to increase or decrease the effect of the contextualisation. The assumption is that a higher p makes the individual more 'unique' but less like its kind (see Erk and Padó, 2008 for a similar use of powers).

The name vector for N is the sum of the contextualisations with respect to all characteristic contexts in C:

$$\sum_{c' \in C} \sum_{d' \in D} cos(c', d')^p w(K, d').\boldsymbol{e}_{d'} \tag{3}$$

The following parameters can be tuned: a) the number m of characteristic contexts used for describing the name; b) the p value. We consider 10-30 characteristic contexts and p = 1-10.

5.2 Analysis

Varying p mostly affects the coherence values used to assess the degree of individuality of a name. We note a general increase in coherence with higher values of p, although it comes to a plateau at $p = 6$ and slowly decreases again. High values of m have the effect that some characters do not satisfy the instantiation property anymore.

In the following, we report our best results, i.e. the system which returns the highest individuality (coherence) figures while leaving the names in the expected instantiation relation with the relevant concepts. This is obtained using $m = 20$ and $p = 6$. We should note that a large quantitative survey would be needed to ascertain which parameter combination best models the cognitive individuation process. We leave this for further work and focus here on a illustrative evaluation of the procedure.

We first note that the instantiation property is straightforwardly satisfied by the model (see Table 4). The shape of the initial kind vector is retained throughout the contextualisation, so that names remain instances of their respective kinds. Interestingly, however, we note that the *WitW* characters also move

Darcy	Elizabeth	Bingley	Jane	Toad	Badger
0.97 **man**	0.97 **woman**	0.98 **man**	0.98 **woman**	0.97 **toad**	0.97 **badger**
0.91 girl	0.90 girl	0.91 boy	0.82 girl	0.75 sea	0.72 sight
0.91 face	0.89 eye	0.90 girl	0.82 man	0.74 desert	0.72 dog
0.91 boy	0.88 man	0.88 eye	0.81 other	0.73 rock	0.71 boy
0.90 smile	0.88 face	0.88 face	0.79 eye	0.73 mountain	0.71 fox

Table 4: Top invCL scores for various characters – contextualised individuals

	Individual coherence	Kind coherence								
		woman	lady	man	gentleman	toad	rat	mole	badger	animal
Darcy	**0.42**	-	-	0.24	0.25	-	-	-	-	-
Elizabeth	**0.40**	0.24	0.28	-	-	-	-	-	-	-
Bingley	**0.42**	-	-	0.24	0.25	-	-	-	-	-
Jane	**0.34**	0.24	0.28	-	-	-	-	-	-	-
Collins	**0.34**	-	-	0.24	0.25	-	-	-	-	-
Denny	**0.40**	-	-	0.24	0.25	-	-	-	-	-
Toad	**0.28**	-	-	-	-	0.24	-	-	-	0.22
Rat	**0.32**	-	-	-	-	-	0.24	-	-	0.22
Mole	**0.24**	-	-	-	-	-	-	0.22	-	0.22
Badger	**0.28**	-	-	-	-	-	-	-	0.23	0.22

Table 5: Coherence values for some characters and the concepts they instantiate – contextualised distributions

towards human concepts: Badger, for instance, has *boy* as its third most likely kind. This tendency gets stronger as p increases, with Mole returning the kinds *mole, human, adult* at $p = 10$. This indicates that in cases where the initial named entity type turns out to be incorrect or partially correct (as in the case of anthropomorphised animals), the model has the potential to rectify the representation.

Further, the produced vectors strongly assert the individuality of the modelled names, in particular for the *P&P* characters. Table 5 shows that all names have higher coherence than their respective kinds (all differences are statistically significant). The names from *WitW* are generally less coherent than those in *P&P*, which can perhaps be explained by the fact that the characters combine properties from two separate areas of the semantic space (animal- and human-related features).

5.2.1 Discussion

A visualisation of the semantic space is provided in Fig. 2. Due to layout restrictions, we show the space for $m = 20$ and $p = 3$. Our best model ($p = 6$) results in essentially the same configuration, but with the names much further apart from the concepts. It is however clear from the illustration that individuals are separated from kinds and occupy their own subspace.

If it is true that kind distributions are a rough representation of the linguistic contexts generally associated with individual members of a group (i.e. if we consider kinds as supremums – see §3.2), existential plurals should be situated somewhere between individuals and kinds in the semantic space. That is, we would assume that the distribution of '*Darcy, Bingley, Collins and Denny*' would highlight some properties common to the individuals but also lose some coherence in virtue of representing their differences, i.e. be closer to a kind. We can in fact illustrate this property by adding name vectors together and inspecting the position of the resulting plural in the semantic space.

Fig. 2 shows that indeed, the plurals '*Darcy and Bingley*', '*Darcy, Bingley and Collins*' and '*Darcy, Bingley, Collins and Denny*' come progressively closer to the kind *man*. Although this result is very tentative and should be shown to be replicable, we take it as support for the idea that there is a principled relation between the distributions of individuals, plurals and kinds (seen as supremums).

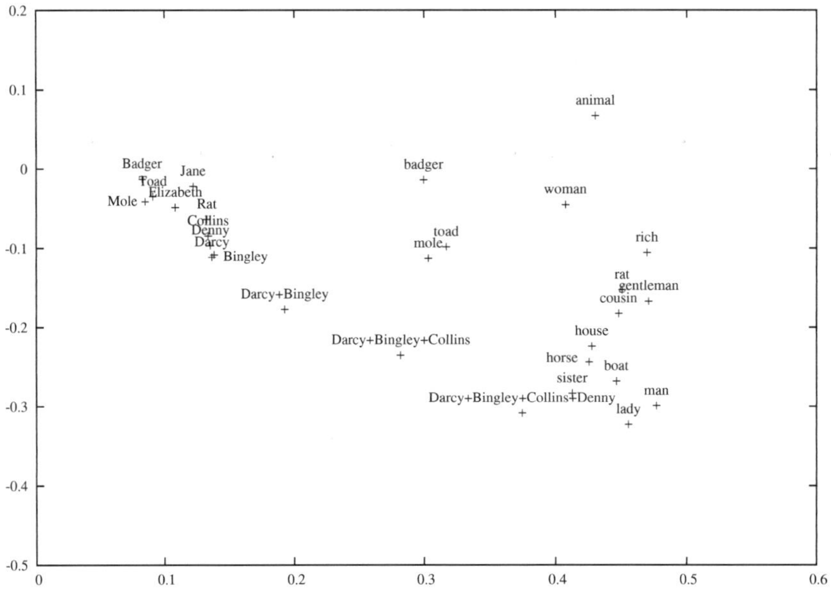

Figure 2: The BNC space with names as contextualised kind distributions. The names have clustered on the left of the space, kinds on the right. Plurals consisting of men's names are roughly situated on a line between the individuals and the concept *man*.

6 Conclusion

In this paper, we have investigated the notion of a distributional proper name and proposed a model which satisfies some natural properties of individuals.

We would like to conclude by adding that we have preliminary results indicating that our contextualisation method can be applied to any type of individual in a co-reference chain with similar effect. That is, the technique can be applied to instances of common nouns (*boat, car, letter*). We intend to pursue this work further, and provide a large-scale evaluation of our proposal involving different types of individuals. We will also integrate the system in a pipeline involving co-reference resolution and test the robustness of this setup.

We believe that having a distributional model of individuals is crucial for several reasons. First, if distributional semantics is to claim psycholinguistic validity, it should account for the fact that many of the words/phrases we use repeatedly (and therefore might build a distribution for) refer to individuals. Consider the name of the city a speaker lives in, the company he/she works for, phrases such as *my boss, Kim's dog*, etc. Second, having access to distributional individuals may help us solve problems that DS has been struggling with. For instance, we may make progress on the topic of antonymy, as (static) antonyms cannot be applied to the same individual (e.g. a city cannot be small and large at the same time). We have also briefly shown that there is potential for developing distributional theories of plurality and genericity by studying the principled relationships between individual, plural and kind distributions.

More generally, we note that our considerations on proper names lead to a less static view of the semantic space. While it is fair to extract distributions from large corpora as lexical representations, the exercise does not teach us much about the way people attribute meaning to new linguistic entities, whether they refer to individuals or concepts (see unknown words, neologisms, second language acquisition, etc). We hope that by viewing the semantic space as a dynamic system, where prior knowledge combined with new linguistic input produces new and updated representations, we can make progress on those issues.

References

Baroni, M., R. Bernardi, and R. Zamparelli (2014). Frege in space: A program of compositional distributional semantics. *Linguistic Issues in Language Technology 9*.

Bruni, E., G. Boleda, M. Baroni, and N.-K. Tran (2012). Distributional semantics in technicolor. In *Proceedings of the 50th Annual Meeting of the Association for Computational Linguistics*, pp. 136–145.

Carlson, G. N. and F. J. Pelletier (1995). *The generic book.* University of Chicago Press.

Chierchia, G. (1998). Reference to kinds across languages. *Natural Language Semantics 6*, 339–405.

Cumming, S. (2013). Names. In E. N. Zalta (Ed.), *The Stanford Encyclopedia of Philosophy*.

Dinu, G., S. Thater, and S. Laue (2012). A comparison of models of word meaning in context. In *Proceedings of the 2012 Conference of the North American Chapter of the Association for Computational Linguistics: Human Language Technologies (NAACL-HLT2012)*, pp. 611–615.

Erk, K. (2013). Towards a semantics for distributional representations. In *Proceedings of the Tenth International Conference on Computational Semantics (IWCS2013)*, Potsdam, Germany.

Erk, K. (2014). What do you know about an alligator when you know the company it keeps? Draft.

Erk, K. and S. Padó (2008). A structured vector space model for word meaning in context. In *Proceedings of the 2008 Conference on Empirical Methods in Natural Language Processing (EMNLP2008)*, Honolulu, HI, pp. 897–906.

Frege, G. (1892). Über Sinn und Bedeutung. *Zeitschrift für Philosophie und philosophische Kritik 100*, 25–50.

Harris, Z. (1954). Distributional structure. *Word 10*(2-3), 146–162.

Herbelot, A. and A. Copestake (2011). Formalising and specifying underquantification. In *Proceedings of the Ninth International Conference on Computational Semantics (IWCS 2011)*, Oxford, UK.

Lenci, A. and G. Benotto (2012). Identifying hypernyms in distributional semantic spaces. In *Proceedings of the First Joint Conference on Lexical and Computational Semantics (*SEM)*, pp. 75–79.

Leslie, S.-J. (2008). Generics: Cognition and acquisition. *Philosophical Review 117*(1), 1–47.

McNally, L. (2014). Kinds, descriptions of kinds, concepts, and distributions. Draft.

Mill, J. S. (1843). A system of logic, ratiocinative and inductive. In J. Robson (Ed.), *Collected Works of John Stuart Mill*, Volume 7-8. Toronto: University of Toronto Press.

Newman, D., J. H. Lau, K. Grieser, and T. Baldwin (2010). Automatic evaluation of topic coherence. In *Human Language Technologies: The 2010 Annual Conference of the North American Chapter of the Association for Computational Linguistics (ACL-HLT2010)*, pp. 100–108.

Rapp, R. (2004). A practical solution to the problem of automatic word sense induction. In *Proceedings of the ACL 2004 on Interactive poster and demonstration sessions.*

Russell, B. (1911). Knowledge by acquaintance and knowledge by description. In *Proceedings of the Aristotelian Society*, pp. 108–128.

Searle, J. R. (1958). Proper names. *Mind 67*(266), 166–173.

Thater, S., H. Fürstenau, and M. Pinkal (2011). Word meaning in context: A simple and effective vector model. In *Proceedings of the 5th International Joint Conference on Natural Language Processing*, Chiang Mai, Thailand.

Feeling is Understanding: From Affective to Semantic Spaces

Elias Iosif
School of ECE, National Technical University of Athens, Greece
"Athena" Research Center, Greece
iosife@central.ntua.gr

Alexandros Potamianos
School of ECE, National Technical University of Athens, Greece
"Athena" Research Center, Greece
potam@central.ntua.gr

Abstract

Motivated by theories of language development we investigate the contribution of affect to lexical semantics in the context of distributional semantic models (DSMs). The relationship between semantic and affective spaces is computationally modeled for the task of semantic similarity computation between words. It is shown that affective spaces contain salient information for lexical semantic tasks. We further investigate specific semantic relationships where affective information plays a prominent role. The relations between semantic similarity and opposition are studied in the framework of a binary classification problem applied for the discrimination of synonyms and antonyms. For the case of antonyms, the use of affective features results in 33% relative improvement in classification accuracy compared to the use of semantic features.

1 Introduction

Mainstream distributional semantic models (DSMs) rely solely on linguistic data, being ungrounded to the real world, i.e., features from other modalities and experiential information that are related to the acquisition of semantic knowledge are ignored. Motivated by findings from the literature of language development, according to which language acquisition is (also) grounded on communication episodes where partners exchange feelings (Tomasello et al., 2005), we consider emotion as part of lexical semantics. We argue that emotion conveys salient information, relaxing the view of emotion as "pathos" (Salovey and Mayer, 1990) that was ostracized by (traditional) models of semantics/logic.

In this paper, the affective content of words is investigated within a network-based framework regarding its contribution to lexical semantics tasks. This framework is motivated by cognitive models that rely on the distributed representation of semantic attributes (features) (Rogers and McClelland, 2004). Given a stimulus (e.g., a word), local areas (sub-spaces) are activated, triggering a number of attributes that are (semantically) related with the stimulus. The activation of attributes can be explained in the context of semantic priming according to which the presence of a word facilitates the cognitive processing of another word (McNamara, 2005). Affective priming constitutes the emotional analogue of semantic priming (Ferré and Sánchez-Casas, 2014). The key machinery of the used network is a two-tier system. The first layer constitutes a local representation scheme for encoding the semantics of target words simulating the aforementioned activation models. The activation models enable the definition of various similarity metrics in the second layer. In this work, we investigate the creation of activation models using both lexical and affective features, which are used for the computation of word semantic similarity. To the best of our knowledge this is the first computational model investigating the role of affect in semantics.

Proceedings of the 11th International Conference on Computational Semantics, pages 162–172,
London, UK, April 15-17 2015.

2 Related Work

Semantic similarity is the building block for numerous applications of natural language processing, such as affective text analysis (Malandrakis et al., 2013). There has been much research interest on devising data-driven approaches for estimating semantic similarity between words. Distributional semantic models (DSMs) (Baroni and Lenci, 2010) are based on the distributional hypothesis of meaning (Harris, 1954) assuming that semantic similarity between words is a function of the overlap of their linguistic contexts. DSMs can be categorized into unstructured that employ a bag-of-words model and structured that employ syntactic relationships between words (Baroni and Lenci, 2010). DSMs are typically constructed from co-occurrence statistics of word tuples that are extracted on existing corpora or on corpora specifically harvested from the web. In (Iosif and Potamianos, 2015), a language-agnostic DSM was proposed as a two-tier system motivated by cognitive considerations such as network activation and priming.. The first layer, encodes the semantics of words via the creation of lexical neighborhoods. In the second layer, similarity metrics are defined on these semantic neighborhoods. The extension of DSMs for representing the compositional aspects of lexical semantics constitutes an active research area (Baroni et al., 2014).

Analysis of text to estimate affect or sentiment is a relatively recent research topic that has attracted great interest, as reflected by a series of shared evaluation tasks, e.g., analysis of tweets (Nakov et al., 2013). Relevant applications deal with numerous domains such as news stories (Lloyd et al., 2005) and product reviews (Hu and Liu, 2004). Affective analysis is also useful for other application domains such as dialogue systems (Lee and Narayanan, 2005). Several resources enable the development of these computational models, ranging from flat lexica (e.g., General Inquirer (Stone et al., 1966) and Affective norms for English Words (Bradley and Lang, 1999)) to large lexical networks (e.g., SentiWordNet (Esuli and Sebastiani, 2006) and WordNet Affect (Strapparava and Valitutti, 2004)). Text can be analyzed for affect at different levels of granularity: from single words to entire sentences. In (Turney and Littman, 2003), the affective ratings of unknown words were predicted using the affective ratings for a small set of words (seeds) and the semantic relatedness between the unknown and the seed words. An example of sentence-level approach was proposed in (Malandrakis et al., 2013) applying techniques from n-gram language modeling.

3 Lexical Features and Metrics of Semantic Similarity

Co-occurrence-based (CC). The underlying assumption of co-occurrence-based metrics is that the coexistence of words in a specified contextual environment indicates semantic relatedness. In this work, we employ a widely-used co-occurrence-based metric, namely, Dice coefficient D (co-occurrence is considered at the sentence level).
Context-based (CT). The fundamental assumption behind context-based metrics is that *similarity of context implies similarity of meaning* (Harris, 1954). A contextual window of size $2H+1$ words is centered on the word of interest w_i and lexical features are extracted. For every instance of w_i in the corpus the H words left and right of w_i formulate a feature vector x_i. For a given value of H the context-based semantic similarity between two words, w_i and w_j, is computed as the cosine of their feature vectors: $Q^H(w_i, w_j) = \frac{x_i . x_j}{||x_i||\,||x_j||}$. The elements of feature vectors can be weighted according to various schemes, while, here we use a binary scheme.

4 Affective Features and Metric of Affective Similarity

A word w is characterized regarding its affective content in a continuous (within the $[-1, 1]$ interval) space consisting of three dimensions (affective features), namely, valence (v), arousal (a), and dominance (d). For each dimension, the affective content of w is estimated as a linear combination of its' semantic similarities to a set of K seed words and the corresponding affective ratings of seeds (for the corresponding dimension), as follows (Malandrakis et al., 2013).

$$\hat{u}(w) = \lambda_0 + \sum_{i=1}^{K} \lambda_i \; u(t_i) \; S(t_i, w), \tag{1}$$

where $t_1...t_K$ are the seed words, $u(t_i)$ is the affective rating for seed word t_i with u denoting one of the aforementioned dimensions, i.e., v, a, or d. λ_i is a trainable weight corresponding to seed t_i. $S(t_i, w)$ stands for a metric of semantic similarity (see Section 3) between t_i and w. The affective distance between two words, w_i and w_j, can be computed as the Euclidean distance over the three-dimensional space, which can be transformed into similarity.

5 Semantic and Affective Networks

In this section, we summarize the main ideas of DSMs that were proposed in (Iosif and Potamianos, 2015) for building semantic networks, which are extended here for the creation of affective networks. An overview of the semantic and affective networks is presented in Fig. 1. Each network type consists

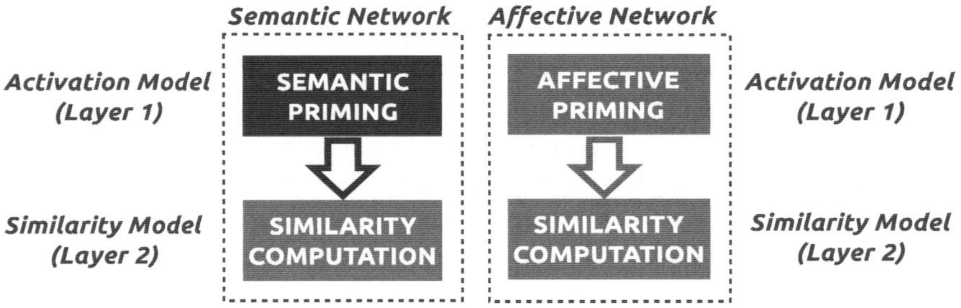

Figure 1: Overview of semantic and affective networks. Each network consists of two layers, namely, activation and similarity.

of two layers, namely, activation and similarity layer. For a target word, w_i, the first layer is used for the activation of a set of other words that are semantically/affectively related with the target. The second layer is used for the computation of semantic/affective similarity between two words for which the respective activation layers have been computed. Regardless of the network type (i.e., semantic or affective), the network is defined as an undirected (under a symmetric similarity metric) graph $F = (V, E)$ whose the set of vertices V are all words in a lexicon O, and the set of edges E contains the links between the vertices. The links (edges) between words in the network are determined and weighted according to the pairwise (semantic of affective) similarity of the vertices. For each word (target word) that is included in the lexicon, $w_i \in O$, we consider a sub-graph of F, $F_i = (N_i, E_i)$, where the set of vertices N_i includes in total n members of O, which are linked with w_i via edges E_i.

5.1 Layer 1: Activation Models

Semantic Activation Model. The computation of the semantic activation model for a target word w_i is motivated semantic priming (McNamara, 2005). The model can be represented as a F_i sub-graph, which is also referred to as the semantic neighborhood of w_i. The members of N_i (neighbors of w_i) are selected according to a semantic similarity metric (in this work, D or Q^H defined in Section 3) with respect to w_i, i.e., the n most similar words to w_i are selected. The semantic neighborhood of target w_i with size n is denoted as $L_i(n)$.

Affective Activation Model. The computation of the affective activation model for a target word w_i is motivated affective priming (Ferré and Sánchez-Casas, 2014). The model can be represented as a F_i sub-graph that denotes the affective neighborhood of w_i. The members of N_i (neighbors of w_i) are selected according to an affective similarity metric (e.g., as defined in Section 4) with respect to w_i, i.e., the n

most similar words to w_i are selected. The affective neighborhood of target w_i with size n is denoted as $A_i(n)$.

5.2 Layer 2: Similarity Model

Here, we describe two network-based similarity metrics proposed in (Iosif and Potamianos, 2015) for computing the similarity between two (target) words w_i and w_j. The metrics are defined on top of the activations models (semantic of affective) of w_i and w_j that were computed in the previous layer of the network[1].

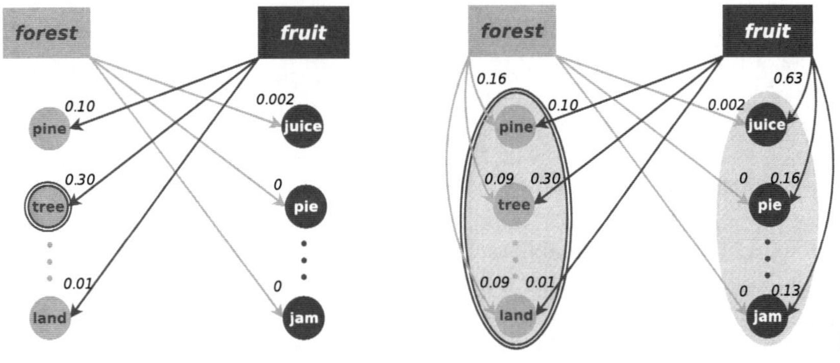

Figure 2: Example of network similarity metrics based on the activation models of two target words. The targets, "forest" and "fruit", are depicted along with their neighbors (Layer 1): {pine, tree, ..., land} and {juice, pie, ..., jam}, respectively. Arcs represent the similarities between targets and neighbors. The similarity between "forest" and "fruit" (Layer 2) is computed according to (a) maximum similarity of neighborhoods, and (b) correlation of neighborhood similarities.

Maximum Similarity of Neighborhoods. This metric is based on the hypothesis that the similarity of two words, w_i and w_j, can be estimated by *the maximum similarity of their respective sets of neighbors*, defined as follows:

$$M_n(w_i, w_j) = \max\{\alpha_{ij}, \alpha_{ji}\}, \tag{2}$$

where

$$\alpha_{ij} = \max_{x \in N_j} S(w_i, x), \quad \alpha_{ji} = \max_{y \in N_i} S(w_j, y).$$

α_{ij} (or α_{ji}) denotes the maximum similarity between w_i (or w_j) and the neighbors of w_j (or w_i) that is computed according to a similarity metric S: for semantic neighborhoods one of the metrics defined in Section 3, or the metric defined in Section 4 for affective neighborhoods. N_i and N_j are the set of neighbors for w_i and w_j, respectively. For the case of semantic neighborhoods the definition of M_n is motivated by the maximum sense similarity assumption (Resnik, 1995) hypothesizing that the most salient information in the neighbors of a word are semantic features denoting senses of this word. An example illustrating the computation of similarity between targets "forest" and "fruit" is depicted by Fig.2(a). M_n(*"forest"*, *"fruit"*) $= 0.30$ because the similarity between "fruit" and "tree" (among all neighbors of "forest") is the largest.
Attributional Neighborhood Similarity. The similarity between w_i and w_j is defined as follows:

$$R_n(w_i, w_j) = \max\{\beta_{ij}, \beta_{ji}\}, \tag{3}$$

where

$$\beta_{ij} = \rho(C_i^{N_i}, C_j^{N_i}), \quad \beta_{ji} = \rho(C_i^{N_j}, C_j^{N_j}).$$

[1]Similarity metrics can be applied over the semantic and affective neighborhoods of w_i and w_j. In the metric definitions we use the (generic) notations N_i and N_j to refer to the neighborhoods of w_i and w_j, respectively, regardless of the type (i.e., semantic or affective) of those neighborhoods.

$C_i^{N_i} = (S(w_i, x_1), S(w_i, x_2), \ldots, S(w_i, x_n))$ and $N_i = \{x_1, x_2, \ldots, x_n\}$. The vectors $C_j^{N_i}$, $C_i^{N_j}$, and $C_j^{N_j}$ are defined similarly as $C_i^{N_i}$. The ρ function stands for the Pearson's correlation coefficient, N_i is the set of neighbors of word w_i, and S is a similarity metric: for semantic neighborhoods one of the metrics defined in Section 3, or the metric defined in Section 4 for affective neighborhoods. The motivation behind this metric is attributional similarity, i.e., we assume that neighborhoods encode semantic or affective features of a word. Semantically/affectively similar words are expected to exhibit correlated similarities with respect to such features. The similarity computation process is exemplified in Fig.2(b) for the target words w_i ="forest" and w_j = "fruit". The similarity vectors between the neighbors N_i of "forest" and each of the words are computed: $C_i^{N_i} = (0.16, 0.09, \ldots, 0.09)$, $C_j^{N_i} = (0.10, 0.30, \ldots, 0.01)$. Similarly, $C_i^{N_j}$, $C_j^{N_j}$ are computed for the neighbors of "fruit" and combined to estimate R_n(*"forest"*, *"fruit"*) $= -0.04$.

5.3 Fusion of Lexical and Affective Activation Models

In this section, we propose two schemes for the unsupervised fusion of semantic and affective activation models defined in Section 5.1. The motivation behind this idea is the hypothesis that both semantic and affective activations are triggered given lexical stimuli, e.g., the target words for which similarity is computed. In addition, for the task of similarity computation we assume that the two activation models are fused rather being exploited independently. Two types of fusion are proposed, namely, local and global. The local scheme is based on the fusion of semantic and affective neighborhoods of relatively small size. The largest possible sizes of semantic and affective neighborhoods (i.e., equal to the number of network nodes) are used for the case of global fusion.

Local. A hybrid neighborhood $N_i^{\Psi(n)}$ for a target word w_i is computed based on its lexical and affective neighborhoods, $L_i(n)$ and $A_i(n)$ of size n, as follows:

$$N_i^{\Psi(n)} = f(L_i(n), A_i(n)), \tag{4}$$

where f stands for a set operator given that $L_i(n)$ and $A_i(n)$ are represented as sets.
Global. A hybrid neighborhood $N_i^{\Omega(n)}$ of size n for a target word w_i is computed based on its lexical and affective neighborhoods, $L_i(|O|)$ and $A_i(|O|)$ of size $|O|$ (i.e., equal to the size of the lexicon O) as:

$$N_i^{\Omega(n)} = g(S(w_i, L_i(|O|)), S(w_i, A_i(|O|)); n), \tag{5}$$

where $S(w_i, L_i(|O|))$ and $S(w_i, A_i(|O|))$ stand for the vectors including the semantic and affective similarity scores between target w_i and the members of $L_i(|O|)$ and $A_i(|O|)$, respectively. Before the application of the g fusion function the two vectors should be normalized and aligned. The fusion results into a single vector of size O from which the n top-ranked values are selected and the corresponding n lexicon entries are considered as members of the neighborhood $N_i^{\Omega(n)}$.

Fusion level: function	Examples		
	Lexical model	Affective model	Fused
Local: $L_i \cup A_i$	L_i ={pine, tree,...}	A_i ={taste, sugar,...}	{pine, tree, taste, sugar,...}
Global: $\zeta_i^L \cdot \zeta_i^A$	$\zeta_i^L = [0.5, 0.3, \ldots]$	$\zeta_i^A = [0.2, 0.8, \ldots]$	$[0.1, 0.24, \ldots]$
Global: $\max\{\zeta_i^L, \zeta_i^A\}$	$\zeta_i^L = [0.5, 0.3, \ldots]$	$\zeta_i^A = [0.2, 0.8, \ldots]$	$[0.5, 0.8, \ldots]$

Table 1: Fusion functions for the lexical and affective activation models.

We present results for a number of simple functions for the fusion of L_i and A_i shown in Table 1. For the case of local fusion, the hybrid neighborhood is built by taking the union of semantic and affective neighborhoods. Denoting vectors $S(w_i, L_i(|O|)$ and $S(w_i, A_i(|O|)$ as ζ_i^L and ζ_i^A, respectively, two functions are used for the case of global fusion: $\zeta_i^L \cdot \zeta_i^A$ and $\max\{\zeta_i^L, \zeta_i^A\}$. The first stands for the product of ζ_i^L and ζ_i^A. The second function gives the maximum element-wise value, i.e, for each lexicon entry and the target w_i the respective maximum semantic or affective similarity score is selected.

6 Features of Semantic Semantic Opposition

Here, we propose two feature sets that are relevant to the relations of synonymy and antonymy (also referred to as semantic opposition (Mohammad et al., 2013)). Antonymy constitutes a special lexical relation, since it embodies both the notion of (semantic) proximity and distance (Cruse, 1986). These features are based on the affective content of words and features of semantic similarity. Unlike people that can easily distinguish synonyms and antonyms, this is a challenging problem for the framework of DSMs. Both synonyms and antonyms exhibit strong associations which can be empirically verified via standard psycholinguistic experiments, as well as within the computational framework of DSMs. For example, in free association norms antonyms are frequently given as responses. Regarding DSMs, the corpus-derived statistics for synonyms and antonyms are correlated leading to comparable similarity scores. For example, in (Mohammad et al., 2013) the relatedness (similarity) scores of semantically similar (SW) and antonymous (AW) words were analyzed. Interestingly, it was found that the average score for AW was slightly higher compared to SW. The affective content of words can be considered as connotations that are added to the respective semantics. The emotional similarity between synonyms and antonyms is expected to have a contribution regarding their discrimination. For this purpose, the following features are proposed:

1) **Lex1 (lexical).** Similarity score based on direct co-occurrence counts. This can be regarded as a coefficient of semantic priming.
2) **Lex2 (lexical).** Similarity score computed according to (2) (max-based network metric). Lexical features are used for both network layers.
3) **Lex3 (lexical).** Similarity score computed according to (3) (correlation-based network metric). Lexical features are used for both network layers.
4) **Aff1 (affective).** Affective distance computed on the three-dimensional space (valence–arousal–dominance). This can be thought as a coefficient of affective priming.
5) **Aff2 (affective).** Similarity: score computed according to (2) (max-based network metric). Affective features are used for both network layers.
6) **Aff3 (affective).** Similarity score computed according to (3) (correlation-based network metric). Affective features are used for both network layers.

In essence, for each feature set (lexical and affective) there two types of similarity. The first type considers the direct similarity of the words of interest, while for the second type, the similarity is estimated via the respective neighborhoods.

7 Experiments and Evaluation Results

In this section, we investigate the role of semantic and affective features for two tasks of lexical semantics. Semantic and affective activation models are used in combination with the aforementioned network-based similarity metrics for the computation of word semantic similarity. This is presented in Section 7.1, while the fusion of the two activation types is shown in 7.2. In Section 7.3, semantic and affective features are evaluated in the framework of semantic opposition. This is done as a binary classification problem for the discrimination of synonyms and antonyms.

7.1 Word Semantic Similarity Computation

Creation of Networks. A lexicon consisting of $8,752$ (single-word) English nouns was taken from the SemCor3 corpus. For the extraction of the textual features a web harvested corpus was created as follows.

For each lexicon entry an individual query was formulated and the $1,000$ top ranked results (document snippets) were retrieved using the Yahoo! search engine and aggregated. The affective ratings (v, a and d) for these nouns were computed using as seeds the manually annotated ANEW lexicon (Bradley and Lang, 1999) (600 seeds were used) and estimating the λ weights of (1) according to (Malandrakis et al., 2013). Regarding $S(.)$ used in (1), the context-based (CT) similarity metric exploiting text features was applied. The network creation consisted of two main steps: 1) computation of semantic and affective neighborhoods as described in Section 5, 2) computation of similarity scores using M_n and R_n defined by (2) and (3), respectively. For the case of semantic neighborhoods two types of similarity metrics (in conjunction with the respective textual features) were applied: co-occurrence-based (CC), and context-based (CT) with $H = 1$.

Evaluation. The task of noun semantic similarity computation was used for evaluation purposes with respect to the following datasets (i) MC (Miller and Charles, 1998),(ii) RG (Rubenstein and Goodenough, 1965), and (iii) WS353 (Finkelstein et al., 2002), retaining those pairs that were included in the network. The Pearson's correlation coefficient against human ratings was used as evaluation metric.

Type of feature for		Network-	Number of neighbors (n)				
Selection of neighbors (1st layer)	Similarity computation (2nd layer)	based metric	10	30	50	100	150
MC dataset							
Lexical (CC)	Lexical (CT)	M_n	0.48	0.80	0.83	**0.91**	0.90
Lexical (CT)	Lexical (CC)	R_n	0.83	0.78	0.80	0.78	0.76
Affective	*Lexical (CC)*	R_n	0.85	**0.91**	0.88	0.85	0.83
RG dataset							
Lexical (CC)	Lexical (CT)	M_n	0.57	0.74	0.78	**0.86**	0.82
Lexical (CT)	Lexical (CC)	R_n	0.65	0.71	0.72	0.72	0.72
Affective	*Lexical (CC)*	R_n	0.78	**0.80**	0.79	0.77	0.74
WS353 dataset							
Lexical (CC)	Lexical(CT)	M_n	0.42	0.55	0.59	0.64	**0.65**
Lexical (CT)	Lexical(CC)	R_n	0.63	0.58	0.59	0.56	0.55
Affective	*Lexical (CC)*	R_n	0.63	**0.68**	**0.68**	0.65	0.63

Table 2: Correlation for word similarity computation.

The performance for various neighborhood sizes is presented in Table 2 for two approaches regarding the activation model (Layer 1) followed by the neighborhood-based similarity estimation (Layer 2). Two types of activation models are used for the computation neighborhoods, namely, lexical and affective. Once the neighborhoods are computed, the network metrics M_n and R_n are employed for the similarity computation based on lexical features. Overall, there are two basic settings: *Lexical+Lexical* and *Affective+Lexical*. The core novelty of this work is on the exploitation of affective features for the activation model, i.e., the Affective+Lexical approach. For the sake of completeness, the results when using textual features only (Lexical+Lexical) are presented for the respective best performing metrics and feature types (according to (Iosif and Potamianos, 2015)): CC/CT for M_n and CT/CC for R_n. Regarding the Affective+Lexical approach, the performance is reported only for R_n that was found to outperform the (omitted) M_n metric. It is notable[2] that the Affective+Lexical combination performs very well being competitive[3] against the best Lexical+Lexical approach, as well as other state-of-the-art approaches (Agirre et al., 2009). Specifically, the Affective+Lexical combination achieves higher (0.68 vs. 0.65)

[2]This was experimentally verified using the affective word ratings given by human annotators (ANEW affective lexicon (Bradley and Lang, 1999)), instead of the automatically estimated ratings produced by (1).

[3]The detailed comparison of the proposed affective models with other lexical DSMs is beyond the scope of this study.

and equal (0.91) correlation scores -compared to the Lexical+Lexical combination- for the WS353 and MC datasets, respectively. The Affective+Lexical combination consistently achieves higher (or equal) performance compared to both Lexical+Lexical combinations when few (10-50) neighbors are used.

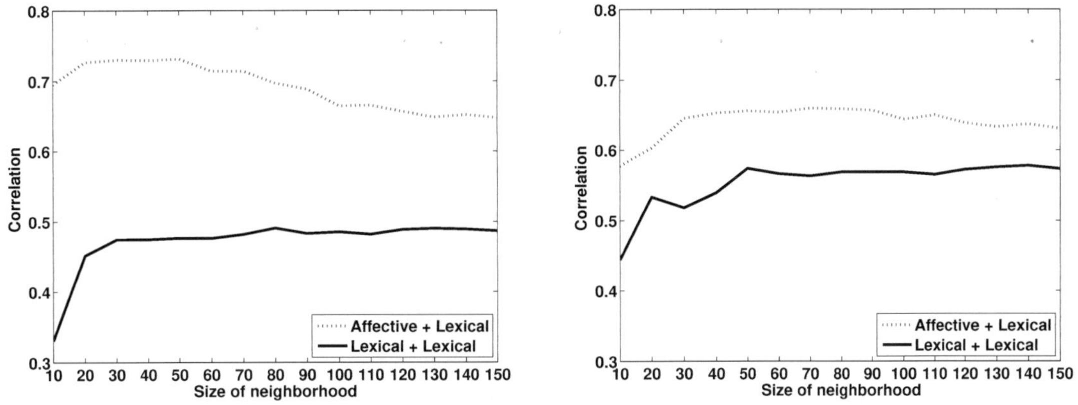

(a) (b)

Figure 3: Correlation for word similarity computation as a function of neighborhood size for pairs consisting of words with: (a) distant affective magnitude (150 pairs from WS353), and (b) comparable affective magnitude (122 pairs from WS353). Results are shown for Lexical+Lexical (solid line) and Affective+Lexical (dotted line) approaches.

Motivated by the very good performance of the Affective+Lexical approach, we conducted further investigation regarding the role of affective information with respect to the affective relation of the words for which the similarity is computed. For this purpose, the pairs of the largest experimental dataset (WS353) where distinguished into two groups according to the affective magnitude of their constituents words. The first group includes pairs whose both constituents have high or low affective magnitude (i.e., words with comparable magnitude), e.g., (king, queen). The remaining pairs were included in the second group (i.e., words with distant magnitude), e.g., (psychology, depression). The discrimination resulted into 122 and 150 pairs consisting of words with comparable and distant affective magnitude, respectively. The performance of the Lexical+Lexical and Affective+Lexical approaches using the R_n similarity metric is shown as a function of the neighborhood size in Fig. 3(a) for words with distant affective magnitude, and in Fig. 3(b) for words with comparable affective magnitude. We observe that the Affective+Lexical approach consistently achieves higher correlation compared to the Lexical+Lexical approach for both groups. The superiority of the Affective+Lexical approach is shown more clearly for the case of words with distant affective magnitude (Fig. 3(a)).

7.2 Fusion of Lexical and Affective Activation Models

Fusion level	Fusion function	Number of neighbors				
		10	30	50	100	150
Best individual model		0.63	**0.68**	**0.68**	0.65	0.63
Best lexical model		0.42	0.55	0.59	0.64	0.65
Local	$L_i \cup A_i$	0.45	0.47	0.44	0.47	0.46
Global	$\zeta_i^L \cdot \zeta_i^A$	0.46	0.48	0.50	0.49	0.48
	$\max\{\zeta_i^L, \zeta_i^A\}$	0.63	**0.68**	**0.68**	0.65	0.63

Table 3: Correlation for word similarity computation (WS353 dataset).

In this section, the evaluation results for the fusion of semantic and affective models (Layer 1) are presented. The fusion schemes shown in Table 1 were used for the computation of hybrid neighbor-

Semantic relation	Baseline (random)	Feature types	
		Lexical (Lex1,Lex2,Lex3)	Affective (Aff1,Aff2,Aff3)
Synonymy	50%	61%	62%
Antonymy	50%	61%	**82%**

Table 4: Classification accuracy for synonymy and antonymy: lexical vs. affective feature sets.

Semantic relation	Baseline (random)	Lexical features			Affective features		
		Lex1	Lex2	Lex3	Aff1	Aff2	Aff3
Synonymy	50%	51%	61%	59%	61%	61%	51%
Antonymy	50%	55%	61%	61%	**81%**	**82%**	50%

Table 5: Classification accuracy for synonymy and antonymy for individual lexical and affective features.

hoods. The network-based similarity metric R_n was applied over the hybrid neighborhoods for the computation of semantic similarity between words (Layer 2). The performance is presented in Table 3 for the largest dataset (WS353) with respect to various neighborhood sizes. The correlation achieved by the best performing individual model (Affective+Lexical using R_n) is included for comparison purposes. The performance of the best model based solely on lexical features (Lexical+Lexical using M_n) is also presented. Regarding the different fusion schemes, the highest performance is obtained for the global approach using the maximum-based function ($\max\{\zeta_i^L, \zeta_i^A\}$). This scheme yields performance that is identical to the best individual model. Also, we observe that the best fusion scheme consistently outperforms the Lexical+Lexical approach for $10 - 100$ neighbors.

7.3 Synonymy vs. Antonymy

Here, we compare the performance of semantic and affective features (described in Section 6) for the discrimination of word pairs the fall into two categories, synonyms and antonyms. The word pairs were taken from two sets of WordNet synonyms and opposites[4] We retained those pairs that were included in the networks described in Section 7.1. In total, 172 pairs are contained in each category for a total of 344 pairs. The experimental dataset include pairs such as (happiness, felicity) and (comedy, tragedy) that correspond to synonyms and antonyms, respectively. Support Vector Machines[5] with linear kernel were applied for classification. For evaluation purposes, 10-fold cross validation (10-FCV) was used, while classification accuracy was used as evaluation measurement.

The classification accuracy is shown for each category in Table 4 with respect to two feature sets: 1) all lexical features (Lex1–Lex3), and 2) all affective features (Aff1–Aff3)[6]. The baseline performance (yielded by random classification) is also presented. Both features types exceed the baseline for synonyms and antonyms. The main observation is that the set of affective features outperforms the lexical feature set for the case of antonyms, i.e., 82% vs. 61% classification accuracy. Regarding synonyms, lexical and affective features yield almost identical performance. The moderate discrimination ability of lexical features was expected since both synonyms and antonyms exhibit high similarity scores as measured in the framework of DSMs. These observations suggest that the affective information is a major contributor for the case of antonyms, which is not surprising since such words are emotionally distant. The performance for all individual features in presented in Table 5 for each category. It is observed that the similarities based on word co-occurrence (Lex1) give the lowest performance for both synonyms and antonyms, while the network-based similarities (Lex2 and Lex3) yield slightly higher results. The key observation is that the top performance, i.e., greater than 80%, can be achieved either using the simple

[4]`http://www.saifmohammad.com/WebPages/ResearchInterests.html\#Antonymy.`

[5]Similar results were obtained with other classifiers, e.g., Naive Bayes.

[6]For the network metrics we used $n = 30$, however, similar results were achieved for other values of n, e.g., 10, 50, 100.

affective similarity (Aff1) or the maximum-based network similarity metric (Aff2). Given the lack of a standard dataset for this task, the comparison of different DSMs is not easy. A corpus-based algorithm was evaluated with respect to similar a task (synonym/antonym discrimination for 136 pairs[7]) achieving 75% classification accuracy under 10-FCV (Turney, 2011).

8 Conclusions

The affective spaces were shown to contain salient information for estimating semantic similarity. The Affective+Lexical approach achieved competitive performance compared to (an example of) the mainstream paradigm of distributional semantic models (i.e., the Lexical+Lexical approach). Moreover, the affective models were found to be more appropriate for the first network layer (compared to the lexical models) when the words for which similarity is computed exhibit distant affective magnitude. To the best of our knowledge, this is the first empirical indication that the affect can be regarded as another source of information that plays a role for the task of semantic similarity estimation between words. Correlation-based similarity metrics and smaller neighborhoods were shown to perform better for Affective+Lexical DSMs. Another major finding is that the affective features are superior to the lexical ones for the case of antonym identification. Regarding the fusion of lexical and affective activation models, the global scheme (i.e., across the entire network) was found to outperform the local one. Further research is needed for understanding the complementarities of affective and semantic spaces, which is important for the design of improved fusion schemes. Last but not least, the role of affective features should be investigated with respect to more semantic tasks (e.g., paraphrasing) and other types of semantic relations and linguistic phenomena (e.g., figurative language).

Acknowledgments. This work has been partially funded by the SpeDial project supported by the EU FP7 with grant number 611396, and the BabyAffect project supported by the Greek General Secretariat for Research and Technology (GSRT) with grant number 3610.

References

Agirre, E., E. Alfonseca, K. Hall, J. Kravalova, M. Pasca, and A. Soroa (2009). A study on similarity and relatedness using distributional and WordNet-based approaches. In *Proc. of NAACL: HLT*, pp. 19–27.

Baroni, M., R. Bernardi, and R. Zamparelli (2014). Frege in space: A program for compositional distributional semantics. *Linguistic Issues in Language Technologies 9*(6), 5–110.

Baroni, M. and A. Lenci (2010). Distributional memory: A general framework for corpus-based semantics. *Computational Linguistics 36*(4), 673–721.

Bradley, M. and P. Lang (1999). Affective norms for English words (ANEW): Stimuli, instruction manual and affective ratings. Tech. report C-1. The Center for Research in Psychophysiology, Univ. of Florida.

Cruse, D. A. (1986). *Lexical Semantics*. Cambridge University Press.

Esuli, A. and F. Sebastiani (2006). SentiWordNet: A publicly available lexical resource for opinion mining. In *Proc. of Conference on Language Resources and Evaluation*, pp. 417–422.

Ferré, P. and R. Sánchez-Casas (2014). Affective priming in a lexical decision task: Is there an effect of words' concreteness? *Psicológica 35*, 117–138.

Finkelstein, L., E. Gabrilovich, Y. Matias, E. Rivlin, Z. Solan, G. Wolfman, and E. Ruppin (2002). Placing search in context: The concept revisited. *ACM Transactions on Information Systems 20*(1), 116–131.

[7]Including verbs, while our network includes only nouns.

Harris, Z. (1954). Distributional structure. *Word 10*(23), 146–162.

Hu, M. and B. Liu (2004). Mining and summarizing customer reviews. In *Proc. of Conference on Knowledge Discovery and Data Mining*, KDD '04, pp. 168–177.

Iosif, E. and A. Potamianos (2015). Similarity computation using semantic networks created from web-harvested data. *Natural Language Engineering 21*(01), 49–79.

Lee, C. M. and S. S. Narayanan (2005). Toward detecting emotions in spoken dialogs. *IEEE Transactions on Speech and Audio Processing 13*(2), 293–303.

Lloyd, L., D. Kechagias, and S. Skiena (2005). Lydia: A system for large-scale news analysis. In *Proc. SPIRE*, Number 3772 in Lecture Notes in Computer Science, pp. 161–166.

Malandrakis, N., A. Potamianos, E. Iosif, and S. Narayanan (2013). Distributional semantic models for affective text analysis. *IEEE Transactions on Audio, Speech, and Language Processing 21*(11), 2379–2392.

McNamara, T. P. (2005). *Semantic priming: Perspectives from Memory and Word Recognition*. Psychology Press.

Miller, G. and W. Charles (1998). Contextual correlates of semantic similarity. *Language and Cognitive Processes 6*(1), 1–28.

Mohammad, S. M., B. J. Dorr, G. Hirst, and P. D. Turney (2013). Computing lexical contrast. *Computational Linguistics 39*(3), 555–590.

Nakov, P., S. Rosenthal, Z. Kozareva, V. Stoyanov, A. Ritter, and T. Wilson (2013). Semeval 2013 task 2: Sentiment analysis in twitter. In *Proc. of Second Joint Conference on Lexical and Computational Semantics (*SEM), Seventh International Workshop on Semantic Evaluation*, pp. 312–320.

Resnik, P. (1995). Using information content to evaluate semantic similarity in a taxonomy. In *Proc. of International Joint Conference for Artificial Intelligence*, pp. 448–453.

Rogers, T. T. and J. L. McClelland (2004). *Semantic Cognition. A Parallel Distributed Processing Approach*. The MIT Press.

Rubenstein, H. and J. B. Goodenough (1965). Contextual correlates of synonymy. *Communications of the ACM 8*(10), 627–633.

Salovey, P. and J. D. Mayer (1990). Emotional intelligence. *Imagination, Cognition and Personality 9*(3), 185–211.

Stone, P. J., D. C. Dunphy, M. S. Smith, and D. M. Ogilvie (1966). *The General Inquirer: A Computer Approach to Content Analysis*. MIT Press.

Strapparava, C. and A. Valitutti (2004). WordNet Affect: An affective extension of WordNet. In *Proc. of Conference on Language Resources and Evaluation*, pp. 1083–1086.

Tomasello, M., M. Carpenter, J. Call, T. Behne, and H. Moll (2005). Understanding and sharing intentions: The origins of cultural cognition. *Behavioral and Brain Sciences 28*, 675–691.

Turney, P. D. (2011). Analogy perception applied to seven tests of word comprehension. *Journal of Experimental and Theoretical Artificial Intelligence 23*(3), 343–362.

Turney, P. D. and M. L. Littman (2003). Measuring praise and criticism: Inference of semantic orientation from association. *ACM Transactions on Information Systems 21*(4), 315–346.

Automatic Noun Compound Interpretation using Deep Neural Networks and Word Embeddings

Corina Dima and Erhard Hinrichs
Collaborative Research Center 833 and Department of Linguistics
University of Tübingen, Germany
{corina.dima,erhard.hinrichs}@uni-tuebingen.de

Abstract

The present paper reports on the results of automatic noun compound interpretation for English using a deep neural network classifier and a selection of publicly available word embeddings to represent the individual compound constituents. The task at hand consists of identifying the semantic relation that holds between the constituents of a compound (e.g. WHOLE+PART_OR_MEMBER_OF in the case of '*robot arm*', LOCATION in the case of '*hillside home*'). The experiments reported in the present paper use the noun compound dataset described in Tratz (2011), a revised version of the dataset used by Tratz and Hovy (2010) for training their Maximum Entropy classifier. Our experiments yield results that are comparable to those reported in Tratz and Hovy (2010) in a cross-validation setting, but outperform their system on unseen compounds by a large margin.

1 Introduction

Recent research in computational semantics has increasingly made use of vector space representations of words in combination with deep neural network classifiers. This recent trend builds on the earlier successes of such representations and classifiers for morphological and syntactic NLP tasks (Collobert et al., 2011), and now also includes semantic tasks such as word similarity, word analogy as well as sentiment analysis (Mikolov et al., 2013; Pennington et al., 2014). The fact that the same type of vector representations can be initially trained for one or more NLP tasks and then be re-used and fine-tuned for a new, seemingly unrelated task suggests that such models can provide a unified architecture for NLP (Collobert and Weston, 2008). The fact that the performance of word embeddings, when combined with deep neural networks, improves in a multi-task learning scenario and can provide state of the art results for NLP further adds to the attractiveness of such methods.

One of the ways to further test the viability of such models and methods is to subject them to a wider range of well-studied NLP tasks and compare the results with previous studies on state-of-the-art NLP datasets.

One such task concerns the automatic interpretation of nominal compounds, a semantic phenomenon that has been widely studied in both theoretical and computational linguistics. This task consists of identifying the semantic relation that holds between the constituents of a compound (e.g. WHOLE+PART_OR_MEMBER_OF in the case of *robot arm*, LOCATION in the case of *hillside home*). Given that noun compounding is a highly productive word formation process in many natural languages, the semantic interpretation of compounds constitutes an important task for a variety of NLP tasks including machine translation, information retrieval, question answering, etc. Due to the productiveness of compounding, an adequate NLP system for the automatic interpretation of compounds will need to be able to generalize well to unseen data, i.e. to compounds that it has not been trained on. Vector space models that are based on very large training corpora and thus have a good coverage of the lexicon of a language provide a good foundation for achieving such generalization behavior. Novel compounds are typically formed of existing words in the language that are recombined to form a new complex word, whose meaning is usually more than the sum of the meaning of its constituents, but which are constrained by the combinatory potential

Proceedings of the 11th International Conference on Computational Semantics, pages 173–183,
London, UK, April 15-17 2015.

of a word. This combinatory potential, i.e. the tendencies to combine with other words, is exactly what is captured in a vector space model, since such models capture the sum of the contexts that a word typically appears in. Hence, vector space models and deep neural network classifiers appear to be well suited for experimenting with this task. Such experiments are facilitated by the availability of a large, annotated dataset of English compounds that is described in Tratz and Hovy (2010); Tratz (2011) and that was used in machine learning experiments.

The present paper reports on the results of experimenting with the Tratz (2011) dataset using four publicly available word embeddings for English and a deep neural network classifier implemented using the Torch7 scientific computing framework (Collobert et al., 2011). These experiments yield results that are comparable to those reported by Tratz and Hovy (2010) and by Tratz (2011), but outperform their system on unseen compounds by a large margin. The remainder of this paper is structured as follows: Section 2 presents previous work related to the automatic classification of compound relations. Sections 3 and 4 present the annotated noun compounds dataset and the four word embeddings that were used in the experiments. These experiments are summarized in Section 5. The paper concludes with a summary of the main results and an outlook towards future work.

2 Related Work

One of the earliest computational approaches to the classification of compound nouns is due to Lauer (1995), who reports an accuracy of 47% at predicting one of 8 possible prepositions using a set of 385 compounds. Rosario and Hearst (2001) obtain 60% accuracy at the task of predicting one of 18 relations using neural networks and a dataset of 1660 compounds. The domain-specific inventory they use was obtained through iterative refinement by considering a set of 2245 extracted compounds and looking for commonalities among them. Girju et al. (2005) use WordNet-based models and SVMs to classify nouns according to an inventory containing 35 semantic relations, and obtain accuracies ranging from 37% to 64%. Kim and Baldwin (2005) report 53% accuracy on the task of identifying one of 20 semantic relations using a WordNet-based similarity approach, given a dataset containing 2169 noun compounds. Ó Séaghdha and Copestake (2013) experiment with the dataset of 1443 compounds introduced in Ó Séaghdha (2008) and obtain 65.4% accuracy when predicting one of 6 possible classes using SVMs and a combination of various types of kernels. Tratz and Hovy (2010) classify English compounds using a new taxonomy with 43 semantic relations, and obtain 79.3% accuracy using a Maximum Entropy classifier and 79.4% accuracy using SVM^{multiclass} on their dataset comprising 17509 compounds and 63.6%(MaxEnt)/63.1%(SVM^{multiclass}) accuracy on the (Ó Séaghdha, 2008) data.

All these efforts have concentrated on English compounds, despite the fact that compounding is a pervasive linguistic phenomenon in many other languages. Recent work by Verhoeven et al. (2012) applied the guidelines proposed by Ó Séaghdha (2008) to annotate compounds in Dutch and Afrikaans with 6 category tags: BE, HAVE, IN, INST, ACTOR and ABOUT. The reported F-Scores are 47.8% on the 1447 compounds Dutch dataset and 51.1% on the 1439 compounds Afrikaans dataset.

3 The Tratz (2011) and Tratz and Hovy (2010) datasets

The experiments reported in this paper use the noun compound dataset described in Tratz (2011)[1]. This dataset, subsequently referred to as the Tratz dataset, is a revised version of the data used by Tratz and Hovy (2010) in their machine learning experiments, subsequently referred to as the Tratz and Hovy dataset. The Tratz dataset is the largest publicly-available annotated noun compound dataset, containing 19158 compounds annotated with 37 semantic relations. Table 1, which is an abbreviated version of Table 4.5 in Tratz (2011), illustrates these relations by characteristic examples and indicates the relative frequency of each relation within the dataset as a whole. The inventory of relations consists of seman-

[1]The dataset is available for download at `http://www.isi.edu/publications/licensed-sw/fanseparser/`

tic categories that resemble but are not identical to the inventories previously proposed by Barker and Szpakowicz (1998) and Girju et al. (2005). Tratz and Hovy (2010) motivate their new inventory by the necessity to achieve more reliable inter-annotator agreement than was obtained for these earlier inventories. The original Tratz and Hovy dataset consisted of 17509 compounds annotated with 43 semantic relations. Tratz (2011)'s motivation for creating a revised noun compound relation inventory with only 37 semantic relations was to create a better mapping between prepositional paraphrases and noun compound relations. The compound classification experiments described in Tratz and Hovy (2010) were, however, not re-run on the revised dataset. Since only the Tratz dataset is publicly available as part of the semantically-enriched parser described in Tratz (2011), this dataset was used in the experiments reported on in the present paper.

4 The embeddings

The automatic classification experiments presented in section 5 use a selection of publicly available word embeddings: the *CW* embeddings[2], decribed in Collobert et al. (2011), the *GloVe* embeddings[3], presented in Pennington et al. (2014), the *HPCA* embeddings[4], described in Lebret and Collobert (2014) and the *word2vec* embeddings[5] introduced by Mikolov et al. (2013). The vector size, the dictionary size, the amount of training data as well as the specific corpora used for creating each of these word embeddings are summarized in Table 2.

A word embedding $W : \mathcal{D} \rightarrow R^n$ is a function that assigns each word from the *embedding dictionary* $\mathcal{D}$ an n-dimensional, real-valued vector. The words in the dictionary $\mathcal{D}$ are *embedded* in a high-dimensional vector space, such that the representations of syntactically and/or semantically similar words are close together in the vector space. Word embeddings are the result of training language models on large amounts of unlabeled, textual data using various learning algorithms.

The *CW* embeddings (Collobert et al., 2011) were obtained by training a language model using a unified neural network architecture. The initial training step used unlabeled data (plain text from the support corpora) for training individual word embeddings. The training procedure uses a context window of size 11. Each context window is considered a positive training example for the word in the middle of the context window, which is called the *target* word. For each positive context window, a corresponding negative context window is generated where the target word is replaced with a random word from the dictionary. The training objective of the neural network can be described as learning to rank the correct context windows higher than the corrupted ones. This initial training step is followed by a supervised training step where the word embeddings are further refined in the context of 4 NLP tasks: part-of-sppech tagging, chunking, named entity recognition and semantic role labeling.

The GloVe model (Pennington et al., 2014) uses statistics of word occurences in a corpus as its primary source of information. It involves constructing a large co-occurence matrix X, where each entry $X_{i}j$ corresponds to the number of times the word j occurs in the context of the word i. The sum of the elements on the i-th row of the matrix represents the number of co-occurences of the word i with any other word in the dictionary in a fixed-size context window (10 words to the left and 10 to the right of the target word). The model uses probability ratios as a mechanism for filtering out "irrelevant words" for a given word-word pair.

Lebret and Collobert (2014) generate the HPCA word embeddings by applying Hellinger PCA to the word co-occurence matrix, a simpler and faster method than training a full neural language model. Word frequencies are obtained by counting each time a word $w \in \mathcal{D}$ occurs after a context sequence of words T. The co-occurence matrix of size N x $|\mathcal{D}|$ contains the computed frequencies for all the words in the dictionary given all the N possible sequences of words. The 10,000 most frequent words in the

[2]The CW embeddings are part of the SENNA NLP suite which can be downloaded from `http://ronan.collobert.com/senna/`

[3]Available at `http://www-nlp.stanford.edu/projects/glove/`

[4]Available at `http://lebret.ch/words/`

[5]Available at `https://code.google.com/p/word2vec/`

Category name	Dataset percentage	Example
Objective		
OBJECTIVE	17.1%	leaf blower
Doer-Cause-Means		
SUBJECT	3.5%	police abuse
CREATOR-PROVIDER-CAUSE_OF	1.5%	ad revenue
JUSTIFICATION	0.3%	murder arrest
MEANS	1.5%	faith healer
Purpose/Activity Group		
PERFORM&ENGAGE_IN	11.5%	cooking pot
CREATE-PROVIDE-GENERATE-SELL	4.8%	nicotine patch
OBTAIN&ACCESS&SEEK	0.9%	shrimp boat
MITIGATE&OPPOSE	0.8%	flak jacket
ORGANIZE&SUPERVISE&AUTHORITY	1.6%	ethics authority
PURPOSE	1.9%	chicken spit
Ownership, Experience, Employment, Use		
OWNER-USER	2.1%	family estate
EXPERIENCER-OF-EXPERIENCE	0.5%	family greed
EMPLOYER	2.3%	team doctor
USER_RECIPIENT	1.0%	voter pamphlet
Temporal Group		
TIME-OF1	2.2%	night work
TIME-OF2	0.5%	birth date
Location and Whole+Part/Member of		
LOCATION	5.2%	hillside home
WHOLE+PART_OR_MEMBER_OF	1.7%	robot arm
Composition and Containment Group		
CONTAIN	1.2%	shoe box
SUBSTANCE-MATERIAL-INGREDIENT	2.6%	plastic bag
PART&MEMBER_OF_COLLECTION&CONFIG&SERIES	1.8%	truck convoy
VARIETY&GENUS_OF	0.1%	plant species
AMOUNT-OF	0.9%	traffic volume
Topic Group		
TOPIC	7.0%	travel story
TOPIC_OF_COGNITION&EMOTION	0.3%	auto fanatic
TOPIC_OF_EXPERT	0.7%	policy expert
Other Complements Group		
RELATIONAL-NOUN-COMPLEMENT	5.6%	eye shape
WHOLE+ATTRIBUTE&FEATURE &QUALITY_VALUE_IS_CHARACTERISTIC_OF	0.3%	earth tone
Attributive and Equative		
EQUATIVE	5.4%	fighter plane
ADJ-LIKE_NOUN	1.3%	core activity
PARTIAL_ATTRIBUTE_TRANSFER	0.3%	skeleton crew
MEASURE	4.2%	hour meeting
Other		
LEXICALIZED	0.8%	pig iron
OTHER	5.4%	contact lense
Personal*		
PERSONAL_NAME	0.5%	Ronald Reagan
PERSONAL_TITLE	0.5%	Gen. Eisenhower

Table 1: Semantic relation inventory used by the Tratz dataset - abbreviated version of Table 4.5 from Tratz (2011). Note that some relations have a slightly different name in the actual dataset than the aforementioned table; this table lists the relation names as found in the dataset.

Name	Embedding size	Dictionary size	Training data size	Support corpora
CW	50	130,000	0.85 bn	enWikipedia + Reuters RCV1
GloVe	300	400,000	42.00 bn	Common Crawl (42 bn)
HPCA	200	178,080	1.65 bn	enWikipedia + Reuters + WSJ
word2vec	300	3,000,000	100.00 bn	Google News dataset

Table 2: Overview of embedding sizes, dictionary sizes, training data sizes and support corpora for the four selected embeddings. The training data size is reported in billions of words.

dictionary were considered as context words, and size of the word sequence T was set to 1.

Mikolov et al. (2013) uses a continuous Skip-gram model to learn a distributed vector representation that captures both syntactic and semantic word relationships. The authors define the training objective of this model as the ability to find "word representations that are useful for predicting the surrounding words in a sentence or a document". The training context for a word is defined as c words to the left and to the right of the word.

For the *GloVe* and *HPCA* embeddings there are multiple sizes of word embeddings available: 50, 100, 200, 300 (6 billion words support corpus) and 300 dimensions (42 billion words support corpus) for *GloVe* and 50, 100 and 200 dimensions for *HPCA*. We have experimented with all the different sizes for each embedding and it was always the highest dimensional embedding that gave the best results in the cross-validation setup. Therefore, due to space limitations we only report results for the maximum size of each embedding.

5 The experiments

This section summarizes the experiments performed on the Tratz dataset using the four embeddings described in the previous section. Section 5.1 describes the pre-processing steps that had to be performed on the Tratz dataset in order to make it inter-operable with the embedding dictionaries. Section 5.2 describes the architecture of the classifier used in all the experiments. Section 5.3 presents the experiments performed using each of the embeddings individually as well as the best performing system that resulted from the concatenation of three out of the four selected word embeddings.

5.1 Dataset pre-processing

In order to make the best use of the word embeddings described in the previous section, several pre-processing steps had to be performed. The Tratz dataset contains about 1% training examples that are person names or titles starting with a capital letter, whereas such names appear in all lowercase in the embedding dictionaries[6]. Therefore all compound constituents of the Tratz dataset were converted to lowercase. This resulted in a *constituent dictionary* $\mathcal{C}$, $|\mathcal{C}| = 5242$ unique constituents for the entire Tratz dataset of 19158 compound instances.

The constituent dictionary $\mathcal{C}$ obtained from the Tratz dataset includes complex words such as '*health-care*' that are themselves compounds and which appear in the dataset as parts of larger compounds such as '*health-care legislation*'. Moreover, such complex words are not uniform in their spelling, appearing sometimes as a single word (e.g. '*healthcare*'), sometimes hyphenated (e.g. '*health-care*') and sometimes as two separate words (e.g. '*health care*'). Therefore such spelling variation had to be adapted to the spelling conventions used by each individual embedding. The same type of adaptation had to be performed in the case of misspelled words in the Tratz dataset and singular/plural forms of the same lemma. In cases where a constituent appears in the embedding dictionary as two separate words we use the average of the individual word embeddings as a representation for the constituent.

[6]On linguistic grounds, it is highly questionable whether personal names should be included in a compound dataset. However, since they are part of the Tratz dataset, we chose not remove them.

The Tratz dataset also contains some infrequent English words such as '*chintz*' (in '*chintz skirt*'), '*fastbreak*' (in '*fastbreak layup*') or '*secretin*' (in '*sham secretin*'), which are not part of the embeddings dictionaries. We used an unknown word embedding for representing such words. This embedding is already part of the dictionary for some embeddings (e.g. the *CW* embedding), and was obtained by averaging over the embeddings corresponding to the least frequent 1000 words for the other embeddings.

The pre-processed Tratz dataset was then partitioned into *train*, *dev* and *test* splits containing 13409, 1920 and 3829 noun compounds, respectively. The combined *train* and *dev* splits were also used to construct a 10-fold cross-validation set.

5.2 Classifier architecture

We used a deep neural network classifier implemented in the Torch7 scientific computing framework (Collobert et al., 2011) for the automatic classification of noun compounds. The classifier is trained in a supervised manner on the examples in the Tratz dataset. A training example pairs the two constituents of a compound (e.g. the individual words '*robot*' and '*arm*' in the case of '*robot arm*') with a semantic relation from the relation inventory (e.g. WHOLE+PART_OR_MEMBER_OF).

Figure 1 displays the architecture of the network which consists of four layers: an input layer, a lookup table, a hidden layer and an output layer. The lookup table (Figure 1a) is a $|\mathcal{C}|$xN matrix which contains an N-dimensional embedding for every entry in the constituent dictionary $\mathcal{C}$.

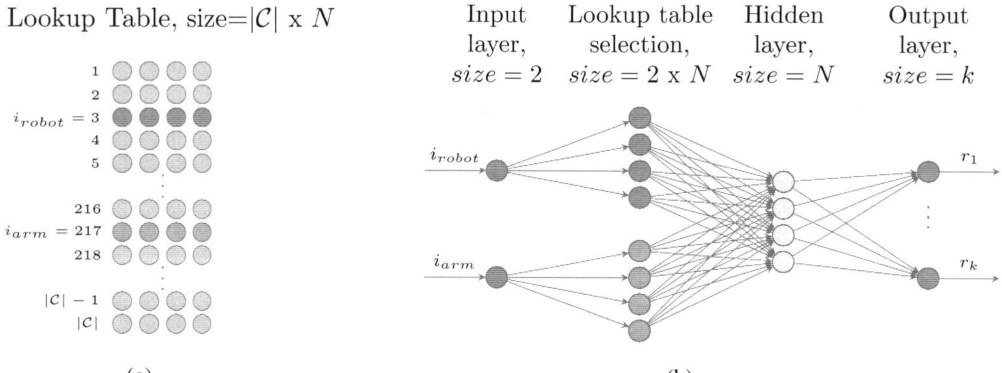

(a) (b)

Figure 1: Classifier architecture

When a training example is presented to the network, the input layer and the lookup table are used to extract the word representations for the two constituents of the example compound. The input layer is used to input two numerical indices that uniquely identify each constituent in the constituent dictionary. These indices are then used to select the individual word representations of the compound constituents from the lookup table. The selected representations are concatenated and the combined representation is fed to the subsequent hidden layer. This hidden layer is intended to capture regularities in the data that are relevant for selecting the correct semantic relation of the example compound. Since the hidden layer is fully connected to the previous layer, such regularities can be drawn from the word representations of both compound constituents, as well as from the relative order of the two constituents. The optimal size of the hidden layer (N, which matches the size of the initial word representation) was determined empirically based on the *dev* split.

The resulting compound representation is then passed through a non-linearity (the logistic function, $\frac{1}{1+exp^{-x}}$) that maps it to the final output layer. The size of the output layer equals the number of semantic relations in the Tratz dataset. A softmax function is used to pick the semantic class which was assigned the highest score by the neural network classifier.

The purpose of the lookup table is to allow the generic word embeddings, which were constructed independently of the compound classification task, to be *fine-tuned* to the current task. This fine-tuning is made possible by having the lookup table as an intermediate layer in the network – and thus modifiable by backpropagation during the training process – as opposed to having the embeddings directly as the input of the network. The fine-tuning of embeddings for a particular task, other than the one they have been initially trained for, has been advocated and proven effective by Collobert et al. (2011); Lebret and Collobert (2014) in the case of several NLP tasks like part-of-speech tagging, named entity recognition and sentiment analysis. In order to gauge the impact of embedding fine-tuning for the present task we compared the results of training a classifier with and without fine-tuning. The classifier without fine-tuning consists of an input layer of size 2 x N, a hidden layer of size N, and the output layer.

The network was trained using the negative log likelihood criterion, using averaged stochastic gradient descent optimization (Bottou, 2012) with a batch size of 5 and an initial learning rate of 0.9. The learning rate is adapted during the training phase, by setting it to 0.3 once the error on the development set is lower then a specified threshold. We used the *dev* split to choose the hyper-parameters of the model, which were used in all the reported experiments.

An early stopping criterion was employed in order to avoid the inherent tendency of neural networks to overfit the training data. We used a criterion proposed by Prechelt (1998), namely stop the training when the generalization error (i.e. the error on the *dev* set) has increased in s successive epochs. We set the number of successive epochs in which the generalization error is allowed to fluctuate to $s = 5$. The final model returned by the training procedure is the model with the best generalization error that was discovered during the training procedure.

5.3 Results

This section discusses the results of the experiments conducted with the neural network classifier presented in the previous section, using the four embeddings described in Section 4. The models are trained using the splits described in Section 3 in three setups: the DEV setup, where the model is trained on the *train* split and tested on the *dev* split; the CV setup, where the model is trained and tested using the 10-fold cross-validation set; the TEST setup, where the model is trained on the combined *train* and *dev* splits and tested on the *test* split. Each model is trained using two architectures: one using fine-tuning (DEV-F, CV-F, TEST-F) and one without fine-tuning (DEV-NO-F, CV-NO-F, TEST-NO-F). The results obtained for these three setups and these two architectures are summarized in Table 3. All the results in this table represent micro-averaged F1 measures[7].

Input embeddings	DEV-NO-F	DEV-F	CV-NO-F	CV-F	TEST-NO-F	TEST-F
CW-50	65.83	78.39	63.59	74.71	66.62	76.03
GloVe-300	74.17	77.81	72.89	76.57	76.05	75.87
HPCA-200	61.45	77.14	70.58	76.66	64.56	76.00
word2vec-300	71.46	73.54	69.07	71.93	71.38	71.59
random embeddings	-	74.17	-	64.54	-	71.43
CW-50+GloVe-300+HPCA-200	**79.01**	**79.48**	**76.20**	**77.70**	**78.14**	**77.12**

Table 3: Results for the task of automatic classification of noun compounds, using the same embeddings with two different architectures: (i) with fine-tuning (F) and (ii) without fine-tuning (NO-F)

The first four rows of Table 3 show the results obtained by the classifier when the individual compound constituents are represented using the four embeddings introduced in Section 4. The cross-validation setup provides the most representative results for the models trained on the Tratz dataset since it is based on different splits of data and averages the results of the individual folds. In all four cases, the models that perform embedding fine-tuning (CV-F) have consistently better results compared to the models that don't change the initial embeddings (CV-NO-F). The improvement brought about by fine-tuning is largest for the *CW* embedding (11.12 increase in F1 score). A plausible explanation for this

[7]The classification task at hand is an instance of *one-of* or *multinomial* classification, therefore micro-averaged F1 is the same as the accuracy.

improvement might be related to the size of the embedding. The *CW* embedding is much shorter than the other three embeddings, and hence the information in the embedding is therefore more coarse-grained. Fine-tuning such relatively coarse-grained word representations to the task at hand is then likely to yield a higher payoff. The importance of fine-tuning is further underscored by the fact that even with an initial random embedding the trained classifier is able to obtain an F1 score of 64.54 in the CV setup.

The classification results can be further improved by using word representations that are obtained by concatenating the word vectors from different embeddings. We experimented with using all the 11 possible combinations of the four embeddings (taken 2,3 and 4 at a time) as the initial representation of a constituent, and both architectures (with/without fine-tuning). The combination of all but the *word2vec* embedding as initial word representations, together with the fine-tuning architecture, empirically yielded the highest results (77.70 F1 score) in the cross-validation setup. Notice also that the size of the network grows considerably when the word representations of different embeddings are concatenated, not only for the input layers but also for the hidden layer, leading to a much more difficult training task when compared to more compact representations. This underscores the importance and effectiveness of good representations for the task at hand, since the performance of the classifier improves despite the more complex training task inherent in such larger networks. It also interesting to note that the training converges faster for the models that fine-tune the initial embeddings than for the ones that don't modify the input embeddings[8].

For completeness, we also report the results obtained for the DEV setup. These results are, as is to be expected, consistently higher than the ones obtained for the cross-validation setup. The improved performance on the DEV set can be explained by the fact that this setup was used to choose the hyper-parameters of the system (learning rate, batch size, optimization method, stopping criterion threshold). The improved performance could additionally be due to idiosyncrasies resulting from the particular split of the data.

The generalization capability to novel compounds of all the models can best be gauged by the results obtained on the unseen data provided by the TEST setup. The *test* split of the dataset contains 3829 compounds with a total of 2479 unique constituents. Almost a fifth of the the total number of constituents in the *test* split (18.23%) appear only in the *test* split, and were thus not seen by the classifier during the training process. As for the other DEV and CV setups, the fine-tuning process has the highest positive effect on the *CW* and *HPCA* embeddings and the performance of the combined embeddings once again outperforms the one of the individual embeddings. When comparing these results to those obtained for the CV setup, the most striking result is that there is almost no degradation in performance for the model with fine-tuning (77.12 TEST vs 77.70 CV F1 score) and actually an increase for the model without fine-tuning (78.14 TEST vs 76.20 CV F1 score).

The results of our experiments also support one empirical observation, namely that the impact of fine-tuning the embeddings decreases as the amount of data they have initially been trained on increases. The embeddings that gain the least from fine-tuning, or even perform slightly better without fine-tuning, are, in our experiments, the *GloVe* and the *word2vec* embeddings, as well as the combinations that include at least one of them. The common denominator of these embeddings is the large amount of data used for their initial training (between 40-100 times more training data than for the other embeddings, see Table 2). The embeddings trained on large support corpora seem therefore to be better suited for direct use in new tasks and have less to gain from fine-tuning, whereas the ones trained on small corpora perform considerably better if they are fine-tuned for new tasks.

Another key aspect underlined by our results is that a neural architecture in combination with the pre-trained, highly-informative word embeddings display a good generalization performance. Due to the high productivity of compounding, which leads to a constant stream of unseen data instances in real-world texts, such generalization ability is particularly important for the task at hand. This generalization ability is in part due to the nature of the word embeddings, which contain implicit information about the lexical semantics of all words in the embedding dictionary $\mathcal{D}$ trained by the initial language model.

[8]For example, in the Test setup, the models with fine-tuning stop, on average, after 15.2 training epochs, while the variants without fine-tuning stop only after an average of 38 training epochs.

While the constituent dictionary C used in the supervised training of the compound classification model is only a small subset of the original embedding dictionary $\mathcal{D}$ (e.g. 5242 vs 130000 words for the *CW* embedding), the lexical information about the remaining (e.g. 124 758) words is still implicitly present in the representation.

robot arm (H) WHOLE+PART_OR_MEMBER_OF	**plastic bag (H)** SUBSTANCE-MATERIAL-INGREDIENT	**birth date (H)** TIME-OF2	**hour meeting (H)** MEASURE	**cooking pot (H)** PERFORM&ENGAGE_IN	**hillside home (H)** LOCATION
dinosaur wing	leather bag	departure date	minute meeting	cooking fork	waterfront home
airplane wing	canvas bag	expiration date	week meeting	fishing pole	patio furniture
mouse skull	cardboard tray	release date	day meeting	recycling bin	fairway bunker
jet engine	gelatin capsule	expiry date	hour course	cooking liquid	beach house
airplane instrument	metal rack	election period	week course	drinking water	basement apartment
pant leg	wire rack	election date	month course	exercise room	ocean water
fighter wing	glass bottle	completion date	week conference	storage bin	cupboard door
bunny ear	tin plate	signing period	year course	fishing town	beach resort
goose wing	glass jar	launch date	hour journey	fishing village	bedroom door
shirt sleeve	wicker basket	redemption date	minute speech	feeding tube	basement vault

Table 4: Nearest neighbors of compounds from the Tratz dataset using **hidden layer representations**.

robot arm (I) WHOLE+PART_OR_MEMBER_OF	**plastic bag (I)** SUBSTANCE-MATERIAL-INGREDIENT	**birth date (I)** TIME-OF2	**hour meeting (I)** MEASURE	**cooking pot (I)** PERFORM&ENGAGE_IN	**hillside home (I)** LOCATION
robot spider	leather bag	delivery date	minute meeting	cooking spray	waterfront home
foot arm	plastic chain	payment date	day meeting	cooking fork	brick home
service arm	plastic pencil	birth weight	night meeting	cooking method	trailer home
mouse skull	garbage bag	election date	week meeting	flower pot	winter home
machine operator	canvas bag	publication date	weekend meeting	cooking liquid	boyhood home
elephant leg	plastic glove	release date	morning meeting	cooking class	retirement home
car body	diaper bag	departure date	afternoon meeting	cooking time	summer home
airplane wing	trash bag	redemption date	hour session	clay pot	family home
property arm	plastic sphere	completion date	evening meeting	cooking show	troop home
rocket system	glass bottle	retirement date	hour event	cooking demonstration	group home

Table 5: Nearest neighbors of compounds from the Tratz dataset using **initial embeddings**.

Additional evidence for the excellent generalization capability of the models reported on in this paper can be gleaned from inspecting the compound representations as constructed by the neural network at the hidden layer level. To this end we loaded the best performing model and removed the output layer, thus being able to isolate the representations constructed by the network for the Tratz compound dataset and to compute cosine similarity measures directly between the compound representations. Table 4 presents a selection of compounds from the Tratz dataset together with their closest 10 neighbors using the *hidden layer representations*. It is quite instructive to compare these 10 nearest neighbors with the 10 nearest neighbors from Table 5, obtained by computing cosine similarities with the *initial compound representations* (taken directly from the best performing combination of embeddings: CW-50+GloVe-300+HPCA-200). For the initial representations, similarity is largely restricted to compounds that share one of the constituents with the compound under consideration. The generalization potential of the initial embedding is thus largely restricted to partial string similarity (e.g. the nearest neighbors to '*cooking pot*' are compounds that contain either '*cooking*' or '*pot*' as one of their constituents). The neighbors obtained via the hidden layer representations display a much greater string variability, and at the same time a much stronger semantic similarity to the target compound. This semantic similarity manifests itself in a remarkable consistency in semantic relation (e.g. the PERFORM&ENGAGE_IN relation in '*cooking pot*' is shared by all of its 10 nearest neighbors when using the hidden layer representation). It is this combination of string variability and strong semantic similarity of the hidden layer representations that allows the network to generalize well to unseen data.

We conclude this section with a comparison of the results obtained for the present experiments with the results obtained by Tratz and Hovy (2010) using a Maximum Entropy (ME) classifier and a large number of boolean features. The features used to represent compounds in the Tratz and Hovy (2010) experiments are based on information from WordNet (synonym, hypernyms, gloss, etc.), from Roget's

Thesaurus, surface-level information (suffixes, prefixes) as well as term usage information in the form of n-grams. The ME classifier takes into account only the most useful 35000 features. Due to differences between the Tratz and Hovy dataset used by Tratz and Hovy (2010) and the Tratz dataset used in the present experiments, a direct comparison is not possible. These differences concern the number of data instances as well as the number of semantic relations – see Section 3 for a more detailed discussion. Such details notwithstanding, it is fair to say that our best result obtained in the cross-validation setting (77.70 F1 score) is close in performance to the reported state of the art (79.3% accuracy obtained by Tratz and Hovy (2010)) for this setting. However, our system outperforms that of Tratz and Hovy (2010) on the classification of unseen compounds by a wide margin (77.12 F1 score vs 51.0% accuracy). While the same disclaimer about the differences in the dataset used by Tratz and Hovy and in the present study applies for the unseen compounds in the *test* set, the fact that we obtained comparable results for the cross-validation (CV) and in the test (TEST) setups speaks well for the robustness of our model.

6 Conclusion

In this paper we have presented a deep neural network classifier approach for the task of automatic noun compound interpretation for English. We have shown that this approach achieves comparable results to the state of the art system trained on a closely-related dataset and significantly outperforms this earlier system when confronted with unseen compounds. Another advantage of our approach derives from the use of pre-trained word embeddings as word representations, rather than using large, manually selected feature sets that are constructed and optimized for a specific task as the initial word representations. Since word embeddings are more generic in nature and allow for re-training in a multi-task scenario, this approach has the potential of being reused, including for related tasks of semantic interpretation of compounds by prepositional paraphrasing, as has been proposed by Lauer (1995), or free paraphrasing, which has been the subject of a shared SemEval task (Hendrickx et al., 2013). However, for the time being, we have to leave such re-purposing to future research. Another direction for future research is to test our approach on other available noun compound datasets for English such as the one provided by Ó Séaghdha (2008). This would allow us to directly compare our approach to earlier systems trained on these datasets. Since the Tratz dataset is considerably larger than all the other publicly datasets, also testing our system on the latter and comparing the relative performance would allow us to better estimate the impact of the training data size as well as the one of the annotation scheme when training deep neural network classifiers for automatic noun compound interpretation.

Acknowledgements

The authors would like to thank the anonymous reviewers for their very useful suggestions. Financial support for the research reported in this paper was provided by the German Research Foundation (DFG) as part of the Collaborative Research Center "Emergence of Meaning" (SFB 833) and by the German Ministry of Education and Technology (BMBF) as part of the research grant CLARIN-D.

References

Barker, K. and S. Szpakowicz (1998). Semi-automatic recognition of noun modifier relationships. In *Proceedings of the 36th Annual Meeting of the Association for Computational Linguistics and 17th International Conference on Computational Linguistics*.

Bottou, L. (2012). Stochastic gradient descent tricks. In *Neural Networks: Tricks of the Trade*, pp. 421–436. Springer.

Collobert, R., K. Kavukcuoglu, and C. Farabet (2011). Torch7: A Matlab-like environment for machine learning. In *BigLearn, NIPS Workshop*, Number EPFL-CONF-192376.

Collobert, R. and J. Weston (2008). A unified architecture for natural language processing: Deep neural networks with multitask learning. In *Proceedings of the 25th international conference on Machine learning*, pp. 160–167. ACM.

Collobert, R., J. Weston, L. Bottou, M. Karlen, K. Kavukcuoglu, and P. Kuksa (2011). Natural language processing (almost) from scratch. *The Journal of Machine Learning Research 12*, 2493–2537.

Girju, R., D. Moldovan, M. Tatu, and D. Antohe (2005). On the semantics of noun compounds. *Computer Speech and Language 19*(4), 479–496.

Hendrickx, I., P. Nakov, S. Szpakowicz, Z. Kozareva, D. O. Séaghdha, and T. Veale (2013). SemEval-2013 Task 4: Free paraphrases of noun compounds. *Atlanta, Georgia, USA*, 138.

Kim, S. N. and T. Baldwin (2005). Automatic interpretation of noun compounds using WordNet similarity. In *Proceedings of the 2nd International Joint Conference on Natural Language Processing*.

Lauer, M. (1995). *Designing Statistical Language Learners: Experiments on Compound Nouns*. Ph. D. thesis, Macquarie University.

Lebret, R. and R. Collobert (2014). Word embeddings through Hellinger PCA. In *Proceedings of the 14th Conference of the European Chapter of the Association for Computational Linguistics (EACL 2014)*, Gothenburg, Sweden, pp. 482–490. Association for Computational Linguistics.

Mikolov, T., I. Sutskever, K. Chen, G. S. Corrado, and J. Dean (2013). Distributed representations of words and phrases and their compositionality. In *Advances in Neural Information Processing Systems*, pp. 3111–3119.

Ó Séaghdha, D. (2008). *Learning compound noun semantics*. Ph. D. thesis, Computer Laboratory, University of Cambridge. Published as University of Cambridge Computer Laboratory Technical Report 735.

Ó Séaghdha, D. and A. Copestake (2013). Interpreting compound nouns with kernel methods. *Natural Language Engineering 19*(03), 331–356.

Pennington, J., R. Socher, and C. D. Manning (2014). GloVe: Global vectors for word representation. In *Proceedings of the Empiricial Methods in Natural Language Processing (EMNLP 2014)*, Volume 12.

Prechelt, L. (1998). Early stopping-but when? In *Neural Networks: Tricks of the trade*, pp. 55–69. Springer.

Rosario, B. and M. Hearst (2001). Classifying the semantic relations in noun compounds. In *Proceedings of the 2001 Conference on Empirical Methods in Natural Language Processing*.

Tratz, S. (2011). *Semantically-enriched parsing for natural language understanding*. Ph. D. thesis, University of Southern California.

Tratz, S. and E. Hovy (2010). A taxonomy, dataset, and classifier for automatic noun compound interpretation. In *Proceedings of the 48th Annual Meeting of the Association for Computational Linguistics (ACL-10)*, Uppsala, Sweden.

Verhoeven, B., W. Daelemans, and G. B. van Huyssteen (2012). Classification of Noun-Noun Compound Semantics in Dutch and Afrikaans. In *Proceedings of the Twenty-Third Annual Symposium of the Pattern Recognition Association of South Africa*, Pretoria, South Africa, pp. 121–125.

Integrating Non-Linguistic Events into Discourse Structure*

Julie Hunter
IRIT, Université Toulouse III
juliehunter@gmail.com

Nicholas Asher
IRIT, CNRS
nicholas.asher@irit.fr

Alex Lascarides
University of Edinburgh
alex@inf.ed.ac.uk

Abstract

Interpreting an utterance sometimes depends on the presence and nature of non-linguistic actions. In this paper, we motivate and develop a semantic model of embodied interaction in which the contribution that non-linguistic events make to the content of the interaction is dependent on their rhetorical connections to other actions, both linguistic and non-linguistic. We support our claims with concrete examples from a corpus of online chats, comparing annotations of the linguistic-only content against annotations in which non-linguistic events in the context are taken into account.

1 Introduction

Embodied conversation enables a speaker to refer to non-linguistic entities in the surrounding situation, using little to no descriptive content. Models of non-linguistic context dependence tend to focus on a fairly well-defined set of expressions, with their reference to entities in the non-linguistic context governed by rules provided by the lexical entry of each expression. Indexical and demonstrative expressions (*I*, *now*, *that*, ...) are the most visible examples (Kaplan, 1989). There are also numerous models of linguistic context dependence, or anaphora, tackling the anaphoric properties of lexical items like *he*, with theories of the *rhetorical structure* of discourse (e.g. Asher (1993), Asher and Lascarides (2003), Hobbs et al. (1993), Mann and Thompson (1987)) that analyze context-dependent relations between entire units of discourse. For example, the eventuality described by one unit might serve to explain the eventuality described by another, or it might stand in contrast to another, and so on.

This paper addresses the discourse interactions between linguistic and non-linguistic events and the resulting contribution of non-linguistic events to semantic content. Situated dialogue makes widespread use of the non-linguistic context, in ways that go beyond demonstrative reference. But comparatively little attention has been dedicated to modeling this interaction, even within theories of discourse. This is perhaps because doing so requires assigning semantic contents to non-linguistic eventualities in the context. Linguistically specified contents carry information about how eventualities should be individuated and conceptualized; contents that are not specified linguistically are left to interpreters to sort out in context. Suppose a waiter approaches you with a bottle of champagne and gives you a certain look. You respond "No, thank you. I'm driving." or you merely shake your head and show him your keys. You have understood that he was offering you champagne and you have coherently responded to his implicit question of whether you would like some. To react appropriately to his action, you not only had to isolate the important features in the visual scene—the look in his eyes, but not the fact that he blinked, for example—you also had to understand that these features came together to produce a *meaningful* act with a particular semantic content and you had to understand that content.

We develop a formally precise pragmatic model of linguistic and non-linguistic interactions by drawing on a corpus of chats taken from an on-line version of the game *Settlers of Catan*. The *Settlers* corpus

*This research was supported by ERC Advanced Grant n. 269427. We thank Eric Kow and reviewers for helpful comments.

Proceedings of the 11th International Conference on Computational Semantics, pages 184–194,
London, UK, April 15-17 2015.

is ideal for our task: firstly, non-linguistic events in the game (dice rolls, card plays, the building of settlements and roads, etc.) are crucial for understanding many of the comments made in the chats; and secondly, the controlled, task-oriented environment minimizes interlocutors' differences in conceptualizing non-linguistic events. The meaning of each non-linguistic event in the game is determined by the game rules and set up. For example, when a blue building appears on the game board, it is clear to all players that the player who was designated as blue at the game's start has just built a settlement on that portion of the board. Minimizing conceptualization problems allows us to examine how non-linguistic events affect the structure of discourse—in particular, how they affect the structures posited by Asher and Lascarides' (2003) *Segmented Discourse Representation Theory* (SDRT), which we adopt as our starting point. Not only do we feel that SDRT is a promising semantic model of discourse, but the *Settlers* corpus is annotated with SDRT's coherence relations. We nevertheless recognize that other approaches to the study of situated dialogue are possible, though we reserve a larger discussion for another occasion.

After introducing our corpus in §2, §3 discusses examples that both highlight the importance of non-linguistic events in our corpus and complicate the task of building discourse structures for our chats. §4 extends SDRT to handle these. §5 addresses some questions that arise from treating non-linguistic events as semantic elements, while §6 situates our project with respect to related work.

2 The *Settlers* Corpus

Settlers is a win-lose game in which players use resources (e.g. wood and sheep) to build roads and settlements. Players build on a game board that is divided into multiple regions, each associated with a certain type of resource and a number between 2 and 12. Players acquire resources in various ways: e.g., through trades with other players or the bank and through rolling two dice. A roll of a 4 and a 2, for example, gives any player with a settlement on a 6 region that region's resource. A player who rolls 7, however, moves the *robber* to a region of her choice (there is no region marked with a 7) and she can then steal from a player whose buildings are on that region. Players with settlements on the region occupied by the robber don't receive its associated resources, whatever the dice rolls.

Trades involve moves that we call *offers*, in which one player proposes to exchange particular resources with another. A successful trade involves an explicit acceptance of an offer. In the original online version of *Settlers*, trades take place non-linguistically, via mouse-clicks, etc. But in our corpus, each player was instructed to negotiate the trade via the online chat interface (see Afantenos et al. (2012) for details). In fact, players chatted not only about trades, but about many aspects of the game state, including building actions and dice rolls. The corpus consists of 59 games, and each game contains dozens of individual negotiation dialogues, each consisting of anywhere from 1 to over 30 dialogue turns. The corpus was collected in three distinct phases: a pilot phase, and two seasons of competitions, the second culminating in a "master's league," with the best players of the second season playing an eliminatory competition to choose an overall winner.

Our corpus manifests a wide variety of examples, including (1)-(3) below, in which linguistically specified contents anaphorically depend on contents of non-linguistic events, and vice versa. When we consider the linguistically specified content alone (b-examples), it is highly ambiguous—*Woo* on its own could be a comment on practically anything, for example—but when the b-examples are taken with their non-linguistic antecedents (a-examples), their interpretations are constrained.

(1) a. [i offers 1 wheat for 1 sheep from j]
b. i: if you have one

(2) a. [i offers 1 wheat for 1 sheep from j]
b. i: or an ore

(3) a. [i rolled a 2 and a 1.] [j gets 2 sheep, 2 wheat. i gets 1 wheat.]
b. i: Woo!

The *Settlers* corpus was originally designed as a tool for studying strategic conversation, not the non-linguistic context, so annotators were given only the verbal exchanges from the chats and told to annotate them for discourse structure in the style of SDRT. A little over 1000 dialogues have been annotated so far. Observations of the effects of excluding non-linguistic events from the annotations (see section 3) have prompted a second round of annotations that includes non-linguistic events. This involves importing descriptions of the non-linguistic events (dice rolls, card plays, etc.) from the game log into the annotation files. The full game log temporally orders all linguistic and non-linguistic game events, yielding an automatic alignment of each utterance with the current game state and an explicit numbering of each turn in the game. Because not all turns from the game log were originally assigned numbers, some server turns are given decimal numbers (e.g. 222.4, *vide infra*) to preserve the original numbering.

Many descriptions of non-linguistic events from the game log are public to the players. These descriptions, whose interpretations are determined by the game rules and state, give the *Settlers* corpus a major advantage for the study of non-linguistic events in discourse: they minimize the effects of the individuation and conceptualization problems, and they also allow us to presuppose joint attention of the players, ensuring that all information can be considered to have entered the common ground.[1]

One might worry, however, that because the server produces these descriptions it should really be considered a conversational participant and the events that we are treating as non-linguistic should really count as linguistically-specified. We do not think this is a concern. First of all, the fact that the non-linguistic events in the game are assigned a semantic content does not make them any less non-linguistic. Reasoning about any non-linguistic events, not just those in our corpus, requires that they be conceptualized. This blurs the line between linguistic and non-linguistic events, but we think this is called for by the nature of situated dialogue. Second of all, the players do not need to rely on the server messages to know what is going on in the game; the messages are helpful only as a record for annotators and for players who might have a lapse in attention. Players can tell by looking at the game board where the robber is located and can see if he moves; they can tell when the dice have been passed to a new player because a pointer on the screen will move to the part of the screen dedicated to that player; and so on. Consider an analogy with a sports game in which player A pushes player B and B yells, "Hey, you can't do that!". The fact that there may be a sports announcer who described the pushing does not make the pushing any less non-linguistic and does not mean that the B's reaction was a reaction to a linguistically-specified event, even if B can hear what the announcer is saying.

3 Analysis of the data

3.1 Crossover

To see how the non-linguistic context affects the discourse structure of our chats, we re-examined 5 games from different parts of the *Settlers* corpus: two from the pilot phase, one from season 1 of the competition, and two from season 2 including one Master's League game. We found many examples in which linguistic moves depend in various ways on non-linguistic events; e.g., examples (1)-(3). Conversely, there are numerous examples in which linguistic moves serve as antecedents to non-linguistic actions. This is common after trade negotiations: a successful linguistic negotiation will result in the non-linguistic action of offering a trade through the game interface; an unsuccessful negotiation will generally result either in an alternative type of trade, such as a trade with the bank, or with the player leading the negotiation ending his turn, thus passing the dice to the next player.

(4)	234	18:55:02:745	gotwood4sheep	anyone got wheat for a sheep?
	235	18:55:10:047	inca	sorry, not me
	236	18:55:18:787	CheshireCatGrin	nope. you seem to have lots of sheep!
	237	18:55:23:428	gotwood4sheep	yup baaa
	238	18:55:32:308	dmm	i think i'd rather hang on to my wheat i'm afraid
	239	18:55:47:845	gotwood4sheep	kk I'll take my chances then...

gotwood4sheep's (GWS) decision to take his chances (239) is the result of the failed negotiation (234-238); turns 234-239 then together result in his ending his turn. On its own, 239 doesn't make much sense—what chances would he be taking? and why is he taking them now? It is the connection between 234-239 and the non-linguistic move of GWS ending his turn, as well as the risks of end-turn moves in

[1]Thank you to an anonymous reviewer for raising this last point and the worry that follows.

the larger game state, that restrict the interpretation of 239: in passing the dice, GWS risks the possibility that another player might roll a 7, causing him to lose precious resources.

Because non-linguistic events were ignored, the first-round of annotations on the *Settlers* corpus contains numerous incorrect attachments and thus incorrect discourse logical forms for the associated chats. In (5), for example, 564 is incorrectly attached to 561 as a Comment.

	561	17:47:24:638	Euan	Ooh! Clay :D
	562	17:47:25:424	Server	jon rolled a 4 and a 4.
(5)	563	17:47:25:426	Server	Cardlinger gets 3 wood. Joel gets 2 ore. Euan gets 1 ore.
	564	17:47:26:064	Cardlinger	that was an easy turn for me :D
	565	17:47:39:875	Euan	I like this "getting resources" business.

The linguistic clues used to guide attachment for 564 were misleading: 561 suggests that someone, probably Euan (E), received clay and that E was happy about it. In 564, Cardlinger (C) expresses a positive attitude about a turn and his comment suggests that he benefited from the turn without doing anything, which is common with resource distributions. E's comment in 565 seems to confirm a resource distribution. Similarities between 561 and 564 and the fact that 562-3 are missing in the original annotation file, led annotators to conclude that C was commenting on the same turn and resource distribution as E.

Treating 564 as a comment on 561 is problematic in part because even if E and C had been commenting on the same event, 561 and 564 should have been either related by a relation like Parallel or understood as two independent comments and so not related at all. Moreover, 564 is, of course, a comment on a completely different event: the mistaken annotation of (5) entails that the token of *that* in 564 refers to an event other than the one that it actually refers to.

The first round of annotations also suffers from missing rhetorical links, which means that the discourse logical forms that result from these annotations do not provide enough information to disambiguate the interpretations of 'orphan' turns, i.e. turns with no incoming rhetorical links. In the vast majority of cases, looking at the surrounding non-linguistic events constrains the interpretation of these turns considerably. (6) illustrates this problem: 344 was an orphan in the first round of annotations, meaning that the annotators did not see a coherent relation between 344 and any previous linguistic turns. The result is that the discourse logical form for (6) leaves the interpretation of 344 far more unconstrained than it intuitively is, with no indication that 344 is even a coherent move in the game.[2]

	341	19:05:26:615	Server	gotwood4sheep rolled a 6 and a 3.
(6)	342	19:05:26:616	Server	inca gets 2 wheat. dmm gets 1 wheat.
	344	19:05:29:595	gotwood4sheep	9 nooo!

Once we consider the non-linguistic context, it is clear that GWS is unhappy because he rolled a 9. It is also clear that 344 is a coherent move in the game because it is rhetorically related to another game move which is itself coherently related to the rest of the game state. Adding non-linguistic turns does not eliminate all ambiguity; in (6), 344 might be a comment only on the roll (341) or on both the roll plus the resource distribution (341 + 342). It is likely a comment on both—the robber is probably occupying a 9 hex on which GWS has a settlement—but there is also a possibility that GWS has another reason for being upset. Still, considering the non-linguistic events reduces the space of possibilities considerably.

3.2 Attachments

Re-examination of the *Settlers* corpus also revealed anaphoric links that yield surprising discourse structures. For instance, linguistic moves can depend simultaneously on a non-linguistic event and a previous linguistic move. Consider (7), which continues (6):

	345	19:05:34:924	Server	inca rolled a 1 and a 3.
(7)	346	19:05:34:926	Server	gotwood4sheep gets 2 wood.
	347	19:05:39:655	gotwood4sheep	4 better :)

(6) and (7) together yield the graph below, foreign to existing theories of rhetorical structure. The dashed line represents some sort of sequential relation that binds the unit [341,342] to [345,346]; we leave aside its nature here to focus on linguistic/non-linguistic links.

[2]Throughout, we skip turns, e.g. 343, to save space when those turns are irrelevant to our main point.

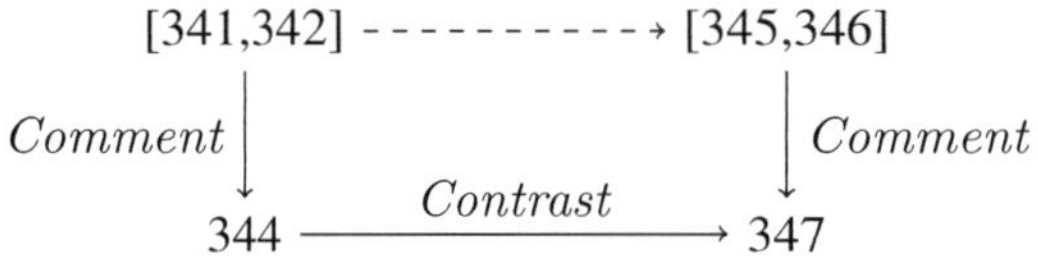

347 is a highly context sensitive fragment that becomes coherent—we understand *what* is better—only once we see its connection to [345,346]. At the same time, *better* signals a contrast with something comparatively worse. In the first round of annotations, annotators used this signal to link 344 (*9 nooo!*) and 347 with Contrast. This is intuitively correct: 344 expresses a negative attitude about the thing that is "comparatively worse", namely events described in [341,342], so the attitudes are in contrast.[3]

Example (8) likewise exhibits simultaneous linguistic and non-linguistic dependence, but it also shows that attachments can span across several game-state changing events, even when those events are related to the linguistic context via coordinating relations like Result, which SDRT predicts should render previously accessible nodes (here [234-239]) inaccessible for future anaphora.

	240	18:55:53:749	Server	inca rolled a 6 and a 2.
	243	18:56:06:835	Server	dmm rolled a 1 and a 6.
(8)	243.1	18:56:06:835	Server	gotwood4sheep needs to discard.
	243.2	18:56:10:630	Server	gotwood4sheep discarded 4 resources.
	245	18:56:13:443	gotwood4sheep	chance fail

(4)+(8) involves a causal chain that passes through 234–239 to a sequence of non-linguistic events, including multiple rolls/turn changes, which update the game state. The last roll (243) results in GWS's losing the gamble (239) that resulted from the failed negotiation (234-238) in (4). 245 was attached to 239 in the first round of annotations and this connection is important for the interpretation of 245. But here again, this link yields a surprising discourse structure because 245 links to 239 despite the presence of Result([234,238],240), which should block accessibility of all events before 240.

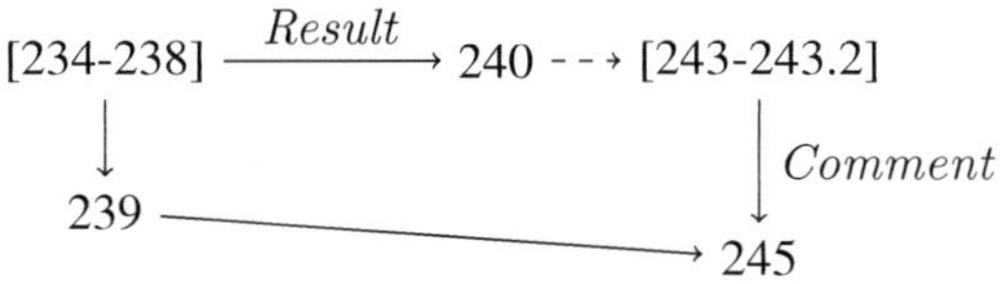

The kind of structures that we see once we incorporate non-linguistic events are unlike the dependency trees familiar from *Rhetorical Structure Theory* (RST; Mann and Thompson (1987)) or the directed graphs from SDRT. Given that the shapes of dependency trees and directed graphs are meant to constrain available attachment points, this raises the question: how does the introduction of non-linguistic events affect the set of available attachment points for a given turn? To answer this question, we must investigate the extent to which a set of non-linguistic events has an internal structure and how this structure effects that of the linguistically specified contents in a situated conversation. The examples in our corpus show that treating the non-linguistic events in *Settlers* as forming an unstructured set or a mere sequence of game-changing events, in which either all events are accessible or only the last one is, is insufficient. (6)+(7) and (4)+(8) show that the last turn is not the only available one, and (9) suggests that this is true regardless of whether there is a previous linguistic antecedent facilitating anaphoric dependence on past non-linguistic events.

	154.1	20:21:09:163	Server	gotwood4sheep played a Soldier card.
	154.3	20:21:10:230	Server	gotwood4sheep stole a resource from ljaybrad123
	155	20:21:12:395	Server	gotwood4sheep rolled a 5 and a 1.
	157	20:21:15:027	Server	gotwood4sheep built a settlement.
(9)	158	20:21:19:939	gotwood4sheep	sorry laura
	159	20:21:23:907	gotwood4sheep	needed clay the mean way :D
	159.1	20:21:24:241	Server	ljaybrad123 played a Soldier card.
	159.4	20:21:35:323	Server	ljaybrad123 stole a resource from gotwood4sheep
	163	20:21:40:457	gotwood4sheep	touché

[3]The intuitive connection between 347 and [341,342]—i.e. the comment *4 better :)* expresses the attitude that the roll of the 4 is better than the roll described in 341—should follow at the level of interpretation from the fact that 347 contrasts with 344, which describes an attitude about 341, so there is no reason to draw an extra arc in the discourse graph from [341,342] to 347.

GWS's utterance in 158 ignores his roll in 155 and building in 157, referring back to his steal in 154.3. To make sense of 163, one needs to consider the relation between the steal in 154.3 and that in 159.4, but it is not the linguistic moves in 158 and 159 that give us this structure; even if we ignore these two moves, 163 is coherent given the non-linguistic context.

On the other hand, a fragment like *sorry laura* is highly anaphoric and needs a salient antecedent; therefore, while 158 need not depend on the last move (157), it can't pick up on just any move in the game, either. There are limitations on the accessibility of non-linguistic events. In other words, the non-linguistic events in our game have an internal structure just as the linguistic events do; and what's more, the two structures are integrated. §4 looks at the nature of this integrated structure in more detail.

4 Integrated discourse structures

As in Asher and Lascarides (2003), our annotations assign speech act labels to *elementary discourse units*, which may coincide with or be a proper part of a speaker's turn. We use distinguished variables $\pi^i, \pi^i_1, \pi^i_2, \ldots$ to label EDUs, where π^i labels a speech act performed by i. To build integrated structures, we also treat non-linguistic events in the game as entities or *elementary event units* (EEUs). Each EEU is assigned a first-order formula ϕ that characterizes its content; i.e. $\epsilon\colon \phi$ is a discourse formula that characterizes the EEU ϵ with ϕ. The interpretation of ϕ in the relevant model, which in this case is determined by the nature of the *Settlers* game, will determine the conceptualization of ϵ. *Complex discourse units* (CDUs), made up of multiple EDUs, EEUs, or a combination of the two, are labelled like EDUs; however, their subscripts reflect a group of speakers when multiple speakers have contributed to their content.

Building appropriate discourse structures for situated discourse requires us to address three problems that already come up for discourse analysis: (a) the *segmentation problem*, i.e. that of individuating the EDUs and EEUs; (b) *the attachment problem*, i.e. how these units link up via their anaphoric dependencies; (c) *the labelling problem*, i.e. which kinds of relations hold between the units. It also requires addressing (d) *the conceptualization problem*, which does not in general arise for the analysis of text. In our *Settlers* corpus study, (a) is moot; the game server segments the relevant events for us, though in general this is a problem (Lascarides and Stone, 2009b). The server messages also help with (d) by assigning a formula ϕ to each ϵ, though these formulas need an interpretation, which we discuss in §5. The discussion in §3.2 shows that (b) needs a solution. We provide this in §4.1-4.2.

The labelling problem, (c), also needs to be addressed because our data require generalizations of certain rhetorical relations that take EEUs and CDUs containing EEUs as arguments. This includes not only Comment (ex. (3)), Alternation (ex. (2)), and Conditional (ex. (1)), but also Result, Explanation, Elaboration and Question-Answer Pair (QAP). For example, we understand gotwood4sheep's action of ending his turn and passing the dice to be the *result* of his failed negotiation attempt. Had he succeeded in trading, he likely would have built something. And in (10), gotwood4sheep's non-linguistic actions provide an *explanation* of his speech act in 538.

(10)	538	21:03:12:661	gotwood4sheep	it may prove a prudent trade, lj...
	539	21:03:24:209	ljaybrad123	nope
	539.1	21:03:25:530	Server	gotwood4sheep played a Soldier card.
	539.4	21:03:28:353	Server	gotwood4sheep stole a resource from ljaybrad123

In the turns leading up to 538, GWS attempts to trade with lj to get the resources that he wants. When she rejects his offer, he plays a Soldier card, which allows him to steal a resource from her. So lj's outcome is worse than had she traded.

57 and 59 in (11) are *restatements* of the non-linguistic offer (56) and accept (58) moves.

(11)	56	16:38:11:641	Server	Joel made an offer to trade 1 wheat for 1 clay.
	57	16:38:22:445	Joel	I just sent the trade request
	58	16:38:30:436	Server	Joel traded 1 wheat for 1 clay from Euan.
	59	16:38:47:583	Euan	I accepted.

Finally, offers to trade function like polar questions, partitioning the subsequent state into two alternatives: the 'addressee' can either accept or reject the offer. Accordingly, we link offers and their responses via QAP. §5 describes the relevant semantics for offer, accept and reject moves.

4.1 Adding EEUs to discourse graphs

If EEUs enter into rhetorical relations with EDUs—even figuring in mixed CDUs—we cannot simply append a Kaplanian-like context of non-linguistic entities to linguistic discourse structures. Kaplanian contexts are unstructured sets of entities, making them unfit to model the structural relations that we have observed and the accessibility facts discussed in §3.2. Instead, we need to extend our discourse graphs to *situated* discourse graphs with nodes for EEUs and arcs that connect them to other nodes. That is, if a discourse structure for a dialogue d derived only from linguistic utterances is a connected graph $G_d = (V, E_1, E_2)$ where V is the set of EDUs and CDUs, $E_1 \subseteq V \times V$ the set of labelled discourse attachments between elements of V, and $E_2 \subseteq V \times V$ the parenthood relation holding between DUs and their CDU hosts (note that $E_1 \cap E_2 = \emptyset$), then a situated discourse graph G_{sd} for d is the graph: $G_{sd} = (V^{sd}, E_1^{sd}, E_2^{sd})$, where V^{sd} shares with V the same EDUs but also contains EEUs and CDUs that include EEUs, while $E_1^{sd}, E_2^{sd} \subseteq V^{sd} \times V^{sd}$ are the analogues in G_{sd} of E_1 and E_2 in G_d.

Given G_d and G_{sd}, several questions arise. First, is G_d a subgraph of G_{sd} in the following sense: are $V \subseteq V^{sd}$, $E_1 \subseteq E_1^{sd}$, and $E_2 \subseteq E_2^{sd}$? The answer is 'no' for many dialogues: new and different CDUs are created in the presence of non-linguistic events. This happens frequently in our corpus when, for example, a series of linguistic moves *results* in an EEU. For instance, a verbal acceptance of an offer typically leads to a non-linguistic offer to trade, as happens in (12); the non-linguistic offer and its acceptance is how players effect an actual change to the game state so that it matches the agreed trade.

(12)	244	10:55:44:639	mmatrtajova	anyone will trad wheat or sheep?
	245	10:55:52:100	Ash	yes for wood
	246	10:55:52:379	J	nopes
	247	10:56:20:215	mmatrtajova	okay wood for wheat?
	248	10:56:32:205	mmatrtajova	and sheep for ore?
	249	10:56:41:896	Ash	ok
	250	10:56:47:071	Server	mmatrtajova made an offer to trade 1 ore, 1 wood for 1 sheep, 1 wheat.

The semantics of causal discourse relations like Result call for a grouping of all of the linguistic and nonlinguistic events that result in the nonlinguistic offer. Thus, adding the non-linguistic turn 250 from (12) triggers the introduction of the CDU represented by the box in the graph on the right:

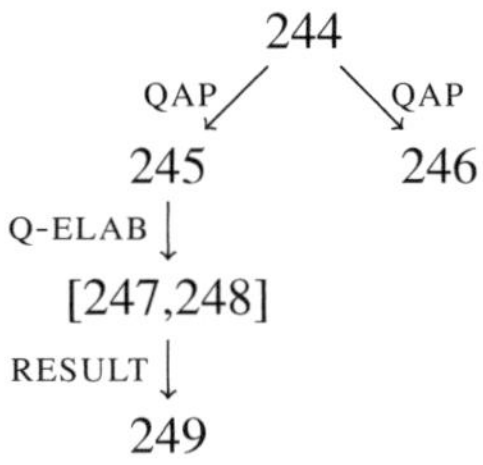

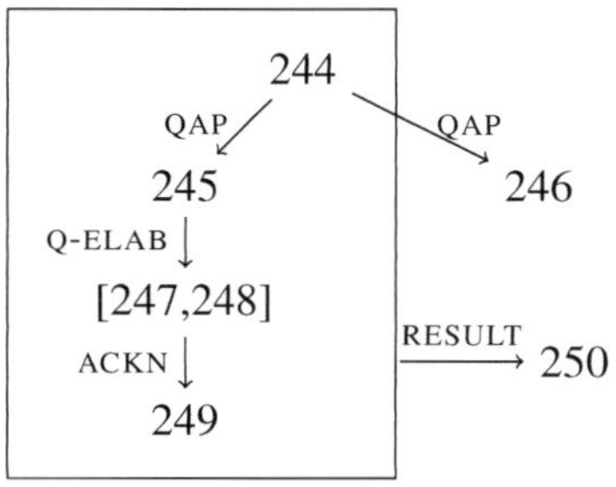

Unsuccessful negotiations, like (4), have a similar effect on the discourse graph, as the negotiation as a whole results in an action such as trading from the bank or ending the turn. Our corpus also provides examples of hybrid (EDU+EEU) CDUs and of CDUs from G_d that disappear once EEUs are added. So in general $V \not\subseteq V^{sd}$, and hence $E_2 \not\subseteq E_2^{sd}$. Our data also show that $E_1 \not\subseteq E_1^{sd}$ (see §4.3).

The next question is: do the new relation instances in the graph G_{sd} obey the same structural constraints as the relation instances in G_d? For example, Venant et al. (2013) argues that CDUs have a *no punctures* property such that if π is a CDU then there are no incoming directed edges to proper elements of π whose source is outside π. In the *Settlers* corpus, all CDUs in the linguistic only graphs G_d have this property. The creation of new CDUs, however, makes it more difficult to verify for the graphs G_{sd}; while we have yet to find any punctures, we need a fuller study. Another constraint that holds for discourse-only graphs G_d is the *Right Frontier Constraint* (RFC) on attachment (Asher, 1993; Asher and Lascarides, 2003), which other theories like RST also adopt. We turn now to a discussion of the RFC.

4.2 The Right Frontier

In SDRT, for a discourse graph $G = (V, E_1, E_2)$, E_1 contains two types of edges, *coordinating* and *subordinating*, and we write $e(x, y)$ for e is an edge with initial point x and endpoint y. The *Right Frontier* (RF) for an EDU y, i.e. the set of available attachment points for y, includes: *Last*, the EDU x just before y in a linear ordering of DUs from the discourse; any node that is super-ordinate to x via a series of subordinating relations; and any CDU in which x figures. More precisely,

Definition 1. Let $G = (V, E_1, E_2)$ be a discourse graph. $\forall x, y, z \in V$, $\text{RF}_G(x)$ iff (i) $x = Last$, (ii) $\text{RF}_G(y)$ and $\exists e \in E_1$, $e(x, y)$ and Subordinating(e), (iii) $\text{RF}_G(z)$, $\text{RF}_G(y)$ and $\exists e, e' \in E_1$ such that $e(x, z)$ and $e'(z, y)$ and Subordinating(e) and Subordinating(e'), or (iv) $\text{RF}_G(y)$ and $\exists e \in E_2$, $e(y, x)$

The RFC is much more complicated in multi-party dialogue than in monologue, even within linguistic-only graphs G_d. For multi-party dialogue, we examined a more complex notion of the RF by considering an RF for the subgraph of the connected contributions of each subgroup of conversational participants in G. This choice reflects the fact that there are often several interwoven conversations between subgroups in a dialogue, and even within a subgroup an agent's contribution can attach to several participants' moves, as observed in Ginzburg and Fernández (2005). On this more complex conception, which we call the *supervaluational* RF, we took an attachment of one discourse unit to another to be an RF violation if and only if the attachment violated the RF of the complete graph and the RF of the subgraph for each subgroup of participants. Our extension of the RFC to subgroups shows that crossing conversations are quite common in our corpus. Of the 8829 relation instances in the corpus, 78% of attachments respected a slightly simplified version of the RF defined above. Manually assessing one representative game, we found that 98% of the attachments respected the supervaluational RF.

Understanding how EEUs affect the RF requires understanding their structure and that of CDUs composed from them. The game structure at a high level is a sequence of large events individuated by moves like dice rolls, bargain initiation and building. Each of these high-level events might have as parts other events: for example, the resource distribution or sequence of robber moves that results from a roll, or the various turns in a trade negotiation, and so on. Prior to any linguistic move any EEU ϵ_1 may be commented on *ad libidem* but a linguistic event, like a new offer or a comment on an EEU, will move the RF on, and we predict that an EEU ϵ_1 preceding the linguistic event is no longer accessible for attachment. Any comment on, say, a roll that precedes a bargaining discussion has to involve a definite description allowing for an RF violation and inducing a so-called *discourse subordination* (Asher, 1993). EEUs that follow the bargaining discussion, e.g. an EEU offer, a resulting EEU acceptance, a new roll and shift in bargaining leader and so on, will *all* remain open so long as no commentary is made on these EEUs. In addition, all of the events on the RF of the preceding discussion will also remain accessible. Once linguistic content is attached to one of these later EEUS ϵ_2, however, the RF of the preceding discussion disappears and all EEUs prior to ϵ_2 become inaccessible. We formalize these observations below in an RF constraint for situated dialogue (ignoring subgroups of participants to simplify), in which the RF is parametrized relative to high-level events ϵ (rolls, bargain initiations, buildings, card plays, etc.); $Acc(x)$ means x is on the the RF as defined in Definition 1; $\prec$ is a linear ordering of EEUs and EDUS in V; and π is an EDU or CDU containing at least one EDU.

Definition 2. Let $G_{sd} = (V, E_1, E_2)$ be a situated discourse graph. $\text{RF}(G_{sd}, \epsilon, Last) = \{Last\} \cup Acc(Last) \cup \{\epsilon' : \epsilon' \prec \epsilon \text{ and } \neg\exists\epsilon''\exists\pi \in V \exists e \in E_1\, (\epsilon' \prec \epsilon'' \wedge e(\epsilon'', \pi))\}$

This definition allows for the "rectangular structures" exhibited by (6)+(7) or (4)+(8) but absent from the linguistic-only graphs G_d produced from the first round of annotations on the *Settlers* corpus.

4.3 Divergences

Differences between situated discourse graphs G_{sd} and linguistic-only discourse graphs G_d provide an indirect measure of how much the non-linguistic context affects the comprehension of linguistic discourse moves, at least for the *Settlers* corpus. It is indirect because we are only able to measure the effects of the non-linguistic context on judgments about attachments and labelling of arcs in the situated discourse graph. Nevertheless, a comparison will be instructive in showing how the non-linguistic context may affect the interpretation of linguistic content.

We categorized the divergences into 5 categories: (i) EEUs missing in G_d that were essential in our judgement for understanding linguistic moves (ME in Table 1); (ii) links missing between EEUs and EDUs (ML); (iii) incorrect links in G_d, which had to be changed in light of the non-linguistic context (IL) (cf. (5)); (iv), missing CDUs in G_d, which the semantics of discourse relations and the presence of EEUs forced us to create (MC) (cf (12)); (v) incorrect dialogue boundaries postulated from the linguistic-only annotations, which changed in light of the non-linguistic context (wrong breaks). Annotators of the linguistic-only part of the dialogue would postulate boundaries when there were two unconnected discourse graphs. These discourse graph boundaries often corresponded to dice rolls but not always. We found two sorts of errors: the first where two distinct discourse graphs G_d and $G_{d'}$ were postulated when in fact there was one connected situated graph, the second where one graph G_d spanned in fact two separate situated graphs G_{sd} and $G_{sd'}$. We counted errors in 3 games: Pilot14, a game with novice players, s1-league1-game3, from season one of the *Settlers* competition, and s2-leagueM-game2, a master's league game. TL and TDU in Table 1 are respectively the total number of links and DUs per game.

game	missing EEU (ME)	missing links (ML)	missing CDU (MC)	incorrect links (IL)	wrong breaks
s1-league1-game3	122	162	26	44	6
s2-leagueM-game2	78	119	15	25	3
pilot14	72	115	6	25	2
game	**total # errors**	**DU error rate (MU/TDU)**	**link error rate in G_d (IL/TL)**	**TL in G_d**	**TDU in G_d**
s1–league1-game3	360	17%	6%	722	687
s2-leagueM-game2	340	21%	7%	369	345
pilot14	220	25%	13%	190	214

Table 1: Error rates on Settlers games

The set of dialogues for a given game provided a variable error rate on the existing annotated links in G_d of between 6% and 13%. On the other hand, our analysis showed that the G_d graphs were often seriously incomplete with respect to events deemed essential to understanding the content of the dialogue. We thus concluded: 1) Non-linguistic events are often crucial for understanding the content of dialogue. While this might not be surprising, it motivates an approach to the study of the semantic content of discourse that embraces its potential for radical context sensitivity and attempts to incorporate this sensitivity into a formal semantic/pragmatic model (cf. Ginzburg (2012)). 2) Despite the radical context sensitivity exhibited by our corpus, linguistic clues for inferential relations were remarkably robust: the linguistic-only annotations were quite incomplete but not hopelessly wrong, given the low error rate of dialogue attachments and labelling in the G_d graphs. Whether these observations generalize to different types of a conversation is an open question, but we hope that the techniques elaborated here can facilitate a comparison of different types of conversation.

5 EEU semantics

Rhetorical relations interact with, and are licensed by inferences about, the *content* of EDUs (Asher and Lascarides, 2003). While EEUs are non-linguistic, their *conceptualization* by conversational participants endows them with a content, $\epsilon : \phi$, that enables them to serve as arguments to rhetorical relations. In the *Settlers* corpus, each such formula ϕ is recorded in a server message; the interpretation of ϕ, the conceptualization of ϵ, is determined by the nature of the *Settlers* game. We illustrate our semantics for EEU contents ϕ by looking at trade moves. For instance, the move *offer*, whether linguistic or non-linguistic, has the semantics of a question at an abstract level. *Accept* and *reject* moves, whether linguistic or not, function as answers. (13) is an example.

(13) $\epsilon : \mathit{offer}(i, 1\mathit{wheat}, 1\mathit{sheep}, j) \rightarrow_{\text{qap}} \pi^j$: I DON'T HAVE ANY SHEEP.

More formally, let g be an initial segment of a game; $g.V^*$, the game tree of all legal sequences given g; and E, the Linear Temporal Logic operator *eventually*. We write '$g < g'$' where the sequence g' extends g, and '$g \models \phi$' where the end state of g satisfies the formula ϕ. We note the fact that some actions depend on prior actions—e.g., '$\epsilon' : acc(a, \epsilon)$' depends on ϵ—with the notation, $\epsilon' \mapsto \epsilon$.

$g \| \epsilon$: $\mathit{offer}(a, c, d, b) \| g'$ iff $g. \| \epsilon \| = g'$ and $\forall g'' > g', g'' \in g'.V^* \rightarrow (g' \| E(acc(b, \epsilon)) \| g'' \vee g' \| E(rej(b, \epsilon)) \| g'')$

$g \| acc(b, \epsilon) \| g'$ iff ϵ: $\mathit{offer}(a, c, d, b) \in g$ and $\exists e \in g'(e \mapsto \epsilon$ and $g.e \models b\ gets\ c\ and\ a\ gets\ d)$

$g \| rej(b, \epsilon) \| g'$ iff ϵ: $\mathit{offer}(a, c, d, b) \in g$ and $\neg \exists e \in g'(e \mapsto \epsilon$ and $g.e \models b\ gets\ c\ and\ a\ gets\ d)$

where $\mathit{offer}(a, c, d, b)$ stands for 'a offers to give c to player b in exchange for d'. Thus (13) holds just in case all continuations of the game include the event of the offer specified in ϵ followed by an event of refusing that offer. We get this by noting that π^j entails that j can't give sheep to i because she has none. The relation QAP ensures the dependency of the linguistic refusal on the non-linguistic offer ($e \mapsto \epsilon$).

6 Related Work

The current work complements prior research on rhetorical dependencies between linguistically specified arguments and co-verbal gestures (Lascarides and Stone, 2009a,b) to model how non-linguistic events affect the overall architecture of discourse. Our project also goes beyond existing work on the non-linguistic context. Aside from semantic and philosophical work on indexicality, projects like TACoS (Regneri et al., 2013) and The Restaurant Game (Orkin et al., 2010) use non-linguistic events to refine event descriptions or to automatically learn scriptal information, but do not engage in the kind of theoretical investigation of the discourse interactions and their semantics that we have undertaken. Finally, corpus based studies of dialogue, e.g. Ginzburg (2012), posit that incomplete utterances (e.g. *Woo!* and *Yay!*) have as a part of their semantics a kind of anaphoric dependency like that studied in rhetorical theories—a requirement for interaction with the discourse situation. Yet this work does not look at how we interact with non-linguistic events in such situations. Our work complements research in these separate fields to give a more complete picture of how the semantic content of discourses depends on interactions with the situations in which our discourses take place.

There has been much recent progress in interpreting multimodal actions within the field of human robot interaction (Perzanowski et al., 2001; Chambers et al., 2005; Foster and Petrick, 2014). The task is to map the outputs of 'low-level' signal processors into a representation of speaker meaning. This work uses planning or reinforcement learning and holds that reasoning about the cognitive states of the participants is a primary and irreducible source of information for parsing multimodal actions. We take a slightly different view: instead of always exploiting reasoning about cognitive states directly, we infer speaker meaning via constraints afforded by models of discourse coherence. Discourse coherence has proved useful for predicting anaphoric dependencies and implicatures in purely linguistic discourse. Our hypothesis is that it will play much the same role in resolving the meanings of multimodal actions.

7 Conclusion

Interaction between non-linguistic and linguistic events extends well beyond the context of a shared task like that in *Settlers*. Suppose a driver does something dangerous in passing you. Whether you respond by yelling at him or by giving him the finger, your response anaphorically depends on and rhetorically connects to the driver's action. The *Settlers* data give us an interesting insight into the seamless web of linguistic and non-linguistic events. Because non-linguistic events are already segmented and described in our corpus, we have been able to ignore the segmentation problem—a problem that in general renders the study of the non-linguistic context dauntingly complex—and examine how non-linguistic events effect discourse structure. We have developed a model of situated conversation to capture these effects, giving us a better understanding of how the non-linguistic context affects semantic content.

References

Afantenos, S., N. Asher, F. Benamara, A. Cadilhac, C. Dégremont, P. Denis, M. Guhe, S. Keizer, A. Lascarides, O. Lemon, P. Muller, S. Paul, V. Popescu, V. Rieser, and L. Vieu (2012). Modelling strategic conversation: model, annotation design and corpus. In *Proceedings of the 16th Workshop on the Semantics and Pragmatics of Dialogue (Seinedial)*, Paris.

Asher, N. (1993). *Reference to Abstract Objects in Discourse*. Kluwer Academic Publishers.

Asher, N. and A. Lascarides (2003). *Logics of Conversation*. Cambridge University Press.

Chambers, N., J. Allen, L. Galescu, and H. Jung (2005). A dialogue-based approach to multi-robot team control. In *Proceedings of the 3rd International Multi-Robot Systems Workshop*, Washington, DC.

Foster, M. E. and R. P. A. Petrick (2014, June). Planning for social interaction with sensor uncertainty. In *Proceedings of the ICAPS 2014 Scheduling and Planning Applications Workshop (SPARK)*, Portsmouth, New Hampshire, USA, pp. 19–20.

Ginzburg, J. (2012). *The Interactive Stance: Meaning for Conversation*. Oxford University Press.

Ginzburg, J. and R. Fernández (2005). Scaling up from dialogue to multilogue: some principles and benchmarks. In *Proceedings of the 43rd Annual Meeting on Association for Computational Linguistics*, pp. 231–238. Association for Computational Linguistics.

Hobbs, J. R., M. Stickel, D. Appelt, and P. Martin (1993). Interpretation as abduction. *Artificial Intelligence 63*(1–2), 69–142.

Kaplan, D. (1989). Demonstratives. In J. Almog, J. Perry, and H. Wettstein (Eds.), *Themes from Kaplan*. Oxford.

Lascarides, A. and M. Stone (2009a). Discourse coherence and gesture interpretation. *Gesture 9*(2), 147–180.

Lascarides, A. and M. Stone (2009b). A formal semantic analysis of gesture. *Journal of Semantics 26*(4), 393–449.

Mann, W. C. and S. A. Thompson (1987). Rhetorical structure theory: A framework for the analysis of texts. *International Pragmatics Association Papers in Pragmatics 1*, 79–105.

Orkin, J., T. Smith, and D. K. Roy (2010). Behavior compilation for ai in games. In *Proceedings of the 6th Artificial Intelligence and Interactive Digital Entertainment Conference (AIIDE)*.

Perzanowski, D., A. Schultz, W. Adams, E. Marsh, and M. Bugajska (2001). Building a multimodal human-robot interface. *Intelligent Systems 16*(1), 16–21.

Regneri, M., M. Rohrbach, D. Wetzel, S. Thater, B. Schiele, and M. Pinkal (2013). Grounding action descriptions in videos. *TACL 1*(2), 25–35.

Venant, A., N. Asher, P. Muller, and P. D. S. D. Afantenos (2013). Expressivity and comparison of models of discourse structure. In *Proceedings of Sigdial 2013*, Metz, France.

A Discriminative Model for Perceptually-Grounded Incremental Reference Resolution

Casey Kennington
CITEC, Bielefeld University
ckennington@cit-ec.uni-bielefeld.de

Livia Dia
University of York
lad507@york.ac.uk

David Schlangen
Bielefeld University
david.schlangen@uni-bielefeld.de

Abstract

A large part of human communication involves referring to entities in the world, and often these entities are objects that are visually present for the interlocutors. A computer system that aims to resolve such references needs to tackle a complex task: objects and their visual features must be determined, the referring expressions must be recognised, extra-linguistic information such as eye gaze or pointing gestures must be incorporated — and the intended connection between words and world must be reconstructed. In this paper, we introduce a discriminative model of reference resolution that processes incrementally (i.e., word for word), is perceptually-grounded, and improves when interpolated with information from gaze and pointing gestures. We evaluated our model and found that it performed robustly in a realistic reference resolution task, when compared to a generative model.

1 Introduction

Reference to entities in the world via definite description makes up a large part of human communication (Poesio and Vieira, 1997). In task-oriented situations, these references are often to entities that are visible in the shared environment. In such co-located settings, interlocutors can make use of extra-linguistic cues such as gaze or pointing gestures. Furthermore, listeners resolve references as they unfold, often identifying the referred entity before the end of the reference (as found, *inter alia*, by Tanenhaus and Spivey-Knowlton (1995); Spivey (2002)). Computational research on reference resolution, however, has mostly focused on offline processing of full, completed referring expressions, and not attempted to model this online nature of human reference resolution. On a more technical level, most of the models making use of stochastic information (see discussion below) have been generative models; even though such models are known to often have certain disadvantages compared to discriminative models.[1]

In this paper, we introduce a discriminative model of reference resolution that is *incremental* in that it does not wait until the end of an utterance to process, rather it updates its interpretation at each word. Moreover, the semantics of each word is *perceptually grounded* in visual information from the world. We evaluated our model and found that it works robustly when compared to a similar generative approach.

In the following section we explain the task of reference resolution and discuss related work. That is followed by an explanation of our model and evaluation experiment. We end with some analyses of the model's strengths and areas of improvement.

2 Background and Related Work on Reference Resolution

Reference resolution (RR) is the task of resolving referring expressions (henceforth REs; e.g., *the red one on the left*) to the entity to which they are intended to refer; the *referent*. This can be formalised as a function f_{rr} that, given a representation U of the RE and a representation W of the (relevant aspects

[1] But see the nuanced discussion by Ng A.Y. & Jordan M. I. (2002).

Proceedings of the 11th International Conference on Computational Semantics, pages 195–205,
London, UK, April 15-17 2015.

of the) world (which can include aspects of the discourse context), returns I^*, the identifier of one the objects in the world that is the intended referent of the RE.

$$I^* = f_{rr}(U, W) \tag{1}$$

This function f_{rr} can be specified in a variety of ways. A number of recent papers have used stochastic models using the following approach: given W and U, the goal of RR is to obtain a distribution over a specified set of candidate entities in that world, where the probability assigned to each entity represents the strength of belief that it is the referred one. The referred object is then the argmax of that distribution:

$$I^* = \underset{I}{\operatorname{argmax}}\, P(I|U, W) \tag{2}$$

We have worked in this area before. Kennington and Schlangen (2013) we applied Markov Logic Networks (Richardson and Domingos, 2006) to the task of computing the distribution over I. The world W, a virtual game board of puzzle pieces, was represented symbolically (e.g., objects were represented by their properties such as colour and shape). The utterance U was represented by its words. We repeated the experiments later in Kennington et al. (2013) where the utterance and world were represented in the same way, but the model that produced the distribution over the candidate objects was generative; it modeled the joint distribution over the objects and their properties, and the words in the utterance. (This model will be further discussed and used as a baseline for comparison below.) In Kennington et al. (2014); Hough et al. (2015) we used that same generative model and representation of W, but U was represented as a semantic abstraction.

Funakoshi et al. (2012) used a Bayesian network approach. The world W (in their case, a set of tangram puzzle pieces) was represented as a set of *concepts* (e.g., shape type), and U was represented by the words in the REs, in an interctive human-human setting. The Bayesian network was used to learn a mapping between concepts and U. The model could handle various types of REs, namely definite references, exophoric pronoun references, and deictic (pointing) references to objects. Similar data was used in Iida et al. (2011), but the mapping between U and W was done with a support vector machine classifier. We recently applied our generative model to this data, with improved results in some areas Kennington et al. (2015).

Engonopoulos et al. (2013) also used a generative approach; W was modeled as an *observation model* (i.e., a set of features over the objects in a 3D scene), and U was a *semantic* model that abstracted over the referring expression.

In Matuszek et al. (2014), W was represented as a distribution over properties (e.g., color and shape) of real-world objects (small wooden blocks of various shapes and colors) as represented by computer-vision output. U was represented as a semantic abstraction in the form of a Combinatory Categorical Grammar parse. Resolving I amounted to generatively computing a joint distribution over the representation of U and W.

In all of these approaches, the objects are distinct and have specific visual *properties*, such as color, shape, and spatial placement. The set of properties is defined and either read directly from the world if it is virtual, or computed (i.e., discretised) from the real world objects. In this paper, we take a different approach to representing the world W and how the distribution for I is computed. Instead of representing the world as a set of discrete properties or concepts, we represent the world with a set of more low-level visual features (e.g., color-values) and compute the distribution over objects discriminatively, as will be explained in Section 3. This represents a kind of perceptually-grounded learning of how visual features connect to words in the RE, where the meaning of the word is represented by a classifier, as explained below.

Treating words as classifiers working with perceptual information has been explored before. Steels and Belpaeme (2005) used neural networks to connect language with colour terms. Their model learned the way colours were used by interacting with humans. Larsson (2013) addressed integrating perceptual meaning into a formal semantics by a model that was tested in a game where participants described a simple object as being on the *left* or *right* side of the game board. Both of these approaches focused on a very limited lexicon of words that are used to described visual objects, namely colours or left/right, and these approaches only took limited perceptual information into account. In this paper, we don't limit the lexicon to a certain class of words, rather we attempt to learn a perceptually-grounded meaning of all the words in a corpus (described below).

Situated RR is a convenient setting for learning perceptually-grounded meaning, as objects that are referred to physically exist, are described by the RE, and have visual features that can be computationally extracted and represented. Kelleher et al. (2005) approached RR using perceptually-grounded models, focusing on saliency and discourse context. The task of RR was also used in Gorniak and Roy (2004); descriptions of objects were used to learn a perceptually-grounded meaning with focus on spatial terms such as *on the left*. However, unlike our approach, these approaches did not model the meaning of words directly, nor are they incremental.

3 A Model of Reference to Visible Objects

Our model interpolates information from the referring expression proper and from other, multimodal information sources such as gaze and pointing gestures. We will describe the parts of the model in turn.

3.1 A Discriminative Model of Linguistic Evidence

Overview As explained with formula (2), we want our model to give us a probability distribution over the candidate objects, given a referring expression (or, to be more precise, given possibly just a prefix of the expression). Instead of trying to learn a mapping between full referring expressions and objects, we break the problem down into one of learning a mapping between individual words and objects, and of composition of the evidence into a prediction for the full expression (or expression prefix).

The Word Model At the basis of the model then is a prediction for a given word and a given object of how well the object fits the word. To compute this, we trained for each word w from our corpus of referring expressions a binary logistic regression classifier that takes a representation of a candidate object via visual features ($\mathbf{x}$) and returns a probability p_w for it being a good fit to the word (where $\mathbf{w}$ is the weight vector that is learned and σ is the logistic function):

$$p_w(\mathbf{x}) = \sigma(\mathbf{w}^\intercal \mathbf{x} + b) \quad (3)$$

This model is shown in Figure 1 as a one-layer neural network.

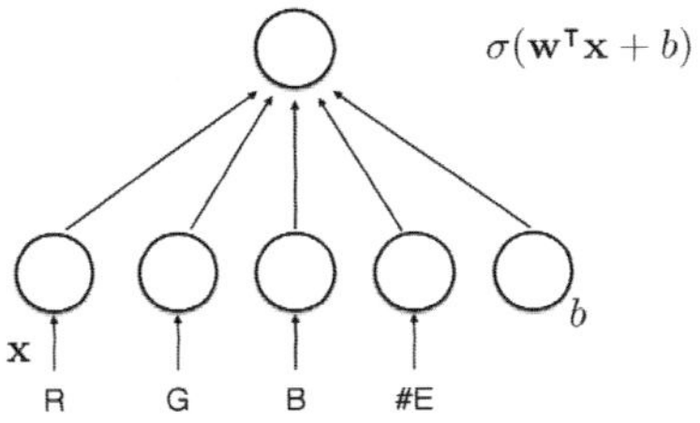

Figure 1: Representation as 1-layer NN

hue, saturation, value
red, green, blue
number of detected edges
x,y coordinates
horizontal skewness
vertical skewness
orientation value

Figure 2: List of features used in our model (total of 12 features).

We train these classifiers using a corpus of REs (further described below), coupled with representations of the scenes in which they were used and an annotation of the referent of that scene. The setting was restricted to reference to single objects. To get positive training examples, we pair each word of a RE with the features of the referent. To get negative training examples, we pair the word with features of (randomly picked) other objects present in the same scene, but *not* referred to by it. This process is shown in Algorithm 1. This selection of negative examples makes the assumption that the words from the RE apply only to the referent. This is wrong as a strict rule, as other objects could have similar visual features as the referent; for this to work, however, this has to be the case only more often than it is not. This is so for our domain, and in general seems a plausible thing to assume that often words used in REs do indeed uniquely single out their referent.

Algorithm 1 Training algorithm for our model, each word classifier receives a set of positive and negative training examples, then maximum likelihood is computed for each word.

```
procedure TRAIN(frame)
    for each RE in corpus do
        for each word in RE do
            pair word with features of object referred to by RE; add to positive examples
            pair word with features of n objects not referred to by RE; add to negative examples
        end for
    end for
    for each word in vocabulary do
        train word binary classifier
    end for
end procedure
```

Application and Composition This model gives us a prediction for a pair of word and object. What we wanted, however, is a distribution over all candidate objects, and not only for individual words, but for (incrementally growing) full REs. To get the former, we apply the word/percept classifier to each candidate object, and normalise (where $\mathbf{x}_i$ is the feature vector for object i):

$$P(I = i|U = w, W) = \frac{p_w(\mathbf{x}_i)}{\sum_{k \in I} p_w(\mathbf{x}_k)} \tag{4}$$

In effect, this turns this into a multi-class logistic regression / maximum entropy model—but only for application. The training regime did not need to make any assumptions about the number of objects present, as it trained classifiers for a 1-class problem (how well does this given object fit to the word?). The multi-class nature is also indicated in Figure 3, which shows multiple applications of the network from Figure 1, with a normalisation layer on top.

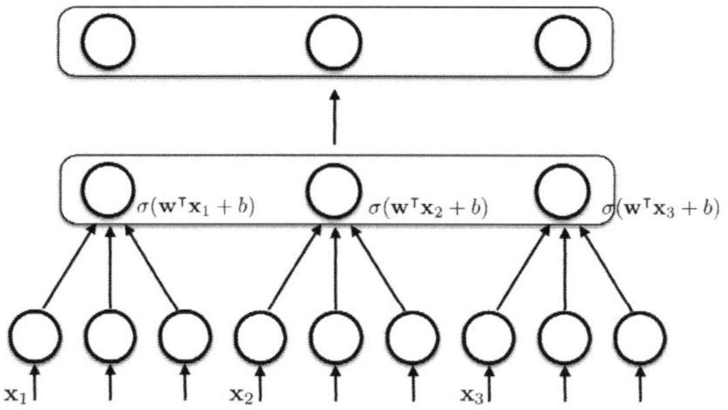

Figure 3: Representation as network with normalisation layer.

To compose the evidence from individual words into a prediction for the whole (prefix of the) referring expression, we chose the simplest possible approach, namely simply to average the previous distribution with the new one. This represents an incremental model where new information from the current increment is added to what is already known. Such a simple model represents an intersective way of composing the words (or, rather, their denotations). More sophisticated approaches can be imagined (e.g., using syntactic structure); we leave exploring them to future work.

$$P(I = i|U_1^k, W) = [P(I = i|U_1^{k-1}, W) + P(I = i|U^k, W)] * \frac{1}{2} \tag{5}$$

3.2 Evidence from Gaze and Deixis

The full model combines the evidence from linguistic information with evidence from other information sources such as the speaker's gaze and pointing gestures. For each, we calculate a reference point (R) on the scene: for gaze, the fixated point as provided by an eye tracker; for deixis, the point on the scene that was pointed at based on a vector calculated from the shoulder to the hand (as described in Kousidis et al. (2013), using the Microsoft Kinect). The centroids of all the objects (I) can then be compared to that reference point to yield a probability of that object being 'referred' by that modality (i.e., gazed at or pointed at) by introducing a Gaussian window over the location of the point:

$$p_{distance}(R_i, I_j; \sigma) = \exp - \frac{(x_i - x_j)^2}{2 * \sigma^2} * \exp - \frac{(y_i - y_j)^2}{2 * \sigma^2} \tag{6}$$

where the mean is R and σ is set by calculating the standard deviation of all the object centroids and the reference point. This can then be normalised over all the $p_{distance}$ scores to produce a distribution over I for each modality where the closer the object is to the reference point, the higher its probability. (We implicitly make the somewhat naive assumption here that the referred object will be looked at by the speaker most of the time during and around the RE. This is in general not true (Griffin and Bock, 2000), but works out here.)

Our final model of RR fuses the the three described modalities of speech, gaze, and deixis using a linear interpolation, where the α parameters are learned from held-out data by ranging over values such that the α values sum to one, and computing the average rank (metric explained below), retaining the α values that produced the best score for that set:

$$P(I|S) = P(I|S_1)\alpha_1 + P(I|S_2)\alpha_2 + P(I|S_3)(1 - \alpha_1 - \alpha_2) \tag{7}$$

4 Evaluation

We will now explain our evaluation experiment, including the data we used, the pre-processing performed on it, a generative model that we will compare to, and the metrics that we will use in our evaluation. We end this section with the results.

4.1 Data

We used data from the Pentomino puzzle domain as described by Kousidis et al. (2013). In this Wizard-of-Oz study, the participant was confronted with a game board containing 15 randomly selected Pentomino puzzle pieces (out of a repertoire of 12 shapes, and 6 colors). The positions of the pieces were randomly determined, but in such a way that the pieces grouped in the four corners of the screen, an example is shown in Figure 4. The participants were seated at a table in front of the screen. Their gaze was then calibrated with an eye tracker (*Seeingmachines FaceLab*) placed above the screen and their arm movements (captured by a Microsoft Kinect, also above the screen) were also calibrated. They were then given task instructions: (silently) choose a Pentomino tile on the screen and then instruct the computer system to select this piece by describing and pointing to it. When a piece was selected (by the wizard), the participant had to utter a confirmation (or give negative feedback) and a new board was generated and the process repeated. In this paper, we denote each of these instances as an *episode*. The utterances, board states, arm movements, and gaze information were recorded in a similar fashion as described in Kousidis et al. (2012). The wizard was instructed to elicit pointing gestures by waiting to select the participant-referred piece by several seconds, unless a pointing action by the participant had already occurred. When the wizard misunderstood, or a technical problem arose, the wizard had an option to flag the episode. In total, 1214 episodes were recorded from 8 participants (all university students). All but one were native speakers of German; the non-native spoke proficient German.

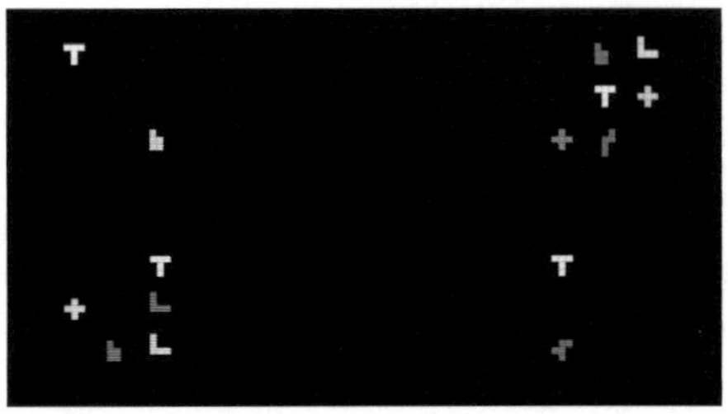

Figure 4: Example Pentomino board for gaze and deixis experiment; the yellow T in the top-right quadrant is the referred object.

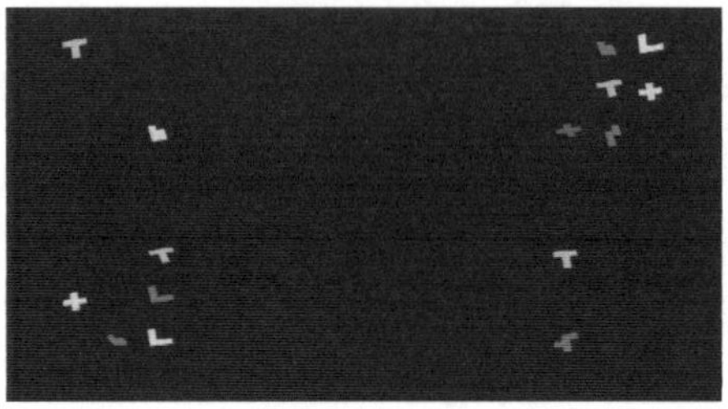

Figure 5: Pentomino Board that has been distorted from its original form (Figure 4); all objects have distorted shapes and colors.

For each episode, the corpus contains two transcriptions of the utterance (one performed by expert transcribers, as well as one created by Google Web Speech; WER 49.8% when compared to expert transcription), deixis and gaze information, as well as an image of what the board looked like to the participant, see Figure 4. Removing episodes that were flagged by the Wizard yielded 1049 episodes with corresponding data. We also have a version of each board image that has been processed in a more involved way, which will now be explained.

Scene Processing We want our model to work with images of real objects as input, even though for our particular data the scenes are represented symbolically (that is, we know without uncertainty each piece's shape, color, and position). Using the images that were generated from these symbolic descriptions and performing computer vision on them does not introduce much uncertainty, as there is no variation in color or appearance of individual shapes, and so the data cannot serve to form generalisations. To get closer to conditions as they would hold when working with camera images (e.g., variations of color due to variations in lighting, distortion of shapes due to camera angles, etc.), we pre-processed these images:[2] We shifted the color spectrum as follows: the hue channel by a random number between -15 and 15 and the saturation and value channels by a random number between -50 and 50. For the object shapes, we apply affine transformations defined by two randomly generated triangles and warp the image using that transform. This generates more complex shapes that retain some notion of their original form. Figure 5 shows a game board that has been distorted from its original in Figure 4.

Using these distorted images, we processed each image using the Canny Edge Detector (Canny, 1986) and used mathematical morphology to find closed contours of the objects, thereby segmenting the objects from each other. We acquired the boundary of the objects (always 15 of them), following the inner contours as identified by a border tracing algorithm (Suzuki and Abe, 1985). For each individual object we then extract the number of edges, RGB (red, green, blue) values, HSV (hue saturation value), and from the object's *moments*: its centroid, horizontal and vertical skewness (third order moments measuring the distortion in symmetry around the x and y axis), and the orientation value representing the direction of the principal axis (combination of second order moments). Taken together, this set of features represents a single object, which can be used for the word-object classifiers described earlier.

Procedure Using 1000 episodes, we evaluate our model across 10 folds (900 episodes for training, 100 for evaluation). Our baseline model is a generative model of RR that will be described below (random baseline is 7%). We also incorporate gaze and deixis by treating them as individual RR models and interpolating their distributions with the distribution given by the model. We ran the experiments twice, once with hand-transcribed utterances as basis for U, and once with automatic speech recogniser (ASR) output. The α weights (Equation 7) for hand-transcribed data were for speech, deixis and gaze: 0.72, 0.16, and 0.12 respectively, and for ASR 0.53, 0.23, 0.24, respectively (note that for ASR, more weight was given to the non-speech models).

[2]This approach also allows us to keep control over the degree of noisiness and systematically study its effect; this is something, however, that we leave for future work.

Task The task is RR, as described earlier. At each increment, the model returns a distribution over all objects; the probability for each object represents the strength of the belief that it is the referred one. The argmax of the distribution is chosen as the hypothesised referent.

A Stronger Baseline Model for Comparison To be able to judge the performance of our model better, we compare its results to a generative model we developed for the same domain, the *simple incremental update model* (SIUM) described in Kennington et al. (2013, 2014). SIUM is a good candidate to compare with this approach because it is also meant to work incrementally and it can accommodate uncertainty in the world representation. As a generative model SIUM learns the joint distribution between RE U and the world W, and it adds as a latent variable R, the properties of the object. This is formalised as follows (following (Kennington et al., 2013); see there for further details):

$$P(I|U,W) = \frac{1}{P(U)} P(I) \sum_{r \in R} P(U|R) P_W(R|I) \tag{8}$$

Here, $P_W(R|I)$ models the connection between objects and properties that are picked out for verbalisation. In the version described in Kennington et al. (2013, 2014), this model is read off the symbolic representation of the scene: the assumption is made that every property that a given object has is equally likely to be verbalised. This is where uncertainty about properties can be inserted into the model, which we do here. We trained an SVM classifier to classify the objects (pre-processed and segmented as described above) with respect to colors (e.g., classes like `red`, `blue`, etc.) and for shapes (e.g., `X`, `T`, etc.). The spatial placement of objects was determined by rules; the board was segmented into 4 quadrants and an object received a `left/right`, and `top/bottom` property with a probability of 1 if the object was in that corresponding area of the board. Where in Kennington et al. (2013, 2014) there was exact knowledge about the properties of objects, we now have distributions over properties, and the changed assumption now is that the likelihood of a property being verbalised is proportional to the strength of belief in it having this property. Other than that, SIUM remained unchanged.

4.2 Metrics for Evaluation

To give a picture of the overall performance of the model, we report *accuracy* (how often was the argmax the intended referent) after the full referring expression has been processed and *average rank* (position of intended referent among the 15 candidates on ordered distribution; ideal would be an average rank of 1, which would also correspond to 100% accuracy). Together, these metrics give an impression of how interpretable the full distribution is, beyond just the argmax. We report results for testing the model only given speech information (and no interpolation with the other models), and the other modalities added separately and jointly. We also computed results for SIUM given speech information.

We also look into how the model performs incrementally. For this, we followed previously used metrics (Schlangen et al., 2009; Kennington et al., 2013), where the predicted referent is compared to the gold refererent at each increment:

- **first correct**: how deep into the RE (%) does the model predict the referent for the first time?
- **first final**: if the final prediction is correct, how deep into the RE was it reached and not changed?
- **edit overhead**: how often did the model unnecessarily change its prediction (the only *necessary* prediction change happens when it first makes a correct prediction)?

4.3 Results

As Figures 6 and 7 show, our model performs well above the SIUM baseline, for all settings. (The *random selection baseline* sits at 7%.) We assume that it performs better not only because as a discriminative model it does not need to model the full joint distribution, but also because it directly learns a connection between words and visual features and does not need to go through a set of pre-determined features, which could be considered as a "lossy" compression of information. The Figures also show that using

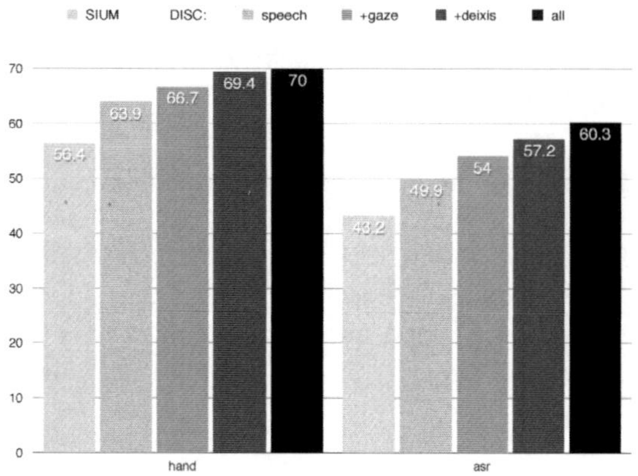

Figure 6: Results of our model in accuracies; higher numbers denote better results.

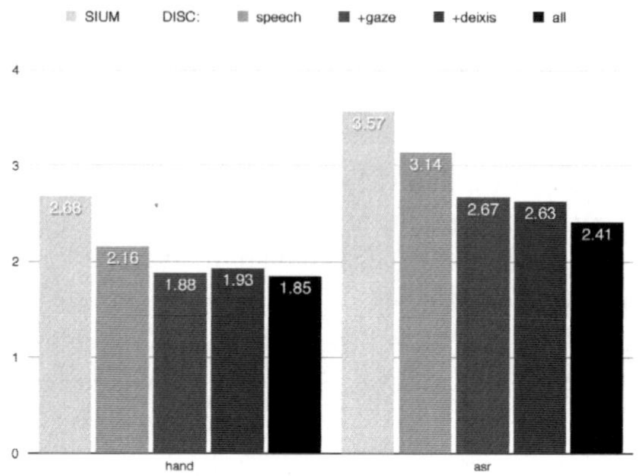

Figure 7: Results of our model in average rank; lower numbers denote better results.

ASR output does have an impact on the performance, as expeced. The speech+deixis models tend to work better than speech+gaze models in terms of accuracy; we speculate that this is due to the (naive) assumption implicit in our setup that participants gaze at the referred object most of the time, where in fact they often look at distractors, etc., making gaze a noisier model of predicting the referent. The story, however, is slightly different for the average rank: speech+deixis is slightly worse than speech+gaze at least for hand-transcribed data; this simply means that though speech+deixis gets the referred object into the argmax position more than speech+gaze, it doesn't always mean a better overall distribution. As expected, the best-scoring average rank is when all models are interpolated, both for hand-transcribed and ASR. Overall, there is about a 6% increase when both modalities are included when using hand-transcribed data. The increase when including both modalities is slightly larger (10%) with ASR. This nicely shows that when given noisier linguistic information, the model can partially recover by taking more benefit from interpolating with other information sources.

4.4 Incremental Results

Figure 8 gives an overview of the incremental performance of our model, compared to that of SIUM. (Results here are for the hand-transcribed utterances.) As the metrics talk about "% into expression", these metrics can of course only be computed when the eventual length of the expression is known, that is, after the fact. Moreover, to make these units comparable (as "10% into the utterance" is very different in terms of words for an utterance that consists of 2 words than for one that is 12 words long), we bin REs into the classes *short, normal, long* (1-6, 7-8, 9-14 words, respectively, as to group together REs that are of similar length).

Ideally for use downstream in a dialogue system, the reference resolver would make a first correct decision quickly, and this would also be the final decision (that is, in the graph the two bars would be close to each other, and at a low value). As the Figure shows, DISC is somewhat earlier than SIUM and on average that decision is very close to the final decision it makes, but it pays for this in a higher edit-overhead. When looking at first-final, SIUM is not that far away from DISC, but nevertheless, the new model beats the baseline across the board (and, as shown in Table 1, is also correct more often). DISC produces less stable predictions, which is presumably due to its response to the expression being a simple summation of the responses to its component words, whereas SIUM is a proper update model.

5 Further Analysis

We analysed several individual word classifiers to determine how well their predictions match assumptions about their lexical semantics. For example, the classifier for the word *links* (*left*) should yield a high

% edit overhead		
utt length	DISC	SIUM
1-6	11.5	3.8
7-8	19.76	17.2
9-14	41.0	27.5
% never correct		
utt length	DISC	SIUM
all lengths	19.5	32.0

Table 1: % edit overhead and never correct

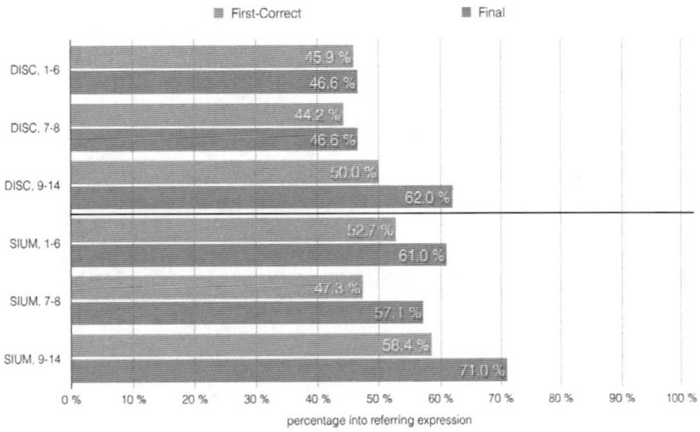

Figure 8: Incremental Performance

probability when given an object representation where the x-coordinate values are small (i.e., on the left of the screen), and lower probabilities for x values that are high. This was indeed the case, as shown in Figure 9. This is a nice feature of the model, as objects that are in the middle of the scene can still be described as *on the left*, albeit with a lower probability. We also tested how well classifiers were learned for colour words. In Figure 10 we show how changing the H S V features (representing colors) across the spectrum, keeping all other object features stable, yielded different responses from the classifier for the word *gelb* (yellow), where the y-axis on the figure represents probability for that particular colour value.[3]

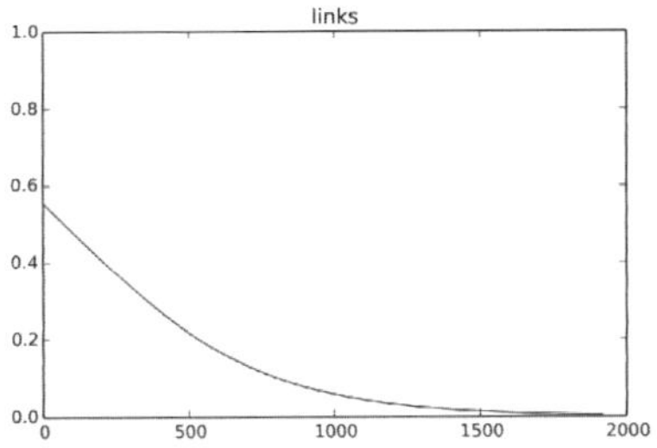

Figure 9: Strength of word *links* (German for *left*) predicting when given different x-coordinate values, the y-axis represents the probability of that point being *left*.

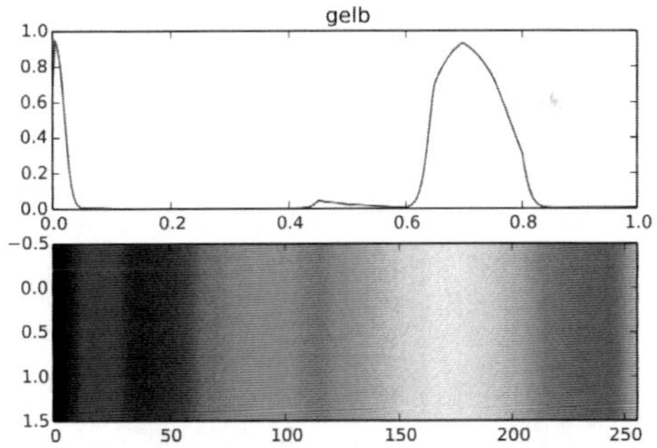

Figure 10: Strength of word *gelb* (German for *yellow*) predicting when given different color (HSV) values.

We further looked into shape words. Figure 11 shows the response of the classifier for *kreuz* (cross) when given object representations where only the shape-related features (number of edges, skewness) were varied across all possible shapes (the x-axis uses here the standard labeling of pentomino pieces with letters whose shapes are similar). Interestingly, the classifier generalised the word to apply not only to objects with the cross shape, but also the Z-shape piece (the red piece in the bottom of the top right group in Figure 4) and others which also intuitively seem to be more similar. For a sanity check, we looked at the responses to change in colour for the word *kreuz*. As Figure 12 shows, this classifier does not pick out any specific color, as it should be. This shows that the word classifier managed to identify those features that are relevant for its core meaning, ignoring the others.

[3]There is also a high probability in the black region. It could be the case that the yellow classifier learned that a low value for B is highly discriminative (black is 0 for all RGB values).

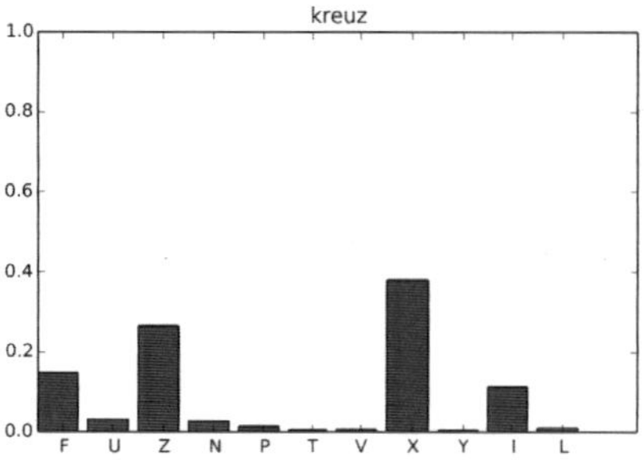

Figure 11: Strength of word *kreuz* (German for *cross*) predicting when given different values of number of edges.

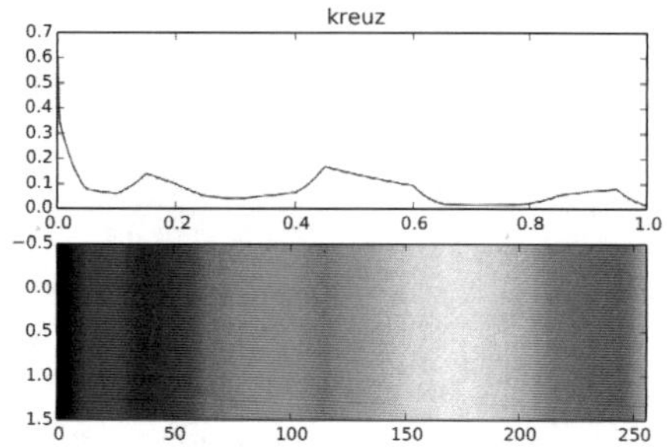

Figure 12: Strength of word *kreuz* (German for *cross*) predicting when given different color (RGB) values.

6 Conclusion

We presented a model of reference resolution that learns perceptually-grounded semantics from relatively low-level, computer vision-based features, rather than from pre-defined sets of object properties or ontologies. We tested the model and found that it worked well for the Pentomino corpus, despite having a very simple notion of compositionality. The model is discriminative and outperforms a generative approach applied the same data. The model fused well with additional modalities, namely gaze and deixis, providing improved results in a reference resolution task. Perhaps best of all, the model is simple: besides the scenes and referring expressions, one only needs to know what object was referred in each scene in order to train the model, which is generally easy to annotate.

For future work, we will apply more principled methods of compositionality. We also plan to apply the model to a more systematic test of how well it performs under varied strengths of image distortion. We further plan on applying the model in a real-time multimodal learning scenario, using video images of real objects.

Acknowledgements We would like to thank the anonymous reviewers for their comments. We also want to thank Spyros Kousidis for his help with the data collection.

References

Canny, J. (1986, June). A computational approach to edge detection. *IEEE transactions on pattern analysis and machine intelligence 8*(6), 679–698.

Engonopoulos, N., M. Villalba, I. Titov, and A. Koller (2013). Predicting the resolution of referring expressions from user behavior. In *Proceedings of EMLNP*, Seattle, Washington, USA, pp. 1354–1359. Association for Computational Linguistics.

Funakoshi, K., M. Nakano, T. Tokunaga, and R. Iida (2012, July). A Unified Probabilistic Approach to Referring Expressions. In *Proceedings of SIGdial*, Seoul, South Korea, pp. 237–246. Association for Computational Linguistics.

Gorniak, P. and D. Roy (2004). Grounded semantic composition for visual scenes. *Journal of Artificial Intelligence Research 21*, 429–470.

Griffin, Z. M. and K. Bock (2000). What the eyes say about speaking. *Psychological science : a journal of the American Psychological Society / APS 11*, 274–279.

Iida, R., M. Yasuhara, and T. Tokunaga (2011). Multi-modal Reference Resolution in Situated Dialogue by Integrating Linguistic and Extra-Linguistic Clues. In *Proceedings of IJCNLP*, Number 2003, pp. 84–92.

Kelleher, J., F. Costello, and J. Van Genabith (2005). Dynamically structuring, updating and interrelating representations of visual and linguistic discourse context. *Artificial Intelligence 167*(1–2), 62–102.

Kennington, C., R. Iida, T. Tokunaga, and D. Schlangen (2015). Incrementally Tracking Reference in Human/Human Dialogue Using Linguistic and Extra-Linguistic Information. In *Proceedings of NAACL*, Denver, U.S.A. Association for Computational Linguistics.

Kennington, C., S. Kousidis, and D. Schlangen (2013). Interpreting Situated Dialogue Utterances: an Update Model that Uses Speech, Gaze, and Gesture Information. In *Proceedings of SIGdial 2013*.

Kennington, C., S. Kousidis, and D. Schlangen (2014). Situated Incremental Natural Language Understanding using a Multimodal, Linguistically-driven Update Model. In *Proceedings of CoLing 2014*.

Kennington, C. and D. Schlangen (2012). Markov Logic Networks for Situated Incremental Natural Language Understanding. In *Proceedings of SIGdial*, Seoul, South Korea, pp. 314–322. Association for Computational Linguistics.

Kousidis, S., C. Kennington, and D. Schlangen (2013). Investigating speaker gaze and pointing behaviour in human-computer interaction with the mint.tools collection. In *Proceedings of SIGdial 2013*.

Kousidis, S., T. Pfeiffer, Z. Malisz, P. Wagner, and D. Schlangen (2012). Evaluating a minimally invasive laboratory architecture for recording multimodal conversational data. In *Interdisciplinary Workshop on Feedback Behaviors in Dialog, INTERSPEECH 2012 Satellite Workshop*, pp. 39–42.

Larsson, S. (2013). Formal semantics for perceptual classification. *Journal of Logic and Computation*.

Matuszek, C., L. Bo, L. Zettlemoyer, and D. Fox (2014). Learning from Unscripted Deictic Gesture and Language for Human-Robot Interactions. In *Proceedings of AAAI Conference on Artificial Intelligence*. AAAI Press.

Ng A.Y. & Jordan M. I. (2002, December). On Discriminative vs. Generative Classifiers: A comparison of Logistic Regression and Naive Bayes, Neural Information Processing Systems. . In *Machine Learning*, Vancouver, Canada.

Poesio, M. and R. Vieira (1997, June). A Corpus-Based Investigation of Definite Description Use. *Comput. Linguist. 24*(2), 47.

Richardson, M. and P. Domingos (2006). Markov logic networks. *Machine Learning 62*(1-2), 107–136.

Schlangen, D., T. Baumann, and M. Atterer (2009). Incremental Reference Resolution: The Task, Metrics for Evaluation, and a Bayesian Filtering Model that is Sensitive to Disfluencies. In *Proceedings of SIGdial*, London, UK, pp. 30–37. Association for Computational Linguistics.

Spivey, M. (2002). Eye movements and spoken language comprehension: Effects of visual context on syntactic ambiguity resolution. *Cognitive Psychology 45*(4), 447–481.

Steels, L. and T. Belpaeme (2005). Coordinating perceptually grounded categories through language: a case study for colour. *The Behavioral and brain sciences 28*(4), 469–489; discussion 489–529.

Suzuki, S. and K. Abe (1985). Topological structural analysis of digitized binary images by border following. *Computer Vision, Graphics, and Image Processing 29*(30), 396.

Tanenhaus, M. K. and M. J. Spivey-Knowlton (1995). Integration of visual and linguistic information in spoken language comprehension. *Science 268*, 1632.

Incremental Semantics for Dialogue Processing: Requirements, and a Comparison of Two Approaches

Julian Hough, Casey Kennington, David Schlangen
Bielefeld University
{julian.hough,ckennington@cit-ec, david.schlangen}@ uni-bielefeld.de

Jonathan Ginzburg
Université Paris-Diderot
yonatan.ginzburg@ univ-paris-diderot.fr

Abstract

Truly interactive dialogue systems need to construct meaning on at least a word-by-word basis. We propose desiderata for incremental semantics for dialogue models and systems, a task not heretofore attempted thoroughly. After laying out the desirable properties we illustrate how they are met by current approaches, comparing two incremental semantic processing frameworks: Dynamic Syntax enriched with Type Theory with Records (DS-TTR) and Robust Minimal Recursion Semantics with incremental processing (RMRS-IP). We conclude these approaches are not significantly different with regards to their semantic representation construction, however their purported role within semantic models and dialogue models is where they diverge.

1 Introduction

It is now uncontroversial that dialogue participants construe meaning from utterances on at least as fine-grained a level as word-by-word (see Brennan, 2000; Schlesewsky and Bornkessel, 2004, *inter alia*). It has also become clear that using more fine-grained incremental processing allows more likeable and interactive systems to be designed (Skantze and Schlangen, 2009; Skantze and Hjalmarsson, 2010). Despite these encouraging results, it has not been clearly stated which elements of incremental semantic frameworks, either formally or implementationally, are desirable for dialogue models and systems; this paper intends to spell these requirements out clearly.

1.1 The need for incremental semantics in situated dialogue

While traditional computational semantics models the meaning of complete sentences, for interaction this is insufficient for achieving *the construction of meaning in real time as linguistic information is processed*. The motivation for incremental semantics becomes clear in situated dialogue systems, which we illustrate here with a real-world scenario. Imagine interacting with a robot capable of manipulating objects of different colours and shapes on a board, where you can direct the robot's action verbally, and the robot also has the ability to direct your actions. When talking to the robot, natural interactions like the following should be possible (the utterance timings and actions of the two participants are represented roughly at the relative time indicated by their horizontal position):

(1)	You:	Take...		the red cross	
	Robot:		[turns head to board]		
(2)	You:	Take the red cross ...		and the blue square	
	Robot:		mhm [takes red cross]		[takes blue square]
(3)	You:	Take the red cross, uh no, that's green.			
	Robot:			[takes green cross]	

Proceedings of the 11th International Conference on Computational Semantics, pages 206–216,
London, UK, April 15-17 2015.

(4) You: The big red cross uh no, the one in the corner
Robot: [moves hand over nearby cross] [retracts, moves hand over cross in corner]

(5) You: Take the red ...
Robot: cross?

(6) You: Take the red ...
Robot: what?

(7) You: Take the blue uh ... yes, sorry, the red cross
Robot: Did you mean red?

(8) Robot: What's your name? [makes puzzled face]
You: Take the red cross

However we may not desire the following interactions:

(9) You: Take every no, wait, take every red cross!
Robot: [moves hand over green cross]

(10) You: Take the ...
Robot: okay!

Here we propose incremental semantics should be motivated by modelling and implementing this highly interactive, realistic behaviour, putting immediate requirements in focus. (1) shows the robot should begin signalling attention before the command is over, (2) shows backchannel acknowledgements should be driven by incremental semantic understanding, (3) and (4) show how computing the meaning of a repaired utterance even when the repair is elliptical ('that's green') or anaphoric ('the one') is crucial. The compound contribution (5) shows the need for semantic construction to go across dialogue partners (this does not mean string completion), while in (6), the WH-sluice from the robot relies on the (potentially defeasible) inference that you wanted it to take something. The mid-utterance clarification request (7) and mid-utterance reaction to irrelevant user behaviour in (8) show the possibility for immediate reaction to pragmatic infelicity. While we would like the maximal amount of information possible on a word-by-word basis, (9) shows this should not result in bad predictions. (10) shows how human-robot interaction relying on acoustic cues such as silence detection for 'end-pointing' utterances alone is clearly insufficient– silence is not always an indicator of semantic or dialogue-level completeness, nor is its absence good evidence for a continuation of a unit of meaning (see Schlangen and Skantze, 2011).

We address how to meet these requirements in semantics as follows: Section 2 outlines our proposed desiderata, 3 technically overviews two approaches to incremental semantics, 4 compares the approaches in terms of the desired properties theoretically and practically, and Section 5 concludes with the implications of our findings.

2 Desiderata

We take as our point of departure Milward (1991), who points out the difference between a system's capacity for *strong incremental interpretation* and its ability to access and produce *incremental representation.* While these are important and we still consider them central requirements in terms of *semantic representation construction properties*, there are others we propose below, some directly related to these and others orthogonal to them. We also discuss *semantic model*, *dialogue*, and *computational* desiderata. We explain these in turn and the connections between them. Figure 1 shows some of the desiderata visually for the utterance 'take the red cross' as it is interpreted by a rudimentary interpretation module reasoning about a real-word scene: the action SELECT is inferred upon processing the first word and the referent set indicating the possible objects the user is selecting narrows thereafter word-by-word when relevant information specifies the referent. The parts we are principally concerned with are those on levels two and three in grey, in addition to their interfaces to the rest of the model.

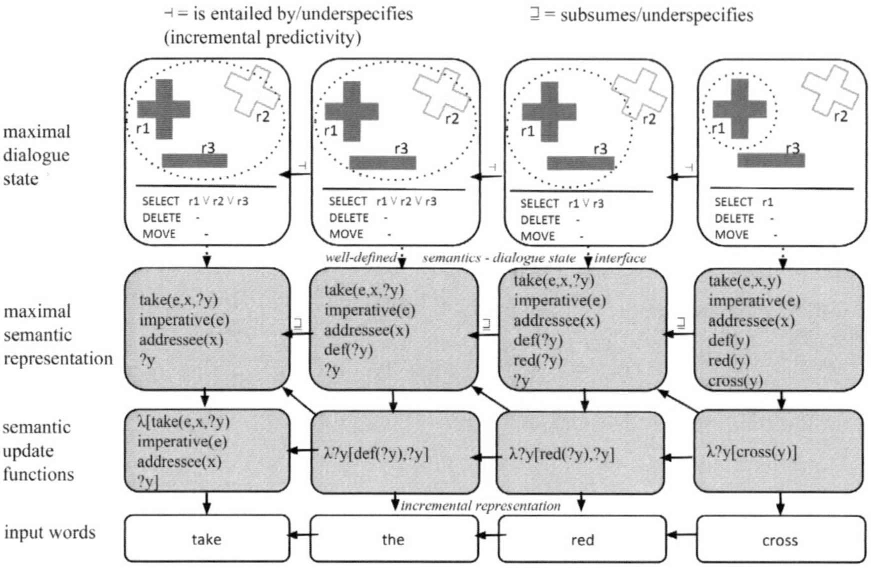

Figure 1: The desired incremental properties of semantics in terms of a dialogue state (level 4, top) idealised scopeless FOL maximal semantic representation with underspecified variables marked '?' (level 3) the update functions (level 2) triggered by input words (level 1). Arrows mean 'triggered by input'.

2.1 Semantic representation construction properties

Strong incremental interpretation In line with Milward (1991), the maximal semantic representation possible should be constructed on a word-by-word basis as it is being produced or interpreted (e.g. a representation such as $\lambda x.like'(john', x)$ should be available after processing "John likes"). The availability of such a representation may, though not necessarily, rely on an interfacing incremental syntactic parsing framework. This is relevant to all examples (1)-(10) for achieving natural understanding and generation. Figure 1 shows the maximal semantic representation at the third level from bottom as idealised scopeless First Order Logic (FOL) formulae with underspecified elements indicated with a '?'.

Incremental representation Again as per (Milward, 1991), assuming a word contributes a minimal amount of semantic representation, the exact contribution each word or substring makes should be available as an increment. However this need not necessarily include all possible information such as semantic dependencies available (e.g. $john'$ attributed to "John" and $\lambda y.\lambda x.like'(y, x)$ attributed to "likes" should be available after processing "John likes"). While strong incremental interpretation is more obviously required for dialogue, the incremental representation requirement becomes stronger when considering the possibility of elements of the input string being revoked in real-time practical dialogue systems– i.e. previous word hypotheses from an ASR output may change (Schlangen and Skantze, 2011). This is also relevant in clarification and repair situations (3), (4) and (7), where on-line computation of the meaning of repaired material relies on identifying its antecedent's semantic representations precisely: access to *how* the incremental information was constructed is essential. Incremental representations are shown as time-linear update functions to the maximal semantic representation as in the second level in Figure 1.

Incremental underspecification and partiality Well-founded underspecification of representation is required– more specifically, structural underspecification, such as that developed in CLLS (Constraint Language for Lambda Structures, Egg et al., 2001). Underspecification should be derivable with incremental representation such as in Steedman (2012)'s Combinatorial Categorial Grammar (CCG) lexicalised model of quantifier scope resolution. As time-linear semantic construction is our central motivation, while we want to capture scope-ambiguous readings of utterances such as 'Every linguist attends a workshop', we add the stipulation that this underspecification be derivable word-by-word. After directly processing a quantifier like 'every' such as in (9), the representation should be as semantically informative as possible, but no more so; representations should be underspecified enough so as not to make bad predictions for the final structure. Incremental underspecification also means having suitable placeholders for anaphoric and elliptical constructions before they get resolved to their final representation.

Subsumption Dialogue models and systems require well-defined subsumption for incrementally checking representations against domain knowledge, both in understanding and in checking against a semantic goal when generating utterances. One computationally tractable and suitable candidate is Description Logic subsumption, where for two semantic concepts A and B, A *is subsumed by* B, i.e. $B \sqsupseteq A$, iff there is no object belonging to concept A that does not belong to B. The semantic framework should allow subsumption checking from the representation alone– in Figure 1 subsumption holds between maximal semantic representations after each prefix.

2.2 Semantic model properties

While the appropriate representation should be available word-by-word as just described, a suitable model and valuation function must reflect their intuitive semantics incrementally, again providing additional desiderata beyond the valuation of fully specified representations.

Interpretation of partial or underspecified representations The partial representations constructed must be evaluable in a consistent way in a given interpretation system. This applies to all examples (1)-(10): for example if the robot responds appropriately before an instruction is over as in (1) it must have computed a meaning representation to the effect *this is a taking event* early in parsing. In recent type-theoretic approaches in computational semantics this kind of valuation is possible if semantic representations are considered types in a type system: inference can be characterized as subtype relation checking either by theorem proving (Chatzikyriakidis and Luo, 2014) or by checking the existence and ordering relations of types on a model (partial order) of types (Hough and Purver, 2014).[1]

Incremental predictivity Related to subsumption is monotonicity (in the sense of monotonic entailment in logic). In general, one would not want the valuation function after the first word to return more specific information than that returned after the second word, nor at the second word evaluate expressions as having a true value which were evaluated as false after the first word, and so on. In general, the total information made available after having consumed a new word should entail the information inferred by the prefix consumed before it is processed– see the top level in Figure 1. However, from a semantic parsing perspective, maintaining robustness while preserving monotonicity for each interpretation requires allowing multiple parse paths due to possible lexical and structural ambiguity, most notably in 'garden path' sentences, and so the output of a semantic parser can update its output non-monotonically, so long as there is a good notion of *predictivity* of future states in time afforded by the semantic model.

Interface and consistency with well-founded reasoning system Well studied logical inference systems like FOL may not be adequate for natural language inference, as evidenced by the logical form equivalence problem (Shieber, 1993).[2] Having said this, consistent logical systems should be in place which reason with the representations.

2.3 Dialogue properties

Incremental illocutionary information Where available syntactically and lexically, information about the type of dialogue move, or illocutionary effects the utterance causes should be made available as soon as possible, as evidenced by (1), in support of Ginzburg (2012)'s approach. This may not generally be lexicalised, and therefore appropriate underspecification should be used instead to interface with the dialogue model. Also, closely related to strong incremental interpretation is the need to allow for *default existential inference*, as in sluices like (6).

[1]Also, while not immediately a natural language model, computationally incremental interpretation can be modelled in terms of projection algebras (Sundaresh and Hudak, 1991), which allow evaluation of partial programs that are consistent with complete programs.

[2]Roughly, Shieber (1993) shows how FOL can have different logical forms equivalent in meaning within a reasoning system, but these equivalences may not ramify in a comparable way in natural language.

Completion and repair potential In dialogue, it is not rare that one participant begins an utterance and another completes it, in the case of compound contributions such as (5)– according to Howes et al. (2011), this happens in 3% of all dialogue contributions (turns). Furthermore (11) from the same authors shows that concatenating contiguous utterances where a speaker completes another's can be ungrammatical, however felicitous at such turn boundaries in real dialogue.

(11) A: Did you burn...
B: myself?

Potential for clarifying semantic content made central in the dialogue framework KoS (Ginzburg, 2012) is another desirable property. Clarification and repair of semantic information requires incremental representation as described above, as parsers and generators must have access to the information as to which part of the semantic construction was triggered by which word.

Interchangeability between parsing and generation Ideally, the representations built up in parsing should be usable by a generation process and vice-versa; akin to the reversible representation approach in (Neumann, 1998). This is not just to deal with compound contributions, but also to be commensurate with the self-monitoring required in generation (Levelt, 1989) without extra overhead.

Well-founded interface to dialogue or discourse models For extrinsic usefulness, incremental semantics should interface with incremental models of discourse and dialogue. While these models are rare, PTT (Poesio and Traum, 1997) and recent extensions of KoS (Ginzburg, 2012) are candidates. For the sub-task of reference resolution, a suitable semantic model should provide word-by-word reference information, relevant to all interactions in our toy domain in (1)-(10). Also, word-by-word access to the dialogue state to compute relevance or coherence allows inferences of pragmatic infelicity like (8).

2.4 Computational properties

Semantic construction stability Related to the predictivity requirement, semantic content already constructed should not be removed and replaced as processing continues unless triggered by revoked input such as a word hypothesis change from ASR input. Stability affects the rest of the dialogue system served by the semantics. This is pertinent in an automatic system which may have different interpretations stored in a beam, where frequent top hypothesis changes may have undesirable effects.

Minimisation of re-computation and efficiency When faced with changing input, one wants to minimise the re-computation of already evaluated parts of the input (the prefix). There are great efficiency benefits if something only has to be evaluated once. For example chart parsing with the Cocke-Younger-Kasami (CYK) algorithm exhibits this property, as it incrementally hypothesises the syntactic structure of a sentence, where partial results of the computation can be stored on a word-by-word basis to maximise efficiency in a dynamic programming chart, and no computation is done more than once. Top-down parsing approaches such as Roark (2001) also have this property.

Well-founded information and probability theoretic properties For training automatic systems, well-understood information theoretic properties of the semantic construction process aid induction of rules from data. This relies on a well understood probability model of the framework in terms of its distributions of structures and update rules.

We now describe two current incremental semantic parsing frameworks to illustrate how the above desiderata are met.

3 Two Current Attempts

3.1 DS-TTR

DS-TTR (Purver et al., 2011) integrates Type Theory with Records (TTR, Cooper, 2005) *record type* ('RT' largely from now on) representations with the inherently incremental grammar formalism Dynamic Syntax (DS, Kempson et al., 2001) to provide word-by-word semantic construction. DS-TTR is an action-driven interpretation formalism which has no layer of syntax independent of semantic construction. The trees such as Figure 2 are constructed monotonically through sequences of tree-building

IF	$?Ty(e)$
THEN	put($Ty(e)$)
	put($[\ x = john\ :\ e\ ]$)
ELSE	abort

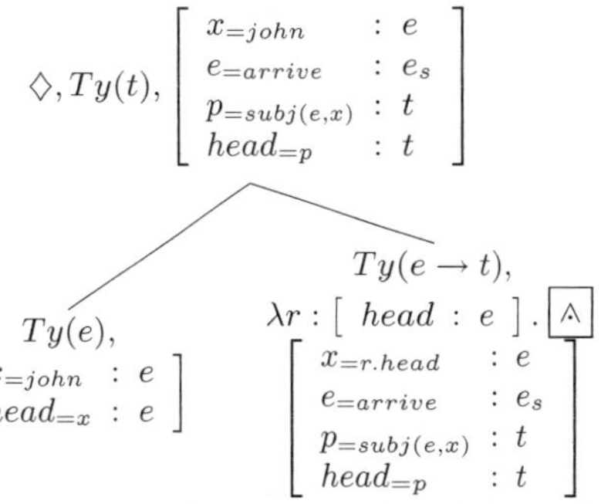

Figure 2: Left: DS-TTR lexical action for 'john'. Right: Final DS-TTR tree for "John arrives"

actions consistent with Logic of Finite Trees (LOFT). The DS lexicon comprises *lexical actions* keyed to words, and also a set of globally applicable *computational actions* (equivalent to general syntactic rules), both of which constitute packages of monotonic update operations on semantic trees, and take the form of IF-THEN-ELSE action-like structures. DS-TTR does not change the LOFT backbone of the DS tree building process, nor does it currently augment the computational actions directly. However, RT formulae are introduced into the lexical actions; for example the lexical action for the word "John" has the preconditions and update effects as in the left-side of Figure 2.

As can be seen on the right side of Figure 2, the DS node types (rather than the RT formulae at the nodes) are terms in the typed lambda calculus, with mother-daughter node relations corresponding to semantic predicate-argument structure. The pointer object, $\diamondsuit$, indicates the node currently under development. Parsing begins by an initial prediction step on an axiom of a single node with requirement $?Ty(t)$ and then the set of computational actions are Kleene star iterated over to yield a tree set. When a word is consumed, it triggers all possible parses in the current tree set (or those within a given beam-width), and then the set of computational actions are then again iterated over to yield a new tree set.

DS parsing yields an incrementally specified, partial semantic tree as words are parsed or generated, and following Purver et al. (2011) DS-TTR tree nodes are decorated not with simple atomic formulae but with RTs, and corresponding lambda abstracts representing RT λ-functions of type $RT \rightarrow RT$. Using TTR's affordance of *manifest* fields, there is a natural representation for underspecification of leaf node content of DS trees, e.g. $[x : e]$ is unmanifest whereas $[x_{=john} : e]$ is manifest and the latter is a subtype of the former. After every word a RT is compiled to the top node with a simple bottom-up algorithm (Hough and Purver, 2012). DS-TTR tree nodes include a field *head* in all RTs. Technically, the range of the λ-functions at functor nodes is the asymmetric merge $\boxed{\wedge}$ of their domain RT(s) with the RT in their range. This allows the $head$ field of argument node RTs in β-reduction operations to be replaced by the $head$ field of the function's range RT at the sister functor node in their resulting mother node RT or RT function. On functor nodes semantic content decorations are of the form λr: $[\, l_1 : T_1\,].r \boxed{\wedge} [\, l_{2=r.l_1} : T_1\,]$ where $r.l_1$ is a path expression referring to the label l_1 in r – see the functor node with DS type label $Ty(e \rightarrow t)$ of Figure 2.

Briefly, in DS-TTR generation (Hough and Purver, 2012), surface realisation is done by generating from a goal TTR RT concept. This requires a notion of subsumption which is given by the TTR subtype relation. Generation is driven by parsing and subtype relation checking the goal concept against each tree's top node RT, and consequently meets the desideratum of interchangeability between parsing and generation described above.

3.2 RMRS-IP

While DS-TTR treats both syntactic and semantic construction as one process, Robust Minimal Recursion Semantics with incremental processing (RMRS-IP, Peldszus et al., 2012) splits the task into a top-down PCFG parse followed by the construction of RMRS (Copestake, 2006) formulae using semantic construction rules, operating strictly word-by-word. The current RMRS-IP implementation uses standard top-down non-lexicalised PCFG parsing in the style of Roark (2001), however uses left-factorization of the standard PCFG grammar rules to delay certain structural decisions as long as possible, employing a beam search over possible parses.

Logical RMRS forms are built up by semantic construction actions operating on the derived CFG trees. In RMRS, meaning representations of a FOL are underspecified in two ways: First, the scope relationships can be underspecified by splitting the formula into a list of *elementary predications* (EP) which receive a label ℓ and are explicitly related by stating scope constraints to hold between them (e.g. qeq-constraints). This way, all scope readings can be compactly represented. Second, RMRS allows underspecification of the predicate-argument-structure of EPs. Arguments are bound to a predicate by anchor variables a, expressed in the form of an *argument relation* ARGREL(a,x). This way, predicates can be introduced without fixed arity and arguments can be introduced without knowing which predicates they are arguments of. RMRS-IP makes use of this form of underspecification by enriching lexical predicates with arguments incrementally– see the right of Figure 5.

Combining two RMRS structures involves at least joining their list of EPs and ARGRELs and of scope constraints. Additionally, equations between the variables can connect two structures, which is an essential requirement for semantic construction. A semantic algebra for the combination of RMRSs in a non-lexicalist setting is defined in Copestake (2007). Unsaturated semantic increments have open slots that need to be filled by what is called the *hook* of another structure. Hook and slot are triples $[\ell{:}a{:}x]$ consisting of a label, an anchor and an index variable. Every variable of the hook is equated with the corresponding one in the slot. This way the semantic representation can grow monotonically at each combinatory step by simply adding predicates, constraints and equations. RMRS-IP extends Copestake (2007) in the organisation of the slots to meet the requirement of strong incremental interpretation, constructing a proper semantic representation for every single state of growth of the syntactic tree. Typically, RMRS composition assumes that the order of semantic combination is parallel to a bottom-up traversal of the syntactic tree. However RMRS-IP proceeds with semantic combination in synchronisation with the syntactic expansion of the tree, i.e. in a top-down left-to-right fashion. This way, no underspecification of projected nodes and no re-interpretation of already existing parts of the tree is required. This, however, requires adjustments to the slot structure of RMRS. Left-recursive rules can introduce multiple slots of the same sort before they are filled, which is not allowed in the classic (R)MRS semantic algebra, where only one named slot of each sort can be open at a time. Thus slots are organized as a stack of unnamed slots, where multiple slots of the same sort can be stored, but only the one on top can be accessed. A basic combination operation equivalent to forward function composition (as in standard lambda calculus, or in CCG) allows combination of substructures in a principled way across multiple syntactic rules without the need to represent slot names.

Each lexical item receives a generic representation derived from its lemma and the basic semantic type (individual, event, or underspecified denotations), determined by its POS tag. This makes the grammar independent of knowledge about what later (semantic) components will actually be able to process ("understand"). Parallel to the production of syntactic derivations, as the tree is expanded top-down left-to-right, semantic macros are activated for each syntactic rule, composing the contribution of the new increment. This allows for a monotonic semantics construction process that proceeds in lock-step with the syntactic analysis. The stack of semantic slots is always synchronized with the parser's stack.

4 Comparison

We now compare DS-TTR and RMRS-IP in terms of how they meet the desiderata set out in Section 2 and compare their incremental performance extrinsically in a proof-of-concept reference resolution task.

Semantic representation construction properties Figure 5 shows the representation constructed by both formalisms for the utterance 'take the red cross' based on hand-crafted grammars. As can be seen both allow *strong incremental interpretation* after each word. DS-TTR is more predictive after processing 'take' by predicting a second (object) argument, however the RMRS-IP grammar in principle could also have this if its PCFG were extended appropriately. *Underspecification and partiality* in representation is good for both as they exhibit incremental extension of their output formulae word-by-word. The DS tree

$$
\begin{array}{ll}
\text{IF} & ?Ty(e), r : \left[\ ctxt : \left[\begin{array}{lcl} u & : & utt \\ x & : & e \\ spkr(u,x) & : & t \end{array}\right]\ \right], \\
 & \uparrow_0\uparrow_{1*}\downarrow_0 \mathrm{r1} : \left[\ cont : \left[\ x1_{=r.ctxt.x} : e\ \right]\ \right] \\
\text{THEN} & \mathtt{put}(Ty(e)), \\
 & \mathtt{put}(r \boxed{\wedge} \left[\ cont : \left[\ x_{=r.ctxt.x} : e\ \right]\ \right]) \\
\text{ELSE} & \mathtt{abort}
\end{array}
$$

Figure 3: DS-TTR lexical action for 'myself' checks the formula at the subject $Ty(e)$ node, which may not have been constructed by current speaker x but can still reference them

model	metric	**1-6**	**7-8**	**9-14**
RMRS-IP	first-correct (FC)	35.1	23.5	18.4
DS-TTR	(% into utt.)	20.1	20.1	33.1
NGRAM		39.0	23.4	31.7
RMRS-IP	first-final (FF)	43.0	25.5	29.3
DS-TTR	(% into utt.)	23.5	23.3	42.8
NGRAM		46.9	35.5	41.4
RMRS-IP	edit overhead (EO)	7.2	3.3	18.8
DS-TTR		5.8	2.9	17.5
NGRAM		10.4	18.6	9.5

Figure 4: Incremental reference resolution results for utterances of different lengths

keeps a record of the requirements still unsatisfied on its nodes, while in RMRS-IP this is done through the stack of semantic slots (shown in the curly brackets in Figure 5). Both DS-TTR and RMRS-IP allow word-by-word specification of entities (i.e. of the definite description 'the red cross').

In terms of the suitability of the underspecification for ellipsis and anaphora, in DS-TTR the interpretation of strict readings of verb phrase ellipsis (VPE) such as "John likes his donkey and Bill does too" $\rightarrow$ *Bill likes John's donkey* and sloppy VPE readings, where "John likes his donkey and Bill does too" $\rightarrow$ *Bill likes his own donkey* is possible incrementally, by different strategies outlined in Kempson et al. (2015). *Wh*-pronouns such as 'who' can be automatically resolved where possible. RMRS has sufficient underspecification to yield similar readings, however this is not operationalised in RMRS-IP parsing.

The semantic increment each word contributes is computed as a difference between the formula computed after a given word and that computed at its previous word in both formalisms, therefore both satisfy *incremental representation*. The subtype relation in TTR is *subsumptive* rather than cohersive, giving DS-TTR another one of our desired properties– see Cooper (2005). Subsumption is not defined in RMRS-IP, but due to its monotonicity in valuation it should exhibit similar properties.

Semantic model properties Both formalisms potentially exhibit *incremental predictivity* in terms of valuation in a semantic model. DS-TTR permits the subtype relation to hold between the current RT and the one constructed at the previous word. This allows valuation on a type lattice whereby type judgements hold from one word to the next but become more specified. RMRS formulae can be flattened to FOL with sortal variables, and given this interpretation can be interpreted monotonically. In terms of *interpretation of partial or underspecified representations* and an *interface and consistency with a well-founded reasoning system*, in DS-TTR, supertypes (the dual of subtypes) allow well-defined underspecified RTs, however more work needs to be done on incorporating underspecified scope relations. As RMRS is defined in a semantic algebra allowing underspecification (Copestake, 2007), it is currently more strongly positioned here. Furthermore, the extensive history of reasoning with FOL logical forms puts RMRS-IP at an advantage to work with well understood semantic models.

Dialogue properties DS-TTR makes claims about dialogue modelling beyond those of RMRS-IP to date. For instance, as regards *interchangeability between parsing and generation*, compound contributions are modelled with speaker-hearer switches which build the same RT, which can be further specified by subtyping to a new goal during the speaker switch. The example (5) can also be accounted for in designing lexical actions which interact with context. By assuming a simple dialogue context is maintained that records who is speaking, this allows interaction-oriented lexical actions to be created, such as that for 'myself' as in Figure 3. This also makes self-monitoring and self-repair in generation possible incrementally, including generating repairs in the face of changing goal concepts (Hough and Purver, 2012). Having said this, these are largely made possible by the well-defined subsumption and monotonicity in subtype relations, so this is in principle re-producible in RMRS. In terms of a *well-founded interface to dialogue models*, while DS-TTR has been used as a dialogue model itself, given DS-TTR's output of RTs, other popular models of dialogue can interface with it, most notably KoS (Ginzburg, 2012). RMRS-IP is well positioned to interface with a variety of formalisms that use FOL, and again, well-founded logical inference in these models puts it at an advantage.

Computational properties Un-enriched PCFGs have well studied information-theoretic properties and complexity, and are learnable from data, however DS-TTR semantic grammars have been proven to be learnable with semantic targets for short utterances (Eshghi et al., 2013), which has not been attempted yet in RMRS-IP. We discuss both formalisms' *semantic construction stability* below.

4.1 Implementation comparison: Reference Resolution task performance

We also compare the frameworks' current parsing implementations in a real-world inference task contingent on the desiderata. This was done in an incremental reference resolution (RR) task using Kennington et al. (2013)'s statistical SIUM model, which learns to associate words (or in our case, semantic representations) with properties belonging to objects in a virtual scene. Both semantic grammars were hand-crafted to achieve coverage of our test corpus of German spoken instructions directed at a manipulator of blocks in the scene. Word-by-word representations from the parsers were used by SIUM to learn which object properties were likely to be in the referred object. Evaluating using a 10-fold cross validation, in addition to utterance-final **RR accuracy** (where the referent hypothesis was the argmax in the distribution over objects produced by SIUM), to investigate incremental performance we use metrics used by the same authors: **first correct (FC)**: how deep into the utterance (in %) does the model predict the referent for the first time?, **first final (FF)**: how deep into the utterance (in %) does the model predict the correct referent and keep that decision until the end?, and **edit overhead (EO)**: how often did the model unnecessarily change its prediction (the only *necessary* prediction happens when it first makes a correct prediction)? Good *semantic construction stability* would mean low EO, and, good *predictivity* should mean short distance between FC and FF (once correct it does not revoke the referent), and in terms of *strong incremental representation* we would want it to make this final choice early on (low FF).

The utterance-final RR accuracy was 0.876 for SIUM using RMRS-IP, out-performing DS-TTR (0.832), and both out-performing a base-line using n-gram features (0.811). In terms of incremental metrics, DS-TTR had good performance in short utterances up to 8 words long, but RMRS-IP, with more robust PCFG parsing strategies and flexible RMRS composition yields better results overall, particularly in longer utterances. DS-TTR showed good stability and predictivity, on average making correct final predictions earlier than RMRS-IP for utterance lengths 1-6 (FF: 23.5% into the utterance vs 43.0%), and lengths 7-8, however falling back significantly for lengths 9-14 (FF: DS-TTR: 42.8% vs. RMRS-IP: 29.3%), which is likely due to bad parses for long utterances. DS-TTR makes more stable choices as the difference between FF and FC is lowest for all but lengths 7-8, and DS-TTR also achieves the lowest edit overhead across all utterance lengths– see Figure 4. Practically, currently RMRS-IP is more robust for long utterances and for utterance-final meaning, while DS-TTR performs better incrementally.

5 Conclusion

We have proposed desiderata for incremental semantic frameworks for dialogue processing and compared two frameworks. RMRS-IP and DS-TTR meet semantic representation construction criteria very similarly, however their semantic model, dialogue properties and practical robustness differ currently. In terms of parsimony and familiarity for researchers, RMRS with PCFG parsing combined constitute more widely studied formalisms, however DS takes Montague grammar-like structures with a dynamic tree logic as its backbone, and TTR is a well developed rich type system, so is also semanticist-friendly.

We conclude that the *remit* of incremental semantics for dialogue is what needs to be explored further: the dialogue phenomena that DS-TTR models directly may not be desirable for all applications, while RMRS-IP, although cross-compatible with different well-studied reasoning systems and grammars could be seen as not doing enough dialogical semantics and needs enriching.

Acknowledgements We thank the three IWCS reviewers for their insightful comments. This work is supported by the DUEL project, supported by the Agence Nationale de la Research (grant number ANR-13-FRAL-0001) and the Deutsche Forschungsgemeinschaft (grant number SCHL 845/5-1).

word	DS-TTR top record type	RMRS-IP formula
take	$\left[\begin{array}{ll} e_{=take} & : es \\ x1 & : e \\ x_{=addressee} & : e \\ p2_{=object(e,x1)} & : t \\ p1_{=subject(e,x)} & : t \\ p_{=imperative(e)} & : t \\ head_{=e} & : es \end{array}\right]$	$[\ell_0{:}a_0{:}e_0]$ $\{ [\ell_0{:}a_0{:}e_0] \}$ $\ell_0{:}a_0{:}$_take(e_0), $\mathsf{ARG}_1(a_0, x_2)$, $\ell_2{:}a_2{:}$addressee(x_2)
the	$\left[\begin{array}{ll} e_{=take} & : es \\ r & : \left[\begin{array}{ll} x & : e \\ head_{=x} & : e \end{array}\right] \\ x1_{=\iota(r.head,r)} & : e \\ x_{=addressee} & : e \\ p2_{=object(e,x1)} & : t \\ p1_{=subject(e,x)} & : t \\ p_{=imperative(e)} & : t \\ head_{=e} & : es \end{array}\right]$	$[\ell_0{:}a_0{:}e_0]$ $\{ [\ell_7{:}a_7{:}e_4], [\ell_0{:}a_0{:}e_0] \}$ $\ell_0{:}a_0{:}$_take(e_0), $\mathsf{ARG}_1(a_0, x_2)$, $\mathsf{ARG}_2(a_0, x_4)$, $\ell_2{:}a_2{:}$addressee(x_2), $\ell_4{:}a_4{:}$_def_q(), $\mathsf{BV}(a_4, x_4)$, $\mathsf{RSTR}(a_4, h_1)$, $\mathsf{BODY}(a_4, h_2)$, $h_1 =_q \ell_7$
red	$\left[\begin{array}{ll} e_{=take} & : es \\ r & : \left[\begin{array}{ll} x & : e \\ p_{=red(x)} & : t \\ head_{=x} & : e \end{array}\right] \\ x1_{=\iota(r.head,r)} & : e \\ x_{=addressee} & : e \\ p2_{=object(e,x1)} & : t \\ p1_{=subject(e,x)} & : t \\ p_{=imperative(e)} & : t \\ head_{=e} & : es \end{array}\right]$	$[\ell_0{:}a_0{:}e_0]$ $\{ [\ell_7{:}a_7{:}e_4], [\ell_0{:}a_0{:}e_0] \}$ $\ell_0{:}a_0{:}$_take(e_0), $\mathsf{ARG}_1(a_0, x_2)$, $\mathsf{ARG}_2(a_0, x_4)$, $\ell_2{:}a_2{:}$addressee(x_2), $\ell_4{:}a_4{:}$_def_q(), $\mathsf{BV}(a_4, x_4)$, $\mathsf{RSTR}(a_4, h_1)$, $\mathsf{BODY}(a_4, h_2)$, $h_1 =_q \ell_7$, $\ell_7{:}a_{10}{:}$_red(e_{10}), $\mathsf{ARG}_1(a_{10}, x_4)$
cross	$\left[\begin{array}{ll} e_{=take} & : es \\ r & : \left[\begin{array}{ll} x & : e \\ p1_{=cross(x)} & : t \\ p_{=red(x)} & : t \\ head_{=x} & : e \end{array}\right] \\ x1_{=\iota(r.head,r)} & : e \\ x_{=addressee} & : e \\ p2_{=object(e,x1)} & : t \\ p1_{=subject(e,x)} & : t \\ p_{=imperative(e)} & : t \\ head_{=e} & : es \end{array}\right]$	$[\ell_0{:}a_0{:}e_0]$ $\{ \}$ $\ell_0{:}a_0{:}$_take(e_0), $\mathsf{ARG}_1(a_0, x_2)$, $\mathsf{ARG}_2(a_0, x_4)$, $\ell_2{:}a_2{:}$addressee(x_2), $\ell_4{:}a_4{:}$_def_q(), $\mathsf{BV}(a_4, x_4)$, $\mathsf{RSTR}(a_4, h_1)$, $\mathsf{BODY}(a_4, h_2)$, $h_1 =_q \ell_7$, $\ell_7{:}a_{10}{:}$_red(e_{10}), $\mathsf{ARG}_1(a_{10}, x_4)$, $\ell_7{:}a_7{:}$_cross(x_4)

Figure 5: Incremental semantic construction by DS-TTR and RMRS-IP

References

Brennan, S. E. (2000). Processes that shape conversation and their implications for computational linguistics. In *Proceedings of the 38th annual meeting of the ACL*, pp. 1–11. ACL.

Chatzikyriakidis, S. and Z. Luo (2014). Natural language reasoning using proof-assistant technology: Rich typing and beyond. In *EACL 2014 TTNLS Workshop*, Gothenburg, Sweden, pp. 37–45. ACL.

Cooper, R. (2005). Records and record types in semantic theory. *Journal of Logic and Computation 15*(2), 99–112.

Copestake, A. (2006). Robust minimal recursion semantics. Technical report, Cambridge Computer Lab.

Copestake, A. (2007). Semantic composition with (robust) minimal recursion semantics. In *Proceedings of the Workshop on Deep Linguistic Processing*, DeepLP '07, Stroudsburg, PA, USA, pp. 73–80. ACL.

Egg, M., A. Koller, and J. Niehren (2001). The constraint language for lambda structures. *Journal of Logic, Language and Information 10*(4), 457–485.

Eshghi, A., J. Hough, and M. Purver (2013). Incremental grammar induction from child-directed dialogue utterances. In *The Fourth Annual CMCL Workshop*, Sofia, Bulgaria, pp. 94–103. ACL.

Ginzburg, J. (2012). *The Interactive Stance: Meaning for Conversation*. Oxford University Press.

Hough, J. and M. Purver (2012). Processing self-repairs in an incremental type-theoretic dialogue system. In *Proceedings of the 16th SemDial Workshop (SeineDial)*, Paris, France, pp. 136–144.

Hough, J. and M. Purver (2014). Probabilistic type theory for incremental dialogue processing. In *Proceedings of the EACL 2014 TTNLS Workshop*, Gothenburg, Sweden, pp. 80–88. ACL.

Howes, C., M. Purver, P. G. Healey, G. Mills, and E. Gregoromichelaki (2011). On incrementality in dialogue: Evidence from compound contributions. *Dialogue & Discourse 2*(1), 279–311.

Kempson, R., R. Cann, A. Eshghi, E. Gregoromichelaki, and M. Purver (2015). Ellipsis. In S. Lappin and C. Fox (Eds.), *Handbook of Contemporary Semantic Theory* (2nd ed.)., Chapter 3. Wiley.

Kempson, R., W. Meyer-Viol, and D. Gabbay (2001). *Dynamic Syntax: The Flow of Language Understanding*. Oxford: Blackwell.

Kennington, C., S. Kousidis, and D. Schlangen (2013). Interpreting Situated Dialogue Utterances: an Update Model that Uses Speech, Gaze, and Gesture Information. In *SIGdial 2013*.

Levelt, W. J. (1989). *Speaking: From intention to articulation*. MIT press.

Milward, D. (1991). *Axiomatic Grammar, Non-Constituent Coordination and Incremental Interpretation*. Ph. D. thesis, University of Cambridge.

Neumann, G. (1998). Interleaving natural language parsing and generation through uniform processing. *Artificial Intelligence 99*, 121–163.

Peldszus, A., O. Buß, T. Baumann, and D. Schlangen (2012). Joint Satisfaction of Syntactic and Pragmatic Constraints Improves Incremental Spoken Language Understanding. In *Proceedings of the 13th EACL*, Avignon, France, pp. 514–523. ACL.

Poesio, M. and D. Traum (1997). Conversational actions and discourse situations. *Computational Intelligence 13*(3).

Purver, M., A. Eshghi, and J. Hough (2011). Incremental semantic construction in a dialogue system. In J. Bos and S. Pulman (Eds.), *Proceedings of the 9th IWCS*, Oxford, UK, pp. 365–369.

Roark, B. (2001). *Robust Probabilistic Predictive Syntactic Processing: Motivations, Models, and Applications*. Ph. D. thesis, Department of Cognitive and Linguistic Sciences, Brown University.

Schlangen, D. and G. Skantze (2011). A General, Abstract Model of Incremental Dialogue Processing. *Dialoge & Discourse 2*(1), 83–111.

Schlesewsky, M. and I. Bornkessel (2004). On incremental interpretation: Degrees of meaning accessed during sentence comprehension. *Lingua 114*(9), 1213–1234.

Shieber, S. M. (1993). The problem of logical-form equivalence. *Computational Linguistics 19*(1), 179–190.

Skantze, G. and A. Hjalmarsson (2010). Towards incremental speech generation in dialogue systems. In *Proceedings of the 11th Annual Meeting of SIGDIAL*, pp. 1–8. ACL.

Skantze, G. and D. Schlangen (2009). Incremental dialogue processing in a micro-domain. In *Proceedings of the 12th Conference of the EACL*, pp. 745–753. ACL.

Steedman, M. (2012). *Taking scope: The natural semantics of quantifiers*. MIT Press.

Sundaresh, R. S. and P. Hudak (1991). A theory of incremental computation and its application. In *Proceedings of the 18th ACM SIGPLAN-SIGACT symposium*, pp. 1–13. ACM.

Semantic Dependency Graph Parsing Using Tree Approximations

Željko Agić[♠♡] Alexander Koller[♡] Stephan Oepen[♣♡]
[♠]Center for Language Technology, University of Copenhagen
[♡]Department of Linguistics, University of Potsdam
[♣]Department of Informatics, University of Oslo
pgm115@hum.ku.dk koller@ling.uni-potsdam.de oe@ifi.uio.no

Abstract

In this contribution, we deal with *graph parsing*, i.e., mapping input strings to graph-structured output representations, using tree approximations. We experiment with the data from the SemEval 2014 Semantic Dependency Parsing (SDP) task. We define various tree approximation schemes for graphs, and make twofold use of them. First, we statically analyze the semantic dependency graphs, seeking to unscover which linguistic phenomena in particular require the additional annotation expressivity provided by moving from trees to graphs. We focus on *undirected base cycles* in the SDP graphs, and discover strong connections to grammatical control and coordination. Second, we make use of the approximations in a statistical parsing scenario. In it, we convert the training set graphs to dependency trees, and use the resulting treebanks to build standard dependency tree parsers. We perform *lossy graph reconstructions* on parser outputs, and evaluate our models as dependency graph parsers. Our system outperforms the baselines by a large margin, and evaluates as the best non-voting tree approximation–based parser on the SemEval 2014 data, scoring at just over 81% in labeled F_1.

1 Introduction

Recent years have seen growing interest in the development of parsing systems that support graph-structured target representations, notably various forms of *semantic* dependency graphs, where it is natural to move beyond fully connected trees, as are dominant in *syntactic* dependency parsing. The SemEval 2014 and 2015 tasks on Semantic Dependency Parsing (SDP; Oepen et al., 2014) have made available large training and test corpora, annotating the Wall Street Journal (WSJ) corpus of the Penn Treebank (PTB; Marcus et al. 1993) with three different representations of predicate–argument structure.

Participating systems in the SDP tasks can be broadly classified into one of the two groups. They either (1) developed dedicated graph parsers, mainly by adapting existing dependency parsers to perform graph parsing, or (2) applied tree approximations, lossily converting graphs to trees in pre-processing, trained standard dependency tree parsers, and finally converted their outputs to graphs in post-processing.

Contributions All submissions for the SDP shared task are short and to the point, i.e., they focus exclusively on describing and evaluating the systems. We note an interesting underlying theme in the tree approximation–based systems, which constitute a majority of the SDP submissions. This theme is the apparent practical utility of using dependency trees instead of graphs, despite the formal mismatch in target representations. In our paper, we contribute with the following main points.

First, we take the standpoint of using dependency tree parsers for graph parsing via tree approximations, because:

1. These parsers are well-tested in syntactic parsing on numerous languages and datasets, and are shown to be accurate, efficient, and robust.
2. By probing the feasibility and limits of tree approximations, we inquire into the nature of the underlying representations. We implicitly ask why and where are graphs needed to encode semantic relations, and are graph-specific structures used by convention or with strong linguistic support.

Proceedings of the 11th International Conference on Computational Semantics, pages 217–227,
London, UK, April 15-17 2015.

Second, we expose the underlying properties of the semantic graph representations in SDP from a more linguistically informed, though still quantitative and empirical viewpoint. Third, we use these insights to design better tree approximations. Namely, we empirically pinpoint a tree approximation which offers a good balance between graph coverage, i.e., reduced lossiness, and at the same time, it provides improvements in statistical graph parsing. For this, we submit detailed evaluation. Finally, the system we create is currently the best non-voting tree approximation–based parser for dependency graphs in the SDP evaluation framework. This system implements a tree approximation that strikes a good and linguistically plausible empirical balance between loss minimization and parsing accuracy.

Outline We provide a detailed account of the properties of SDP graphs (§2), introduce approaches to tree approximations (§3) and evaluate them (§4). We use this linguistic insight to produce a linguistically motivated tree approximation–based parsing framework, which we evaluate as the top-performing non-voting parser based on tree approximations on the SDP data (§5).

Related work In the SDP 2014 campaign, Kuhlmann (2014) adapted the tree parsing algorithm of Eisner (1996), while Thomson et al. (2014) implement a novel approach to graph parsing. Martins and Almeida (2014) adapt TurboParser (Martins et al., 2013) for graph processing, and Ribeyre et al. (2014) utilize the parser of Sagae and Tsujii (2008).

Graph parsing by tree approximations and post-processing was most notably performed by the top-performing system of the competition, the one by Du et al. (2014). Their tree approximations are obtained by depth-first and breadth-first graph traversals, possibly changing the edge directions in the direction of the traversal. However, this was not sufficient to win the competition, since two other teams – Schluter et al. (2014) and Agić and Koller (2014) – also implemented a similar approach and scored in the mid range. For overall premium accuracy, Du et al. (2014) applied voting over the outputs of 17 different tree approximation–based systems, which arguably makes for a computationally inefficient resulting system.

The single top-performing tree approximation system was the one by Schluter et al. (2014), which is closely followed by Agić and Koller (2014). The latter one are the only to provide some linguistic insight into the SDP graphs.

2 Semantic Dependency Graphs

In this section, we take a closer look at the semantic dependency graphs from SDP 2014. The three SDP annotation layers over WSJ text stem from different semantic representations, but all result in directed acyclic graphs (DAGs) for describing sentence semantics. The three representations can be characterized as follows (Oepen et al., 2014; Miyao et al., 2014).

1. DM semantic dependencies stem from the gold-standard HPSG annotations of the WSJ text, as provided by the LinGO English Resource Grammar (ERG; Flickinger, 2000; Flickinger et al., 2012). The resource was converted to bi-lexical dependencies in preparation for the task by Oepen and Lønning (2006) and Ivanova et al. (2012) by a two-step lossy conversion.
2. PAS bi-lexical dependencies are also derived from HPSG annotations of PTB, which were originally aimed at providing a training set for the wide-coverage HPSG parser Enju (Miyao and Tsujii, 2008). As noted in the task description, while DM HPSG annotations were manual, the annotations for training Enju were automatically constructed from the Penn Treebank bracketings by Miyao et al. (2004).
3. PCEDT originates from the English part of the Prague Czech–English Dependency Treebank. In this project, the WSJ part of PTB was translated into Czech, and both sides were manually in accordance with the Prague-style rules for tectogrammatical analysis (Cinková et al., 2009). The dataset is post-processed by the task organizers to match the requirements for bi-lexical dependencies.

Nodes in SDP DAGs are single words, and an edge can be drawn between any two words, provided that no cycles are introduced. The graphs allow for disconnected (singleton) nodes, which represent

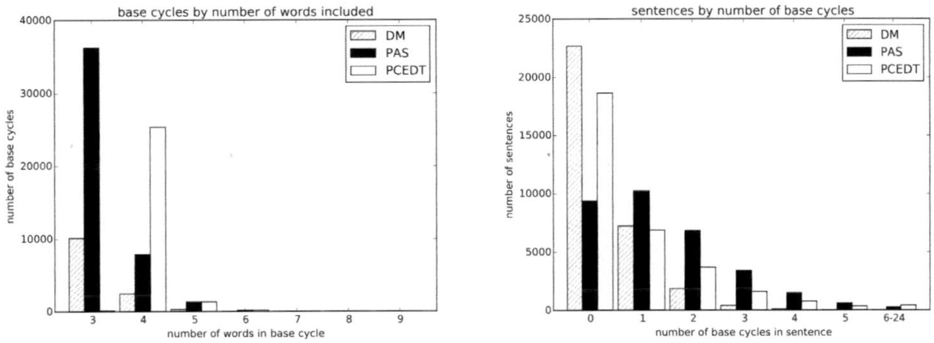

Figure 1: Distributions of (a) base cycles by the number of words in the base cycle, and of (b) sentences by the number of base cycles per sentence.

semantically empty words. Each graph typically has one top node which represents the semantic head of the sentence. By virtue of bi-lexical dependencies, a single node (argument) might have multiple heads (predicates). We call this phenomenon reentrancy, and refer to nodes with indegree of 2 and more as reentrant nodes. Reentrancies and disconnected nodes are the two properties that contrast SDP DAGs from 'standard' dependency trees, where a fixed indegree of 1 is required for all nodes.

The core problem of using a tree parser to generate graphs is to investigate the structural properties that distinguish graphs from trees. Setting aside the singletons, the difference between SDP DAGs and trees amounts to the phenomenon of reentrancy. Reentrancy may also be necessary to capture certain semantic relationships, and it is thus worth studying whether we can correlate its various types with different semantic phenomena. For these reasons, we now take a closer look into reentrant SDP graphs.

Prior to our work, Agić and Koller (2014) provide a short overview of the SDP data. They show the distribution of node indegrees for all nodes, and for source nodes of edges participating in reentrancies, showing that a very large number of the latter nodes have zero indegree themselves. They also show that the frequency mass for other nodes in reentrancies is rather small, but still not negligible, even if their approach does not address these.

2.1 Base Cycles

Reentrancies caused by non-content source nodes with zero indegree arguably do not amount to much in terms of meaning representations. One typical example from DM is given in Figure 2: it is the edge *Cray* $\longrightarrow$ *Computer* in the top left corner graph. From the viewpoint of tree approximations, these would be easily accounted for, as we sketch in the following section.

What interests us much more are the reentrancies originating from connected nodes. By definition, DAGs do not contain directed cycles. However, the reentrancies that involve connected nodes might constitute undirected cycles in the graph. There are two such examples in Figure 2: in the top left graph, *Computer* is the argument of both *applied* and *trade*, while in the top right graph, *cultural* and *economic* are the arguments of both *and* and *forces*. These two are typical examples of control in DM, and coordination in PCEDT. At the same time, they constitute undirected cycles: one spans 3 nodes of the graph, and the other one 4 nodes.

Further, we gain insight on the quantitative properties of such undirected cycles. For this, we introduce the notion of a cycle base. A cycle base of an undirected graph is a minimal set of simple cycles of a graph with respect to cardinality. Cycle base of an undirected graph can be detected in polynomial time by Paton's algorithm (Paton, 1969). Thus, for each SDP graph, we create an undirected copy, retrieve its cycle base using Paton's algorithm, and then extract all its base cycles. We then look into their distributional properties.

There is a total of 12,970 base cycles in DM, 45,119 in PAS, and 27,026 in PCEDT. Their distribution

Table 1: Distributions of coarse-grained parts of speech for nodes participating in base cycles.

DM			PAS			PCEDT		
	#	%		#	%		#	%
N V V	3843	29.63	N V V	15541	34.44	CC N N V	4789	17.72
PRP V V	1208	9.31	MD N V	5005	11.09	CC N N N	3418	12.65
N TO V V	1203	9.28	PRP V V	4012	8.89	, N N V	2512	9.29
J N V	1059	8.16	J N V	3544	7.85	CC V V V	1633	6.04
IN N V	962	7.42	CC N V V	2155	4.78	CC N V V	1614	5.97
J J N	506	3.90	MD PRP V	1622	3.59	N N N V	805	2.98
CD CD N	324	2.50	IN N V	1087	2.41	N N V V	752	2.78
PRP TO V V	277	2.14	J PRP V	877	1.94	N V V V	665	2.46
J PRP V	228	1.76	CC N N N	676	1.50	, N N N	495	1.83
N N V	202	1.56	CC V V	561	1.24	CC J J N	447	1.65

by the number of containing nodes is given in Figure 1 (left side). We can tell that for DM, a large majority of base cycles span 3 nodes, as well as for PAS, while PCEDT cycles dominantly consist of 4 nodes. Further in the text, we refer to these base cycles as *triangle* and *square* cycles.

As for the distribution of sentences by the number of base cycles contained (Figure 1), in DM and PCEDT, most sentences have no cycles, while the sentences with cycles mostly have 1 or 2. In PAS, the distribution is more evenly split for 0-2 cycles, and decreases afterwards.

Control and coordination We proceed to look into the distributions of base cycles per parts of speech (POS) of the containing nodes, and per edge labels of the containing edges. We also look into the node lemmas, and we extract a number of distributions. One of these, the one with POS tags of nodes in cycles, is given in Table 1 for the top 10 most frequent cycles. For DM and PAS, we see that the most frequent POS pattern includes two verbs (V) and a noun (N), and in PCEDT coordinators (CC) are present in a large majority of cases. By further insight into the distributions of edge label patterns and lemma patterns, which we omit here due to space limitations, we conclude the following. In DM and PAS, more than 70% of the cycles address the linguistic phenomena of control and coordination, while in PCEDT, a large majority of the cycles encodes exclusively coordination. PCEDT coordination commonly involves 4 nodes in base cycles, while both control and coordination in DM and PAS result in 3-node cycles.

We depart from the quantitative analysis of SDP data with the following main observation. If we exclude semantically empty singleton nodes, graph representations of sentence meaning involve reentrancies. Setting aside the simple reentrancies caused by annotation conventions rooted in meaning representation theories, we focus on the reentrancies explained through undirected base cycles. Through this lens, we isolate the linguistic phenomena of control and coordination, which govern the cycles. This in turn confirms that cycle types do correlate with specific semantic phenomena, and we proceed to utilize this fact in the process of designing linguistically informed tree approximations of dependency graphs.

3 Tree Approximations

In this section, we define tree approximations. First, we address some general considerations. Then, we introduce three linguistically uninformed baseline tree approximations, and an informed approximation based on our observations from the SDP data.

Outline The general framework of the tree approximation parsers for SDP is outlined as follows. First and foremost, these systems all rely on standard dependency tree parsers for performing the parsing. These are trained on dependency trees, and they output dependency trees. Thus, in order to utilize a tree parser in SDP, these systems have to implement pre-processing and a post-processing, which are respectively related to the training and testing procedures of the standard parser.

Prior to training, the SDP training sets are pre-processed, i.e., converted from DAGs to dependency trees, and these trees are provided as input for the parser training procedure. In the application phase, the models that were trained on these approximated trees are applied on the evaluation data, producing the trees on top of which post-processing is run. Typically, in post-processing, lossy heuristics are applied to the output trees, expanding them into graphs.

Deletion and trimming Converting reentrant graphs to trees requires edge removal. The basic idea of removing edges in pre-processing and trying to reconstruct them in post-processing is at the core of tree approximations. Before proceeding, we make an important distinction between two types of edge removal, which we name *deletion* and *trimming*. In deletion, it is not possible to reconstruct the removed edge in post-processing, i.e. the removed edge is permanently lost. In trimming, by contrast, the removed edge can be reconstructed – or *untrimmed* – in post-processing, either deterministically or with a certain success rate. In the shared task, a number of systems approached trimming through *label overloading*. In label overloading, a deletion of one edge is recorded in another kept edge, similar to encoding non-projective dependency arcs in pseudo-projective tree parsing (Nivre and Nilsson, 2005). In post-processing, the information stored in overloaded labels is used to attempt edge untrimming.

We proceed to explore several ways of performing tree approximations, which include a mixture of edge removals via deletion and trimming.

3.1 Baselines

Three baselines are used in this research. We re-implement the official SDP shared task baseline, and the local edge flipping and depth-first flipping systems of Agić and Koller (2014).

OFFICIAL: The official baseline tree approximation only performs deletions and artificial edge insertions to satisfy the dependency tree constraints. No trimming is performed. For reentrancies, all edges but one are deleted: we keep the edge from the closest predicate measured by surface distance, preferring leftward predicates in ties. Singletons are attached to the immediately following node, or to the artificial root node if the singleton ends the sentence, by using the `dummy` label. Any remaining nodes with no incoming edges are attached to the root and the edge is labeled as `root`.

LOCAL: In the OFFICIAL system, all reentrancies are treated uniformly. However, as previously addressed, Agić and Koller (2014) observe there are lots of reentrancies caused by zero indegree sources. LOCAL system simply detects such edges and flips them around by changing their direction. These changes are marked by overloading the label using the prefix `flipped`. After flipping, OFFICIAL is run to delete all the remaining reentrancies and meet the tree constraints. Thus, LOCAL combines trimming in the form of edge flipping and label overloading with OFFICIAL deletion.

DFS: Similar to a number of systems from the SDP shared task, we take the idea of edge flipping further, and perform depth-first graph traversal. We traverse the undirected copy of the graph starting from its top node, i.e., the semantic head of the sentence. For each edge traversal, we compare the traversal direction to the direction of the edge in the original graph. If the directions are identical, we insert the edge to the tree. If they are reversed, we insert a reversed edge to the tree and denote this reversal by appending the `flipped` label to the original label, just like in LOCAL. Any surplus reentrancies are deleted by the depth-first traversal, and the removals are governed by the traversal order: the first edge through which a node was visited is preserved, and its label possibly overloaded, while the other edges are removed. Any remaining disconnected nodes or top-level predicates are connected by applying OFFICIAL. As for LOCAL, DFS also combines trimming with deletion, generalizing the idea of LOCAL flipping and likely trimming more edges and deleting less than OFFICIAL and LOCAL.

The two baselines that perform trimming, LOCAL and DFS, are paired with very straightforward untrimming. Any edge with a label prefixed by `flipped` is simply flipped back by changing the edge direction, and the label suffix is removed. Since both approaches also use OFFICIAL, post-processing also includes `dummy` and `root` edge removal. This post-processing scheme results in reconstructing

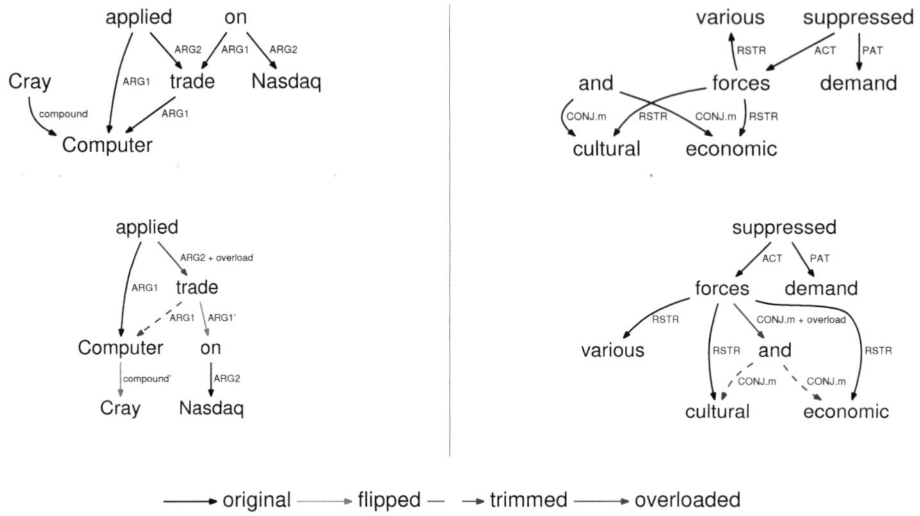

Figure 2: An illustration of triangle (▽) and square (□) base cycle trimmings, and subsequent DFS traversals for example sentences with DM and PCEDT semantic dependency graph representations. Singleton nodes are omitted. DM sentence #20018026: *Cray Computer has applied to trade on Nasdaq.* PCEDT sentence #20445047: *Various cultural and economic forces have suppressed demand.*

reentrancies, and re-introducing singletons to the resulting graph. Since all three approaches delete at least some edges, they are by definition lossy.

DFS trimming and deletion is illustrated in the top part of Figure 2 on a DM graph. The traversal starts in top node *applied*. First, we visit *Computer*, where traversal direction matches edge direction, and the edge is inserted to the tree. Then, we depart *Computer* towards *Cray*, and this time the traversal direction does not match original edge direction, and we insert the flipped edge to the tree (red in the figure). Traversal by depth continues until all nodes are visited. The resulting tree has two flipped edges, and one edge (blue, dashed) is permanently lost in the traversal as DFS visits each node only once.

3.2 Base Cycle Trimming

LOCAL and DFS only manage to trim selected subsets of edges participating in reentrancies. In LOCAL, the selection is due to indegree filtering of source nodes in reentrancies, and in DFS, it is governed by the order of graph traversal. In both cases, some edges in reentrancies get deleted. Here, in base cycle trimming, we define a procedure that accounts for these remaining edges, and attempts to trim them as well, rather than deleting them.

As we learned from Figure 1, a large majority of base cycles have either 3 or 4 nodes, and we name them triangles and squares. Building on that, we define two base cycle trimming approaches: one for the triangles, and the other one for the squares. Before introducing these trimmings, we suggest that they come in two distinct forms; we first describe these forms, and then proceed with outlining the trimmings.

Radical and conservative trimming Our *radical trimming* of base cycles amounts to label edge overloading. Namely, as LOCAL and DFS approached trimming by flipping and label overloading to systematically account for a large portion of edges in reentrancies, radical trimming attempts to systematically account for all base cycles. It does so by trimming all cycles and overloading a possibly large number of edge labels with traces of these trimmings. As we expect this will significantly expand the edge label set, we consider a more moderate approach, which we call *conservative trimming*. In it, we do not overload the edge labels at all. Instead, we perform the trimmings only if linguistic cues, or more precisely, lemmas and edges in the base cycles allow for it. This is to say that we only trim a subset of base cycles

Table 2: Upper bound evaluation for the tree approximations. Radical and conservative triangle ($\bigtriangledown$) and square ($\square$) base cycle trimming and untrimming are compared with the baselines. Scores are provided for the whole SDP training set as no parsing is performed.

	DM				PCEDT			
	P	*R*	*LM*	# labels	*P*	*R*	*LM*	# labels
OFFICIAL	100.00	55.28	2.54	52	100.00	90.35	54.33	71
LOCAL	100.00	87.50	17.35	79	100.00	92.33	54.65	124
DFS	100.00	97.30	65.43	79	100.00	94.03	54.58	133
radical trimming								
$\bigtriangledown$ + LOCAL	100.00	88.33	21.07	101	–	–	–	–
$\bigtriangledown$ + DFS	100.00	98.89	85.07	154	–	–	–	–
$\square$ + LOCAL	–	–	–	–	100.00	93.59	56.02	382
$\square$ + DFS	–	–	–	–	100.00	95.21	66.33	413
conservative trimming								
$\bigtriangledown$ + LOCAL	98.98	87.93	19.66	79	–	–	–	–
$\bigtriangledown$ + DFS	99.12	98.07	83.83	79	–	–	–	–
$\square$ + LOCAL	–	–	–	–	98.83	92.88	54.99	124
$\square$ + DFS	–	–	–	–	98.96	94.65	65.57	133
radical – DFS	0.00	+1.59	+19.64	+75	0.00	+1.18	+11.75	+280
conservative – DFS	-0.88	+0.77	+18.40	0	-1.04	+0.62	+10.99	0

which falls within our linguistically motivated pattern, and that we only reconstruct edges when such patterns are observed in post-processing. In this approach, we do not cover as many base cycles as in radical trimming, but we avoid the need for large artificial expansions of label sets. Now we proceed to triangle and square removal, and for each, we describe the radical and the conservative instance.

$\bigtriangledown$ **TRIANGLE:** We start off by creating an undirected copy of the graph, in which we detect the undirected base cycles. For each of these, we identify its corresponding subgraph in the directed graph. This subgraph consists only of the edges and nodes that are present in the undirected base cycle, the only difference between the two being the (un)directedness. All undirected base cycles only contain nodes with a degree of 2. Their corresponding directed subgraphs also always follow a certain pattern, which we define as follows. Let x, y and z be the 3 triangle nodes in the directed subgraph. Since the SDP graphs are DAGs, the triangles are never directed cycles. Consequently, there is only one way to construct such a triangle regarding in- and outdegree: there will be a governing predicate x (indegree 0, outdegree 2), a controlled predicate y (1, 1), and an argument z (2, 0). In terms of edges, we would observe $x \rightarrow \{y, z\}$ and $y \rightarrow z$. We proceed to trim the edge $y \rightarrow z$. In radical trimming, we overload the label $l(x, y)$ of the edge $x \rightarrow y$ by prefixing it with (a) the label of the trimmed edge $l(y, z)$, and (b) the label of $l(x, z)$ in order to find the target for subsequent untrimming. In conservative trimming, we trim the same edge, but only if a pattern is detected. The pattern requires that $l(x, z) = l(y, z)$ and that the lemmas of x and y are in the list of allowed lemmas collected from the corpus by observing base cycles at training. After base cycle trimming, we run DFS to ensure we meet the tree constraints.

There is an example of triangle trimming in Figure 2 for the DM graph. The triangle represents verb control, where x = *applied*, y = *trade*, and z = *Computer*. The base cycle is detected and the edge is trimmed. In radical trimming, edge overloading also occurs.

$\square$ **SQUARE:** Similar to triangles, in trimming these base cycles, we also focus on a specific square structure that we observed in the SDP data. In this structure, there are typically two predicate nodes, x and y (indegree 0, outdegree 2), and two argument nodes, w and z (2, 0). There are edges $x \rightarrow \{w, z\}$ and $y \rightarrow \{w, z\}$. We delete the latter ones, and insert a new edge $x \rightarrow y$. In radical trimming, we overload the label of the newly-introduced edge with information for subsequent reconstruction of the two deleted edges in post-processing. This information includes the labels for all four edges in the square: two for reinserting the deleted edges, and two for detecting the arguments. As for the triangle case, in conservative trimming, we only trim the edge if a lemma pattern is fired, and if $l(x, w) = l(x, z)$ and $l(y, w) = l(y, z)$, i.e., if the edge labels are symmetrical.

This is also illustrated by Figure 2, in the PCEDT graph. In it, the predicates are x = *forces* and y = *and*, while w = *cultural* and z = *economic* are arguments. The edges are trimmed, and a new edge $x \longrightarrow y$ is introduced. In radical trimming, this edge is assigned a label with trace information.

4 Upper Bounds for Trimming

In this section, before applying our tree approximations in graph parsing, we test them for upper bound accuracy. At this point, we exclude PAS from further consideration, and focus on DM and PCEDT. This is motivated by focusing the contribution, since PAS is shown to be the easiest dataset to parse in the shared task, and thus we put our efforts into improving on the two more difficult datasets.

Upper bound accuracy is a loss metric for trimming and subsequent processing. We evaluate by (1) performing $\bigtriangledown$ trimming for DM and $\square$ trimming for PCEDT, and (2) converting the resulting trees back to graphs right away, i.e., with no parser training or dependency tree parsing in-between. Then we (3) evaluate the converted graphs against the original ones using standard metrics. By this, we measure the edge preservation capabilities of the approximations, or the maximum graph parsing score that would be obtained if the parsing step provided perfect accuracy. We measure labeled precision *(LP)*, recall *(LR)* and labeled graph exact match *(LM)*.

The results are given in Table 2. OFFICIAL is very lossy, since it only performs deletions. Its precision is perfect as the preserved edges match the original ones, while all the rest are absent from the graph. The absence shows in recall: for DM, 45% of the original edges are lost, while we lose 10% in PCEDT. At around 2%, exact match scores are extremely low. LOCAL flipping preserves a more edges than OFFICIAL, and so does DFS over the both. For DM, LOCAL is 30-40 points better than OFFICIAL in terms of recall, while DFS beats LOCAL on these two datasets by approximately 10 points. In PCEDT, the improvements are smaller because OFFICIAL was more competitive to begin with, but the recall still improves by 4 points from OFFICIAL to DFS. To conclude this first comparison batch, we observe that the edge loss of DFS is quantified at 2.7% and 5.97% for DM and PCEDT. Thus, whatever improvements might result from applying the base cycle trimmings, they fall within these margins.

The radical trimmings maintain perfect precision, as untrimming is deterministic given the overloaded labels. Combining them with LOCAL tree approximation improves their recall by up to 1 point over using just LOCAL. Once again, the improvements are more substantial for DM, than for PCEDT. For radical trimming with DFS, we observe virtually the same improvement pattern over just using the DFS approximation However, the differences in exact match scores *(LM)* really outline the benefits of trimming, with absolute improvements of almost 20 points in DM, and 12 points in PCEDT. In absolute terms, combining radical trimming and DFS manages to fully reconstruct 85% of DM graphs, and 65% of PCEDT graphs. Thus, a small 1-1.5 point improvement in recall accounts for large improvements in exact matching. This is supported by our earlier quantitative assessments of the datasets, as edges that form undirected cycles and that were previously lost to DFS are now reachable through label overloading. As they are comparatively infrequent phenomena, untrimming these edges improves DFS recall by a small margin, but the overall gains in upper bound performance are much more significant.

In the conservative mode, the trimmings and untrimmings are triggered by linguistic cues. The untrimmings therefore don't necessarily have to result in perfect precision. This is due to the fact that the untrimming triggers can also be activated by the linguistic cues where not required. We can see this in Table 2: conservative trimming with LOCAL and DFS decreases precision by approximately 1 point in DM and PCEDT. As before, combining the trimming with DFS is a bit better than with LOCAL. The recall of the conservative approach improves over the baselines, and lands between DFS and radical trimming on the absolute recall and exact match scales. This is expected, as conservative trimming accounts for a subset of the cycles accounted for by radical trimming.

To conclude the discussion, we observe an ordering of tree approximations by growing upper bound performance. Basic DFS is followed by conservative trimming, and the highest upper bounds are reached through radical trimming. However, this comes at a price, which is payed in edge label set increases. We can see in Table 2 that the label sets increase substantially: 75 extra labels are added over the DFS DM label sets, and in PCEDT, the increase amounts to 280 new artificial labels. We expect this to influence the performance of the tree parser substantially. At the same time, we trust that the rather small decrease in upper bound precision, paired with an increase in recall for conservative trimming will pay off in higher graph parsing scores after tree parsing and untrimming, since conservative trimming does not increase the label sets.

5 Graph Parsing

We proceed to evaluate our tree approximations in graph parsing. Here, our previously outlined parsing pipeline is applied: training graphs are converted to trees using different pre-processing approximations, parsers are trained and applied on test data, outputs are converted to graphs and evaluated against the gold standard graphs. We observe the labeled F_1 scores *(LF)* and exact matches *(LM)*.

Experiment Setup For dependency tree parsing, we use the `mate-tools` state-of-the-art graph-based parser of Bohnet (2010). As in the shared task, we experiment in two tracks: the open track, and the closed track. In the closed track, for training the parser, we use only the features available in the SDP training data, i.e., word forms, parts of speech and lemmas. In the open track, we also pack additional features from the SDP companion dataset – automatic dependency and phrase-based parses of the SDP training and testing sets – as well as the Brown clustering features (Brown et al., 1992).

For top node detection, we use a sequence tagger based on conditional random fields (CRFs). To guess the top nodes in the closed track, we use words and POS tags as features, while we add the companion syntactic features in the open track.

5.1 Results

The evaluation results are listed in Table 3. The overall performance of our basic DFS tree approximation parser is identical to the one of Agić and Koller (2014) in the closed track. In the open track, however, we improve by 2-3 points in *LF* due to better top node detection, and improved tree parser accuracy due to the introduction of additional features in the form of Brown clusters, which were shown to also improve other systems in the SDP task (Schluter et al., 2014).

The radical approach to trimming and untrimming, both $\bigtriangledown$ for DM and $\square$ for PCEDT, significantly decreases the overall parsing accuracy in comparison with DFS. The score drops by 1.62 points for DM, and 2.44 points for PCEDT in the closed track, and even more in the open track, by 2.59 and 4.10 points. This is apparently due to big drop in the dependency tree parsing *LAS* scores prior to graph reconstruction, since our radical approach introduces large numbers of new edge labels in the training stage, and then attempts to parse using these large label sets, which severely undermines the performance. Still, even with this decrease, the exact match scores actually still improve around 3 points *LM* for DM, and 1 point for PCEDT. Since the upper bound *LM* scores were much higher for the radical trimmings in comparison with basic DFS, this is expected behavior: even with the large numbers of additional erroneous outputs of the tree parser, more complete graphs still get reconstructed by the untrimmings.

Conservative trimmings and untrimmings provide the most interesting set of observations when it comes to our evaluation. For them, the tree parsing scores either remain virtually the same as for DFS, or even slightly increasing. This as a direct consequence of not introducing extra edge labels while trimming: we simply remove the cycles using linguistic cues, and attempt to reconstruct them after parsing; thus, the DFS pre-processing and subsequent parsing are only slightly influenced. The slight increase can be attributed to the linguistically informed trimmings as well, since with them we don't rely on blind deletions of DFS, in turn making the resulting trees linguistically more plausible.

The impact of the conservative approach becomes apparent in post-processing, when we use the same linguistic clues for untrimming the edges, i.e., reconstructing the undirected cycles. We see the positive impacts of conservative untrimmings in both evaluation metrics, for both datasets, and in both the closed and the open track scenario. The *LF* scores increase 0.70 and 0.55 points over DFS in the

Table 3: Graph parsing results. The radical and conservative, triangle (▽) and square (□) trimmings are compared with DFS in closed and open track evaluation scenarios. We evaluate for labeled F_1 score *(LF)*, and for labeled exact match *(LM)*. The tree parsing labeled attachment score *(LAS)* is also provided.

	closed track						*open track*					
	DM			PCEDT			DM			PCEDT		
	LF	*LM*	*LAS*	*LF*	*LM*	*LAS*	*LF*	*LM*	*LAS*	*LF*	*LM*	*LAS*
DFS	79.35	9.05	78.99	67.92	5.86	81.01	83.00	10.46	84.00	70.24	5.79	85.44
radical												
▽ + DFS	77.73	12.15	75.62	–	–	–	80.56	13.44	80.23	–	–	–
□ + DFS	–	–	–	65.33	6.67	77.47	–	–	–	66.14	6.98	83.37
conservative												
▽ + DFS	80.05	18.91	79.04	–	–	–	83.55	20.01	83.96	–	–	–
□ + DFS	–	–	–	68.82	11.53	81.05	–	–	–	71.18	12.09	85.53
radical – DFS	-1.62	3.10	-3.37	-2.59	0.81	-3.54	-2.44	2.98	-3.77	-4.10	1.19	-2.07
conservative – DFS	0.70	9.86	+0.05	0.90	5.67	+0.04	0.55	9.55	-0.04	0.94	6.30	0.09

closed an open track for DM, and around 0.90 points for PCEDT. Exact graph matching improves even more significantly, 5-10 points for both datasets. We attribute the increase in *LF* to not impeding the tree parser by introducing new labels, while at the same time managing to reconstruct a portion of undirected cycle edges in post-processing.

At this point, it is worth comparing the parsing evaluation to the upper bound performance of DFS, radical and conservative trimming. In terms of upper bound scores, our conservative trimming scored slightly higher than DFS, and slightly lower than radical trimming. However, this elaborate design decision to sacrifice a small fraction of upper bound precision and recall not to introduce additional edge labels to the dataset turns out to pay off substantially in graph parsing. Overall, including our open track DFS PAS score of 88.33, our system scores an average *LF* score of 81.02, which makes it the top-performing single-parser system based on tree approximations on the SDP shared task data.

6 Conclusions

We conducted an exhaustive investigation of semantic dependency graph parsing using tree approximations. In this framework, dependency graphs are converted to dependency trees, introducing loss in the process. These trees are then used for training standard parsers, and the output trees of these parsers are converted back to graphs through various lossy conversions. In the paper, we provide an account on the various properties of several tree approximations. We measure their lossiness, and evaluate their effects on semantic dependency graph parsing in the framework of the SemEval 2014 shared task (SDP).

Our main findings pertain to linguistic insights on the properties of directed acyclic graphs as used in SDP to provide meaning representations for English sentences, and to the impact of linguistically motivated tree approximations to data-driven graph parsing. We manage to attribute the arguments of multiple predicates to verb control, and to coordination across three different graph representations, and we use this observation to develop a tree approximation that produces a top-performing tree approximation–based system on SDP data.

References

Agić, Ž. and A. Koller (2014). Potsdam: Semantic Dependency Parsing by Bidirectional Graph-Tree Transformations and Syntactic Parsing. In *SemEval*.

Bohnet, B. (2010). Top Accuracy and Fast Dependency Parsing is not a Contradiction. In *COLING*.

Brown, P. F., P. V. Desouza, R. L. Mercer, V. J. D. Pietra, and J. C. Lai (1992). Class-based n-gram Models of Natural Language. *Computational Linguistics 18*(4).

Cinková, S., J. Toman, J. Hajič, K. Čermáková, V. Klimeš, L. Mladová, J. Šindlerová, K. Tomšů, and Z. Žabokrtský (2009). Tectogrammatical Annotation of the Wall Street Journal. *The Prague Bulletin of Mathematical Linguistics 92*.

Du, Y., F. Zhang, W. Sun, and X. Wan (2014). Peking: Profiling Syntactic Tree Parsing Techniques for Semantic Graph Parsing. In *SemEval*.

Eisner, J. (1996). Three New Probabilistic Models for Dependency Parsing. In *COLING*.

Flickinger, D. (2000). On Building a More Efficient Grammar by Exploiting Types. *Natural Language Engineering 6*(1).

Flickinger, D., Y. Zhang, and V. Kordoni (2012). DeepBank: A Dynamically Annotated Treebank of the Wall Street Journal. In *TLT*.

Ivanova, A., S. Oepen, L. Øvrelid, and D. Flickinger (2012). Who Did What to Whom? A Contrastive Study of Syntacto-Semantic Dependencies. In *Linguistic Annotation Workshop*.

Kuhlmann, M. (2014). Linköping: Cubic-Time Graph Parsing with a Simple Scoring Scheme. In *SemEval*.

Marcus, M., M. A. Marcinkiewicz, and B. Santorini (1993). Building a Large Annotated Corpus of English: The Penn Treebank. *Computational Linguistics 19*(2).

Martins, A., M. Almeida, and N. A. Smith (2013). Turning on the Turbo: Fast Third-Order Non-Projective Turbo Parsers. In *ACL*.

Martins, A. F. T. and M. S. C. Almeida (2014). Priberam: A Turbo Semantic Parser with Second Order Features. In *SemEval*.

Miyao, Y., T. Ninomiya, and J. Tsujii (2004). Corpus-oriented Grammar Development for Acquiring a Head-Driven Phrase Structure Grammar from the Penn Treebank. In *IJCNLP*.

Miyao, Y., S. Oepen, and D. Zeman (2014). In-House. An ensemble of pre-existing off-the-shelf parsers. In *SemEval*, Dublin, Ireland.

Miyao, Y. and J. Tsujii (2008). Feature Forest Models for Probabilistic HPSG Parsing. *Computational Linguistics 34*(1).

Nivre, J. and J. Nilsson (2005). Pseudo-Projective Dependency Parsing. In *ACL*.

Oepen, S., M. Kuhlmann, Y. Miyao, D. Zeman, D. Flickinger, J. Hajic, A. Ivanova, and Y. Zhang (2014). SemEval 2014 Task 8: Broad-Coverage Semantic Dependency Parsing. In *SemEval*.

Oepen, S. and J. T. Lønning (2006). Discriminant-Based MRS Banking. In *LREC*.

Paton, K. (1969). An algorithm for finding a fundamental set of cycles of a graph. *Communications of the ACM 12*(9).

Ribeyre, C., E. Villemonte de la Clergerie, and D. Seddah (2014). Alpage: Transition-based Semantic Graph Parsing with Syntactic Features. In *SemEval*.

Sagae, K. and J. Tsujii (2008). Shift-Reduce Dependency DAG Parsing. In *COLING*.

Schluter, N., A. Søgaard, J. Elming, D. Hovy, B. Plank, H. Martínez Alonso, A. Johanssen, and S. Klerke (2014). Copenhagen-Malmö: Tree Approximations of Semantic Parsing Problems. In *SemEval*.

Thomson, S., B. O'Connor, J. Flanigan, D. Bamman, J. Dodge, S. Swayamdipta, N. Schneider, C. Dyer, and N. Smith (2014). CMU: Arc-Factored, Discriminative Semantic Dependency Parsing. In *SemEval*.

Semantic construction with graph grammars

Alexander Koller
University of Potsdam
koller@ling.uni-potsdam.de

Abstract

We introduce *s-graph grammars*, a new grammar formalism for computing graph-based semantic representations. Semantically annotated corpora which use graphs as semantic representations have recently become available, and there have been a number of data-driven systems for semantic parsing that can be trained on these corpora. However, it is hard to map the linguistic assumptions of these systems onto more classical insights on semantic construction. S-graph grammars use graphs as semantic representations, in a way that is consistent with more classical views on semantic construction. We illustrate this with a number of hand-written toy grammars, sketch the use of s-graph grammars for data-driven semantic parsing, and discuss formal aspects.

1 Introduction

Semantic construction is the problem of deriving a formal semantic representation from a natural-language expression. The classical approach, starting with Montague (1974), is to derive semantic representations from syntactic analyses using hand-written rules. More recently, semantic construction has enjoyed renewed attention in mainstream computational linguistics in the form of *semantic parsing* (see e.g. Wong and Mooney, 2007; Zettlemoyer and Collins, 2005; Chiang et al., 2013). The idea in semantic parsing is to make a system learn the mapping of the string into the semantic representation automatically, with or without the use of an explicit syntactic representation as an intermediate step. The focus is thus on automatically induced grammars, if the grammar is not left implicit altogether.

Training such data-driven models requires semantically annotated corpora. One recent development is the release of several corpora in which English sentences were annotated with *graphs* that represent the meanings of the sentences (Banarescu et al., 2013; Oepen et al., 2014). There has already been a body of research on semantic parsing for graphs based on these corpora, but so far, the ideas underlying these semantic parsers have not been connected to classical approaches to semantic construction. Flanigan et al. (2014) and Martins and Almeida (2014) show how to adapt data-driven dependency parsers from trees to graphs. These approaches do not use explicit grammars, in contrast to all work in the classical tradition. Chiang et al. (2013) do use explicit Hyperedge Replacement Grammars (HRGs, Drewes et al., 1997) for semantic parsing. However, HRGs capture semantic dependencies in a way that is not easily mapped to conventional intuitions about semantic construction, and indeed their use in linguistically motivated models of the syntax-semantics interface has not yet been demonstrated.

But just because we use graphs as semantic representations and learn grammars from graph-banks does not mean we need to give up linguistic insights from several decades of research in computational semantics. In this paper, we address this challenge by presenting *s-graph grammars*. S-graph grammars are a new synchronous grammar formalism that relates strings and graphs. At the center of a grammatical structure of an s-graph grammar sits a *derivation tree*, which is simultaneously interpreted into a string (in a way that is equivalent to context-free grammar) and into a graph (in a way that is equivalent to HRGs). Because of these equivalences, methods for statistical parsing and grammar induction transfer from these formalisms to s-graph grammars. At the same time, s-graph grammars make use of an explicit inventory of semantic argument positions. Thus they also lend themselves to writing linguistically interpretable grammars by hand.

Proceedings of the 11th International Conference on Computational Semantics, pages 228–238,
London, UK, April 15-17 2015.

The paper is structured as follows. In Section 2, we will briefly review the state of the art in semantic parsing, especially for graph-based semantic representations. We will also introduce Interpreted Regular Tree Grammars (IRTGs) (Koller and Kuhlmann, 2011), which will serve as the formal foundation of s-graph grammars. In Section 3, we will then define s-graph grammars as IRTGs with an interpretation into the *algebra of s-graphs* (Courcelle and Engelfriet, 2012). In Section 4, we will illustrate the linguistic use of s-graph grammars by giving toy grammars for a number of semantic phenomena. We conclude by discussing a number of formal aspects, such as parsing complexity, training, and the equivalence to HRG in Section 5.

2 Previous Work

We start by reviewing some related work.

2.1 Semantic construction and semantic parsing

In this paper, we take "semantic construction" to mean the process of deriving a semantic representation from a natural-language string. Semantic construction has a long tradition in computational semantics, starting with Montague (1974), who used higher-order logic as a semantic representation formalism.

Under the traditional view, the input representation of the semantic construction process is a syntactic parse tree; see e.g. Blackburn and Bos (2005) for a detailed presentation. One key challenge is to make sure that a semantic predicate combines with its semantic arguments correctly. In Montague Grammar, this is achieved by constructing through functional application of a suitably constructed lambda-term for the functor. Many unification-based approaches to semantic construction, e.g. in the context of HPSG (Copestake et al., 2001), TAG (Gardent and Kallmeyer, 2003), and CCG (Baldridge and Kruijff, 2002) use explicit argument slots that are identified either by a globally valid name (such as "subject") or by a syntactic argument position. Copestake et al. (2001), in particular, conclude from their experiences from designing large-scale HPSG grammars that explicitly named arguments simplify the specification of the syntax-semantics interface and allow rules that generalize better over different syntactic structures. Their *semantic algebra* assigns to each syntactic constituent a semantic representation consisting of an MRS, together with *hooks* that make specific variable names of the MRS available under globally available names such as "subject", "object", and so on. The algebra then provides operations for combining such representations; for instance, the "combine with subject" operation will unify the root variable of the subject MRS with the variable with the name "subject" of the verb MRS. Like this standard approach, and unlike the HRG approach described below, this paper identifies semantic argument positions by name as well, and extends this idea to graph-based semantic representations.

Recently, semantic construction has resurfaced in mainstream computational linguistics as "semantic parsing". Here the focus is on directly learning the mapping from strings to semantic representations from corpora, with or without the use of an explicit syntactic grammar. The mapping can be represented in terms of synchronous grammars (e.g. Wong and Mooney, 2007) or CCG (e.g. Zettlemoyer and Collins, 2005). Both of these lines of research have so far focused on deriving lambda terms, and are not obviously applicable to deriving graphs.

2.2 Graphs as semantic representations

The recent data-driven turn of semantic parsing motivates the development of a number of semantically annotated corpora ("sembanks"). Traditional semantic representations, such as higher-order logic, have shown to be challenging to annotate. Even the Groningen Meaning Bank (Bos et al., 2014), the best-known attempt at annotating a corpus with traditional semantic representations (DRT), uses a semi-automatic approach to semantic annotation, in which outputs of the Boxer system (Curran et al., 2007) are hand-corrected. A larger portion of recent sembanks use *graphs* as semantic representations. This strikes a middle ground, which is mostly restricted to predicate-argument structure, but can cover phenomena such as control, coordination, and coreference. In this paper, we will take the hand-annotated graphs of

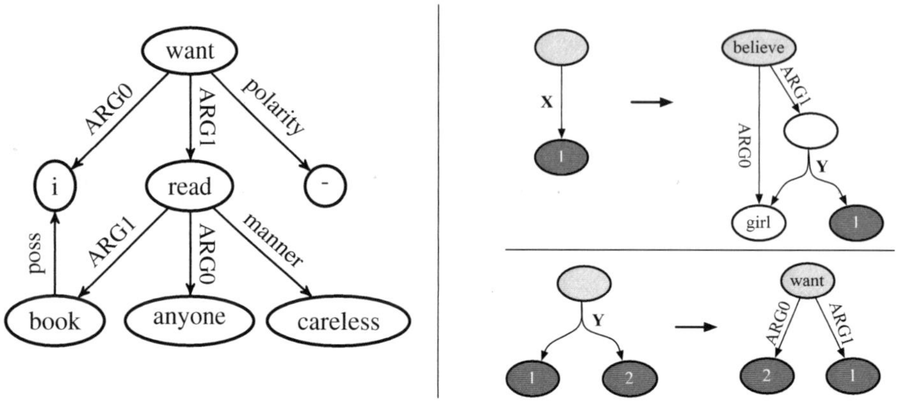

Figure 1: Left: an AMR for the sentence "I do not want anyone to read my book carelessly"; right: two example HRG rules.

the AMR-Bank (Banarescu et al., 2013) as our starting point. These *abstract meaning representations* (AMRs; see the example in Fig. 1) use edge labels to indicate semantic roles, including ones for semantic arguments (such as "ARG0", "ARG1", etc.) and ones for modification (such as "time", "manner", etc.). Graphs are also used as semantic representations in the *semantic dependency graphs* from the SemEval-2014 Shared Task (Oepen et al., 2014). These are either manually constructed or converted from deep semantic analyses using large-scale HPSG grammars.

The recent availability of graph-based sembanks has triggered some research on semantic parsing into graphs. Flanigan et al. (2014) and Martins and Almeida (2014) do this by adapting dependency parsers to compute dependency graphs rather than dependency trees. They predict graph edges from corpus statistics, and do not use an explicit grammar; they are thus very different from traditional approaches to semantic construction.

Chiang et al. (2013) present a statistical parser for synchronous string/graph grammars based on *hyperedge replacement grammars* (HRGs, Drewes et al., 1997). HRGs manipulate hypergraphs, which may contain hyperedges with an arbitrary number k of endpoints, labeled with nonterminal symbols. Each rule application replaces one such hyperedge with the graph on the right-hand side, identifying the endpoints of the nonterminal hyperedge with the "external nodes" of the graph. Jones et al. (2012) and Jones et al. (2013) describe a number of ways to infer HRGs from corpora. However, previous work has not demonstrated the suitability of HRG for linguistically motivated semantic construction. Typical published examples, such as the HRG rules from Chiang et al. (2013) shown in Fig. 1 on the right, are designed for succinctness of explanation, not for linguistic adequacy (in the figure, the external nodes are drawn shaded). Part of the problem is that HRG rules take a primarily top-down perspective on graph construction (in contrast to most work on compositional semantic construction) and combine arbitrarily complex substructures in single steps: the Y hyperedge in the first example rule is like a higher-order lambda variable that will be applied to three nodes introduced in that rule. The grammar formalism we introduce here builds graphs bottom-up, using a small inventory of simple graph-combining operations, and uses names for semantic argument positions that are much longer-lived than the "external nodes" of HRG.

2.3 Interpreted regular tree grammars

This paper introduces synchronous string/graph grammars based on *interpreted regular tree grammars* (IRTGs; Koller and Kuhlmann, 2011). We give an informal review of IRTGs here. For a more precise definition, see Koller and Kuhlmann (2011).

Informally speaking, an IRTG $\mathbb{G} = (\mathcal{G}, (h_1, \mathcal{A}_1), \ldots, (h_k, \mathcal{A}_k))$ derives a language k-tuples of objects, such as strings, trees, or graphs (see the example in Fig. 2). It does this in two conceptual steps. First, we build a *derivation tree* using a *regular tree grammar* $\mathcal{G}$. Regular tree grammars (RTGs; see

RTG rule	homomorphisms
S → r_1(NP, VP)	1: $x_1 \bullet x_2$
	2: $x_1 \bullet x_2$
VP → r_2(V, NP)	1: $x_1 \bullet x_2$
	2: $x_2 \bullet x_1$
NP → r_3	1: John
	2: Hans
NP → r_4	1: the box
	2: die Kiste
NP → r_5	1: opens
	2: öffnet

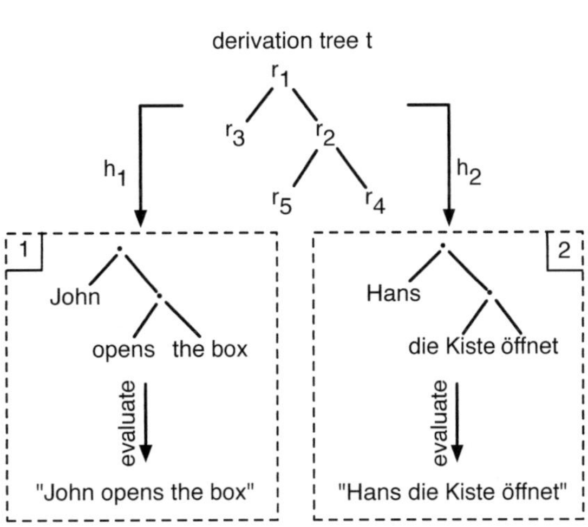

Figure 2: An IRTG (left) with an example derivation (right).

e.g. Comon et al., 2008, for an introduction) are devices for generating trees by successively replacing nonterminals using production rules. For instance, the RTG in the left column of Fig. 2 can derive the derivation tree t shown at the top right from the start symbol S.

In a second step, we can then *interpret* t into a tuple $(a_1, \ldots, a_k) \in \mathcal{A}_1 \times \ldots \times \mathcal{A}_k$ of elements from the *algebras* $\mathcal{A}_1, \ldots, \mathcal{A}_k$. An algebra $\mathcal{A}_i$ is defined over some set A_i, and can evaluate *terms* built from some signature Δ_i into elements of A_i. For instance, the *string algebra* T^* contains all strings over some finite alphabet T. Its signature contains two types of operations. Each element a of T is a zero-place operation, which evaluates to itself, i.e. $[\![\text{John}]\!] = \text{John}$. Furthermore, there is one binary operation $\bullet$, which evaluates to the binary concatenation function $[\![\bullet(t_1, t_2)]\!] = w_1 w_2$ where $w_i = [\![t_i]\!]$. Each term built from these operation symbols evaluates to a string in T^*; for instance, at the lower right of Fig. 2, the term (John $\bullet$ (opens $\bullet$ the box)) evaluates to the string $[\![$John $\bullet$ (opens $\bullet$ the box)$]\!]$ = "John opens the box".

An IRTG derives elements of the algebras by mapping, for each interpretation $1 \leq i \leq k$, the derivation tree t to a term $h_i(t)$ over the algebra using a *tree homomorphism* h_i. The tree homomorphisms are defined in the right-hand column of the table in Fig. 2; for instance, we have $h_1(r_2) = x_1 \bullet x_2$ (which concatenates the V-string with the NP-string, in this order) and $h_2(r_2) = x_2 \bullet x_1$ (which puts the NP-string before the V-string). It then evaluates $h_i(t)$ over the algebra $\mathcal{A}_i$, obtaining an element of $\mathcal{A}_i$. Altogether, the language of an IRTG is defined as

$$L(\mathbb{G}) = \{\langle [\![h_1(t)]\!]_{\mathcal{A}_1}, \ldots, [\![h_k(t)]\!]_{\mathcal{A}_k} \rangle \mid t \in L(\mathcal{G})\}.$$

In the example, the pair $\langle$John opens the box, Hans öffnet die Kiste$\rangle$ is one element of $L(\mathbb{G})$. Generally, IRTGs with two string-algebra interpretations are strongly equivalent to synchronous context-free grammars, just as IRTGs with a single string-algebra interpretation represent context-free grammars. By choosing different algebras, IRTGs can also represent (synchronous) tree-adjoining grammars (Koller and Kuhlmann, 2012), tree-to-string transducers (Büchse et al., 2013), etc.

3 An algebra of s-graphs

We can use IRTGs to describe mappings between strings and graph-based semantic representations. Let an *s-graph grammar* be an IRTG with two interpretations: one interpretation (h_s, T^*) into a string algebra T^* as described above, and one interpretation $(h_g, \mathcal{A}_g)$ into an algebra $\mathcal{A}_g$ of graphs. In this section, we define a graph algebra for this purpose.

The graph algebra we use here is the *HR algebra* of Courcelle (1993), see also Courcelle and Engelfriet (2012). The values of the HR algebra are *s-graphs*. An s-graph G is a directed graph with node

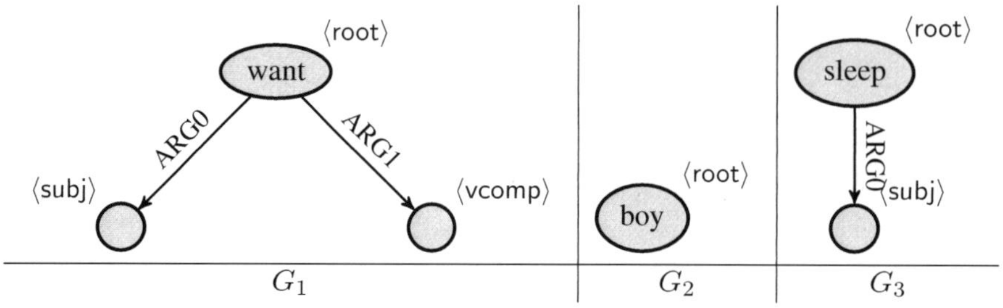

Figure 3: Example s-graphs.

labels and edge labels in which each node may be marked with a set of *source names* $s \in S$ from some fixed finite set S.[1] At most one node in an s-graph may be labeled with each source name s; we call it the *s-source of G*. We call those nodes of G that carry at least one source name the *sources* of G.

When we use s-graphs as semantic representations, the source names represent the different possible semantic argument positions of our grammar. Consider, for example, the s-graphs shown in Fig. 3. G_3 comes from the lexicon entry of the verb "sleep": It has a node with label "sleep", with an ARG0-edge into an unlabeled node. The "sleep"-node carries the source name root, indicating that this node is the "root", or starting point, of this semantic representation. (We draw source nodes shaded and annotate them with their source names in angle brackets.) We will ensure that every s-graph we use has a root-source; note that this node may still have incoming edges. The other node is the subj-source of the s-graph; this is where we will later insert the root-source of the grammatical subject. Similarly, G_1 has three sources: next to the labeled root, it has has two further unlabeled sources for the subj and vcomp argument, respectively.

The HR algebra defines a number of operations for combining s-graphs which are useful in semantic construction.

- The *rename* operation, $G[\mathsf{a}_1 \to \mathsf{b}_1, \ldots, \mathsf{a}_n \to \mathsf{b}_n]$, evaluates to a graph G' that is like G – except that for all i, the a_i-source of G is now no longer an a_i-source, but a b_i-source. All the n renames are performed in parallel. The operation is only defined if for all i, G has a a_i-source, and either there is no b_i-source or b_i is renamed away (i.e., $\mathsf{b}_i = \mathsf{a}_k$ for some k). Because we use the source name root so frequently, we write $G[\mathsf{b}]$ as shorthand for $G[\mathsf{root} \to \mathsf{b}]$.

- The *forget* operation, $\mathsf{f}_{\mathsf{a}_1,\ldots,\mathsf{a}_n}(G)$, evaluates to a graph G' that is like G, except that for all i, the a_i-source of G is no longer an a_i-source in G'. (If it was a b-source for some other source name b, it still remains a b-source.) The operation is only defined if G has a a_i-source for each i. [2]

- The *merge* operation, $G_1 \mid\mid G_2$, evaluates to a graph G' that consists of all the nodes and edges in G_1 and G_2. As a special case, if G_1 has an a-source u and G_2 has an a-source v, then u and v are mapped to the same node in G. This node then has all the adjacent edges of u and v in the original graphs.

By way of example, Fig. 4 shows the results of applying some of these operations to the s-graphs from Fig. 3. The first s-graph in the figure is $G_3' = G_3[\mathsf{vcomp}]$, which is shorthand for $G_3[\mathsf{root} \to \mathsf{vcomp}]$. Observe that this s-graph is exactly like G_3, except that the "sleep" node is now a vcomp-source and not a root-source. We then merge G_1 with G_3', obtaining the s-graph $G_1 \mid\mid G_3'$. In this s-graph, the vcomp-sources of G_1 and G_3' have been fused with each other; therefore, the ARG1-edge out of the "want" node (from G_1) points to a node with label "sleep" (which comes from G_3'). At the same time, the subj-sources of the two graphs were also fused. As a consequence, the ARG0 edge of the "want" node (from G_1) and the ARG0 edge of the "sleep" node (from G_3') point to the same node.

[1]Courcelle and Engelfriet's definition is agnostic as to whether the graph is directed and labeled.

[2]Note that Courcelle sees *rename* and *forget* as special cases of the same operation. We distinguish them for clarity.

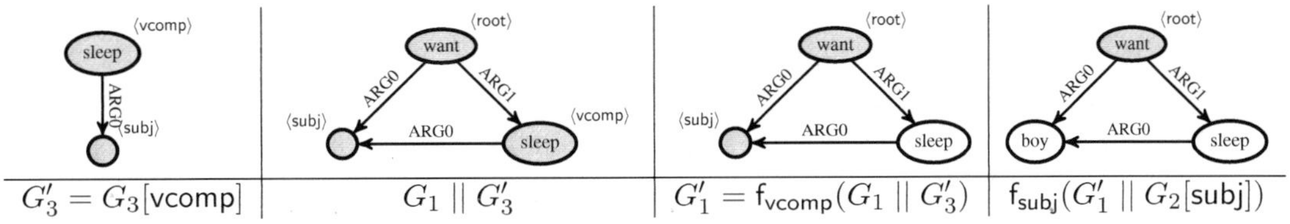

Figure 4: Combining the s-graphs of Fig. 3.

RTG rule	homomorphisms
S $\rightarrow$ comb_subj(NP, VP)	s: $x_1 \bullet x_2$ g: $\mathsf{f}_{\mathsf{subj}}(x_2 \parallel x_1[\mathsf{subj}])$
VP $\rightarrow$ sleep	s: sleep g: G_3
NP $\rightarrow$ boy	s: the boy g: G_2
VP $\rightarrow$ want$_1$(VP)	s: wants to $\bullet\, x_1$ g: $\mathsf{f}_{\mathsf{vcomp}}(G_1 \parallel x_1[\mathsf{vcomp}])$
VP $\rightarrow$ want$_2$(NP, VP)	s: wants $\bullet\, x_1 \bullet$ to $\bullet\, x_2$ g: $\mathsf{f}_{\mathsf{vcomp}}(G_1 \parallel \mathsf{f}_{\mathsf{obj}}(x_1[\mathsf{obj}] \parallel x_2[\mathsf{subj} \rightarrow \mathsf{obj}, \mathsf{root} \rightarrow \mathsf{vcomp}]))$

Figure 5: An s-graph grammar that illustrates complements.

Next, we decide that we do not want to add further edges to the "sleep" node. We can therefore forget that it is a source. The result is the s-graph $G_1' = \mathsf{f}_{\mathsf{vcomp}}(G_1 \parallel G_3')$. Finally, we can merge G_1' with $G_2[\mathsf{subj}]$, and forget the subj-source, to obtain the final graph in Fig. 4. This s-graph could serve, for instance, as the semantic representation of the sentence "the boy wants to sleep".

4 Semantic construction with s-graph grammars

We will now demonstrate the use of s-graph grammars as a grammar formalism for semantic construction. We will first present a grammar that illustrates how functors, including control and raising verbs, combine with their complements. We will then discuss a second grammar which illustrates modification and coordination.

4.1 Complements

Consider first the grammar in Fig. 5. This is an s-graph grammar that consists of an RTG with start symbol S whose rules are shown in the left column, along with a string and a graph interpretation. The right column indicates the values of the homomorphisms h_s and h_g on the terminal symbols of the RTG rules; for instance, $h_g(\mathsf{comb\_subj}) = \mathsf{f}_{\mathsf{subj}}(x_2 \parallel x_1[\mathsf{subj}])$.

As a first example, let us use this grammar to derive a semantic representation for "the boy sleeps", as shown in Fig. 6. We first use the RTG to generate a derivation tree t, shown at the center of the figure. Using the homomorphism h_s, this derivation tree projects to the term $h_s(t)$ (shown on the left), which evaluates to the string "the boy sleeps" in the string algebra. At the same time, the homomorphism h_g projects the derivation tree to the term $h_g(t)$, which evaluates to the s-graph shown on the far right. Observe that the "boy" node becomes the ARG0-child of the "sleep" node by renaming the root-source of G_2 to subj; when the two graphs are merged, this node is then identified with the subj-source of G_3. These operations are packaged together in the homomorphism term $h_g(\mathsf{comb\_subj})$.

The grammar in Fig. 5 can also analyze sentences involving control verbs. Fig. 7 shows a derivation of the sentence "the boy wants to sleep". We can use the same rule for "sleep" as before, but now we use it as the VP argument of want$_1$. The grammar takes care to ensure that all s-graphs that can be

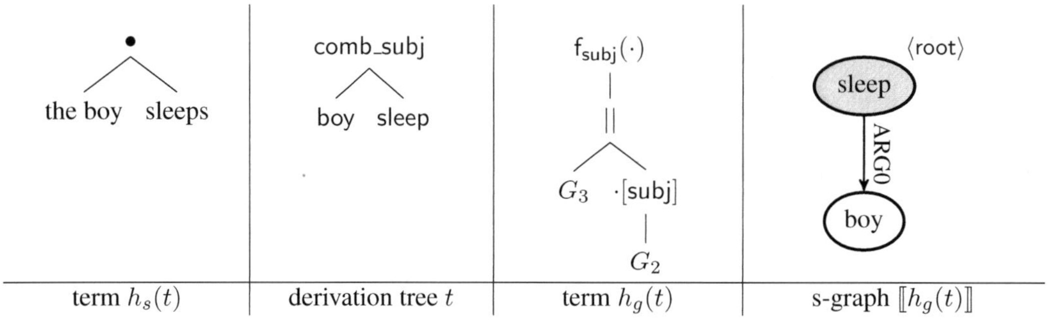

Figure 6: A derivation for "the boy sleeps", using the grammar in Fig. 5.

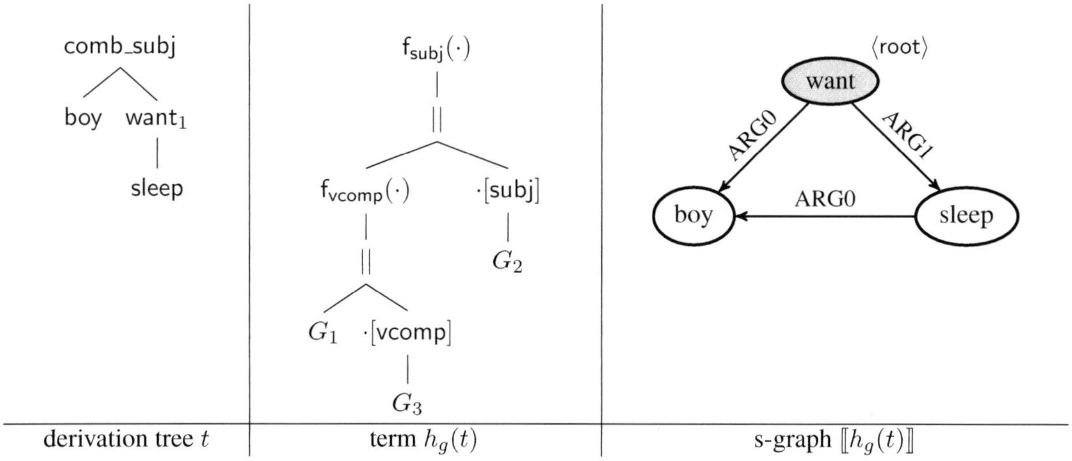

Figure 7: A derivation of "the boy wants to sleep" using the grammar in Fig. 5.

derived from VP have a subj-source along with the root-source that all derivable s-graphs have. Before we merge G_1 and G_3, we rename the root-source to vcomp to fill that argument position. By leaving the subj-source of G_3 as is, the merge operation fuses the subj-arguments of "sleep" and "wants", yielding the s-graph G_1' from Fig. 4. Notice that we did not explicitly specify the control behavior in the grammar rule; we just "let it happen" through judicious management of argument names.

The grammar also has a second rule for "wants", representing its use as a raising verb. The rule passes its grammatical object to its verb complement, where it is made to fill the subject role by renaming subj to obj. We omit the detailed derivation for lack of space, but only note that this rule allows us to derive AMRs like the one on the left of Fig. 1.

4.2 Modifiers

We now turn to an analysis of modification. The AMR-bank models modification with modification edges pointing from the modifier to the modifiee. This can be easily represented in an s-graph grammar by merging multiple root-sources without renaming them first.

We illustrate this using the grammar in Fig. 8. In the grammar we use shorthand notation to specify elementary s-graphs. For instance, the rule for coord merges its (renamed) arguments with an s-graph with three nodes, one of which is a root-source with label and and the other two are unlabeled sources for the source names 1 and 2, respectively; and with edges labeled op1 and op2 connecting these sources. In the examples below, we abbreviate this graph as G_{coord}; similarly, G_{snore} and $G_{\text{sometimes}}$ are the elementary s-graphs in the "snores" and "sometimes" rules.

Consider the derivation in Fig. 9, which is for the sentence "the boy who sleeps snores" using the s-graph grammar from Fig. 8. The subtree of the derivation starting at "rc" represents the meaning of the

RTG rule	homomorphisms
$\text{NP} \rightarrow \mathsf{mod\_rc}(\text{NP}, \text{RC})$	s: $x_1 \bullet x_2$ g: $x_1 \,\|\|\, x_2$
$\text{RC} \rightarrow \mathsf{rc}(\text{RP}, \text{VP})$	s: $x_1 \bullet x_2$ g: $(\mathsf{f}_{\mathsf{root}}(x_2 \,\|\|\, x_1[\mathsf{subj}]))[\mathsf{subj} \rightarrow \mathsf{root}]$
$\text{RP} \rightarrow \mathsf{who}$	s: who g: $\langle \mathsf{root} \rangle$
$\text{VP} \rightarrow \mathsf{coord}(\text{VP}, \text{VP})$	s: $x_1 \bullet \text{and} \bullet x_2$ g: $\mathsf{f}_{1,2}((\langle 1 \rangle \xleftarrow{\text{op1}} \mathsf{and}\langle \mathsf{root} \rangle \xrightarrow{\text{op2}} \langle 2 \rangle) \,\|\|\, x_1[1] \,\|\|\, x_2[2])$
$\text{VP} \rightarrow \mathsf{sometimes}(\text{VP})$	s: sometimes $\bullet\, x_1$ g: $((\langle \mathsf{root} \rangle \xrightarrow{\text{time}} \mathsf{sometimes}) \,\|\|\, x_1$
$\text{VP} \rightarrow \mathsf{snore}$	s: snores g: $\mathsf{snore}\langle \mathsf{root} \rangle \xrightarrow{\text{ARG0}} \langle \mathsf{subj} \rangle$

Figure 8: An s-graph grammar featuring modification.

relative clause. It combines the s-graph for "sleep" from the grammar in Fig. 5 with the s-graph for the relative pronoun, which is just a single unlabeled node, using the ordinary renaming of the root-node of the relative pronoun to subj. However, the rule for the relative clause then differs from the ordinary rule for combining subjects with VPs by forgetting the root-source of the verb and renaming subj to root. This yields the s-graph "sleep $\xrightarrow{\text{ARG0}}$ $\langle \mathsf{root} \rangle$". The "mod_rc" rule combines this with the s-graph for "the boy" by simply merging them together, yielding "sleep $\xrightarrow{\text{ARG0}}$ $\mathsf{boy}\langle \mathsf{root} \rangle$". Finally this s-graph is combined as a subject with "snores" using the ordinary subject-VP rule from earlier.

This derivation illustrates the crucial difference between complements and adjuncts in the AMR-Bank. To combine a head with its *complements*, an s-graph grammar will rename the roots of the complements to their respective argument positions, and then forget these argument names because the complements have been filled. By contrast, the grammar assumes that each s-graph for an *adjunct* has a root-source that represents the place where the adjunct expects the modifiee to be inserted. Adjuncts can then be combined with the heads they modify by a simple merge, without any renaming or forgetting.

One challenge in modeling modification is in the way it interacts with coordination. In a sentence like "the boy sleeps and sometimes snores", one wants to derive a semantic representation in which the boy is the agent of both "sleeps" and "snores", but "sometimes" only modifies "snores" and not "sleeps". Fig. 10 shows how to do this with the grammar in Fig. 8. The subtree below "sometimes" (which projects to the string "sometimes snores" on the string interpretation) is interpreted as the s-graph "$\mathsf{snore}\langle \mathsf{root} \rangle \xrightarrow{\text{time}}$ sometimes". This is because the grammar rule for "sometimes" simply adds an outgoing "time" edge to the root-source of its argument, and leaves all sources in place. The coordination rule then combines this s-graph with G_3 from Fig. 3. This rule renames the root-sources of these two s-graphs to 1 and 2 respectively, but does not change their subj-sources. Thus these are merged together, so an ordinary application of the subject rule yields the s-graph shown at the right of Fig. 10.

5 Formal aspects

We conclude the paper by discussing a number of formal aspects of s-graph grammars.

First of all, this paper has focused on illustrating s-graph grammars using hand-written toy grammars for a number of semantic phenomena. We believe that s-graph grammars are indeed a linguistically natural grammar formalism for doing this, but ultimately one obviously wants to exploit the recent availability of meaning-banks to automatically induce and train statistical grammars. It is straightforward to make IRTGs a statistical grammar formalism, and to adapt algorithms for maximum likelihood and EM estimation, Viterbi parsing, etc. to statistical IRTGs (see Koller and Kuhlmann (2011) for a sketch of a

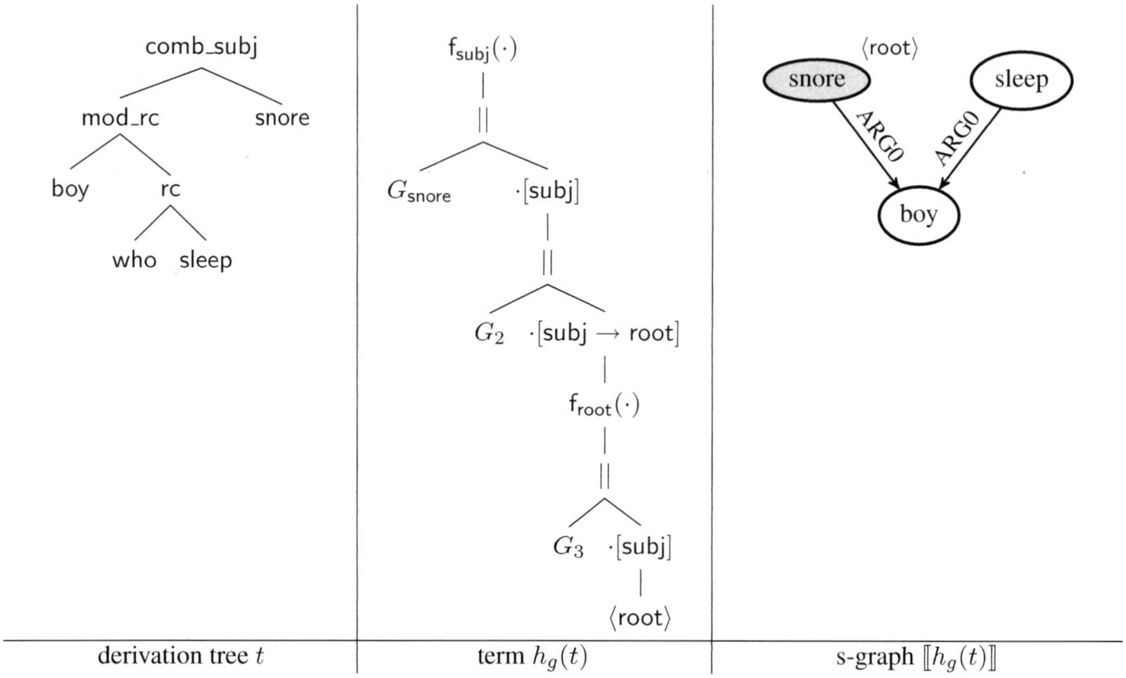

Figure 9: A derivation for "the boy who sleeps snores" using the grammar in Fig. 8.

PCFG-style probability model and Chiang (2003) for a discriminative probability model that transfers easily to IRTGs).

We have focused here on using s-graph grammars for semantic construction, i.e. as devices that map from strings to graphs. Algorithmically, this means we want to compute a parse chart from the string, extract the best derivation tree from it, and then compute its value in the graph interpretation. However, it is sometimes also useful to take a graph as the input, e.g. in an NLG or machine translation scenario, where one wants to compute a string from the graph.

We can adapt the IRTG parsing algorithm of Koller and Kuhlmann (2011) to graph parsing by showing how to compute *decomposition grammars* for the HR algebra. A decomposition grammar for an input object a is an RTG whose language is the set of all terms over the algebra that evaluate to a. We do not have the space to show this here, but the time complexity of computing decomposition grammars in the HR algebra is $O((n \cdot 3^d)^s \cdot ds)$, where n is the number of nodes in the graph, d is the maximum degree of the nodes in the graph, and s is the number of sources that are used in the grammar. This is also the overall parsing complexity of the graph parsing problem with s-graph grammars.

There is a close formal connection between s-graph grammars and Hyperedge Replacement Grammars (HRGs), which we reviewed in Section 2. Every HRG can be translated into an equivalent s-graph grammar; this follows from the known encoding of HRG languages as equational sets over the HR algebra, see e.g. Section 4.1 of Courcelle and Engelfriet (2012). More concretely, one can adapt the tree-decomposition construction of Chiang et al. (2013) to encode each HRG whose rules have maximum *treewidth* k into an equivalent s-graph grammar with $s = k + 1$ sources. Thus the parsing complexity of s-graph grammars coincides with Chiang et al.'s parsing complexity for HRGs of $O((n \cdot 3^d)^{k+1} \cdot d(k+1))$.

One key difference between HRGs and s-graph grammars is that the "sources" that arise in the translation of HRGs to IRTGs are meaningless, abstract names, which are forgotten after each rule application. By contrast, s-graph grammars can use linguistically meaningful source names which can persist if they are not explicitly forgotten in a rule. By managing the lifecycle of the subj-sources explicitly, we were able to write succinct rules for control verbs in Section 4.1. Similarly, the coordination rule in Section 4.2 fuses whatever sources the coordinated elements have, and thus it can be applied verbatim to other syntactic categories beyond VP. This reflects Copestake et al.'s (2001) observation that the use of

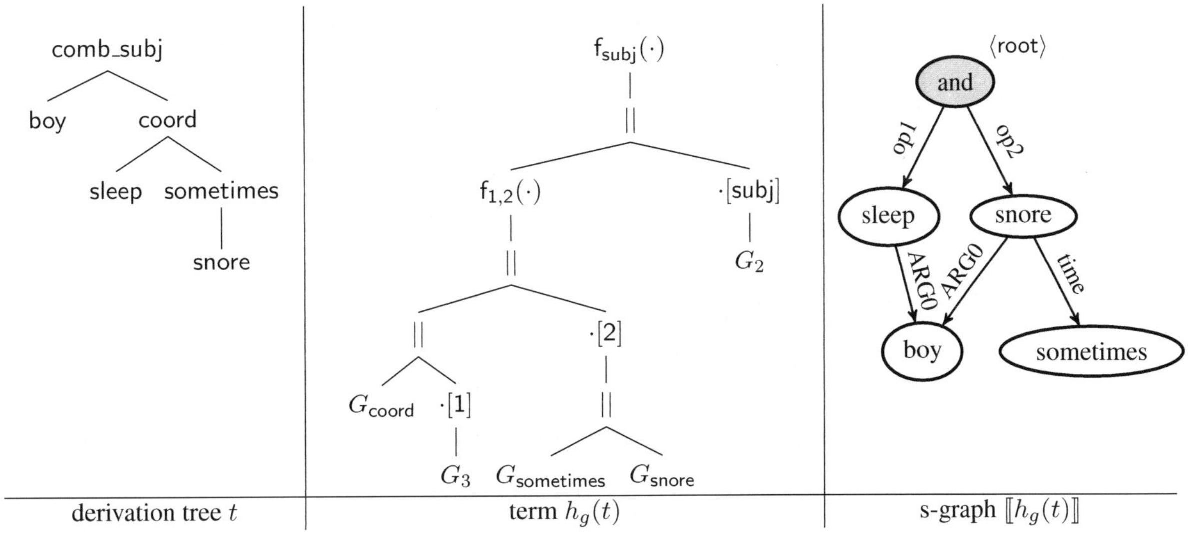

Figure 10: A derivation for "the boy sleeps and sometimes snores" using the grammar in Fig. 8.

explicit argument names can support more general semantic construction rules than are available when arguments are identified through their position in an argument list (as e.g. in HRG).

6 Conclusion

We have introduced s-graph grammars, a synchronous grammar formalism that describes relations between strings and graphs. We have also shown how this formalism can be used, in a linguistically principled way, for graph-based compositional semantic construction. In this way, we hope to help bridge the gap between linguistically motivated semantic construction and data-driven semantic parsing.

This paper has focused on developing grammars for semantic construction by hand. In future work, we will explore the use of s-graph grammars in statistical semantic parsing and grammar induction. A more detailed analysis of the consequences of the choice between argument names and argument positions in semantic construction is also an interesting question for future research.

Acknowledgments. The idea of using an IRTG over the HR algebra for semantic graphs was first developed in conversations with Marco Kuhlmann. The paper was greatly improved through the comments of a number of colleagues; most importantly, Owen Rambow, Christoph Teichmann, the participants of the 2014 Fred Jelinek Memorial JHU Workshop in Prague, and the three reviewers.

References

Baldridge, J. and G.-J. Kruijff (2002). Coupling CCG and hybrid logid dependency semantics. In *Proceedings of the 40th ACL*.

Banarescu, L., C. Bonial, S. Cai, M. Georgescu, K. Griffitt, U. Hermjakob, K. Knight, P. Koehn, M. Palmer, and N. Schneider (2013). Abstract meaning representation for sembanking. In *Proceedings of the Linguistic Annotation Workshop (LAW VII-ID)*.

Blackburn, P. and J. Bos (2005). *Representation and Inference for Natural Language. A First Course in Computational Semantics*. CSLI Publications.

Bos, J., V. Basile, K. Evang, N. Venhuizen, and J. Bjerva (2014). The Groningen Meaning Bank. In N. Ide and J. Pustejovsky (Eds.), *Handbook of Linguistic Annotation*. Berlin: Springer. Forthcoming.

Büchse, M., A. Koller, and H. Vogler (2013). General binarization for parsing and translation. In *Proceedings of the 51st ACL.*

Chiang, D. (2003). Mildly context-sensitive grammars for estimating maximum entropy parsing models. In *Proceedings of the 8th FG.*

Chiang, D., J. Andreas, D. Bauer, K. M. Hermann, B. Jones, and K. Knight (2013). Parsing graphs with hyperedge replacement grammars. In *Proceedings of the 51st ACL.*

Comon, H., M. Dauchet, R. Gilleron, F. Jacquemard, D. Lugiez, C. Löding, S. Tison, and M. Tommasi (2008). Tree automata techniques and applications. `http://tata.gforge.inria.fr/`.

Copestake, A., A. Lascarides, and D. Flickinger (2001). An algebra for semantic construction in constraint-based grammars. In *Proceedings of the 39th ACL.*

Courcelle, B. (1993). Graph grammars, monadic second-order logic and the theory of graph minors. In N. Robertson and P. Seymour (Eds.), *Graph Structure Theory*, pp. 565–590. AMS.

Courcelle, B. and J. Engelfriet (2012). *Graph Structure and Monadic Second-Order Logic*, Volume 138 of *Encyclopedia of Mathematics and its Applications.* Cambridge University Press.

Curran, J., S. Clark, and J. Bos (2007). Linguistically motivated large-scale NLP with C&C and Boxer. In *Proceedings of the 45th ACL: Demos and Posters.*

Drewes, F., H.-J. Kreowski, and A. Habel (1997). Hyperedge replacement graph grammars. In G. Rozenberg (Ed.), *Handbook of Graph Grammars and Computing by Graph Transformation*, pp. 95–162.

Flanigan, J., S. Thomson, J. Carbonell, C. Dyer, and N. A. Smith (2014). A discriminative graph-based parser for the abstract meaning representation. In *Proceedings of ACL*, Baltimore, Maryland.

Gardent, C. and L. Kallmeyer (2003). Semantic construction in feature-based TAG. In *Proceedings of the 10th Meeting of the European Chapter of the Association for Computational Linguistics.*

Jones, B. K., J. Andreas, D. Bauer, K. M. Hermann, and K. Knight (2012). Semantics-based machine translation with hyperedge replacement grammars. In *Proceedings of the 24th COLING.*

Jones, B. K., S. Goldwater, and M. Johnson (2013). Modeling graph languages with grammars extracted via tree decompositions. In *Proceedings of the 11th FSMNLP.*

Koller, A. and M. Kuhlmann (2011). A generalized view on parsing and translation. In *Proceedings of the 12th IWPT.*

Koller, A. and M. Kuhlmann (2012). Decomposing TAG algorithms using simple algebraizations. In *Proceedings of the 11th TAG+ Workshop.*

Martins, A. F. T. and M. S. C. Almeida (2014). Priberam: A turbo semantic parser with second order features. In *Proceedings of SemEval 2014.*

Montague, R. (1974). The proper treatment of quantification in ordinary english. In R. Thomason (Ed.), *Formal philosophy: Selected papers of Richard Montague.* New Haven: Yale University Press.

Oepen, S., M. Kuhlmann, Y. Miyao, D. Zeman, D. Flickinger, J. Hajic, A. Ivanova, and Y. Zhang (2014). SemEval 2014 Task 8: Broad-coverage semantic dependency parsing. In *Proceedings of the 8th International Workshop on Semantic Evaluation (SemEval 2014).*

Wong, Y. W. and R. J. Mooney (2007). Learning synchronous grammars for semantic parsing with lambda calculus. In *Proceedings of the 45th ACL.*

Zettlemoyer, L. S. and M. Collins (2005). Learning to map sentences to logical form: Structured classification with probabilistic categorial grammars. In *Proceedings of the 21st UAI.*

Layers of Interpretation: On Grammar and Compositionality

Emily M. Bender
University of Washington
ebender@uw.edu

Dan Flickinger
Stanford University
danf@stanford.edu

Stephan Oepen
University of Oslo and Potsdam University
oe@ifi.uio.no

Woodley Packard
University of Washington
sweaglesw@sweaglesw.org

Ann Copestake
University of Cambridge
aac@cl.cam.ac.uk

Abstract

With the recent resurgence of interest in semantic annotation of corpora for improved *semantic parsing*, we observe a tendency which we view as ill-advised, to conflate sentence meaning and speaker meaning into a single mapping, whether done by annotators or by a parser. We argue instead for the more traditional hypothesis that sentence meaning, but not speaker meaning, is compositional, and accordingly that NLP systems would benefit from reusable, automatically derivable, task-independent semantic representations which target sentence meaning, in order to capture exactly the information in the linguistic signal itself. We further argue that compositional construction of such sentence meaning representations affords better consistency, more comprehensiveness, greater scalability, and less duplication of effort for each new NLP application. For concreteness, we describe one well-tested grammar-based method for producing sentence meaning representations which is efficient for annotators, and which exhibits many of the above benefits. We then report on a small inter-annotator agreement study to quantify the consistency of semantic representations produced via this grammar-based method.

1 Introduction

Kate and Wong (2010) define 'semantic parsing' as "the task of mapping natural language sentences into complete formal meaning representations which a computer can execute for some domain-specific application." At this level of generality, semantic parsing has been a cornerstone of NLU from its early days, including work seeking to support dialogue systems, database interfaces, or machine translation (Woods et al., 1972; Gawron et al., 1982; Alshawi, 1992, inter alios). What distinguishes most current work in semantic parsing from such earlier landmarks of old-school NLU is (a) the use of (highly) task- and domain-specific meaning representations (e.g. the RoboCup or GeoQuery formal language) and (b) a lack of emphasis on natural language syntax, i.e. a tacit expectation to map (more or less) directly from a linguistic surface form to an abstract representation of its meaning.

This approach risks conflating a distinction that has long played an important role in the philosophy of language and theoretical linguistics (Quine, 1960; Grice, 1968), viz. the contrast between those aspects of meaning that are determined by the linguistic signal alone (called 'timeless', 'conventional', 'standing', or 'sentence' meaning), on the one hand, and aspects of meaning that are particular to a context of use ('utterer', 'speaker', or 'occasion' meaning, or 'interpretation'), on the other hand. Relating this tradition to computational linguistics, Nerbonne (1994, p. 134) notes:

> Linguistic semantics does not furnish a characterization of the *interpretation* of utterances in use, which is what one finally needs for natural language understanding applications—rather, it (mostly) provides a characterization of *conventional content*, that part of meaning determined by linguistic form. Interpretation is not determined by

Proceedings of the 11th International Conference on Computational Semantics, pages 239–249,
London, UK, April 15-17 2015.

form, however, nor by its derivative content. In order to interpret correctly, one must exploit further knowledge sources and processes that ... probably are not linguistic at all: domain knowledge, common sense, communicative purpose, extralinguistic tasks, assumptions of interlocutors about each other.

In the currently widespread approach to semantic parsing, the results of linguistic research in semantics are largely disregarded in favor of learning correlations between domain-typical linguistic forms and task-specific meaning representations, using the linguistic signal as well as domain-specific information (e.g. a database schema) as sources of constraint on the search space for the machine action that is most likely the one desired. We see two interrelated drawbacks to such an approach: First, to the extent that grammatical structure is taken into account, the same problems must be solved anew with each new task. Second, as a result, such task-specific solutions seem unlikely to scale to general-purpose natural language understanding. In order to reach that lofty goal, we argue, there must be some task-independent model of the conventional content of linguistic utterance types which can be paired with domain-specific knowledge and reasoning in order to reach appropriate interpretations of utterances in context.

Success in many semantically-sensitive NLP tasks requires algorithms that can glean a representation of at least a subset of speaker meaning. But what machines have access to is not any direct representation of a human interlocutor's intended speaker meaning, but rather only natural language utterances. Such utterances involve tokens of sentence (or sentence fragment) types, which in turn have computable sentence meaning. While sentence meaning does not determine situated speaker meaning, it is an important cue to it (Quine, 1960; Grice, 1968; Reddy, 1979; Clark, 1996). We argue here that sentence meaning, but not speaker meaning, is compositional (see Grice 1967), and accordingly that NLP systems would benefit from reusable, automatically derivable, task-independent semantic representations which target sentence meaning, in order to capture exactly the information in the linguistic signal itself. Furthermore, we argue that such sentence meaning representations are best built compositionally, because the compositional approach affords better consistency, more comprehensiveness, and greater scalability.

In this position paper we begin by providing a working definition of compositionality and briefly survey different types of semantic annotation with an eye towards classifying them as compositional or not (§2). §3 provides an overview of the English Resource Grammar (ERG; Flickinger 2000, 2011), a resource for producing semantic representations, covering most of what falls within our definition of compositional, at scale. §4 articulates the three main benefits of a compositional approach to producing semantic annotations, viz. comprehensiveness, consistency and scalability. In §5, we present a small inter-annotator agreement study to quantify the consistency of semantic representations produced via grammar-based sembanking. Finally, in §6, we consider how ERG-based semantic representations can be used as the backbone of even richer annotations that incorporate information which is not compositionally derivable.

2 Compositionality

In this section we explore which aspects of meaning among those captured by annotation projects serving NLP work (and thus presumably of interest to the NLP community) can be seen as compositional. Our purpose in doing so is two-fold: On the one hand, it illuminates the claim that sentence meaning is compositional by delineating those aspects of meaning representations admissible as sentence meaning by that criterion. On the other hand, it sheds light on the range of possible contributions of a grammar-based approach to semantic annotation.

As Szabó (2013) points out, there are many different interpretations of the principle of compositionality in the literature. Since we are concerned with annotation, the issue is compositionality of meaning representations (rather than denotation, for instance). In order to ask which aspects of meaning are compositional, we provide the following working definition:[1]

[1]In Szabó's terms, our definition of compositionality is local, distributive, and language-bound and furthermore consistent with the rule-to-rule principle. It is also consistent with the notion of compositionality from Copestake et al. (2001) and implemented in the ERG, which furthermore adds the constraint that the function for determining meanings of complex expressions must be monotonic in the sense that it cannot remove or overwrite any information contributed by the constituents.

(1) A meaning system (or subsystem) is compositional if:

- it consists of a finite (but possibly very large) number of arbitrary atomic symbol-meaning pairings;
- it is possible to create larger symbol-meaning pairings by combining the atomic pairings through a finite set of rules;
- the meaning of any non-atomic symbol-meaning pairing is a function of its parts and the way they are combined;
- this function is possibly complex, containing special cases for special types of syntactic combination, but only draws on the immediate constituents and any semantic contribution of the rule combining them; and
- further processing will not need to destructively change a meaning representation created in this way to create another of the same type.

Applying this definition to layers of semantic annotation attested in various projects within NLP, we find that they include both compositional and non-compositional aspects of meaning.

Perhaps the clearest candidate for an annotation layer that is compositional is predicate-argument structure, which appears to be fully grammar-derived: Lexical entries (atoms) provide predicates and argument positions; grammar rules dictate the linking of arguments across predicates. Note, however, that there may be disagreement as to whether particular linkings (e.g. between the subject of a participial modifier and the subject of the clause it modifies) are required by the grammar or simply anaphoric in nature. Beyond predicate-argument structure, the grammars of particular languages also provide at least partial constraints on the scope of negation and other operators, the restriction of quantifiers, modality, tense/aspect/mood, information structure, discourse status of referents of NPs, and politeness. These subsystems we consider partially compositional. There are also layers of annotation that may be considered compositional, but not according to sentence grammar, such as coherence relations/rhetorical structure.

Turning to types of semantic annotation which are not compositional, we first find layers that concern only atoms. These include fine-grained word-sense tagging, named entity tags and so on. According to the definition we have given, there may be an indefinite number of atom-meaning pairings, but these are outside the scope of the compositionality principle. What is built compositionally, on our account, is the relationships between the pieces of meaning contributed by the words.[2] There is an additional principle, often tacitly assumed, that word-meaning pairings should not be multiplied beyond necessity: in the strictest form of this, word senses are only distinguished if the distinction interacts with the syntax and morphology. A compositional representation that is consistent with this principle can be further specialized with finer-grained word sense and semantic role information without changing its structure, and hence this amounts to a form of underspecification, rather than a strong claim about lexical meaning.

Another kind of non-compositional meaning layer is that which requires some sort of further computation over linguistic structure. This can be seen as purely monotonic addition of further constraints on underspecified meaning representations, but it is not compositional in the sense that it is never (strictly) constrained by grammatical structure. In this category, we find quantifier scope ambiguity resolution (e.g. Higgins and Sadock 2003), coreference resolution (e.g. Hobbs 1979), and the determination of the focus of negation (e.g. Blanco and Moldovan 2011). All of these build on partial constraints provided by the grammar, but in all cases, the interpretation of particular sentences in context will correspond to one (or a subset) of the possibilities allowed by the grammar.

The next layer of meaning annotation to consider corresponds to discourse processing. This includes the calculation of presupposition projection (e.g. Van der Sandt 1992; Zaenen and Karttunen 2013; Venhuizen et al. 2013), coherence relations/rhetorical structure (e.g. Marcu 1997), and the annotation of discourse moves/adjacency pairs (Shriberg et al., 2004). These aspects of meaning clearly build on information provided during sentence-level processing, including lexically determined veridicality contexts (e.g. (2a) vs. (2b)) as well as discourse connectives. In both cases, the grammatical structure links embedded clauses to the relevant lexical predicates.

[2]We assume here that word sense is a property of roots, rather than fully inflected forms. Productive derivational morphology supports compositionally built-up meanings for morphologically complex words. Semi-productive morphological processes and frozen or lexicalized complex forms complicate any conventional grammar-based treatment, however.

(2) a. They forgot to vote. [⇒ They didn't vote.]

b. They forgot that they had voted. [⇒ They did vote.]

As this level of processing concerns relationships both within and across sentences, it is clearly not compositional with respect to sentence grammar. We consider it an open question whether there are compositional processes at higher levels of structure that constrain these aspects of meaning in analogous ways, but we note that in presupposition processing at least, a notion of defeasibility is required (Asher and Lascarides, 2011).

Finally, there are semantic annotations that attempt to capture what speakers are trying to do with their speech acts. This includes tasks like hedge detection (Vincze et al., 2008) and the annotation of social acts such as authority claims and alignment moves (Morgan et al., 2013) or the pursuit of power in dialogue (Swayamdipta and Rambow, 2012). While in some cases there are keywords that have a strong association with particular categories in these annotation schemes, these aspects of meaning are clearly not anchored in the structure of sentences but rather relate to the goals that speakers have in uttering sentences. Lacking a firm link to the structure of sentences, they do not appear to be compositional.

We have seen in this (necessarily brief) section that existing annotation projects span both compositional and non-compositional aspects of meaning, and we have furthermore identified those that are constrained, in whole or in part, by (sentence-level) grammatical structures as well as those that build on such structures. In the following section we describe how the English Resource Grammar relates to the broader project of creating rich representations of sentence meaning.

3 The English Resource Grammar

We have categorized layers of meaning annotation according to whether they are compositional, and if not, in what way they fail to demonstrate compositionality. The majority of those identified as compositional are compositional according to sentence grammar. In this section, we briefly describe the English Resource Grammar (ERG; Flickinger 2000, 2011) an open-source, domain-independent, linguistically precise, broad-coverage grammar for English that encapsulates the linguistic knowledge required to produce many of the types of compositional meaning annotations described above, at scale.

The ERG is an implementation of the grammatical theory of Head-driven Phrase Structure Grammar (HPSG; Pollard and Sag 1994), i.e. a computational grammar that can be used for both parsing and generation. Development of the ERG started in 1993, building conceptually on earlier work on unification-based grammar engineering at Hewlett Packard Laboratories (Gawron et al., 1982). The ERG has continuously evolved through a series of research projects (and two commercial applications) and today allows the grammatical analysis of most running text across domains and genres. In the most recent stable release, version '1214', the ERG contains 225 syntactic rules and 70 lexical rules for derivation and inflection. The hand-built ERG lexicon of some 39,000 lemmata, instantiating 975 leaf lexical types providing part-of-speech and valence constraints, aims for complete coverage of function words and open-class words with 'non-standard' syntactic properties (e.g. argument structure). Built-in support for light-weight named entity recognition and an unknown word mechanism typically enable the grammar to derive full syntactico-semantic analyses for 85–95% of all utterances in standard corpora, including newspaper text, the English Wikipedia, or bio-medical research literature (Flickinger et al., 2012, 2010; Adolphs et al., 2008). Each of these analyses includes both a derivation tree recording the grammar rules and lexical entries that were used, and the associated semantic representation produced compositionally via this derivation, within the Minimal Recursion Semantics (MRS) framework (Copestake et al., 2005). We refer to these ERG-derived MRS objects stored in Redwoods treebanks as English Resource Semantics (ERS) expressions.

Using the annotation methodology described by Oepen et al. (2004), for each roughly annual release of the ERG, a selection of development corpora is manually annotated with the 'intended' analysis among the alternatives provided by the grammar. For those utterances which either do not receive a full parse or where no correct analysis can be found by the annotator in the available parse forest, partial analyses can be assigned during annotation by making use of a recursively applicable binary *bridging* rule which preserves the semantic contributions of its two daughter constituents at each application of the rule. Alternatively, the annotator may record that no analysis is available. The automatic exports of the correct derivation tree and ERS for each of these sentences are made available as the Redwoods Treebank; at the end of 2014, the current version of Redwoods encompasses gold-standard ERG analyses for 85,000 utterances ($\sim$1.5 million tokens) of running text from half a dozen different genres and domains.

In more detail, the task of annotation for a sentence consists of making binary decisions about the set of *discriminants* each of which partitions the parse forest into two: all of the analyses which employ the particular rule or lexical entry, and the rest of the analyses which do not. This method, originating with Carter 1997, enables the human annotator to rapidly discard analyses in order to isolate the intended analysis, or to conclude that the correct analysis is unavailable. As a reference point for speed of annotation using this method, an expert treebanker using the current '1214' version of the ERG annotated 2400 sentences (37,200 words) from the Brown corpus in 1400 minutes, for an average rate of 1.7 sentences per minute.[3]

Annotations produced by this method of choosing among the candidate analyses licensed by a grammar will thus record those components of sentence meaning which are constrained by the grammatical structure and lexical items used in the intended analysis. In the next section we review some of the desired benefits of this method for producing and maintaining semantically annotated corpora which are sufficiently detailed, consistent, and numerous to be of use in non-trivial NLP applications that require the computation of semantics either for parsing or for generation.

4 Benefits of Compositionality

We are concerned here with the goal of designing task-independent semantic representations and deploying them at scale to create a large sembank including diverse genres. Such representations can be created compositionally, where the content and internal structure of the representations is constrained by syntactic structure, or non-compositionally, where annotators encode their understanding of a sentence directly. The latter category is exemplified by Abstract Meaning Representation (AMR; Langkilde and Knight 1998; Banarescu et al. 2013). In the former category, we find both manual annotation projects, such as PropBank (Kingsbury and Palmer, 2002) and FrameNet (Baker et al., 1998), which annotate semantic information with reference to syntactic structure, and grammar-based annotation initiatives such as the Redwoods Treebank (Oepen et al., 2004), TREPIL (Rosén et al., 2005), and the Groningen Meaning Bank (Basile et al., 2012).

We argue here that a grammar-based, compositional approach is critical to achieving this long-range goal, in particular because it supports more comprehensive representations (§4.1), produced with better consistency (§4.2) and greater scalability (§4.3). The drawback to a grammar-based approach is that it cannot, in itself, include information that is not compositional, but as we will develop further in §6 below, it is possible to have the best of both worlds, adding non-compositional information as additional annotation layers over grammar-produced semantic representations.

4.1 Comprehensiveness

Where task-specific meaning representations are free to abstract away from task-irrelevant details of linguistic expression, task-independent representations only have that luxury when the variation is truly (sentence) meaning preserving. A task-independent semantic representation should capture exactly the meaning encoded in the linguistic signal itself, as it is is not possible to know, *a priori*, which parts of that sentence meaning will be critical to determining speaker meaning in any given application.

[3]This rate is roughly consistent with an earlier experiment using the same Redwoods treebanking method where annotation times were noted: MacKinlay et al. (2011) report a somewhat slower mean annotation time by an expert annotator of 0.6 sentences per minute, but this difference can be attributed to the greater average sentence length (and hence increased number of discriminants to be determined) for that biomedical corpus: 23.4 tokens compared with 15.5 for the Brown data.

$\langle h_1,$
h_4:person$\langle 0:6 \rangle$(ARG0 x_5),
h_6:_no_q$\langle 0:6 \rangle$(ARG0 x_5, RSTR h_7, BODY h_8),
h_2:_eat_v_1$\langle 7:11 \rangle$(ARG0 e_3, ARG1 x_5, ARG2 i_9)
$\{ h_1 =_q h_2, h_7 =_q h_4 \} \rangle$

$\langle h_1,$
h_4:_every_q$\langle 0:5 \rangle$(ARG0 x_6, RSTR h_7, BODY h_5),
h_8:_person_n_1$\langle 6:12 \rangle$(ARG0 x_6),
h_2:_fail_v_1$\langle 13:19 \rangle$(ARG0 e_3, ARG1 h_9),
h_{10}:_eat_v_1$\langle 23:27 \rangle$(ARG0 e_{11}, ARG1 x_6, ARG2 i_{12})
$\{ h_1 =_q h_2, h_7 =_q h_8, h_9 =_q h_{10} \} \rangle$

```
(e / eat-01
 :polarity -
 :ARG0 (p / person
   :mod (e / every)))
```

Figure 1: ERS and AMR representations of (3a,b).

A grammar-based, compositional approach requires that each word and syntactic structure in a sentence be accounted for, either by contributing its piece to the overall semantic representation or by being explicitly determined to be semantically vacuous.[4] As a result, the paraphrase sets in a grammar-based approach tend to be narrower than those produced by non-compositional, free-hand annotation. For example, the AMR annotation guidelines (Banarescu et al., 2014) present the examples in (3) and (4) as paraphrase sets, as they are likely be true in many of the same real-world circumstances and/or have the same practical interpretation in a given task.

(3) a. No one ate.
b. Every person failed to eat.

(4) a. The boy is responsible for the work.
b. The boy is responsible for doing the work.
c. The boy has the responsibility for the work.

Nonetheless, these sentences intuitively differ in nuances of meaning. Compare these to (5), which gives a (partial) set of strings analyzed as exact paraphrases by the ERG:

(5) a. Kim thinks Sandy gave the book to Pat.
b. Kim thinks that Sandy gave the book to Pat.
c. Kim thinks Sandy gave Pat the book.
d. Kim thinks the book was given to Pat by Sandy.
e. The book, Kim thinks Sandy gave to Pat.

The members of the paraphrase sets identified by the ERG, while varying in interesting ways in their syntax, remain very close in their lexical content and share semantic dependencies. In contrast, the ERG assigns distinct representations to the different items in (3) and (4), as shown in Figure 1.

To summarize, compositionally constructed meaning representations are comprehensive in the sense that they account for every meaningful component of the string. We note that natural languages feature meaningful elements whose contribution is orthogonal to questions of truth conditions, for example, politeness markers (e.g. the word *please* in English, or grammaticized elements such as pronoun choice in many other languages) and markers of speaker attitude towards what is being expressed (e.g. adverbs like *frankly*). A comprehensive meaning representation should also capture both the contributions of these types of elements and their relations to the meaning of the rest of the sentence.

4.2 Consistency

A compositional approach to semantic annotation promotes consistency in the first instance by imposing constraints on possible semantic representations. Requiring meaning representations to be grounded in both the lexical items and syntactic structure of the strings being annotated significantly reduces the space of possible annotations. Grammar-based compositional approaches add to this the ability to encode design decisions about the annotations in machine-readable form and thus automatically produce only representations that conform to the design decisions. For example, the two arguments of the subordinating conjunction *when* are relatively similar in their relationship to the predicate. A grammar-based approach can with complete consistency always map the clause immediately after *when* to the same one of those arguments.

[4]Determining which elements are semantically vacuous can be non-trivial, but generally turns on testing paraphrase candidates for truth-conditional equivalence.

This does not mean that no human effort is required in grammar-based annotation, but the annotation task is simpler.[5] In grammar-based sembanking, discussed further in §5 below, the annotators are choosing among representations created by the grammar, rather than creating the representations themselves. One way to quantify the relative simplicity of such an approach is in the length of the annotation guidelines. For the study reported in §5, we relied on a set of heuristics explained in <1,000 words, along with documentation of the grammar explaining the purpose of each grammar rule and type of lexical entry. This contrasts with the AMR annotation guidelines (Banarescu et al., 2014), which run to 57 pages, or the PropBank annotation guidelines (Babko-Malaya, 2005), at 38 pages. The more human annotators can rely on their linguistic intuitions (here, in judging whether the grammar-produced semantic representations match their understanding of the most likely intended sentence meaning in context) rather than trying to track and apply a wide range of rules or heuristics, the more we can expect them to produce consistent results. A second way in which a compositional approach promotes consistency is by providing 'guide rails' to help annotators adhere to sentence meaning as opposed to speaker meaning. In human annotation of linguistic data, annotators will always be working in the context of their own interpretation of the intended speaker meaning. A sentence-meaning annotation task requires annotators to separate out their intuitions about the one from the other. If the target annotations are grammatically constrained (with or without the aid of a computational grammar), it should be more feasible for annotators to restrict themselves to annotating those parts of the meaning which are due to the linguistic signal itself.

4.3 Scalability

A third benefit of a compositional approach is that, by enabling grammar-based annotation, it gains great scalability, in terms of the amount of text annotated, genre diversity and long-term refinement of the annotations. While the initial effort required to create an implemented grammar exceeds the (still not inconsiderable) effort required to create and pilot annotation guidelines, once an implemented grammar has reached an interesting level of coverage, it can be used to annotate text very quickly. This makes it inexpensive to incorporate new genres into the collection of annotated text. Flickinger (2011) observes that the ERG has fairly consistent coverage across quite divergent genres (including tourist brochures, Wikipedia articles, online user forum posts, and chemistry papers) since the higher-frequency, core phenomena are the same.

However, even the most complete linguistically precise grammar will still lack complete coverage over naturally occurring texts, if only because of ungrammatical or extragrammatical strings in those texts. This is the familiar trade-off between accuracy (or, more relevantly here, consistency) and robustness. However, for many applications, complete annotation of the input text is not required, but merely a sufficiently large sample of annotated in-domain items. Furthermore, a precision grammar can be augmented with robustness strategies, at a cost in annotation detail and/or consistency. This 'bridging'-rule approach to this problem is discussed further in §5 below.

Finally we observe that grammar-based semantic annotation also scales particularly well in the complexity of the annotations themselves. Specifically, discriminant-based treebanking/sembanking (Carter, 1997) supports a dynamic approach to annotation that allows the annotated resources to be updated largely automatically when the grammar underlying the annotations is improved (Oepen et al., 2004). In the present context, this means that any refinements to the analysis of particular semantic phenomena or additions of layers of grammar-based annotation (e.g. information structure) that are added to the grammar can be swiftly applied throughout the corpus.

4.4 Summary

In this section we have elaborated on what we consider the three main benefits to a compositional approach to semantic annotation: comprehensiveness, consistency and scalability. In the following section, we provide a quantitative study of consistency as well as some quantitative indicators of scalability.

[5] The development of a grammar in the first place represents a lot of human effort, but this effort is captured in an artifact—the grammar—that allows it to be reused within and across domains indefinitely; see §4.3.

5 Inter-Annotator Agreement in Grammar-Based Sembanking

We carried out a small-scale experiment to quantify the consistency achievable with grammar-based sembanking specifically using the English Resource Grammar. For comparability with results reported by the AMR project (Banarescu et al., 2013), we drew our text from Antoine de Saint-Exupéry's *The Little Prince*. The annotations were produced by three of the authors, according to the Redwoods discriminant-based treebanking methodology (see §3 above), with some extensions (discussed below). We first triply annotated a 50-sentence trial set and then produced an adjudicated gold standard for that set, refining and documenting our annotation heuristics in the process. We then proceeded to independently annotate a 150-sentence sample. It is on this larger sample that we report inter-annotator agreement.

In our study, we used revised annotation software, allowing two key improvements over the classical Redwoods procedure: The first of these enhancements makes unbiased annotation possible even in cases where the level of ambiguity makes complete enumeration of the space of candidate analyses computationally prohibitive. In the original Redwoods set-up, annotators are only presented with the top N (usually 500) analyses, according to a parse selection model trained on previously annotated data. In the revised approach (Packard, 2015), we compute discriminants directly from a packed parse chart which preserves all of the parses in the forest, rather than by comparing a subset of the individual analyses to each other. Second, where previously Redwoods-style treebanking was limited to those sentences for which the grammar could produce a correct analysis, we have adopted a technique that allows us to produce meaning representations for all sentences in the input—though these representations will be incomplete in cases where the grammar does not find a correct spanning analysis. The technique involves augmenting the grammar with two pseudo-grammatical rules, one which projects any grammatical constituent to an 'island', and one which bridges two adjacent islands. The semantic representations within each island will be consistent with the standards of the grammar, though the connections between islands are left vague. Since this extension is not intended to produce additional analyses for items which are correctly analysed, sembanking is done in two passes: first, with the robust analyses suppressed, and then on a second pass, only for items without satisfactory analyses, with the bridging rules turned on. In our sample sembank, these robust analyses allowed us to increase the coverage from between 79% and 88% of sentences (depending on the annotator) to 100% (for all three annotators).

We also produced an adjudicated gold standard version of all 200 annotated sentences.[6] This was achieved by comparing the annotations selected by each annotator (with or without bridges), for each item on which there was disagreement (71 items, including 55 of the 150 item sample), discussing the differences, and either selecting one of the three as fully correct or creating a hybrid representing the consensus decision for each choice point. When we felt that the decisions were not already fully guided by the existing annotation guidelines, we worked to articulate an extension to the guidelines that would support the decision.

Table 1 summarizes inter-annotator agreement for the 150 item sample, using three different metrics:[7] (a) *exact match*, i.e. wholly identical ERSs, and F_1 scores for (b) *argument identification* (EDM_a) and (c) for *predicate naming and argument identification* (EDM_{na}). The latter two metrics quantify what Dridan and Oepen (2011) call Elementary Dependency Match, i.e. F_1 computed over sets of triples extracted from a reduction of each full ERS into a variable-free Elementary Dependency Structure (EDS; Oepen and Lønning 2006), i.e. a labeled, directed graph that is formally very similar to AMRs. Here, we consider two types of triples, viz. ones associating a predicate name with a node and ones relating two nodes in an argument relation. From the leftmost ERS in Figure 1, for example, three predicate name triples would be extracted, including ⟨7:11⟩ – NAME – _eat_v_1, and three argument triples (discarding unexpressed arguments), including ⟨7:11⟩ – ARG1 – ⟨0:6⟩.[8] Slightly higher EDM_{na} than EDM_a suggests that predicate naming is easier to annotate than argument identification, which is plausible seeing that

[6] The adjudicated gold standard, together with the annotation guidelines, is available from www.delph-in.net/lpp.

[7] None of these correct for chance agreement as that is currently an unsolved methodological problem in graph-structured annotations

[8] For increased comparability with AMR, we ignore a third type of triple, corresponding to so-called variable properties, i.e. information about tense, mood, aspect, number, or person.

	Annotator Comparison			
Metric	A vs. B	A vs. C	B vs. C	Average
Exact Match	0.73	0.65	0.70	0.70
EDM_a	0.93	0.92	0.94	0.93
EDM_{na}	0.94	0.94	0.95	0.94

Table 1: Exact match ERS and Elementary Dependency Match across three annotators.

the only sense distinctions drawn in the ERG are those that contrast in their syntactic distribution.

In general, the statistics in Table 1 strongly support our expectations regarding consistency of annotation: In at least two out of three cases, any pair of annotators arrives at exactly the same representation of sentence meaning; in the granular EDM metrics, pairwise inter-annotator agreement ranges consistently in the mid-nineties F_1. Although not directly comparable due to methodological differences in the interpretation of the task of sembanking, formal differences in the nature of target representations, and the annotation of web texts rather than *The Little Prince*, we observe that Banarescu et al. (2013) report triple-based F_1 scores for inter-annotator agreement in AMR sembanking of 0.71. This, in our view, clearly suggests that a well-defined target representation at the level of sentence meaning (or, in other words, all and only the grammaticized contributions to interpretation) affords comparatively high levels of annotation quality at relatively moderate costs per additional items annotated.

6 Conclusion: Further Layers of Annotation

In this position paper, we have argued that NLP systems would benefit from task-independent semantic representations which capture the information in the linguistic signal (i.e. sentence meaning), as a basis from which to map to task-dependent hypotheses about speaker intentions. Some of the information we would like to see in such annotations is grammatically constrained, and we have argued that representations of those aspects of meaning are best built compositionally. However, there are further aspects of meaning which are closely tied to the linguistic signal but are not constrained by sentence-level grammar (or only partially so constrained). We agree here with Basile et al. (2012) and Banarescu et al. (2013) that a single resource that combines multiple different types of semantic annotations, all applied to the same text, will be most valuable (see also Ide and Suderman 2007). However, just because some aspects of the desired representations cannot be created in a grammar-based fashion does not mean that what can be done with a grammar has no value. To get the best of both worlds, one should start from grammar-derived semantic annotations and then either add further layers of annotation (e.g. word sense, coreference) or, should larger paraphrase sets be desired, systematically simplify aspects of the grammar-derived representations, effectively 'bleaching' some of the contrasts.

In moving from the current state of the art towards more comprehensive representations, we envision several kinds of enrichment: First, there are extensions to the grammar, supporting ever greater coverage and more detailed information about sentence-level, compositional meaning representations (e.g. partial constraints on coreference, reflecting binding-theoretic configurations or partial constraints on information structure). Second, the output of a grammar like the ERG might serve as the input to another sort of grammar to compute structure-sensitive, cross-sentential phenomena such as presupposition propagation. Third, the atoms of the grammar-derived semantic representations could be further annotated with links to word-sense inventories, ontological resources, and the like. Similarly, phenomena such as (non-grammatically constrained) coreference could be annotated over the semantic representations, as links between semantic variables, including those representing syntactically null anaphora.

Critically, this layered approach builds on top of compositional meaning representations. As we have argued, the compositional approach supports the development of more comprehensive representations (capturing more detail at each layer considered), more consistent deployment of the annotations (as design decisions are coded directly into the grammar and the task for the human annotator is simplified), and greater scalability of annotations, across texts, genres, and in the addition of layers and other refinements to the annotations themselves.

References

Adolphs, P., S. Oepen, U. Callmeier, B. Crysmann, D. Flickinger, and B. Kiefer (2008). Some fine points of hybrid natural language parsing. In *Proceedings of the 6th International Conference on Language Resources and Evaluation*, Marrakech, Morocco.

Alshawi, H. (Ed.) (1992). *The Core Language Engine*. Cambridge, MA, USA: MIT Press.

Asher, N. and A. Lascarides (2011). Reasoning dynamically about what one says. *Synthese 183*(1), 5 – 31.

Babko-Malaya, O. (2005). PropBank annotation guidelines. Available from `http://verbs.colorado.edu/~mpalmer/projects/ace/PBguidelines.pdf`.

Baker, C. F., C. J. Fillmore, and J. B. Lowe (1998). The Berkeley FrameNet project. In *Proceedings of the 17th International Conference on Computational Linguistics and the 36th Meeting of the Association for Computational Linguistics*, Stroudsburg, PA, USA, pp. 86 – 90.

Banarescu, L., C. Bonial, S. Cai, M. Georgescu, K. Griffitt, U. Hermjakob, K. Knight, P. Koehn, M. Palmer, and N. Schneider (2013). Abstract meaning representation for sembanking. In *Proceedings of the 7th Linguistic Annotation Workshop and Interoperability with Discourse*, Sofia, Bulgaria, pp. 178 – 186.

Banarescu, L., C. Bonial, S. Cai, M. Georgescu, K. Griffitt, U. Hermjakob, K. Knight, P. Koehn, M. Palmer, and N. Schneider (2014). Abstract Meaning Representation (AMR) 1.1 specification. Version of February 11, 2014.

Basile, V., J. Bos, K. Evang, and N. Venhuizen (2012). Developing a large semantically annotated corpus. In *Proceedings of the 8th International Conference on Language Resources and Evaluation*, Istanbul, Turkey, pp. 3196 – 3200.

Blanco, E. and D. Moldovan (2011). Semantic representation of negation using focus detection. In *Proceedings of the 49th Meeting of the Association for Computational Linguistics*, Portland, OR, USA, pp. 581 – 589.

Carter, D. (1997). The TreeBanker. A tool for supervised training of parsed corpora. In *Proceedings of the Workshop on Computational Environments for Grammar Development and Linguistic Engineering*, Madrid, Spain, pp. 9 – 15.

Clark, H. H. (1996). *Using Language*. Cambridge: Cambridge University Press.

Copestake, A., D. Flickinger, C. Pollard, and I. A. Sag (2005). Minimal Recursion Semantics. An introduction. *Research on Language and Computation 3*(4), 281 – 332.

Copestake, A., A. Lascarides, and D. Flickinger (2001). An algebra for semantic construction in constraint-based grammars. In *Proceedings of the 39th Meeting of the Association for Computational Linguistics*, Toulouse, France, pp. 140 – 147.

Dridan, R. and S. Oepen (2011). Parser evaluation using elementary dependency matching. In *Proceedings of the 12th International Conference on Parsing Technologies*, Dublin, Ireland, pp. 225 – 230.

Flickinger, D. (2000). On building a more efficient grammar by exploiting types. *Natural Language Engineering 6 (1)*, 15 – 28.

Flickinger, D. (2011). Accuracy vs. robustness in grammar engineering. In E. M. Bender and J. E. Arnold (Eds.), *Language from a Cognitive Perspective: Grammar, Usage, and Processing*, pp. 31–50. Stanford: CSLI Publications.

Flickinger, D., S. Oepen, and G. Ytrestøl (2010). WikiWoods. Syntacto-semantic annotation for English Wikipedia. In *Proceedings of the 7th International Conference on Language Resources and Evaluation*, Valletta, Malta.

Flickinger, D., Y. Zhang, and V. Kordoni (2012). DeepBank. A dynamically annotated treebank of the Wall Street Journal. In *Proceedings of the 11th International Workshop on Treebanks and Linguistic Theories*, Lisbon, Portugal, pp. 85 – 96. Edições Colibri.

Gawron, J. M., J. King, J. Lamping, E. Loebner, E. A. Paulson, G. K. Pullum, I. A. Sag, and T. Wasow (1982). Processing English with a Generalized Phrase Structure Grammar. In *Proceedings of the 20th Meeting of the Association for Computational Linguistics*, Toronto, Ontario, Canada, pp. 74 – 81.

Grice, H. P. (1967). Logic and conversation. In P. Cole and J. L. Morgan (Eds.), *Syntax and Semantics 3: Speech Acts*, pp. 41 – 58. New York: Academic Press.

Grice, H. P. (1968). Utterer's meaning, sentence-meaning, and word-meaning. *Foundations of Language 4*(3), 225 – 242.

Higgins, D. and J. M. Sadock (2003). A machine learning approach to modeling scope preferences. *Computational Linguistics 29*(1), 73 – 96.

Hobbs, J. R. (1979). Coherence and coreference. *Cognitive Science 3*(1), 67 – 90.

Ide, N. and K. Suderman (2007). GrAF: A Graph-based Format for Linguistic Annotations. In *Proceedings of the Linguistic Annotation Workshop*, pp. 1 – 8.

Kate, R. J. and Y. W. Wong (2010). Semantic parsing. The task, the state of the art and the future. In *Tutorial Abstracts of the 20th Meeting of the Association for Computational Linguistics*, Uppsala, Sweden, pp. 6.

Kingsbury, P. and M. Palmer (2002). From TreeBank to PropBank. In *Proceedings of the 3rd International Conference on Language Resources and Evaluation*, Las Palmas, Spain, pp. 1989 – 1993.

Langkilde, I. and K. Knight (1998). Generation that exploits corpus-based statistical knowledge. In *Proceedings of the 17th International Conference on Computational Linguistics and the 36th Meeting of the Association for Computational Linguistics*, Montréal, Canada, pp. 704 – 710.

MacKinlay, A., R. Dridan, D. Flickinger, S. Oepen, and T. Baldwin (2011). Using external treebanks to filter parse forests for parse selection and treebanking. In *Proceedings of the 2011 International Joint Conference on Natural Language Processing*, Chiang Mai, Thailand, pp. 246 – 254.

Marcu, D. (1997). The rhetorical parsing of unrestricted natural language texts. In *Proceedings of the 35th Meeting of the Association for Computational Linguistics and the 7th Meeting of the European Chapter of the Association for Computational Linguistics*, Madrid, Spain, pp. 96 – 103.

Morgan, J. T., M. Oxley, E. M. Bender, L. Zhu, V. Gracheva, and M. Zachry (2013). Are we there yet? The development of a corpus annotated for social acts in multilingual online discourse. *Dialogue & Discourse 4*, 1 – 33.

Nerbonne, J. (1994). Book review. Computational linguistics and formal semantics. *Computational Linguistics 20*(1), 131 – 136.

Oepen, S., D. Flickinger, K. Toutanova, and C. D. Manning (2004). LinGO Redwoods. A rich and dynamic treebank for HPSG. *Research on Language and Computation 2*(4), 575 – 596.

Oepen, S. and J. T. Lønning (2006). Discriminant-based MRS banking. In *Proceedings of the 5th International Conference on Language Resources and Evaluation*, Genoa, Italy, pp. 1250 – 1255.

Packard, W. (2015). Full forest treebanking. Master's thesis, University of Washington.

Pollard, C. and I. A. Sag (1994). *Head-Driven Phrase Structure Grammar*. Studies in Contemporary Linguistics. Chicago, USA: The University of Chicago Press.

Quine, W. V. O. (1960). *Word and Object*. Cambridge, MA, USA: MIT Press.

Reddy, M. J. (1979). The conduit metaphor. A case of frame conflict in our language about language. In A. Ortony (Ed.), *Metaphor and Thought*, pp. 164 – 201. Cambridge, UK: Cambridge University Press.

Rosén, V., P. Meurer, and K. De Smedt (2005). Constructing a parsed corpus with a large LFG grammar. In M. Butt and T. H. King (Eds.), *Proceedings of the 10th International LFG Conference*, Bergen, Norway.

Shriberg, E., R. Dhillon, S. Bhagat, J. Ang, and H. Carvey (2004). The icsi meeting recorder dialog act (mrda) corpus. In M. Strube and C. Sidner (Eds.), *Proceedings of the 5th SIGdial Workshop on Discourse and Dialogue*, Cambridge, Massachusetts, USA, pp. 97 – 100.

Swayamdipta, S. and O. Rambow (2012). The pursuit of power and its manifestation in written dialog. In *ICSC*, pp. 22 – 29.

Szabó, Z. G. (2013). Compositionality. In E. N. Zalta (Ed.), *The Stanford Encyclopedia of Philosophy* (Fall 2013 ed.).

Van der Sandt, R. A. (1992). Presupposition projection as anaphora resolution. *Journal of semantics 9*(4), 333 – 377.

Venhuizen, N., J. Bos, and H. Brouwer (2013). Parsimonious semantic representations with projection pointers. In *Proceedings of the 10th International Conference on Computational Semantics (IWCS 2013) – Long Papers*, Potsdam, Germany, pp. 252–263.

Vincze, V., G. Szarvas, R. Farkas, G. Móra, and J. Csirik (2008). The BioScope corpus. Biomedical texts annotated for uncertainty, negation and their scopes. *BMC Bioinformatics 9(Suppl 11)*.

Woods, W. A., R. M. Kaplan, and B. L. Nash-Webber (1972). The lunar sciences natural language information system. Final report. BBN Report 2378, Bolt Beranek and Newman Inc., Cambridge, MA, USA.

Zaenen, A. and L. Karttunen (2013). Veridicity annotation in the lexicon? A look at factive adjectives. In *Proceedings of the 9th Joint ISO–ACL SIGSEM Workshop on Interoperable Semantic Annotation*, Potsdam, Germany, pp. 51 – 58.

Pragmatic Rejection*

Julian J. Schlöder and Raquel Fernández
Institute for Logic, Language and Computation
University of Amsterdam
julian.schloeder@gmail.com, raquel.fernandez@uva.nl

Abstract

Computationally detecting the accepting/rejecting force of an utterance in dialogue is often a complex process. In this paper we focus on a class of utterances we call *pragmatic rejections*, whose rejection force arises only by pragmatic means. We define the class of pragmatic rejections, present a novel corpus of such utterances, and introduce a formal model to compute what we call *rejections-by-implicature*. To investigate the perceived rejection force of pragmatic rejections, we conduct a crowdsourcing experiment and compare the experimental results to a computational simulation of our model. Our results indicate that models of rejection should capture partial rejection force.

1 Introduction

Analysing meaning in dialogue faces many particular challenges. A fundamental one is to keep track of the information the conversing interlocutors mutually take for granted, their *common ground* (Stalnaker, 1978). Knowledge of what is—and what is not—common ground can be necessary to interpret elliptical, anaphoric, fragmented and otherwise non-sentential expressions (Ginzburg, 2012). Establishing and maintaining common ground is a complicated process, even for human interlocutors (Clark, 1996). A basic issue is to determine which proposals in the dialogue have been *accepted* and which have been *rejected*: Accepted proposals are committed to common ground; rejected ones are not (Stalnaker, 1978). An important area of application is the automated summarisation of meeting transcripts, where it is vital to retrieve only mutually agreed propositions (Galley et al., 2004).

Determining the acceptance or rejection function of an utterance can be a highly nontrivial matter (Walker, 1996; Lascarides and Asher, 2009) as the utterance's surface form alone is oftentimes not explicit enough (Horn, 1989; Schlöder and Fernández, 2014). Acceptance may merely be inferable from a *relevant next contribution* (Clark, 1996), and some rejections require substantial contextual awareness and inference capabilities to be detected—for example, when the intuitive meaning of *'yes'* and *'no'* is *reversed*, as in (1), or when the rejection requires some *pragmatic enrichment*, such as computing presuppositions in (2):[1]

(1) A: TVs aren't capable of sending.
B: Yes they are.
$\rightsquigarrow$ *rejection*

(2) A: You can reply to the same message.
B: I haven't got [the] message.
$\rightsquigarrow$ *presupposition failure*

Our main concern in this paper are rejections like (2) whose rejection force can only be detected by pragmatic means. Aside from presupposition failures, we are particularly concerned with rejections related to implicatures: either rejections-of-implicatures or rejections-by-implicature as in the following examples of scalar implicatures:[2]

*The research presented in this paper has been funded by the European Community's Seventh Framework Programme (FP7/2007-2013) under grant agreement no. 567652 *ESSENCE: Evolution of Shared Semantics in Computational Environments* (http://www.essence-network.com/).

[1]Examples from the AMI Meeting Corpus (Carletta, 2007).

[2]Examples from the British National Corpus (BNC) (Burnard, 2000).

Proceedings of the 11th International Conference on Computational Semantics, pages 250–260,
London, UK, April 15-17 2015.

(3) A: That's brilliant.
B: Well I thought that was quite good.
$\rightsquigarrow$ *good, not necessarily brilliant*

(4) A: It was good weren't it?
B: It's brilliant.
$\rightsquigarrow$ *not merely good*

In both examples, B's utterances do not seem to (fully) agree with their antecedent: In (3) B can be taken to implicate *'good $\rightsquigarrow$ not brilliant'*, thereby disagreeing with A's assertion; in (4), B can be taken to reject the same implicature attributed to A. We consider both examples to be what we call *pragmatic rejections:* utterances whose rejection force is indeterminable by purely semantic means. A particular feature of such rejections is that they are *prima facie* not in logical contradiction with their antecedent. Yet, as pointed out by Walker (2012), a widespread consent identifies rejection force with contradicting content.

We proceed as follows: In the next section, we give a more comprehensive account of what we introduced in the previous paragraph, offer a precise definition of the term *pragmatic rejection*, and discuss some associated problems. Afterwards, we review related literature, both on the topic of rejection computing and on the pragmatics of positive and negative answers. The main contributions of our work are a novel corpus of pragmatic rejections (Section 4), a formal model to compute rejections-by-implicature (Section 5), and a crowdsourcing experiment to gather agreement/disagreement judgements. In Section 6, we present the results of this experiment and compare them to a computational simulation of our model. We summarise our findings and conclude in Section 7.

2 Pragmatic Rejection

A commonly held view on rejection states that a speech event constitutes a rejecting act if and only if it is inconsistent in the dialogue context (*e.g.*, in the formal model of Schlöder and Fernández, 2014). Under that conception, rejection is typically modelled as asserting the negative of a contextually salient proposition. However, as observed by Walker (1996, 2012), this does not give the full picture. A perfectly consistent utterance can have rejection force by a variety of *implicated* inconsistencies:[3]

(5)	A: We're all mad, aren't we?	$\forall x : M(x)$
	B: Well, some of us.	$\exists x : M(x)$
	$\rightsquigarrow$ *not (necessarily) all of us*	$\rightsquigarrow \exists x : \neg M(x)$
(6)	A: Check to see if your steak's burning.	$B(s)$
	B: Well something's bloody burning.	$\exists x : B(x)$
	$\rightsquigarrow$ *not (necessarily) my steak*	$\rightsquigarrow \neg B(s)$
(7)	A: Maybe three days.	$t = 3$
	B: Three or four days.	$t = 3 \vee t = 4$
	$\rightsquigarrow$ *not (necessarily) three*	$\rightsquigarrow \neg(t = 3)$
(8)	A: [Abbreviations are used] now in narrative and dialogue.	$N \wedge D$
	B: Well, in dialogue it's fine.	D
	$\rightsquigarrow$ *not (necessarily) in narrative*	$\rightsquigarrow \neg N$

What is remarkable about these rejections is that they are not only consistent with their antecedent, but are in fact *informationally redundant*—they are mere implications of the antecedent and as such intuitively innocuous. On the other hand, it is unexpected that a contradicting implicature[4] can arise at all: Since implicatures can be cancelled by prior context, the occurrence of an inconsistent implicature is unexpected from a theoretical standpoint (Walker, 1996).

[3]Examples from the BNC (Burnard, 2000).

[4]Walker (1996) called these *implicature rejection*; we cannot adopt the terminology, as we need to discern rejection-by-implicature from rejection-of-implicature below.

Already Horn (1989) observed that some rejections are not semantic in nature, leading him to coin the term *metalinguistic negation*. Examples include rejections of implicatures, as in (9) and (10), or of presuppositions as in (11):[5]

(9) A: It's your job.
$\rightsquigarrow$ *your job alone*
B: It's our job.

(10) A: Three or four days.
$\rightsquigarrow$ *exact value unknown*
B: Well, four.

(11) A: Put a special colour of the buttons.
$\rightsquigarrow$ *there are buttons*
B: But we don't have any buttons.

Rejections of implicatures are also (semantically) consistent with their antecedent, though they need not be informationally redundant, and rejections of presuppositions only become inconsistent once the presupposition has been computed. These examples are also not accounted for by the standard approach: neither can their rejection force be determined by a simple search for inconsistency, nor do these rejections amount to asserting the negative of their antecedent. In (9), B cannot be said to assert that it is not her job, she just takes offence to the connotation that it is her's alone, and in (11), B also cannot be taken to assert that there should *not* be a special colour on the buttons. An interesting case of rejections-of-implicatures are utterances that are taken to be more general than their addressee is willing to accept. In the following examples, the offending implicature arises because B expected (or wanted) A to be more specific; the lack of specificity gives rise to a generalising implicature:[6]

(12) A: You like country. $\rightsquigarrow$ *country in general*
B: But not all country.

(13) A: You love soap. $\rightsquigarrow$ *soaps in general*
B: I love lovely soaps. $\rightsquigarrow$ *not all soaps*

Example (13) is a particular case where it is both an implicature that is rejected, and an implicature that does the rejecting: A's utterance is pragmatically enriched to a general interpretation by B, exactly as in (12), but instead of explicitly rejecting this, A *implicates* the rejecting *'not all'*.

In general, when we speak of a *rejection* (or more generally of *rejection force*), we mean an answer to an earlier assertion or proposal that signals the speaker's refusal to add the assertion/proposal's content to the common ground. In particular, we exclude replies to questions from our study, since a negative answer to a polar question has a different influence on the common ground: it adds the negative counterpart of the question's propositional content. From now on we say that an utterance is a *pragmatic rejection* if it has rejection force, but is semantically consistent with what it is rejecting. We restrict our discussion to the three types exemplified above: rejection-by-implicature, rejection-of-implicature and rejection-of-presupposition.[7] We are concerned with the task of determining which utterances are (pragmatic) rejections, *i.e.*, given a (consistent) utterance, how can we determine if it has rejecting force?

3 Related Work

A typical area of interest for rejection computing is the summarisation of multiparty meeting transcripts (Hillard et al., 2003; Hahn et al., 2006; Schlöder and Fernández, 2014) and online discussions (Yin et al., 2012; Misra and Walker, 2013). This body of work has identified a number of local and contextual features that are helpful in discerning agreement from disagreement. However, their models—if explicated—rarely take pragmatic functions into account. Also, the task of retrieving rejections remains a computational challenge; Germesin and Wilson (2009) report high accuracy in the task of classifying utterances into *agreement / disagreement / other*, but have 0% recall of disagreements.

Walker (1996, 2012) first raised the issue of *implicature rejection*. Building on Horn's (1989) landmark exposition on negation and his discussion of *metalinguistic* rejections, she describes a new class of utterances which are not in contradiction with their antecedent, but nevertheless have rejection force. Her prototypical example is *'A: There's a man in the garage.'* – *'B: There's something in the garage.'* (similar to our (6)), where B's utterance is clearly implied by A's, but rejecting by virtue of a Quantity

[5] Examples (9) and (11) from the AMI Corpus (Carletta, 2007), and (10) from the BNC (Burnard, 2000).

[6] Example (12) from the Switchboard Corpus (Godfrey et al., 1992) and (13) from the BNC (Burnard, 2000).

[7] We do not claim that this is an exhaustive categorisation. In particular, we think that rejection-by-presupposition is also possible, as in the constructed example *'A: John never smoked.'* – *'B: He stopped smoking before you met him.'*

implicature. An example where the rejecting speaker adds a disjunction, similar to our (7) (*'A: Maybe three days.' – 'B: Three or four days.'*), was already discussed by Grice (1991, p. 82), though he did not make an explicit connection to rejections *by* implicatures,[8] even though he mentions that there are rejections *of* implicatures. Walker (2012) is concerned with the question of why a rejecting implicature is not cancelled by prior context, and proposes to stratify the grounding process into different levels of *endorsement*, where a tacit endorsement does not have cancellation force.

Potts (2011) and de Marneffe et al. (2009) have investigated a phenomenon similar to pragmatic rejection: They study answers to polar questions which are *indirect* in that they do not contain a clear *'yes'* or *'no'* and therefore their intended polarity must be inferred—sometimes by pragmatic means. They describe answers that require linguistic knowledge—such as salient scales—to be resolved; these are similar to our examples (3) and (4). Potts (2011) reports the results of a crowdsourcing experiment where participants had to judge whether an indirect response stood for a *'yes'* or a *'no'* answer. He then analyses indirect responses by their relative *strength* compared to the question radical. His experimental data shows that a weaker item in the response generally indicates a negative answer (*'A: Did you manage to read that section I gave you?' – B: 'I read the first couple of pages.'*), while a stronger item in the response generally indicates a positive answer (*'A: Do you like that one?' – 'B: I love it.'*). The former result corresponds to our rejection-by-implicature, while the latter is in contrast to our intuitions on rejection-of-implicature. As mentioned, our focus lies with rejections of assertions rather than answers to polar questions. Since the results of Potts and colleagues do not straightforwardly generalise from polar questions to assertions, we have adapted their methodology to conduct a study on responses to assertions; we return to this in Section 6.

4 A Corpus of Pragmatic Rejections

To our knowledge, there is currently no corpus available which is suitable to investigate the phenomenon of pragmatic rejection. We assembled such a corpus from three different sources: the AMI Meeting Corpus (Carletta, 2007), the Switchboard corpus (Godfrey et al., 1992) and the spoken dialogue section of the British National Corpus (Burnard, 2000). Since, generally, rejection is a comparatively rare phenomenon,[9] pragmatic rejections are few and far between. As indicated above, we consider an utterance a *pragmatic rejection* if it has rejection force, but is not (semantically) in contradiction to the proposal it is rejecting. As it is beyond the current state of the art to computationally search for this criterion, our search involved a substantial amount of manual selection. We assembled our corpus as follows:

- The AMI Meeting Corpus is annotated with relations between utterances, loosely called *adjacency pair* annotation.[10] The categories for these relations include `Objection/Negative Assessment (NEG)` and `Partial Agreement/Support (PART)`. We searched for all `NEG` and `PART` adjacency pairs where the first-part was *not* annotated as a question-type (`Elicit-*`) dialogue act, and manually extracted pragmatic rejections.
- The Switchboard corpus is annotated with dialogue acts,[11] including the tags `ar` and `arp` indicating (partial) rejection. We searched for all turn-initial utterances that are annotated as `ar` or `arp` and manually extracted pragmatic rejections.
- In the BNC we used SCoRE (Purver, 2001) to search for words or phrases repeated in two adjacent utterances, where the second utterance contains a rejection marker like *'no'*, *'not'* or turn-initial *'well'*; for repetitions with *'and'* in the proposal or *'or'* in the answer; for repetitions with an existential quantifier *'some*'* in the answer; for utterance-initial *'or'*; and for the occurrence of scalar

[8] His (mostly unrelated) discussion centres on the semantics and pragmatics of the conditional *'if.'* He remarks in passing that replying *'X or Y or Z'* to *'X or Y'* rejects the latter, although "not as false but as *unassertable*" (his emphasis).

[9] Schlöder and Fernández (2014) report 145 rejections of assertions in Switchboard, and 679 in AMI; as the BNC contains mainly free conversation, rejections are expected to be rare dispreferred acts (Pomerantz, 1984). We also note that Walker (1996) did not report any "implicature rejections" or rejections-of-presupposition from her dataset.

[10] See `http://mmm.idiap.ch/private/ami/annotation/dialogue_acts_manual_1.0.pdf`.

[11] See `http://web.stanford.edu/~jurafsky/ws97/manual.august1.html`.

implicatures by manually selecting scales and searching for the adjacent occurrence of different phrases from the same scale, *e.g.*, *'some – all'* or *'cold – chilly'*. We manually selected pragmatic rejections from the results.

Using this methodology, we collected a total of 59 pragmatic rejections. We categorised 16 of those as rejections-of-implicature, 33 as rejections-by-implicature, 4 as both rejecting *an* implicature and rejecting *by* one, and 6 as rejections-of-presupposition. All examples used in Section 2 are taken from our corpus.[12] While this small corpus is the first collection of pragmatic rejections we are aware of, we note that it is ill-suited for quantitative analysis: On one hand, we cannot be sure that the annotators of the Switchboard and AMI corpora were aware of pragmatic rejection and therefore might have not treated them uniformly—in fact, that we found pragmatic rejections in AMI annotated as NEG and as PART supports this. On the other hand, our manual selection might not be balanced, since we cannot make any claims to have surveyed the corpora, particularly the BNC, exhaustively. In particular, that we did not find any rejections-by-presupposition should not be taken as an indication that the phenomenon does not occur.

5 Computing Rejections-by-Implicature

In this section we focus on the rejections-*by*-implicature. We contend that rejections-of-implicatures and rejections-of-presuppositions can be adequately captured by standard means to compute implicatures and presuppositions. For example in van der Sandt's (1994) model, a rejection can address the whole informational content, including pragmatic enrichment, of its antecedent utterance. However, it is a challenge to formally determine the rejection force of a rejection-by-implicature (Walker, 2012). We present a formal model that accounts for rejections-by-implicature and directly generalises on approaches that stipulate *rejection as inconsistency*. As a proof of concept, we discuss an implementation of our model in a probabilistic framework for simulation.

5.1 Formal Detection

The examples for rejection-by-implicature we found share some common characteristics: they are all informationally redundant, and they are all rejections by virtue of a Quantity implicature (Grice, 1975).[13] The crucial observation is that they are in fact not only informationally redundant, but are *strictly less* informative than their antecedent utterance, if we were to consider both individually. Recall the examples from Section 2, *e.g.*:

(8)	A: [Abbreviations are used] now in narrative and dialogue.	$N \wedge D$
	B: Well, in dialogue it's fine.	D
	$\rightsquigarrow$ *not (necessarily) in narrative*	$\rightsquigarrow \neg N$

Now, the Quantity implicature can be explained by the loss of information: The less informative utterance expresses that the speaker is unwilling to commit to any stronger statement. The rejecting implicature is not cancelled because the rejecting speaker does not ground the prior utterance—does not make it part of her individual representation of common ground—and hence it has no influence on the implicatures in her utterance. This is partially modelled by theories making use of structured contexts, *e.g.*, KoS (Ginzburg, 2012) or PTT (Poesio and Traum, 1997). In such models, an utterance would be marked as pending until grounded (or rejected) by its addressee. However, this raises a complication in how exactly the pending utterances influence implicature computation: For the implicature *'not in narrative'* to arise in example (8) above, A's utterance must be taken into account. Hence the utterance's informational content is available to compute an implicature, but unable to cancel it. Instead of resolving this tension,

[12]The corpus, our classification, as well as the results of our experiment described in Section 6, will be made freely available.

[13]In principle, rejections by Quality or Relation implicatures seem possible: A Quality implicature could arise if someone says something absurd, which our model would consider a rejection by semantic means. A sudden change of topic, flouting the Relation Maxim, might be used as a rejection. However, detecting topic changes is far beyond the scope of our work.

we present an account that sidesteps the problem of cancellation altogether by utilising the informational redundancy of rejections-by-implicature.

An informationally redundant utterance serves *a priori* no discourse function, therefore some additional reasoning is required to uncover the speaker's meaning (Stalnaker, 1978). In particular, an utterance may *appear* to be informationally redundant, but only because the speaker's context has been misconstrued: If we attribute too narrow a context to the utterance, it might just *seem* redundant. Hence we propose the following: If an utterance is informationally redundant, its informational content should be evaluated in the (usually wider) *prior context*, *i.e.*, in the context where the preceding utterance was made. If, then, the utterance turns out to be less informative than its antecedent, it is a pragmatic rejection. We call the enlargement of the context the *pragmatic step*. Note that the pragmatic step itself makes no reference to any implicatures or to the rejection function or the utterance, thereby avoiding the cancellation problem.

We claim that this easily extends current models that adhere to a *rejection as inconsistency* paradigm. As a demonstration, we present the appropriate account in possible world semantics. Let $[\![\cdot]\!].$ stand for the context update function, mapping sets of possible worlds to smaller such sets: $[\![u]\!]_c$ is the information state obtained by uttering u in c. We now describe when utterance u_2 rejects the previous utterance u_1. For brevity, write c_1 for the context in which u_1 is uttered, and $c_2 = [\![u_1]\!]_{c_1}$ for u_2's context. Then we can attempt a definition:

$$u_2 \text{ rejects } u_1 \text{ if } ([\![u_2]\!]_{c_2} = \emptyset) \vee ([\![u_2]\!]_{c_2} = c_2 \wedge [\![u_2]\!]_{c_1} \supsetneq [\![u_1]\!]_{c_1}).$$

That is, u_2 has rejecting force if it is a plain inconsistency (reducing the context to absurdity), or if it is informationally redundant (does not change the context) and is properly less informative than its antecedent (would result in a larger context set if uttered in the same place). If we stipulate that the context update function captures pragmatic enrichment, *i.e.*, computes implicatures and presuppositions, then we capture the other pragmatic rejections by the inconsistency condition.

However, a technicality separates us from the complete solution: The rejecting utterance u_2 might be—and frequently is—non-sentential and/or contain pronominal phrases relating to u_1. That means that it actually cannot be properly interpreted in the prior context: the informational content of u_1 is required after all. Consider for example the following rejection-by-implicature:

(14)	A: Four. Yeah.	$x = 4$
	B: Or three.	$x = 4 \vee x = 3$
	$\rightsquigarrow$ *not (necessarily) four*	$\rightsquigarrow \neg(x = 4)$

Here, B's utterance requires the contextual information of A's previous turn to have the meaning *'four or three.'* To account for this, we need to separate the context into a *context of interpretation* (the discourse context, including everything that has been said) and a *context of evaluation* (the information against which the new proposition is evaluated) and only do the pragmatic step on the evaluative context. Now, our model for rejection in possible world semantics reads as:

$$u_2 \text{ rejects } u_1 \text{ if } ([\![u_2]\!]_{d_2,e_2} = \emptyset) \vee ([\![u_2]\!]_{d_2,e_2} = e_2 \wedge [\![u_2]\!]_{d_2,e_1} \supsetneq [\![u_1]\!]_{d_1,e_1}).$$

Where d_1 and d_2 are the interpretative contexts in which u_1 and u_2 are uttered, respectively, and e_1 and e_2 are the corresponding evaluative contexts. Here, $[\![u]\!]_{d,e}$ maps an utterance u, an interpretative context d and an evaluative context e to an evaluative context: The context obtained by interpreting u in d and updating e with the result.

This is not a new—or particularly surprising—approach to context. Already Stalnaker (1978) proposed a two-dimensional context to discern interpretation from evaluation, though his concern was not mainly with non-sentential utterances, but rather with names and indexicals. Also, the aforementioned theories of dialogue semantics employing structured information states characteristically make use of multi-dimensional representations of context to solve problems of anaphora resolution or the interpretation of non-sentential utterances. Typically, such systems keep track of what is *under discussion* separate from the *joint beliefs* and use the former to facilitate utterance interpretation. This roughly corresponds to our separation of interpretative and evaluative context.

This characterisation of rejection describes all semantic rejections, understood as inconsistencies, and adds the rejections-by-implicature via the pragmatic step. It does not overcommit either: An acceptance, commonly understood, is either more informative than its antecedent (a relevant next contribution), or informationally redundant when mirroring the antecedent utterance,[14] but then not *less* informative in the prior context. This includes the informationally redundant acceptance which puzzled Walker (1996):

(15) A: Sue's house is on Chestnut St.
B: on Chestnut St.

Walker (1996) claims that (15) is informationally redundant and less informative than the antecedent, hence it is expected to be an implicature rejection—but factually is a confirmation. Our model solves the issue: If B's non-sentential utterance is enriched by the interpretative context in the aftermath of A's utterance, it has *exactly* the informational content of its antecedent, and therefore is correctly predicted to be accepting.

5.2 Computational Simulation

The probabilistic programming language Church (Goodman et al., 2008) has been put forward as a suitable framework to model pragmatic reasoning. As a proof of concept, we have implemented our formal model on top of an implementation of Quantity implicatures by Stuhlmüller (2014). The implementation models two classically Gricean interlocutors: Speakers reason about rational listener behaviour and vice versa. Stuhlmüller's (2014) original model simulated scalar implicatures; we adapted his model to capture the *'and'/'or'* implicatures of examples (7) and (8).

The world in our model has two states, p and q, that can each be true or false. The speaker's vocabulary is {`neither`, `p`, `q`, `not-p`, `not-q`, `p-or-q`, `p-and-q`}. The listener guesses the state of the world as follows: Given a message, the listener reasons by guessing a rational speaker's behaviour given a rational listener; 'guessing' is done via sampling functions built into the programming language. For example, the message `p-and-q` unambiguously communicates that $p \wedge q$, because no rational listener would conclude from `p-and-q` that $\neg p$ or $\neg q$. On the other hand, `p-or-q` is taken to communicate $p \wedge \neg q$ and $\neg p \wedge q$ in about 40% of samples each and $p \wedge q$ in about 20% of samples, since all three states are consistent with the message, but a rational speaker would rather choose `p-and-q` in $p \wedge q$ because it is unambiguous.

Message	Response	Rejection
`p`	`not-p`	100%
`p-and-q`	`not-p`	100%
`p`	`p`	0%
`p-or-q`	`p-and-q`	0%
`p-or-q`	`p`	0%
`p`	`p-and-q`	0%
`p-and-q`	`p-or-q`	**78%**
`p-and-q`	`p`	**65%**
`p`	`p-or-q`	**64%**
`p`	`q`	59%

Table 1: Probabilities (1000 samples) that a pragmatically reasoning speaker would recognise a rejection.

The message `p` induces the belief that $p \wedge \neg q$ in roughly 65% of samples, and $p \wedge q$ in the remaining 35%. Again this is due to the fact that $p \wedge \neg q$ is indeed best communicated by `p`, whereas $p \wedge q$ is better communicated by `p-and-q`—the listener cannot exclude that q holds but thinks it less likely than $\neg q$ because different speaker behaviour would be expected if q were true.

For the implementation of rejection-by-implicature, we proceed as follows: Given a proposal and a response, obtain a belief by sampling a state of the world consistent with rational listener behaviour when interpreting the *response*: this is evaluating the response in the prior context, *i.e.*, computing what would happen if the speaker would utter the response instead of the proposal. Then check if this belief could have also been communicated by the proposal; if *not*, then the response is less informative (because it is consistent with more beliefs) than the proposal, and the model judges the response as rejecting. In each sample, the model makes a binary choice on whether it judges the response as rejecting or accepting.

We report some test runs of the simulation in Table 1, where for each proposal–response pair we computed 1000 samples. We observe that semantic rejections (*i.e.*, inconsistencies) are assigned rejection

[14] Either by repeating a fragment of the antecedent, or by a particle like *'yes,'* which is understood to pick up the antecedent.

In the following dialogues, speaker A makes a statement and speaker B reacts to it, but rather than simply agreeing or disagreeing by saying Yes/No, B responds with something more indirect and complicated. For instance:

A: It looks like a rabbit.
B: I think it's like a cat.

Please indicate which of the following options best captures what speaker B meant in each case:

- B definitely meant to agree with A's statement.
- B probably meant to agree with A's statement.
- B definitely meant to disagree with A's statement.
- B probably meant to disagree with A's statement.

In the sample dialogue above the right answer would be "B definitely meant to disagree with A's statement."

Cautionary note: in general, there is no unique right answer. However, a few of our dialogues do have obvious right answers, which we have inserted to help ensure that we approve only careful work.

Figure 1: CrowdFlower prompt with instructions, adapted from Potts (2011).

force with 100% confidence, and utterances intuitively constituting acceptances are never considered rejections. Some of the acceptances might be rejections-of-implicatures (being strictly more informative than the message they are replying to), but since our model does not pragmatically enrich the message, these are not found. In fact, it is not clear to us when, without further context or markers, replying `p` (or `p-and-q`) to `p-or-q` is an acceptance-by-elaboration or a rejection-of-implicature:[15], are required to make the distinction; this also fits our experimental results below. An implicature like `p-or-q` $\rightsquigarrow \neg p$ needs to be computed elsewhere if at all.

Implicature rejections are not assigned 100% rejection force due to the probabilistic model for pragmatic reasoning. Since, per the model, the utterance `p-or-q` induces the belief that $p \wedge q$ in at least some samples, the listeners cannot always recognize that `p-or-q` is an implicature rejection of `p-and-q`. In fact, the confidence that something is an implicature rejection scales with how well—how often—the implicature itself is recognized. Replying `q` to `p` is computed to be a rejection, because in the model `q` implicates that $\neg p$, as every utterance is taken to be about the state of both p and q.[16] In fact, replying `q` to `p` is also a rejection-*of*-implicature, as `p` also implicates $\neg q$. However, as pointed out above, our model does not capture this.

6 Annotation Experiment

In order to investigate the perceived rejection force of pragmatic rejections, we conducted an online annotation experiment using the corpus described in Section 4.

6.1 Setup

We adapted and closely followed the experimental setup of Potts (2011). The annotators were asked to rank the dialogues in our corpus on a 4-point scale: *'definitely agree'*, *'probably agree'*, *'probably disagree'* and *'definitely disagree'*. The instructions given to the participants, recruited on the crowdsourcing platform CrowdFlower,[17] are recorded in Figure 1. Like Potts (2011), we curated our corpus for the purposes of the annotation experiment by removing disfluencies and agrammaticalities to ensure that the participants were not distracted by parsing problems, as well as any polarity particles (including *'yeah'* and *'no'*) in the response utterance.

To ensure the quality of the annotation, we included some agreements and semantic disagreements as control items in the task.[18] Participants who ranked a control agreement as disagreeing or vice versa were excluded from the study. Some control items were chosen to require a certain amount of competence

[15]We hypothesise that more subtle cues, particularly intonation and focus

[16]Due to this closed world assumption, we cannot say that this is a Relevance implicature.

[17]`http://www.crowdflower.com`

[18]Drawn from the AMI Corpus from items annotated as `Positive Assessment` and `Negative Assessment` respectively.

Rejection-	by-implicature					of-implicature			both	of-presupp.	**Total**
	or	*and*	*generalise*	*restrict*	*scalar*	*or*	*generalise*	*scalar*			
Raw number	12	5	2	3	11	1	8	7	4	6	59
Judged disagreeing	58%	17%	0%	26%	51%	21%	61%	42%	40%	68%	47%
Std. deviation	0.31	0.22	0	0.10	0.38	–	0.30	0.35	0.34	0.37	0.34

Table 2: Average percentage of *'probably/definitely disagreeing'* judgements by category.

in discerning agreement from disagreement. For example, (16) is an agreement despite the negative polarity particle *'no'* appearing, and (17) is an agreement move that requires an inference step with some substantial linguistic knowledge; (18) is an example for clear-cut agreement.

(16) A: I think wood is not an option either.
B: No, wood's not an option.

(17) A: We can't fail.
B: We fitted all the criterias.

(18) A: It's a giraffe.
B: A giraffe okay.

We added 20 control agreements and 10 control disagreements to our corpus of pragmatic rejections, and presented each participant 9 dialogues at a time: 6 pragmatic rejections and 3 control items. Thereby we constructed 10 sets of dialogues, each of which was presented to 30 different participants. We filtered out participants who failed any of our control items from the results. The amount of filtered judgements was as high as 33% on some items. Polarity reversals like (16) were particularly effective in filtering out careless participants: Failure to recognise a polarity reversal shows a lack of contextual awareness, which is vital to judge pragmatic rejections.

6.2 Results and Discussion

For each item, we computed the percentage of participants who judged it as having rejecting force, *i.e.*, as either *'probably disagree'* or *'definitely disagree'*; see Table 2 for an overview of the results by category. To better understand our results, we classified the rejections-by/of-implicatures further by the implicature that gives rise to the rejection. We found the following sub-types in our dataset:

Rejections by means of an implicature:

- *or*-implicature as in (7): *'A: Maybe three days.' – 'B: Three or four days.'*
- *and*-implicature as in (8): *'A: ... in narrative and dialogue.' – 'B: Well, in dialogue.'*
- *generalising* implicature as in (6): *'A: ... your steak's burning.' – 'B: Well, something's burning.'*
- *restricting* implicature as in (5): *'A: We're all mad.' – 'B: Some of us.'*[19]
- *scalar* implicature as in (3): *'A: That's brilliant.' – 'B: [it] was quite good.'*

Rejections of an implicature:

- *or*-implicature as in (10): *'A: Three or four days.' – 'B: Well, four.'*
- *generalising* implicature as in (12): *'A: You like country' – 'B: But not all country.'*
- *scalar* implicature as in (4): *'A: It was good weren't it?' – 'B: It's brilliant.'*

Overall, about half of all judgements we collected deemed an item to have rejection force. These judgements were again split roughly 50-50 into *'probably disagree'* and *'definitely disagree.'* When a judgement did not indicate rejection force, *'probably agree'* was the preferred category, chosen in 78% of *'agree'* judgements. However, we saw substantial variation in the judgements when categorising the pragmatic rejections as above.[20]

Most notably, the two rejections by generalising implicature were never judged to have rejection force. Our hypothesis is that this is due to the fact that the surface form of these implicatures repeats some central phrase from their antecedent, and they are therefore taken to agree *partially*, which leads

[19]While this example could technically be considered a scalar implicature, we take *all-some* to be a special case of removing information; one can also restrict by adding adjectives to disagree with a universal statement, as in (13): *'A: You love [all] soap.' – 'B: I love lovely soaps.'*

[20]In contrast, we could not find any relation between our experimental results and previous annotations of the utterances in our corpus (if they were previously annotated, *i.e.*, taken from the AMI or Switchboard corpora).

them to be judged as *'probably agree.'* For example, in the rejection by a generalising implicature (6), the interlocutors are apparently considered to agree on 'something *burning*.' The same observation holds for rejections by *and*-implicature, *e.g.*, in (8) the interlocutors might be judged to agree on the 'usage *in dialogue*.' In contrast, rejections by *or*-implicature and by scalar implicature stand out as being judged disagreeing more often: 58% and 51%, respectively. In our corpus, the surface form of such implicatures does not typically involve the repetition of a phrase from their antecedent. As a case in point, the rejection by *or*-implicature (14) *'A: Four. Yeah.'* – *'B: Or three.'* was judged to have rejection force much more frequently (86%) than the similar (7) *'A: Maybe three days.'* – *'B: Three or four days.'* (40%) where B repeats part of A's proposal.[21] We think that other linguistic cues from the utterances' surface forms, as well as the information structure the subjects read off the written dialogue, also had an influence on the perceived force of the responses. In particular, we attribute the high percentage of judged disagreements in the rejections of generalising implicatures (61%) to them being typically marked with the contrast particle *'but'*—a well known cue for disagreement (Galley et al., 2004; Misra and Walker, 2013)

The rejections-of-presuppositions received the overall largest amount of rejection force judgements (68%). This is in accordance with previous work that has treated them in largely the same way as typical explicit rejections (Horn, 1989; van der Sandt, 1994; Walker, 1996). In particular, all rejections-of-presuppositions in our corpus correspond to utterances annotated as `Negative Assessment` in the AMI Corpus. That even these utterances received a substantial amount of *'probably agree'* judgements puts the overall results into context: The subjects show a noticeable tendency to choose this category.

The experimental results in Table 2 should not be compared quantitatively with the simulation outcome in Table 1, Section 5.2. The judgement scale in the experiment is in no direct relation with the probabilistic reasoning in the simulation. Qualitatively speaking, however, the experiment shows a difference in how rejections by *or*- and *and*-implicatures are perceived, whereas the simulation yields nigh-identical results for these two. This could be due to linguistic cues simply not present in the simulation, and due to participants in the experiment choosing *'probably agree'* when they perceived *partial* agreement in a dialogue. In contrast to such 'partial' judgements, our formal model considers agreement/disagreement as a binary distinction and infers full disagreement from slight divergences in informational content. We conclude from the experiment that this binary assumption should be given up, also in the probabilistic implementation, where the probabilities represent uncertainty about the world rather than the kind of partial agreement/disagreement that seems to be behind our experimental results.

7 Conclusion and Further Work

We have laid out the phenomenon of pragmatic rejection, given it a general definition, and assembled a small corpus of such rejections. While we cannot give a full formal treatment of pragmatic rejection here, our formal model improves over extant work by capturing rejections-by-implicature. A simulation of the model has shown that it yields theoretically desirable results for agreements and semantic disagreements and predicts rejection force of rejections-by-implicature. Compared to our annotation experiment, however, the model lacks sophistication in computing what is apparently perceived as partial agreement/disagreement. The pragmatic rejections we collected were judged to have rejection force only about half of the time, and otherwise our subjects showed a preference for the category *'probably agree.'* We tentatively attribute this to linguistic cues, related to the surface form of some pragmatic rejections, which led the annotators to consider them partial agreements. We leave a deeper investigation into these cues, including intonation and focus, to further work

In sum, while our model accounts for more data than previous approaches, we conclude that a more sophisticated model for rejection should give up the agree/disagree binary and account for utterances that fall inbetween; the data and analysis we presented here should be helpful to guide the development of such a model. Computing partial rejection force, particularly *which part* of an antecedent has been accepted or rejected, is part of our ongoing work.

[21]The hedging *'maybe'* in A's utterance might also had an influence: Taking *'maybe'* as a modal operator, A is saying $\Diamond d = 3$ which is not in contradiction with B's implicature *'possibly not three,'*, *i.e.*, $\Diamond d \neq 3$.

References

Burnard, L. (2000). *Reference Guide for the British National Corpus (World Edition)*. Oxford University Computing Services.

Carletta, J. (2007). Unleashing the killer corpus: experiences in creating the multi-everything AMI Meeting Corpus. *Language Resources and Evaluation 41*(2), 181–190.

Clark, H. H. (1996). *Using language*. Cambridge University Press.

Galley, M., K. McKeown, J. Hirschberg, and E. Shriberg (2004). Identifying agreement and disagreement in conversational speech: Use of Bayesian networks to model pragmatic dependencies. In *Proceedings of ACL'04*.

Germesin, S. and T. Wilson (2009). Agreement detection in multiparty conversation. In *Proceedings of the 2009 international conference on Multimodal interfaces*.

Ginzburg, J. (2012). *The Interactive Stance*. Oxford University Press.

Godfrey, J. J., E. C. Holliman, and J. McDaniel (1992). SWITCHBOARD: Telephone Speech Corpus for Research and Development. In *Proceedings of ICASSP'92*.

Goodman, N. D., V. K. Mansinghka, D. M. Roy, K. Bonawitz, and J. B. Tenenbaum (2008). Church: a language for generative models. In *Proceedings of Uncertainty in Artificial Intelligence*.

Grice, H. P. (1975). Logic and conversation. In *Syntax and Semantics,* Vol. 3, pp. 41–58. Acad. Press.

Grice, H. P. (1991). *Studies in the Way of Words*. Harvard University Press.

Hahn, S., R. Ladner, and M. Ostendorf (2006). Agreement/disagreement classification: Exploiting unlabeled data using contrast classifiers. In *Proceedings of HLT-NAACL 2006*.

Hillard, D., M. Ostendorf, and E. Shriberg (2003). Detection of agreement vs. disagreement in meetings: training with unlabeled data. In *Proceedings of HLT-NAACL 2003*.

Horn, L. R. (1989). *A Natural History of Negation*. University of Chicago Press.

Lascarides, A. and N. Asher (2009). Agreement, disputes and commitments in dialogue. *Journal of Semantics 26*(2), 109–158.

de Marneffe, M.-C., S. Grimm, and C. Potts (2009). Not a simple yes or no: Uncertainty in indirect answers. In *Proceedings of the SIGDIAL 2009 Conference*.

Misra, A. and M. Walker (2013). Topic independent identification of agreement and disagreement in social media dialogue. In *Proceedings of the SIGdial 2013 Conference*.

Poesio, M. and D. Traum (1997). Conversational actions and discourse situations. *Computational Intelligence 13*(3), 309–347.

Pomerantz, A. (1984). Agreeing and disagreeing with assessments: Some features of preferred/dispreferred turn shapes. In *Structures of Social Action*. Cambridge University Press.

Potts, C. (2011). The indirect question-answer pair corpus. `http://compprag.christopherpotts.net/iqap.html`. Accessed: 2014-11-24.

Purver, M. (2001). SCoRE: A tool for searching the BNC. Technical Report TR-01-07, Department of Computer Science, King's College London.

van der Sandt, R. A. (1994). Denial and negation. *Unpublished manuscript, University of Nijmegen*.

Schlöder, J. J. and R. Fernández (2014). The role of polarity in inferring acceptance and rejection in dialogue. In *Proceedings of the SIGdial 2014 Conference*.

Stalnaker, R. (1978). Assertion. In *Syntax and Semantics,* Vol. 9, pp. 315–332. Academic Press.

Stuhlmüller, A. (2014). Scalar Implicature. `http://forestdb.org/models/scalar-implicature.html`. Accessed: 2014-11-24.

Walker, M. A. (1996). Inferring acceptance and rejection in dialogue by default rules of inference. *Language and Speech 39*(2-3), 265–304.

Walker, M. A. (2012). Rejection by implicature. In *Proceedings of the Annual Meeting of the Berkeley Linguistics Society*.

Yin, J., P. Thomas, N. Narang, and C. Paris (2012). Unifying Local and Global Agreement and Disagreement Classification in Online Debates. In *Proceedings of the 3rd Workshop in Computational Approaches to Subjectivity and Sentiment Analysis*.

Feedback in Conversation as Incremental Semantic Update*

Arash Eshghi
Heriot-Watt University
a.eshghi@hw.ac.uk

Christine Howes
University of Gothenburg
christine.howes@gu.se

Eleni Gregoromichelaki
King's College London
eleni.gregor@kcl.ac.uk

Julian Hough
Bielefeld University
julian.hough@uni-bielefeld.de

Matthew Purver
Queen Mary University of London
mpurver@qmul.ac.uk

Abstract

In conversation, interlocutors routinely indicate whether something said or done has been processed and integrated. Such feedback includes *backchannels* such as 'okay' or 'mhm', the production of a next relevant turn, and repair initiation via *clarification requests*. Importantly, such feedback can be produced not only at sentence/turn boundaries, but also sub-sententially. In this paper, we extend an existing model of incremental semantic processing in dialogue, based around the Dynamic Syntax (DS) grammar framework, to provide a low-level, integrated account of backchannels, clarification requests and their responses; demonstrating that they can be accounted for as part of the core semantic structure-building mechanisms of the grammar, rather than via higher level pragmatic phenomena such as intention recognition, or treatment as an "unofficial" part of the conversation. The end result is an incremental model in which words, not turns, are seen as procedures for contextual update and backchannels serve to align participant semantic processing contexts and thus ease the production and interpretation of subsequent conversational actions. We also show how clarification requests and their following responses and repair can be modelled within the same DS framework, wherein the divergence and re-alignment effort in participants' semantic processing drives conversations forward.

1 Introduction

In conversation, interlocutors provide frequent feedback about whether something said can be taken as understood. For Clark (1996), a crucial point of advancing the joint project of dialogue is establishing that we are sufficiently coordinated to continue, a process called "grounding", which uses, for example, backchannel responses (such as 'mm', example 1:2127, or 'yeah') and non-linguistic cues (e.g. nods and smiles).[1] Alternative responses indicate processing difficulties or lack of coordination and signal a need for clarification or repair (example 1:2112).

Clark and Schaefer (1989) present a model of *contributions* in dialogue that consist of both a *presentation* and an *acceptance* phase. In the acceptance phase, listeners can display evidence of understanding at various levels, from continued attention to verbatim repetition, with backchannels being one possible type (see also Allwood et al., 1992). The acceptance phase can also be used to clear up sources of misunderstanding, as with clarification requests. Traum (1994) develops a formal model of grounding in which *grounding acts* at the level of individual utterances build up *discourse units*, at which level core speech acts are realised through being grounded. More recently, Ginzburg (2012) provides a substantial dialogue model based on embedding the grammar under an utterance processing protocol, modelling updates of interlocutors' information states. Grounding or clarification processes rely on a notion of

*We would like to thank Ruth Kempson and the anonymous IWCS reviewers for their comments. Eshghi is supported by the EPSRC BABBLE project (grant number EP/M01553X/1) and Hough by the DUEL project funded by the ANR (grant number ANR-13-FRAL-0001) and the DFG (grant number SCHL 845/5-1). We thank them for their financial support. Purver is partially supported by ConCreTe: the project ConCreTe acknowledges the financial support of the Future and Emerging Technologies (FET) programme within the Seventh Framework Programme for Research of the European Commission, under FET grant number 611733.

[1]We focus on verbal feedback here; however, we believe that the analysis also applies to non-verbal feedback e.g. nodding.

Proceedings of the 11th International Conference on Computational Semantics, pages 261–271,
London, UK, April 15-17 2015.

"locutionary proposition", a linguistic sign, specified with an appropriate illocutionary force through the grammar. Such propositions become the elements manipulated during the grounding process, resulting in either acceptance in the common ground or the generation of clarification. Elements providing feedback or repair are assigned lexical entries or construction types that presuppose the derivation of such propositions in the context.

However, importantly, such feedback can be produced sub-sententially and during an ongoing turn (as with the backchannels in (1) lines 2127 and 2129), illustrating the crucially incremental nature of coordination in human interaction, without the need to invoke propositional contents at all stages.

(1) Example dialogue from the British National Corpus (BNC) KPU[2]

Gearoid	2111	We went to see something called the Wedding Banquet.
Anne-Marie	2112	Called the Wedding [Banquet]?
Gearoid	2113	[Banquet].
Anne-Marie	2114	Really?
⋮	⋮	
Gearoid	2126	It's about these two chaps living in New York ⟨pause⟩ one is American and the other is er ⟨pause⟩ Hong Kong, no Chinese ⟨pause⟩ and they're an affair, they're [living]
Anne-Marie	2127	[Mm].
Gearoid	2128	together, very [sort of]
Anne-Marie	2129	[Mm].
Gearoid	2130	you know, kind, one is an architect and the other ⟨pause⟩ the Chinese guy is a property dealer.

Moreover, in most dialogue models, grounding or clarification generation introduce a speaker/hearer asymmetry in their representations in that speakers are assumed to be omniscient regarding their own utterances (which seems to preclude backchannels/clarifications addressed to self), as a result of complete, clear plans/intentions guiding their production (e.g. Poesio and Rieser, 2010). However, the joint nature of dialogue actions becomes evident in the fact that, besides listenership, turn-managing, understanding, and acceptance backchannel feedback and its elicitation, like any mechanism in interaction, have perlocutionary effects in conversation, post-hoc characterisable both as "intended" and "unintended" (2):

(2)

A: John...uh... yes, John, yeah?
B: mhm, mhm
A: he went to the party yest....
B: yeah, yes, ok.
A: He saw your sister with.
B: yes, yes.
A: W ? I'll tell the story at my own pace.

Similarly, repetitions of phrases/sentences in dialogue serve various feedback functions (both for self and other) besides clarification. These range from surprise or disbelief indicators to delaying functions, and, like backchannels, their content cannot always be explicated as a full propositional intention without some loss of the impression or effect shared in context (example 3).

(3)

A:	1	Nirma was at the party.
A:	2a	Nirma! / Nirma? / Who? (Why Nirma? / Sorry, I meant Irma.)
B:	2b	Nirma eh? I knew it.
B:	2c	Nirma! Oh how nice.
B:	2d	Nirma... Wait, I know this name.
B:	2e	Nirma, Nirma, I see.

[2] Overlapping talk is shown in aligned square brackets.

Models of grounding have been recently explored in practical dialogue systems. However, these systems either explore the positioning of backchannels based on low-level features (e.g. Cathcart et al., 2003; Gravano and Hirschberg, 2009); or rely on a notion of feedback that incorporates reasoning about the intentions, mental states or goals of one's interlocutor (e.g. Visser et al., 2014; Buschmeier and Kopp, 2013; Wang et al., 2011). The former type of system may allow a dialogue model to sound 'more human', but do not give any insight into why feedback occurs where it does; and, in the latter, full intention recognition requires a level of complexity that corpus studies on repair (Purver et al., 2003; Colman and Healey, 2011), backchannels (Kjellmer, 2009), and conversational analysis of multiparty dialogue (Goodwin, 1979; Koschmann and LeBaron, 2003) suggest are unnecessary as a prerequisite in natural conversation. In contrast, under the view pioneered by Ginzburg (2012) and Poesio and Rieser (2010), all such phenomena require an account that integrates their linguistic features with their functions in dialogue because of various form-content constraints. However, even if this is the general perspective assumed here, examples (1)-(3) show that the grammar needs to be able to provide an account of such feedback and repair mechanisms that remains flexible enough to be put to various situated uses without requiring specific propositional contents to be derived for single words or phrases. This is a significant requirement given that both the content (Clark, 1996) and the scope of a feedback contribution is highly underspecified (as also pointed out by an anonymous IWCS reviewer), rather than determinable through use of fixed constructions. Moreover, backchannels and clarification requests, like anaphora and ellipsis antecedents, can be provided through actions employing various modalities, like eye-gaze, posture, head movement and bodily gestures (Goodwin, 1986). For this reason the grammar model needs to be able to integrate input from various sources without rules that confine such input to linguistic signs (cf Ginzburg (2012) whose locutionary propositions preclude such unification).

In this paper we first outline the formal model of Dynamic Syntax with Type Theory with Records (DS-TTR); we then present an extension to the model and show how it can provide a low-level, semantic model of feedback phenomena, in particular backchannels and clarification interaction, without recourse to dialogue moves/acts or reasoning about intentions. The model is illustrated using variations on example (4).

(4) Example dialogue from BNC KPY

A	1006	Er, the doctor
B	1007	Chorlton?
A	1008	Chorlton, mhm, he examined me, erm, he, he said now they were on about a slide ⟨unclear⟩ on my heart.

2 Dynamic Syntax and Type Theory with Records (DS-TTR)

Dynamic Syntax is an action-based grammar formalism, which models the word-by-word incremental processing of linguistic input. Unlike many other formalisms, DS models the incremental linear construction of *interpretations* without recognising an independent level of syntactic representation. Thus, the output for any given string of words is a purely *semantic* tree representing its predicate-argument structure; tree nodes correspond to terms in the lambda calculus, decorated with labels expressing their semantic type (e.g. $Ty(e)$) and logical formulae as record types of the Type Theory with Records framework (TTR, see below); beta-reduction determines the type and formula at a mother node from those at its daughters (Figure 1).

These trees can be *partial*, containing unsatisfied *requirements* potentially for any element, for example, node labels (e.g. $?Ty(e)$, a requirement for future development to $Ty(e)$), and contain a *pointer*, $\diamond$, labelling the node currently under development. Grammaticality is defined as processability in a context: the successful incremental word-by-word construction of a tree with no outstanding requirements (a *complete* tree) using all information given by the words in a string.[3]

[3]In this paper, we exclude all considerations of tense/aspect for simplicity. But see Cann (2011).

2.1 Actions in DS

The parsing process is defined in terms of conditional *actions*: procedural specifications for monotonic tree/string development. These can be either general structure-building principles (*computational actions*) or language-specific actions induced by parsing particular lexical items (*lexical actions*).

Computational actions These form a small, fixed set of IF..THEN..ELSE action specifications. Some merely encode the properties of the lambda calculus and the logical tree formalism (LoFT, Blackburn and Meyer-Viol, 1994): e.g. T (removal of satisfied requirements), C (moving the pointer up and out of a lower sub-tree once all requirements therein are satisfied, see Figure 1), and E - (beta-reduction of daughter nodes at the mother). Others reflect the fundamental predictivity and dynamics of DS: *A introduces a single unfixed node with underspecified tree position (replacing feature-passing concepts for phenomena like long-distance dependency); L -A builds a paired ("linked") tree corresponding to semantic conjunction (licensing relative clauses, apposition and more). These actions represent possible processing strategies, applying optionally at any stage of a parse if their preconditions are met.

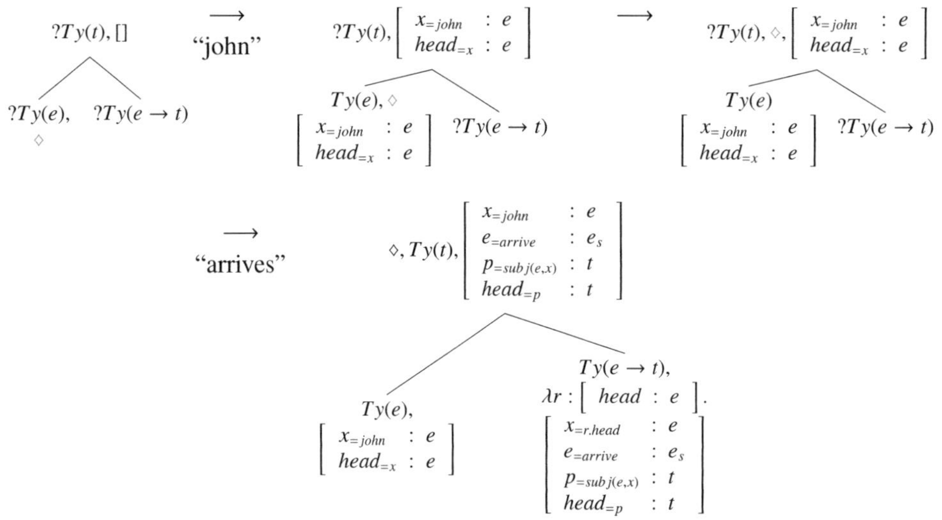

Figure 1: Incremental parsing in DS-TTR: *"John arrives"*

Lexical actions The lexicon associates word forms with lexical actions; like computational actions, these are also sequences of tree-update actions in an IF..THEN..ELSE format, composed of *atomic* tree-building actions such as `make`, `go`, `put`. `make` creates a new daughter node, `go` moves the pointer, and `put` decorates the pointed node with a label. Figure 2 shows an example for a proper noun, *John*. The action checks whether the pointed node (marked as $\diamond$) has a requirement for type *e*; if so, it decorates it with type *e* (thus satisfying the requirement), formula *John′* and the bottom restriction $\langle\downarrow\rangle\bot$ (meaning that the node cannot have any daughters). Otherwise (if no requirement $?Ty(e)$), the action aborts, meaning that the word *'John'* cannot be parsed in the context of the current tree.

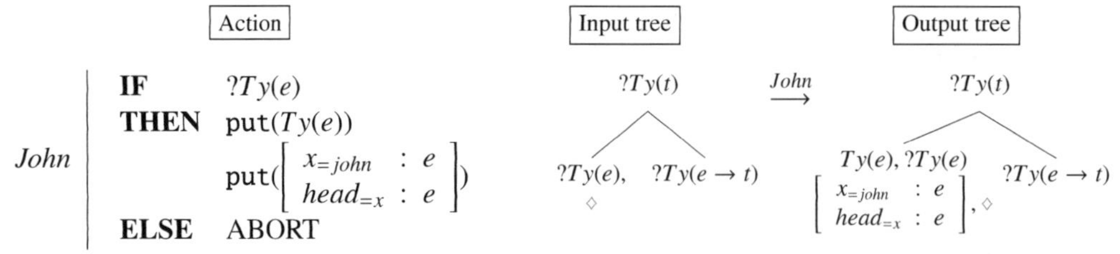

Figure 2: Lexical action for the word 'John'

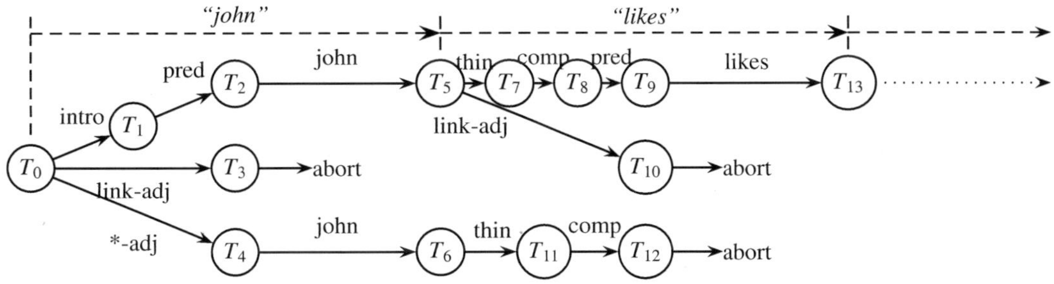

Figure 3: DS parsing as a graph: actions (edges) are transitions between partial trees (nodes).

2.2 Type Theory with Records

Type Theory with Records (TTR) is an extension of standard type theory shown useful in semantics and dialogue modelling (Cooper, 2005; Ginzburg, 2012). For us here, it provides the logical formalism in which meanings are expressed (Purver et al., 2011; Hough and Purver, 2012; Eshghi et al., 2012). Given its fine-grained, structured representations (see below), it has also been used to encode the linguistic, and non-linguistic context of an utterance (Purver et al., 2010; Dobnik et al., 2012). This is important for us here since such an integration provides for non-linguistic elicitations and provisions of feedback.

In TTR, logical forms are specified as *record types* (RTs), sequences of *fields* of the form $[\, l : T \,]$ containing a label l and a type T. RTs can be witnessed (i.e. judged true) by *records* of that type, where a record is a sequence of label-value pairs $[\, l = v \,]$. $[\, l = v \,]$ is of type $[\, l : T \,]$ just in case v is of type T.

Fields can be *manifest*, i.e. given a singleton type e.g. $[\, l : T_a \,]$ where T_a is the type of which only a is a member; here, we write this using the syntactic sugar $[\, l_{=a} : T \,]$. Fields can also be *dependent* on fields preceding them (i.e. higher) in the record type – e.g. in $\begin{bmatrix} l_1 & : T_1 \\ l_{2=a} & : T_2 \\ l_{3=p(l_2)} & : T_3 \end{bmatrix}$. Importantly for us here, the standard subtype relation $\sqsubseteq$ can be defined for record types: $R_1 \sqsubseteq R_2$ if for all fields $[\, l : T_2 \,]$ in R_2, R_1 contains $[\, l : T_1 \,]$ where $T_1 \sqsubseteq T_2$.

Following Purver et al. (2011), we assume that DS tree nodes are decorated with RTs, and corresponding lambda abstracts representing functions from RT to RT (e.g. $\lambda r{:}\, [\, l_1 : T_1 \,].[\, l_{2=r.l_1} : T_1 \,]$ where $r.l_1$ is a *path* expression referring to the label l_1 in r) – see Figure 1. TTR's subtype relation allows a record type at the root node to be inferred for any partial tree, and incrementally further specified via subtyping as parsing proceeds (Hough and Purver, 2012).

2.3 Graph-based Parsing & Generation

In parsing, given a sequence of words $(w_1, w_2, ..., w_n)$, the parser starts from the *axiom* tree T_0 (a requirement to construct a complete propositional tree, $?Ty(t)$), and applies the corresponding lexical actions $(a_1, a_2, \ldots, a_n)$, optionally interspersing computational actions. This can be modelled as a directed acyclic graph (DAG) rooted at T_0, with partial trees as nodes, and computational and lexical actions as edges (i.e. transitions between trees) (Sato, 2011). Figure 3 shows an example: here, *intro*, *pred* and **adj* correspond to the computational actions I , P and *-A respectively; and 'john' is a lexical action. Different DAG paths represent different parsing strategies, which may succeed or fail depending on how the utterance is continued. Here, the path $T_0 - T_5$ will succeed if *'John'* is the subject of an upcoming verb ("John upset Mary"); $T_0 - T_6$ will succeed if *'John'* turns out to be a left-dislocated object ("John, Mary upset").

This incrementally constructed DAG makes up the entire *parse state* at any point. The rightmost nodes (i.e. partial trees) make up the current maximal semantic information; these nodes with their paths back to the root (tree-transition actions) make up the *linguistic context* for ellipsis and pronominal construal (Purver et al., 2011).

This fine-grained DAG can also be seen as subsumed by a coarser-grained DAG at the word level; at this level, edges represent words, with nodes representing sets of (partial) trees, which are the right-most nodes in the more fine-grained parse state DAG after processing that word. For Figure 3, this level would consist of two edges: one for *"john"* connecting a node $\{T_0\}$ to a node $\{T_5, T_6\}$; and one for *"likes"* connecting that node $\{T_5, T_6\}$ to a node $\{T_{13}\}$. This higher-level representation obscures grammatical parsing details, but is more compatible with speech recogniser input and dialogue manager output in a practical system. In our explanations below, we will use this coarser-grained representation.

3 A semantic model of feedback

The extension to DS-TTR we make here is to represent the state of multiple dialogue participants as they jointly construct and negotiate meaning in dialogue by providing different forms of feedback. To model grounding states, we make use of the parser/generation context DAG (see Figure 3) for a given dialogue participant, augmented with two coordination pointers (different to the tree pointer mentioned above): one pointer, dubbed the *self-pointer*, ♦, indicates the node in the DAG which that dialogue participant has provided evidence for reaching (by producing any contributing output, including backchannelling, answering a question, extending another participant's utterance, or repair initiation). The operation of this pointer can also be regarded as a self-monitoring device, which can trigger self-addressed backchannels and repairs. The second coordination pointer, which we term the *other-pointer*, ◇, indicates the node in the DAG which one's interlocutor(s) have provided evidence for reaching.

This allows us to model feedback in the form of backchannels, CRs, continuations and answers to questions, or indeed any local use of context-dependency. Table 1 shows some of the forms this feedback might take. The model is defined within the incremental process of joint semantic construction, without recourse to higher-level pragmatic reasoning, dialogue acts, or intention recognition.

On this account, if the two coordination pointers are on the same DAG node, any (sub-)utterance on the DAG path from this doubly pointed node back to the root can be taken to be grounded. More generally, the intersection of the ♦ $\rightarrow$ root path and ◇ $\rightarrow$ root path is grounded; the remaining ◇ $\rightarrow$ root path is as yet ungrounded; and other paths are *repaired* (see below). Divergence of the two pointers represents the source for forward momentum in dialogue: something must be done by either of the parties in order to align these pointers. This is conceptually analogous to Matheson et al. (2000)'s notion of *obligation* or Ginzburg (2012)'s *discursive potential*, but operates without recourse to dialogue acts such as acceptance, or rejection. As will become clear below, linguistic signs of rejection here do not necessarily correspond to denying, or discussing a proposition, but instead indicate abandonment of a DAG branch. Under this general view, linguistic elements can unproblematically operate sub-propositionally, for instance, establishing a referent before the proposition involving that referent is complete.

	Local			Non-Local		
Confirmed	(a)	A: B: A:	The doctor Chorlton? Chorlton, mhm, he examined me	(b)	A: B: A:	The doctor examined me Chorlton? Chorlton, mhm, he examined me
Repaired	(c)	A: B: A: B:	The doctor Chorlton? no, Fitzgerald uh-huh	(d)	A: B: A: B:	The doctor examined me Chorlton? no, Fitzgerald uh-huh

Table 1: Local & Non-Local Clarification Interaction

3.1 Backchannels

Backchannels as DAG pointer movement As shown in Figure 4, producing any utterance has the effect of moving one's self-pointer ♦ along the DAG; parsing something someone else says moves one's other-pointer ◇. As one person speaks and the other listens, the two pointers diverge in position; the intervening material is ungrounded (see Poesio and Traum (1997)'s *ungrounded discourse units*). An analysis of backchannels as signs associated with null parsing actions (actions which contribute no new

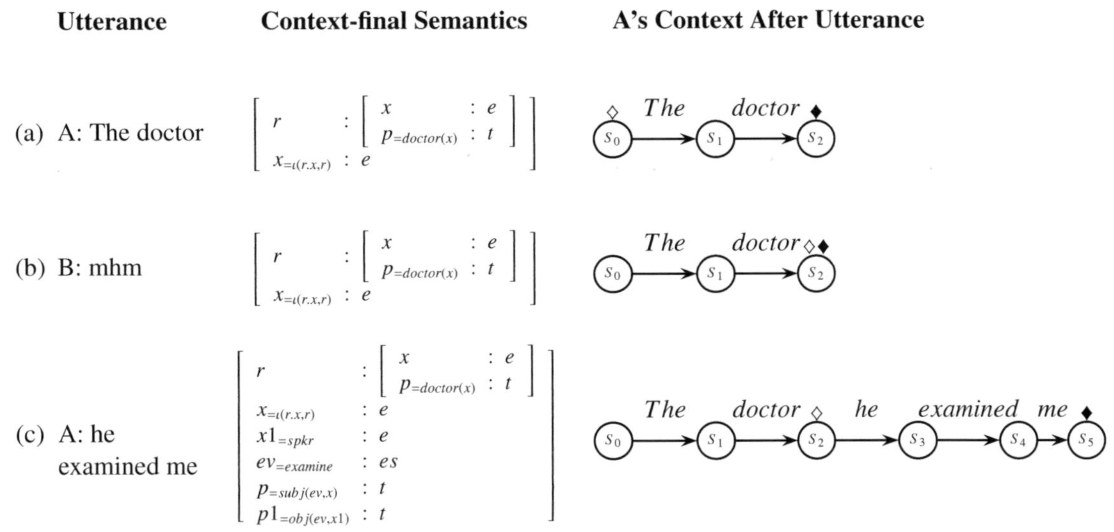

Figure 4: Backchannels as movement of context DAG coordination pointers. From A's perspective.

semantic information to the partial DS tree under construction) would therefore provide a minimal account: parsing such a trivial action produced by an interlocutor after producing some output will move the other-pointer to catch up with the self-pointer; generating such an action after hearing an interlocutor's input will move the self-pointer to catch up with the other-pointer (see Figure 4(a-b)). Backchannels can therefore be seen as minimal utterances to carry out this pointer convergence; they act as grounding signals by ensuring that both pointers are at the same node in the DAG.

Backchannels as semantic compilation Such a simple account, however, fails to capture the distribution of backchannels: it would predict that they should be equally likely at any point, and this is not the case. A richer account is available if we also take backchannels to be associated with non-trivial lexical entries which apply the standard DS computational action of - the movement of the DS tree pointer from a daughter node with no outstanding semantic requirements to its mother (see Fig. 1). This action is taken to be freely available in DS, as a necessary part of the basic tree compilation process (see Kempson et al., 2001); however, additionally associating it with particular lexical entries will ensure that it is applied if it can be, whenever such a word is parsed or generated.

Under this account, parsing or generating a backchannel causes the action to be run; backchannels are therefore useful at points in the parse where a sub-tree (semantic constituent) has just been completed. Not only does this have the coordinating effect of aligning DAG pointers (as above), it also reduces parse-state ambiguity, reducing the partial-tree set currently under consideration to the subset where has been carried out (if such a subset exists). For example, in the dialogue, "A: Mary, my friend B: mhm A: …", B's backchannel will cause A to eliminate DAG paths (or make them less likely to be followed) that are not compatible with , thus hindering, e.g. further qualifications of 'Mary', such as a relative clause (because the DS tree pointer has moved out of the 'Mary' sub-tree). Although the existence of such preferences is an empirical question, it seems intuitive because B has presumably resolved the 'Mary' reference successfully.

Backchannel-relevance spaces (Heldner et al., 2013) are therefore predicted to be places where - is possible, without having to postulate this as a separate pragmatic rule, or see them as associated with a specified dialogue update function. It is also predicted that use of such processing strategies carries risks, in that they can be misconstrued, misused or abused. For example, if a backchannel is produced where, from the perspective of the speaker, should not be available (e.g. mid-NP constituent), this may indicate that a participant's DAG is not coordinated with their interlocutor's. In various sociolinguistic studies, uncoordinated feedback is taken to indicate lack of attention, rapport or interest. On the other hand, this flexibility can also be exploited for various effects. Kjellmer (2009) discusses in-

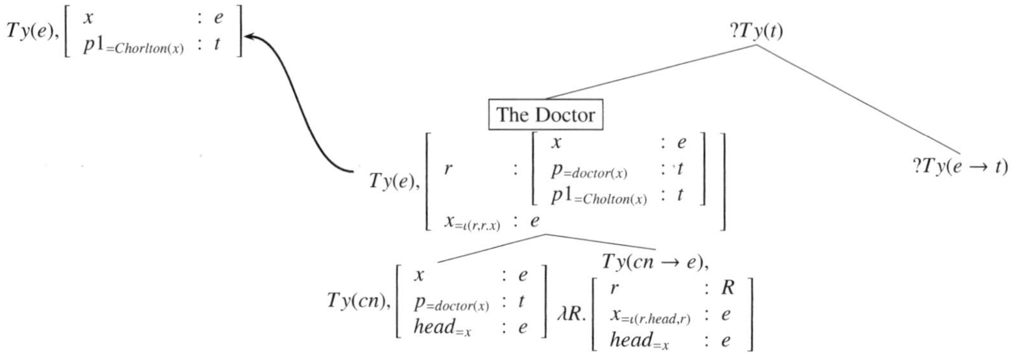

Figure 5: Processing *Chorlton?* in "A: *the doctor* B: *Chorlton?*"

terruptive feedback cases where the next element (after which would be available) is highly predictable. In our DS modelling this would indicate that the listener, through the grammar's generation of predictions, is able to achieve conceptual access and has reached the point at which can apply without all the words being articulated (analogously to Howes et al., 2012, which showed that people responded to incomplete utterances as if what was in the surface had been completed if the 'missing' material was highly predictable). This might give the surface appearance of an abandoned but, nevertheless, grounded utterance.[4] These possibilities highlight important points. Firstly, due to the situatedness of interaction, feedback has an open-ended range of functions resulting in potential participant mismatches. Consequently, a "feedback" mechanism may be used as a tool to perform another (implicit) dialogue act that moves the conversation forward or achieves particular perlocutionary effects (see, e.g., (2) earlier). Finally, from a modelling point of view, these effects emphasise that, not only incremental parsing, but also predictive processing, when incorporated as part of the grammar, can provide for a wider range of effects and generalisations across phenomena.

3.2 Clarification Interaction

Processing Clarification Requests In DS-TTR, elliptical clarification requests (CR), taking the form of NP-repetitions, or appositions that aim to clarify an NP's content, are processed as *extending* a semantic tree in context. This is done using the L - computational action (see Section 2) motivated independently for processing relative clauses and adjuncts (Cann et al., 2005). This leads to the creation of a paired LINKed tree of root node type *e* ($Ty(e)$), which is linked to the $Ty(e)$ node annotated with the content of the NP being clarified (see Fig. 5). Once the LINKed tree is complete, its content is combined through record type *extension* (TTR variant of conjunction, see Section 2.2) with the content of the NP being clarified. NP content is modelled in DS-TTR as the compilation of terms of the epsilon calculus. This provides the potential of indefinitely extending the restrictors of such terms, which is exploited here for accumulating contents (sometimes trivially) resulting from clarification sequences.

CRs can appear both locally, as in Table 1, (a,c), or non-locally from their antecedent, as in (b,d). Nevertheless, we model both in the same way, as extensions of the relevant NP's content. As Fig. 5 shows, processing *Chorlton?* locally involves building a LINKed tree from its antecedent, "the doctor". Once this LINKed tree is complete, the Record Type (RT) representing the content of *the doctor* is extended with that of "Chorlton", leading to an annotation on that node marked as The Doctor (which designates a unique individual who is a doctor and whose name is Chorlton). Parsing/production can then continue as normal, thus setting up the context in which the CR response is processed (whether that response is positive as in Table 1 (a,b) or negative as in (c,d)).

Non-local CRs require backtracking along the current DAG branch to a point where the CR can be parsed in the same way (see Fig. 6 and for further details Hough and Purver's (2012) model of self-repairs). This backtracking is triggered by the inability to parse/produce in the local context (or a very

[4]Thanks to an anonymous IWCS reviewer for pointing out this phenomenon, which, in our view, parallels our DS modelling of compound contributions in Purver et al. (2010).

low probability path having to be taken). The actions backtracked over (the DAG edges traversed) are then re-applied once the CR has been parsed or produced (i.e. when suitably indicated by punctuation or intonation). This "action replay", independently motivated for other forms of ellipsis (Kempson et al., 2014; Gargett et al., 2009), leads to the full content of the CR being established as before.

Contextual divergence The above account of how CRs are parsed and produced does not sufficiently capture all aspects of a clarificational exchange. What is also needed is an account of negative or positive responses to CRs, and the modelling of speaker/hearer context divergence during a clarification sequence. Having introduced the self- and other-coordination DAG pointers motivated earlier for an account of backchannels, we can now provide an incremental model of speaker/hearer interaction during a clarificational exchange in terms of how these pointer positions initially diverge to process a CR, and then converge again, thus re-establishing grounding, once the CR and its response have been integrated.

Figure 6 shows the incremental updates arising in the clarifier B's context in example (d) in Table 1, a case of a non-local CR which requires backtracking.[5] Initially, B successfully parses A's utterance, thus moving the other-pointer to the right-most node of his DAG. Not having secured a referent for "the doctor" with enough certainty, he then aims to produce the CR, *Chorlton?*, which involves backtracking to "the doctor" node in order to produce it. At this juncture A and B's contexts have diverged: A's self-pointer appears at the rightmost DAG edge while B has not grounded that edge. B's production of the CR causes A to have to parse it. This serves to re-align pointer positions for A and B, the result of which is both of them focussing on "the doctor"-sub-tree as the source of the misalignment. A can now offer a confirmatory or a negative response to the CR. (c), in Fig. 6 illustrates the latter case, with the utterance of *no* reflecting the abandonment of the "Chorlton?" branch, rather than the denial or rejection of a propositional content. This is followed by a correction of B's CR, thus forcing B's white other-pointer out of the "Chorlton?" branch, and inducing the construction of the new, "Fitzgerald" branch. At this juncture, B's self- and other-pointers are on different branches. This can be taken as representing the requirement for further action to be taken in order to realign pointer positions. Especially for B, whose pointer is now on an abandoned repaired branch, this can constitute an obligation to ground the new information provided by A's repair *Fitzgerald*, thus accounting for the forward momentum created by the negative response. Note how the repaired branch is still part of the context, as like Ginzburg et al. (2014) we take the repaired material as grounded. B's final backchannel, in 6(d), then serves to realign his two pointers, signalling acceptance to A, who, having processed the backchannel moves her white, other-pointer to the same node, $s10$, thus ending the clarification sequence with the achievement of a realignment of A's and B's contexts.

An alternative parsing path is illustrated in (e) of Figure 6. It represents the case where A, after the clarification in 6(b), confirms that the doctor is in fact Chorlton. This simply involves, for B, moving his other-pointer to the end of the "Chorlton?" branch, thus confirming the referent of *the doctor* as Chorlton. This, unlike the negative response in 6(c) which necessitated rejecting already established branches and pointer divergence, ends the clarification sequence. Both alternatives end up with A's and B's contexts aligned as the result of repair and backchannelling and set for the continuation of the dialogue.

4 Conclusions

We have presented a word-by-word incremental account of the coordination phenomena backchannels and clarification interaction within a semantic parsing framework. Given a psychologically realistic time-linear processing model must maintain multiple live options in parallel, such phenomena can provide substantial gains for a coupled parser/generator system by ensuring localisation of possible repair points within recent, ungrounded material. However, such gains can only be modelled if the system supports fully incremental processing, without necessary recourse to sentential or propositional constructs or pre-specified illocutionary forces. Such an approach explains not only the pervasiveness of coordination strategies, but their availability for flexible, creative use by interlocutors at the pragmatic level to express and elicit various social and affective effects.

[5]For space reasons we do not here include the clarification recipient A's point of view.

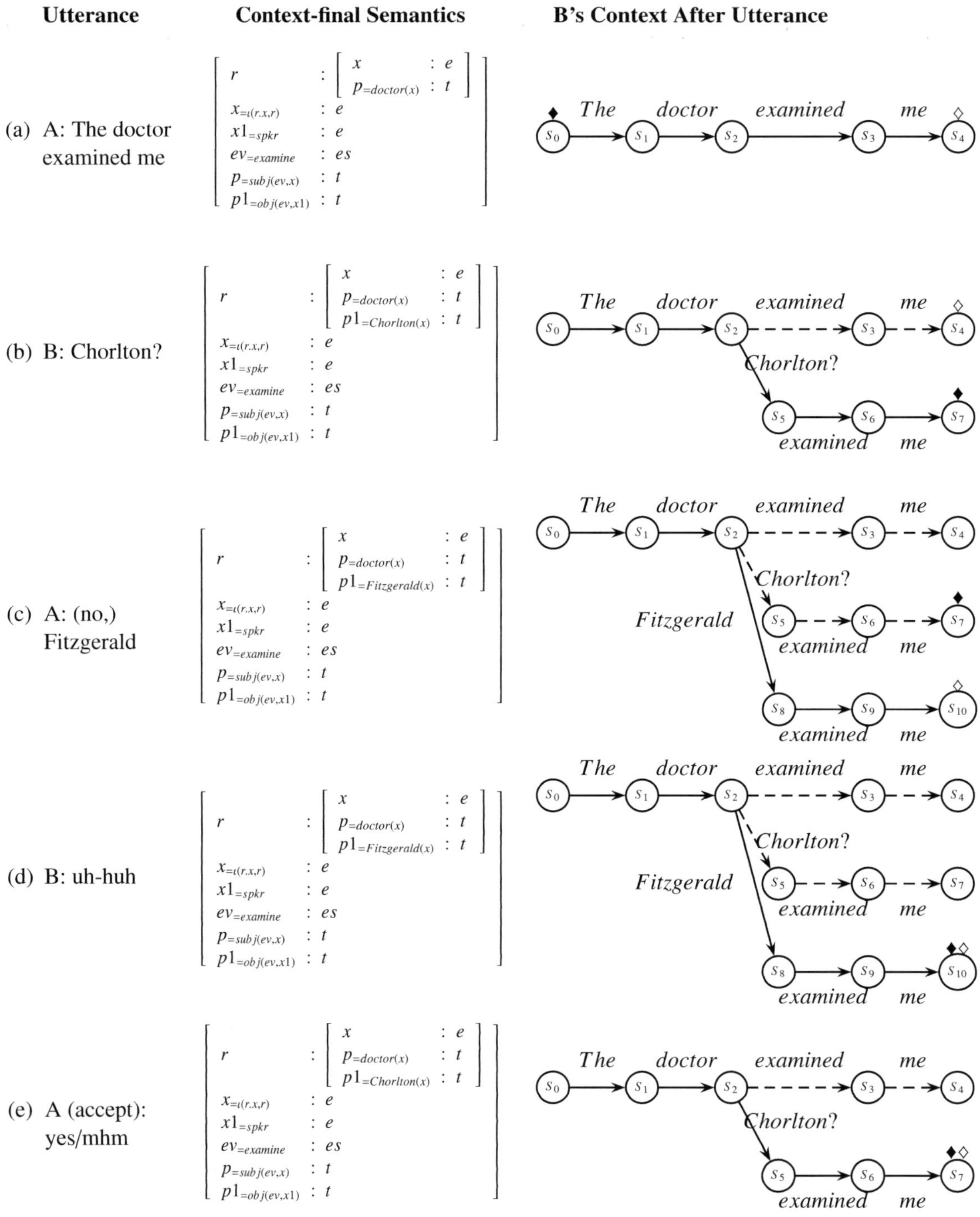

Figure 6: Clarification Interaction in DS-TTR from B's perspective. Turn (e) comes after (b)

References

Allwood, J., J. Nivre, and E. Ahlsén (1992). On the semantics and pragmatics of linguistic feedback. *Journal of Semantics 9*(1), 1–26. Also published as Gothenburg Papers in Theoretical Linguistics 64.

Blackburn, P. and W. Meyer-Viol (1994). Linguistics, logic and finite trees. *Logic Journal of the Interest Group of Pure and Applied Logics 2*(1), 3–29.

Buschmeier, H. and S. Kopp (2013). Co-constructing grounded symbols–feedback and incremental adaptation in human-agent dialogue. *KI-Künstliche Intelligenz 27*(2), 137–143.

Cann, R. (2011). Towards an account of the English auxiliary system: building interpretations incrementally. In R. Kempson, E. Gregoromichelaki, and C. Howes (Eds.), *Dynamics of Lexical Interfaces*. Chicago: CSLI Press.

Cann, R., R. Kempson, and L. Marten (2005). *The Dynamics of Language*. Oxford: Elsevier.

Cathcart, N., J. Carletta, and E. Klein (2003). A shallow model of backchannel continuers in spoken dialogue. In *Proceedings of the 10th conference of the European Chapter of the Association for Computational Linguistics (EACL)*, pp. 51–58.

Clark, H. H. (1996). *Using Language*. Cambridge University Press.

Clark, H. H. and E. F. Schaefer (1989). Contributing to discourse. *Cognitive Science 13*(2), 259–294.

Colman, M. and P. Healey (2011, July). The distribution of repair in dialogue. In C. Hoelscher and T. Shipley (Eds.), *Proceedings of the 33rd Annual Conference of the Cognitive Science Society*, Boston, MA, pp. 1563–1568.

Cooper, R. (2005). Records and record types in semantic theory. *Journal of Logic and Computation 15*(2), 99–112.

Dobnik, S., R. Cooper, and S. Larsson (2012). Modelling language, action, and perception in type theory with records. In *Proceedings of the 7th International Workshop on Constraint Solving and Language Processing (CSLP-12)*, pp. 51–63.

Eshghi, A., J. Hough, M. Purver, R. Kempson, and E. Gregoromichelaki (2012). Conversational interactions: Capturing dialogue dynamics. In *From Quantification to Conversation*, Volume 19 of *Tributes*, pp. 325–349. College Publications.

Gargett, A., E. Gregoromichelaki, R. Kempson, M. Purver, and Y. Sato (2009). Grammar resources for modelling dialogue dynamically. *Cognitive Neurodynamics 3*(4), 347–363.

Ginzburg, J. (2012). *The Interactive Stance: Meaning for Conversation*. Oxford University Press.

Ginzburg, J., R. Fernández, and D. Schlangen (2014, June). Disfluencies as intra-utterance dialogue moves. *Semantics and Pragmatics 7*(9), 1–64.

Goodwin, C. (1979). The interactive construction of a sentence in natural conversation. In G. Psathas (Ed.), *Everyday Language: Studies in Ethnomethodology*, pp. 97–121. New York: Irvington Publishers.

Goodwin, C. (1986). Audience diversity, participation and interpretation. *Tex 6*(3), 283–316.

Gravano, A. and J. Hirschberg (2009). Backchannel-inviting cues in task-oriented dialogue. In *INTERSPEECH*, pp. 1019–1022.

Heldner, M., A. Hjalmarsson, and J. Edlund (2013). Backchannel relevance spaces. In *Nordic Prosody: Proceedings of XIth Conference, Tartu 2012*, pp. 137–146.

Hough, J. and M. Purver (2012, September). Processing self-repairs in an incremental type-theoretic dialogue system. In *Proceedings of the 16th SemDial Workshop on the Semantics and Pragmatics of Dialogue*, Paris, pp. 136–144.

Howes, C., P. G. T. Healey, M. Purver, and A. Eshghi (2012, August). Finishing each other's ... responding to incomplete contributions in dialogue. In *Proc. 34th Annual Meeting of the Cognitive Science Society*, Sapporo, Japan, pp. 479–484.

Kempson, R., R. Cann, A. Eshghi, E. Gregoromichelaki, and M. Purver (2014). Ellipsis. In S. Lappin and C. Fox (Eds.), *Handbook of Contemporary Semantic Theory*. Willey-Blackwell Publications.

Kempson, R., W. Meyer-Viol, and D. Gabbay (2001). *Dynamic Syntax: The Flow of Language Understanding*. Blackwell.

Kjellmer, G. (2009). Where do we backchannel? on the use of mm, mhm, uh huh and such like. *International Journal of Corpus Linguistics 14*(1), 81–112.

Koschmann, T. and C. D. LeBaron (2003). Reconsidering common ground: Examining Clark's contribution theory in the OR. In *Proceedings of the 8th European Conference on Computer Supported Cooperative Work*, pp. 81–98. Kluwer.

Matheson, C., M. Poesio, and D. Traum (2000, April). Modeling grounding and discourse obligations using update rules. In *Proc. 1st Meeting of the North American Chapter of the Association for Computational Linguistics (NAACL)*, Seattle.

Poesio, M. and H. Rieser (2010). Completions, coordination, and alignment in dialogue. *Dialogue and Discourse 1*, 1–89.

Poesio, M. and D. Traum (1997). Conversational actions and discourse situations. *Computational Intelligence 13*(3), 309–347.

Purver, M., A. Eshghi, and J. Hough (2011, January). Incremental semantic construction in a dialogue system. In J. Bos and S. Pulman (Eds.), *Proceedings of the 9th International Conference on Computational Semantics*, Oxford, UK, pp. 365–369.

Purver, M., J. Ginzburg, and P. G. T. Healey (2003). On the means for clarification in dialogue. In R. Smith and J. van Kuppevelt (Eds.), *Current and New Directions in Discourse & Dialogue*, pp. 235–255. Kluwer Academic Publishers.

Purver, M., E. Gregoromichelaki, W. Meyer-Viol, and R. Cann (2010, June). Splitting the 'I's and crossing the 'You's: Context, speech acts and grammar. In *Proc. 14th SemDial Workshop on Semantics and Pragmatics of Dialogue*, Poznań, pp. 43–50.

Sato, Y. (2011). Local ambiguity, search strategies and parsing in Dynamic Syntax. In E. Gregoromichelaki, R. Kempson, and C. Howes (Eds.), *The Dynamics of Lexical Interfaces*, pp. 205–233. CSLI.

Traum, D. (1994). *A Computational Theory of Grounding in Natural Language Conversation*. Ph. D. thesis, U. Rochester.

Visser, T., D. Traum, D. DeVault, and R. op den Akker (2014). A model for incremental grounding in spoken dialogue systems. *Journal on Multimodal User Interfaces 8*(1), 61–73.

Wang, Z., J. Lee, and S. Marsella (2011). Towards more comprehensive listening behavior: beyond the bobble head. In *Intelligent Virtual Agents*, pp. 216–227. Springer.

Dynamics of Public Commitments in Dialogue

Antoine Venant
Université Toulouse 3, IRIT
antoine.venant@irit.fr

Nicholas Asher
CNRS, IRIT
asher@irit.fr

Friday 20th March, 2015

Abstract

In this paper, we present a dynamic semantics for dialogue in terms of commitments. We use this to provide a model theoretic treatment of ambiguity and its effects on the evolutions of commitments as a dialogue proceeds. Our first semantics ensures common commitments and has a simple logic for which we provide a complete axiomatization. On the other hand, our semantics poses difficulties for the analysis of particular dialogue moves, in particular acknowledgments, and of disputes. We provide a second semantics that addresses these difficulties.

1 Introduction

Ambiguity arises in dialogue content at various levels of granularity—lexical, syntactic, semantic levels and at the level of discourse structure. In context, these ambiguities trigger pragmatic inferences. These different mechanisms interact in an especially complex way in computing a semantics in terms of commitments, which is for many reasons an attractive idea (Hamblin, 1987; Traum and Allen, 1994; Traum, 1994). To see why, assume as most do that conversation is a rational activity designed to achieve certain goals that the dialogue's participants aim to accomplish by talking with their interlocutors. Pragmatic inferences are drawn by rational conversationalists by reasoning on the basis of these conversational objectives and the dialogue context. Assume further that the *coherence* of a dialogue agent i's contribution is tied to the possibility of inferring coherence relations between i's utterances which often constrain in return the possible disambiguisation of those utterances, and force or cancel scalar implicatures (Asher, 2013). More particularly, a particular discourse move m typically presupposes a particular commitment on the part of m's agent concerning the commitments that *other* agents have made on a move n. This commitment may not be what the the author of n intended for innocuous or strategic reasons. Here is an example (from Venant et al., 2014).

(1) a. C: N. isn't coming to the meeting. It's been cancelled.
b. A: That's not why N. isn't coming. He's sick.
c. C: I didn't say that N. wasn't coming because the meeting was cancelled. The meeting is cancelled because N. isn't coming.

C's initial contribution contains a discourse ambiguity. A has taken C to be committed one of its possible disambiguations when C turns out to have committed to the other. But A is not wrong to take C to be committed to what he takes him to commit to, we think; and so there is a question of how to represent the meaning of this exchange (Venant et al., 2014).

We address these considerations by providing a *dynamic* notion of public commitments. By performing a dialogue act X, an agent A *commits* to some content, potentially ambiguous. By responding with another dialogue act Y, a second agent B might commit to having interpreted X in a particular way. (or else to be incoherent). What is central in putting this notion of meaning at work, and the object of this paper is the dynamics of such commitments. We provide an axiomatization for a simple, first kind

Proceedings of the 11th International Conference on Computational Semantics, pages 272–282,
London, UK, April 15-17 2015. ©2015 Association for Computational Linguistics

of dynamics, look at some problems this simple dynamics has with the semantics of dialogue acts like acknoweldgments, and produce a second dynamics that resolves the problems of the first.

2 Public Commitments, Ambiguities and Strategic Context

A conversation is (ideally at least) a sequential exchange of messages. As stated in the introduction, it is also a rational activity. Messages are exchanged for some purpose; conversationalists expect something out of the conversation. In a fully cooperative settings, they typically seek an exchange of information and update their beliefs accordingly with the information they receive. In such case the conversational process closely follows the process of successive belief-state updates. It can nonetheless not be *equated* with such cognitive updates even in the cooperative case. Agents can pretend to believe in the responses of others for various purposes, even when they know their contributions are incorrect. In (partially) non-cooperative settings, nothing guarantees that a message will be believed. One can add uncertainty to the picture and, for instance, model the effect of a message as modifying a probability distribution over possible states of the world. However in a fully non-cooperative setting, *e.g.* where one agent i does not believe anything that agent j says, and this is known by everyone else, the reception of any message from j should leave the i's uncertainty exactly as it was. Nevertheless, some conversations actually take place in such settings (political debates or discussions between adversaries with opposing views). Thus, even if conversationalists' interests are opposed in these cases, there must be additional constraints that i) make it rational for them to have the conversation and ii) provide some effect to the sending of a message. Following (Venant et al., 2014), we formulate a general theory of dialogue content even for such cases using public commitments: even when agents do not communicate beliefs to their interlocutor, they communicate commitments. Performing an utterance publicly commits its author to the content of that utterance (Hamblin, 1987). Therefore, the conversational objectives of an agent are not solely expressed in terms of the sole informational content of the messages, but in terms of the public commitments of every participants as well. Typically, i may ask j "Did you eat all of my cookies?", knowing perfectly well that j did and has no incentive to tell the truth anyway, but with a conversational objective of just having i commit to an answer (either have him admit the fact, or gather material that will allow to confront him later.

Sending or not sending a message may thus have strategic consequences while leaving the agents' belief states unchanged. While much of game theory applied to language assigns utilities and thus preferences to belief states, we can also think of preferences over commitments. Player i's goal may be to extract a certain commitment from j; that is, i will be happy with her conversational performance if j commits to some proposition φ—for instance, in a philosophical debate, i might hope to show that j commits to a contradiction or some absurd proposition. Conversely, it may then be part of j's *winning condition* to avoid a commitment to φ. This makes ambiguity an essential strategic tool: by uttering an ambiguous message j may on one reading not commit to φ, while on another reading she does. Our example (1) from the introduction already reveals how ambiguities lead to different commitments. (1-b) reveals that A takes C in (1-a) to have committed to a particular rhetorical connection between N's not coming to the meeting and the meetings cancellation—namely, one of explanation: that N isn't coming *because* the meeting's been cancelled. We know this because A's contribution in (1-b) has the form of a Correction (Asher and Lascarides, 2003). However, (1-a) is genuinely ambiguous: it also has the reading on which N isn't coming and so *as a result* the meeting's been cancelled. And (1-c) reveals that C commits to having committed to the result reading with (1-a). Now suppose A's goal was to get C to commit to an attackable, thereby perhaps impugning his credibility. C's message looks like it satisfied A's goal, but because it was ambiguous, C can avoid the attack that A might have planned.

In light of this discussion, our analysis of commitments must involve commitments to ambiguous propositions. On the other hand, our informal analysis of (1) show that a proper analysis of the dynamic of commitments must also involve *nested commitments*. For instance, (1-b) implies that A commits that C commits to the explanation reading of (1-a). In fact Venant et al. (2014) show that such nested commitments are a consequence of the semantics of rhetorical relations. In what follows we develop a dynamic account of nested commitments with ambiguous signals. Our approach is compatible with but does not assume any compact representation of the ambiguous signal as in, e.g., Reyle (1993), as we represent all disambiguations model-theoretically. We hope in future work to investigate compact representations of our models.

3 A Language for the Dynamics of public Commitment with Ambiguities

To model the dynamic of public commitment with ambiguous signals, we assume here an abstract, simplified view of conservations as sequences of $\langle (linguistic) action, speaker\rangle$ pairs. We will build ambiguity into the linguistic actions recursively: in the base case, an action is an unambiguous utterance, whose content we simplify to be a propositional formula. Ambiguous actions are recursively constructed from a set of (lower-level) actions (representing its possible disambiguations). In order to explain this in more formal terms, we introduce some preliminary definitions: Let PROP denote a set of propositional variables (at most countably infinite) and I a set of agents. We define simultaneously the set of actions $\mathcal{A}$ and formulas $\mathcal{L}_0$:

Definition 1 (Actions and formulas)**.** $\mathcal{A}$ and $\mathcal{L}_0$ are the smallest sets such that:

$\forall p \in \text{PROP}\ p \in \mathcal{L}_0$	$\forall \varphi \in \mathcal{L}_0\ \varphi! \in \mathcal{A}$
$\forall \varphi, \psi \in \mathcal{L}_0\ \forall i \in I\ \neg\varphi, C_i\varphi, \varphi \wedge \psi \in \mathcal{L}_0$	for any finite collection of actions $(\alpha_s)_{s=1\ldots n}$ in $\mathcal{A}$
$\forall \varphi \in \mathcal{L}_0\ \forall \alpha \in \mathcal{A}\ \forall i \in I\ [\alpha^i]\varphi \in \mathcal{L}_0$	$(\sim \alpha_s)_{s=1\ldots n} \in \mathcal{A}$

Additional logical constants and connectors are defined as usual: $\varphi \vee \psi \equiv \neg(\neg\varphi \wedge \neg\psi)$, $\varphi \rightarrow \psi \equiv \neg\varphi \vee \psi$, $\bot \equiv p \wedge \neg p$, $\bot \equiv p \vee \neg p$.

The semantics of our language is based on that for Public Announcements logic (PAL) with private suspicions introduced in Baltag et al. (1998). More specifically, we translate each of our actions in (Baltag et al., 1998)'s *action structures* and then rely on their semantics.

Recalling some basic definitions, a *frame* is a tuple $\langle W, (R_i)_{i\in X}\rangle$ with W a set of worlds and for each $i \in I$, R_i is a binary relation over W, and a *model* $\mathcal{M}$ is a pair $\langle \mathcal{F}, \nu\rangle$ with $\mathcal{F}$ a Kripke frame and $\nu : W \mapsto \wp(\text{PROP})$ an assignment at each world w of propositional variables true at w. We will sometimes use models as superscripts for set of worlds $W^{\mathcal{M}}$, or accessibility relations $R_i^{\mathcal{M}}$ to refer to the set of worlds or the relation of that particular model or frame. We will also abuse notation and write $w \in \mathcal{M}$ as a shortcut for $w \in W^{\mathcal{M}}$. A *pointed model* is a pair $\langle \mathcal{M}, w\rangle$ with $w \in W^{\mathcal{M}}$.

The semantics of action-free formulas is as usual with respect to a pointed model:

Definition 2 (Semantics of static formulas)**.**

$$\langle \mathcal{M}, w\rangle \models p \text{ iff } p \in \nu^{\mathcal{M}}(w)$$
$$\langle \mathcal{M}, w\rangle \models \neg\varphi \text{ iff } \langle \mathcal{M}, w\rangle \not\models \varphi$$
$$\langle \mathcal{M}, w\rangle \models \varphi \wedge \psi \text{ iff } \langle \mathcal{M}, w\rangle \models \varphi \text{ and } \langle \mathcal{M}, w\rangle \models \psi$$
$$\langle \mathcal{M}, w\rangle \models C_i\varphi \text{ iff } \forall w', R_i^{\mathcal{M}}(w, w') \rightarrow \langle \mathcal{M}, w'\rangle \models \varphi$$

In order to provide a semantics for terms with actions, we need (Baltag et al., 1998)'s definition of an *action structure*:

Definition 3 (Action Structures)**.** An action structure is a pair $\langle \mathcal{F}, pre\rangle$ where $pre : W^{\mathcal{F}} \mapsto \mathcal{L}_0$ associates to each world in $\mathcal{F}$ a formula, called the *precondition* of this world.

Interpreting formulas with actions require us to first update the model with the action, then to evaluate the formulas with respect to the updated model. As mentioned earlier, we proceed in two steps; we first associate a pointed action-structure with each action in $\mathcal{A} \times I$, and then classically update the model with this action. We first recall (Baltag et al., 1998)'s informal definition of the update operation. The update of a model $\mathcal{M}$ through an action a is obtained by taking, for each world in a's structure a different copy of $\mathcal{M}$'s world that satisfy the precondition, then allowing a transition for agent i from a world to another iff i)the two worlds were initialy i-related and ii)the two copies they belong to are i-related in a's structure. More precisely:

Definition 4 (Action updates). Let $S = \langle \mathcal{F}, pre \rangle$ be an action structure. Let $k \in S$ and let $\langle \mathcal{M}, w_0 \rangle$ be a pointed model. Let $|\varphi|^{\mathcal{M}} = \{w \in \mathcal{M} \mid \mathcal{M}, w \models \varphi\}$. If $w_0 \notin pre(k)$, the update $\langle \mathcal{M}, w_0 \rangle \star \langle S, k \rangle$ *fails*. Otherwise, it is defined as $\langle \mathcal{M}^S, (w_0, k) \rangle$ the model with $W^S = \bigcup_{l \in S} |pre(l)|^{\mathcal{M}} \times l$ as set of worlds, accessibility relations defined as $R_i^{\mathcal{M}^S}((w,l),(w',l'))$ iff i)$R^{\mathcal{M}}(w,w')$ and ii) $R_i^S(l,l')$, and valuations left unchanged *i.e.* $\nu((w,l)) = \nu(w)$.

We now provide the translation of conversational moves of our language (*i.e.* elements of $\mathcal{A} \times I$) into pointed action-structures:

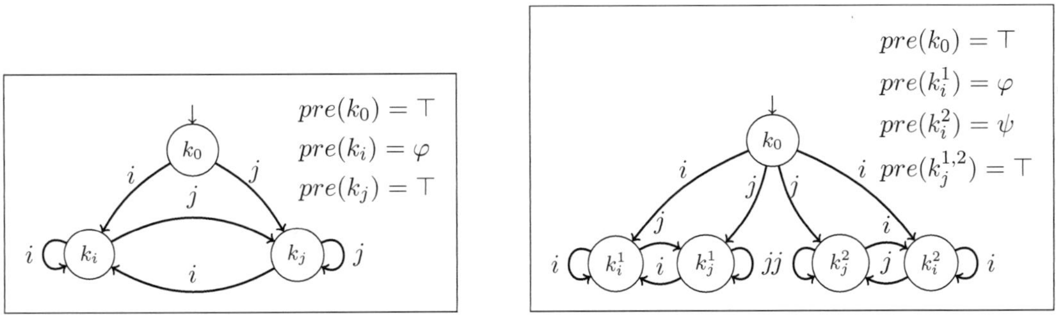

(a) Unambiguous move $\varphi!^i$

(b) Ambiguous move $(\varphi! \sim \psi!)^i$

Figure 1: Some action structures

A simple unambiguous discourse move by i will generate a *common commitment* to $C_i\varphi$. An ambiguous move, on the other hand, will not but will involve a disjunction of common commitments. A common commitment for a group G towards a proposition φ, $C_G^*\varphi$, has the effect that $C_G\varphi \wedge C_G C_G \varphi \wedge \ldots C_G(C_G)^n\varphi \wedge \ldots$ (analogously to common knowledge). Semantically, we define common commitments for a group G, $C_G^*\varphi$, as

$$\langle \mathcal{M}, w \rangle \models C_G^*\varphi \text{ iff } \forall w' (\bigcup_{x \in G} R_x)^+(w,w') \rightarrow \langle \mathcal{M}, w \rangle \models \varphi,$$

where the union $\cup$ of two relations is defined as $(R \cup R)(w,w')$ iff $R(w,w')$ or $R'(w,w')$, and R^+ denotes the transitive closure of the binary relation R ($R^+(w,w')$ iff $\exists n > 0\, \exists w_1, \ldots w_n\; w_n = w' \wedge R(w,w_1) \wedge \ldots R(w_{k-1},w_k) \ldots R(w_{n-1},w_n)$).

Definition 5 (Interpretation of conversational moves). The interpretation function $[\![\cdot]\!]$ interprets conversational moves of $\mathcal{A} \times I$) as pointed action-structures. Let $m = \alpha!^i \in \mathcal{A} \times I$. $[\![m]\!]$ is defined inductively over α:

- If $\alpha = \varphi!$ then $[\![\alpha]\!] = \langle K, pre, k_0 \rangle$ with $K = \{k_0, k_i, k_j\}$, accessibility relation is defined as $R_i^K(k_{\{0,i,j\}}, k_i)$, $R_j^K(k_{\{0,i,j\}}, k_j)$ and no other transitions; preconditions are defined as $pre(k_0) = pre(k_j) = \top$ and $pre(k_i) = \varphi$. The pointed world is k_0 and the action-structure is depicted in figure 1a.
- If $\alpha = (\sim \alpha_s)_{s=1\ldots n}$, let $\langle K^s, pre^s, k_0^s \rangle = [\![\alpha_s!^i]\!]$ be the action structure recursively computed for $\alpha_s!^i$. Assuming the K^s- and $K^{s'}$-worlds are disjoint for $s \neq s'$ (otherwise, first take disjoint copies of the K^ss), define $[\![\alpha_m]\!] = \langle K, pre, k_0 \rangle$ with $K = \bigcup_s K^s \setminus \{k_0^s\}$, accessibility relations defined as i)$\forall k \in K^s\; x \in \{i,j\}\quad R_x^K(k_0,k)$ iff $R_x^{K^s}(k_0^s,k)$, ii) $\forall k,k' \in K_s \setminus \{k_0^s\}\; R_x^K(k,k')$ iff

$R_x^{K^s}(k, k')$ and iii) there are no other transitions than the one previously listed. pre is defined as $pre(k_0) = \top$ and for $pre(k) = pre^s(k)$ for $k \in K^s$. The pointed world is k_0. Figure 1b shows the action-structure $[\![(\varphi! \sim \psi!)^i]\!]$ for a move by i which is ambiguous between a commitment to φ and one to ψ.

Note that given this definition, $\sim$ is "associative" in the sense that

$$[\![((\alpha_1 \sim \alpha_2) \sim \alpha_3)^i]\!] = (\alpha_1 \sim (\alpha_2 \sim \alpha_3))^i]\!] = [\![(\alpha_1 \sim \alpha_2 \sim \alpha_3)^i]\!] \text{ (up to renaming of the worlds).}$$

Armed with these definitions, we can now complete the semantics of $\mathcal{L}_0$ providing the semantics for action terms:

Definition 6. Semantics of dynamic formulas:

$$\langle \mathcal{M}, w \rangle \models [\alpha^i]\varphi \text{ iff } \langle \mathcal{M}, w \rangle \star [\![\alpha^i]\!] \models \varphi$$

Note that due to the fact $[\![\alpha^i]\!]$'s pointed world always has $\top$ as precondition, the update $\langle \mathcal{M}, w \rangle \star [\![\alpha^i]\!]$ cannot fail and the definition is correct.

Worked out example We illustrate our dynamics by providing an abstract but principled view of the evolving commitments in (2):

(2) a. i : I have my piano lesson in ten minutes. When I get back the shop will be closed.
b. i : And there is no more beer.
c. j : I am not going to get you beer. Go get it yourself.
d. i : I did not say that. I am not asking you to get it.
e. j : Oh yes you did.

What is central to the picture here? i commits to some proposition (we abbreviate it as p), and then to something else, that in its context of utterance might be interpreted as a commitment on a request for j to get beer. i makes an utterance that entails that he takes j to be committed to the request. j then this dispute this commitment of his. i refuses the correction. Assume that we can refer to an external semantic/pragmatic theory that licenses or rejects possible interpretations of a sentence in context, and that such a linguistic theory tells us that (2-b) as (at least) an assertion that there is no more beer ($\neg b$) licenses a pragmatic inference to a request for i to get some beer ($\neg b \wedge r$). We can then correctly describe (2) as involving these action sequences:

(3) a. $i : p!^i$
b. $i : (\neg b! \sim (\neg b \wedge r)!)^i$
c. $j : (C_i r)!^j$
d. $i : (C_j C_i r \wedge \neg C_i r \wedge \neg r)!^i$
e. $j : (C_i(C_j C_i r \wedge \neg C_i r) \wedge C_i r)!^i$

Figures 2, show how the dynamics transform the initial model. In order to keep the figures readable, we graphically group nodes into clusters, edges going in and out of these clusters are to be understood as distributing over each inner node. We also omit some isolated worlds that therefore have no impact (*i.e.* they are present in the definition of action update, but not reachable from any other world). Nodes are labelled by their valuations, except for the actual world labelled as w_0. The initial model of the conversation is depicted in figure 2a.

The initial model in figure 2a shows that neither speaker commits to anything. Figure 2 shows how i's assertions in (3-b)–(3-d) have transformed the commitment space for j and i: after updating with (3-b), i's public commitments and j's commitments concerning i's commitments are ambiguous as to whether the implicature to go get beer holds; but after the update with (3-c), only i's commitments remain ambiguous. j's commitments concerning i''s commitments are no longer ambiguous; he commits

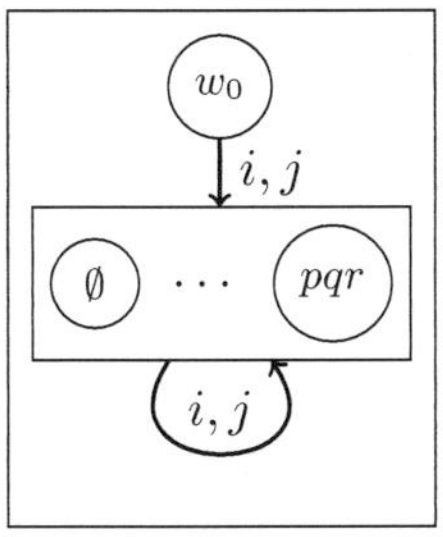

(a) Initial Model for example (3)

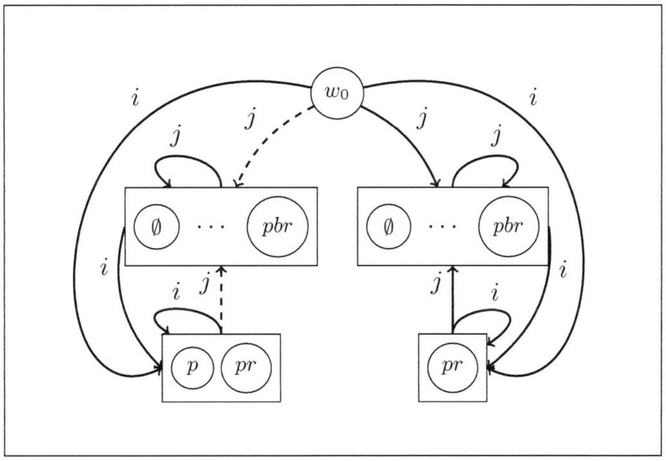

(b) Models after (3-b) and (3-c), respectively with and without the dashed edges.

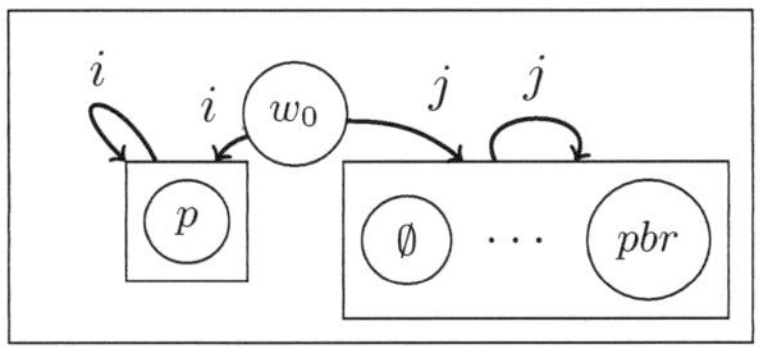

(c) Model after (3-d)

Figure 2: Models at different stages of example (3). Arrows should be understood as distributing over all inner nodes.

to i's having committed to the implicature that he should go get the beer. After (3-d), j's commitments concerning i have become inconsistent. This is a consequence of our strong modeling assumptions about a perfect communication channel leading to common commitments. We will see in section 5 yet another reason to weaken our proposal.

4 Complete Deduction System for $\mathcal{L}_0$

One of the interests in keeping the base language of our analysis simple is to be able to investigate the logical properties of the dynamics of commitments. Accordingly, in this section, we present a complete deduction system for $\mathcal{L}_0$. The system and completness proof follow from the general picture drawn in (Baltag et al., 1998), where the authors provide a complete deduction system for the language allowing any kind of action-structure. It turns out however, that the restricted action-structures that are the interpretations of our conversational moves $\mathcal{A}$(see definition 5) allow nice simplifications, most notably the elimination of any reference to action-structures in the syntactic rules. This allows us to have deduction system for L_0 which does not require embedding of L_0 into an larger language with additional syntactic constructions. The deduction system is presented on figure 3.

In order to proof completeness of the above system, we adapt step by step (Baltag et al., 1998)'s proof to the simplified system. The proof function by reduction of the logic to the static logic K. The idea behind the proof is, once soundness is established, to see our system's axioms as rewrite rules (rewriting the left-hand sides of the equivalences into the right-hand sides), and show that the system is able to proof the equivalence of any given formula to an action-free formula. From there it is quite straightforward to reduce provability of a formula to provability of an action free formula, which is granted as $K-$axioms are part of our system.

Lemma 1. *The deduction rules are sound.*

All propositional validities	
from $\vdash \varphi \rightarrow \psi$ and $\vdash \varphi$ to infer $\vdash \psi$	(MP)
$\vdash [\alpha^i](\varphi \rightarrow \psi) \rightarrow ([\alpha^i](\varphi) \rightarrow [\alpha^i](\psi))$	($[\alpha^i]$-normality)
$\vdash C_i(\varphi \rightarrow \psi) \rightarrow (C_i(\varphi) \rightarrow C_i(\psi))$	(C-normality)
from $\vdash \varphi$ to infer $\vdash C_i\varphi$	(C-necessitation)
from $\vdash \varphi$ to infer $\vdash [\alpha^i]\varphi$	($[\alpha^i]$-necessitation)
$\vdash [\alpha^i]p \leftrightarrow p$	(rw1)
$\vdash [\alpha^i]\neg\psi \leftrightarrow \neg[\alpha^i]\psi$	(rw2)
$\vdash [\alpha^i](\psi_1 \wedge \psi_2) \leftrightarrow [\alpha^i]\psi_1 \wedge [\alpha^i]\varphi_2$	(rw3)
$\vdash [\varphi!^i]C_j\psi \leftrightarrow C_j[\varphi!^i]\psi \qquad (\text{for } j \neq i)$	(rw4)
$\vdash [\varphi!^i]C_i\psi \leftrightarrow C_i(\varphi \rightarrow [\varphi!^i]\psi)$	(rw5)
$\vdash [\sim(\alpha_s)^i_{s\in S}]C_x\varphi \leftrightarrow \bigwedge_S [\alpha^i_s]C_x\varphi$	(rw6)

Figure 3: Deduction system for $\mathcal{L}_0$
$i, j, x \in I$, $p \in$ PROP

Proof. The proof is trivial for Modus Ponens, necessitation and normality rules. (rw1)'s, (rw2)'s and (rw3) soundness follows directly from definitions (and the fact that our actions never fail). (rw4),(rw5) and (rw6) requires a little more work:

- Let for a world $w \in \mathcal{M}$ $\langle \mathcal{M}^\alpha, (w_0, k_0)\rangle$ denote $\langle \mathcal{M}, w\rangle \star [\![\varphi!^i]\!]$, the update of $\mathcal{M}$ by action φ^i at w (recall that the set of worlds and relations of $\mathcal{M}^\alpha$ does not depend on w). Notice first that the following is true for any formula γ, $k \in \{k_0, k_i, k_j\}$ and w such that $(w, k) \in \mathcal{M}^\alpha$:

  $$\langle \mathcal{M}^\alpha, (w, k_0)\rangle \text{ and } \langle \mathcal{M}^\alpha, (w, k)\rangle \text{ are bissimilar.}$$

  by definition the valuations of (w, k_0) and (w, k) are the same. Since the worlds accessible from k_0 in $[\![\varphi]\!]$ are exactly those accessible from k, it follows from the definition of $\mathcal{M}^\alpha$ that the worlds accessible from (w, k_0) are exactly those accessible from (w, k) which is sufficient to establish the bissimulation.

  Let us now prove the soundness of (rw5). The proof for (rw4) is similar. Let $\langle \mathcal{M}, w_0\rangle$ be a pointed model. $\langle \mathcal{M}, w\rangle \models [\varphi!^i]C_i\psi$ iff $\langle \mathcal{M}^\alpha, (w_0, k_0)\rangle \models C_i\psi$ iff $\forall (w, k) \in \mathcal{M}^\alpha\ R_i((w_0, k_0), (w, k)) \rightarrow \langle \mathcal{M}^\alpha, (w, k)\rangle \models \psi$. Since we have shown that $\langle \mathcal{M}^\alpha, (w, k)\rangle$ is bissimilar to (w, k_0) and using the definition of $\mathcal{M}^\alpha$, we find the above to be further equivalent to $\langle \mathcal{M}, w\rangle \models \varphi$ and $R_i^{\mathcal{M}}(w_0, w) \rightarrow \langle \mathcal{M}^\alpha, (w, k_0)\rangle \models \psi$. But since by definition $\langle \mathcal{M}, w\rangle \models [\varphi!^i]\psi$ iff $\langle \mathcal{M}^\alpha, (w, k_0)\rangle \models \psi$, satisfaction of the initial formula is finally equivalent to $\langle \mathcal{M}, w_0\rangle \models C_i(\varphi \rightarrow [\varphi!^i]\psi)$.

- Let $\alpha = ((\sim \alpha_s)_{s\in S})$ and $x \in I$. by construction, for any world k x-accessible from k_0 in $[\![\alpha]\!]$ there is world k_s in $[\![\alpha_s]\!]$ x-accessible from k_0 and such that $\langle K^\alpha, k\rangle$ and $\langle K^{\alpha_s}, k_s\rangle$ are bissimilar. This implies that for any world in (w, k) x-accessible from (w_0, k_0) in $\mathcal{M}^\alpha$ there is a $s \in S$ and a world (w, k_s) in $\mathcal{M}^{\alpha_s}$ such that $\langle \mathcal{M}^\alpha, (w, k)\rangle$ and $\langle \mathcal{M}^{\alpha_s}, (w, k_s)\rangle$ are bissimilar. Conversely, for any world $(w, k_s) \in \mathcal{M}^{\alpha_s}$ x-accessible from (w_0, k_0) there is a bissimilar world $(w, k) \in \mathcal{M}^\alpha$ x-accessible from (w_0, k_0).

  Assume that for each α_s, $\langle \mathcal{M}^{\alpha_s}, (w_0, k_0)\rangle \models C_x\varphi$. Let (w, k) be x-accessible from $(w_0, k_0) \in \mathcal{M}^\alpha$. We me must have $\langle \mathcal{M}^{\alpha_s}, (w, k_s)\rangle \models \varphi$ and by bissimilarity $\langle \mathcal{M}^\alpha, (w, k)\rangle \models \varphi$, hence $\langle \mathcal{M}^\alpha, (w_0, k_0)\rangle \models C_x\varphi$.

Conversely, assume that $\langle \mathcal{M}^{\alpha}, (w_0, k_0)\rangle \models C_x\varphi$. Let $(w, k_s) \in \mathcal{M}^{\alpha_s}$ be a world x-accessible from (w_0, k_0), there is a $(w, k) \in \mathcal{M}^{\alpha}$ bissimilar to (w, k_s) and therefore $\langle \mathcal{M}^{\alpha_s}, (w, k_s)\rangle \models \varphi$ and $\langle \mathcal{M}^{\alpha_s}, (w_0, k_0)\rangle \models C_x\varphi$.

All together we can conclude to $\langle \mathcal{M}, w_0\rangle \models [(\sim \alpha_s)_{s\in S}]C_x\varphi$ iff $\langle \mathcal{M}, w_0\rangle \models \bigwedge_S[\alpha_s]C_x\varphi$, *i.e.* (rw6) is sound.

□

Lemma 2. *Rules* (rw1)–(rw6) *seen as rewrite rules rewriting the left-hand sides of the equivalences into the right-hand sides form a terminating rewriting system.*

This is classicaly obtained from (for instance) the technique of lexicographic path ordering. We do not detail the proof here for sake of space.

Since a rewrite-rule can always be applied to a formula starting with an action, a direct corollary of lemma 2 is that any formula can be rewritten into an action-free formula by the by the rewrite system obtained from the deduction rules.

Lemma 3. *If* $\vdash \varphi \leftrightarrow \psi$ *then for all well formed formula* γ *of* $\mathcal{L}_0$, $\vdash \gamma[\varphi/p] \leftrightarrow \gamma[\psi/p]$.

This can be achieved by induction over the length of γ.

Proposition 1. *The deduction system is strongly complete.*

Together with lemma 2, lemma 3 yields through a quick induction over the rewrite steps, that for any formula $\varphi \in \mathcal{L}_0$, there is an action-free formula φ_0 (one of φ normal forms w.r.t the rewrite system) such that $\vdash \varphi \leftrightarrow \varphi_0$, from there the strong completeness is reduced to the one of modal logic K.

5 Acknowledgments and corrections

Next we look at two particular dialogue moves that affect commitments in complex ways: acknowledgments and corrections. For many researchers Clark (1996); Ginzburg (2012); Traum and Allen (1994), *inter alia*, an acknowledgment as in (4)c by 0 of a discourse move m by 1 can signal that 0 has understood what 1 has said, or that 0 has committed that 1 has committed to a content p with m, and serve to "ground" or to establish a mutual belief that 1 has committed to p. Corrections, and self-corrections, as in (4)d, on the other hand, serve to remove commitments.

(4)
a. 0: Did you have a bank account in this bank?
b. 1: No sir.
c. 0: OK. So you're saying that you did not have a bank account at Credit Suisse?
d. 1: No. sorry, in fact, I had an account there.
e. 0: OK thank you.

We believe that acknowledgments perform an important grounding function in a commitment based semantics for dialogue: they serve to produce *common commitments*, the commitment analogue to mutual beliefs. There is, however, a problem with our semantics when it comes to treating acknowledgments: grounding acknowledgments are semantically superfluous; if m entails p, then i's making m entails $C^*_G C_i p$. Rational speakers should never acknowledge in a grounding sense; i's acknowledgment of j can only mean that i agrees with the content of j's move, which manifestly it does not, as in (4)c (such acknowledgments are often present in legal questioning).

We have other indications that our dialogue semantics so far is not quite right. For instance, saying "φ" is not the same as saying "I commit to φ", and simply i's saying "φ" should not induce via the logic alone a common commitment that $C_i\varphi$. Of course if i says "φ" and then "I did not say φ" he his ultimately saying something *false*. But this is not the same as him committing to an *absurdity*, *i.e.* an inconsistency not just with the actual state of the world, but in its own right. As already illustrated, the dynamics of sections 4 and 5 validates $\langle \mathcal{M}, w\rangle \models [\varphi^i]C^*_{i,j}C_i\psi$ which indeed makes it impossible for one to consistently perform such a sequence of utterances. This hypothesis can be seen either as a consequence of perfect linguistic knowledge and a communication channel, and mutual commitment of the agents thereto.

To treat acknowledgments, we first enrich our language into a language $\mathcal{L}_{ack}$ with actions for acknowledgments. We do that by adding the recursive construction $Ack(\alpha^x)$ to the set of linguistic action $\mathcal{A}$, for any $\alpha \in \mathcal{A}$ and $x \in I$. Defining the semantics of $\mathcal{L}_{ack}$ just requires us to define the interpretation of acknowledgment-actions into action-structures. Let $\alpha \in \mathcal{A}$ be a linguistic action. Let $\langle K^\alpha, k_0^\alpha, pre^\alpha\rangle = [\![\alpha^x]\!]$. Let k_0 and k_j be "fresh" symbols not appearing in K^α.

$$[\![Ack(\alpha^x)^i]\!] = \langle\{k_0, k_j\} \cup K_\alpha, k_0, pre\rangle$$

Accessibility relations are defined as $R_i(k_0, k_0^\alpha)$, $R_j(k_0, k_j)$, $R_{i,j}(k_j, k_j)$, $\forall k, k' \in K^\alpha, \forall x \in \{i, j\}\ R_x(k, k')$ iff $R_x^{K^\alpha}(k, k')$ and no other transitions. $pre(k_0) = pre(k_j) = \top$ and pre coincide with pre^α on K^α.

It is easy to check that effects of action $Ack(\alpha^x)^i$ commit i to the effects of α^x and that, given the dynamics of sections 4 and 5, acknowledgments of previous actions have no effect in the sense that $\langle \mathcal{M}, w\rangle \models [\alpha^x][Ack(\alpha^x)^i]\varphi$ iff $\langle \mathcal{M}, w\rangle \models [\alpha^x]\varphi$. This formalizes the problem. To address the problem, we provide an alternative semantics for $\mathcal{L}_{ack}$, in which we redefine the interpretation of linguistic actions as action structures. Only unambiguous utterance-actions need a new definition, as the recursive computation mechanism of action-structures for ambiguous utterances- and acknoledgments-actions stays the same.

Definition 7 (Weak action interpretation)**.** Define $[\![\cdot]\!]^1$ by

$$[\![\varphi!^i]\!]^1 = \langle k_0, k_i, k_1, k_0, pre\rangle$$

with $R_i(k_0, k_i), R_j(k_0, k_1), R_{i,j}(\{k_i, k_1\}, k_1)$ and no other transitions. $pre(k_0) = pre(k_1) = \top$ and $pre(k_i) = \varphi$

$$[\![\sim(\alpha_s)^i_{s\in S}]\!]^1 \text{ and } [\![Ack(\alpha^x)]\!]^1 \text{ are computed as before}$$

Define finally $\models^1$ as the new truth-maker operator defined as $\models$ was, but this time based on the interpretation $[\![\cdot]\!]^1$ of linguistic actions.

Under $\models^1$ action $[\varphi!^i]$ has i commits to φ, but changes neither i's second order commitments (in general $\langle \mathcal{M}, w\rangle \not\models^1 C_iC_i\varphi$) nor anyone else's commitments. This now fixes our problem of the liar who denies commitments he has previously made; someone can now commit to φ but then later say *I never said* φ and remain consistent.

This weaker semantics, however, makes grounding impossible in finite conversations. The situation is analogous in other models where a discourse move m by i entails only (a)C_ip and (b)that all the conversational participants believe C_ip, see for instance (Traum, 1994; Ginzburg, 2012). Then j's acknowledgment of m would entail $C_jC_ip \wedge Bel_GC_jC_ip$. We can show using a game theoretic framework, that common commitments are achievable only after an infinite sequence of acknowledgment moves between i and j.

Can we do without common commitments in conversation? We think not; common commitments are essential (see also Clark (1996)) for strategic reasons and can be present even when mutual beliefs about a shared task are not. Suppose that i's goal is that $C_j\varphi$ and that j cannot consistently deny the commitment. If i only extracts from j a move m that $C_j\varphi$, j has a winning strategy for denying i victory. She simply denies committing to φ (*I never said that*), since $C_j\neg C_j\varphi$ is consistent with $C_j\varphi$, even if $Bel_jC_j\varphi$. Player j lies, but she is consistent. If i manages to achieve $C_jC_j\varphi$, j can still similarly counter i maintaining consistency. *Only if* i achieves the *common commitment* $C^*_GC_j\varphi$, with G the group of conversational participants) does j not have a way of denying her commitment without becoming inconsistent, as $C^*C_j\varphi \rightarrow (C_jC_j\varphi \wedge C_jC_jC_j\varphi \wedge \cdots)$.

Our proposal is that a particular sort of acknowledgment and confirming question licenses the move to common commitment. It is the one in (4)c, where 0 asks a confirming question after an acknowledgment of a move m. If 1's answer to the confirming question is consonant with m, then $C^*_{\{0,1\}}C_1\varphi$, and 0 has achieved her goal. We can explain this using our notion of ambiguous commitments. An acknowledgment is in fact ambiguous. One reading comes from our simple semantics where an acknowledgment adds one layer of commitment—i.e. if j acknowledges i's commitment to φ with a simple *OK*, we have $C_j C_i \varphi$. The other reading is that it indeed implies a common commitment of the form $C^*_{i,j} C_j \varphi$, following our second semantics for assertions. The clarification question, when answered in the affirmative, selects the common commitment formulation. (Clark and Brennan, 1991) acknowledges that grounding may seem to require conversationalist to give infinitely many positive bits of evidence—(*Requiring positive evidence of understanding seems to lead to an infinite regress*), and claims that some form of evidence such as *continued attention* solves the situation as it can occur continuously and does not require a separate presentation. Our proposal is compatible but distinct from Clark's (ours is also formally worked out), and interestingly survives in non-cooperative settings.

We quickly now turn to corrections. Speakers can not only deny prior commitments but also "undo" or "erase" them with *self-corrections*. For instance, if in (4)b 1 commits to not having a bank account; in (4)d 1 no longer has this commitment (See Ginzburg (2012) for a detailed account of repair). Conversational goals of the form $C^*_G C_i p$ are unstable if i may correct herself; they may be satisfied on one finite sequence but not by all its continuations. j's being able to correct a previous turn's commitments increases the complexity of i's goalsSerre (2004), which affects the existence of a winning strategy for i; an unbounded number of correction moves will make any stable $C^*_G C_i p$ goal unattainable, if p is not a tautology. We observe, however, a sequence of self-corrections is only a good strategy for achieving j's conversational goals if she is prepared to provide an explanation for her shift in commitments (and such explanations must come to an end). As (Venant et al., 2014) argues, conversationalists are constrained to be credible in a certain sense if they are to achieve their conversational goals. Constantly shifting one's commitments with self-corrections leads to non-credibility, thus avoiding the problem of unbounded erasures.

To provide a semantics for corrections, we begin from Lascarides and Asher (2009), who provide a *syntactic* notion of revision over the logical form of the discourse structure. Using the correction of m as an action update on the commitment slate prior to m yields a semantics for corrections. Our formal semantics captures the dynamic effects of announcements, corrections and acknowledgments; common commitments are important conversational goals and that particular conditions must obtain if they are to be achieved.

6 Conclusions

We have presented two semantics for dialogue in terms of commitments that is general enough to handle non-cooperative and cooperative dialogues. The first one is conceptually simple and has a straightforward axiomatization but fails to give a sensible semantics for acknowledgments and is also too restrictive concerning denials of commitments, which our semantics makes inconsistent instead of simply a lie. Finally, we discussed corrections as another problem for the semantics of dialogue and offered a solution.

References

Asher, N. (2013). Implicatures and discourse structure. *Lingua 132*(0), 13 – 28. SI: Implicature and Discourse Structure.

Asher, N. and A. Lascarides (2003). *Logics of Conversation.* Cambridge University Press.

Baltag, A., L. S. Moss, and S. Solecki (1998). The logic of public announcements, common knowledge, and private suspicions. In *Proceedings of the 7th Conference on Theoretical Aspects of Rationality and Knowledge*, TARK '98, San Francisco, CA, USA, pp. 43–56. Morgan Kaufmann Publishers Inc.

Clark, H. (1996). *Using Language.* Cambridge, England: Cambridge University Press.

Clark, H. H. and S. E. Brennan (1991). Grounding in communication. In L. Resnick, J. Levine, and S. Teasley (Eds.), *Perspectives on Socially Shared Cognition*, pp. 127–149. American Psychological Association.

Ginzburg, J. (2012). *The Interactive Stance: Meaning for Conversation.* Oxford University Press.

Hamblin, C. (1987). *Imperatives.* Blackwells.

Lascarides, A. and N. Asher (2009). Agreement, disputes and commitment in dialogue. *Journal of Semantics 26*(2), 109–158.

Reyle, U. (1993). Dealing with ambiguities by underspecification: Construction, interpretation and deduction. *Journal of Semantics 10*, 123–179.

Serre, O. (2004). Games with winning conditions of high borel complexity. In *ICALP*, pp. 1150–1162.

Traum, D. (1994). *A Computational Theory of Grounding in Natural Language Conversation.* Ph. D. thesis, Computer Science Department, University of Rochester.

Traum, D. and J. Allen (1994). Discourse obligations in dialogue processing. In *Proceedings of the 32nd Annual Meeting of the Association for Computational Linguistics (ACL94)*, Las Cruces, New Mexico, pp. 1–8.

Venant, A., N. Asher, and C. Degremont (2014). Credibility and its attacks. In V. Rieser and P. Muller (Eds.), *The 18th Workshop on the Semantics and Pragmatics of Dialogue*, pp. 154–162.

Simple Interval Temporal Logic for Natural Language Assertion Descriptions

Reyadh Alluhaibi
The University of Manchester, UK
alluhair@cs.man.ac.uk

Abstract

SystemVerilog assertion (SVA) is widely used for verifying properties of hardware designs. This paper presents a new method of generating SVAs from natural language assertion descriptions. For capturing the temporal semantics in natural language descriptions, we develop a new logical form called *simple interval temporal logic* ($\mathcal{SITL}$) which can deal formally with temporal constructions such as temporal prepositions. Furthermore, $\mathcal{SITL}$ makes the transformations from natural language descriptions to SVAs possible. Thus, we build transformation rules to map our logic into SVAs. Our systematic experimental investigation on AXI bus protocol in ARM (2010) suggest that our method is applicable for generating SVAs from natural language descriptions.

Keywords: Temporal semantics; temporal prepositions; natural language descriptions; SystemVerilog assertions

1 Introduction

Formal verification is the process of checking whether a design fulfils certain requirements (properties). In the last decade, one major challenge in the area of formal verification has been to reduce the effort required to design hardware systems (Darringer, 1988; Milne, 1993). SVA is one of the formal verification tools used for verification finite state concurrent systems such as sequential circuit designs. SVA is a linear temporal logic which can express temporal behaviours of the system designs. In fact, SVA allows complex temporal relations between signals to be expressed in a concise and accurate way. However, capturing the required temporal behaviours of the design requires a precise temporal description in SVA.

Therefore, several attempts have been made to generate formal system requirements from natural language specifications in (Clarke et al., 1986; Holt, 1999; Grover et al., 2000; Harris, 2013). The motivations of these approaches are to reduce design time and errors and also to help us to have early identifications of incomplete and inconsistent specifications. Unfortunately, generating formal requirements from natural language specifications is still limited because most such approaches fail to capture certain temporal expressions commonly occurring in natural language specifications such as tenses, aspects, and temporal prepositions.

Of course, various linguists have attempted to provide formal semantics for certain temporal expressions in natural language (e.g. Reichenbach, 1947; Vendler, 1967; Dowty, 1972). Most approaches, (such as in Reichenbach (1947)), focus on tenses and are not readily applicable to hardware specifications, since, most of such specifications must be written in the present tense. Admittedly, the studies of aspectual classes (Vendler, 1967; Dowty, 1972) are useful when considering the temporal behaviours of natural language descriptions; however, in practice, these aspectual classes are not an essential requirements for generating SVAs.

In contradistinction to these linguistic studies, there is a logical form that can provide the formal semantics for temporal proposition phrases — *temporal preposition logic* ($\mathcal{TPL}$) which is one of the more recent interval logics as introduced in Pratt and Francez (2001). However, $\mathcal{TPL}$ is more expressive than SVA. Thus, this paper seeks to remedy these problems by finding a simpler way to translate natural language assertion descriptions featuring temporal expressions to SVAs directly. Our new logic $\mathcal{SITL}$

Proceedings of the 11th International Conference on Computational Semantics, pages 283–293,
London, UK, April 15-17 2015.

under some assumptions can be translated to SVA. $\mathcal{SITL}$ is a subset of $\mathcal{TPL}$. Although $\mathcal{TPL}$ is more expressive than $\mathcal{SITL}$, $\mathcal{SITL}$ can capture most temporal constructions that are described in natural language assertion descriptions. We hope in this paper to provide a method that is more precise and efficient in formal verifications than the previous attempts of Harris (2013).

The structure of the paper as follows. Section 2 introduces the basic definitions and notation of $\mathcal{TPL}$ and SVA. Section 3 introduces the syntax and semantics of $\mathcal{SITL}$ as well as its benefits of capturing temporal expressions. Section 4 shows a method for generating SVAs from natural language descriptions. The experimental methods and results are presented in Section 5. Section 6 reviews the techniques for generating formal specifications from natural language specifications and the effects of aspectual classes on the semantics of SVAs and Section 7 concludes the paper.

2 Preliminaries

2.1 Temporal Preposition Logic ($\mathcal{TPL}$)

In this section, we recall the semantics of $\mathcal{TPL}$ presented in Pratt-Hartmann (2005). $\mathcal{TPL}$ is a first-order language having variables which range over time-intervals and predicates corresponding to event-types and temporal order-relations. In this paper, the letters I, J with or without decorations, range over time intervals, where an interval is closed, bounded, non-empty subset of real numbers. Let us review the semantics of $\mathcal{TPL}$ using examples from natural language assertion descriptions. Consider the sentences:

(1) *Awid* is asserted

(2) *Awid* is asserted during every cycle

(3) *Awid* is asserted during every cycle until *Awvalid* goes high.

Sentence (1) states that, within the temporal context, there is an interval over which *Awid* is asserted. The meaning of (1) can be represented as follows:

(4) $\exists \mathrm{J}_0(\text{asserted}(\text{Awid}, \mathrm{J}_0) \wedge \mathrm{J}_0 \subseteq \mathrm{I})$.

Notice that the quantification of J_0 is limited to the temporal context which represented by the free variable I. Sentence (2) states that, within the temporal context I, every interval over which a cycle occurs includes an interval over which *Awid* is asserted. The meaning of (2) can be represented as follows:

(5) $\forall \mathrm{J}_1(\text{cycle}(\mathrm{J}_1) \wedge \mathrm{J}_1 \subseteq \mathrm{I} \rightarrow \exists \mathrm{J}_0(\text{asserted}(\text{Awid}, \mathrm{J}_0) \wedge \mathrm{J}_0 \subseteq \mathrm{J}_1))$.

Notice that *cycle* is considered in Pratt and Francez (2001) as a temporal noun which has an interval time such as *meeting*, *Monday*, and *1995*. Thus, the meaning of *cycle* should be as follows:

(6) $\lambda \mathrm{J} \lambda \mathrm{I}[\text{cycle}(\mathrm{J}) \wedge \mathrm{J} \subseteq \mathrm{I}]$,

Intuitively, the word "cycle" picks out those intervals J over which a cycle occurs with some temporal context I as shown in Formula (5).

Some events take place not during, but before or after various time-intervals. Thus, we need to define some functions that can express these relationships.

Definition 2.1. Let I = [a,b] and J = [c,d] be intervals. If a $<$ c $<$ d $<$ b, we let the terms init(J,I) and fin(J,I) denote the intervals [a,c] and [d,b], respectively, where init and fin are partial functions to denote the initial segment of I up to the beginning of J, and the final segment of I from the end of J, respectively. Finally, we denote the definite quantifier $\imath$ with the standard (Russellian) semantics $\imath(\psi, \psi')$.

Now, we can expresses sentence (3) in $\mathcal{TPL}$ as follows:

(7) $\iota J_2(\text{high}(\text{Awvalid}, J_2) \wedge J_2 \subseteq I,$
$\forall J_1(\text{cycle}(J_1) \wedge J_1 \subseteq \text{init}(J_2,I) \rightarrow \exists J_0(\text{asserted}(\text{Awid},J_0) \wedge J_0 \subseteq J_1)))$.

This formula states that, within the temporal context I, there is a unique interval J_2 such that *Awvalid* goes high at J_2 and every interval J_1 such that J_1 is a cycle and J_1 is contained init(J_2,I), which in turn includes an interval J_0 over which *Awid* is asserted.

In this section, we have given a flavour of the language $\mathcal{TPL}$. For a complete specification, we refer the reader to Pratt and Francez (2001).

2.2 SystemVerilog Assertions (SVA)

SVA is a subset of SystemVerilog which combines hardware descriptions and formal verifications. Assertions formally verify the correctness of the specifications. SVA has the ability to define sequential expressions with clear temporal relationships between them. These temporal relationships are expressed by one or more clocks. For example, assertion (8) checks that the signal "AWID" is high at every posedge clock. If the signal "AWID" is not high at any posedge clock, the assertion will fail.

(8) sequence s1;
@(posedge clk) AWID;
endsequence.

In SVA, the clock cycle delays are defined by a "##" sign and there are two types of delays possible, a single delay or a range of delays. Consider

(9) AWID ##2 AWVALID

(10) AWID ##[1:4] AWVALID.

Assertion (9) states that the signal "AWID" is true at the point of evaluation, and must remain true for next clock cycle before the single "AWVALID" will be true, while assertion (10) states that the signal "AWID" is true, and may remain true for up to 3 further clock cycles, directly after which the single "AWVALID" will be true. Note that we can specify an assertion with infinite repetition range such as in (11) where the $ symbol indicates that the signal "AWVALID" will eventually occur.

(11) AWID ##[1:$] AWVALID.

Furthermore, there are two types of implication in SVA: an overlapped implication and a non-overlapped implication. The overlapped implication is denoted by the symbol |-> while the non-overlapped implication is denoted by the symbol |=> as shows, respectively.

(12) AWID |-> AWVALID

(13) AWID |=> AWVALID.

Assertion (12) states that if the antecedent "AWID" holds, then the consequent expression "AWVALID" starts in the same clock cycle. On other hand, assertion (13) states that if the antecedent "AWID" holds, then the consequent expression "AWVALID" starts in the next clock cycle. Note that assertion (13) can be expressed differently using a "##" sign as shown below in (14) where ##1 means a delay of one clock cycle before the consequent expression "AWVALID" is started.

(14) AWID |-> ##1 AWVALID.

Moreover, SVA has sequential binary operators such as "and" and "or" operators which works with two sequences or boolean expressions. The "and" operator means that if both two sequences or boolean expressions are true, then the result of "and" operation is true. However, the resultant of the "or" operands is true whenever at least one of sequences boolean expressions is true. Consider

(15) AWID and AWVALID

(16) AWID or AWVALID.

Assertion (15) will be only true if both signals "AWID" and "AWVALID" are true; on other hand, the result of assertion (16) is true when either signal AWID or signal AWVALID is true.

All of the above-mentioned operators will be used for constructing transformation rules between $\mathcal{SITL}$ and SVA. For a more detailed account of SVA refer to Vijayaraghavan and Ramanathan (2006).

3 Simple Interval Temporal Logic ($\mathcal{SITL}$)

We define $\mathcal{SITL}$ as a subset of $\mathcal{TPL}$. Both logics work well for capturing temporal expressions in English. However, we choose $\mathcal{SITL}$ over $\mathcal{TPL}$ because it is more applicable for generating SVA.

A $\mathcal{SITL}$ language L is a triple (C,P,F) of sets of constant symbols, predicate symbols, and functional symbols. Note, each predicate symbol and functional symbol must be assigned to non-zero natural number which represents its arity. A term is a variable or a constant. Also, if f is a function symbol of arity n and $t_1, \ldots, t_n$ are terms, then $f(t_1, \ldots, t_n)$ is a term.

$\mathcal{SITL}$-formula ψ is defined by the Backus-Naur Form production rule as follows.

$\psi := \top \mid \bot \mid \neg\psi \mid \psi \wedge \psi' \mid \psi \vee \psi' \mid P(t_1, \ldots, t_n) \mid Q.TP(\psi, \psi')$.

Here $\top$, $\bot$, $\neg$, $\wedge$, and $\vee$ have the same meaning as in first-order logic, P is a predicate symbol of arity n and $t_1, \ldots, t_n$ are terms; TP is a binary predicate symbol that only corresponding to temporal prepositions such as *when*, *after*, *before*, and *until*. Note, TP is not a standard formulation of logic which means here if ψ and ψ' are formulas, then $Q.TP(\psi, \psi')$ are formulas too where Q denotes any type of quantifiers (such as universal, existential or definite quantifier) and "$TP(\psi, \psi')$" is restricted by Q. For example, a formula like "$\imath.when(\psi, \psi')$" means that ψ and ψ' are bounded by the definite quantifier $\imath$.

3.1 Semantics

We define $\mathcal{SITL}$ based on $\mathcal{TPL}$ introduced by Pratt-Hartmann (2005) as follows:

(17) $[\imath.when(\psi, \psi')]^{\#}(I) = \imath J([\psi]^{\#}(J) \wedge J \subseteq I, [\psi']^{\#}(J))$;

(18) $[\imath.before(\psi, \psi')]^{\#}(I) = \imath J([\psi]^{\#}(J) \wedge J \subseteq I, [\psi']^{\#}(fin(J,I))$;

(19) $[\imath.after(\psi, \psi')]^{\#}(I) = \imath J([\psi]^{\#}(J) \wedge J \subseteq I, [\psi']^{\#}(init(J,I))$;

(20) $[\imath.until(\psi, \psi')]^{\#}(I) = \imath J([\psi]^{\#}(J) \wedge J \subseteq I, [\psi']^{\#}(init(J,I))$;

(21) $[\imath.until\ after(\psi, \psi')]^{\#}(I) = \imath J([\psi]^{\#}(J) \wedge J \subseteq I, [\psi']^{\#}(init(J,fin(J,I))))$;

(22) $[Q.during(\psi, \psi')]^{\#}(I) = QJ([\psi]^{\#}(J) \wedge J \subseteq I, [\psi']^{\#}(J))$;

(23) $[\exists.for(\psi, \psi')]^{\#}(I) = \exists J([\psi]^{\#}(J) \wedge J \subseteq I \wedge [\psi']^{\#}(J))$.

First of all, the temporal prepositions in (17-21) require their complements to be definitely quantised since these readings are suitable for many cases in natural language descriptions. Second, the temporal preposition *during* in (22) is located ψ' to be within the interval of ψ where the quantification to restrict its complement is not decided. Finally, the temporal preposition *for* in (23) enforces its complement to be existentially quantified. These quantification restrictions on temporal preposition phrases have been discussed in Pratt and Francez (2001), which drew attention to the fact that some temporal prepositions impose restrictions on the temporal quantification appearing in their complements.

Taking the prepositions *until* and *until after* into consideration as expressed in (20) and (21), it is worth noting that out interpretation are different from $\mathcal{TPL}$. In $\mathcal{TPL}$, the preposition *until* universally quantifies its modificands explicitly. We leave this quantification implicit for simplification purpose which as stated before facilitates the generation of SVA. $\mathcal{SITL}$ is therefore constructed to consider interpretation of temporal prepositions that are required for the generation of correct SVAs.

3.2 Interpretation of $\mathcal{SITL}$ in English

In this section, we provide an interpretation of $\mathcal{SITL}$ in English involving temporal constructions. The purpose of $\mathcal{SITL}$ is to have a subset of $\mathcal{TPL}$ that is closer in expressive power to common constructions encountered natural language specifications. Consider

(24) *Awid* must remain stable when *Awvalid* is asserted.

which can be expressed in $\mathcal{SITL}$ and $\mathcal{TPL}$, respectively, as follows:

(25) $\imath$.when(asserted(Awvalid), stable(Awid))

(26) $\imath J_1($ asserted(Awvalid, $J_1) \wedge J_1 \subseteq I, \exists J_0($ stable(Awid, $J_0) \wedge J_0 \subseteq J_1))$.

Both formulas have the same meaning, namely, that, within the temporal context I, there is a unique interval J over which *Awvalid* is true which includes an interval over which *Awid* is true. However, $\mathcal{SITL}$ formula (25) is less expressive than $\mathcal{TPL}$ formula (26) in which $\mathcal{SITL}$ can easily transform to SVA such as (27) for formula (25). The transformations from $\mathcal{SITL}$ to SVA will be discussed later.

(27) *AWVALID* |-> $stable(*AWID*).

More interpretations can be provided here with temporal prepositions such as *after* and *before*. Consider the following sentences

(28) *Awid* must be low after *Awvalid* goes high

(29) *Awid* must be low before *Awvalid* goes high.

Both sentences can be expressed in $\mathcal{SITL}$ as follows, respectively.

(30) $\imath$.after(high(Awvalid), low(Awid))

(31) $\imath$.before(high(Awvalid), low(Awid)).

Formula (30) states that when the signal Awvalid goes high, the signal Awid must be low in the next cycle. Formula (31) states that before the signal Awvalid goes high, the signal Awid must be low. Thus, $\mathcal{SITL}$ defines events and their temporal locations correctly which enable us to easily map $\mathcal{SITL}$ formula into SVA as shown in (32) and (33) for (30) and (31), respectively.

(32) *AWVALID* |-> ##1 !*AWID*

(33) !*AWID* |-> ##1 *AWVALID*.

Furthermore, $\mathcal{SITL}$ can interpret complex temporal expressions that occur in natural language assertion descriptions. Consider

(34) When *Awvalid* is asserted, Awid must remain low until *Awready* goes high.

Sentence (34) has a complicated meaning since it includes two temporal prepositions *when* and *until*. Thus, we need to interpret it based on the most natural reading which here means the semantics of *until* must be restricted by the semantics of *when* as follows.

(35) $\overbrace{\imath.\text{when(asserted(Awvalid), } \overbrace{\imath.\text{until(high(Awready), low(Awid))}}^{until}\text{)}}^{When}$.

In order to explain our interpretation in $\mathcal{SITL}$, consider the following $\mathcal{TPL}$ formula

(36) $\imath J_2($ asserted(Awvalid, $J_2) \wedge J_2 \subseteq I, \imath J_1($high(Awready, $J_1) \wedge J_1 \subseteq$fin$(J_2, I),$
$\forall J_0(J_0 \subseteq$ init$(J_1,$ fin$(J_2, I)) \rightarrow$ low(Awid, $J_0)))),$

which states that within the temporal context I, there is a unique interval J_1 such that *Awvalid* is asserted at J_1 and there is a unique interval J_0 such that J_0 is a subset of fin(J_1,I) and *Awready* is high at J_0 and *Awid* must be low during init(J_0,fin(J_1,I)). Notice, (36) is not constructed of using rules (17) and (20) in Section 3.1. The complexities of *when* in conjunction with *until* require us to define a special rule as shown in (37), where locates the temporal relation between them correctly.

(37) $[\imath.\text{when}(\psi, \imath.\text{until}(\psi', \psi''))]^{\#}(I) = \imath J_1([\psi]^{\#}(J_1) \wedge J_1 \subseteq I, \imath J_0([\psi']^{\#}(J_0) \wedge$
$J_0 \subseteq \text{fin}(J_1,I), [\psi'']^{\#}(\text{init}(J_0,\text{fin}(J_1,I))))).$

Even if we change the order of sentence (34) as in the following example, we can only have the interpretation (35), that in which the semantic of *when* has wider scope than the semantic of *until* because in our method we do not intend to embed temporal prepositions; therefore we will allow them in ordering which they appear.

(38) Awid must remain low until *Awready* goes high when *Awvalid* is asserted.

In the end, we have shown the interpretations of $\mathcal{SITL}$ in requirement examples that were taken from ARM (2010) and how precise $\mathcal{SITL}$ is for specifying these requirements including temporal constructions. Then, we have explained how $\mathcal{SITL}$ can eliminate the complexity which can be caused by temporal prepositions. In the next section, we will show how can be possible to translate $\mathcal{SITL}$ to SVA using transformations rules.

4 Generating SystemVerilog Assertions

In this section, we describe a method for generating SVA from natural language descriptions. Our method will be divided into two distinct steps. First, we extract $\mathcal{SITL}$ from a parse tree using semantic rules and then we generate SVA from $\mathcal{SITL}$ using transformation rules.

4.1 Semantic Rules for Extracting $\mathcal{SITL}$

We build our semantic rules based on combining typed logic with lambda abstraction. This method defined in Montague (1974), which has been used globally to build semantic representations for a fragment of English. First of all, we use a wide coverage parser that produces *Penn tree-bank* style parse trees. Then, we take parse trees from the adopted parser and we apply our semantic rules to extract $\mathcal{SITL}$ from the parse trees such as in Figure 1 for sentence (24).

Notice that in Figure 1, the modal auxiliary (MD), the verb in base form (VB), and the auxiliary verb (AUX) are ignored when followed by the "VP" or "ADJP" because such constructions lead to redundancy if we attempt to represent every category. More importantly, most existing parsers attach the "SBAR" category to the "VP" category instead of the "S" category, which causes difficulties when handling the scope of temporal quantifications. Therefore, we handle this issue by moving up the "SBAR" category as shown in Figure 1 to be combined with the "S_0" category to extract $\mathcal{SITL}$ precisely.

We have constructed 176 semantic rules to extract $\mathcal{SITL}$. Each terminal or non-terminal node has a semantic rule based on its part of speech tag. These rules are limited to our case study which might be extended in the future work. This step was made specifically to support our theory about how easy it can be to generate SVA from $\mathcal{SITL}$ than other logical forms as explained in Section 3.2.

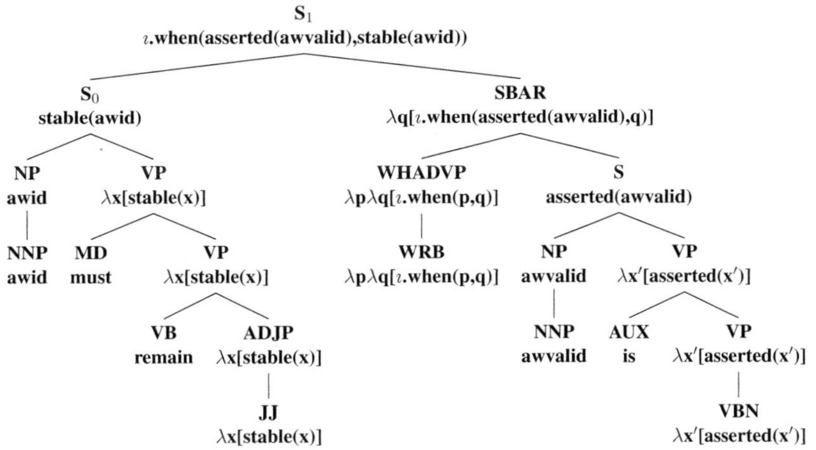

Figure 1: The annotated parse tree corresponds to semantic rules

4.2 Transforming $\mathcal{SITL}$ to SVA

This step is about generating SVA from $\mathcal{SITL}$ using transformation rules. These rules were constructed using all the possible interpretations of temporal expressions in SVA from ARM (2010) and Vijayaraghavan and Ramanathan (2006). The transformation rules take $\mathcal{SITL}$ as an input and produce its equivalent in SVA. Generating SVA from $\mathcal{SITL}$ will turn out to be straightforward because using $\mathcal{SITL}$ helps to reduce the difficulties of mapping natural language assertion descriptions to SVAs. The transformation rules are defined as follows:

1. $[\imath.\text{when}(\psi, \psi')]^{\#} = ([\psi]^{\#} \ |\text{->}\ [\psi']^{\#})$;
2. $[\imath.\text{before}(\psi, \psi')]^{\#} = ([\psi']^{\#} \ |\text{->}\ \#\#1\ [\psi]^{\#})$;
3. $[\imath.\text{after}(\psi, \psi')]^{\#} = ([\psi]^{\#} \ |\text{->}\ \#\#1\ [\psi']^{\#})$;
4. $[\imath.\text{until}(\psi, \psi')]^{\#} = ([\psi']^{\#}[{*}0:\$]\ \#\#1\ [\psi]^{\#})$;
5. $[\imath.\text{until after}(\psi, \psi')]^{\#} = ([\psi']^{\#}[{*}0:\$]\ \#\#0\ [\psi]^{\#})$;
6. $[\exists.\text{for}(\mathbb{N}, \psi)]^{\#} = ([\psi]^{\#}[{*}\mathbb{N}]^{\#})$.

The transformation rule (1) maps ψ and ψ' into SVA as an overlap relation. In the transformation rule (2), ψ and ψ' maps into SVA where ψ' must occur a cycle before ψ is true, while the transformation rule (3) is inverse of (2). The transformation rule (4) maps ψ and ψ' into SVA where ψ' must occur until the cycle before ψ is true, while in the transformation rule (5), ψ' must remain true until ψ is completed. In addition to transformation rules (4) and (5), the temporal preposition $until$ frequently comes with another temporal prepositions such as $when$, $during$, and $after$. For example, assertion (39) is constructed by combining the transformation rule (3) with the transformation rule (4) which here means after ψ comes true, ψ'' must remain true until ψ' occurs.

$$\text{(39)}\quad \overbrace{([\psi]^{\#}\ |\text{->}\ \#\#1\ \overbrace{[\psi'']^{\#}[{*}0:\$]\ \#\#1\ [\psi']^{\#}}^{until}}^{after}).$$

Finally, the transformation rule (6) is related to the preposition *for* which takes only numerical expressions as its complement such as one cycle, two cycles, and etc which denote number of repetitions. For example, sentence (40) indicates that after the signal "Awid" is true, Awvalid must be low for two consecutive cycles as shown in assertion (41).

(40) Awvalid is low for two cycles after Awid goes high.

(41) AWID |-> ##1 !AWVALID[*2].

Having discussed how to translate $\mathcal{SITL}$ into SVA involving temporal prepositions, there are other categories need to be translate into SVAs such verbs, adjectives, and noun phrases. Thus, we have collected the most common words in natural language descriptions from ARM (2010). Then, we assigned each word a link to a particular SVA's term. For example, the adjectives "stable" and "constant" are linked to a keyword "$stable". Table 1 shows some common words in $\mathcal{SITL}$ and their formal terms in SVA.

#	*SITL*	SVA	#	*SITL*	SVA
	verb			Conjunction and Disjunction	
7	has/have/use/require(ψ, ψ')	ψ |-> ψ'	19	$\psi \vee \psi'$	(ψ or ψ')
8	$\neg$exceed(ψ, ψ')	ψ <= ψ'	20	$\psi \wedge \psi'$	(ψ and ψ')
9	be/set(ψ, ψ')	(ψ==ψ')		Preposition	
10	asserted/permitted(ψ)	ψ	21	on(ψ, ψ')	(ψ==ψ')
11	$\neg$de-asserted/$\neg$permitted(ψ)	!ψ	22	with(ψ, ψ')	(ψ==ψ')
12	$\neg$be(ψ, ψ')	(ψ!=ψ')		Noun phrases or signals	
	Adjectives		23	write burst	(AWBURST==AXI_ABURST_INCR)
13	stable/constant(ψ)	$stable($\psi$)	24	read burst	(ARBURST==AXI4PC_ABURST_INCR)
14	high(ψ)	ψ	25	write transaction	AWBURST
15	low(ψ)	!ψ	26	read transaction	ARBURST
16	greater(ψ, ψ')	($\psi > \psi'$)	27	data_width parameter	DATA_WIDTH
17	equal(ψ, ψ')	(ψ=ψ')	28	awvalid	AWVALID
18	less(ψ, ψ')	($\psi < \psi'$)	29	awid	AWID

Table 1: Transformation rules for some common words.

As shown in Table 1, it is necessary that we link each word with its SVA's term in our transformation rules; otherwise the output will not have the correct transformations.

What follows is a description of how our transformation rules can be an efficient method for generating SVAs. To illustrate how we perform our transformations, we execute it on example (25). The steps below show how SVA can be generated from $\mathcal{SITL}$ formula using our transformation rules.

[$\imath$.when(asserted(Awvalid), stable(Awid))]$^{\#}$ = [asserted(Awvalid)]$^{\#}$ |-> [stable(Awid)]$^{\#}$ (rule 1);
[asserted(Awvalid)]$^{\#}$ |-> [stable(Awid)]$^{\#}$ = [Awvalid]$^{\#}$ |-> [stable(Awid)]$^{\#}$ (rule 10);
[Awvalid]$^{\#}$ |-> [stable(Awid)]$^{\#}$ = AWVALID |-> [stable(Awid)]$^{\#}$ (rule 28);
AWVALID |-> [stable(Awid)]$^{\#}$ = AWVALID |-> $stable([Awid]$^{\#}$) (rule 13);
AWVALID |-> $stable([Awid]$^{\#}$) = AWVALID |-> $stable(AWID) (rule 29).

In summary, we described a method for translating $\mathcal{SITL}$ to SVA. This method enables us to translate most $\mathcal{SITL}$s into SVAs. Next section will show experimental results that demonstrate the performance of our method.

5 Experimental Methods and Results

To evaluate the ideas discussed in this paper empirically, we collected documents from ARM (2010) for verification of the AXI bus protocol. These documents contain a large number of SVAs specifying system requirements together with English comments explaining their meaning. We took the English comments and we parsed them using Charniak's parser (Charniak, 2000) to produce parse trees. Then, we extracted $\mathcal{SITL}$ from parse trees via semantic rules as explained in Section 4.1. Finally, we generated SVAs from $\mathcal{SITL}$ using our transformation rules that described in Section 4.2. The total number of such comments is 397 SVAs. Our program contains 83 transformation rules and approximately 2374 words with their logical forms in SVA. Most of these words are noun categories where approximately 65% of the words are automatically generated, and approximately 35% are manually written such as words (23-27) in Table 1.

In this paper, we compare our results with those obtained by ARM (2010). We consider our assertion results are true when they are identical to the originals or having the same meaning but different expressions since temporal behaviour sequences can be expressed in more than one way. As outcomes, we found our program successfully generated SVAs for 297 out of 397, or 74.81% of all assertions. Thus, our method can be useful for generating SVA which reduces design time and errors. A second point to make is that by observing the given results, the relation between the English comments and their equivalent meaning in SVA is not complex, but rather is straightforward mapping that only need a proper formal logic featuring temporal expressions such as $\mathcal{SITL}$.

Of course, our program does not work in every case. Consider

(42) A sequence of locked transactions must use a single ID.

where the expression "a sequence of locked transactions" corresponds to multiple signals which must use the "single ID" in a special order which can not be defined from a theoretical standpoint; unless if we use a practical approach which would not be sufficient here. Thus, our program failed to generate SVAs in three circumstances, (i) when it is difficult to determine the meaning of their lexical items in SVA as shown in (42), (ii) when sentences contain words that are not introduced in the transformation rules before running our system as explained in Section 4.2, and finally (iii) when the adopted parser gives a wrong parse tree in which case no result is computed. Note that the third limitation is due to the chosen parser which can be solved with a better parser.

6 Related Work

6.1 Specifications in Natural Languages

One of common ways to generate formal specifications from natural language specifications is to use natural language processing techniques which help engineers to express system requirements with unrestricted language such as in (Osborne and MacNish, 1996; Lamar, 2009). However, although natural language processing techniques provide very respectable accuracies for real-world texts by using part-of-speech taggers and syntactic parsers, these approaches may produce multiple syntactical parses which may not be plausible at the interpretation level to eliminate the ambiguous one.

Therefore, Grover et al. (2000) and Fuchs et al. (2008) use a controlled natural language (CNL) to deal with ambiguities of natural languages. CNL is a subset of natural language with a restricted syntax and semantics in order to reduce or eliminate ambiguity and complexity of natural languages. CNL based-tools have been used in many areas such as software and hardware specifications, specifications of legal contracts, and business rule specifications. For example, Fuchs et al. (2008) uses CNL to provide a knowledge representation language in several application domains and to translate CNL's texts to *discourse representation structures* and *first-order logic*. However, most of such approaches fail to cope with natural language specifications featuring temporal constructions.

In the case of expressing temporal constructions, Clarke et al. (1986) uses a controlled English tool to convert English specifications into computation tree logic (CTL) which is used as a logical representation for hardware verification. Although CTL is commonly used for specifying temporal properties of finite-state systems, most of these approaches are not expressive enough to capture the semantics of temporal prepositions in natural language descriptions.

A more practical approach for capturing SVAs from natural language descriptions is presented in Harris (2013). This approach uses an attribute grammar approach (Engelfriet, 1984) to generate SVA. However, it fails to discuss the issues of temporal constructions in natural language descriptions. This approach offers generally a suitable way to generate SVAs from natural language requirements. On other hand, our method aims to be more focused on specifying temporal expressions in natural language assertion descriptions and provides an efficient method for generating SVAs involving temporal behaviours.

6.2 Aspectual Class

Over the past decade researchers have investigated the effects of aspectual classes of verb phrases in natural language semantics. Vendler (1967) and Dowty (1972) have worked to build a taxonomy of temporal-event descriptions to provide better descriptions of how people describe events in our language. For example, Vendler (1967) has classified verbs into four aspectual classes – states, activities, achievements and accomplishments – in order to provide the way in which verbs can be viewed with respect to time. However, the effects of these aspectual classes on generating SVAs are limited because any temporal expression at verb phrase level is restricted by the semantics of temporal prepositions. Moreover, in practice, any SVA must be checked in every clock cycle regardless what its value in the previous clock cycle. Consider

(43) When Awid is low, Awvaild is high.

(44) When Awid goes low, Awvaild goes high.

Sentence (43) has a state verb in *when*'s complement, whereas sentence (44) has an event verb. The meanings of both sentences are different in literature. In sentence (43), "Awid is low" means that it is started before the current interval, while in sentence (44), "Awid goes low" means that it is started at the current interval. However, in SVA, both mean the same since both antecedent expressions will be checked at every posedge clock. Therefore, there is not going to be any gain from the studies of aspectual classes since state and event verbs are treated similarly in the domain of interest.

However, by examining the temporal semantics of some natural language descriptions, we found some surprising insights from the semantics of temporal prepositions with aspecual classes. For example, some temporal prepositions are constrained in respect of the event types (activities, achievements or accomplishments) they can take as arguments. Consider

(45) * Awid is low after Awvaild is high.

(46) Awid goes low after Awvaild goes high.

Sentence (45) is odd because *after* preposition resists to take a state verb in its complement. However, sentence (46) is a correct statement because *after* preposition can take an event verb in its complement. Note, these restrictions are also applied to *until*, *until after*, and *before* prepositions. On other hand, *when* or *while* does not have these restrictions in which both can have either a state or an event in their complements such as in (43) and (44). Finally, we can say aspectual classes can help us to provide legal grammatical constructions of various sentence forms and their interactions with different temporal prepositions. In this paper, we do not intend to take aspectual classes into consideration in our tool because our goal is to eliminate any unnecessary complexity for usability purposes.

7 Conclusion

We presented a method for translating natural language assertion descriptions into SVAs based on $\mathcal{SITL}$. We have constructed $\mathcal{SITL}$ using $\mathcal{TPL}$. We first showed some interpretations of $\mathcal{SITL}$ in English and then we presented transformation rules for mapping $\mathcal{SITL}$ to SVAs. We developed a small program for verifying our method on AXI bus protocol in ARM (2010). Our experimental results suggest that using $\mathcal{SITL}$ as a logical representation for capturing SVAs featuring temporal expressions can enable us to have more accurate and effective results than existing tools.

In the future, we plan to extend $\mathcal{SITL}$ to handle other temporal constructions such as prepositions specifying durations – e,g. *in*, *within*, or *throughout* – or prepositions specifying particular points in time – e,g. *by* or *since*. This extension will enhance the performance of our method by representing more temporal constructions, and generate their equivalent meaning in SVA.

References

ARM, A. (2010). Axi protocol specification (rev 2.0). *Available at http://www. arm. com.*

Charniak, E. (2000). A maximum-entropy-inspired parser. In *Proceedings of the 1st North American chapter of the Association for Computational Linguistics conference*, pp. 132–139. Association for Computational Linguistics.

Clarke, E. M., E. A. Emerson, and A. P. Sistla (1986). Automatic verification of finite-state concurrent systems using temporal logic specifications. *ACM Transactions on Programming Languages and Systems, 8*(2), 244–263.

Darringer, J. A. (1988). The application of program verification techniques to hardware verification. In *Papers on Twenty-five years of electronic design automation*, pp. 373–379. ACM.

Dowty, D. R. (1972). *Studies in the logic of verb aspect and time reference in English.* Department of Linguistics, University of Texas at Austin.

Engelfriet, J. (1984). Attribute grammars: Attribute evaluation methods. *Methods and tools for compiler construction*, 103–138.

Fuchs, N. E., K. Kaljurand, and T. Kuhn (2008). Attempto Controlled English for knowledge representation. In *Reasoning Web*, pp. 104–124. Springer.

Grover, C., A. Holt, E. Klein, and M. Moens (2000). Designing a controlled language for interactive model checking. In *Proceedings of the Third International Workshop on Controlled Language Applications*, pp. 29–30.

Harris, I. G. (2013). Capturing assertions from natural language descriptions. In *Natural Language Analysis in Software Engineering (NaturaLiSE), 2013 1st International Workshop on*, pp. 17–24. IEEE.

Holt, A. (1999). Formal verification with natural language specifications: guidelines, experiments and lessons so far. *South African Computer Journal*, 253–257.

Lamar, C. (2009). Linguistic analysis of natural language engineering requirements.

Milne, G. J. (1993). *Formal specification and verification of digital systems.* McGraw-Hill, Inc.

Montague, R. (1974). Formal philosophy; selected papers of Richard Montague.

Osborne, M. and C. MacNish (1996). Processing natural language software requirement specifications. In *Requirements Engineering, 1996., Proceedings of the Second International Conference on*, pp. 229–236. IEEE.

Pratt, I. and N. Francez (2001). Temporal prepositions and temporal generalized quantifiers. *Linguistics and Philosophy 24*(2), 187–222.

Pratt-Hartmann, I. (2005). Temporal prepositions and their logic. *Artificial Intelligence 166*(1), 1–36.

Reichenbach, H. (1947). The tenses of verbs.

Vendler, Z. (1967). *Linguistics in Philosophy.* Cornell University Press.

Vijayaraghavan, S. and M. Ramanathan (2006). *A practical guide for SystemVerilog assertions.* Springer.

How hard is this query? Measuring the Semantic Complexity of Schema-agnostic Queries

André Freitas[1], Juliano Efson Sales[2], Siegfried Handschuh[1], Edward Curry[2]
[1]Department of Computer Science and Mathematics
University of Passau
[2]Insight Centre for Data Analytics
National University of Ireland, Galway
[1]firstname.lastname@uni-passau.de
[2]firstname.lastname@insight-centre.org

March 25, 2015

Abstract

The growing size, heterogeneity and complexity of databases demand the creation of strategies to facilitate users and systems to consume data. Ideally, query mechanisms should be *schema-agnostic*, i.e. they should be able to match user queries in their own vocabulary and syntax to the data, abstracting data consumers from the representation of the data. This work provides an information-theoretical framework to evaluate the semantic complexity involved in the query-database communication, under a schema-agnostic query scenario. Different entropy measures are introduced to quantify the semantic phenomena involved in the user-database communication, including structural complexity, ambiguity, synonymy and vagueness. The entropy measures are validated using natural language queries over Semantic Web databases. The analysis of the semantic complexity is used to improve the understanding of the core semantic dimensions present at the query-data matching process, allowing the improvement of the design of schema-agnostic query mechanisms and defining measures which can be used to assess the semantic uncertainty or difficulty behind a schema-agnostic querying task.

Semantic Complexity, Entropy, Schema-agnostic Queries, Database Queries, Databases

1 Introduction

The growing data availability on Big Data environments demands the creation of strategies to facilitate the interaction between data consumers and databases. As the number of available data sources grows and schemas increase in size and complexity, the effort associated with matching an *information need* to a database schema, intrinsic to the creation of structured queries such as SPARQL and SQL, becomes prohibitive. Ideally, data consumers, being them humans or intelligent agents, should be able to be abstracted from the representation of the data by using a *schema-agnostic query mechanism* [6].

However, structured queries are still the primary way to interact with databases. Despite the evolution of natural language interfaces (NLIs), and the empirical evaluation behind different NLI approaches, relatively little attention is given to the analysis of the semantic phenomena behind the user-database communication (UDC). The construction of semantic models for databases brings the potential of improving UDC and the design of more principled schema-agnostic query mechanisms.

In this work information theoretic models are used to define measures of *semantic complexity* for *schema-agnostic queries*. The measures of semantic complexity are used to quantify the role of core semantic phenomena such as *ambiguity*, *synonymy* and *matching complexity* in the *semantic interpretation*

Proceedings of the 11th International Conference on Computational Semantics, pages 294–304,
London, UK, April 15-17 2015.

of schema-agnostic queries. The contributions of this paper are: (i) to provide a principled and comprehensive analysis of existing semantic measures of semantic complexity in the UDC context, (ii) to validate these measures over a realistic query scenario based on natural language queries over large-schema RDF graph datasets, (iii) to introduce novel semantic complexity measures based on distributional semantic models and (iv) to use the semantic complexity models to support the design of schema-agnostic queries.

This paper is organized as follows: section 2 introduces schema-agnostic queries; section 3 introduces the concept of semantic complexity and entropy; section 4 describes the schema-agnostic queries and the associated semantic entropy model and measures; section 5 validates the model and discusses design principles derived from the entropy measures which can be used on schema-agnostic query mechanisms; section 6 describes conclusions and future works.

2 Mapping Schema-agnostic Queries

Schema-agnostic queries are queries which assume that users do not know the terminology and the structural relations inside a dataset while expressing their information needs [6, 5]. Since the query information can be represented in the database using different terms and relations, schema-agnostic queries are intrinsically associated with a *semantic matching* and *interpretation* model. Schema-agnostic queries can follow a natural language, keyword or a structured query syntax.

In the Information Retrieval space, different works evaluated the query performance by providing predictors based on language models applied in the estimation of vagueness and ambiguity (clarity score in [3]), and by improving query performance using selective pruning [15]. Sullivan [14] uses effectiveness measures to classify 50 question narratives over unstructured text as easy or hard.

Previous works have investigated the formal conditions for mapping a natural language query to a database. The work of Popescu et al. [12] provides a formal description of *natural language interfaces to databases*, concentrating on the definition of the concept of *semantic tractability*. Essentially, the concept of *semantic tractability* provides a description of soundness and completeness conditions for mapping natural language queries to database elements. Comparatively, this work focuses on evaluating query performance predictors for schema-agnostic queries on structured data, targeting addressing schema-agnostic queries over heterogeneous databases.

3 Semantic Complexity & Entropy

The concept of *entropy* in information theory is defined as a measure of uncertainty or surprise associated with a random variable. The random variable represents possibilities over the possible *states* or *configurations* that a specific symbolic system can be in, where the entropy is directly proportional to the number of states.

In order to transport the concept of entropy to the UDC problem, four symbolic sets are introduced: (i) a *word set* W, which expresses the set of words used to describe the domain of discourse shared by the user and database, (ii) a *word sense set* WS, which describes the possible senses associated with the words, (iii) a *proposition set* S, to describe the possible (syntactically valid) compositions of words senses and (iv) a *concept set* C, to describe the set of concepts associated with the possible interpretation for all the compositions. The unambiguous *semantic interpretation* of a query $I(q)$ or database statement $I(s)$ is a concept c_i in the concept domain. Figure 1 depicts the relationship between the sets in the query/database interpretation process. Ambiguity, vagueness and synonymy are defined as mappings patterns between the four sets.

It is possible to define a set M for the semantically valid mappings between W and C under a specific query database matching $m_\Sigma(Q, G)$ for a specific semantic model Σ. The semantic entropy associated with the query-DB matching is proportional to the cardinality of M.

In the context of schema-agnostic queries, the concept of entropy can be interpreted under four main perspectives:

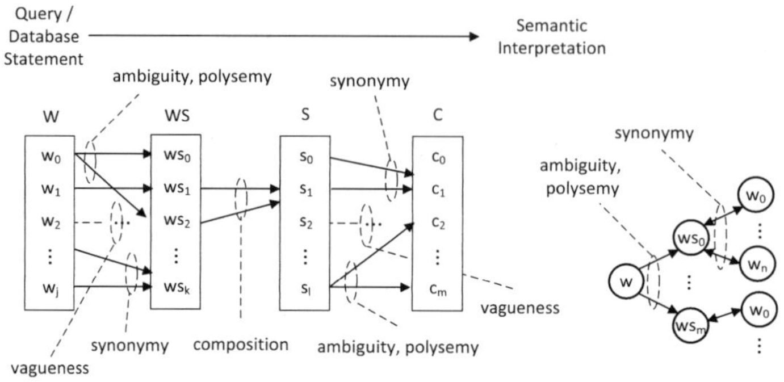

Figure 1: Mapping from words in a query to meaning (w_j) to word sense (ws_k), syntactic composition (s_l) and the associated concept (c_m) for the statement.

- (i) **structural/conceptual complexity:** Databases which express a large number of concepts have larger semantic entropy values. The number of interpretations is usually correlated to the number of distinct entities in the database and the number of possible compositions between them (propositions).
- (ii) **level of ambiguity:** Words/propositions can convey different meanings. The degree of ambiguity (number of possible interpretations) varies for different words and propositions. Depending on the domain of discourse and on the selection of the words, queries and databases can have different levels of associated ambiguity.
- (iii) **vocabulary gap/indeterminacy/vagueness:** The interpretation of a query or of a database statement is dependent on the ability of the data consumer (receiver) to interpret the expressed information. Query and databases may not be expressed in the same vocabulary (synonymy phenomenon) or in the same abstraction-level. Additionally, query and data may not be mapped with the contextual information available in the query or in the database. Indeterminacy/vagueness are semantic phenomena where words, entities or propositions fail to map to the exact meaning intended by the transmitter.
- (iv) **novelty:** Semantic entropy is usually associated with the degree of novelty/informativeness/-surprise associated with the communication process. The more informative the result returned by a query in relation to the specific background knowledge of the query issuer, the larger the entropy value. This dimension is not the focus of this work.

The process of mapping a schema-agnostic query Q to a database associated interpretation $I_G(Q)$ depends on the semantic entropy associated with each entropy dimension and involves coping with the semantic phenomena of structural complexity, term ambiguity, structural ambiguity, vagueness and synonymy. The next section introduces *semantic entropy measures* for each of these dimensions. In the definition of the entropy measures, a practical perspective was adopted (which focuses on the computation of these measures instead of a purely formal model) where the definition of approximate measures take place wherever the application of the complete model is not viable or practical.

4 Semantic Entropy Measures

A generic interpretation process for a schema-agnostic query Q can be defined as a set of steps which map a sequence of words $<w_0, w_1, ..., w_n>$into a set of possible database interpretations $I_G(Q)$. It is assumed that both query and database terminologies are defined under the same language L and that database entities are described using natural language labels. The generic process of interpreting the query can be summarized into the following steps with a set of associated entropy measures:

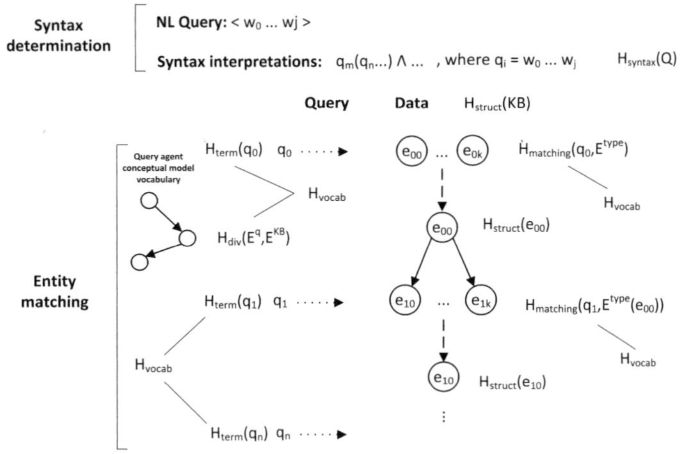

Figure 2: Generic steps for the query processing and associated entropy measures for each step.

- **Syntactic matching:** Consists in the possible interpretations for the syntactic structure of the query under the database syntax. This step consists in the segmentation of the query Q into a set of terms $<q_0, q_1, ..., q_n>$. The entropy H_{syntax} expresses the syntactic uncertainty/ambiguity in the determination of the syntactic mapping.
- **Vocabulary matching:** Consists in the matching/alignment between query entities and database entities, once a syntactic structure was defined. The entropy H_{vocab} is the uncertainty/ambiguity associated with the matching between query entity candidates and database entities.

Figure 2 depicts the steps in the query interpretation process and the associated entropies, while Figure 3 depicts an example for a specific query example. In this section, to maximize generalizability a logical (constant, predicate) terminology is used to express database statements and queries. In the evaluation section the model is specialized into the RDF/SPARQL model.

4.1 Measures of Semantic Entropy

4.1.1 Syntactic Entropy (H_{syntax})

The syntactic entropy of a query is defined by the possible syntactic configurations in which a query can be interpreted under the database syntax. Figure 2 and Figure 3(2) depicts H_{syntax} within the query interpretation model. The syntactic interpretation of a query Q is a tuple $T = <C, \Pi, R, L, Op>$, where C and Π are the set of constants and predicates in the database, $R \rightarrow \Pi \times C \times \cdots$ is the ordered set of syntactic n-ary associations between C and Π, L is the set of logical operators $\wedge, \vee$ and Op a set of functional operators.

The syntactic entropy is given as a function of the probability of the syntactic interpretation of a query. Let Syn be the *lexical categories* and *constituent categories* associated with the set of query words w_i and terms q_i. Let DM be the data model categories (e.g. C, Π, R, L, Op) in which the set of Syn categories can be mapped. Let $N_{syntax}(q_i)$ be the number of possible data model categories DM in which the query term q_i was observed to be mapped in a reference alignment corpus, and $count(q_i \rightarrow DM)$ the number of observed instances of the mapping to a specific alignment $q_i \rightarrow DM$. The probability of a term q_i syntactic mapping is given by:

$$P_{syntax}(Q) = \prod_{i=0}^{n} \frac{count(q_i \rightarrow DM)}{N_{syntax}(q_i)}$$

where $q_i \rightarrow DM$ are specific mappings. $H_{syntax}(Q)$ is computed by applying P_{syntax} into Shannon's entropy formula [13].

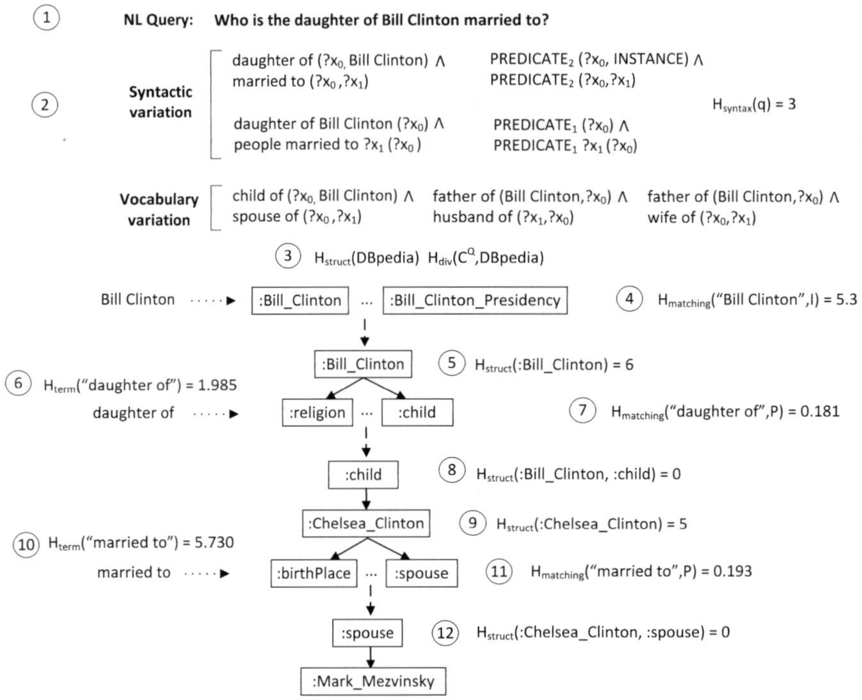

Figure 3: Instantiation of the query-entropy model for an example query.

4.1.2 Structural Entropy (H_{struct})

The *structural entropy* defines the complexity of a database based on the possible propositions that can be encoded under its schema. It provides a numerical description of the amount of information expressed in the database, independent of the query. Pollard & Biermann [11] proposed a structural entropy measure to quantify the entropy of a structured database. The entropy is computed by taking into account the number of predicates and constants and their syntactic combination. Figure 2 and Figure 3(5,8,12) depicts H_{struct}. The entropy of a constant c or a predicate π are defined as a function of the cardinality of the set of tuples in which the constant or the predicate is inserted. Further details are available in [11].

4.1.3 Terminological Entropy (H_{term})

The *terminological entropy* focuses on quantifying an estimate on the amount of *synonymy* and *vagueness* for the query or database terms. Let t be a query or database term containing the sequence of words $<w_0, w_1, ..., w_n>$. The terminological entropy is defined as a function of $P_{term}(w_i, w_j)$, i.e. the probability of a word w_i being expressed as a w_{j-th} related word for the associated ws sense (Figure 1). Under the query-database semantic matching problem, the relation between w_i and w_j can easily transcend the synonym relation, expressing a broader *semantic relatedness relationship*. Semantic relatedness will include both taxonomic (including different abstraction levels) and non-taxonomic relationships. As an absolute number of relationships cannot be enumerated, approximate entropy measures can be used to estimate the terminological entropy of a term. Figure 2 and Figure 3(6,10) depicts H_{term}.

One example of approximate terminological entropy measures is the *translational entropy* (Melamed, 1996) [10] which uses the coherence in the translation of a word (translational distribution) as an entropy measure. Given a set of word pairs of a set of ordered word pairs (s, t), respectively coming from a source language and a target language, an iterative process is used to determine the frequency $F(s, t)$ in which a word s is translated to a word t where $F(s)$ is the absolute frequency of the source word in the text. The probability that s translates to t is defined as $P(t|s) = F(s, t)/F(s)$. The notion of probability is defined by the translational distribution, the term $H(T|s)$ is generated, calculating the entropy of a

Measure	Semantic Measure Category	Type	Semantic Phenomena	Application
Pollard & Biermann [11]	Structural	Precise	Possibilities	Query-Data Alignment or Data
Translational Entropy (Melamed [10])	Terminological	Approximate	Ambiguity, Synonymy, Vagueness	Query or Data
Distributional Entropy	Terminological	Approximate	Ambiguity, Vagueness	Query or Data
Matching Entropy	Terminological	Approximate	Ambiguity, Vagueness	Query-Data Entity Alignments

Table 1: Classification of entropy measures according to associated features.

given word s against the target words set T: $H_{trans}(T|s) = -\sum_{t \in T} P(t|s)\ \log\ P(t|s)$.

4.1.4 Matching Entropy ($H_{matching}$)

Consists of measures which describe the uncertainty involved in the query-data matching/alignment between query terms and dataset entities. While terminological entropy measures provide an isolated estimate of the entropy, providing a prospective estimate of the matching complexity, the query-data matching entropy provides an estimate based on the set of potential alignments. These measures compute the uncertainty/ambiguity of an alignment under a semantic model Σ. Let q be an entity candidate in the query and let e_i be an i-th alignment candidate in the dataset. The *query-data matching entropy* can be estimated using the complement of a similarity metric $1 - sim_{space}(\vec{\mathbf{q}}, \vec{\mathbf{e_i}})$ such as cosine similarity, over a $word = \{w_0, \cdots, w_m\}$ or $concept = \{c_0, \cdots, c_n\}$ (e.g. distributional semantic model [8]) vector spaces. Distributional semantic models, semantic models based on the statistical patterns of co-occurrence of words within a large corpora can provide practical estimators for $H_{matching}$. Figure 2 and Figure 3(4,7,11) depicts the $H_{matching}$. In this case the entropy is not defined as a function of a probability but it is associated with a score.

5 Validation & Analysis

This section focuses on the validation and analysis of the proposed semantic complexity model. The model is validated using the Question Answering over Linked Data (QALD) 2011/2012 test collection [2], which is used as a challenge for the comparative evaluation of question answering systems over Linked Datasets. The performance of the participating Question Answering (QA) systems in addressing the schema-agnostic natural language queries is used as a gold standard for the validation of the semantic entropy model. The assumption is that queries with lower entropy positively correlate with the precision and recall performance of the system.

The QALD 2011/2012 test collections consist of 150 natural language queries over DBpedia 3.6 and DBpedia 3.7[1] as datasets. The QALD test collection was generated as a set of queries created by users around entities described in DBpedia. The set of questions covers different answer types and topics (e.g. proteins, countries, cities, companies, artists, planets, politicians, music, etc). QALD natural language queries explore different query patterns in the database.

The approximate entropy measures were setup using the following parameters:

- *Translational Entropy:* used the *European Parliament Parallel Corpus* for the generation of the translational corpus. The measure employed seven bitexts translating from English to Spanish, French, Portuguese, Italian, Greek, Swedish and Dutch, which were averaged to generate the final score.

[1] http://dbpedia.org/

- *Matching Entropy:* Generated as a set of vectors using the Explicit Semantic Analysis (ESA) [7] distributional semantic model over the Wikipedia 2013 corpus.

The *correlation* between each entropy measure and the *f-measure* of the participating QA systems was calculated taking into account the 150 queries in the test part of the QALD 2011 and 2012 test collections. Four top-performing QA systems were used in the evaluation: PowerAqua [9], Freya [4] for QALD 2011 and QAKis [1] and MHE for QALD 2012. The inter-annotator agreement between the PowerAqua [9] and Freya [4] is κ = 0.501 (95% confidence interval, 'moderate' agreement) and between QAKis [1] and MHE is κ = 0.236 (95% confidence interval, 'fair' agreement). A multiple linear regression model based on H_{syntax}, H_{term} (H_{trans}), $H_{matching}$ (H_{dist}) and H_{struct} was built.

The regression model parameters are shown in Table 2. H_{syntax} has a *significant negative correlation* with f-measure showing that the number of possible syntactical interpretations have a significant impact in the query interpretation process. Another *significant correlation is given by the terminological entropy measure* over the terms in the query which map to predicates (H_{term}, calculated by the translational entropy H_{trans}) The correlation shows that the translational entropy provide a valid estimator which reflect the higher level of ambiguity, synonymy and vagueness for predicate-type elements (the higher semantic gap for predicates is confirmed in Table 3). The $H_{matching}$ instantiated as H_{dist} *also presents a significant correlation for predicates*, confirming its suitability as an estimator for the vocabulary gap.

The *structural entropy* H_{struct} *of instances and classes showed a negative correlation with the f-measure*. The correlation is not significant for the structural entropy of the properties. This assymetry can be explained by the fact that in RDF the class or instance in most of the cases define the topic of the query (What is the highest *mountain*?, Who is the wife of *Barack Obama*?) having a *higher specificity* and being *more discriminative* in the definition of the data search space, while the properties tend to be more generic and reused across different contexts. The average structural entropy of instances (5.93) is significantly lower than the average structural entropy of properties (27.18). A query over a structurally more complex / better described entity (Barack Obama, with 505 associated triples) tend to be more difficult to resolve when compared to a less structurally complex entity (Michelle Obama, 268 associated triples).

Entropy Measure	**Estimate**	**Std. Error**	**t-value**	**Pr(>—t—)**
H_{syntax}	-0.05632	0.01697	**-3.317**	0.0011
H_{struct} Inst/Class (Sum)	0.00016	0.00599	0.027	0.97868
H_{struct} Prop (Sum)	-0.00013	0.00155	-0.086	0.93146
H_{trans} Pred (Sum)	-0.01330	0.01666	**-0.798**	0.42610
H_{dist} Pred (Sum)	-0.00202	0.00810	**-0.249**	0.80348

Table 2: Linear regression model between the evaluated entropy measures and the average f-measure of QA systems. Multiple R-squared = 0.1094 and adjusted R-squared = 0.0771

In addition to the entropy analysis, the queries were analyzed and categorized according to three dimensions (Figure 4): (i) query-term entity alignments, (ii) query features and (iii) query structure. This categorization supports a more in depth analysis of the impact of semantic complexity in the querying process.

All the 150 query-database alignments were analysed according to the type of their lexical alignment (*semantically related*, *similar string* (Dice coefficient >0.5), *substring*, *identical*). The distribution of query-database alignments is shown in Table 3. The proportion of *instances* which are *identical* to the query term is significantly larger compared to other categories, showing that the *lexical variability for instances (constants) is much smaller*. This is explained by the fact that instances usually map to named entities, which are less bound to synonymy, abstraction-level variations and vagueness. In contrast, *properties and classes (predicates)* tend to map to less specific terms, and *are more bound to ambiguity, synonymy and vagueness*. This is confirmed by the larger proportion of alignments for properties and classes under the *semantically related* category.

The queries were also analysed and categorized according to a set of query features: *contains in-*

Vocabulary Alignment Type	Vocabulary Type	Value
Semantically Related	Class	0.294
String Similar	Class	0.117
Identical	Class	0.117
Substring	Class	0.470
Identical	Complex Class	0.5
String Similar	Complex Class	0.1
Semantically Related	Complex Class	0.4
Semantically Related	Instance	0.098
Identical	Instance	0.696
Substring	Instance	0.147
String Similar	Instance	0.049
Missing Vocabulary Match	Instance	0.009
Missing Vocabulary Match	Null	1
Substring	Predicate	0.168
Missing Vocabulary Match	Predicate	0.109
Semantically Related	Predicate	0.411
Identical	Predicate	0.168
String Similar	Predicate	0.142
Identical	Value	0.25
Substring	Value	0.75

Table 3: Distribution of vocabulary gap types for each entity type (QALD 2011/2012).

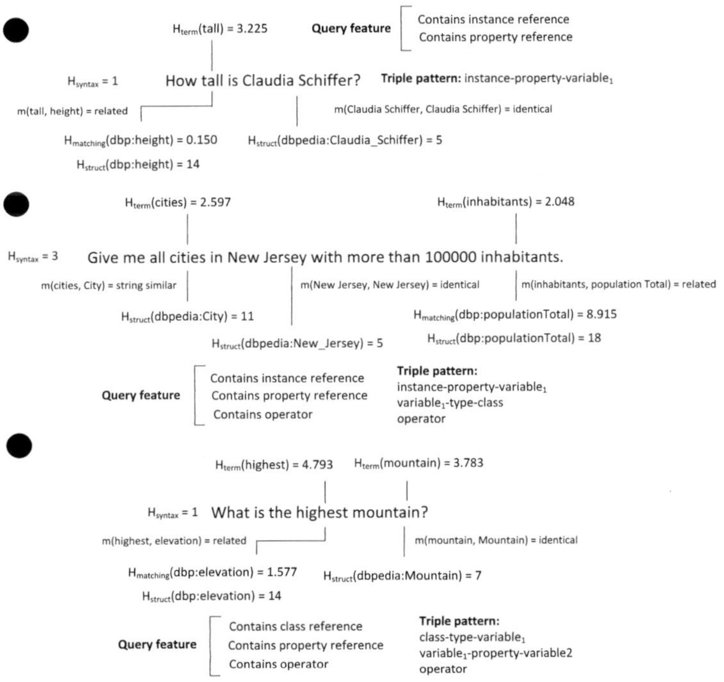

Figure 4: Entropy and query features for example queries.

stance reference, contains class reference, contains property reference, contains complex class reference (a complex class is a class with more than two words), *contains value reference contains operator reference, is a Yes/No question.* The features express the core natural language query - database mappings that need to be addressed by the query mechanism. The correlation between the query features and the average f-measure for the QA systems was also calculated and a multiple linear regression model was built (Table 4). Queries containing references to instances were positively correlated to the f-measure, while queries not containing instances were negatively correlated. This can be interpreted by combining this analysis with the alignment information from Table 3: predicate-type alignments are more bound to vocabulary variation (higher H_{term}, H_{vocab}) and are more difficult to resolve when compared to instance/value alignments.

Entropy Measure	Estimate	Std. Error	t-value	Pr(>—t—)
Instance	0.0750	0.1177	**0.638**	0.5247
Class	-0.0083	0.0816	-0.102	0.9189
Complex Class	-0.2118	0.1010	**-2.097**	0.0378
Property	0.0737	0.1659	0.444	0.6576
Value	-0.0565	0.1184	-0.478	0.6335
Yes/No	0.0054	0.1138	0.048	0.9615
Operator	-0.1506	0.0740	**-2.036**	0.0437

Table 4: Linear regression model between the query features and the average f-measure of QA systems. Multiple R-squared = 0.1171, adjusted R-squared = 0.09817.

Both *entropy* (H_{syntax}, H_{struct}, H_{term}, $H_{matching}$) and *query features* (*instances*, *complex classes*, *operators*) can be used as estimators for semantic complexity. Queries which were not or were poorly answered by the reference systems showed clear patterns which are correlated with entropy values: (i) high syntactic complexity (high H_{syntax}); (ii) high vocabulary gap (high $H_{matching}$, H_{term}) and (iii) predicate-based query (no instance reference in the query) (H_{struct}, H_{term}). Table 5 provides the classification of the set of unanswered/poorly answered queries according to the presence of high entropy values and also lists the non-trivial query term - database entity alignments. All unanswered queries fall into one (62%) or more (38%) of these categories.

5.1 Reflections on the Design of Schema-agnostic Query Mechanisms

The entropy measures and query feature analysis of the previous section can be used to define heuristics for maximizing the probability of a correct query-data matching in a schema-agnostic query scenario. A list of heuristics for addressing schema-agnostic queries are summarized below, based on the previous analysis:

1. **Prioritize the alignment of constants (instances):** Instances are less bound to vocabulary variation (lower H_{term}, H_{vocab}). The lower structural entropy H_{struct} associated with constants also allows the reduction of the search space.

2. H_{term} **can be used as a heuristic for matching complexity:** Having an estimation of the potential vocabulary variation of query terms predicates can be used to allow the prioritization of alignments with less ambiguity, synonymy and vagueness. H_{term} can be used to prioritize easier mappings.

3. H_{syntax} **is a strong estimator of query complexity:** Queries with complex compositional predicate patterns generate large entropy values which propagates to the matching stage. Schema-agnostic query mechanisms can explore query constraining approaches to minimize high H_{syntax} entropy values.

4. $H_{matching}$ **can be used as an estimator for the quality of the predicate alignment:** This value can be used to estimate the uncertainty of the alignment, supporting, for example, disambiguation mechanisms & clarification dialogs.

6 Conclusions & Future Work

This paper provides an analysis of measures of semantic complexity for schema-agnostic queries. A semantic model was built to understand the semantic dynamics behind the query-database semantic matching. Information theoretic models were used as a quantification model to measure the semantic complexity of mapping queries to database elements. The entropy measures and other query features were evaluated using a set of 150 natural language schema-agnostic queries over DBpedia by comparing the correlation between different Question Answering systems and the entropy measures. Syntactical,

Query	Syntactic compl. (H_{syntax})	Vocab. gap ($H_{matching}$, H_{term})	Pred. Pivot (H_{struct}, H_{term})	Non-trivial alignments
How many monarchical countries are there in Europe?		✓		monarchical countries - governmentType
Give me the capitals of all U.S. states.			✓	
Which states border Utah?		✓		border - east — border - southeast — border - south — border - northeast — border - north — border - west
Which mountain is the highest after the Annapurna?	✓	✓		highest - elevation
Which bridges are of the same type as the Manhattan Bridge?	✓	✓		type - design — type - design
Which state of the United States of America has the highest density?	✓	✓		highest density - densityrank
When did Germany join the EU?		✓		join - accessioneudate
Give me all soccer clubs in Spain.		✓		null - ground
Which German cities have more than 250000 inhabitants?	✓	✓	✓	inhabitants - populationTotal
How many students does the Free University in Amsterdam have?	✓			
What is the longest river?		✓	✓	longest - length
Does the new Battlestar Galactica series have more episodes than the old one?	✓			
Give me all people that were born in Vienna and died in Berlin.	✓	✓		died - deathPlace — born - birthPlace
Do Harry and William, Princes of Wales, have the same mother?	✓			
Give me all Australian nonprofit organizations.			✓	null - null
List all boardgames by GMT.		✓		null - publisher
Which countries are connected by the Rhine?				
Was the Cuban Missile Crisis earlier than the Bay of Pigs Invasion?	✓	✓		earlier - date
Give me all Frisian islands that belong to the Netherlands.	✓	✓		null - country
Which Greek goddesses dwelt on Mount Olympus?		✓		dwelt - abode
Which daughters of British earls died in the same place they were born in?	✓	✓		born - birthPlace — died - deathPlace
Who was called Scarface?		✓		called - nickname
Give me a list of all American inventions.		✓	✓	null - null
Which films starring Clint Eastwood did he direct himself?	✓			
Show me all songs from Bruce Springsteen released between 1980 and 1990.	✓	✓		songs - artist — release - releaseDate
Which movies did Sam Raimi direct after Army of Darkness?	✓			
What is the founding year of the brewery that produces Pilsner Urquell?	✓			founding year - foundation — brewery - brewery
Which country does the creator of Miffy come from?		✓		creator - creator — country - nationality
For which label did Elvis record his first album?		✓		null - releaseDate — label - recordLabel — null - artist —
% of unanswered questions	**51.7%**	**68.9%**	**20.6%**	

Table 5: 'Hard queries', i.e. queries which were nor or were poorly answered by the benchmarking systems. 'Checked' dimensions represent high entropy values.

terminological and matching entropies had a significant correlation with the results (f-measure) of the benchmarked systems. Based on the results, recommendations for the design of schema-agnostic query approaches were suggested. Future work will concentrate on the refinement of the entropy measures.

References

[1] Cabrio, E., Cojan, J., Aprosio, A.P., Magnini, B., Lavelli, A., Gandon, F.: Qakis: an open domain qa system based on relational patterns. In: Proceedings of the ISWC 2012. CEUR Workshop Proceedings, vol. 914 (2012)

[2] Cimiano, P., Lopez, V., Unger, C., Cabrio, E., Ngonga Ngomo, A.C., Walter, S.: Multilingual question answering over linked data (qald-3): Lab overview. In: CLEF (2013)

[3] Cronen-Townsend, S., Zhou, Y., Croft, W.B.: Predicting query performance. In: Proceedings of the 25th Annual International ACM SIGIR Conference on Research and Development in Information Retrieval. pp. 299–306. SIGIR '02, ACM, New York, NY, USA (2002)

[4] Damljanovic, D., Agatonovic, M., Cunningham, H.: Freya: An interactive way of querying linked data using natural language. In: Proc. of the European Semantic Web Conference Workshops. vol. 7117, pp. 125–138 (2012)

[5] Freitas, A.: Schema-agnositc queries over large-schema databases: a distributional semantics approach. In: PhD Thesis (2015)

[6] Freitas, A., Pereira Da Silva, J.C., Curry, E.: On the semantic mapping of schema-agnostic queries: A preliminary study. In: Workshop of the Natural Language Interfaces for the Web of Data (NLIWoD), 13th International Semantic Web Conference (ISWC) (2014)

[7] Gabrilovich, E., Markovitch, S.: Computing semantic relatedness using wikipedia-based explicit semantic analysis. In: Proceedings of the 20th International Joint Conference on Artifical Intelligence. pp. 1606–1611. IJCAI'07, Morgan Kaufmann Publishers Inc., San Francisco, CA, USA (2007)

[8] Harris, Z.: Distributional structure. In: Word, 10(23). pp. 146–162 (November 1954)

[9] Lopez, V., Fernández, M., Motta, E., Stieler, N.: Poweraqua: Supporting users in querying and exploring the semantic web. Semantic Web 3(3), 249–265 (2012)

[10] Melamed, I.D.: Measuring semantic entropy. In: Proceedings of the SIGLEX Workshop on Tagging Text with Lexical Semantics. pp. 41–46 (1997)

[11] Pollard, S., Biermann, A.W.: A measure of semantic complexity for natural language systems. In: Proc. of the 2000 NAACL-ANLP Workshop on Syntactic and Semantic Complexity in Natural Language Processing Systems. pp. 42–46. Association for Computational Linguistics, Stroudsburg, PA, USA (2000)

[12] Popescu, A.M., Etzioni, O., Kautz, H.: Towards a theory of natural language interfaces to databases. In: Proceedings of the 8th International Conference on Intelligent User Interfaces. pp. 149–157. IUI '03, ACM, New York, NY, USA (2003)

[13] Shannon, C.: A mathematical theory of communication. Bell System Technical Journal 27, 379–423, 623–656 (1948)

[14] Sullivan, T.: Locating question difficulty through explorations in question space. In: Proceedings of the 1st ACM/IEEE-CS Joint Conference on Digital Libraries. pp. 251–252. JCDL '01, ACM, New York, NY, USA (2001)

[15] Tonellotto, N., Macdonald, C., Ounis, I.: Efficient and effective retrieval using selective pruning. In: Proceedings of the Sixth ACM International Conference on Web Search and Data Mining. pp. 63–72. WSDM '13, ACM, New York, NY, USA (2013)

Author Index